A CONSTITUTIONAL
AND LEGAL
HISTORY
OF
ENGLAND

A Constitutional and Legal History

OF ENGLAND

by GOLDWIN SMITH, *Professor of History*

WAYNE UNIVERSITY

DORSET PRESS · NEW YORK

This edition published by Dorset Press
a division of Marboro Books Corporation.
1990 Dorset Press

ISBN 0-88029-474-4

Printed in the United States of America
M 9 8 7 6 5 4 3 2 1

TO
EMILY AND GOLDWIN
DOUGLAS
AND BRUCE

"*A nation is an association of reasonable beings united in a peaceful sharing of the things they cherish. Therefore to determine the quality of a nation, you must consider what those things are.*"

ST. AUGUSTINE

"*It were good, therefore, that men in their innovations would follow the example of time itself, which, indeed, innovateth greatly, but quietly, and by degrees, scarce to be perceived.*"

FRANCIS BACON

Preface

ONE of the tasks of able and sympathetic instructors is to try to widen the first thin rays of undergraduate curiosity. The modern college student is interested above all in the present, the here and now. Sometimes the austere scholarship of the professor, as he labors with paleography and pipe rolls, causes him to forget that once, long ago, he was persuaded to adopt "a willing suspension of disbelief" as he hesitantly entered a classroom. Only by slow steps do we learn that "the roots of the present lie deep in the past." The undergraduate student does not usually study English constitutional history, or any other subject, for the same reasons as the professor. Often he "takes" a course because the local authorities require him to do so. Perhaps that is the main reason why he is now reading this book.

It might therefore be desirable to remind the student that the main elements of the British constitution and laws were made in the hot-blooded drama of human history by men toughened in the field of battle, the courts of law, and the cockpits of politics. All were realists, hard-headed fellows like ourselves. And today, in the running hours of world events, the constitution and the laws are changing still, altered by the hands and voices of practical men. Still true are the words of Aristotle: "In practical matters the end is not mere speculative knowledge of what is to be done, but rather the doing of it."

The modern college student, confronted with paragraphs and pages about English constitutional history, may regretfully conclude that much eludes him. He may feel that success does not swiftly attend his attempts to penetrate into the alien world of the curia regis, possessory assizes, crimes against the state and crimes against the person. If he bestows even a cursory glance upon the massive achievements of historians he may flinch and flee to the textbook, his main stockade against the terrors of the unknown.

In 1873 Bishop William Stubbs wrote these words in the preface to his *Constitutional History of England:* "The history of institutions cannot be mastered,—can scarcely be approached,—without an effort." Bishop Stubbs was right. "Learn not," says the proverb, "and know not." The road to knowledge about English constitutional history is hazardous and hard. Truth, as usual, is found among the rocks.

History, says the *Oxford English Dictionary,* is a discipline which records and explains, a discipline which evaluates the character and significance of events. To make history superficial, a watery broth without nourishment, brings no profit. In these days, a reminder of the dangers of the opposite point of view may not come amiss. *Facilis descensus Averni.* All the same, the historian should keep a vigilant sense of reality. He errs if he thinks that the high wisdom historians guard and perpetuate must be unfolded in polysyllabic profundities. Our task is to ignite the minds of students to deeper understanding, and modern students usually prefer simple words, precise and clear. Hence the historian should try to use language that is unambiguous and straightforward. "For if the trumpet gives an uncertain sound, who shall prepare himself for the battle?"

But painful realities confront the professor who asserts his desire to be "unambiguous and straightforward." Even the most deliberate candor, the most careful floodlighting, the most sensible study of the convoled intricacies of the British constitution, do not provide answers that are fixed and final. Today the dust lies thick on the works of many historians of the British constitution once revered as gods for their wisdom. Knowledge advances, judgments change, and the vast emptiness of error is steadily being reduced by the indefeasible desire of the scholar to rescue the truth from obscurity. Frequently, however, it seems to some historians that the hands and minds of their colleagues falter, fumble, swerve aside. Consequently there are often doubts and disputes. Every historian knows that the acreage of description and debate upon several aspects of British constitutional and legal history is now very large.

The student must be prepared to appreciate the fact that although notable advances have been made by scholars in recent years there are still, upon many topics, divergent points of view. The voices of the constitutional historians in the grove where Clio dwells do not always say the same thing. If they did, it would doubtless be "a gross conforming stupidity, a stark and dead congealment of wood and hay and stubble, forced and frozen together." The conclusions of the constitutional historian must always be reached with caution and must frequently contain much that is tentative. "We are moderns," Professor F. W. Maitland once remarked. "Every thought will be too sharp, every word will imply too many contrasts. We must, it is feared, use many words and qualify our every statement until we have almost contradicted it."

Without begging any major questions at issue I have endeavored constantly to avoid discussing at length problems that are yet unresolved. Nor can I pretend that I have treated any subject exhaustively, even in the decades of strategic change. Such a consideration is outside the scope of my intention, which is to describe and illuminate the main features of English constitutional and legal history for the undergraduate and the general reader. It is the work of years to raise in strength and symmetry a full structure, with casemated stories, neat embrasures, finished parapets. My paragraphs in this book range themselves to form a scaffolding, and little more. If in consequence some experts find my treatment of the subjects of their special competence too slight, I can only plead that it is by design and ask them to judge it as such. I would perhaps also remark that I am humbly aware that in many respects my knowledge stands in need of improvement.

My performance has not always kept pace with my desires. Dr. Samuel Johnson said long ago: "There are two things which I am confident I can do well; one is an introduction to any literary work, stating what it is to contain, and how it should be executed in the most perfect manner; and the other is a conclusion, showing from various causes why the execution has not been equal to what the author promised to himself and to the public." For all that professors and students do not approve I ask indulgence.

Many undergraduates may be somewhat less than fully informed about the main features of the history of England. They would be well advised to read one of the standard surveys of English history in order to obtain a more complete understanding of the forces that helped to shape the laws and the constitution. It is also desirable that every student should read and study many of the published sources. The best selection of important documents is *Sources of English Constitutional History,* prepared by Professor Carl Stephenson and Professor Frederick G. Marcham of Cornell University, and published by Harper and Brothers in 1937. The publishers have generously given me permission to quote from this volume.

A number of friends and colleagues have helped me in the writing of these pages. It is a special pleasure to acknowledge my debt to Professor Arthur C. Bining of the University of Pennsylvania, the editor of the Scribner's Historical Series. His meticulous scholarship, his patience and understanding, have saved me from all sorts of errors. The mistakes and heresies that remain are mine alone. Professor Holden Furber of the University of Pennsylvania read every page of the manuscript. For his expert advice and his thoughtful corrections I am more grateful than I can say in a few formal words.

My colleague Professor Frederick C. Hamil has willingly shared his wide knowledge with me and I gratefully record his assistance and advice. The hard-edged mind of Professor Hartley Thomas of the University of Western Ontario has helped me to shape my own ideas and the quiet competence of his colleague Professor Walter Balderston has guided me away from numerous mistakes of interpretation and detail.

Many others have aided me along the way. I feel a special debt of gratitude to Mr. Campbell Calder, Q. C., of London, Canada; Professor George P. Cuttino of Emory University; Mr. John W. Holmes of the Department of External Affairs, Ottawa, Canada; Professor Ernest P. Kuhl of the State University of Iowa; Professor William H. Seiler of Kansas State Teachers College; Professor Francis D. Wormuth of the University of Utah.

My admirable colleagues at Wayne University know how much I appreciate their helpfulness and forbearance.

I must add a special word of appreciation to Professor Geoffrey Bruun, whose words, so well-informed and wise, have contributed more than he knows to whatever salt and stability this volume may possess.

GOLDWIN SMITH

Wayne University
Detroit, Michigan

Contents

xiii

List of Maps

A CONSTITUTIONAL
AND LEGAL
HISTORY
OF
ENGLAND

CHAPTER I

The Anglo-Saxons:

kings and men

HEIRS OF ROME

AT the dawn of the Christian era the Roman legions had subdued the larger part of Europe. Roman rule meant almost universal law, order and peace. Throughout all the Empire there was the Roman culture, the Roman institutions, the Latin language.

Upon the outer edges of the Empire stood the British Isles. Julius Caesar had first attacked the Celts of Britain in 55 B.C. After nearly a hundred years the Emperor Claudius slowly drove the Britons back and established Roman authority over the area we now call England. The Roman Empire brought law and order, town life, roads.

But neither Claudius nor his successors ever subdued Scotland, Ireland, Cornwall, Devon, or Wales beyond the Grampians. Long before the final collapse of Rome the unconquered Celts attacked Roman Britain from Scotland, from the barrier backlands of Wales and Cornwall, from untamed Ireland. From Europe came marauding forces of Angles, Jutes and Saxons to pillage and destroy.

Early in the fifth century the Burgundians, Franks, Goths and Vandals plunged southwards towards Rome, the heart of an enfeebled Empire. In 410 Rome was sacked. From the sprawling Roman provinces the legions had slowly departed. The Roman Empire in the West was at an end. The writ of Caesar ran no more.

After the power of the Empire crumbled, the Picts and Scots and the Angles, Jutes and Saxons increased the pace and strength of their attacks upon Britain. Then, about 450, the European tribesmen began to migrate from their homelands. They travelled to the west and invaded the island areas the Romans could no longer defend.

These events covered a long period of time. At last, in a tangled

1

skein of events but dimly seen today, the invaders conquered and held the larger part of what is now England. Soon, few traces of Roman influence remained, except as memories. As a result, English constitutional history has nothing to do with Roman Britain. It has a great deal to do with the Angles, Jutes and Saxons.

The bold barbarian invaders were not separate, well-organized tribes from distinct Continental areas. Sea-rovers all, and mingled together, they came over the rough North Sea "with a common purpose but little unity of command." They preferred to live away from the Roman town sites and settled in the woodland and the open fields. They lived mainly by hunting and agriculture. Their culture was barbaric. Their religion was pagan. Their social organization was primitive, fluid, indefinite.

Nineteenth century historians used to say, as zealous Montesquieu said in the previous century, that the British constitution was born in the forests of Germany before the Anglo-Saxon tribes invaded England. It is obviously true that the tribes coming from northern Europe brought and maintained, for a time, several customs of German society. Earlier scholars produced studies about the Germanic origins of Anglo-Saxon institutions, often heavily and dangerously bulwarked by quotations from Caesar, Bede and Tacitus. In fact, despite valuable investigations by many scholars, we have little precise knowledge about the Angles and Saxons in their early European settlements. For the practical purposes of study, the constitutional and legal history of England begins in England and it begins with the Anglo-Saxon settlement.

The period of Anglo-Saxon rule lasted more than six hundred years, a considerable timespan. These centuries were filled with wars. Kingdoms rose and fell. By the year 600 there were seven large, separate kingdoms, usually called the Heptarchy: Northumbria, Mercia, East Anglia, Essex, Wessex, Kent and Sussex. These, and several smaller tribal units, were often ruled by strong and ambitious kings. At first the most powerful state was Kent, heavily populated by Jutes. It was Ethelbert of Kent (560–616) who accepted Christianity when Augustine came from Rome in 597. It was Ethelbert who became lord of the East Saxons and East Angles. In the seventh and eighth centuries the northern states of Mercia and Northumbria battled for supremacy. Northumbria won first and Mercia won last. Under Offa II (757–796) Mercia reached the summit of her power. Offa drove back the

Welsh and made the west country from Cumberland to Devon part of England.

The ninth century saw the rise of Wessex. In 825 Wessex conquered Mercia. The able Egbert (802–839) seized Cornwall; even the Northumbrians called him overlord. Then, as the wars among the Anglo-Saxon kingdoms ended, a new conflict began. The Danes came from Norway and Denmark seeking battle and booty. When Alfred (871–899), famous son of the house of Wessex, became king of all England he found almost half of his kingdom already conquered by the Danes. After several defeats, Alfred drove back his enemies and by the treaty of Wedmore (878) the Danes agreed to stay in the region called the Danelaw, north and east of London.

Alfred's son, Edward the Elder (899–925), and seven successors slowly pushed back the Danes beyond the Humber. Meanwhile, the blood of Dane and Saxon slowly mingled as the generations passed and the process of assimilation continued. In 1002 Sweyn, king of Denmark, attacked England. When Edmund Ironside died in 1016 the English had no leader and Sweyn's son Canute was chosen king of all England. He also ruled Denmark and Norway. Thus political unification came not from Alfred of Wessex but from Canute, the Dane.

Five years after Canute's death his line died out. The English then turned back to the Saxon family of Alfred. In 1043 Edward the Confessor was crowned at Winchester. Twenty-three years later William of Normandy was to conquer England in the red day of Hastings.

The student need read no more than this summary statement to conclude that during the six rough centuries of the Anglo-Saxon period there would inevitably occur numerous shocks and jars and changes in custom and practice, varying from region to region. There were many contrasts in types of settlement, in methods of landholding, in laws, in complicated custom. Changes and innovations in institutions increased. That is the reason why the historian finds it impossible to make fixed and final statements about many aspects of the Anglo-Saxon period. Of course, to any generalization exceptions multiply. It is always impossible to reduce a complex piece of history to an easy and accurate formula or to impose uniformity upon unyielding and different materials.

Anglo-Saxon records are often fragmentary and ambiguous. Nevertheless, the night watches of diligent scholarship and usually acute

THE BRITISH
ISLES
PHYSICAL MAP
Miles
0 20 40 60 80

conjecture have produced many books and articles about the numerous local variations in the customs and institutions of Anglo-Saxon
England. It would be impertinence and folly to attempt a complete
and competent summary of many technical conclusions in the brief
compass of this book. In any event, it is beyond the limited scope of
these pages to consider at length the regional variations or to trace in

slow detail the development of Anglo-Saxon legal and political machinery. Here it must suffice to submit to the student reasonably accurate answers to a series of precise and basic questions: What was the nature of the Anglo-Saxon monarchy? Was there a nobility? Who were free to work out their own happiness or misery? Who were the king's servants and advisers and what did they do? What were the units of local government and how did they function? What kind of legal system did the people possess and how was the law enforced? How was the land held? What was the role of the church? What foundations were laid by the Anglo-Saxons for the structure to be erected by the creative builders of the Middle Ages?

THE KINGSHIP

For fifteen hundred years the institution of monarchy has been an essential part of British polity. The old Anglo-Saxon kingship, however, bears little resemblance to the feudal monarchy of the Middle Ages or to the constitutional monarchy of the present. An Anglo-Saxon of Alfred's day would find our modern idea of limited monarchy quite unintelligible. It is always wise for the student to remember that our ancestors frequently did not see things as we do. Between the Anglo-Saxons and ourselves lie more than a thousand years of history. Their ways were not our ways, their ideas not ours. Hence the words we employ to describe Anglo-Saxon attitudes and actions must be used with discrimination. We must always be aware of the slippery and deceiving dangers of attributing to the Anglo-Saxons, to the men of the Renaissance age, or to the Jeffersonians, ideas, distinctions, reasons and attitudes that they never possessed and would not understand.

The first source of kingship was military ability. When the Anglo-Saxon tribes came to England they were led by war chiefs, men who could carve out kingdoms from the land of the Celts and battle with rival tribes. As some kingdoms were swallowed up the monarchs who survived grew more powerful. The reader has noted how the units of the uneasily balanced Heptarchy gradually yielded to the armed demands of conquerors and how the early eleventh century saw the emergence of an England at last united under the statesman-warrior Canute. The meaning of kingship expanded.

Anglo-Saxon kings were formally selected from a particular family by the leading strong and sagacious men of the state. Thus the monarchy was hereditary in the sense that it was confined to a certain family, elective in the sense that any male member of the royal family might be chosen. Very often a strict line of succession from father to son was followed. Sometimes kings were deposed. Sometimes, in hours of emergency, new dynasties were established.

Kings, weak or strong, had considerable moral power. They were often hailed as heroes and frequently regarded as being hedged with divinity, first in a pagan and then in a Christian sense. After Christianity returned to England the church helped to increase the strength of the monarchy. The foundations of a long alliance were being laid. Churchmen, of course, wanted monarchs strong enough to defend the faith, to give them lands and wealth, to assist them in providing the people with the means of grace and the hope of glory. Naturally enough, the church preferred large and stable states and thus aided the slow progress towards a united kingdom. Certain things, said the church, must be rendered unto Caesar. At the same time, kingship was invested with strong religious sanctions. The consecration of a king was a religious ceremony of high importance. The coronation oath of Edgar (946) indicates the importance of the moral power and responsibility of the king. "In the name of the Holy Trinity I promise three things to the Christian people my subjects: first, that God's Church and all Christian people of my realm shall enjoy true peace; second, that I forbid to all ranks of men robbery and all wrongful deeds; third, that I urge and command justice and mercy in all judgments, so that the gracious and compassionate God who lives and reigns may grant us all His everlasting mercy."

In both pagan and Christian days the king was a symbol, a representative of his nation, a being who embodied the national ideals. Men, past and present, do not easily find in abstractions a focus for their emotions. They desire something concrete: personality, flesh and blood, coherence, continuity. If networks of loyalty are loosely attached to abstract ideals, they collapse. The Anglo-Saxon king was the symbol of courage and national prowess in war; he was king "by the grace of God"; he was the defender of the law; he was often the driving force in the defense of his people. "In the king's righteousness," wrote Alcuin in 793, "is the common weal, victory in war, mildness of the seasons, abundance of crops, freedom of pestilence. It is for the king to atone with God for his whole people." In the long chapters of the Anglo-Saxon period the moral authority of the crown seldom diminishes and is not easily impaired.

The inquiring reader will now ask what were the practical powers of the Anglo-Saxon kings. In the material sphere the status and strength of the monarchy steadily increased from the pagan settlement days to the Norman Conquest. The pace of increase was particularly rapid after the accession of Alfred in 871.

At no time did Anglo-Saxon rulers obtain absolute authority. They were limited in scores of ways, several of which will be pointed out later. Above all, they were limited by custom, the stream of life-habit. In primitive phases of organization the "cake of custom" inevitably assumed a significant place: the traditional and complex weight of obligation, of privilege, of status, of kindred, of lordship, of all the rules of personal association. Law was tribal custom or folkright. The king, and all his subjects, were subordinate to custom. With the advice and consent of the great and wise men of his kingdom the monarch might occasionally declare what the law was, but he never gave or made it. As Professor Edward Jenks well says, "Law was not legislation, but record." The directive force of precedent came from the past, from the well-springs of the communal mind of the folk, from the remembered folkright. What was placed in written record was merely a "settling" or "fastening" of ancient customs. Much will be said later about Anglo-Saxon law but it is imperative at this point to stress the continuous significance of fettering custom upon the royal power.

The king held large areas of land. His various resources were larger than those of the greatest of his subjects. He obtained his income from tenants on the royal lands; from the king's share of penal fines imposed in local courts (wite, which in the twelfth century becomes a discretionary money payment called amercement); from certain levies and tolls in money and kind; from the emergency tax called the Danegeld, levied in 991 to buy off the Danes; from the maintenance due the king and his retinue in journeys through the kingdom (purveyance); from the forfeited property of outlaws; from wrecks and treasure trove; from mines, saltworks and the like. So innocent was the age of any theoretical or "constitutional" elements that there was no distinction between the personal purse of the king and the public treasury, between the king's land and the land of the state.

The king commanded the army, the fyrd. He appointed the important officials in his household, men whose duties will be described later. He controlled the appointment of many higher officials in the church. He summoned and presided over the council of the wise and great of his realm.

Any offense committed against the king or on his property was heavily punished. This special protection (mundborg) of the "king's peace" was the tendril of a concept destined later to provide a legal method by which the state increased its authority. The "king's peace" was often extended to include certain places, persons or times. In the period of the feud-truce neither an individual nor his kindred might do any violence without affronting the king and incurring heavy penalties. Individuals usually protected were members of the royal family, the king's servants, and other persons under the royal protection. Special occasions, such as feast days, court or public assembly days, festival days, and coronation days were also protected by the "king's peace." Places protected included the king's property and presence, highways and waterways, roads from the king's boroughs, military roads, markets, forests, walled towns, centers where the fyrd was gathering, and the like.

The king, like all individuals, had a fixed value set by the law upon his life (wergeld) and payable to his kin in the event of his death by violence. In his case, the sum was set so high that nobody could pay it and hence the fate of the regicide was death. There had not yet developed any law of treason.

The king also had jurisdiction (sac) over persons of high rank. The reader will find numerous examples of these and other royal prerogatives in the promulgated laws (dooms) of Anglo-Saxon kings cited in numerous collections of English constitutional documents. For instance, the dooms in the great code of Canute (1017–1035) list items that are later to be pleas of the crown: "These are the rights which the king enjoys over all men in Wessex: namely [compensations for] breach of his personal protection (mundbryce), housebreaking (hamsocne), assault by ambush (forsteal), and neglect of military service (fyrdwite)."

When the Normans came after the reign of King Edward the Confessor, many changes occurred to alter the nature and content of the royal authority. On the other hand, some Anglo-Saxon elements remained essentially unshaken and endure to the present day. In later chapters the reader will see the successive mergings of the streams of continuity and change so characteristic of the growth of the crown and of all the institutions and laws of England.

CLASSES AND CUSTOMS

It is often said that Anglo-Saxon society was like a pyramid. The king and the princes of the blood stood at the apex. Below were ranged the nobles, the freemen, and, at the base, the serfs, slaves and rightless men. This simile is useful if the reader recognizes that it is intended to convey an impression, no more. As an accurate description it fails because it takes no account of the fact that there were numerous regional variations in time and place; that before the tenth century we have only fragmentary records; that a fluid society contained many men who were being carried by events and forces up and down the class scale.

The nobles obtained personal nobility by birth, service to the king, or wealth in land. In the early stages of the Anglo-Saxon conquest the nobility of blood were called eorls. These eorls are not to be confused with the later "earls" who appeared by the eleventh century when the Danish word "earl" (jarl) was widely substituted for "ealdorman," a term originally applied to a noble named by the king to command the militia and preside in the courts of one or more shires.

There were also the gesiths (companions or comites), mentioned only in early records. These gesiths, close associates and personal followers of the king, obtained their position by military service. Large estates were usually ceded to them. Their leader was indeed the "loaf-giver" (hlaford) famed in song and story.

Soon the thegns (retainers or servants) took the place of the gesiths as a noble caste deriving its rank from service to the king, bishop, or ealdorman. Real property became so important that a freeman who obtained a certain amount of land moved to the higher status of a thegn. Thegnage was never a closed estate. The word "thegn" is an elusive term. Particularly because of his variable functions the tangible marks of a thegn's status are often difficult to find, define and classify.

About 850 the higher thegns were becoming a landed aristocracy more interested in their local affairs than in court service. By the tenth century they were widely used by the king to see to the royal interests in the provinces. Some of them became great local magnates. "The king's thegn," says Professor J. E. A. Jolliffe, "was becoming the knight of the shire of his day." At the end of the Anglo-Saxon age, land is slowly superseding race and kin in importance.

In a law court the oath of an eorl, a gesith or a thegn was usually worth six times that of an ordinary freeman. The noble was protected by a wergeld, his valuation in terms of money to be paid by the guilty party if he should be slain. His wergeld was about six times that of an ordinary freeman. The higher offices of church and state went to men of the noble class. Many sat in the witan or great council of the kingdom. By the tenth and eleventh centuries excessive power was silently moving into the hands of the noble and the wealthy.

The non-noble freemen or peasant landholders were the most numerous class in the state. In many respects these ordinary freemen, called ceorls, formed the real basis of the whole Anglo-Saxon social system. As the dooms of Canute say, the freemen were the "law-worthy" men, the lawful men, solid and respectable. They were commanded by the king to perform many duties. Their responsibilities were numerous. So, too, were their rights, enshrined in immemorial custom, the law of the folk, the folkright.

Ever since Professor J. M. Kemble stressed, a hundred years ago, the importance of the family group (maegth) and Professor Frederick Seebohm opposed him, much learned controversy has occurred. In 1937 Professor J. E. A. Jolliffe raised once more the problem of the nature and significance of kinship. For excellent reasons many scholars have felt that the position taken by Professor Jolliffe cannot be adequately defended. Professor Jolliffe has concluded that the rights of the freeman were an essential outcome of the primitive idea of the kindred or blood-tie. He has claimed that a man's whole position as a freeman depended upon his association with his kin, those of a common blood with him, proved in a descent through at least four generations. It is certainly true that in early Anglo-Saxon England the acts of every man apparently involved his kindred. His blood relations shared his responsibility. If one man killed another the family of the slayer was legally open to revenge and the family of the slain man was committed to taking it unless the appeasement of the set blood-price or wergeld was paid by the slayer's kindred to "buy off the spear." Apparently the man who could find no kin was an outlaw. In a court of law an individual could not be considered reputable unless he had the support and testimony of his kin, given in a fashion to be described later. Some authorities are of the opinion that a man's folkright was effective only when he acted as a member of his family group.

The touchstone principles and basic rules of kinship have perhaps been unduly stressed in recent years. In any event, they receded in significance when a later pattern of social organization by territory, neighborhood, and lordship waxed strong in the decades before the Normans came.

All freemen were apparently responsible for meeting the triple demands of the so-called *trinoda necessitas:* fyrd or military service; repairing strongholds; and building and repairing bridges. Freemen were also required to contribute to the public burden of the food-rent or feorm, by which it was mandatory for villages to supply at certain times fixed amounts of provisions for the king and his retinue. Finally, it was necessary for all freemen to attend and take part in the sessions of the local law courts in the hundred and shire.

At this point it becomes impossible to say that there are any further characteristics common to all freemen in Anglo-Saxon England. By what modern physicists call "operational definition" we can ascertain some rights and duties of freemen in one district. In an adjoining area these rights and duties are slightly different. In a more distant locality the picture is altered still more. Thus the whole class of freemen varied in character from region to region. The grades of freemen were numerous and blurred and shaded at the edges. Different levels of freedom and servility are suggested by the welter of names: the ceorl, the sokeman of the north and east, the villani, including the bordari, the cotari and others, on and on.

Let us suppose that a student hears or reads somewhere a brief definition of a villein, the meanest of free men who holds his land by flimsy tenure. If he then reads Professor F. W. Maitland's classic *Domesday Book and Beyond* he will discover that master historian analyzing with caution and care the complex structure of the freeman stratum of Anglo-Saxon society, including what he calls "the heterogeneous villein class." For Professor Maitland there were no brief definitions of villeins or any other groups. His knowledge was too vast for that. Always there were the exceptions, always the qualifications.

A student may ask: "Does not the freeman, whoever he may be, have a fixed wergeld?" A glance at the dooms published in collections of documents will show that wergelds are often stated there. "A Welsh horseman," say the dooms of Ine (688–695), "who rides in the king's service has a wergeld of 200 shillings." The student will find that there are many wergelds within the broad freeman class. In the Kent of Ethelbert's day, for instance, the wergeld of a ceorl was 100 golden shillings to the kinsfolk of the slain man (2,000 silver pieces) and 50 to the king. At the same time, however, the wergeld of a villein, also a freeman, was only 200 small Saxon shillings to his kinsfolk and 30 shillings to his lord (man-bot).

Textbooks frequently say that the normal holding or tenement of a common free man was one hide of land; that a hide usually contained 120 acres; and that a hide was used as a basis of taxation. This statement is precise and neat and final, but it is not quite true. The student who turns to his well-thumbed sources will find that after the seventh century the normal holding of a fully free man is indeed the hide in many parts of England. But in Wiltshire the hide contains only 40 acres, not 120. In Kent there is no hide at all. The men of Kent use as a land measure the "sulung," which is said by Professor F. M. Stenton and others to be the amount of land that can be kept in cultivation by a plough-team of eight oxen. At this point a farmer's son may rightly remark that eight oxen are a lot for one plough-team. Like many definitions, this one of the "sulung" is wholly satisfactory only if we let it pass without scrutiny.

Readers who prefer daring and fearless generalizations may feel that these comments are too academic, too illustrative of the results of the professors' earthworm research. Others will understand that those who wish to be scholars must follow without evasion the clues and facts they find. In any event, enough has been said to suggest the difficulties in "defining" the ordinary freeman class beyond very narrow limits.

Below those who were free were the serfs, economically dependent. The serf still had a small wergeld. When a serf was slain his kinfolk were paid 40 pence and his lord 20 Saxon shillings. By this reckoning the value of a serf to his lord was the equivalent of the price of 16 sheep or 3 oxen. The lord could not sell or mistreat the serf. All serfs were free to marry. They worked for their lords and paid by labor and produce for the land they held. About 25,000 serfs were listed in Domesday Book. Finally, there were the slaves (theows), mere chattels, who could be bought and sold as livestock. This class was small. Many were freed from full slavery in Anglo-Saxon days and became serfs.

On the eve of the Norman Conquest bad harvests, war and cattle plagues aided in causing the once strong position of the freemen to deteriorate until it had become essentially servile. As members of unfree classes the peasants now had drifted into dependence upon local lords. There they were bound by personal ties that involved the performance of customary service, almost invariably agricultural. In 1066 there were fewer slaves and fewer freemen; and the various grades of unfree serfs had greatly increased.

Nineteenth century historians pictured an Anglo-Saxon village filled with freemen, warrior-peasants singing at their work and sleeping more soundly than princes. It is a pity that modern scholarship has so effectively exploded that delightful idea.

THE WITAN

At least once a year for more than four hundred years the king's major advisers, both lay and clerical notables, met together. They formed the witan or witenagemot, the aristocratic assembly of the great and wise of the realm. Ine of Wessex (688–726) called them "the most eminent of my people." In an early meeting a contemporary found men "such as most surely knew how all things stood in the land of their forefathers' days. . . . And many ancient men told how the law was laid down soon after Augustine's day."

The witan was regarded as vaguely representing the national will. This fact must not tempt today's reader to look upon the witan as a representative body in anything like the modern sense. The members of the witan did not stand for "the people" except, perhaps, against a tyrant. Doubtless on such occasions the aristocrats would be protecting their own skins and coins as well as those of the lower classes. The witan was always composed of men of wealth, wisdom and prestige. It was indeed an aristocratic assembly and it looked after its own aristocratic interests and privileges. Some nineteenth century historians saw several democratic elements in the witan. They were mistaken and the student is warned against placing too much reliance upon this aspect of their scholarship.

Rumbles of scholarly controversy still are heard about the extent to which the witan can be called a formal council. It certainly had no sense of unity, no fixed membership, no determinable composition. There is also some doubt about several of the positive functions earlier attributed to it in the twelve canons of J. M. Kemble and elsewhere. Although nobody possessed any official right to attend the witan there were several essential members such as the royal family, the archbishops, bishops, abbots, royal chaplains, the ealdormen and earls so powerful in the local shires, and several officials of the royal household. Apparently the king also summoned any eorls, gesiths, or king's thegns he wished to attend. Today the attendance at a meeting of the witan can be determined only by a study of the list of witnesses with which royal charters end; but the length of a list of witnesses was decided by the length of the parchment on which the charter was written. Thus there are few full lists of those attending a witan. In the tenth century it seems that between fifty and a hundred men witnessed the kings' grants. A witan of Ethelstan in 931 included "Celtic princes, Danish earls and the thegns and ealdormen of all England." To a witan in 1005 came the king and queen, the king's 7 sons, 14 bishops, 16 abbots, 3 ealdormen and 44 thegns.

The witan, like any other primitive body, performed several functions which, as Professor Chadwick said long ago, were never clearly defined or classified. Men of the witan selected and deposed the king, subject to the laws of selection described earlier. While the king reigned the witan met and was dissolved at his command. When it was in session the witan advised the king in important matters of state and shared his responsibility for what we call today public or state acts: the imposition of taxes; negotiations with foreign powers; defense measures; prosecution of traitors; royal gifts of estates; ecclesiastical patronage. On occasion, too, the witan seems to have controlled certain appointments, as in the case of the election of an abbot by the witan in 1044. In connection with all of these operations the witan obviously had a deliberative function, illustrated further by Bede's account of the meeting called in 626 by Edwin of Northumbria to consider the adoption of Christianity and by the discussions about the payment of the Danegeld in the years after 991.

The witan also acted as a high court, not of appeals but of first instance. It tried the cases of great men and causes important to the kingdom. In doing so, the witan of course interpreted and added to the body of customary law. We have noted earlier that the witan assisted the king in preparing the dooms and in safeguarding and amending custom. The dooms of the Anglo-Saxon kings, several of which are easily available in the standard collections of documents, should be consulted by the reader.[1] These dooms, which are documents similar to the Carolingian capitularies, pronounced and declared the right law. Law was, of course, always the domain of the community. King and witan (let us stress the fact again) did not make law. They stated what it had been and what it was. The preamble to the dooms of Alfred shows how Alfred and his witan accepted or rejected dooms of the past: "I, then, King Alfred, have collected these [dooms] and ordered [them] to be written down . . . and those which were not pleasing to me, by the advice of my witan I have rejected.

[1] See Carl Stephenson and F. G. Marcham, *Sources of English Constitutional History* (1937), pp. 2-22.

. . . I, then, Alfred, King of the West Saxons, have shown these dooms to all my witan, who have declared it is the will of all that they should be observed."

A strong king dominated the witan. A weak king bowed before the magnates who sat about him. Without consciously intending to do so, the witan thus kept alive the principle that the king must govern with advice. It was unfortunate for the Anglo-Saxons that the power and place of both king and witan were to be progressively weakened on the eve of the Norman Conquest. This enfeeblement resulted from the accumulation of excessive power in the hands of a few earls, local potentates who guarded and extended their controls with jealous eyes. These and other national weaknesses tempted William of Normandy, a strong ruler and a mighty robber.

THE ROYAL HOUSEHOLD

No administrative system can work successfully unless it is under-pinned by trained men, capable of active adjustment and constant vigilance. In the courts of Anglo-Saxon kings there were several men whose tasks were essentially administrative. From the days of Ethelstan (924–939) we can see some of their names and functions. It would be unwise to belittle them. They are England's first civil servants.

Even Anglo-Saxon government, a quite modest business by mod-ern standards, could not wait upon the periodical comings and go-ings of the witan. There were daily jobs to be done. It was inevitable that the kings should turn to their companions and servants in the royal household. About many of the household officials we know very little. About the important individuals we know more, especially for the century immediately preceding the Norman Conquest.

Let us first consider the chamberlain (burthegn). He was originally the keeper of the royal chamber, including the wardrobe and the royal treasure. The keeping, accounting, and expenditure of the king's treasure obviously formed a part of the routine of the house-hold. Both Edgar and Edward the Confessor had three chamberlains in office at the same time. The later Anglo-Saxon kings often had more than one officer for each office of state. There is no evidence of a specialized growth of the fiscal aspects of royal government under the Anglo-Saxons. Nevertheless, the foundations of the British Treas-ury were being laid.

A second official of the household was the chancellor. There is no evidence that the title, probably imported from the Continent, was actually used before the reign of Edward the Confessor. The office, in contrast, arose very early because Anglo-Saxon kings, usually illiterate, needed servants to act as secretaries, to compose charters and letters. Literate priests were the obvious choice for the royal clerical staff. We know the names and have the records of several of them. These ecclesiastics, or mass priests, were the forerunners of the staffs of the later chancellors. The chancellor himself kept the great seal, which first appeared in the time of Edward the Confessor and was henceforth used to authenticate the king's documents.

There were several officials of lesser importance. The stewards (disc thegns, dapiferi, seneschals) supervised the arrangements for royal food supplies and aided in collecting the royal feorm. Both stewards and butlers (byrele) attended the king's table. The stallers (later called Constables, Masters of Horse, and Marshals) first appeared in a document of 1032 and Professor L. M. Larson tells us that the office is Norse in origin. The staller originally had charge of the royal stables. His name and functions, as shown above, changed considerably in the following centuries.

Beyond the list of these officials of the household stood another servant of the king, a man of high importance called the sheriff (scir gerefa, scirman, reeve of the shire). The sheriff, by that name, does not appear until the reign of Canute (1017–1035) but we know that the office, like that of the chancellor, existed much earlier.

There were several reasons why the sheriffs came rather swiftly to power and prominence once their opportunity opened before them. All Anglo-Saxon kings wanted to maintain reliable links between the central government and the local regions, some of them far from London. At first the landed thegns, a nobility not of blood but of service, provided the kings with the linch-pins they needed between court and country. From the ranks of these thegns the king frequently appointed ealdormen, who presided over the shires or counties. As the ealdormen and later the earls grew in pride and power, they came to care less for royal interests and more for their own in both national and regional affairs. Their viceregal sway covered large areas, sometimes several counties. Political events late in the Anglo-Saxon period show clearly how the earls were becoming rapidly more powerful. They commanded the militia units of the shires; they jointly presided with the bishops over the shire courts; they obtained a third of the profits in the shire court and a third of the customs of the boroughs within their earldoms. The famous "earl's third penny" has a dark and fascinating history. These earls were thus great lords, too powerful for the safe unity of the realm. It was an ominous development.

On the eve of the Norman Conquest the king turned to the sheriffs and ordered them to perform specific duties in specific counties. If the thegns and the earls would not effectively serve the king and the central government, then the sheriffs most certainly would.

The sheriff was always a leading man in the shire. He understood local affairs and knew the people who lived in the community. Many of his changing functions will emerge more clearly later. Here it is important to note that as a royal servant, appointed by the king and responsible to him alone, the sheriff became in fact the king's main representative and administrative officer in the shire. In the absence of the earl, the sheriff presided with the bishop in the local shire court. He took over some of the duties of the earls and ealdor-men, especially the command of the local militia units. As an agent of the king he was responsible for the execution of justice in the shire, for the carrying out of the king's commands, the watching of the royal interests. He collected the king's share of court fines and fees and all other revenues due the crown. He supervised the lands and buildings of the crown. He kept the king in touch with local affairs. No matter how proud the great earls might be the sheriff reminded the lofty and the low that the shire was ruled in the name of the king alone.

In this chapter we have swiftly described the fierce and clumsy combats that finally led through crimson stains to a politically united Anglo-Saxon England. Here, at last, one king ruled over blended races and controlled diverse local loyalties. Looking back, we have also studied the nature and powers of Anglo-Saxon kingship. We have weighed the importance of custom, that accumulated wisdom which the Anglo-Saxons were certain no one man and no one hour could supply. We have written, with a brevity unfortunately not corresponding to the scale of the subject, about the nobles warmed by the rays of the king's bounty and the freemen, serfs and slaves. We have reviewed the powerful witan, the vigorous royal household, and the strength and duties of the busy and formidable sheriff. Against this background we are brought to examine such things as the local territorial divisions, the structure of local government, and the administration of law in Anglo-Saxon England. It is time now to turn to the shire, the hundred, the village and the borough.

CHAPTER II

The Anglo-Saxons:
land and law

SHIRE AND HUNDRED

WHEN students consider a fluid society such as that of the Anglo-Saxons there is always the danger that they may get lost in its details, its intricacies and obstacles, its scribblings in the corridors of time. The writer has resolutely tried to avoid confronting the reader with a recitation of too many featureless and unrelated facts. He has doubtless affronted those who still confidently believe that there is some virtue in the determined accumulation of unanchored footnotes. It was an evil hour when the serpent first tempted men to memorize lists of rigid and static statements in the blinkered belief that they were fertilizing understanding. Poor foundling facts detached from their proper patterns and processes neither confirm nor refute anything. The dominant problems of relation, of fitting things into place, of seeing what men can make happen, these alone unite to yield purpose and meaning from the midst of apparent turmoil.

The reader has now seen how a reasonably coherent state emerged after the weary wars of the Heptarchy and Danish periods. He has studied the nature of the monarchy, the class structure of society, the witan and the royal household. The trends and tempo that prevailed in the central government were also evident upon the local stages of the shire and hundred, the village and borough. Some of the decisive drives of later Anglo-Saxon influence are to be found in local government. Here, as elsewhere, the Anglo-Saxons, through disturbed and fluctuating centuries, brought into being a range of possibilities which the Normans later saw and seized upon. Almost everything the Normans achieved in local government was conditioned by influences and events from the Anglo-Saxon past. This has been of great advantage to England.

18

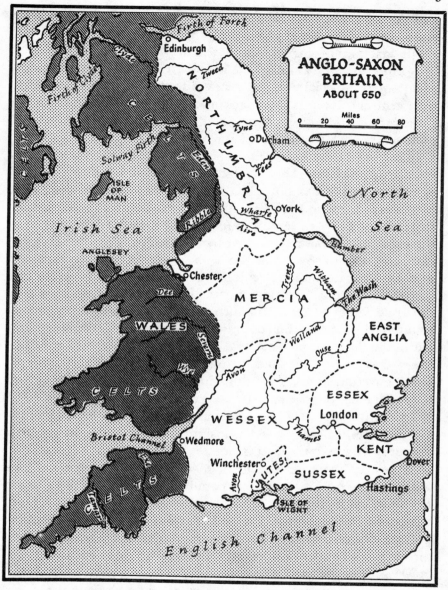

Before the Normans came several Anglo-Saxon kingdoms had gradually been divided into units called shires, mentioned earlier in these pages. With but few changes the basic structure of these local divisions has continued to the present day. The practice of creating shires, later called counties after the Norman equivalent comtés, probably began in Wessex in the seventh century. It was extended first to the eastern and western midlands, then slowly to the rest of England. Kent, Essex and Sussex today cover approximately the same territory as the ancient Anglo-Saxon kingdoms bearing those names. The East Anglian areas of Norfolk and Suffolk follow the boundaries of early tribal divisions. Many shires, especially in the east and west, take their names from their central and capital boroughs or fortress towns. In the north, the shires carved from ancient Mercia and Northumbria were quite large; some did not appear until after the Norman Conquest.

In each shire the head of the community, the commander of the militia, the official chief of the local judicial system was the ealdorman, appointed from the nobility by the king, who sometimes recognized hereditary claims to the office. By the tenth century the ealdorman frequently supervised several counties. Then, in the days of Canute, the ealdorman came to be called by the Danish name "earl." In an earlier section it was explained how the power of the earls expanded in a way dangerous to the central government. Their viceregal controls increased and the earldoms began to be passed in hereditary fashion from father to son. This menace, as we have seen, was partly countered by the extension of the powers of the sheriff, the king's servant in the shire, who took several of the duties earlier performed by the ealdorman or earl. Thus, before the Norman Conquest, the pillars of government and law in the shires were the ealdorman or earl, the sheriff, and the bishop, who declared ecclesiastical law.

The shires were used for numerous administrative, fiscal and judicial purposes. In each shire was a shire court, an assembly that met at least twice a year, the most important court below the witan. It may have been a lineal descendant of the earlier tribal folkmoot. The folkmoot had been a thoroughly popular assembly, something which the shire court, despite the opinions of some nineteenth century writers, decidedly was not. To the shire court came only the most important men of the shire, the large landowners. For many lesser freemen it was a burden to travel far and stay for long when the fields grew weedy or the harvest ripened.

The shire court dealt with both secular and ecclesiastical matters. There were no independent church courts in Anglo-Saxon England. Hence the local bishop, as mentioned earlier, sat at the sessions with the earl and the sheriff. It will be recalled that in the later Anglo-Saxon days the attendance of the earl at the shire court was becoming increasingly irregular and the sheriff was inheriting much of the earl's work in the county. Therefore the sheriff and the bishop were in fact more and more the twins of local power and prestige.

When the earl, or earlier the ealdorman, was present at the court he usually presided. If he was absent, the sheriff was chairman. If ecclesiastical cases were tried it seems that the bishop became president. The nouns "chairman" and "president" have been used above because neither the earl, sheriff, or bishop was ever a judge in a shire court. It was the assembly itself, or sometimes a part of it, that decided upon, or awarded, the method of proof. Decisions were based upon the unwritten customary law. No appeal from a decision was possible. The procedure by which the judicial decisions were obtained in the local courts is described later in the section on crime and punishment.

Below the shire, and above the village and the borough, was the territorial unit of the hundred, in the north of England known by the Danish name wapentake and in Kent and Sussex called lathe and rape. The origin of this subdivision is one of the most difficult problems of Anglo-Saxon history. Many interesting conjectures and theories have been ably presented during the last century and it is unfortunate that we cannot pause to consider them here.[1] The hundred is not mentioned by name before the reign of Edgar (959–975). Recently, scholars have inclined to the view that the hundred was deliberately developed as an administrative, financial and judicial unit intermediate between the county and the village. It was "a deliberate remodelling of administrative geography" at least in the midland regions where the hundreds were neatly divided and symmetrical. In the midlands the hundred usually contained about a hundred hides of land, or 12,000 acres. Elsewhere the shapes were irregular and the size varied considerably, from less than 20 to more than 150 hides, with the hides themselves of shifting acreage. One county contained sixty-one hundreds, another but four.

The hundred had a court that normally met every four weeks. An official appropriately called the hundredman usually presided in the hundred court. He was the agent of the earl or sheriff and probably was the direct descendant of the king's local reeve who had been very important in the history of the early Anglo-Saxon kingdoms. Most collections of documents contain the dooms of Edgar which prescribe

[1] The best discussions known to the author are in F. M. Stenton's *Anglo-Saxon England* in the *Oxford History of England* series (1943) and F. W. Maitland's classic *Domesday Book and Beyond* (1897).

several rules for the hundred courts. The student is strongly urged to read these dooms. In fact, of course, he is urged to read as many documents as possible in the whole range of English legal and constitutional history.

Like the shire court the hundred assembly administered and interpreted the customary law. Apparently any case that might be brought in the shire court might also be brought in the hundred or, as we say today, the two courts had concurrent jurisdiction. The hundred court settled local pleas and kept local order. It punished thieves and those who had been slack in their pursuit. It checked upon delinquent taxpayers and adjusted taxation. Like a modern police court, the hundred court also dealt with numerous petty cases.

In the early years of this very active and popular court all free landholders were apparently required to attend. But at the end of the Anglo-Saxon period, as in the case of the county courts, the obligation seems to have been attached only to certain large landholdings. Thus, as the number of freemen progressively declined in the kingdom, even the small local courts that once were popular assemblies were passing into the hands of those wealthy few who had laid field to field in large estates.

VILLAGE AND BOROUGH

Most Anglo-Saxons lived in small villages in the midst of agricultural areas. There were several kinds of villages and several descriptive names. There were, for example, the hams (Birmingham, Durham, Nottingham—originally a cluster of huts or homes), the tuns (Preston, Towton, etc.—tun is a word originally meaning enclosure), and the hagae (fenced tenements). The word "chester" (Chester, Manchester, Worcester) originally was the Latin castra (camp). It therefore refers to Roman settlements. The suffix "by" is Danish (Whitby, Derby); it remains in the modern "by-law."

In the villages, the basis of Anglo-Saxon social organization, there usually lived ten to thirty families, their thatched huts standing in clusters. Beyond the huts stretched the open fields, pastures, and woods. In those areas where the "open field" system existed the arable unenclosed land was divided into strips, usually separated by unploughed turf. A villager might have several strips scattered in different parts of a great open field. In free villages the villagers had individual ownership of the land they cultivated. The pasture and the woods were shared by the villagers in common and they often cut their hay from a common meadowland. In unfree villages the villagers depended upon the lord who owned all the land. They cultivated the part of the arable land not used by their lord and paid him rents and services. On the eve of the Conquest most of the villagers had ceased to be free, engulfed by the advance of the great landowners. Freemen in large numbers passed into an unfree status. Private jurisdiction and private lordship crept forward. Dependent land-holding methods multiplied. The villages were on their way to disappear for centuries in the post-Conquest manor.

Twentieth century historians perhaps realize more fully than their predecessors how tentative are the conclusions at which they arrive. Eager questions still intrude. Today there is a deep scholarly interest in the government of Anglo-Saxon villages. There is also strong disagreement among the scholars about the conclusions they have reached. The Anglo-Saxon evidence is slender, the contemporary language vague. The infallible crutches of the "facts" are too few. One famous historian ascribed considerable importance to the meetings of the villagers in a "village moot" in terms of later governmental development. A second has doubted that there was any assembly of villagers at all for economic, judicial or political purposes. A third has contented himself with saying that village agricultural policy was probably determined in an annual meeting. It is certain that in the twelfth century a priest, a reeve and four men attended some of the local hundred courts in behalf of village interests, but no one knows when this development began. In writing about Anglo-Saxon courts and assemblies Professor F. M. Stenton has stated a fact which those who have argued brilliantly by inference have sometimes forgotten: "One of the anomalies of Anglo-Saxon history is the extreme rarity of early reference to these fundamental institutions."

In the hundred and the shire also stood the urban municipality called the borough. In England today the name remains the same and the word "city" is used only to identify a borough that possesses, or has possessed, a cathedral church. Contemporary historians, especially Professors James Tait and Carl Stephenson, have debated warmly the origin and growth of these English boroughs. Professor Stephenson has concluded that there was little Anglo-Saxon commerce and but small-scale urban development; that such Anglo-Saxon boroughs as there were really had no urban character; that the origin of commercial and industrial towns was essentially a later Danish and Norman development. The conclusions of Professor Stephenson have not been accepted by the late Professor Tait or by Professors Helen Cam, F. M. Stenton and others.[2]

It has been argued by some historians, including Professor F. W. Maitland, that the original burhs (places fortified by a wall or palisade: Edinburgh, Canterbury, Salisbury, Scarborough) were royal boroughs established by Anglo-Saxon kings. These boroughs contained a special king's house where the stringent provisions of the king's peace prevailed. Later some of these boroughs were absorbed into the lands of strong nobles, among whom were such men as the mighty earls of Lincoln and Warwick. Other boroughs, such as the market town "ports," also appeared as "old" boroughs long before 1066. It seems probable that the borough had several different kinds of origin.

Whatever their several origins, the boroughs became military stations, places of refuge, avenues of opportunity for craftsmen and other laborers, profit spots for merchants, centers where borough "moots" or courts were held three times a year. Almost every borough was also a minting place. All dies were cut in London and minters or moneyers could go up to get them there. Stamped on each coin was the name of the borough where it was struck and the name of the moneyer. Some boroughs had several minters. London had more than 20; York had 12; Chester, Lincoln and Worcester had 9 each; Gloucester had 6 and Norwich 5. The coins circulated throughout the shires.

These centers with their shifting populations thus became alien communities within the shire and hundred. Professor Maitland wrote wisely of the "heterogeneous" nature of the boroughs and well noted that there was apparently little idea of corporate development and no essential principle of cohesion except the "king's peace" and the moot and the market place, where the king's sagacious agents kept their eyes on market scales. The historical development of each borough needs to be studied separately. In recent years much progress has been made by several able scholars.

Every burgess apparently held his house or his place of business in the borough directly from the king or the earls or thegns of the shire. To the king or the lord went the court tolls. The holder of a royal tenement regularly paid the "gafol" tax to the king. A "geld" was paid annually to the king by the whole borough. Sometimes the king "farmed" the tolls and profits of the market and the court to the sheriff

---

[2] See Carl Stephenson's *Borough and Town* (1933) and James Tait's *Medieval English Boroughs* (1936).

for an agreed sum. There was a very complex system of intermingled tenures, many kinds of service by which the burgess held his tenements, many tolls, taxes, rents, profits and miscellaneous "customs." Often old elements faded away and new ones appeared. Mayors and aldermen arose. On the eve of the Norman Conquest the borough was gradually tending to become a self-governing unit.

As the towns increased in wealth and prestige kings and lords were prepared to barter and to grant royal charters that made specific concessions to the burgesses. Most of the borough charters were showered down in the Norman and Angevin periods, especially during times of stern financial pressure on the crown such as those that occurred in the reigns of Richard I (1189–1199) and John (1199–1216).

A common concession was burgage tenure, entitling the burgesses to make one annual payment for the right to hold their houses, shops and the like. Sometimes the charter provided that the sheriff must not enter the borough on official business. The sums due to the king or lord were handed to the sheriff or his agent in a lump sum (the "firma burgi" or "farm" of the borough). Many other provisions will be found in the charters available in several standard collections of English constitutional and legal documents. Especially commended to the student's attention is the famous charter of Henry I (1100–1135) to the City of London, the earliest known grant of a borough in fee-farm to the burgesses. The reader is of course aware that many of the peculiar powers and privileges of several English boroughs have their legal strength and justification in the ancient charters granted by kings or powerful lords.

CRIME AND PUNISHMENT

"Modern law," said Dean Roscoe Pound, "seeks for its immediate end the administration of justice. Primitive law seeks for its immediate end the preservation of the peace. Modern law suppresses revenge; primitive law buys off revenge." The system of laws of any tribe or nation reflects the civilization, the values and attitudes of those who live under it, the shields of defense they raise against snipers within and hostile hosts without. We have already seen that Anglo-Saxon law was an involved mass of the detailed and inelastic rules of primitive and immemorial custom. Law was something that nobody made, not even the king or witan. By tradition and custom alone was the law binding. Generations of men kept in their memories the law and the judgments. By the Middle Ages immutable custom was replaced by "natural law." Later it was asserted that law existed to preserve "natural equality." Then, later still, law became the reasonable ideal of "natural rights." This concept, in turn, laid the foundations of individualism. "Let the government leave me alone while I do what I can."

Thus Anglo-Saxon law was formal, mechanical, limited in scope. It was mainly concerned in a rough age with violent wrongs to property or persons: homicides, woundings, thefts of cattle. The modern student should be sharply reminded that he is accustomed to a different kind of attitude, a different kind of law. He can then more easily remember with profit a number of points that follow from the fact that the Anglo-Saxon system was primitive and rigid, with little detailed theory.

In the childhood of the race the fettering rules of the law bound men to the savage wheel of their destinies. Obvious and formidable weaknesses inevitably resulted. No rigid legal system can prevent injustices from seeping or surging through the chinks in the barriers. Its machinery is powerless to provide remedies for more than a limited number of wrongs, and these must be of certain kinds and qualities. For instance, no inflexible system of law can ever make allowance for intent: what happens in a man's mind before he acts. English law moved with hesitation towards the crucial concept of liability directly related to such elements as intention and negligence.

A young man who enters a law school today will rapidly discover that there is a wide province of modern law called "torts," a field concerned with intention, negligence, and a large part of the whole region of civil wrongs and liabilities. More precisely, a tort may be defined as a civil wrong other than a breach of contract for which an action now lies at common law. Massive volumes on torts and contracts are ranged along the corridors through which the student moves towards his law degree. It must be admitted with melancholy that there is no *general principle* of liability in modern law and probably none can ever be established. The law of torts can never be codified. But today, at least, we have moved far beyond the narrow perimeters set by the complex mechanical rules, the "iron laws" that stood at the very core of Anglo-Saxon society.

Nor were these the only elements in Anglo-Saxon law that maimed or sapped the idea and practice of justice. For instance, there was no distinction between what later came to be called civil and criminal cases. All were fused together. Secondly, Anglo-Saxon courts never sought to investigate "the facts in the case," to use the tools of evidence, to hear witnesses (except in certain cases of property transfers such as cattle sales). By crude tests or ordeals the judgment of God was obtained. There was never room for discretion. The root of the trouble was the cumbersome rigidity of the law. No one dared challenge the rules. Were they not the sacred product of custom, of slow time? The voice of the law was final, supremely positive and often very wrong.

The reason for the existence of any court is the enforcement of certain legal principles or general doctrines. The rules based upon these principles form the essential substance of the law and hence unite to make what is called substantive law. Thus the substantive law of the Anglo-Saxons consisted of the dooms plus unwritten remembered custom. In addition to substantive law there must be rules determining the structure of the courts and the procedure to be used to enforce the commandments of substantive law. These rules are called adjective law, because they stand outside the substance of the law itself like an adjective stands outside a noun.

Let us now examine more closely the substantive law of the Anglo-Saxons and the complicated pattern of the procedural activities of the courts. The written laws of Anglo-Saxon England begin with the dooms of Ethelbert of Kent (560–616) and end with those of Canute (1017–1035). Within the five centuries between these two events several strong kings like Ine (688–726), Alfred (871–899), and Edgar (959–975) brought together a series of rules, written fragments of the great body of customary law. Rescued from oblivion by scholars, these dooms tell us much about the organs and usages of Anglo-Saxon government and law.

Anglo-Saxon justice was administered in several places: the central witan and the local county, hundred, borough, and lords' courts. The reader will recall that earlier passages have described and explained the basic functions and composition of both the witan and the regional assemblies. It must be emphasized again that in Anglo-Saxon England there were none of the modern distinctions between the executive, legislative and judicial aspects of government. All courts were both judicial and administrative bodies. All courts were in theory, and usually in practice, courts of first instance. There was no appeal from one court to another. Sometimes, however, as shown in the dooms of Canute, the shire court heard a case when men claimed that they were unable to obtain justice in a hundred court. Similarly, the king and the witan occasionally heard cases allegedly blocked in the county courts. But these were unusual events. Most of the time the courts moved along the separate paths marked out by hallowed custom.

It has been held by some scholars that beyond the shire and hundred courts there were effective deterrents to crime in the local arrangements, sometimes rather haphazard, for the detection and apprehension of criminals. In early Anglo-Saxon days, as these pages have shown, a kindred was often regarded as legally responsible for the behavior of all its members. The lot of the "kinless" man was hard before the kindred control was replaced by territorial and lordship surveillance and protection. In the middle of the tenth century a widely quoted law of King Edgar (759–775) provided that "men shall ride forth in pursuit of thieves. If there is pressing need, notice shall be given to the hundred-man and he shall then inform the tithing-men; and they shall all go forth, whither God may direct them, to find [the criminals]." The law also required that every man "shall be under surety," being placed in pledge by someone of good reputation who would be responsible for bringing him into court if he should be accused of a crime.

Professor Felix Liebermann and others have seen in the "tithing" passage of the dooms of Canute a reference to a group of ten or twelve men from one settlement united for mutual surety and held to collective responsibility for the apprehension of criminals. ("It is our will that every freeman above the age of twelve shall be brought within hundred and tithing if he wishes to be law-worthy. . . .") Professor W. A. Morris and several other scholars are strongly of the opinion that the "tithing" referred to in the dooms of Edgar and Canute was entirely territorial and had nothing to do with what was a later protective measure imposed upon Englishmen by the occupying Normans. Other authorities assert that the tithing foreshadows the Norman frankpledge system by which neighbors within a township were mutually obliged to report to the hundred court all crimes committed within their territory and to produce the men accused. Whether or not there is any final answer to these questions, it is certainly true that to an increasing extent the communal voice of the neighborhood and the responsibility of the lord for members of his household provided more surety for the lawful man "worthy of his law and his wer," and made harder the way of the transgressor.

Most cases were settled in shire and hundred courts and there the procedure was inflexible, incapable of expansion. First of all, the defendant was called into court by the accuser, who followed a carefully prescribed formula of summons. If the defendant refused to come he was fined. If he still refused to come he might be outlawed and then slain on sight.

Let us now suppose that Wulf, accused by Breca of stealing a cow, did not evade the summons but came at once to court. The plaintiff Breca would then state his case, swearing a formal and customary fore-oath: "By the Lord before whom this holy thing is holy, I thus bring my charge with full folk-right, without deceit and without malice and without any guile whatsoever, that stolen from me was this cow, which I claim and which I seized in the possession of Wulf."

After Breca had thus sworn, the defendant Wulf would in turn swear a formal oath of rebuttal: "By the Lord . . . I am guiltless, both in thought and deed, of the accusation made against me by Breca."

The oaths of charge and denial had to be delivered according to the set form, with verbal accuracy and without stammering. If a slip occurred and "the oath burst" then clearly God was pointing to the swearer's guilt. *Qui melius probat melius habet.* In a deeply religious age the whole court procedure was a solemn affair. He was a brazen fellow who could lie before his assembled neighbors, affront God and imperil his soul.

If the two oaths described above had been taken successfully the men assembled in the courts usually settled upon further measures designed to reveal the guilt or innocence of the accused. The only "judgment" the court ever gave was the decision as to what method of "proof" should be used. Once the "proof" process was stipulated and set in train the court did nothing but watch to see that the rules of procedure were followed.

In the next phase, guilt or innocence was revealed by the use of oaths or ordeals. Let us now suppose that the court decided to "award the proof" to the defendant Wulf and required him to find oath-helpers to a certain number who would swear that Wulf's oath was true. In early Anglo-Saxon days only a man's kinsmen could be his oath-helpers. Later all law-worthy men might swear. The oath-helpers who swore their oaths need not know anything about the facts of the case. In this method of settlement, later called compurgation, the oath-helpers had to be willing to endanger their souls by swearing with the accused: "By the Lord . . . the oath which Wulf has sworn is clean and without falsehood." Fear of God's punishment was supposed to make a man reluctant to swear in support of a bad or doubtful character. If a man could not get a sufficient number of men to support his oath he lost his case. Usually a man making proof in this fashion was asked to produce six, twelve or twenty-four oath-helpers. The value of an oath varied according to a man's rank in society. The oath of a thegn, as noted earlier, was equal to the oath of six ceorls.

In later Anglo-Saxon days, when communities became enlarged and life grew more complex, the oath-helping system was badly abused. Perjury flourished. Despite these facts, there were appeals to compurgation—the clearing of an accused person by the oaths of others—until the seventeenth century, especially in the ecclesiastical courts. Since then the oath-helping procedure has been used but once in England: in the case of Rex *v.* Williams in 1824.

Anglo-Saxon courts also used the ordeal, a deliberate appeal to God to show where the guilt lay. There was no place for modifying pleas. Nor could there be any debate about questions of law and questions of fact, so important in the later growth of the common law. Several kinds of ordeals were used. In each case solemn religious ceremonies were conducted by the priest who prayed that God "disclose the fullness of truth." In the ordeal of hot iron a man carried a piece of hot iron in his hand a certain number of feet, the distance usually varying with the seriousness of the charge. The hand was then bound and sealed. "And after the third day it shall be inspected to see whether within the sealed wrapping, it is foul or clean." If a hand was healing cleanly, the man was innocent; if not, he was guilty. "And if anyone breaks these provisions, the ordeal shall be a failure for him, and he shall pay a fine of 120 shillings to the king."

In the ordeal of hot water a man was required to pick a stone out of a pot of boiling water; then his hand was bound and the same procedure followed as in the case of the ordeal by hot iron. Another type of ordeal was by cold water. An accused man was bound and thrown into a pool blessed by a priest. If he sank in the consecrated water, he was innocent. If he floated he was guilty because the pure water had refused to accept him. In the ordeal of cosned, a piece of bread was adjured to choke the swearer of a false oath. This, "the ordeal of the cursed morsel," was not widely used. All such methods of determining guilt or innocence may seem to the modern student to be quite irrational. And yet, in the Anglo-Saxon age, there were probably few guilty men who would refuse to confess their guilt when the alternative appeared to be a direct challenge to God or the eternal damnation of their souls through a combination of guilt and perjury.

At this point the reader may ask why no reference has been made to ordeal by battle. The answer can be swiftly given. Battle tests, like the ordeals by fire and water, were considered appeals to God. Christian missionaries were opposed to the wager of physical combat. They refused to bless the weapons. Obviously no appeal could be made to God with unblessed tools of slaughter. Hence ordeal by battle ended in England with the coming of Christianity. After 1066 it came back again from Normandy. In Norman and Angevin days wager by battle became a familiar method of proof in disputes about the ownership of land. Great landowners sometimes hired professional champions to do battle for them. As a matter of fact, however, not many disputes went all the way to the final step of blood and battle. Very few combats actually took place. By the middle of the thirteenth century it is quite clear that the method of proof by the battle ordeal is seldom thought of, seldom used. Not until 1819 was ordeal by battle abolished by statute.

Students who consult the texts of dooms in standard collections of documents will find that many of the clauses provided for fines and compensations for certain crimes of violence. For serious crimes the punishment was often mutilation. "Counterfeiters," state the dooms of Ethelred (978–1016), "shall [each] lose a hand." About 690 the dooms of Ine declared: "If a ceorl has often been accused of theft and is finally proved guilty he shall have his hand or foot cut off."

Imprisonment was seldom used as a method of punishment. Few buildings were solid enough to be adequate jails. Usually, as the dooms show, the punishment was in the form of fines. By this procedure the injured party obtained compensation. The carefully calculated compensation for damages or injuries of any kind was called a bot. For example, by the dooms of Ethelbert of Kent (560–616) it was provided that compensation for minor injuries should be as follows: one eye, 50 shillings; one ear, 12 shillings; a front tooth, 6 shillings; a big toe, 10 shillings; for hitting a man on the nose with a fist, 3 shillings; for seizing a man by the hair, 2½ shillings.

In another context references have been made to the importance of the idea of kindred, the basic blood-tie among men. In early Anglo-Saxon days this concept was highly significant. Later, as has been explained, new ideas of lordship, of territory and neighborhood, reduced the importance of the bonds of kinship. For several centuries, however, crimes against the person of an individual often involved his whole family. Thus the kin of a man killed by violence were compensated by a wergeld, supposed to represent the value of the slain man's life. Reference has been made to the fact that the higher a man's rank in society the higher was his wergeld. Sometimes, if found guilty of a major crime, an individual was required to pay a fine equal to his wergeld to redeem his own life. "If a thief is captured in the act of thieving," say the dooms of Ine, "let him suffer death or redeem his life through payment of his wergeld."

There was also a fine called a wite, mentioned earlier. This was a penal fine payable to the king or some other public authority because the state had been sinned against. Sometimes, by the process of outlawry, the whole community waged war on an offender. Sometimes, too, legal permission was given to an injured man or his kindred to begin a blood-feud and thus obtain self-redress and vengeance. In the later Anglo-Saxon period both blood-revenge and outlawry were being gradually replaced by the less savage solutions provided by wergeld, bot and wite.

LAND AND LORDSHIP

In the latter part of the Anglo-Saxon period all land was held by folkland or bookland title. Folkland was once defined as the common property of the nation. Nineteenth century authorities concluded that folkland was held without any written title but by the folkright, the remembered laws or customs of the community. In the 1890's Professor Paul Vinogradoff and others were certain that folkland might be finally defined as land held under common or folk law. Professor F. W. Maitland stated clearly that folkland did not mean that there were any particular attributes attached to the land itself, only that the land was held by unwritten title. It was pointed out that the term "folkland" occurs only in one doom and two charters. It was clear that the written law had little to say about it. Disputes about possession were settled by the process of oath and ordeal in the folkmoots, the local courts of the shire and hundred. Folkland could not be given away by will or testament of any kind; it could not be alienated without the permission of the witan; its inheritance was determined by custom and custom alone.

This explanation of folkland seems simple enough. The reader who has digested it may be troubled to learn that several problems of folkland are still perplexing scholars. Much doubt has been expressed about the dovetailed explanations of earlier authorities.

It is always difficult to avoid seeing in a landscape or a document what you have been taught to look for or what you wish to find. Students of history are human beings. They may be certain themselves that they are making inferences from the documents before them but in reality they may be selecting facts to illustrate conclusions their minds and emotions have reached long before. That may be the root of the errors we find in the writing and research of our forefathers. Our grandsons may find the same kind of thing afoot in our assumptions and settled conclusions. In any event, the conclusions of Professor Vinogradoff and Professor Maitland on the subject of folkland are not fully accepted today. There are too many obstructions in the framework of the earlier ideas. The arguments are not clinched to our satisfaction.

Recently Professor F. M. Stenton has provided some answers that have hitherto been lacking. What he says possesses an advantage modern scholars prize: the merit of establishing after an examination of all the available evidence a calculated explanation that apparently fits all the known facts. After declining to accept the heavy paragraphs that have weighted textbooks for sixty years Professor Stenton puts forward, with delightful economy of words, his definition of folkland: "Folkland is land subject to the rents and services (feorm) by which the whole people once maintained its king." Here, it seems, concreteness has been loaded back into the problem and the answer. Moreover, as Professor J. E. A. Jolliffe has shown, by the tenth and eleventh centuries the holder of folkland seems to have been increasingly free from customary rules hindering the free disposal of land. He is of the opinion that the Saxons' folkland rights, on the eve of the Norman Conquest, were very close to absolute property rights. These new conclusions about the nature of folkland may be destroyed tomorrow but they stand today.

The nature of bookland differed considerably from folkland. The latter stock of English land law comes from Teutonic custom. Bookland, on the other hand, was foreign, Latin and clerical. As the name shows, bookland was land held by a written title recorded in a royal book or charter. Professor W. H. Stevenson has proved that the written Anglo-Saxon charters that created and governed bookland were derived from private charters used in the later Roman Empire. About forty charters issued in Anglo-Saxon England between 600 and 750 still exist and are clearly based upon the Roman form of conveyance. The introduction of these written instruments to show land grants was probably the work of the famous theologian and archbishop of Canterbury, Theodore of Tarsus (668–690). The oldest English charter of which we have any knowledge was made in May, 674. There is abundant evidence that the practice of using charters to record land conveyance spread rapidly through southern England and then, more slowly, into the north.

It is unlikely that much will be added to the results produced by Professor F. W. Maitland's solid and circumspect scholarship in the intricate passages about bookland published in *Domesday Book and Beyond*. When the king gave bookland, said Professor Maitland, he gave it "for good and all." As Maitland has also noted, the gift of land was usually a reward for a thegn's faithful and obedient service. No question could be raised about bookland except in the witan itself. Bookland was under the protection of the king, the witan and the church. Damnation waited upon him who violated a charter. "Whereas the fashion of this world **passeth away**," runs the language of one land grant, "but the joys of heaven are eternal, therefore I give land to my thegn so that he may enjoy it during his life and leave it on his death to whomever he pleases, and if anyone come against this charter may he perish forever. I have confirmed this gift with the sign of Christ's holy cross."

If the donee ever fled in battle or otherwise failed in his duty or committed a crime, the land went back to the king. The Normans later were to say that the land "escheated." Such sad events seldom occurred. The book or charter usually stated that the land was given in perpetuity or, to repeat Maitland's phrase, "for good and all." Bookland could be alienated and inherited without let or hindrance from anybody. Normally it was exempted from all public burdens except the *trinoda necessitas*, that triple duty of primitive origin mentioned earlier (the responsibility for army service, repairing strongholds, building and repairing bridges). As a matter of minor interest it may be noted here that the term *trinoda necessitas* was brought into the language of historians by John Selden's mis-reading of a forged tenth century document.

Future scholars may decide that the removal of numerous obligations from bookland was a matter of high importance. The position of Professor F. M. Stenton today may be taken by others tomorrow. He says: "It still remains an open question whether the distinction between bookland and folkland may not after all turn on the simple fact that bookland, unlike folkland, was land exempt from the heaviest of public burdens by royal charter."

Many Anglo-Saxon kings gave large tracts of land to that great landlord, the church. They may have felt that land devoted to the service of God would bring spiritual benefits and perhaps pave the royal way to paradise. Several hundred ecclesiastical title deeds or charters exist to show how much land was conveyed to the church. For example, when the Normans came to England in 1066 the church held one-quarter of the county of Worcester. It should be noted, however, that bishops, abbots and other men of the church usually did not have the same free right of alienation as laymen. Much church land was in the form of rigid permanent endowments for sacred purposes. The rules of the bequests could not be broken although sometimes they could be made elastic. Of course the church did not depend solely upon the land for its economic power. Although there was no abundance of liquid capital in Anglo-Saxon England the church still had many sources of income. For instance, most free men made "church-scot" payments in kind (such as grain, chickens, and hogs) in proportion to their land holdings. This custom later yielded to the tithing system. There was also the "soul-scot" levy whereby a portion of a dead man's goods was given to the parish priest in return for prayers. For each team in the parish one penny ("plough alms") was paid to the church after Easter. These are only three examples of the numerous ways in which the body economic of the church was nourished.

There are technical reasons why no fully adequate and accurate definition can be given here of the form of land tenancy called laenland or loanland. We can pause to say only that laenland was originally a tenancy at will, a temporary gift on condition of service, or a loan for a term of lives, usually three or five. The church frequently used the device of laenland to grant for a limited period property that it could not alienate. Sometimes, to give greater stability to a laen, kings and bishops converted laenland into bookland for a specified term. They used, like the famous Bishop Oswald of Worcester, the clumsy but delightful fiction of conveying "eternal inheritance for three lives," at the end of which period the land reverted to the grantor.

These paragraphs about methods of landholding help to explain a parallel development. We have already seen how the fluid class structure of Anglo-Saxon England was based on land, birth and service.

Many tribal customs, some of them stretching back into ancient mists, doubtless contributed to the rise of Anglo-Saxon lords on the one hand and the various dependent classes on the other. Several scholars have carefully examined the Continental bodyguard arrangement usually called the *comitatus* or comradeship and some have concluded that here are to be found the roots of the personal relationship between lords and dependents that later grew into the practice of lordship and vassalage. In this book we need not explore the possible sources of Anglo-Saxon lordship. It is enough to say that it was quite natural that in the long years of disturbance and conflict some lords would steadily extend their economic, military and political power by laying field to field and increasing the number of their followers. Freemen and small landowners, bruised by war and disorder, often sought the protection of powerful magnates. Men who put themselves by private transactions under the leadership and protection of the lords were said to "commend" themselves. The lord received personal service and in return he gave security. This process of commendation was obviously a source of mounting strength to the lordship system. Private power grew.

There was a second way in which the strength, stature, and superiority of the lords increased. Slowly they multiplied and extended their private jurisdictions, their franchises, their immunities at the expense of the crown on the one hand and the free landowners on the other. There appeared the royal custom of granting specific rights, franchises, or immunities to bishops, abbots, thegns and earls. Favored subjects of the king obtained charters that provided for the alienation of several public rights such as tolls, market fees, forest privileges, rents, profits of justice, and sometimes jurisdiction itself. These mighty subjects thus proceeded to exercise powers hitherto possessed only by the king or the "state." Whole hundreds were sometimes conveyed to certain lords. In 904, for instance, King Edward gave the Bishop of Winchester very great "liberties" in the large and famous estate at Taunton. Such franchises or immunities were to become the main roots of private jurisdiction in England.

Among the rights frequently given to the lords were those called "sake" and "soke." (Sake: A. S. *sacu,* a cause, a matter in dispute, hence the right to have a court and do justice; soke: A. S. *socn,* a "seeking" or "making suit," hence the duty of tenant to "seek" or "sue" at his lord's court and the right of the lord to hold a court.) The lord's right of "sake and soke" (or "sac and soc") might be exercised over a village or a group of villages: all depended on the terms of the royal grant. Of course, as Professor F. W. Maitland and others have remarked, the right to hold a court was really a fiscal rather than a jurisdictional right. After all, the lord was not the judge in the court; it was the tenants or "suitors" who made the judgments. But the lord did preside and he did take the profits.

These "sake and soke" rights could only be claimed by virtue of a specific royal grant. Such rights never arose as a result of relations between a lord and his tenants. For instance, a lord often did not have "sake and soke" rights over his villeins; they were frequently, of course, under the jurisdiction of the hundred court. But if the lord did possess "sake and soke" rights by charter over the region in which the tenants lived, then the tenants were indeed "sokemen" bound to attend the "hall-moot" or manorial or seignorial court of their lord. If the lord held "soke" over a whole hundred, then the hundred court became the lord's court, a place where the king's sheriff might not come, a place where all the profits went to the lord. It was generous of Canute to give his wife Emma "sake and soke" rights over eight of the hundreds of England.

Thus a man might be bound to a lord by a personal bond, by a tenurial bond, and by a justiciary bond. On the other hand, he might be linked to a lord by only one of those bonds and not by the others.

There were other specific powers often granted by royal charter to certain lords. For example, the right of "toll and team" meant the right of the lord to take a percentage or payment from the sale of cattle or other goods made on the lord's estate (toll) and to hold a court in which accused men could prove their rightful possession of cattle or other goods (team). Lords who did not possess full "sake and soke" rights were sometimes given the specific authority to do justice upon thieves seized within their estates while in possession of stolen property. These are but a few of the many kinds of franchises and immunities bestowed by royal charter upon the lords of Anglo-Saxon England.

This brief description of bookland, folkland, commendation and immunities should show that the changes in late Anglo-Saxon England were even more remarkable than earlier passages suggested. It is clear that these changes were essentially feudal in character. The use of the word "feudal" in this connection will remind several readers of the modern scholarly controversies about the "feudal elements" in the England of Edward the Confessor's day. From the point of view of the scholar such problems and disputes are neither trivial nor temporary. The body of evidence that has been discovered by the probing expert is growing larger and learned conjecture and conflict proceed apace.

The average undergraduate student may not consult any of the standard works describing in detail the numerous alterations in the structure of Anglo-Saxon England. Nevertheless, he should be sharply aware of the swift pace of change in the decades before the Normans came to conquer England in 1066. Secondly, he should recognize the fact that these changes were creating disastrous situations within the state. On the eve of the Norman Conquest, the Anglo-Saxon kingship was being steadily weakened by the unabated challenge of the nobles, by the desperate frailty of Edward the Confessor, by the creeping paralysis of the administrative machinery. We have already remarked that the freeman class, so long the spine of the social, political and economic body, was being silently eroded. In an hour of crisis the leaders of Anglo-Saxon England joined the great and discouraging company of those who failed. There is no mistaking the incessant currents of peril swirling about the forlorn foundations of the state.

Such was the setting of the stage, such the cast of the players, when the Normans came in 1066. It would be imprudent to speculate on what might have happened had William of Normandy not crossed the narrow seas. Such facile speculation belongs to an already overcrowded realm. The important fact is that in 1066 the first period of English constitutional and legal history ended abruptly. The Normans brought new forces, new ideas and new power. Sir Maurice Amos once called the Norman Conquest "that fundamental mercy which secured for England, long before any European country, a united kingdom under a vigorous and gifted race of rulers." Perhaps the quotation of this distinguished scholar's words is to look at the distant mountains before we have found our path through the lower forests. It is to these lower forests, to the story of the constitutional and legal achievements of the Normans, that we must now turn.

CHAPTER III

The Normans:

peace by power

FEUDAL FOUNDATIONS

THE Norman Conquest of 1066 opened new and significant phases of constitutional development. William the Conqueror (1066–1087), that grandchild of the Northland fiord, systematically established strong royal powers and found able servants to make that strength effective.

Led by William, the vigorous and capable Normans succeeded in bringing about a new order, a revolution in the social structure. The conquerors had the power to make radical changes. They had rather precise conceptions of what they wanted. Because they were mature and practical men, trained in the skills of the Continent, they lost no time in moving towards their goals. The chief servants of the royal household were Normans. No Anglo-Saxon was appointed to any high office in the church. When William died there were only two English bishops and two English abbots. Only a few sheriffs were Englishmen. The sullen north was cowed. Great Norman castles were built at strategic points in England and along the Welsh border. The result of all this was an immense profit in lives and time.

Now the hour was at hand for the introduction of customs and institutions prevalent in the duchy of Normandy and common to Western Europe. From their homeland the Normans brought the ideas of full-grown feudalism and all the peculiar implications contained in the flexible concept of the feudal contract. In Anglo-Saxon England there had indeed been approaches to feudal arrangements, as in the practice of "commendation." But there had been no genuine feudalism, no national tenurial and social organization in which duties and rights were precisely defined. Society in England was now to be organized according to a man's relation to the land, then the chief source of power, wealth and prestige. Before we consider the tangled skein of events that were about to be spun into history it is wise to examine, step by step, something of the nature of the feudal institutions now imported from Normandy and destined to be so significant in English history. The Normans were no amateurs in the art of war. Nor were they amateurs in the strategy of government.

The term "feudalism" clearly implies a scheme of things based upon fiefs (feuda): lands held of a superior in fee or on conditions of military service. Long before the eleventh century the ancient Frankish ceremony of homage, soon to be linked to the Christian oath of fealty, created the binding ties of vassalage and lordship. In this sacred act of homage the man about to become a vassal knelt bareheaded in fidelity and reverence and placed his hands between those of his lord. In becoming a vassal an individual swore that he would be the lord's "man" and would "bear faith to you of life and members and earthly honor against all other men, saving the faith I hold to our Lord King." The lord, for his part, bound himself to give his vassal justice and protection.

Thus lord and man were presumably bound in mutual and honorable loyalty. By the eleventh century the act of homage usually meant that the vassal received lands from his lord in return for which he gave special services. Hence the contract of homage almost invariably set up land tenure. Of course, a man who had not been given a fief might be a vassal still. But there could never be a fief without a vassal to hold it. In England, in William's day and for long after, there was to be no man without his lord and almost every man held land of his lord, on certain fixed and specified conditions.

Once, not so long ago, historians could write freely about "the feudal system," quite unhampered by doubts as to the wisdom of using such a term. Today we know that the so-called "feudal system" was in fact very unsystematic indeed, even though it does not deserve to be called, as it has been, "legalized anarchy." Feudal contracts varied from country to country, from region to region, from age to age. Feudalism was a growing thing; it was lively and flexible; it was never fixed and frozen; it never stood still. There were many kinds of local arrangements, diverse local customs, individual agreements reached by particular negotiations. Such variations are characteristic of all proliferating organic growths.

One feudal principle, already mentioned, remained intact and constant: the principle that tenants held land from their lords under a system of primogeniture in return for certain services. These services, despite the diverse kinds of contracts, were always carefully defined. Lords and vassals in a feudal community were bound together not only by social, military and economic ties but also by the legal bonds that made these ties precise and effective. This was the very essence of feudalism.

For more than two centuries the institution of feudalism worked in England and it worked with considerable success. One of the main reasons for its long survival was the active idea it contained of the mutual obligations of all men. In the intricate network of rights and duties everybody was responsible to somebody else. Nobody was entirely free. The custom was the community custom and nobody had a right to change it. In those days custom, law and right were usually held to be synonymous. One result of these customary and contractual relationships was a more closely integrated society than England had ever known. The mental attitude born of this scheme of things became a powerful force in shaping the actions of Englishmen for many centuries. It is no accident that the ideas of contracts, rights and duties appear again and again in the tide of English affairs.

William the Conqueror, so "stark, stern, and wrathful," held that the Anglo-Saxons had forfeited their lands. A large part of those confiscated acres he kept for himself. The crown was the largest landowner in every county. Included in the royal demesne of William and his successors were about seventy forests, carefully protected by kings who liked to hunt the royal stags. In these royal forests, the forest laws, forerunners of the later obnoxious game laws, were enforced by special courts, odious to the people. Under William I a king's subject who killed a deer was blinded; under his successors the penalty was death. In addition to the broad forest lands thousands of acres of fields and meadows remained in the royal hands.

Out of these lands the king obtained large revenues. They were his, and his alone. This fact helped the king and his government to remain independent so long as the royal revenues kept pace with the ordinary costs of government. In a distant future day the expenses of government were to outrun the royal income from land and other sources. Then the crown was to discover that its strength was being steadily drained away. The power of the purse, always of massive importance, had passed to other hands. But this development came long after William I had been buried in his church at Caen.

The land not retained by William for himself was parcelled out among his principal followers in pieces large and small. All these grants were made by feudal contracts. A tenant's "ownership" of land was always limited by his obligations. For instance, the tenants-in-chief, those holders of land directly of the king (*in capite*), very commonly held their lands by military tenure alone. These great and powerful vassals were obliged, as holders of "knights' fees," to supply the king with a specified number of fully equipped mounted soldiers or knights once a year for a designated length of time, usually forty days.

Churchmen, on the other hand, sometimes held land by a kind of legal fiction called frankalmoign, or free alms, tenure. By this arrangement land was held without any services attached except religious tasks, such as prayers for the soul of the grantor or those of his ancestors. But most of the broad fields enjoyed by bishops and abbots, the lords spiritual of England, were held under the same conditions of tenure as the lands of the lay barons. After all, great churchmen were indeed the king's vassals and for the "baronies" of their endowments they were as much responsible to the king as anybody else. A special agreement exempted them from personal military service and they gathered their quotas of knights to aid the king from their own sub-tenants on the fief.

The lower holdings within the royal grants to nobles were often held by tenures that involved some kinds of non-military service, including the payment of several feudal dues, such as the aids and reliefs to be described later. One of the most important of these was called "socage" tenure, where money payments and certain non-military services were rendered to the lord in return for land.

As in Anglo-Saxon days, many a man in Norman England obtained and held "soke" rights—the power to hold court and do justice with the franchise to receive the fees or fines arising from his jurisdiction over certain territories or certain men (sokemen). Under the Anglo-Saxon kings, free socage had been the most common and important of free, non-noble tenures. After the Conquest the freeholders of England normally held land by one of the numerous socage tenures and of these free socage (or fee farm), the predecessor of the modern freehold, remained most significant and popular. In medieval England the word "socage" thus meant the status, holding or tenure of a

sokeman. Later, the meaning of the word changed and for a very good reason.[1]

In feudal England the same individual might hold different pieces of land by many different tenures. A great noble, for instance, some-

---

[1] See F. W. Maitland, *Domesday Book and Beyond*, pp. 66 ff.

times held land on socage tenure of a lesser lord. As a result of this "divorce of tenure and personal status" it was not possible to describe an acreage of land by referring to the status of the tenant. Gradually, therefore, pieces of land began to be identified by the services attached to them. "Service due from each particular piece of land," as Professor D. J. Medley once remarked, "came to be everything." So it was that "socage" ceased to mean the "status, holding or tenure of a sokeman." Instead, it came to mean any tenure having the incidents of such tenure: fealty, relief and escheat, with freedom from scutage, wardship, and marriage payments and obligations. The road was thus clear to the freehold or "fee simple" estate concepts described later in this chapter.

Very frequently we observe the form of non-military service called "serjeanty." This kind of tenure usually involved the performance of some duty at court. It might require, for example, the filling of an office in the royal household or administration. These serjeanties (called "grand" serjeanties for honorable service and "petty" serjeanties for menial) increased steadily in the Norman and Angevin period as the machinery of government expanded. Side by side with the manors that were feudal endowments for military purposes stood the manors granted for various administrative activities. The serjeanties, as Professor George Burton Adams once remarked, "endowed the civil servants of the feudal age."

William directly controlled the granting of land to his barons. He distributed the main allotments so that there were few large compact territorial units. Most of the holdings of his tenants-in-chief consisted entirely of isolated manors or groups of manors scattered widely over England. In some cases this was perhaps less the result of policy than of accident. It is significant, however, that William did not revive the great Anglo-Saxon earldoms of Wessex and Northumbria.

William was at once both the king of England and the head of the feudal hierarchy. He did not propose to see his great power diminish. For instance, he kept the Anglo-Saxon fyrd, the old militia or general levy of the ordinary freemen, to supplement and be independent of the mercenary warriors and the knights' fee services provided by his barons. If the barons became refractory, as they did in 1173, for example, the fyrd could be mobilized by the monarchy. William was determined to be master in his kingdom. He would not have his barons behaving like the "tall trees of the feudal forest" in France. He clearly understood the natural feudal tendency towards rebellion, the natural ambitions of some of the great and powerful men of his realm. He knew that effective government could only be maintained if the barons never dared to disobey or defy the king. A weak central government always meant strong and often irresponsible barons. The result in later days was frequently revolt, lawlessness, and all the chaotic evils attendant upon the rise of unbridled power among the local magnates. But so long as William ruled in England there was small chance of feudal disorder.

On rare occasions the Conqueror departed from his custom of keeping full control of the lands of his feudal barons. Norman and Angevin kings often found it a difficult task to defend the border areas in the west and north. Hence it seemed desirable to set up strong "buffer states" in the marches. In a few of these regions feudal magnates were given prerogatives elsewhere kept by the king. For many centuries such territories have been called "palatine" lands, and the word "palatine" still denotes an unusual position in the national scheme of government, an exercise of local sovereignty in a large area.

The word "palatine" is derived from the Latin *palatium,* a palace. In Merovingian and Carolingian France important governors and judges were often called "palatine counts." When the Frankish Empire disintegrated several nobles, swift in usurping power, obtained the same title. In England the name was used from the reign of William I.

Several English regions became distinguished as palatinates. In the county of Durham, for example, palatine powers were claimed by the bishops of Durham. These claims, confirmed by Norman and Angevin kings in the interests of defense against the Scotsmen, still survive in altered form in the twentieth century. The county of Cheshire, another palatinate created by William the Conqueror, has not passed away. The Earl of Chester owed William allegiance but otherwise, like the Bishop of Durham, the earl was a sovereign ruler. In 1351 Edward III made Henry, the fourth Earl of Lancaster (who became Henry IV in 1399) a duke with palatine rights and liberties. The ducal dignity and palatinate have descended through Henry IV to the present House of Windsor.

What was the nature and scope of the palatine powers once fully possessed by the Bishop of Durham, the Earl of Chester, the Duke of Lancaster and others? The holders of palatinates, those subordinate regalities within a larger franchise, could levy taxes and raise armies (except Lancaster). They had their own courts of justice exercising the same jurisdiction as did the king's courts in other parts of the realm. In Lancaster, for instance, no writs could run in the county except those issued by the Duke's chancellor. The royal justices held no courts there. The judges were appointed under the Duke of Lancaster's seal and all cases were tried in his courts of common law, chancery or exchequer. Such were some of the palatine powers.

The revolution of 1399, as noted earlier, brought the Duchy of Lancaster under royal control. The duchy is still considered an entity separate from the estates of the crown proper, still independently administered by a Duchy Council and a Court of Duchy Chamber. In recent years a few changes have been made. The powers of the Court of Duchy Chamber were reduced in 1873 when civil and criminal jurisdiction in the county were transferred to the national High Court of Justice. The Chancellor of the Duchy is now but a political appointee, far fallen from his once high estate. Nevertheless, he still possesses many unusual powers. For instance, he appoints all justices of the peace for the whole county. "The roots of the present lie deep in the past."

RIGHTS AND OBLIGATIONS

The reader will remember that in Anglo-Saxon England many men "commended" themselves to strong leaders. Land and protection were better, surely, than the profitless dangers of independence. In Norman England, too, the facts were clear: a few strong men of the aristocracy had large grants of land and, on the other hand, many landless men wanted land, protection, security and justice. The latter gravitated to the lords who would give them these things in return for loyalty and specified service.

When England was partitioned by William the Conqueror his tenants-in-chief obviously could not keep and operate all their holdings. Some land they did hold for themselves and kept the income. Usually they let out a large part of their acres to lesser tenants or rear vassals. This process of subletting or enfeoffing vassals is usually called subinfeudation. It continued downwards through the social strata from the great baron who held a hundred manors to the knight who held but one. At the end of the eleventh century there were about 8,000 subtenants in England. All the vassals from top to bottom assumed the obligations of the feudal contract into which they had entered.

Under feudal arrangements, as explained earlier, the man who held a fief held it as a vassal from his lord to whom he owed allegiance, homage and service. However, it sometimes happened that a man held land from several lords. In such cases he acknowledged one of these lords as his liege lord. Then the tenant might swear allegiance and do homage to the other lords only insofar as he did not violate his obligations to his liege lord.

It is necessary to word such statements as these very carefully. To do otherwise is dangerous. Often feudal arrangements did not develop in a fashion amenable to easy definition; rather they have had it sometimes thrust upon them. We cannot here consider the numerous details of varying feudal contracts and habits. We must be concerned only with certain broad facts. In summary, we have thus far stated that throughout the fabric of tenurial contracts, so tightly knit in complex patterns, every man was another man's vassal; all land had its lord; each tenant received both a fief and personal protection; every tenant owed personal loyalty to his immediate lord and to his overlord; and both lord and vassal had rights and duties that had to be fulfilled. Let us now examine some of these powers and obligations.

Earlier pages have shown that the tenants-in-chief usually held their lands by military tenure. They provided knights for the king's army, usually for forty days a year. The king probably never obtained more than 5,000 knights but, after all, rebellious barons or foreign foes would find this a formidable force. Sometimes, as we have also seen, the barons held land by socage or serjeanty tenure, in which cases they paid cash or performed non-military services.

There was also the obligation of the tenants to aid the lords by giving counsel. The king, or any feudal lord or baron, had the feudal right to the counsel of his tenants. Hence the king frequently summoned his tenants-in-chief to meet with him. It was their duty to give advice, to help in formulating policy, to participate in judicial decisions, to discuss the affairs of the realm. By the same token vassals throughout England were required to go to their lords' court to give counsel, to aid in problems of administration, to help in the administration of justice. Thus tenants-in-chief went to the king's court; those who held land from the tenants-in-chief went to the baronial courts of those magnates; and so down the scale. If the most humble knight had free tenants enough he might hold a court in which the cases of his tenants would be judged by the feudal law and the custom of the manor. Much will be said later about the nature and functions of the king's court and the baronial courts of Norman England.

On certain fixed occasions a vassal was required to pay feudal "aids" (*auxilia*) to his lord. These were payments by which the vassal gave assistance when the lord was faced by unusual expenses. The feudal relation between lord and vassal made such an arrangement just and necessary. Thus "aids" were to be paid for "the ransoming of our body, for the making of our eldest son a knight and for the once marrying of our eldest daughter." In these three special cases the king, or any other lord, had a legal right to exact and collect the feudal obligation. Of course, a vassal was expected to help his lord in any time of need. However, apart from the three cases listed above, the tenant was not legally obliged to give aid at his lord's request. If he did consent to help, the sum given was always called a "gracious aid" (*gratis*) because it was voluntary. No lord, not even the king, could collect such aids unless those who were liable to pay them had given their consent. Some kings and lords later ignored this rule. When they broke the feudal law the result was trouble. In the need for consent to noncustomary feudal aids lies part of the origin of the modern principle and practice of taxation. It should, of course, be noted also that William I kept and trebled the Danegeld, that direct Anglo-Saxon tax on land. He thus made it possible to impose non-feudal national taxes on land and, later, on movables.

There were many other feudal obligations, usually called "incidents" because they were incident or attached to the status of the tenant. The customary feudal incidents due the lord included, for example, a sum of money called a "relief," payable when the heir of a deceased vassal wished to succeed to his father's estate (*relevium*). This taking up again of a fief was a feudal custom based upon the idea of abiding proprietorship of land, the theory that the regranting of the land was an act of grace on the part of the lord and hence to be paid for. In the case of tenants-in-chief the king's officers did take actual possession of the land on a vassal's death. This is the right of *primer seisin* (first possession). The vassal's heir obtained recognition after he had paid the relief and created a new legal and moral bond by doing homage and swearing fealty. It may be noted in passing that fealty existed in all free tenures. Homage was confined to military tenures. Hence fealty was far more important in the laws of treason and allegiance than it ever was in the laws of feudal tenure.

The lord also had the right of wardship for minor heirs, in which case he took all the income from the lands of the fief until the heir could give the military and other services that might be called for under the feudal contract. It was the lord's duty to support and educate all of the deceased vassal's minor children. It was sometimes fortunate that the lord was forbidden to touch the dower rights of the widow. If the fief fell to a minor heiress, she was forbidden to marry without the lord's consent. The theory supporting this practice was that the lord must be sure that the ward's husband would be able and willing to meet the obligations involved in the holding of the fief. Frequently the lord simply sold his right of selection to the highest bidder. This right was clearly a valuable perquisite. Sometimes heiresses were in fact auctioned and bartered in a most unchivalrous fashion.

There were other incidents, hallmarks of duty that remained until feudal tenure was abolished in the late seventeenth century. For example, if a vassal died without heirs the land of the grantee went back by escheat to his lord. Before the statute of *Quia Emptores* (1290) "revert" and "escheat" were synonymous terms. If a vassal was convicted of felony his land was forfeit to his lord. In some cases the king, if the felon was a vassal below the level of a tenant-in-chief, had the right to possession of the land for a year and a day. If a vassal broke his contract the land might also go back to his lord. If the lord broke his contract after one year of attempts to obtain redress the vassal might defy the lord by an established ritual form (*diffidatio*), "put him out of his faith," coerce him, become absolved from the bonds of vassalage. This was the path followed by the barons who opposed King John in the thirteenth century.

These contracts and conventions were often less precise than the preceding paragraphs might suggest. It is almost always impossible to state with exactness and brevity many of the intangible and imponderable things which help to form a "theory of society" and a climate of opinion. Some of the feudal obligations were in fact not sharply defined. Feudal problems and disputes were multiplied in the Middle Ages. Oaths were not always kept. Vassals were not always given warranty and protection. Who was to control a strong king who wanted to be far more than a universal landlord? How could a weak king control overweening and rival barons? Who, sometimes, could determine what abuses, sins and errors had been committed and by whom? What, indeed, was a "just" relief? What was a "just" aid? How impartial could a lord's court be when the lord himself was a party to the suit? Sets of feudal undertakings were often complex, varying according to place and time, clogged by a multiplicity of local customary practices. It is not surprising that points in dispute were often not capable of a satisfactory settlement.

MANORS AND TENANTS

Because the Norman and Angevin society was basically agrarian, the fiefs were composed of one or more rural agricultural settlements called manors. These manors were the normal units of land division for purposes of feudal landholding. "This brings us face to face with a question we have hitherto evaded," says Professor F. W. Maitland in his classic *Domesday Book and Beyond*. The question is: "What is the manor?" In twenty-one pages, with his usual skill, Professor Maitland presents a definition of a manor as it existed in England in the late eleventh century. We discover that the word "manor" (*manerium:* house) is in fact a vague word. Manors in England varied in structure, in size, in the nature of their ends and operations. There is no single type. Sometimes we find there is not even a manor house. Sometimes, too, there is no lord's demesne land on the manor. With this cautious introduction let us note some general facts about which all scholars are agreed.

In feudal days the manor was an estate controlled and supervised by a lord for his profit. Part of the estate the lord of the manor usually kept for his own use and that part of the total manorial land was called the demesne. Dominating the manor's village usually stood the wooden manor house. Here lived either the lord or his agent. About the manor house there usually stretched the lord's orchard, meadow, garden, stables, storehouses, implement sheds, and a part of the arable land of the great fields where the lord's strips intermingled with those of his tenants.

A system of rigid economic feudalism controlled the manor and its tenants. The tenants held the land outside the lord's demesne. They lived in a village in the clay and wattle huts known to generations of men. Each tenant held scattered strips of land in a large open field. He held "rights of common," including the right to pasture cattle on common meadow land, to let his hogs range in the common woods.

Most of the men who were freemen in 1066 were swiftly forced into the ranks of the unfree villeins. Those few who did remain free held various amounts of land in permanent tenure for which they paid rents of money or produce. They could sell or alienate their holdings. They seldom owed the lord any "servile" or base labor.

So long as they kept up the specified services and payments due the lord they could not be ousted.

The largest group of workers on the manor were the villeins. In return for his holdings in the arable open field (usually about thirty acres) the villein did heavy "base" services on the land of his lord. This was usually two or three days a week. In planting or harvest time he did extra, or "boon" work. He was also required to pay rent, usually in kind, to his lord. If he wanted to use the lord's mill, bridges, or oven he had to pay a heavy fee. On certain special occasions he had to pay other charges. For instance, when a villein's daughter married he had to pay a fee called the *merchet* to his lord. When he died his heir had to give the lord a *heriot*, corresponding to the relief in higher society. This would be paid by giving the lord the best ox or some other valuable gift. The villein might not marry without the lord's permission. He was not allowed to leave the village unless the lord gave approval. He was indeed "bound to the soil." For justice he depended upon the manor court, controlled by the lord's steward.

Below the villeins were the cottars and the bordars, whose holdings were sometimes five acres, often only a hut and a garden plot. They, too, owed labor services and payments to the lord. Occasionally there were men of lower status still, the bondsmen who held no land but who did chores for the lord of the manor or worked as swineherds or beekeepers.

It is true that all of these tenants on the manor had a core of rights, protected by law. The lord's power was not absolute. And yet the bailiffs and stewards, the lord's chief administrative officers, frequently were harsh, ruthless, careless of the local or national law. The lives of most of the people were poor and short. In the pages of Domesday Book we discover that 79 per cent of the heads of families in the rural population were listed as unfree. It was upon these unfree men that the manorial income ultimately depended and upon the manorial income depended the survival of feudalism.

THE DOMESDAY INQUEST

Thus the Conqueror and his Normans elbowed out much that was Anglo-Saxon on the local as well as the national scene. Perhaps the best light on the whole economic and social situation is in the passages of William's unique Domesday Book, a landmark in early British history.

Prominent among the importations of the Normans was the prerogative institution called "the sworn inquest of lawful men." William did not create the inquest procedure (*inquisitio*) when he used it in making Domesday Book. As European documents show, the practice was very old. Reliance upon the sworn testimony of the neighborhood runs back through the Franks to the Romans. In Europe and England the inquest was used through long centuries for a variety of administrative and judicial purposes. The procedure was simple: certain individuals, carefully selected because they were likely to know the answers to the questions asked, were summoned before royal commissioners, called the king's *missi, legati,* barons or justices. The persons thus assembled were put on oath and queried about facts in dispute or facts about which the king wanted more information. For instance, inquests were held at Ely to establish what lands the church in fact held there at the time of the Conquest.

William used this method of inquiry to compile information about the population and resources of all the manors of England. In 1085 and 1086 the Conqueror set up royal commissions and sent agents on circuit to undertake a detailed and unprecedented survey and census. Normally in each hundred the sworn men were asked specific questions such as these: What is the name of the manor? Who held it in King Edward's time? Who holds it now? How many hides does it contain? How many ploughs? How many freemen, villeins, sokemen, cottars, serfs? How much woods? How much meadow? How many pastures? How many mills? How many fishponds? What was the value of the manor in King Edward's time? How much is it worth now?

The extraordinary Domesday Book, as Professor V. H. Galbraith has shown, was essentially a feudal survey. William wanted to know the main facts about his kingdom. He wanted to obtain a comprehensive mass of information from a reluctant people about national economic conditions so that, if possible, a heavier Danegeld might be assessed. He wanted a collection of facts useful in settling outstanding pleas. "So narrowly did he cause the survey to be made," wrote a monk at Peterborough in the *Anglo-Saxon Chronicle,* "that there was not one single hide or rood of land, nor—it is a shameful thing to tell but he thought it no shame to do—was there an ox, cow, or swine that was not set down in the writ."

The perambulating inquisitors of the king, with the authority of royal justices, collected the facts. They relied especially upon the men between the nobles and the serfs, the "responsible, well-informed and honest" men who were soon to be important in the new glories of the jury system. William and his agents did not want the survey to degenerate into an accumulation of useless information. In the final abstract of the original returns the statistical details obtained in the survey were drastically curtailed. The condensed and rearranged remainder was divided into the two volumes of Domesday Book, later so named because none could escape its judgment. The two volumes are usually called *Great Domesday* and *Little Domesday*. One volume was devoted to Essex, Norfolk, and Suffolk; the second to the rest of England. The completed work remains as an ordered and permanent record of England's economic resources in William's day, the royal rights over them, the social condition of Englishmen in the eleventh century. It was all a great triumph for the sworn inquest, an institution of massive importance in later English history. These manuscripts were often used in medieval law courts, and in their published form are occasionally used today in cases involving topography or genealogy. The earnest student is urged to consult the text of some of the illuminating returns of the Domesday Inquest. Most easily available are the selections from returns made from Cambridgeshire, Herefordshire, Cheshire, Berkshire, and other counties quoted by Professor Carl Stephenson in *Sources of English Constitutional History*.

THE LAW OF PROPERTY

The reader will easily understand how the introduction of feudalism made necessary the slow emergence of new concepts and new developments in the laws of England, particularly in the laws relating to property. Before we proceed to discuss these things, however, it would be well, perhaps, if we made a few preliminary comments about some facts of importance throughout this volume.

Those who are innocent of any legal knowledge or conceptions often ask why the language of the law seems to be only partly intelligible, abstruse, repetitive and in general bulged with verbosity. The answer is that the words of the law do not merit such adverse criticism. The lawyer must be as precise as a surgeon. Legal language and legal logic meet in one. It is usually impossible to translate or alter legal words and phrases and at the same time preserve the meaning inherent in the original text. So it is that the student may find in the pages of this book some passages that bring bewilderment, dismay, or the dead weight of indifference. Not all readers of books about laws and constitutions persist to the end. Those who do not find the pages burdensome and comfortless usually achieve a new understanding and a new perspective. The law is the daughter of slow time. Generations of men have labored to create the structure that now exists. Tomorrow's heirs are our wards now.

In the western world there are two main systems of law: the Roman or civil law and the English or common law. Today the law that once prevailed in the Roman Empire still rules in modern Continental Europe. It is the main bulwark of the legal systems of Central and South America, of the Dutch, French, Portuguese, and Spanish colonies, of Quebec and Louisiana, of many other lands beyond the ken of Caesar. The common law, developed slowly by the kings and courts of England, is rooted now in the United States, in Australia, Canada, New Zealand, and in many other areas outside the British seas. In these chapters about the Normans and Angevins we see emerging some of the basic principles and practices of the English legal system.

It would be wrong to imagine that the Norman Conquest immediately pointed the way to a sharp departure from Anglo-Saxon law and a swift embracing of the laws of the Normans and the Continent. Professor F. W. Maitland once called 1066 "the midnight of legal history" and emphasized how little written law the Normans had of their own. William did not suddenly impose a large body of laws upon England. He promised to maintain the laws of Edward the Confessor, by which he meant the general laws accepted by the courts in contact with local customs. There were, as we have seen, multiple and varying threads of custom in England. Only slowly were they moulded and massaged into the growing patterns of court procedure and royal law. In 1066 these developments were in the unguessed future.

Nevertheless, a few swift changes were inevitable after the impact of the Conquest. The most important of them were related to feudalism. All feudal arrangements, as we have seen, rested upon law and custom. It is no accident that real estate law is today essentially feudal, or that personal property is often governed by a different set of rules, or that the distinction between movable and immovable goods is so important.

In Anglo-Saxon England the usual method of creating or transferring interest in land was by a public ceremony known as livery of seisin—the phrase may be roughly translated as delivery of possession, although the serious student will discover that what Professor F. W.

Maitland called "the mystery of seisin" does not necessarily mean actual physical possession. The ceremony was normally held on or within sight of the land that was being formally put into an individual's possession. It was also held in the presence of witnesses who would remember the transaction. As a symbol of the corporeal delivery or transfer of the land the donor or seller usually gave the new holder a clod of earth, a twig, a key, a ring or a cross. In this mode of conveyancing there were also stated clearly the "words of limitation" that carefully delimited the rights or interests of the possessor. Sometimes, particularly after the lordship system developed, the grants or sales were accompanied by the written documents earlier described in the paragraphs about bookland. But most land in Anglo-Saxon England was not held by written record or charter of witnesses. In fact, it was not legally necessary to possess deeds or other written evidence of land rights before the passage of the Statute of Frauds in 1677.

We have already seen that after 1066 the Anglo-Saxon distinctions between bookland, folkland and laenland ceased to have any meaning. Under the Normans and Angevins all land was held directly or indirectly of the crown under specific sets of arrangements. The basis of the land law was now the feudal contract. The type of service alone determined the type of tenure by which the land was held.

In the complex "feudal system" the rights and seisins of overlords and lords were numerous. When their legal claims were answered several collective rights still remained to the vassal. These collective rights were called estates. The vassals usually divided up these rights and the divisions were also called estates. The emergence of the "estate" idea is very important in the history of English law.

The type of tenure determined the quality of a person's legal interest in a piece of land. The nature of an "estate" determined the quantity of a person's legal interest in it. Subsequent chapters will show that in later days estates could take several forms and be subdivided in many ways. The growth of legal concepts about estates was gradual until the blaze of developments of the thirteenth century. It is a long road from William the Conqueror to the Law of Property Act of 1925. Here, at the beginning of the feudal age, let us consider the forms of estates that emerged first. How did they develop? What were their characteristics?

The basic estate was called a freehold or fee simple and the term was used to describe the vassal's collective and undivided rights in his property. The estate was called a "fee" because it was a fief held of a lord and "simple" because it was uncomplicated. After a routine fee had been paid to the feudal lord the land could be freely bought or sold. Only in one major respect was the vassal limited: he might not dispose of the land by will. This limitation was universally imposed because the right of free testamentary disposition would explode the principle of primogeniture, so essential to feudalism. It might also take away from the lord his rights of wardship. The normal estate was the fee simple and originally it seems to have been almost identical in form with its direct ancestor free socage tenure. In the beginning, too, it apparently lasted no longer than the lifetime of the grantee.

A second form of estate was called the fee simple conditional. This kind of estate arose because many a landed proprietor desired to determine how his lands would be held after his death. It was quite natural that the heads of prominent families would want their successors to continue to be prominent and wealthy far into the future. Thus the holder of a fee simple estate frequently tried to tie the hands of his heir by passing the land along with conditions attached to the holding of it. For two hundred years after 1066 one method was widely used to prevent an heir from dividing his estate and thus weakening his family: the land was sold or given to the son by the father on condition that it descend in turn to the son's heirs. Thus, for instance, a wastrel or black sheep could have and use the land but he could not alienate it. The broad acres had to pass as a bloc to his heirs.

No medieval king liked to see local families becoming too strong in land and wealth. Hence royal courts usually supported the claim of free alienation, the right of a man to sell his land without let or hindrance no matter what the limiting condition of an original grant or sale might be. The words in such a document usually said that the donor was giving the land or the seller was selling the land to a man "and his heirs." By the reign of Edward I (1272–1307) royal courts were saying that the words "and his heirs" were but "words of art," words of limitation or description and not an integral part of a purchase or gift agreement.

The courts thus held that when the fee simple conditional estate was first set up the words "and his heirs" were used merely to define the estate (interest) which had been transferred from the father to the son. After all, the sole beneficiary of the original transfer was the son. The heirs of that son had not purchased any right or interest in the property and they were mentioned, said the courts, for the sole purpose of helping to describe or delimit or define both the estate and the person to whom the sale or gift was made. Therefore, asserted the royal courts, as soon as an heir is born to the man who now holds the estate the description of limitation is complete, the fee simple conditional becomes a fee simple, and the holder may convey the estate to a third party in fee simple whenever he wishes.[2]

As Chapter IX will show, some of the famous statutes of Edward I's reign related directly to the fee simple conditional problem. The great *Quia Emptores* of 1290 played a major part in giving definition to the theory of estates. Many enactments helped to fix in English land law more feudal elements than can be found in any other country. The chapter about the achievements of Edward I in the field of law will describe, for example, how the Statute of Westminster II—that *De Donis Conditionalibus* document praised and damned through the centuries—created entailed estates, thus adding the new fee tail to the estates held by the older fee simple and the fee simple conditional arrangements.

This chapter has been chiefly concerned with feudalism in England. We have noted some of the problems of lordship and vassalage, contract and obligations, the classes of men and the nature of the land law. With these developments a change took place in the processes of central and local government, in the administrative system, and in the relations of church and state. Here, of course, we find the usual standard medieval problems and ideas appearing again. Who is going to dominate whom? Can the king control the feudal magnates of his court and country? How effective can a Norman or Angevin ruler make the local courts and the local administration? How can the increasingly divergent interests of church and state be reconciled? What interests must give way to hold England together?

The next chapter is designed to give the reader an outline of the means William the Conqueror and his successors used to answer these and other questions in an age of enterprise and then of decay. We must always remember that our British ancestors did not know what we know. Like ourselves, they moved forward into the unknown and the unforeseen.

---

[2] For a detailed discussion of the complex ramifications of fee simple conditional arrangements see W. S. Holdsworth, *A History of English Law,* vol. III, pp. 106–111 or F. Pollock and F. W. Maitland, *A History of English Law before the Time of Edward I,* vol. II, pp. 17 ff.

CHAPTER IV

Enterprise

and decay

COURT AND HOUSEHOLD

THERE were found Norman kings of England: William I (1066–1087), William II (1087–1100), Henry I (1100–1135), and Stephen (1135–1154). The ablest of these were William I, some of whose achievements have already been described, and his talented son Henry I. William II was evil and reckless and he constructed nothing. The reign of Stephen, following the shining chapters of Henry I's enterprise, brought decay and disintegrating feudal anarchy. This chapter describes the main features of legal and constitutional development in the years before Stephen's death in 1154. We begin with an examination of the structure of central government.

At the three annual feasts when the king wore his crown the great council of England assembled. The members met at Easter in Winchester, at the festival of Whitsuntide (seven weeks after Easter) in Westminster, and at Christmas in Gloucester. This council was the king's feudal court, the *curia regis,* the nucleus of future parliaments, the ancestor of the modern House of Lords and the departments of state. In this impressive council the whole nation was conceived to be present. Membership in a feudal age was based upon landholding, not upon the criterion of personal importance as in the case of the Anglo-Saxon witan. The principle of composition was thus new to England, an importation from the Frankish world quite dissimilar to Saxon arrangements.

The king was lord of all the vassals in a kingdom that was, after all, the greatest of feudal honors. He summoned the mighty barons, including the abbots and bishops, and the duty to attend was sometimes enforced by penalties. The king, of course, could summon to the great court whomever he wished, and in a later day he also called knights and burgesses. But for nearly two centuries the feudal magnates alone were ordered to come. "We command and pray you that as you cherish us and our honour, avoiding all excuse and delay," runs a summons of 1205, "you come to us at London on Sunday next before the Ascension of our Lord, with us to consider our great and arduous concerns and the common good of our kingdom."

Thus the feudal barons were brought together to form the *curia regis* of England. They discussed the affairs of the realm. They advised the king. They took decisions on great matters of state and the king was glad to have them commit themselves to policy. Here, indeed, were the rudiments of legislation. The barons also altered existing law. They made new laws. They were habitually active in performing the executive and administrative tasks of the state. They formed the highest court of law in the land.

As the Norman government became more centralized and efficient the advisory, legislative and judicial functions and duties of the king's great feudal court increased, sometimes almost to flood level. In early days, as we have seen, it was the duty of the great barons to perform the service of attending the *curia regis*. In later days, these barons insisted that their attendance and participation was a right not to be limited or taken away by the king. The consequences of the baronial demands form a significant chapter in the growth of the law of the constitution. It suffices here to describe the *curia regis* as it existed in Norman days and to remark in passing that no fixed and final and clear ideas about the nature of the legal powers of either the crown or the *curia regis* had yet appeared. As Professor A. B. White once remarked, the facts preceded the theory. They often do.

In the intervals between the great court assemblies the king, faced with the day-to-day business of government, relied upon a small number of personal advisers, usually from the ranks of the baronage and from the royal servants in the king's household. This small permanent council was in constant attendance upon the king. It was not by any means a committee of the great council. In fact, its functions were the same as those of the larger group. The smaller body in the king's entourage could do anything the larger body could do. Its powers, though the size was shrunken, were not one whit diminished. Contemporaries called the small council by the same name as the larger body, the *curia regis*. In the following pages, for the sake of convenience, a purely arbitrary distinction will be made between the two councils: the full feudal assembly will be called the great council and the smaller group will be referred to as the *curia regis*.

As the controls of the Norman government became more extensive and intensive the routine business of the state inevitably increased. Royal household officials frequently became busy executive officers of the king. The first and most important of these was the Chancellor, whose power became very great.

In Chapter I it was explained that there was an official in the court of Edward the Confessor known as the Chancellor, or king's secretary. At first the Chancellor was the head of the king's chapel, the chief of the chaplains, the king's spiritual adviser or "keeper of the king's conscience," the holder of the great seal. In early Norman days most of his spiritual duties were taken over by the king's almoner and the chaplains of the court. Nevertheless, the Chancellor, always a churchman in the Norman period because of the literary tasks of his office, continued to advise the monarch on several ecclesiastical matters, especially on those church appointments over which the king had control. Meanwhile, the more secular duties of the Chancellor's office increased. His responsibilities, soon to be difficult to measure, included the preparation of all royal documents. This had been true in Edward the Confessor's day, and it was true still. The Chancellor continued to hold the great seal and he alone could authenticate court papers. So it was that the Chancellor and his corps of learned clerks, who were usually the chaplains of the royal household, soon formed a secretariat of the government later known as the Chancery.

By the reign of Henry I (1100–1135) the Chancellor's officials had begun to develop several kinds of records, afterwards clearly distinguished as the charter, patent, and close rolls. About a hundred years later (1204) all documents (except judicial writs) issued by the Chancery clerks were enrolled on one of these three great Chancery rolls. These were the predecessors of the cross-indexed files kept in the steel filing cases of modern government departments. Each roll contained copies of the communications sent out from the Chancellor's offices. The charter rolls recorded such things as royal grants of land, franchises and privileges. The patent rolls, their name suggesting rightly that they were open to public scrutiny, covered various matters of public interest. The close rolls, as the adjective indicates, were not open to inspection because they contained papers whose publication would serve no desirable purpose. All of these rolls, of course, were of great value to the clerks in an expanding and busy Chancery.

Here the clerks could check upon fees due the king. Their notations on the rolls showed who was responsible for the issuing of a royal letter.

It may also be noted that the various memoranda of these long departed clerks are of incalculable value to expert scholars today. A large number of the early rolls still exist in England's archives. They testify across the centuries to the careful and effective supervision and control exercised by the Chancellor and his subordinates over the operations of government. In the reign of Henry II, as we shall see, the development of the writ in the judicial system still further enhanced the power and prestige of the Chancellor and his officials. From such beginnings grew a major law court and the post of the Lord Chancellor, today the highest officer of the crown.

Those who are familiar with the scholarship of Professor J. E. A. Jolliffe and others will be aware that the office of a second official, the Justiciar, can be described in brief compass only at the risk of over-simplification. Let us here leave aside the vexed question as to whether or not the title and office of the Justiciar were continuing and permanent in the Norman period. For our purposes it is enough to state that the Justiciar was included in the ranks of the royal servants. He was not technically a member of the king's household at all but a special royal agent. By the reign of Henry I he had become the king's chief administrative and legal assistant. He was the head of the royal judicial system. He was the king's deputy who shared with the Chancellor the duty of directing the administration of government. He sometimes served as viceroy when the king was absent in France. Usually the Justiciar, like an increasing number of government officers, stayed in London and did not follow the ambulant court. It was quite obvious, as the tasks of government increased, that many officials could not go about with the king on his travels within and without the kingdom. The process of settling in a permanent location is usually called, in an excellent phrase, "going out of court."

The starting point of the Justiciar's office was certainly as promising as that of the Chancellor. But in the years when the Chancellor's restless empire expanded, the Justiciar was a victim of the decisive pressure of fates beyond his control. When Henry II was king (1154–1189) all went well. Indeed, for a time, there were two Justiciars. During the reigns of Richard I (1189–1199) and John (1199–1216) several able Justiciars helped to bridge those troubled years. But John lost Normandy and afterwards the king usually stayed home in

England. Hence there was no need for a Justiciar-viceroy. Then, too, by the thirteenth century there was a permanent body of king's justices and on this score there was no longer any major purpose in having a Justiciar to head the royal judicial system. The office, once so powerful, completely disappeared in the reign of Edward I (1272–1307).

A third officer of importance was the Treasurer. To understand the origin of the Treasurer's office we must look for a moment at the Chamberlain. The reader will recall that the major functions of the Chamberlain included the doing of much confidential royal business. He was the chief of the king's chamber. He looked after the king's private treasure and the royal wardrobe. He was responsible for the pay and provision of troops, for matters of protocol and ceremony, for meeting the daily expenses of the court. Under the Normans many of the Chamberlain's powers gradually passed to other officials. One of the men who occupied a province of the Chamberlain's collapsing empire was the Treasurer.

Before the Conquest the king's treasure usually travelled about with the king and the Chamberlain guarded it. After 1066 most of the king's treasure was stowed for safety at Winchester. The custodian there was the Treasurer, then a subordinate of the Chamberlain. Early in the twelfth century the Treasurer became directly responsible to the king. Thus, at last, he was independent of the Chamberlain.

Upon the Treasurer soon devolved the task and craft of keeping account of receipts and expenditures. So arose the institution of the Exchequer, a body whose duties came to include the protection of the royal treasure, the receipt and auditing of accounts, the holding of a court to settle fiscal cases. The term *scaccarium* (chessboard) or exchequer is derived from the system of accounting and first appears about 1118.

The variable staff of the Exchequer included the Treasurer, two assistant Chamberlains, and certain other members of the Treasury personnel. Besides these men, the Chancellor and several members of the *curia regis*, including the Constable, sat in the composite body of the Exchequer to watch, advise, and check. The Chancellor's clerk, for instance, copied and checked the Treasurer's accounts. Aides of the Chancellor drafted all writs issued from the Exchequer. In practice the Chancellor, as the king's secretary, accounted for all of the king's personal and casual income and the Treasurer accounted for the legal crown revenue.

The Treasurer was the chief professional officer or secretary of this large committee called the Exchequer. He directed and controlled the mechanical details and administration of the accounting system. The upper Exchequer (*scaccarium superius*) was in fact a kind of division of accounts because it kept records of the collection and disposal of the royal revenues and heard and settled pleas and problems about these activities. This body corresponds to the present Exchequer in England. The lower Exchequer (*scaccarium inferius*) was a subordinate division concerned with the physical operations of receipt and disbursement of money. This "exchequer of receipt" is the ancestor of the modern Treasury.

In the upper Exchequer a new method of computation came to be used. The *scaccarium,* from which we noted the Exchequer took its name, was a squared cloth divided into columns showing tens of thousands, thousands, hundreds, etc., of pounds, shillings, and pence. Upon these squares counters or tokens were placed to make clear, especially to illiterate fellows like some sheriffs, the totals of amounts calculated in an abacus fashion. The final annual reports were compiled in documents called pipe rolls. There was one pipe roll for each year. This pipe roll system was the result of the labors of Nigel, Bishop of Ely under Henry I. It was a mature method of financial calculation and reporting. Fortunately for scholars of today a minute description of the operations and improvements was recorded in the famous *Dialogue on the Exchequer,* an essay in Latin attributed to Richard Fitz-Nigel, illegitimate son of Nigel and Treasurer of the Exchequer. This treatise, written about 1177, is the first essay to appear in England on the subject of public administration.[1]

Men of law and business who worked in the English government eight hundred years ago seemed to have liked efficiency and order. That is as good an explanation as any we can find for the first appearance of the Exchequer. It was clearly desirable to consolidate and centralize in one control center the numerous offices and divisions of government that were getting and spending money. This is probably the reason why so many diverse elements are found gathered together in the Exchequer, especially in the early days of its development. The process of differentiation within the supervising *curia regis* was slow.

---

[1] The student interested in the early history of the Exchequer system should read Professor R. L. Poole's *The Exchequer in the Twelfth Century.* Extracts from the first famous pipe roll of Henry I (1130) are printed in *Sources of English Constitutional History* edited by Professor Carl Stephenson and Professor F. G. Marcham (pp. 49–54).

As we shall note later, such differentiation always came about as a result of the need for the specialization of function that is basic to good government. In the early chapters of the story of the Exchequer we see a typical illustration of the way new bodies arose, usually with provoking gradualness, out of the small council.

If we depart from technical language we can still say with considerable accuracy that the Exchequer really began as a kind of special session of the *curia regis* summoned to consider financial matters. In such a session men like the Treasurer, the hereditary assistant Chamberlains, and the Chancellor's officers had a special prominence because they had a special financial job to do. Then, in the slow tide of long years, the Exchequer began to divide from the *curia regis* and to divide within itself. Between 1110 and 1127, for instance, the Court of Exchequer appeared. Financial disputes are frequent in any age. "No system of audit," said a wise man, "is possible without a court."

Sometimes, of course, financial cases continued to be dealt with in the full *curia regis*. This is especially true in the years before the Exchequer Court became a fixed and separate office of the Crown. Until the hour when the Exchequer Court appeared as a separate common law court either the king or some barons of the *curia regis* had to sit in it. Otherwise there would not have inhered in the Exchequer Court any legal authority. Power had to flow from the king. The authority of the king's *curia regis* had to lie in any commission, any devolution of control. A later chapter will show how the functions and power of the Exchequer as an administrative body and a court altered, expanded, and sharpened in a day when the Norman kings were gone. In both Norman and Angevin days the Exchequer was one of the major pivots of the state.

The Chancellor, the Justiciar and the Treasurer were the three most important household officials of the Norman reigns. In examining the structure of medieval government the student can distinguish many more royal servants. In the recesses of the household they performed numerous functions. A number of these lesser officials are listed in a survey apparently prepared shortly after the death of Henry I. This document, preserved today in two rather badly jumbled texts, sets forth the constitution and arrangements of the royal household. Students who read the English version published by Professor Carl Stephenson in *Sources of English Constitutional History* (pp. 65–70) will agree with him that "it is a most remarkable document, revealing graphically how, in a feudal age, matters of government and domestic economy were intimately combined."

Among the royal household servants was the chief forester, whose duties were so extensive in the reigns of Richard (1189–1199) and John (1199–1216). He was a royal agent, master of all the lands and lodges in the royal forests, responsible directly to the king. There were the steward and the royal butler, very busy but not very important. There was the constable, successor to the Anglo-Saxon staller, with the marshals who were his aides. Finally, there were the numerous lesser servants: the carters, the cooks, the falconers, the grooms, the purveyors, the keepers of the king's bed and the servants of his bath.

Most of these minor officials and servants were not important in English legal and constitutional history. When the administrative machine of the state slowly separated from the royal household and "went out of court" these men stayed behind. Their offices, even when they did not fade and disappear in the household, possessed no major place in the broad tide of national history. The most important men, the most important offices evolving out of the permanent royal household in the Anglo-Saxon and Norman periods were the Chancellor, the Treasurer, and, to a lesser degree, the Justiciar. The first seeds of the modern departments of state were planted, took root and grew.[2]

THE CHARTER OF LIBERTIES, 1100

Beyond the machinery of government there are always ideas and principles. In Norman and Angevin times these patterns of value were inevitably connected with feudal law and feudal contract.

In several places these chapters stress the moderation of William I's reign and the strains and excesses of the rule of William II, his evil successor. William I was himself accused by his barons of violating the feudal contract by suppressing their "rights" to engage in private warfare. They led a futile revolt against William in 1075. When William II was king he really did abuse and break the feudal contract despite his frequent promises of reform. William II was killed in 1100 and Henry I filched the throne from his elder brother Robert. Then Henry tried to tighten his grasp on the crown by meeting the demands

[2] See Anthony Steel, "The Place of the King's Household in English Constitutional History," *History*, XV, January, 1931. See also David C. Douglas and George W. Greenaway (eds.), *English Historical Documents 1042–1189*, Part II, Section B.

of the barons. The barons insisted that Henry abandon the wicked and arbitrary ways of William II. He promised to do so and put his promise in a famous coronation charter. This charter was probably never intended to be enforced and its main importance lies in the fact that it became a precedent for Magna Carta.

But it is not enough to dismiss "the charter of liberties" with the comment that it was a precedent for the more famous document of 1215. The student who looks at the text will note that there runs throughout the paragraphs the thread of an important principle: William II's deeds had been unjust and illegal and Henry I admitted that there were certain things that even a king might not do under the feudal contract. The king had his rights. But the barons had their rights too, from Westminster to the edge of the utmost marches of the island.

Henry I agreed to limitations on arbitrary power. Then, and only then, did the barons agree to support him within the broad feudal contract. Kings must not be tyrants, said the barons of England, because tyranny is illegal. There was no place for it in the contractual legalities of feudalism. Thus the first stretch of the road to limited monarchy was being built long before the workmen had any idea of direction or goal. It is in this sense that Henry's charter is important in English constitutional and legal history. It is an early signpost on a highway of time that leads through progress and peril to the civil wars of the seventeenth century, the Revolution of 1688, the birth of the Cabinet system and the years beyond.

We must often disregard the impressive verbiage characteristic of such medieval documents as Henry's coronation charter. We must rather remember that Henry I did not mean all he said. And we must not forget that Henry was a tyrant in a legal and methodical way. Nevertheless, there still stand forth the specific ideas and recognized principles stressed in the previous paragraphs. "The kingdom has been oppressed by unjust exactions," said Henry, "and I henceforth remove all the bad customs through which the kingdom of England has been unjustly oppressed; which bad customs I here in part set down." Again and again in the document appear such words as "just," "legitimate," "the counsel of my barons," "let justice be done," "rightful," "firm peace," "as was done before the time of my father, in the time of my other predecessors." The barons were looking after their interests. Henry I was doing what seemed to him expedient. And both barons and monarchs spoke in terms of principle and contract, justice and law. Such ideas, once held and stated, are not easily abandoned. Even feckless Stephen confirmed "the liberties and good laws" of the past. The barons of John's day found that these ideas were both right and convenient.

THE LOCAL SCENE: LAWS AND COURTS

We have seen how the royal government was steadily strengthened in the Norman period by the growth of the central administration. In these days feudalism and custom did not prevent the expansion of royal power. They did not yet stand athwart the road of progress. On the contrary, the early achievements of the *curia regis* and the king's household proved enduring and decisive.

Meanwhile the winds and currents of other forces were impelling change beyond the seat or ken of the central government. They moved silently over the face of England, shaking the shires and hundreds and boroughs, touching the barons and villeins far from London, shaping the raw mass of custom. Let us now look at the nature of events and the structure of institutions beyond the king's court and household.

There is ample cause for saying that William I and the Normans did not find strong reasons for making many lightning changes in the long-memoried local laws and customs. They did insist that these local institutions must not challenge peace or the efficient operations of government. Their yardstick was a practical one. Early in his reign William the Conqueror disclaimed any intention of "Normanizing" England. In making a grant to Londoners in the form of a charter he declared that he wanted both French and English "to enjoy all the rights that you enjoyed in the days of King Edward."

The student will find the same theme in the unofficial compilation of William's decrees usually called the "Ten Articles." There William said he wanted "peace and security to be maintained between Englishmen and Normans." He clearly stated that "all shall keep and hold the law of King Edward, with the addition of those [amendments] which I have made for the benefit of the English people."

Despite the reassuring quotations in the previous paragraphs the student must not forget that behind the documents are always facts and behind facts are men. There were many difficulties. All is seldom harmony in a conquered state. Lesions had to be cauterized. The Anglo-Saxons had to be persuaded to conduct themselves so as not to give heavy offense to the Normans. Again, the Normans did have some customs and habits that had to be grafted to things English. After all, the initiative was in the hands of the Normans.

So we come to the facts of change. First, there is one question of legal procedure which it is well to mention now. The Normans, as we noted in Chapter II, used the duel as a method of proof, especially in cases involving claims to land or charges of felony. Thus the trial by battle procedure, discarded by the Anglo-Saxons, came back with the conquerors. Nevertheless, it came back delimited by qualifications. In the frequently quoted ordinance concerning trials William I established a series of precise rules which said, among other things, that Englishmen were not compelled to use trial by battle among themselves or in disputes with Normans. An Englishman might use oath-helpers or trial by the ordeal of iron "if that suits him better." Nevertheless, some Englishmen did employ trial by battle and the method did not cease to be legal in England until the early nineteenth century.

A second change was necessary to protect individual Normans from Anglo-Saxon violence. In one of the decrees included in the "Ten Articles" William I stated that "all men whom I have brought with me, or who have come after me, shall be under my peace and protection. And if any one of them is slain, his lord [the slayer's lord] shall take the slayer within five days if he can; if, however, he cannot, he shall make a beginning of paying to me 46m. of silver [and shall continue with his payments] as long as the property of that lord shall last. When, moreover, the property of that lord fails, the entire hundred in which the homicide was committed shall bear the common responsibility of paying what remains [of the debt]." If the slayer's lord or the hundred could prove, by a complex process called "presentment of Englishry," that the slain man was English and not Norman then the heavy fine, called *murdrum,* need not be paid. If it could not be proved that the slain man was English he was considered a Norman and the *murdrum* had to be paid.

There is a third important fact to be stated here. The Normans, naturally zealous about peace and security, established the Norman frankpledge system. The Anglo-Saxons had assumed that lower class men who possessed little or no property were probably unreliable and irresponsible fellows. Hence they were required to have a "pledge" to produce them in court to answer for any alleged misdeeds. Later this practice was extended to include nearly all freemen. A fixed group of a man's neighbors formed his pledge and this group was called a tithing. If any male over twelve years of age was found not to be in a tithing the township was fined. If a tithing did not produce an accused member it was fined. In the south of England the tithing was identical with the township or manor. In the midlands the tithing was usually a group of ten or twelve men. In the northern counties the system did not exist at all. At each hundred court assembly the "tithing man," head of the tithing, reported to the court.

Under the Normans the system of holding fixed groups of men mutually responsible for the appearance of any of them in court came to be called the frankpledge system. Some aspects of these arrangements have already been described. "Every one who wishes to be considered a freeman"—so runs a passage in the Ten Articles—"shall be in pledge, so that his pledge shall hold and keep him for justice should he commit any offense. And should any such [offender] escape, his pledges shall see to the payment of simple compensation toward the claim and shall clear themselves [by oath] of having been cognizant of any fraud in that escape."

In Norman and Angevin days, the practice of frankpledge existed in all of England except the northern and western border areas. In those regions the tasks of frankpledge control were performed by subordinates of the sheriff called sergeants of the peace. In the shires well inside the borders the personal sureties and disciplines of the Norman frankpledge arrangement stayed unchallenged for more than two centuries. Professor W. A. Morris has explained with detailed scholarship how important and constant was the pattern of frankpledge action and power.

One more detail has still to be added. The famous "view of frankpledge," a confusing term often encountered, was the formal survey, or "view," of all the police machinery of the collective responsibility system. In the areas where private franchises included hundred courts the local lords conducted the "view of frankpledge." Elsewhere it was the sheriff's duty to undertake the survey, a process which was an aspect of the sheriff's "turn" of a later age. This assignment was carried out in a full meeting of the hundred court. Were the tithings efficiently organized? Were they truly responsible? Were all males enrolled? Where the answers to questions such as these were unsatisfactory those responsible were punished. Early court records show long lists of fines levied upon tithings and townships for their failure to discharge with unremitting zeal the tasks laid by the law upon them.

The local courts of England were not roughly altered by the Norman Conquest. Nevertheless, some slow and relentless changes did begin. For instance, it was earlier remarked that an increasing number of franchises and immunities were being granted by Anglo-Saxon kings in the years before the Conquest. Private jurisdictions of Anglo-Saxon lords had driven wedges into the regional controls of the local shire and hundred courts. After 1066 Norman lords replaced Saxon lords.

The king was the fountain of justice, the source of law. Thus power could pass to private hands by royal grant and, if need be, it could flow back to the monarch again. So Norman kings frequently confirmed earlier royal grants giving jurisdiction over specified hundred courts to local lords. Such private courts, quite familiar institutions back in Normandy, were multiplied by Norman grants.

In addition to these private hundred courts, controlled by franchisal right or "liberty," there were the manorial courts. There were a large number of manorial courts. After all, the manorial system had absorbed all of the free villages of England. In these assemblies the lord or his steward presided. The law invoked was the customary law. The manorial courts, meeting every three or four weeks, were the ordinary courts for the serf, the villein, and the small freeman living, let us say, on socage tenure on the manor. The serf, entirely under the jurisdiction of his lord, was probably judged by his fellow serfs; the freeman was judged by his fellow freemen. The nonnoble freeman, of course, might be under the jurisdiction of his lord or of the hundred court, depending upon the legal rights of the lord.

Many of the manor court cases were petty, but those whose records have come down to us show events and problems as constant as human nature. "They also say that William Askil, John Parsons, and Godfrey Green furtively carried off four geese from the vill of Horsepoll." "Robert son of Carter by night invaded [the property of] Peter Burgess and feloniously threw stones at his door." "Adam Moses gives half a sester of wine to have an inquest as to whether Henry Ayulf imputed to him the crime of larceny and used vile and insulting words."

With the Normans there came to England the Continental idea that a feudal lord had jurisdiction over his tenants. Hence there appeared a new kind of private court in addition to the manorial courts and the hundred courts in private hands. This was a feudal baronial or "honor" court for the lord's vassals and free tenants. Meeting irregularly, the baronial court held a strictly feudal jurisdiction over questions such as landholding within the lord's fief, the relation of the lord to his free tenants and the tenants to one another, the problems of feudal services due the lord. In all of its procedure this court was of course concerned with the operations of feudal law. The most important of these feudal courts was obviously the king's court, the *curia regis*, the court of the greatest of landlords, composed of the tenants-in-chief.

Thus we see that the realm of England contained many communal and private courts. There were the shire and hundred courts. There were the hundred courts in private hands, each one a "liberty," the result of a franchise grant. There were the baronial or "honor" courts concerned solely with feudal law. There were the manorial courts, the ecclesiastical courts, the forest courts, the borough courts mounting in independence and power. There were the stannary courts, the special courts of the tin miners of Devon and Cornwall. Soon to be clearly distinguishable were the courts merchant, those bodies of summary jurisdiction that settled the cases of seafaring men in the port towns and the problems of peddlers, pickpockets, and quarrelling merchants at the great medieval fairs—the "dusty feet" or "pie powder" courts (*pied poudre*). Besides this list there are many more courts whose character and tasks can be studied in the more lengthy legal histories.

Now at this stage it is interesting, and it is important, to remark that by the middle of the twelfth century many paths had been cleared for the vast expansion of royal justice that was to come with Henry II and his successors. The multiplicity of courts and jurisdictions invited it. The swollen ecclesiastical and baronial powers at the end of Stephen's reign invited it. Such challenges could not help but fix the sensitive glance of the imperious Henry II, so conscious of the demands of a firm and efficient throne. The claws of the great must be clipped. Both the cause for royal action and the means to effect it had been unconsciously prepared. The present can never insulate itself against the future.

Even before the great reign of Henry II there is much evidence to show that the royal authority was being exercised to an increasing extent in local communities. The next section will describe, for example, the growth of the functions of the sheriff, that mighty agent of the king in the shires. When the sheriffs of Henry I's day undertook some dishonest activities in the shire and hundred courts the wrath of the king was swiftly kindled. He showed that he was quite ready to use all of the weapons at his command to achieve his royal ends in the local areas: "Know that I grant and command," states a detailed ordinance of Henry, "that henceforth [the courts of] my counties and hundreds shall meet in the same places and at the same times as they did in the time of King Edward, and not otherwise. And I am unwilling that my sheriff, on account of any business that particularly concerns him, should have them meet in any other way. . . . Also I will and command that all men of the county shall attend the county [court] and the hundred [court] as they did in the time of King Edward." There is no doubting the meaning of language such as that. A strong king will be obeyed, whoever speaks to the contrary.

The judicial work of the *curia regis* was at first restricted to "great men and great causes." But soon the power of the *curia regis* began to be used for other purposes. Its expansive influence radiated over England. After all, the *curia regis* was the king's court and the king's instrument.

There are some passages in what Professor Carl Stephenson called "the wretched compilation misnamed *Leges Henrici Primi*" (1116) that show several of the laws and usages current in the early twelfth century. The attentive student, working with his documents, will note that the list of "pleas" reserved to the king and his royal courts have increased far beyond the Anglo-Saxon total. There is clearly prevalent the idea that anybody who commits a crime offends against the king, and hence it is a "crown plea." And where can crown pleas be dealt with except in royal courts, the courts of the king? Slowly, relentlessly, royal justice is being extended at the expense of the old local court system with its ancient bots and wites.

Several years ago Professor George Burton Adams showed that by Henry I's reign royal justices were being sent out frequently from the *curia regis* to full meetings of the shire courts, thus turning the shire courts into royal courts for the duration of the visit of the justices. We have also seen that hundred courts became king's assemblies when "view of frankpledge" was held. The beginning of the decline of the local communal bodies was at hand. Of course, the men who lived in the early twelfth century did not know that the English legal structure was about to be altered and repaired. Only rarely have institutions been built by calculating men with plans for the far future. As the following chapters unfold the reader will see the first faint beginnings of now firmly established practices in law and government. These early steps were taken for purposes that seemed quite practical at the time. The men who forged the tools were concerned that they should do the job required by the circumstances.

THE LOCAL SCENE: THE SHERIFF

We have now seen that the energy and dynamism of the Normans, loosed upon England in 1066, did not pursue a shattering and irresponsible course. In some cases, particularly in the machinery and operations of central government, there was a speedy extension of Norman habits and ideas. As we have also observed, there were several alterations in the local arena. Of course, many of the Anglo-Saxon traditions and techniques, rooted in the centuries, were not overcome. They were only modified. The Norman system had the capacity to fuse past and present, to weld, or at least interlock, things old and new. There was not unblemished neatness within the confines of the complex Norman state but the Normans did produce an arrangement of vitality and an arrangement that worked.

This mingling of continuity and change can be sharply shown by considering the institution of the Norman sheriff. Norman kings, like Anglo-Saxon rulers, needed a link between the central power and the local authorities. Hence they did not snub or discard the Anglo-Saxon sheriff. They saw that there was no effective alternative to the sheriff, no other adequate institution. As they slowly sorted out the powers and functions of officials they kept the sheriff and for a time left his traditional powers unimpaired.

The Anglo-Saxon earl, on the other hand, rapidly ceased to have any importance as a government official representing the central government in the shires. The earl no longer helped to connect county and capital. He ceased to attend the shire and hundred courts. His title remained, but his governmental powers withered except, of course, in the palatine earldoms.

It was upon the sheriff, so similar to the Norman *vicecomes* on the Continent, that the mantle of local power fell. He was still, as in earlier days, the main local instrument of the king and the central government. Usually the strong central authorities appointed outstanding feudal barons in the shires as sheriffs. William and his successors saw to it that the office seldom became hereditary. It was clearly dangerous to have too much power in the hands of a family that might take advantage of troubled times to throw off dependence upon the king. Sometimes, of course, the picture was altered. For instance, in John's reign (1199–1216) considerable confusion in the counties resulted when no strong man would take the job of sheriff. After all, many barons in John's day were among the king's enemies. But before the early thirteenth century the sheriffs were indeed strong men, supporting pillars of the state.

For his shrievalty the sheriff was required to pay to the Exchequer a definite and annual rental fee called the sheriff's "farm." This fee paid by the king's shire representative was gathered from the regular royal revenue of the king's boroughs and demesne manors in the shire, from the "sheriff's aid" that existed in some counties (a fixed amount of tax per hide), and from the penalties imposed by the local hundred and shire courts. The sheriff was permitted to keep all that he collected above his rental fee. This was his profit. "The sheriff was interested in power and profit and he got both."

To an increasing extent the central government tried, often with ill success, to keep the sheriffs' profit down to a reasonable level and to prevent rapacious scoundrels from commandeering property and extorting money from confused and helpless subjects of the king. Sheriffs were not incorruptible in the Middle Ages. In the fifteenth century, for example, it seems that there were few temptations to which many of them did not succumb.

The sheriff's actual power was increased by an event to which we have made earlier reference. In William I's reign the earl ceased to come to the shire and hundred courts. At the end of this chapter it will be explained why the bishop, too, stayed away. Thus the sheriff or his deputy presided alone and the balance earlier maintained by the presence of earl or ealdorman, bishop and sheriff, was upset. Henry I tried to correct this evil. He removed several sheriffs from their posts. His royal justices were ordered to keep suspicious eyes upon the sheriffs and report any derelictions of duty. This last measure was sometimes rendered less effective than one might suppose because when the king sent out justices from the *curia regis* to do administrative work and hold local king's courts the sheriff frequently became a justice for the duration of the court. Thus a shrewd sheriff was often able to conceal from the other justices the true character of his activities when they were not about his shire to watch and quiz and prowl.

In addition to collecting revenue and presiding at the sessions of the local courts the sheriff had many tasks. He often had official custody of the royal castles in his county. He looked after prisons. He commanded the militia in time of war. He arrested criminals. We have earlier noted that he supervised tithings and presided over the "view of frankpledge" in special sessions of the hundred court. He gave hospitality to royal guests who came to his shire. He was required to serve the royal orders, called writs, sent out from the Exchequer to debtors. In later days, this indispensable agent of the king in the units of the kingdom served the judicial writs sent out from the central courts and collected juries for the assizes.

The next chapter will describe the powers and position of the sheriff in Henry II's reign. In those years (1154–1189) the sheriff's authority was increased in some respects, decreased in more. Before 1300, many voices rose to challenge a power that few but the king could have disputed in the days of the Conqueror. The golden age of the sheriff was in the early part of the twelfth century. The thirteenth century saw many of his duties distributed among other men or abolished entirely. In still later times, especially under the Tudor monarchs (1485–1603), the lords lieutenant of the counties and the justices of the peace, well versed in local affairs, assumed the main burdens of local government. The once proud sheriffs found that their stepping stones to power were cracked and crumbled by new forces and new men.

THE NORMAN CHURCH

Stripped to its essentials, the story of Norman England's development of institutions of law and government has taken little space to tell. It took a long time to happen. There now remains something more, and something important, to say about the Norman period. Man does not live by bread and government alone.

Throughout the centuries of Western civilization the voice and power of the Christian church have united to influence the destinies of men and states. After the missionaries of Rome came in 597 to Ethelbert's Kent the gospel of Christ was slowly spread through all of Anglo-Saxon England. The rising strength and prestige of churchmen is shown in numerous records that have survived the floods of time. Archbishops, bishops and the abbots of great monasteries stood about the king. Some served him in the household. Some sat in the witan. Some sat in the shire and hundred courts to declare the ecclesiastical law and judge clerical offenses. Many of the clergy were great landholders, important sons of the church, proud landed barons in the feudal system, shrewd and busy clerics and statesmen, intimate advisers of the king.

In the years immediately before the Norman Conquest the church, despite the achievements of men like Edgar and Dunstan, became decadent, slovenly, worldly and somnolent. The invasions of the "heathen" Danes destroyed several dioceses in the north. The archbishopric of York drifted away from Canterbury. The monasteries declined in sanctity and learning. England became more isolated from the Continent, more independent of the papacy. The effect of the Cluniac reforms, so important on the Continent, stopped at the English Channel.

Thus the Norman power rolled over England at a moment of critical importance in the history of the church. The exciting and vital forces of the Continent were now unleashed in England. It was an hour when the centralizing and reforming currents of the Cluniac movement were in full flow, always stressing moral elevation, efficient organization and intellectual activity. When Gregory VII became Pope in 1073 the way was apparently prepared for the triumph of his principles of reform. Those principles demanded the creation of an entirely new relationship between church and state. The Pope, said Gregory, was supreme in the church. Secondly, Gregory asserted, the Pope as the Vicar of Christ was superior to all temporal rulers.

William of Normandy conquered England under the consecrated banner of the papacy. It was inevitable that Rome would expect William to aid the church in undertaking major reforms in his island kingdom. Had he not done so in Normandy? It was also natural that Gregory VII, claiming superior temporal power, might even demand that William should hold England, as the Normans held southern Italy, under the feudal overlordship of the successor of St. Peter. Such a demand, phrased in the direct language one would expect from Gregory VII, came to William in 1076. William, said Gregory, must give an oath of fealty to the Pope and do homage for England. Papal taxes, such as Peter's pence, must be diligently collected and sent to Rome.

Here the interests of Gregory VII and William I collided. Wrote William: "To the most excellent pastor of the Holy Church, Gregory, William by the grace of God glorious king of the English and duke of the Normans greeting with affection. Holy Father, your legate, coming to me on your behalf, has admonished me to do fealty to you and your successors, and to take better heed touching the money which my ancestors used to send to the Church of Rome. To the one request I consent, to the other I do not consent. I have refused to do fealty, and I do refuse, because neither did I promise it, nor, as I find, did my predecessors do fealty to your predecessors. As to the money, it was negligently collected for nearly three years when I was in France but now that I have by divine mercy returned to my kingdom what has been collected is sent by the present messenger and the rest will be sent through the messenger of our faithful archbishop Lanfranc when opportunity shall serve. Pray for me and for the estate of our realm, because we have loved your predecessors and desire sincerely to love you before all men and obediently to hear you."

William was glad to be a generous patron of the church. He was willing and eager to undertake reforms and reorganization, to make the church more efficient, to encourage a new zeal and fire new learning, to aid in building churches. William's friend and adviser Lanfranc became archbishop of Canterbury. Lanfranc was a shrewd and famous lawyer and theologian, once prior of the abbey of Bec and later abbot of Caen. The best of the new spirit of Rome and Cluny came across the Channel. King and archbishop united to lift the moral and intellectual power of the church in England. Clerical celibacy was enforced. Simony was abolished. Monastic rules were to be obeyed and monastic life purified. Schools were increased. Cathedral chapter government was reorganized.

There were several other reforms. About 1070, for instance, William took a further step quite acceptable to Gregory VII. He separated the lay and ecclesiastical jurisdictions of the courts. In a famous ordinance William stated that he had "decided to amend the ecclesiastical law which up to my own time has not been rightly observed in England nor in accordance with the holy canons." By William's edict neither a bishop nor an archdeacon was allowed to hold pleas in a hundred court, although some clerics apparently did come to lay courts for a few years. All men "accused in any cause, or of any offense, under ecclesiastical law, shall come to the place named and selected for this purpose by the bishop . . . submitting to the justice of God and of His bishop, not according to the [judgment of the] hundred but according to the canons and to ecclesiastical law. If indeed any one, puffed up with pride, neglects or refuses to come for justice before the bishops, let him be summoned once, twice, and thrice. But if, even then, he will not come to make amends, let him be excommunicated." To strengthen the authority of the spiritual power still further William ordered all lay officers to assist in enforcing the decisions of the church courts.

Thus the ecclesiastical and lay courts were divided. Before 1070, as we have seen, bishop and sheriff sat with the earl or ealdorman in local courts to administer justice jointly to layman and cleric. After about 1070, as we have also noted earlier, the bishop left the hundred court and the power of the sheriff grew. The bishops now began to hold courts of their own concerned with spiritual affairs and the great tract of problems covered by canon law. The decision of William was important, how important he could not know. The separation of the courts led to new and unforeseen conflicts between church and state. The gateway was open and the road was prepared for the long hostilities of a later age, for the murder of an archbishop and the excommunication of a monarch.

At the time of the separation of the courts William's interests seemed guarded with care on every hand. Wherever his advantage and service appeared to be in no jeopardy William met the wishes of the papacy. Beyond that point he refused to travel. He would not permit Gregory VII or anybody else to invade or nibble at his own royal power. The secular arm of the state was to be free and strong.

The intentions and practices of William are clearly shown in the famous set of rules attributed to him by the chronicler Eadmer: (1) no pope was to be acknowledged as true pope without royal authority; (2) no papal letters or legates were to be admitted to England without royal permission; (3) no English barons were to be excommunicated or brought to trial unless the king agreed; (4) the king might veto any acts of ecclesiastical assemblies. We are not certain that these precisely phrased rules were actually formulated by William. The important fact is that Eadmer does state succinctly a major part of William's steady policy.

The protracted struggle between church and state was heralded by another event. Pope Gregory VII demanded that the papacy should control the appointment of bishops and abbots. William replied that all bishops and abbots should be elected in his presence. He also insisted that the king should invest archbishops, bishops, and abbots with the symbols of seisin (see Chapter III) as his barons. Finally, William claimed the right to invest these churchmen with the ring and the staff, symbols of their spiritual offices. Despite the vehement objections of Gregory VII, William continued to do all these things until the end of his reign. The suspicious William watched narrowly the claims of the papacy, so successfully advanced against the Emperor Henry IV. A strong monarch and a strong Pope stood sharply opposed. The result was a stalemate.

All the clergy below the Pope possessed a double character. As officials of the church they belonged to a universal system that knew no nationality; they were subordinate to the Pope. They were also subjects of the king. A feudally loyal man might not be fit to head a diocese. And yet a man fit to head a diocese might be hostile or indifferent to the king's interests. Who, then, should control elections to high offices in the church? Who should invest the higher clergy with the symbols of office?

How far did the state have the right to control the property of the church? Where did the power of the church courts end and that of the secular state courts begin? Did the church, for instance, rightly claim jurisdiction over all cases where a clergyman was a party to the suit, all cases of inheritance, all contracts, all problems of marital relations? Was the king to have no legal authority over his clerical subjects and in many areas none over laymen? Claims and collisions multiplied.

William II, who succeeded William the Conqueror in 1087, was a coarse and debauched ruler. His feudal levies were extortionate. He had little sense of decency or justice. After Lanfranc died in 1089 William left the archbishopric vacant, collecting its revenues for himself. Suddenly, in 1093, the king became ill. Then he repented. "The devil a saint would be." He forced Anselm, famous theologian and consummate fisher of men, to fill the vacant archbishopric.

When William unexpectedly escaped death he discovered two things about the quiet and pious Anselm: the new archbishop sturdily opposed the king's plundering of the church; he believed in the extreme papal claims to power over temporal rulers. Anselm refused to be invested with the symbols of office by the scandal-smirched hands of William. In 1097 he finally succeeded in obtaining William's permission to leave England. He alone of the king's subjects had dared to resist.

In 1100 William was shot, perhaps by accident, in the New Forest his father had made in Hampshire. The king who succeeded him was the shrewd Henry I, several of whose achievements we have earlier discussed. Henry I, that "lion of justice" foretold by King Arthur's magician Merlin, recalled Anselm with honor and restored him to the see of Canterbury. He offered to return all the church lands seized by William II provided that Anselm rendered the customary homage as a direct tenant of the king. But a great church council of 1099 had forbidden any churchman to do homage to a layman. Anselm steadily refused to do homage to Henry I. Moreover, the militant Gregory VII had decided that investiture could only be performed by a church-man. There was to be no "lay investiture." Gregory VII had said, in effect, that kings could no longer control appointments to spiritual offices. Henry I seized the lands of Canterbury and exiled Anselm.

In 1107 a compromise was achieved. An agreement provided that churchmen should give homage for their fiefs, thus admitting that they were feudally vassals of the king. Henry I, for his part, surren-dered his claim to invest with the ring and the staff the churchmen chosen by the cathedral clergy. Through the cathedral chapters Henry and his successors could control the election of churchmen to vacant offices. The king's candidates were usually chosen as prelates and hence the control of the investiture was of little importance. Anselm now ruled his church in peace. The controversy was ended, for a time. It was to leap to flames once more in the reign of Henry II.

THE END OF THE NORMAN AGE

Henry I died in 1135. The barons set aside his daughter Matilda and gave the throne to Stephen, son of William the Conqueror's daughter Adela. Stephen was conscientious, energetic and weak. It was dangerous to have a "soft and good" man for a king. Royal au-thority collapsed and with it went law and justice. The barons, always turbulent under a weak king, grew into anarchy. They pillaged and plundered and fought among themselves. Rapine and disruption flooded over England. Matilda brought more war when she came to claim the throne. "Men said openly that Christ and his saints slept."

This confusion was ended by the skillful diplomacy of Henry, Bishop of Winchester, and Theobald, Archbishop of Canterbury. It was agreed that Stephen should reign unopposed until his death. Matilda's son, Henry of Anjou, was recognized as heir to the throne. Unchecked feudalism was to end. Castles built after 1135 were to be razed. Mercenaries were to go home. Crown lands seized by hungry barons were to be returned.

Stephen died in 1154. The hour was at hand for the coming of Henry II, one of the mightiest monarchs of the Middle Ages. No barons were to break loose from royal control in his reign.

A chapter of English legal and constitutional history began in 1066. It ended with the coming of Henry II in 1154. Of the four Norman kings two were strong and built well: William I and Henry I. William II and Stephen built not at all.

The rings of growth in institutions are often faintly marked. Unless a historian gives a false kind of emphasis he must sometimes confess to seeing but small changes in short time spans. To find intentions where none existed in the minds of our ancestors is unwise. To attribute to them design where they do not declare it is likewise placing firm decision in the place of halting or haphazard experiment. The Norman reigns between 1066 and 1154 saw nothing final, nothing determined and definite. These were decades of slow and unspectacular advance and retreat. The enterprise of William I and Henry I is succeeded by the paralysis of Stephen's reign. The keen eye can but dimly perceive how principles and policies slowly inch forward. Emerging phases of evolution and elaborations of practice united to bridge the century between the battle of Hastings and the death of Stephen.

We now pass to Henry II, the first of the Angevins. There is not a modern problem of government that his influence does not touch. There is no court of common law on which the light of his reign has not fallen.

CHAPTER V

Henry the Second:
the making of order

TASKS OF GOVERNMENT

"NOTHING causes a prince to be so much esteemed," said Machiavelli, "as great enterprise and setting a rare example." Henry II (1154–1189) did both, and left an indelible mark on the history of many lands.

When Henry came to bring security and order to a weary and distracted kingdom in 1154 he was already a skilled politician, preferring the tools of diplomacy to those of force and war. He was twenty-one years old, scholarly, practical, efficient, with an essentially legal turn of mind. Moving with a shrewd and determined energy, Henry tolerated no slackness in others. Contemporaries wrote frequently in amazement of the vitality of "the king who never rested." With him all seemed to move upon an heroic scale. His fits of anger were apparently Hitlerian tempests of fury. His spells of sadness seemed to carry his spirit into almost psychopathic troughs of depression. The business of kingship was the absorbing passion of his restless being. He would be all that his grandfather Henry I had been, and more. He, too, would be an indefatigable "lion of justice."

As a result of mingled matrimonial diplomacies this able Henry held more territory in France than the king of France himself. The vast and hybrid lands of the Angevin Empire stretched from Scotland to the Pyrenees. Despite the fact that Henry II preferred to avoid wars much of his reign was occupied with conflicts and skirmishes in Ireland, Scotland, Wales and France. This book is not concerned with Henry's dramatic and usually profitable deeds in the turbulent lands beyond the borders of England. Our task is to examine what Henry did in his island kingdom and to see why those achievements made

DOMINIONS of HENRY II

- Ruled by Henry II directly as King
- Held by Henry II as Vassal of the King of France
- Held from Henry II by Vassals
- Royal Domain of the King of France
- Lands other than Angevin held by Vassals of the King of France

SCOTLAND

PICTS
SCOTS
DALRIADA

LOTHIAN
ANGLES
STRATHCLYDE
BRITONS

ULSTER

NATIVE IRISH

Irish Sea

ANGLO NORMAN FEUDAL COLONIES

Dublin

Limerick

Cork

Wexford

Pembroke

Snowdon
NORTH WALES

LORDS MARCHERS

Newburgh

Ouse

Trent

Shrewsbury

Peterborough

Northampton

Ouse

Ely

Gloucester

ENGLAND

London

Bath

Clarendon

Salisbury

Canterbury

Winchester

Thames

Severn

ATLANTIC

OCEAN

English Channel

Strait of Dover

FLANDERS

Scheldt

Rouen

Caen

Bec

NORMANDY

Tinchebrai

Seine

PERCHE

ISLE OF FRANCE

Paris

Marne

CHAMPAGNE

BRITTANY

MAINE

ANJOU

BLOIS

Blois

TOURAINE

BOURGES

Loire

BOURBON

BURGUNDY

Saône

POITOU

FRANCE

Vienne

Angoulême

AQUITAINE
(GUIENNE)

Bordeaux

Dordogne

Rhone

Bay of Biscay

GASCONY

Garonne

TOULOUSE

Toulouse

Mediterranean Sea

CASTILE

NAVARRE

ARAGON

Scale of Miles
0   40   80   120   160

him one of the greatest men in English medieval history. For thirty-five years Henry II drove on towards his goals, relentless and almost unimpeded.

The first obvious and immediate task was to recover the order and efficiency that had been shattered and lost in the anarchy of Stephen's reign. Shortly after his coronation Henry sent home the foreign mercenaries Stephen had hired. He ordered the destruction of all castles that had been built by the barons without the king's license. He revoked several royal grants of lands and offices made by Stephen. With the aid of able servants he began to rebuild the central government on the foundations laid by William the Conqueror and Henry I.

Let us first consider the Exchequer. It will be remembered that this body had emerged quite clearly in the reign of Henry I. Here was the first offshoot of the *curia regis,* that fertile source from which were to grow so many royal courts. The important judicial and administrative functions of the Exchequer have been described in Chapter IV. Twice a year it sat in full force to balance accounts before the chequered table. The rest of the time the permanent staff officers performed their mounting tasks.

In Henry II's reign the judicial duties of the Exchequer increased at an accelerated pace. Because it dealt with king's debtors the Exchequer, as we have seen, developed a particular kind of judicial procedure and thus became a court of law as well as an administrative body. But as its judicial business increased there appeared the first sharp evidence that changed emphases on function were to result in an altered structure. Gradually, several of the royal household officials from the *curia regis* concluded that there was no need for them to attend the Exchequer meetings. They saw that many of their functions could be adequately performed by the expert clerks. They also saw that processes of specialization were still further dividing the whole body of the Exchequer.

The Chancery, from which all writs originated, was to become fully separated from the Exchequer in Richard I's reign (1189–1199). By the middle of the thirteenth century the Justiciar and Chancellor no longer attended Exchequer meetings. The Treasurer thus became the main official of the Exchequer and a Chancellor of the Exchequer became the keeper of its official seal. In the thirteenth century, too, the king began to appoint all the members, or "barons," of the Exchequer. Thus, at last, the Exchequer was no longer feudal. It had parted from the parent stem of the *curia regis*. It was well on its way to becoming what it is today: a department of state charged with the receipt and care of the national revenue.

By the seventeenth century the Exchequer as a court became completely separated from the Exchequer as a revenue department headed by the Chancellor of the Exchequer. The Court of Exchequer was finally absorbed in the King's Bench Division of the High Court of Justice created by the Judicature Act of 1873. The Exchequer as a "treasury department" still functions, as every Englishman knows who pays an income tax. These aspects of change and growth will be dealt with more adequately later. They are mentioned swiftly here so that the reader may obtain more than a vague hint of the outcome of some of these events of the Middle Ages.

A further division of function began to appear between the great council and the *curia regis*. In Henry II's reign the whole *curia regis* began to have more judicial business. Because the *curia regis* contained several lawyers and the great council was mainly composed of laymen it was quite natural that most judicial cases should not be tried before the great council at all, but before the smaller *curia regis* or a part of it. With some exceptions, only cases in which the king or barons had a major interest continued to be tried before the great council. These occasions were not numerous. The *curia regis* was thus coming slowly to be considered as a body whose work was mainly judicial and administrative.

We have seen how specialization of functions in Henry II's day was to begin the development of both a common law court and a modern department of state out of the original Exchequer after it had separated from the *curia regis*. Until recently, it was believed that a similar tendency towards differentiation of powers and specialization of functions was neatly and vividly illustrated by an event that occurred in 1178. Some eminent scholars have now cast doubt upon the validity of the interpretation of that event usually given by constitutional historians. Because several complex problems still remain unsolved it is impossible here to state conclusions with a firm confidence that they are final and sure. On the other hand, it is possible to describe, with appropriate caution, a few facts and probabilities.

In 1178 Henry II chose a separate group of about five clerks and laymen to sit permanently at Westminster to transact judicial business other than that covered by Exchequer jurisdiction. Thus the remaining members of the *curia regis* would be left free for other work. The five men Henry II ordered to stay at Westminster were usually called the Bench. It seems that they normally performed their duties without the presence of the king. In the judgment of many scholars, these five men in fact formed a central permanent court and that court was the origin of the Court of Common Pleas. Other authorities feel that this interpretation of the source and rise of the Court of Common Pleas is not entirely correct or complete.

Certain judges, following the king about on his travels, did justice in his presence (*coram rege*). At the same time, however, we know that some judges were still looked upon as *coram rege* men who did not follow the king and who did settle some cases when he was not present at all. Nevertheless, all of these judges did judge cases involving the king: the pleas of the crown. Their activities clearly marked a major aspect of the beginning of another famous court, the Court of King's Bench. In later chapters we will note more precisely how, by 1300, the three great common law courts had divided in amoeba fashion from the *curia regis:* Exchequer, Common Pleas and King's Bench.

The growth of centralization was also speeded by the increase of royal revenues and the steady decline of baronial power. Henry II was well aware that the sinews of central government were strengthened by the rising income from the lands of the king, the feudal incidents, the administration of justice, and any other sources that could be legally tapped. He imposed "shield money" or scutage taxes by which feudal magnates paid money to the king instead of sending military aid. The king used the money thus obtained, or a part of it, to hire mercenaries who could usually be relied upon. There were also extraordinary levies of the tallage, an arbitrary tax upon "the king's demesnes and lands which were then in the king's hands" and upon the boroughs.[1]

There were other significant measures. In 1170 the king held an inquiry into the behavior of sheriffs. The king's object was to depose proud feudal lords from the sheriffdoms and to put efficient agents of the Exchequer in their places. After the reports were submitted Henry saw to it that few barons remained as sheriffs. The new sheriffs were usually more successful tax collectors, at least from the crown's point

---

[1] Students will find in *Sources of English Constitutional History*, edited by Professors Carl Stephenson and F. G. Marcham (pp. 91–93), several entries from the pipe roll of 1187 concerning scutage, tallage, and the profits of justice. They may consult with further profit the baronial returns for 1166 quoted in the same book (pp. 89–91). Important sections of most of the documents mentioned in this chapter will also be found in that useful volume.

of view. In 1166 Henry placed a small income tax upon his subjects to aid in the recovery of Jerusalem from the Mohammedans. In 1184 the Assize of the Forest provided precise and severe penalties for those who committed "any sort of offence" against Henry "touching his venison and his forests."

In 1181 the Assize of Arms ordered all freemen in England to furnish themselves with arms and armor according to their means. "Whoever possesses one knight's fee shall have a shirt of mail, a helmet, a shield, and a lance. . . . And none of them shall keep more arms than he ought to have by this assize . . . no one shall carry arms out of England except by command of the lord king . . . the justices shall have a report." Thus Henry II in fact revived the old fyrd or Anglo-Saxon militia, a useful home guard against foreign invasion or feudal rebellion.

In 1188 Henry levied the famous Saladin tithe. This ordinance provided that "Every one shall give in alms for this year's aid of the land of Jerusalem a tenth of his rents and movables. . . . This money is to be collected within each parish. . . . And if anyone . . . gives less than he should, let there be chosen from the parish four or six lawful men who, being sworn, shall determine the amount that he should have declared; then he must make up the deficiency in his contribution."

By steps such as these Henry II made himself the most powerful king England had yet seen. Nevertheless, his legal mind was troubled. The masterful Henry was slowly bending barons and freemen to the royal will. Could he not make the churchmen subject to the king's law?

HENRY II AND THE CHURCH

There had slowly emerged in Europe the idea of two powers, spiritual and temporal, a dual authority governing the lives of men. Every European had two loyalties, one to the church that had brought its teachings into dark places, the other to the state, that creation of man which had brought organization, a degree of security, and secular power. Every European in this kind of world had to render some things to his temporal rulers, some to the papacy. There was one church, one revelation, one spiritual domination of the church universal. Europe was Christendom; and the spiritual center of Christendom was at Rome.

Because the twin loyalties to church and state imposed upon medieval men were often incompatible, English rulers fought frequently with Rome about the lines of demarcation between papal and royal jurisdiction. Not until the sixteenth century did there arise the new idea that Christian doctrines could be divided by national boundaries. That concept would have been unintelligible to men of the Middle Ages.

During the dislocation of Stephen's reign the clergy had made deep inroads into the powers of the king. Stephen had issued a charter granting privileges to the church that Henry II would have abruptly denied. Bishops had often obeyed the commands of the Pope and ignored the orders of Stephen. The claims of ecclesiastical jurisdiction were being steadily defined and broadened by church lawyers who had profited from the increased study of Roman law.

Extensive areas of law were handled by the church courts. Clerics in orders could be tried for crimes only in these ecclesiastical bodies: the archdeacon's court, a court of first instance; the bishop's court; the two archiepiscopal courts of Canterbury and York; the papal curia at Rome, the final court of appeal. And yet no penalty involving the shedding of blood could be imposed. The most severe penalty the church could inflict was solitary confinement on a restricted diet. For instance, a murderer convicted in a church court was not executed. He might be punished by imprisonment or penance or unfrocked and degraded from his clerical office. Henry said "it took two crimes to hang a priest." By that comment Henry meant that for one crime a priest might be unfrocked. If the ejected priest then committed a second crime he might be hanged because he was no longer protected by the church.

The "criminous clerks" who thus escaped severe sentences were a public scandal. In later centuries, almost any scoundrel who had a sufficient smattering of knowledge to read the so-called "noose verse" at the beginning of Psalm 51 ("Have mercy upon me, O God, according to Thy loving kindness") or who had any connection with a church (a janitor, for instance) might call himself a "clerk." Hence he might demand "benefit of clergy," which included the right to be tried in a church court. It should be noted in passing that in the sixteenth century some statutes included the words "without benefit of clergy," meaning that a man who was "literate" should be punished on the same basis as one who was not.

It was inevitable that Henry II should seek to end the immunity of the church from lay jurisdiction and bring it under the control of the royal courts. In 1161 Henry selected as the archbishop of Canterbury his friend, confidant and Chancellor, Thomas Becket. The king assumed that the archbishop would continue to cooperate with the crown. But Becket abandoned the ways of a courtier and a Chancellor. He put the church before the king and the state. He was determined to be a champion of the church.

The main clash between Henry II and Becket arose over the question of the "criminous clerks" and this dispute of course involved the basic problem of the relations between church and state. From a great council of barons and bishops held at Clarendon in 1164 the king apparently demanded a "recognition" of the ancient customs of the kingdom. A "recognition" was a formal answer required from a jury appointed to make an "inquest." It is possible that in the famous document called the Constitutions of Clarendon we really do have the report of the great council acting as a jury to answer the questions asked of it. In any event, the council listed or declared "a certain portion of the customs and liberties and rights of his [Henry II's] ancestors—namely of King Henry his grandfather—and of other things which ought to be observed and held in the kingdom." The Constitutions stated that "on account of the dissension and disputes that had arisen between the clergy and the justices of the lord king and the barons of this realm this recognition was made. . . ." In sixteen sections the document listed, among other things, the rules that Henry II wanted the church to accept.

The third clause of the Constitutions of Clarendon required that the "clerks" or clergymen should be arrested by the king's officers, accused in a royal court, tried in an ecclesiastical court. If the accused was convicted in a church court "then the Church should no longer protect him." He should therefore be degraded from his orders and sent back to the royal courts for sentence and punishment. There were other clauses. "If the archbishop fails to provide justice, recourse should finally be had to the lord king. . . ." (Clause 8). "No one who holds of the king in chief . . . shall be excommunicated . . . unless first the lord king agrees. . . ." (Clause 7). "When an archbishopric, bishopric, abbey, or priory within the king's gift becomes vacant it shall be in his hands. . . ." (Clause 12). Suits about the rights of presentation to churches and advowson were to be tried in secular courts. Suits about the ownership of land, except land proved to be held by frankalmoign tenure, were also to be tried "in the court of the lord king." No archbishop, bishop, or parson of the kingdom was permitted to go out of England "without the license of the lord king."

In several contexts the feudal position of the archbishops, bishops, and abbots as barons and vassals of the king was clearly stated.

Under heavy pressure Becket and his fellow churchmen "granted and steadfastly promised, *viva voce* and on their word of truth that the said customs . . . should be held and observed for the lord king and his heirs in good faith and without evil intent. . . ." Becket later asserted that his promise conflicted with the "liberties of the church" and obtained a papal dispensation releasing him from any obligation to observe customs contrary to ecclesiastical interests.

Becket at last refused to put the archbishop's seal on any document containing the king's proposals. He fled to France. Henry seized the revenues of the see of Canterbury. Becket replied by excommunicating the king's ministers. Only after six years of broken negotiations did king and archbishop reach a compromise.

But there was to be no peace. When Becket returned to England more difficulties arose. The "turbulent priest" was murdered in Canterbury Cathedral by four of Henry's knights. All Christendom was shaken. Henry II at once sent ambassadors to the Pope to assure him that he had known nothing of the plans of the assassins. The Pope refused to grant absolution until Henry agreed to allow appeals to Rome. Henry agreed on condition that such appeals did not encroach upon the royal prerogative. Henry was also forced to permit "criminous clerks" to be tried and punished by the church. He did succeed in his demand that such clerks who "pled their clergy" must give proof of their status in royal courts. The principles of the Constitutions of Clarendon were gravely weakened by the murder of Becket and the papal wrath. Appeals to Rome increased. Papal authority mounted with them. The death of Becket checked Henry's course. Another bitter chapter in the struggle between church and state was to occur within half a century.

THE KING'S JUSTICES

It is well to keep in mind certain facts about the reign of Henry II. One salient feature of the period of history is the use of old tools for new purposes. Again and again we see that procedures but fitfully employed in earlier years became regular and normal under the shrewd control of the efficient and calculating Henry. In a silent process of great significance there emerged an improved and impartial machinery of government and law. The sinister power of the scrambling barons dwindled. There was more order, more security, more protection of the rights of the subject, so soon to be riveted in the common law.

Of paramount importance, in these days when the power of the central government was felt at the shoulder of every Englishman, was the wide employment of itinerant justices and the rise of the jury system.

William I, Henry I and Henry II wanted order, peace and efficiency. They got these three things by strengthening the power of the central government. Now the effective extension of power always means the increase of executive tasks. At first the primitive *curia regis* was not a many-celled organism. It was undifferentiated and simple. But with the increasing pressures of administrative activity the cells increased, the functions multiplied, and the body of the *curia regis* grew.

Even before the Conquest, special royal agents had sometimes been sent into the shires and hundreds to do various jobs for the king. After 1066 the Norman kings occasionally despatched a few members of the *curia regis* to attend to royal business in the local areas. After all, the members of the *curia regis* who travelled with the king or stayed permanently at Westminster could not keep shrewd eyes upon the sheriffs, look after wardships, see that the king in fact got the property that had escheated to him and all the revenue that was properly his. Nor could they inspect castles and arms and watch over the king's share of court incomes. Personal inspection by royal agents obviously served the royal interests. Hence, more and more, members of the *curia regis* went over England, watching and checking and interfering like the suspicious *missi* of Charlemagne.

We know that Henry I sometimes sent out royal justices to the counties to investigate local conditions, to examine and report upon the work of the sheriffs, and to see that justice was done. It is idle to speculate about the reasons why Henry I only used this machinery in a spasmodic manner. Perhaps he never realized what a potent instrument he had in his hands. Henry II, for his part, began and continued to send justices out from Westminster. Their supervision was strengthened and regularized.

With his genius for order and detail in administration Henry instructed his justices to go about the counties on the circuits, or "iters," at regular intervals. They were required to safeguard the king's rights; to check upon the sheriffs; to inspect the barons' courts and ward off the growth of excessive power there; to preside over the county court; to gather taxes. Henry rightly considered tax collection an important aspect of government. All agents of Henry II were bound to keep keen eyes open to detect any leakages in revenue. "The justices were as busy collecting the king's taxes as enforcing the king's peace."

It is perhaps desirable to pause here to say once more that Henry II and his immediate successors were always concerned about the activities of local officials, especially the sheriffs. After the Inquest of Sheriffs, mentioned earlier, Henry dismissed all but seven from their posts. Under Henry I and Stephen county justiciars had been used to reduce the bulging powers of the sheriff. But the local justiciars, in turn, became too powerful for the king's comfort and Henry II wiped their offices away. The regents of Richard I (1189–1199) decided that each county court should select four men to make duplicate lists of pleas of the crown and other matters to be brought to the attention of the royal justices. They were also to make preliminary inquiries in criminal cases and to place their reports at the disposal of the justices. If the sheriff inadvertently forgot some things the king might want to know, these four men, called coroners, would have recorded them on their coroners' rolls. Thus the sheriffs, it was hoped, would be effectively checked by the watchful coroners.

In later days the functions of the coroners dwindled. As the reader knows, the main tasks of coroners in the twentieth century is to empanel juries and direct investigations into the causes of death by violence and misadventure. But the twelfth century is with us still in this respect: in many parts of the United States there stands the rule that only the coroner can arrest the sheriff.

As the justices went about on their circuits they accomplished many things, some of them beyond what was intended or perceived. It is worthy of note, for instance, that they used the freeholders assembled in the local courts to help them in judicial, financial, and administrative business. Such a procedure was one of the many ways in which traditions of service and cooperation were developed, useful chapters in the background of the growth of local self-government. And here, again, we see another illustration of how Henry II steadily drew the community into greater responsibility to the crown.

In 1194 all sheriffs were forbidden to hold pleas of the crown in their own shires. In 1215 clause 24 of Magna Carta said with brevity and precision: "No sheriff, constable, coroner or other bailiff of ours shall hold the pleas of our crown." Westminster was becoming more and more the capital of the judicial system as well as of the government. Thus, as the age grew in expertness, the whole network of administration and justice was being made to feel and respond to the king's will. Under Henry II many things reached a condition that foreshadowed their final state.

Despite the fact that Henry was a feudal king in a feudal age he did much to narrow the scope of feudalism and its liberties. Over-mighty baronial power, producing lesions in the body politic, was not to Henry's liking. The next chapter will show in what startling fashion the king extended the authority of the royal courts. In this section the reader is asked to observe some of the numerous other ways in which the increase of the crown's strength was achieved at the expense of the thwarted and angry barons.

The mounting habit of using the machinery of the itinerant justice system to find facts and statistics for the complex purposes of finance and administration produced an interesting and permanent result. There soon appeared two kinds of circuits undertaken by the king's justices. The first was the routine trip of the ordinary itinerant jus-tices dealing mainly with judicial matters. Sometimes the judicial commissions issued to them were of a specific nature. Sometimes, too, they were of minor importance. For example, a man who held a commission of gaol (jail) delivery was authorized to try all the prison-ers in a jail specifically named in the commission. Often these com-missions were given to prominent knights in a community. The com-missions of oyer and terminer, usually given only to royal justices, gave authority to hear (oyer) and settle (terminer) criminal cases. The latter was sometimes a general commission. Sometimes, on the other hand, its authority was restricted to one vill, hundred, or county. And sometimes, too, it covered only one kind of offense.

The most frequent kind of commission was that giving authority to hear assizes. The word "assize" at first meant the sitting of a court or assembly and then it came to have specific technical meanings that will be described at length in the next chapter. Here it must suffice to say that the justices holding commissions of assize heard pleas of the crown and a rising number of cases that today we call "civil." Be-cause this work and the results of it were so important it will be dis-cussed in detail in the next chapter.

The second kind of circuit was a much more formidable operation undertaken by royal commissioners and usually called the "General Eyre," the *iter ad omnia placita*. We know that in 1176 England was divided into areas for regular judicial visitation and that six groups, each containing three justices, moved in their designated eyres. The first list of the articles for a general eyre that has survived is that for the year 1194.[2] The student who studies these articles prepared at Westminster will see that the justices had tremendous commissions. They were charged to make long and wide inquiries about almost every matter in the realm that could possibly concern the king. They did hold pleas but that function was secondary. The emphasis was upon their investigative, fiscal, and administrative tasks. They were to investigate, for instance, such things as vacant churches in the gift of the king; wardships, marriages, and escheats; aids due the king but unpaid; "malefactors and their receivers or confederates"; "the slayers of Jews and who they are"; debts and fines; false measures of wine; the enrollment of all debts, pledges and rents of Jews.

In many eyres those who had franchises were ordered to come to claim them. The sheriffs were almost always questioned at length. Representatives elected by the various local units were queried about events and persons in their neighborhoods. These protracted and glutted inquests—Professor F. W. Maitland called them "those tedious old iters"—were naturally quite unpopular. In 1221 the men of Cornwall fled into the forests to avoid meeting the justices who came with long parchments to pry and prowl and point. Henry III was once compelled by an angry hubbub to promise that the "General Eyre" would not be held more frequently than once in seven years.

There are several excellent examples of the wide and detailed investigations of the general eyres. Earlier in this chapter references were made to the Inquest of Sheriffs of 1170. The justices who went on that famous perambulation did not limit themselves to asking questions about sheriffs. They scrutinized such things as the administration of barons and bishops on their estates; the dealings of the foresters; the state of the royal manors, wardships, escheats, farms, and churches; the work of the bailiffs and other minor crown officials. The inquest of 1170 set a precedent for recurrent inquests upon a widening range of subjects. For instance, the following were all prepared as a result of investigations by royal justices: the tallage of 1173, the Assize of Arms, the assessment of the Saladin tithe and, in Richard I's reign, the levy of a carucage (a tax levied on the plough-team or on the plough-land).

---

2 These articles are fortunately quoted at some length (pp. 104–107) in *Sources of English Constitutional History*, a volume frequently referred to in these pages.

We come now to a second important subject inextricably linked to the rise of the itinerant justices. This is the development of the jury.

THE JURY SYSTEM

Since 1066 the English Channel has been a moat defending England against foes from the Continent. But ideas have usually crossed the narrow seas with little let or hindrance. Englishmen have seldom tried to keep them out by guns, quotas, bans or tariffs. The islanders, of course, inevitably rejected some foreign conceptions and customs. What they found of value they kept. The rest they ignored or discarded.

The Normans brought with them many Roman and Frankish ideas and practices. Some articles in the baggage of feudalism were left to rust by the walls or were stowed away and forgotten. Somehow they never got sorted out or fixed or polished at all. At the same time, as the reader is well aware, there were several Norman importations that swiftly became a part of the English tradition. One of the most notable of these was the sworn inquest of lawful men, the jury.

The idea and practice of the sworn inquest is very old. Frankish kings possibly took the procedure from Rome. William the Conqueror brought it directly from his Frankish state to England and there it thrived. Several reasons explain the fruitful growth of the vine's branches.

In the twelfth and thirteenth centuries, as the reader knows, there was a substantial body of men in England who stood above the level of the villeins and below the nobles. These non-noble freemen, urban and rural, were an important class. They were usually responsible men, men of property and integrity. They were also possessed of a wide range of information about local affairs. It was these men who were required to attend the shire, hundred, and borough courts. It was they who served in the militia. They paid a large part of the Danegeld and, later, the carucage and tallage taxes. The knights of the lowest nobility moved down towards these freemen and the freemen moved up towards the knights. Sons and daughters of knights and non-noble freemen married. "Thus England's middle class virtually included all between a very small group of great barons and the villeins." The gentry class of England was being born. In this solid group were found the men who made the sworn inquest system work successfully.

William the Conqueror gathered the information for compiling Domesday Book by using the royal institution called the inquest. In each locality William's commissioners summoned men likely to know the answers to certain specific questions about property and persons in their respective neighborhoods. Through the Norman and Angevin centuries the royal commissioners put men on oath and asked searching questions on crucial points of fact. Did they want to know how well the sheriffs were serving the king? They asked the solid and respectful men, the "lawful men," of the neighborhood. Did they seek information to aid them in assessing and collecting the royal revenues? They quizzed the honest and sober men of the counties and hundreds. Writs ordering sworn inquests for various purposes, especially in matters of land and revenue, multiplied in Norman and Angevin England. All standard collections of constitutional and legal documents contain numerous illustrations of the writs concerning inquests. The primitive sworn inquest or jury was a purely prerogative instrument of royal power. It was a tool of administration. And, in the beginning, it was nothing more.

Henry II used the adaptable sworn inquest for many purposes. Like his predecessors, he found the inquest an admirable means of getting answers to administrative and non-judicial questions. Secondly, as the next chapter will show, the jury performed another function: it became a normal and effective method of dealing with common pleas in "civil" cases.

Henry and his justices did a third thing, something new and important. They used the inquest as a method of getting suspected criminals into the clutches of the royal authorities. They established in the royal court system a jury charged with the task of presenting or accusing criminals. The accusing jury was the direct antecedent of the grand jury, an institution that has thrived through many ages. Only in 1933 was it at last abolished in England for most purposes. Elsewhere in the western world it is found in different forms and with varying degrees of power.

Much learned discussion has occurred on the subject of the accusing jury and some authorities have based interesting conjectures upon such things as the case of the twelve thegns in the reign of Ethelred and the irregular practices of the Frankish kings of the ninth century. It would seem, however, that there is no solid evidence to show that the accusing jury, the jury of presentment, existed anywhere before it was used in England by Henry II. It may be, as Professor F. W.

Maitland believed, that the use of the accusing jury procedure was suggested to Henry II by the frankpledge system, that mutual collective security scheme described in Chapter IV. If we had both time and space we might summarize the various theories, sometimes halting and sometimes bold, that have been put forward about the sources of the accusing jury. The facts, it seems, do not always speak for themselves.

Now we have seen that the members of the inquest were selected because it was presumed that they would know something about the questions asked of them. They were sworn (*jurati*) to give a true answer (*veredictum*). Henry II, as we have said, used the old machinery of the inquest. We have also said that Henry asked something new from the juries of the local communities. He asked them to "present" the names of suspected criminals.

The Assize of Clarendon (1166) was a superb piece of constructive "legislation." By that document Henry II made several of his ideas a part of the regular court procedure. "For the preservation of peace and the enforcement of justice," Henry ordered that "inquiry shall be made in every county and in every hundred through twelve of the more lawful men of the hundred and through four of the more lawful men of each vill, [put] on oath to tell the truth, whether in their hundred or in their vill there is any man accused or publicly known as a robber or murderer or thief, or any one who has been a receiver of robbers, or murderers, or thieves, since the lord king has been king." Ten years later, in the Assize of Northampton, arson and counterfeiting were added to the list of crimes to be investigated. The assizes of Clarendon and Northampton were two ordinances that stood against the erosions of change and time. Unlike several assizes, they did not "sink into the mass of unenacted common law."

Thus the accusing or presenting juries, these neighbors who knew one another, were required to present to the king's justices the names of individuals suspected of crimes. Well-informed about local conditions, they "indicted," or spoke against, the suspected persons. They were not under the immediate control of the presiding justice on the one hand or the accused and his friends on the other. Indeed, in the practical operations of the local courts these selected lawful men in fact prepared the criminal charges, the pleas of the crown. Aided by sheriffs, coroners and the reports of honest neighbors the jurymen tried to find out who committed crimes, to get guilty men and suspects arrested and brought before the court for trial. If members of a jury failed to accuse anyone suspected of a crime they were heavily fined. In cases of common pleas delinquent juries were punished through the writ of attaint procedure.

All the crude and long preliminary trial forms employed earlier in criminal trials, such as oath-taking and compurgation, were almost eliminated. After 1166 there was no road of escape in the pleas of the crown except through the ordeal. Under the second clause of the Assize of Clarendon a man accused of being a robber, murderer or thief was to be seized. "And he shall go to the ordeal of water and swear that, to the value of 5s., so far as he knows he has not been a robber, murderer or thief, since the lord king has been king."

Several accounts of the operations of the accusing jury have been preserved through the centuries. The *Select Pleas of the Crown* volumes edited by Professor F. W. Maitland for the Selden Society contain many cases of crime and tragedy that the student of legal history may consult with profit. For instance, we read the following from the report of a Cornish eyre of 1201: "The jurors say that they suspect Willam Fisman of the death of Agnes of Chilleu, for the day before he had threatened her body and her goods. And the four neighboring townships being sworn, suspect him of it. It is considered that he purge himself by water under the Assize."

We have noted earlier that twelfth century society agreed that facts about such things as taxes, landholding and the number and nature of crimes could be established by the sworn inquest of twelve (the number varied) respectable men. To the king and his justices it also seemed logical that facts about guilt or innocence in criminal cases might be determined by a jury's decision.

The trying jury, sometimes called the jury of verdict, was slowly coming to be used in most cases of common pleas. As the next chapter will show, this jury was at first employed only in the assizes. Then it became the usual instrument in the great majority of other "civil" cases. It is true that in some of the older forms of action, such as debt, compurgation continued to be permissible for several centuries. But such cases were not numerous. The exceptions did not heavily cloud the rule.

In such circumstances it was probably inevitable that shrewd men often asked questions like these: "In criminal cases does God always unequivocally reveal His truth by the speedy ordeals?" "Why can the jury trial not be used in criminal actions, in pleas of the crown?" "Is it impious to believe that the jury method is more efficient and more just than the judgment by fire, water, and the rest?"

For several decades the antique procedures of the ordeals were still used in criminal cases. It was hard to overcome the idea that guilt or innocence was best revealed by God in the ordeal methods familiar to countless generations of men. The umbilical cord of tradition was always strong. It was argued, for example, that men charged with serious crimes and facing mutilation or death were entitled to the divine revelation provided by the ordeal. Was the human tribunal of the jury a sufficient and just instrument when accused men were in such jeopardy?

Only by slow steps did the ordeal yield before the pressure of doubt about its validity. For instance, the fourteenth clause of the Assize of Clarendon provided that a man indicted by an accusing jury should go at once to the ordeal by water. Accused men, "publicly and shamefully denounced" men, who were found innocent by the ordeal still had to "abjure the lands of the king so that they shall cross the sea within eight days unless they are detained by the wind." They were forbidden to return to England. A similar provision is found in the first clause of the Assize of Northampton (1176). "And if he [the accused] should be cleared by the [ordeal of] water, let him find sureties and remain in the kingdom, unless he has been accused of murder or other disgraceful felony by the community of the county and the lawful knights of his own countryside. If [now] he has been accused, in the aforesaid manner of this [sort of crime], although he has been cleared by the [ordeal of] water, let him nevertheless go out of the kingdom within forty days and take with him his chattels, saving the rights of his lords; and let him abjure the realm [on pain of being] in the lord king's mercy." It was clear, then, that if the ordeal failed to oblige with a conviction, the man accused by the lawful testimony of his neighbors still had to get out of the country.

Such enactments clearly show dissatisfaction with the ordeal. There were other grounds for mounting doubts about the wisdom and validity of a strict adherence to existing procedures. It sometimes happened, for instance, that a muscular ruffian was well aware that he could defeat a certain man of property in trial by battle. He would then threaten to accuse the propertied man of a crime and thus force a battle trial. The scoundrel would make it plain, however, that in return for a sum of money he would refrain from laying a false charge.

This, of course, was flagrant blackmail. To stop the iniquitous business Henry II and his justices permitted the accused to buy a writ to have a jury decide if he had been charged in good faith or out of hate and spite (*de odio et atia*). It is clear that this writ allowed many accused men to have a "jury trial" if they wished.

In 1203 Pope Innocent III condemned the judgment by fire and water and in 1215 the Fourth Lateran Council at Rome prohibited priests from taking any further part in ordeals. One of the purposes of the new order was to remove some temptations from the paths of the priests. It was often difficult for priests to refuse when accused men offered sizeable bribes to them to say, for instance, that a burn inflicted by a fire ordeal had healed cleanly enough to prove innocence. Thus the decision of the church brought to an end, or almost so, the trial by the ordeal of fire and water.

And yet there were difficulties. One obstacle stood firmly against the procedure of trial by jury. What was to be done with individuals who were obviously guilty and refused to submit themselves to jury trial, to "put themselves upon the country"? An accused person indicted by the suit of the king might not be tried by the human means of jury trial without his consent. It was counter to the climate of conviction to force jury trial upon anybody. After having been formally accused by a presenting jury many notorious felons felt, and rightly, that they had but small chance of acquittal by a trying jury. If they were convicted, all their property was forfeit to the king. Many men refused absolutely to submit to jury trial. What, then, was to be done with them when the ordeal was no more and no other method of decision but jury trial was available?

Sometimes those who refused to accept jury trial were kept in jail. Here, for instance, is a brief description of an event in the county of Gloucester in the year 1221: "Henry Peterich of Whaddon was held in the castle of the lord king at Gloucester for stolen sheep whereof he was accused; and afterward at the lord king's command by writ he was let out on bail until the coming of the justices; and then comes said Henry and denies the theft . . . but he does not wish to put himself upon the verdict of the twelve jurors and therefore let him be kept in custody."

Often the men who refused to submit to jury trial were not kept in jail. To persuade such recalcitrant persons to consent to be tried by jury rather drastic steps were taken. Weights, stones or heavy chains were loaded upon them. They were frequently given no food. As a result of this treatment, called *peine forte et dure,* many obstinate fellows died. However, as they died legally unconvicted of any crime, their blood was not attainted and their families inherited their property. *Peine forte et dure* was not legally abolished until 1772.

The jury of verdict thus came to be used in nearly all criminal cases. Nevertheless, the student must not conclude that the trying jury of the twelfth century was identical with the pivotal and famous institution of the modern petty jury. The number of jurors varied. Frequently the same individuals sat in both the accusing jury and the trying jury. Sometimes, indeed, the whole trying jury was merely the indicting jury sitting a second time for a different purpose. Several experiments were tried to overcome the obvious weakness of asking a man's indictors to pass upon his guilt or innocence. Not until 1352 did a statute law forbid a man's accusers from sitting upon the jury that tried him.

It must also be remembered that all jurymen were still regarded as sworn witnesses themselves. They were never looked upon as impartial judges of fact before whom witnesses appeared to tell the whole truth. Not until the fourteenth century did their verdict have to be unanimous. There was no such thing as a deadlocked jury in the days of Henry II, or Richard I, or John.

The laws of evidence were still in the future. The procedures of pleading were tangled and ill-defined. As will be explained in later chapters, the tasks confronting judges and lawyers in the courts of successive centuries were often confused and formidable. The solutions reached by bench and bar were no more simple, rational, or elegant than the common law itself. They were often clumsy, creaking and cumbersome. Nevertheless, the machinery worked. It was always a going concern. It grew stronger by the century. The words written by a famous professor about the law may also be said with justice about the court system: "It was ever awkwardly rebounding and confounding the statecraft which tried to control it. The strongest king, the ablest minister, the rudest lord protector could make little of this 'ungodly jumble.' "

Upon these simply stated facts hang many chapters in the history of English freedom under the law. Sometimes, as in the seventeenth century, the stones laid through long decades by kings, judges and lesser men were heavily shaken. But they did not crumble or fall. They remained, as they remain today, strong and necessary units in the pillars of society.

It is not irrelevant to remind the modern reader at this point that the labors and traditions of medieval society were producing far more things than were recorded in assizes and writs. We can clearly see in retrospect that long strides forward were being taken in the minds of vigilant men. New concepts were emerging about the nature of law and the purpose of the courts. Combinations of fates and forces were producing admirable and unique effects.

Sir Maurice Amos is of the opinion that the "moving spirit" of the English constitution is to be found in a characteristic of the English mind that he describes as "attachment to law," the idea that in law there is an authority above any other power in the state. He wisely quotes the words of Sir Francis Bacon: "The people of this Kingdom love the laws thereof, and nothing will oblige them more than assurance of enjoying them." It is of course impossible to say that this characteristic appeared at any particular time in England's history, just as it is inaccurate to say that Englishmen alone possess it. However, we need not hesitate to stress the fact that without the formative and fortunate decades of Henry II's reign the "attachment to law" praised by Sir Maurice Amos and others might not have existed at all. What Henry II and his subjects achieved forms an early chapter in the long tale of progress towards stable freedom under the law.

LEGAL LITERATURE: RANULF DE GLANVILLE

Let us now, for the remainder of this chapter, touch briefly upon another subject. We have seen that many ideas and procedures were being tested in Henry II's age of experiment and new learning. In these years there also appear for the first time interesting illustrations of what men were thinking about law and administration. Students who read Professor W. S. Holdsworth's superb *Sources and Literature of English Law* will find vivid descriptions of the thought and activities of judges and lawyers over several centuries. What they said and did was of high importance.

The ability and enthusiasm of Henry II's higher civil servant Richard Fitz-Nigel, bishop of London and treasurer of the Exchequer, has already been mentioned in Chapter IV. *The Dialogue on the Exchequer,* attributed to him, carefully described the working of the Exchequer, that heart of the machinery of government. About 1187 there appeared a second book, a treatise possibly written by Ranulf de Glanville, soldier, sheriff, and king's Justiciar: the *Treatise on the Laws and Customs of England.*

Perhaps Glanville did not write the book usually ascribed to him. It may have been prepared by his nephew Hubert Walter, later Archbishop of Canterbury, Justiciar, and Chancellor. Nevertheless, these famous pages on laws and customs were certainly done under Glanville's eye and supervision. The important fact is that the treatise is the oldest of the legal classics of England. It was the first of a long series of books systematically recording and interpreting the English law. The name of this famous servant of Henry II stands beside such great jurists as Bracton, Littleton, Coke and Blackstone. "Glanville, who led the way, is still entitled to the veneration always due to those who open the paths of science."

Glanville's volume contained fourteen books about the law practiced and administered in the *curia regis*. It dealt with such subjects as the land law, church and state courts, debts and other contracts, pleas of the crown, and the writ system. For several decades it was a text both widely read and widely praised. Finally, as Professor W. S. Holdsworth and others have remarked, Glanville's volume showed the marked influence of Roman law, an influence that was to increase in England until the fourteenth century. Glanville, of course, was not alone in his interest in the problem of reconciling English customary laws with the rediscovered texts of Justinian.[3]

Glanville's work foreshadowed the form which the literature about the law was to take for several centuries. Pointed questions, asked and answered in the better books, have had no small share in the growth and extension of English law. The law is always living and changing and those who have written about it have often shared in its vitality. The first thing is always the vision.

These bold years of Henry II were of course years of experiment. One thing was clear, and Glanville's book of authority illustrated it well: the day of vague and conflicting laws was departing. A new era was at hand, a period characterized by more efficiency and uniformity than England had ever known. Much of the fabric of the law, as we have noted earlier in this chapter, was being slowly altered. But the threads, as we have also seen, were mainly those of the old customary laws, described by generations of men "so far as they were able, in a straight path, turning neither to the right nor the left, passing over nothing, adding nothing, changing nothing by walking crookedly."

---

[3] The student who is especially interested in this subject may read with great profit Chapter V of Professor C. H. McIlwain's *The Growth of Political Thought in the West*.

That, then, was how Henry II and his assistants pushed forward the frontiers of administration, reached an uneasy settlement about the relations of church and state, deliberately expanded the operations of itinerant justices and jurymen, gave the shrewd Glanville cause to describe and comment. Meanwhile other changes were transforming the patterns of court policy and procedure. They were of such importance that they demand treatment in a separate chapter.

CHAPTER VI

Henry the Second:
the making of law

THE ORIGINAL WRITS

IN Chapter V we discussed the way in which the itinerant justices carried with them on their circuits the mobilized powers of the *curia regis*. They were, indeed, "the *curia regis* on the march." By their presence they turned the local courts into royal courts. They, and they alone, used the jury, a royal judicial instrument.

At first the jury system of inquiry was used only in administrative and criminal cases. But it was obvious that there was, and could be, no legal barrier in the land to prevent the royal justices, as a part of the *curia regis*, from investigating other men and other causes. The jury system offered a reasonably impartial method of settling every case, including what we call today civil cases, or common pleas. It was quite natural that many suitors wanted to make use of the king's court rather than the communal courts of the hundred and shire. In the king's court they could get the facts of the case before a jury. To be able to do this, in their opinion, was manifestly advantageous. Justice is always a desirable commodity.

These suitors obtained the necessary permission to use the royal court, the king's justice, and the jury, by purchasing from the Chancellor's office—to be called the Chancery from the reign of Richard I—a document called a writ. The writ, a royal command based upon the king's authority, opened up frontiers undreamed of in the past. It described the case and authorized the royal justices to try it. Here began the common law principle, of paramount importance, that every case must open with a writ, the original writ. Here also began a profitable source of income for the crown. *Justitia est magnum emolumentum.*

The original writs purchased by the suitors were prepared by the clerks of the Chancellor's office. Different forms of writs to fit frequent types of occurrences and actions were devised. Thus, more and more, the original writs became formal and stereotyped. It was not at all surprising that the neat and logical minds of the Chancellor's clerks liked to follow existing patterns. Change was often abhorrent. "Ask for the old ways and walk therein and ye shall find rest for your souls." Glanville listed thirty-nine types of writs framed in terms used and repeated again and again (hence "writs of course"). At the same time, the judicial writs used during court proceedings (to compel, for instance, a defendant to appear in court) also became fixed in form.

From these facts other facts followed. The original writ purchased by the suitor directed the sheriff to take certain steps, to follow a specified formula of procedure from which no departure was legally possible. Thus each writ of necessity gave rise to a particular form of action in the court. Hence the form of action, the adjective law, heavily influenced the growth of legal principles, so large a part of substantive law. In this way the writs defined, controlled, and slowly developed many of the processes by which the courts gave justice.

This point is important. If a writ did not interlock exactly with a suitor's case the royal justices declared it invalid and threw it out of court. Redress could only be obtained if there was complete adherence to the writs and forms of action. The writs became so stereotyped that if the facts could not be massaged to fit one of the existing writs then there was no recourse to the courts. Judges and lawyers had to remember a massive number of procedural rules. There came to be a forest of about 470 different original writs. Each demanded its own special form of procedural action.

These facts are stated at some length because the student must understand that the rules of procedure or adjective law played a part of overwhelming importance in the early stages of the development of law. Sir Henry Sumner Maine, that great authority of the historical school of jurisprudence, once remarked that "early substantive law has the look of being secreted in the interstices of procedure." Of course, judges extended and modified, through the process of reasoning by example and analogy called "legal logic," the principles upon which the rules were based. That is one reason why professors of law, insisting upon a solid and rational jurisprudence, still require their students to look first for the legal principle involved in specific cases not covered in statute law. "Give me the principle," Mr. Justice Story said to his law students, "even if you find it laid down in the Institutes of Hindu Law."

In a later day, as we shall see, many of the old procedures were abandoned. And yet, in the famous words of Professor F. W. Maitland: "The forms of action we have buried, but they rule us from their graves." For historical reasons a very large part of substantive law is still bound up with procedure.

Henry II and the Chancellor's clerks classified more and more judicial actions and steadily multiplied the number and types of writs by a series of royal ordinances called "assizes." The word "assize" was carried over from enactments setting up new forms of action and used to describe the actions themselves. Thus, the actions were also called "assizes." The royal ordinances themselves were not looked upon as altering the law, which was long regarded as not susceptible to change. Declared by the general agreement of the king and the *curia regis* in the "assize" the ordinances were usually considered as clarifying the existing law. This was certainly true in many decisions that were really normal administrative acts. Elsewhere, as today's student will insist, the major legal reforms of Henry II, brought about by the "assize" methods, were revolutionary in content and scope. Nevertheless, Henry and his contemporaries never regarded their acts as changing the law. They would say, were they with us now, that they were merely "declaring" the law, as in the days of the dooms long past. That is the reason why the barons at Merton in still later days, asked to change the laws of bastardy, could say with sober mien that they were unwilling to change the laws of England.

THE WRITS FOR REAL ACTIONS

Let us now consider the writs for real actions, most of which were available for cases covered by them until 1833. Students will find that Professor Carl Stephenson has included in *Sources of English Constitutional History* copies of several forms of writs occurring in Ranulf de Glanville's *Treatise on the Laws and Customs of England*. Of these writs the oldest and one of the most important was the writ of right, without which no action to recover land could be commenced in the courts. In the Middle Ages land was inevitably the principal cause of litigation. The writ of right recognized that it was within the proper province of the plaintiff's feudal lord to try in his own feudal court a specific case about land. It did not invade the jurisdiction of the feudal court but simply brought it under keener scrutiny and royal supervision. This the writ of right accomplished by commanding the feudal lord to do justice to the plaintiff and threatening that in default the king would do so through the sheriff. (*"Quod nisi feceris, vicecomes meus faciet."*)

Closely related to the writ of right was the writ *praecipe* which went further than the writ of right. It ignored the feudal court and ordered the sheriff to command the defendant to restore to the plaintiff the land in dispute or appear in a royal court to explain his failure to do so. Here was another definite step in royal encroachment upon the jurisdiction of the feudal baronial courts. To many angered barons it seemed that Henry II was ousting and usurping too much. For all contemporaries of Henry these things must have stood in sharp contrast to the litter of disorder in Stephen's reign.

The strong Henry II was thus insisting upon the royal right to supervise all land actions in his kingdom. Before Henry died, the writ of right had become obligatory for all pleas about freehold land. A century later the writ of right had become in fact nothing but a necessary legal preliminary to action in the royal courts because immediately following the issuance of a writ of right a writ of *tolt* was issued pulling the case into the sheriff's court and a writ of *pone* then directed its removal from the sheriff's court into the king's court.

These swift steps were based on the fiction that the lord had refused to do justice. In still later centuries the writ of right served to commence very technical proceedings in a maze of legal operations. There emerged, for instance, the little writ of right close, based on the startling fiction that the feudal lord had waived his right to jurisdiction.

If a legal dispute about land was dealt with in the lord's court it was usually settled through trial by battle. Here it became customary for hired champions to represent the litigants. If the action was commenced or transferred before the justices of the king's court it was tried by a method called the Grand Assize, a procedure available when the appropriate writ was bought from Chancery. Under the provisions of Henry II's ordinance of the Grand Assize the case was settled by four knights summoned by the sheriff. These knights elected twelve or more others who decided who had the right to the property, regardless of who was in actual possession of it. If a man had a good case it was obvious that he would prefer this method of decision.

Even in the reign of Henry II there were several evident weaknesses in the operations of the writ of right. For instance, the courts in the Middle Ages carefully protected individual titles to land and the law provided that no person might be deprived of his land rights unless he had personally been present in the court when the case was tried. Knavish defendants with shaky titles stayed away from court but continued to hold the property in dispute, often for years. A series of technical pleas called essoins (excuses) could also cause actions to lag. The essoin of illness, for example, allowed action to be delayed a year and a day. Fraudulent collusions often heaped delay upon delay. It was not surprising that Henry II and his justices tried to hammer out and use legal tools to bring about speedier remedies. They could never erase the writ of right but they could and did invent ways to achieve more summary actions and more substantial justice.

Once the tendrils of some necessary legal concepts grew, the rest was easy. Shrewd justices, many of whom were among the most efficient lawyers in the land, helped the Chancellor's clerks to devise new and summary forms of action to speed the law, protect justice, and keep the peace. About 1166 they invented the writ *novel disseisin,* a petty or possessory assize as distinct from the Grand Assize. This assize, and others like it, to be described later, provided for a new and special kind of procedure, specifically set forth in the Assize of Northampton (1176). The person who purchased a *novel disseisin* writ from the Chancellor's office got an order to the sheriff requiring that royal agent to summon twelve jurymen. The jury was then asked whether or not the defendant had disseised the plaintiff after a specified date. If the jury replied in the affirmative the land was to be restored to the plaintiff immediately. The fact should be stressed, however, that only seisin had been decided, not right. No possessory assize protected anything but seisin. If the defendant was certain that his right or title stood superior to that of the plaintiff then he might buy a writ of right and start along that long trail.

The reader will recall (see Chapter III) that seisin under the law did not mean the same thing as possession. Because this volume must be brief it is suggested that the serious student may learn more about the tangled problem of seisin by reading Professor F. W. Maitland's essays "The Mystery of Seisin," "The Seisin of Chattels," and "The Beatitude of Seisin" in the first volume of his *Collected Papers.* Of course, some authorities may feel that the questions are now unimportant because the Property Acts of 1925 almost eliminated in England the problems of seisin except as bases for understanding some aspects of estates and conveyancing.

A second possessory assize extended the remedy of *novel disseisin*. This was the *mort d'ancestor* procedure developed about 1176. It was used by heirs who had been prevented from obtaining seisin of lands which they claimed as their just inheritance from a close relative. *Novel disseisin* would obviously be of no use in cases such as this because the plaintiffs had never held seisin and therefore could not claim that they had been recently disseised. The writ *mort d'ancestor* ordered the sheriff to summon a jury. The jury was then asked whether or not a specified immediate relative of whom the plaintiff was the heir had died in seisin of the property in dispute. If the jury answered in the affirmative the plaintiffs were given seisin of the land and their opponents were left to decide whether or not they wanted to buy a writ of right and start that long action to get the land. For technical reasons the original *mort d'ancestor* writs were limited to claims involving close relatives (father, mother, brother, sister, uncle, aunt). In Henry III's reign (1216–1272) three new writs efficiently extended the *mort d'ancestor* procedure to cover earlier ancestors, so that a man could then try to secure seisin of lands left by his grandparents, great-grandparents or cousins.

A third possessory assize was *darrein presentment* (last nomination to a benefice). Because church livings were endowed with land or tithe rights they were regarded as real property. The writ of *darrein presentment* was designed to settle disputes over appointments, or presentments, of clergymen to church livings. Such quarrels were numerous in the Middle Ages. The *darrein presentment* writ provided a jury method for temporary settlement by giving the disputed advowson rights to the patron who had last presented a candidate to the living in question. The rival claimant might then, if he wished, buy a writ of right of advowson and thus begin the necessary form of action leading to a final settlement.

It may be remarked here that if there was ever any preliminary question as to whether an acreage of land in dispute was held by lay or ecclesiastical tenure the problem was settled in the royal courts under the Assize *Utrum* (whether). Specific provisions for the operation of the assize were inserted in the Constitutions of Clarendon of 1164 (article 9). If, as a result of this "parson's writ of right," it was decided by the jury's recognition that the land in dispute was ecclesiastical land then, until the thirteenth century, the case was finally decided in the church courts.

It was inevitable that skillful lawyers would develop new and intricate technical defenses. What Lord Mansfield later called "niceties of pleading" multiplied in the cases of the real actions of the possessory assizes. Sometimes, for instance, cases were defeated on technical grounds because there were verbal inaccuracies or because the possessory assizes were too limited in scope and hence the legal forms did not fit the facts. So it was that another important real property writ appeared in Henry II's reign. This was the writ of entry, which soon provided for new and very flexible forms of real action. The writ of entry is still used in the states of Maine, Massachusetts and New Hampshire. In its early form this writ required a jury to decide whether a tenant had entered upon the land in dispute as the result of a weak and faulty title. Because the writ thus raised the question of title it could be used for kinds of action not hitherto permitted.

The writ of entry has had a long and curious history and at this point it seems desirable to anticipate some subsequent chapters of legal development. Let us look first at the year 1215. In that year the alarmed and angry barons tried to stop the royal encroachments on the feudal courts by barring the continued use of the writ *praecipe* (Magna Carta, clause 34). Much of this check was evaded by the extended use of the writ of *pone,* described earlier. Later the writ of entry was expanded to cover nearly all forms of real action about land and the original intentions of the barons were defeated.

Late in the fourteenth century, when England was in the midst of the Peasants' Revolt and widespread economic distress, Parliament passed two statutes (1382, 1391) of Forcible Entry. These statutes were directed at individuals who forcibly entered private property, even though they might be the rightful possessors. Thus many damaged or aggrieved parties, feeling that the statutes generally forbade all forcible entries, began to take actions upon the basis of the statute law. They began, in other words, to use it as a remedy.

Still another form of action appeared in the late fifteenth century. This was called Ejectment, a form closely coupled to Trespass, an important subject soon to be discussed. To explain the development of the Ejectment process, so far as it can be rendered intelligible in succinct fashion, it is first necessary to underline the fact that leaseholders were never protected by the possessory assizes, which gave redress only when land was held in fee. To an increasing extent, however, leasehold, at first a contract, was becoming a form of estate. By the late fifteenth century the royal justices began to allow leaseholders to assert the particular type of trespass *vi et armis* (by force and by arms) called Ejectment and to collect damages for any interference with their leases. Later the procedure was extended by the king's courts to cover the return of the land from which the plaintiff had been ousted.

Now we have seen that under the writ of right and other early real actions many kinds of collusive delays and evasions and deliberate chicanery were possible. Freeholders saw in Ejectment a swift method, often superior to the forcible entry actions, of getting their claims settled. By the use of an involved series of fictions the road was opened to them.

The following is but one of the elaborate fictions used to serve the ends of the freeholders. Let us assume that A wished to dispute B's title to some land. In these circumstances A proceeded to grant a lease of the land he wanted to recover to his friend C and C entered upon the land. (Here is the entry.) C was ejected by B, who resented this kind of procedure, or by a good friend of A—let us call him D—sometimes known as the "casual ejector." (Here is the ouster.) C then brought action of Ejectment to recover possession against B or the "casual ejector" D, alleging his title by lease from A. At this moment the title of A (the real plaintiff) to grant a lease to C (the nominal plaintiff) was in issue. Was A's title valid? Or was the title of B, the real defendant, a better one? That was the important question, the one that A wanted settled from the beginning.

By this and other curious processes resting upon legal fictions Ejectment came to be applied to freeholds. To initiate an action to recover a freehold it was only necessary that the plaintiff grant a lease for the specific purposes of the action; that the lessee should be ejected; and that either the real defendant or the "casual ejector" should defend right or title in court. Lease, entry, ouster, these were the recurring steps in all the Ejectment proceedings. Soon the names in the formal court records show that the lessee and the "casual ejector" became fictitious persons. Fictitious, too, were the events because few troubled to go through the actual steps before bringing action. That is the reason why so many actions recorded by the seventeenth century contained the names of John Doe as the lessee and Richard Roe as the "casual ejector." The Ejectment process, a personal action, gradually replaced the earlier real ones. It continued to be the usual remedy for the recovery of land until forms of action were legally abolished in England in 1833.

PROPERTY LAW AND CONVEYANCING

Questions which inevitably arise in connection with the preceding pages about the writs for real action are these: How was conveyancing of real property done after the Conquest? How did men determine the precise interest for which seisin was surrendered? For instance, was the property handed over for life or in perpetuity? The Anglo-Saxon method of livery of seisin, earlier described, was widely replaced after the Conquest by detailed charters that described the property transactions carefully.

Of course charters might be lost. That is one reason why there slowly developed new methods of recording transfers of land. The first of these was called conveyancing by fine, a complicated way of getting a statement of seisin entered on a court roll. A positive court record was obviously a strong guarantee of title. In Henry II's reign collusive actions came to be permitted in royal courts to enable records of land transfers to be filed. Thus in the history of the conveyancing procedure, as in so many chapters of medieval law, the convenient assistance of collusive actions played a notable part. Indeed, if justices and lawyers had not united to permit such actions to go forward, insisting only that the letter of the law be observed, the whole course of English legal history would have been changed. The advance of the line was achieved by flank attacks as well as by direct assault.

Let us suppose that A sold a parcel of land to B and that B paid him for it. B wanted a court record of title. He started out to get it by entering suit for the land. A, who had been paid, did not defend the case. Then the court awarded B the land under the fine or final agreement (*finalis concordia*).

The fine itself contained five separate parts. The last section, or foot (*pes*), of the fine summarized the whole transaction. The foot of the record was therefore very valuable. One copy of it was made on the upper left hand section of a large sheet of parchment. A second copy was made on the upper right hand side. Below these two copies a third was made that covered the whole lower half of the parchment sheet. The parchment was then cut and each party to the transaction was given one of the two copies of the agreement written at the top of the sheet. The lower part of the sheet, containing the third copy of the record, was placed on the roll of the court.

When the parchment was divided into three parts the cutting was done along irregular lines (hence the word "indenture"). Forged documents could easily be detected because they would not fit into the jagged edges of the original parchment. It was a wise precaution, an excellent insurance. In later days the same kind of protection was given in a more efficient and simple way. Three copies of the foot of the fine were made, each on a separate sheet. One copy was given to each of the two parties involved in a property transfer and the third was put on the permanent court roll. The "Feet of Fines," performing a part of the functions of the modern registry offices, run in an unbroken series from 1195 to 1833.

A second mode of conveyance, called recovery, developed later. It was of considerable importance, as will be seen in Chapter IX, in the history of entailed estates. The process of recovery, like the fine, was a collusive action. It commenced when the plaintiff purchased a writ of right. The defendant appeared before the justice and asked permission to try to reach a settlement out of court (imparl). He did not return and thus lost the case by default. The court then made formal livery of seisin to the plaintiff. All these events were shown in the court records. The transfer of property was complete and the title was guaranteed by the court entries.

THE PERSONAL WRITS

Before the student can appreciate or find intelligible the books or articles he may encounter on the subject of the laws of England or the United States he must be aware that there are several basic differences between the rules operating in the field of the land laws and those that govern property other than land. Now it is time to say something about these things.

The English law of property divides chattels (movable goods) into two parts: (1) the "incorporeal chattels" or things (choses) in actions, such as stocks, bonds, insurance policies, and (2) "corporeal chattels," concrete objects such as cows, horses, automobiles. The rules of personal property law are frequently derived from the Roman law through the canon law. After the battles of the Middle Ages the church courts lost almost all jurisdiction over land. They did continue to include for a long time such subjects as matrimonial causes, testamentary causes, and the administration of estates in their jurisdiction. The last two categories are clearly concerned with personal property. Students today study Wills in their courses on Property. There are separate probate courts in the United States.

It has already been explained that a large part of the real estate law of the British Commonwealth and Empire and the United States is basically feudal. The previous paragraph has briefly stated that personal property law, on the other hand, contains what one writer has aptly called "curious interfusions" of Roman law. The ancient Teutonic rule, for example, says that if Smith wrongfully sells a chattel, then Kelly, the man who really owns it, cannot claim the property from the man who bought it from Smith. Kelly has only a personal claim (*in personam*) against Smith. Strange as it seems, the Code Napoleon and the laws of Spain and Italy have adopted this Teutonic rule. On the other hand, England holds to the ancient Roman rule which distinguishes sharply between ownership and possession. The owner, says the Romano-British rule, may follow his property anywhere. This illustration is one of many that could be used to italicize some fundamental rules that many readers of this book will study at length in the libraries of law schools.[1]

We must now briefly review the development of original writs for personal, as distinct from real actions. Two of these writs need little comment. The first was the writ of covenant. It dealt, like the cumbersome writ of account, with written and formal agreements about such things as the leases of land. There was yet no method of enforcing agreements or contracts unless they were made by sealed covenants. The second writ was the writ of debt. This was a document authorizing the man who purchased it from Chancery to sue in royal courts for the money owed him. A third writ, called detinue, branched from the debt form of action. The common form of this action enabled an individual to start suit for specific recovery against a person or persons illegally withholding chattels that the plaintiff alleged he was entitled to possess. The writ itself was a command to the defendant to stop detaining the chattels and to hand them over to the plaintiff. This form of action was for a time defective because there was yet no provision for any legal remedies in cases where chattels were returned in damaged condition.

Of still greater importance were two famous personal writs called trespass and replevin.

[1] See Edward Jenks, *The Book of English Law*, Chapters XXIII, XXV, XXVI and Harold Potter, *An Historical Introduction to English Law and Its Institutions*, pp. 393–470.

The flexible writ of trespass, called by Professor F. W. Maitland "the fertile mother of actions," has been already referred to in the passages about Ejectment. It was issued to redress wrongs and damages against persons, chattels, or land committed by force and by arms (*vi et armis*). This personal action paralleled the recovery of land in *novel disseisin*. Arrest was a process in this form of action because the defendant was allegedly guilty of violence, a serious offense. A defendant found guilty not only paid damages to the plaintiff but was also punished for committing an offense against the king. Obviously such a form of action was effective and speedy, far superior to the old Anglo-Saxon method of distress. It remained for the lawyers to enlarge and extend the scope of this trespass action.

In later chapters will be discussed the emergence and growth of new actions born of the original trespass procedure, especially the actions of case, trespass on the case, and assumpsit. It will also be explained how the law of wrongs, called torts, became a branch of the common pleas activities of the royal courts, mainly by means of the writ of trespass. As later chapters will show, every personal action must lie today in torts if it does not lie in contracts. At the same time the student will observe how men learned in the laws of England gradually groped towards the significant concept that wrongful intention, the dark malice of the will, must underlie all legal definitions of criminal liability.

Let us now examine the personal writ called replevin. First of all, it will be remembered that reference was made earlier to the self-help, blood feud, and distress remedies of Anglo-Saxon England. For centuries men had held the right to take and hold goods and chattels from other men in certain circumstances, as in the case of a landlord holding a tenant's cattle to force payment of rent. Hence arose the form of action called replevin, a procedure concerned with the problems of goods and chattels wrongfully taken by distress. The writ of replevin provided for a jury to decide whether or not there had been any illegal distress.

This action was sometimes awkward. For example, if a distrainer claimed any ownership in the property distrained, the action immediately ended because the writ of replevin no longer fitted the case. A student may ask: "Why was the distrainer not liable for trespass?" The answer is that although the distrainer had *custody* of the cattle or kettles he did not have *possession* of them. Hence he had committed no legal trespass on personal property. In other words, in a trespass action a plaintiff claimed that he was dispossessed. In a replevin action the plaintiff never claimed that possession was actually his but only that the defendant had illegally taken the goods into his custody. This kind of dispute often arose from the problems of services incident to land tenure in the Middle Ages. If the plaintiff won his case in a replevin action the chattels were surrendered to him. In later years, as a result of several developments, it became possible for replevin frequently to be replaced by trespass. One obvious and practical reason for this step was that damages could be awarded under trespass, something that could never happen in a replevin action.

These briefly described forms of action are the most important of the many invented in the twelfth century. Some were destined to wither and die. Others are with us still, strong sinews of the legal arms of the state.

THE COMMON LAW

Common law is a term used both in medieval and modern times to describe the great body of English unwritten law, as distinguished from Roman civil law, international law, and the system of law administered by courts of equity and admiralty courts. In its less technical sense it denotes the law generally applicable in the absence of special enactments or local custom. It is referred to early, as in the *Dialogue of the Exchequer*. And today its power is felt and its language is heard in many lands.

We have noted how the cumbersome and formal customary laws of the local courts once varied from shire to shire. They were the peculiar inheritance of the people. They were not made by anybody. They were rather "found" in the early mists of the centuries. We have also seen that the feudal law brought by the Normans did not change this pattern. True, the feudal law was in some respects uniform throughout England. But the feudal law was mainly concerned with the conditions of landholding. Then, too, as Professor C. H. McIlwain and others have remarked, there was never any incompatibility between feudalism and the immemorial local customs of the shires and hundreds. "The very essence of feudalism is a territorial principle which makes the ancient custom the law of the fief, a principle no less effective if the community happens to be the whole realm."

Before Henry II died something unexpected and unplanned was happening to local courts and local customs. What was formless and experimental in Henry I's day became regular and normal when Henry II was king. The itinerant justices put trial by inquest at the disposal of suitors. The jury gave a rational method of finding answers to disputed facts. In what Professor F. W. Maitland once called "the formulary period of English law" the justices declared the principle and practices of the central courts at Westminster. As they moved about England in these formative and constructive years they also absorbed the best in local law. They spread the use of the elaborated technical system of forms of action.

To an increasing extent the custom of the realm came to be the custom of the courts. Again and again we can see the interactions between the customary law and the judges and lawyers who interpreted it. The process of reconciliation was slow but it was steady and sure. Thus there came to be forged a common law for a large part of the kingdom. Learned justices and lawyers possessed wide knowledge of decided cases and precedents. The principle of *stare decisis* is very old. It is relevant to note that in Henry II's day Glanville referred to one case decision. About a century later Bracton referred to five hundred in his *De Legibus* and his *Notebook* has references to two thousand. Geoffrey Chaucer's "sergeant of the lawe," so vividly described in the *Canterbury Tales,* was learned in all the cases and dooms from William the Conqueror's day onward.

"Common law" today means a body of customary modes of decision. If there is no statute law to cover a case the court must search to find the precedents created by adjudicated cases, precedents stored in the minds or the books. The courts have usually followed past decisions in like cases (*stare decisis*), looking always to those past decisions (frequently still considered as "solemn ascertainments of the law") for principles to be applied by logic or analogy in new situations.

Today in the British nations and in the United States points of law decided by the courts have become part of the coral growth of the law itself and are held to bind the judges in similar cases. Can a governing statute be found? If not, the rule of common law which is applicable must be discovered. Once the rule is found or decided by the court it henceforth binds that court and all inferior courts. Judgments of courts have often begun chain reactions leading towards new elements and vital principles. Shaped by the directive forces of logic, analogy, tradition, and the pervasive values of particular societies, the common law has slowly grown, the living memory of the social organism.

In France and Germany local differences existed in variegated provincial customs. These countries at last adopted large parts of Roman law to obtain a uniform national code. England had no need for the reception of Roman law because both accident and policy had produced a widely spread English common law, "the common engagement of the republic."

As the courts of common law became separated from the executive center they grew more inelastic. Their formal principles and procedures became stereotyped, less capable of dealing with new kinds of cases. It must be remembered that not until the nineteenth century was there very much simplification of procedure or abolition of technicalities in the old forms of process, pleading and actions. But such events were in the future. Of all these things the age of Henry II knew nothing at all.

The reader may be left with some misapprehensions if no more is said than this. It is not quite true to state that there developed a uniform law for all England. Several scholars have shown that there long remained many variations in law and custom. The immediately following passages, for instance, are mainly based upon the indefatigable scholarship of Professor Nellie Neilson.[2]

Some borough courts administered their own laws with their ancient peculiarities. The semi-independent communities of the tin and lead miners had their very old customs and their own court privileges. In the palatinates and other liberties of the borderlands the king's writ did not run. "If royal justices appeared within their boundaries it was with the lord's consent unless there had been a default of feudal justice." There were also special jurisdictions for the region of the salt marshes and the fenlands. The procedure in forest regions was different from elsewhere and even in the fourteenth century there were still seventy great forests in England. The famous "custom of Kent" resisted the pressure of the common law for many years. The merchant and maritime law used in English coastal towns obviously could not be assimilated by the body of the common law. English ports usually embraced the code of Oléron, a system developed in Barcelona. No courts of Admiralty appeared in clear outline and activity in England until the end of the fourteenth century.

We have perhaps been taught to stress too much the integration of the common law and its utility as an instrument of national cohesion.

---

[2] See, for instance, Professor Neilson's "The Early Pattern of the Common Law," *American Historical Review*, XLIX (1944).

Then, too, it seems that common law lawyers of a later generation probably exaggerated the "dangers" from the civil law of Rome. Further, the English common law was a blend of Roman and feudal law as well as Anglo-Saxon. In the twelfth century, for instance, the Italian Vacarius was one of those who lectured in Roman law at Oxford. Many of the English judges and lawyers who shaped the early structure of the common law were themselves trained and learned in the civil and the canon law. It seems quite probable that they borrowed more than was accidental from the great corpus of Rome. Men who wrote about the English law often showed the effect of Roman influence. Sometimes, indeed, they even plugged the chinks they found in the English structure with material quarried from the rich mines of Rome.

The desire to protect the common law against innovation slowly grew and persisted. It persisted for a long time. For example, in *The Place in Legal History of Sir William Shareshull* (Chief Justice of the King's Bench 1350–1361) Professor Bertha Putnam describes how Shareshull and others repeatedly spoke of "the old law," of "old usage," of "custom in old times." Once, on a question of process, Shareshull said: "We do *not* wish to change our ancient course." Is it true, as we usually say, that before the appearance and growth of equity the justices almost invariably adhered to the common law? It would seem perhaps probable in view of the phrases quoted above (and there are many more) and the general attitude of the men of law. And yet it is often dangerous to argue by quotation and to keep too close to the documents. We must not glibly claim or assert too much. Shareshull and his fellow justices always insisted upon the importance or "right" in the common law. Sometimes "right" and "custom" were not the same thing. As Professor Putnam wisely remarks, there is "ample justification for the opinions of recent writers that equity was at first not strictly separated from law and that in early days the common law courts had an opportunity to administer it."

These, then, are some brief comments about such things as the continued variations of the local law from fenland to forest, the influence of Roman law, and the pervasive idea of "right" in the administration of the courts. They are stated in summary fashion here because the student, however short his textbook, should not be left unaware of some of the altered emphases of modern scholarship in the field of medieval legal history. Numerous ideas about the common law, cherished and repeated for many long years, are now in the process of revision.

Such were some of the achievements of Henry II in the fields of administration and law. In foreign affairs the clouds were usually dark. At the end of Henry's reign the envenomed duel with France moved to a sordid climax. The king was betrayed by Eleanor, his queen. All of his sons conspired and fought against him. "From the devil we came; to the devil we return," said Richard, the best of the lion's brood. Prematurely old, defeated in battle, broken by labor, disease and sorrow, Henry II died in 1189. About him pressed the shadows of treachery and humiliation. He could not foresee the sunlit glory that was to brighten his name in ages yet unborn. He did not know what great things he had done.

CHAPTER VII

Magna Carta
and beyond

YEARS OF DANGER

WHEN Stephen died in 1154 England was full of anarchy and anarchy nourishes nothing. When Henry II died in 1189 a profound revolution had taken place. Fertility had been the constant note of his rule. He had brought order. He had hammered out security. He had temporarily tamed the great feudatories. He had plucked the flower safety from the nettle danger. And soon the prospect was altered again.

The student who is not engrossed in the details of events sees emerging several salient features of law and government towards the end of the twelfth century. The power of the crown had been strengthened into predominance. The machinery of government had been increasingly centralized. The feudal council of great landed vassals was frequently summoned for aid and advice. Certain members of the council and the royal household formed a permanent body of administrators and justices to carry on the daily tasks of central government. From the efficient organs of the administrative offices and the courts the king's authority radiated into the local communities of the hundred and shire. Over the countryside the interests of the crown were guarded and expanded by the itinerant justices, the sheriffs, the coroners, the bailiffs.

In recent chapters we have been discussing the nature and momentum of the changes that brought this situation about before the death of Henry II. His departure marks the end of a phase of constitutional and legal history. Another begins as dark and rapid events loom over the horizons of the thirteenth century. This chapter is mainly about

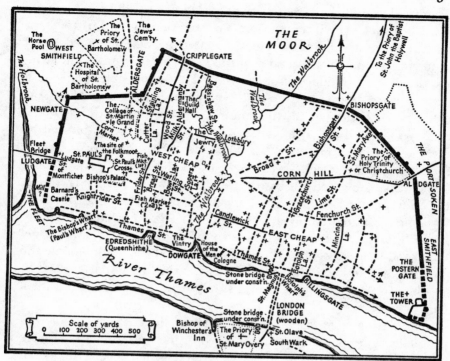

LONDON IN THE YEAR 1200

the attempts of many barons of England to neutralize the royal changes to which they were opposed.

There is no light without a shadow. It was inevitable that many of the feudal barons watched with furrowed brows and wary eyes the relentless extension of royal strength when Henry II was king. All around England the balance of power was shifting. So long as Henry remained upon the throne it seemed probable that nothing could be done to reduce the growing strength of the crown. True, the feudal barons had revolted in 1173. But Henry was both wily and strong and the rebellion had been crushed. The armed clash of interests resulted in defeat for the nobles. Therefore they waited, poising their threats and nursing rancor and resentment. Royal power muted, but did not end, the deep antagonism between crown and barons. The years were not yet come when ideas could be thrashed out by discussion and conflicting issues reconciled by mutual compromise.

After Henry II came Richard I (1189–1199) and after Richard came John (1199–1216). Under these kings the uneasy situation grew worse.

To many barons the alternative to the acceptance of the royal policies was rebellion and civil commotion. To them the new and triumphant royal techniques were abhorrent. Those techniques, it seemed, stood condemned alike by the actions of the king's agents and by the damage done to the feudal contracts which king and nobles were both committed to observe and uphold. Numerous barons of England, denied the enchantment of knowing what were the destinies of the common law and the royal courts, saw the scene as ugly, suffused by royal ambition, unredressed baronial grievances, sinful disregard of the rights of the tenants-in-chief. So often divided by jealousy and faction, a sizeable body of barons were at least united in this conviction. They could not know what lay ahead on the slopes of time.

These frustrated barons thought that they knew what needed doing. Their task, as they saw it, was to rally support and devise a detailed and positive policy of collective action which would enable the crown to be checked in its course. That was the first important target. In some future hour there would surely ripen another chance for a trial of strength.

The cutting edge to policy always lies in the answers to practical problems. The concrete questions asked in the days of Henry II were now asked again and with more cause and vehemence. How could the king be kept to the letter and spirit of the law? How could the administrative authority be made subservient to custom? Was the feudal contract to be broken whenever the king willed? Were the servants of the crown to continue exploiting, imperilling, or filching away the rights of the barons? What should be the defined components of feudalism? One modern scholar has wisely said that "the real problem was one of administration and the character of the king." Professor F. M. Powicke has also remarked in his *Stephen Langton* that it was characteristic of the tide of thought in the early thirteenth century that political expediency should be brought to the test of moral law.

Many objections were now to be gathered up and synchronized into a big one. When John was king, as we shall see, the crown's power was weakened. That weakness invited some barons to believe that the day of their deliverance from the royal yoke was at hand. At last, when the piper played, the barons refused to dance to the royal measure. Whispers gave way to threats and those threats were far more justified under John than they ever were under

Henry II. The disputes, of course, were about very important human problems. Kings and barons were attempting to answer questions as old as government itself. What is the law? Who shall make it? Who shall guard it? Who shall guard the guardian? The old arguments are often still afoot. Through long ages human frailty and ignorance have shared the road with strength and wisdom.

Let us now turn to consider the events that led to the sealing of Magna Carta in 1215. Our first task is to look at the decade when Richard I ruled England.

RICHARD I

Henry II was a statesman. Richard I was a soldier. Only twice during Henry's reign had Richard visited England, for he had lived and fought on the Continent. In an age of waning chivalry Richard, a fiery and reckless adventurer, brought glory to his name but no statecraft to government. To Richard his island kingdom was mainly useful as a source of gold to finance his projects abroad. To obtain money the great knight-errant sold bishoprics, abbotcies, offices of state, earldoms, castles, borough charters, the hands of heiresses who were royal wards, anything that could command a market. He dismissed sheriffs and they paid for their restoration. He saw to it that his half brother Geoffrey was elected to the archbishopric of York. The price that Geoffrey paid was £3,000.

Such were some of the means that Richard used to gather funds to go on the third Crusade. Energetic Christendom was thrusting towards the pink hills of Palestine. Frederick Barbarossa, the aged Holy Roman Emperor, Philip Augustus of France, and Richard of England were the leaders of those who took the Cross. When Richard departed for the Holy Land he left behind his brother John and his half brother Geoffrey. Both were ambitious. Both were bent on treachery. They swore that they would not work ill to Richard's interests when he was busy with his holy enterprise. But neither John nor Geoffrey was precise in promise keeping.

The pages of this book cannot be concerned with the events of the third Crusade, nor with Richard's difficulties in the long journey home. When Richard was absent from England the barons within and without his council disturbed the land with their rivalries. Philip Augustus, pleading ill health, left Palestine for France to begin operations against the Angevin inheritance in France belonging to his ally Richard. The faithless John, deep in intrigue with the French king, further imperilled the Angevin possessions. Such was the situation when Richard came back to England early in 1194.

At once Richard prepared for war with Philip Augustus. He collected all the moneys that he could and in May, 1194, he left England for the last time. In 1199 an enemy's crossbow brought him down and he died, as he had lived, in a soldier's tent.

A fact of major importance in Richard's reign was the steady extension of royal taxation. Because coined money had become more widely available in the twelfth century many feudal payments in kind had been commuted into money settlements. From early in the century, for example, a tenant, "avoiding all excuse and delay," often made a money payment called scutage. This was a cash sum paid in lieu of the military service required of him under the feudal contract. From about 1150 scutage formed an increasingly large part of the state income.

Richard I, busy with foreign and expensive wars, made excessive levies of scutage. He used a large part of the sums collected to buy supplies and hire foreign troops. The barons strongly opposed Richard's extended use of the scutage method of collecting revenue. They claimed that the knight's fee arrangements in the feudal contract required only a forty-day personal service of the stipulated number of fully equipped knights. There was, the nobles asserted, no provision for compelling the vassals to pay regularly for either foreign mercenaries or English knights. It seemed clear to them that Richard was moving beyond the limits of the feudal contract in his exactions. Did not the reports of the Iter of 1194 show clearly what heavy machinery Richard had devised to procure money? Was not the tallage of 1194 followed by the scutage of 1195?

The baronial attitude towards Richard's policies and methods may be easily illustrated. In 1197 Richard ordered his tenants-in-chief to provide three hundred knights to fight under the royal banner in France. The barons, led by the bishops of Lincoln and Salisbury, refused to accede to the royal command. They asserted that the tenants-in-chief were not bound by the feudal contract to render service beyond the shores of England. In this contention the barons were not on sound legal ground. Both feudal law and feudal custom in fact supported Richard's demand. The important consideration, however, is that the barons refused to meet the king's wishes. The crises of feudalism under John and Henry III were foreshadowed in Richard's day.

William the Conqueror and Henry I had collected the Danegeld, that land tax first levied by the Anglo-Saxon kings. Under Stephen, as might be expected, there was no systematic collection of the Danegeld or anything else. Henry II revived the Danegeld and Richard I did not abandon it.

In addition to the scutage and the Danegeld there was available to Richard a third source of taxation income: the tax to support the Crusades in the Holy Land. In 1166 and 1185 Henry II had made this levy. In 1188 the king and great council had imposed the famous "Saladin tithe," described in Chapter V. It will be recalled that this tax was not upon land but upon personal property. Every person was to pay a tenth of his rents and movables, "except the arms, horses, and clothes of knights and likewise the horses, books, clothes, vestments and all sacred furnishings of clergymen, and [except] the precious stones of both clergymen and laymen." The tithe tax was levied, as the above quotation indicates, upon all classes. And at this point the student should be reminded again that the assessment and collection of most of the taxes mentioned here were carried out by men in the local communities working side by side with the local machinery of the jury system. Many traditions and habits united to form the historical roots of the sturdy oak of local self-government.

When Richard had to be ransomed from the Holy Roman Emperor (1194) his tenants were faced with the task of collecting about £100,-000. Three times taxes were levied. Money was obtained from scutage, from personal property taxes like the Saladin tithe, from a tax on land mentioned in Chapter V and called a carucage (the tax was usually five shillings a carucate and a carucate was about a hundred acres of plough-land). One year's crop of wool was taken from the wealthy Cistercians, rich with their fields and their sheepfolds.

In medieval and modern centuries problems of taxation have been subjects of frequent consideration and comment. Solutions devised by governments have seldom been entirely satisfactory from the points of view of those who pay the taxes and watch the spending of revenues. In Richard I's reign there were numerous complaints. It was asserted that taxation was excessive. It was claimed that the royal income was being used carelessly and dissipated for many quite undesirable purposes.

The barons of Richard's day were sharply interested in the feudal contract as they understood it. Despite the successful invasions of baronial jurisdictions and powers by Henry II the tenants-in-chief were still anxious to hold the crown to all aspects of the contract element in feudalism. They were not prepared to ignore or accept what they considered the illegitimate demands and actions of Richard I and John. If the staggering blows suffered by the nobility at the hands of a series of remarkable kings were at long last to be parried, then the time to do it seemed to be at hand. The king must be compelled to keep his contract.

THE ROAD TO MAGNA CARTA

Most professors of history impress upon their students the importance of balance and judgment, focus and perspective. In the fields of their special competence they usually possess those qualities themselves. Modern scholars, working with patience and skill, have often made necessary the revision of many ideas about the past held with tenacity by our fathers. For instance, until recent years successive historians have stressed over and over again the less desirable characteristics of King John, partly because most men find them so repugnant. John was indeed vicious and arbitrary. He was a hard and calculating king in a ruthless age. At the same time, the tale of John and the making of Magna Carta cannot be described with justice as the struggle between an evil king and moral barons looking smugly towards posterity to praise them. This fact the student must constantly keep in mind.

Through windows newly made by several scholars, especially Professor Faith Thompson and Professor Sidney Painter, we can see once more that legal and constitutional history deals with men as well as with trends and institutions.[1] We can see very vividly how the nature of human beings, especially individuals in places of power, sways and alters the course of the world's affairs. In John's reign the traditions and claims of prelates and barons collided directly with the claims and practices of a medieval monarch. Conflicting ideas about the common good have been a fruitful source of discord in the harmony of states. At the crest of the Middle Ages, John and his barons

---

[1] See Faith Thompson, *The First Century of Magna Carta: Why It Persisted as a Document* (1925) and *Magna Carta, Its Role in the Making of the English Constitution 1300–1629* (1948). See also Sidney Painter's article "Magna Carta" in *The American Historical Review* LIII, No. 1 (1947).

were opposed in a struggle of principle and self-interest. Both were stubborn and angry and armed with power.

The barons were in no mood for appeasement. They wanted to put a brake upon royal authority. They wanted to lighten their feudal tasks and taxes. They wanted to protect their jurisdictions against the increasing controls of the crown and its officials. They held that the ancient feudal theory said that the nobles were the king's natural councillors entitled by right to collaborate with him in shaping the policies of government. Always hungry for power, the barons were prepared not only to cooperate but also, if necessary, to control. In the Middle Ages the pendulum of power swings sometimes towards the king and sometimes towards the nobles. The first part of the thirteenth century marked a time when the barons gained a premature victory. The fruits of triumph, as later chapters will show, were to be at first imperilled and then almost completely lost in the squabbles of baronial factions.

It is of very real importance to understand that several events in John's reign combined to prepare the way for the breach between king and barons and the sealing of Magna Carta. The skies abroad grew heavier with menace. Two great struggles now occurred. The first was a major war with France. The second was an unprecedented conflict with Rome.

After John was crowned king of England in 1199 he carried on the war that his brother Richard I had waged with Philip Augustus of France. The assaults and intrigues of Frenchmen resulted in humiliating reverses to British arms. Soon most of John's territories in France were gathered into Philip's eager hands: Normandy, Maine, Anjou, Touraine, Brittany. It was inevitable that many Englishmen should ask how much longer they should pay heavy and profitless taxes to defend territories held under the English flag in France. Were these lands citadels of power and fountains of profit? Or were they liabilities? Why should any attempt be made to recoup John's losses on the fields of battle and about the tables of diplomacy?

When the curtain fell on the drama of disaster in Normandy a second contest began, this time between John and Pope Innocent III, militant and able defender of papal authority.

Hubert Walter, famous Archbishop of Canterbury, died in 1205. King John wanted the bishop of Norwich, a paunchy racketeer, to be the new archbishop. Under canon law, only the monks of the cathedral chapter of Canterbury had the right to choose an archbishop.

The king had no legal power to interfere in the election. The bishops had often participated in the selection of an archbishop but in doing so they had acted without legal justification. The bishops, and probably a majority of the monks too, were prepared to accept John's candidate. Of a different opinion were several of the younger monks about Canterbury. They met secretly at night, elected their sub-prior Reginald to be the successor to Hubert Walter, and sent him to Rome to receive the pallium from Innocent III. When the king discovered what had happened, he confronted the divided ranks of the cathedral chapter. John's candidate was now chosen. Thus the names of two claimants were sent forward to the Pope.

Innocent III, the strongest Pope since Gregory VII, declared both elections irregular. He persuaded some Canterbury monks who were in Rome to elect Stephen Langton, an English cardinal living in Rome, a famous theologian, poet and scholar. John, of course, was neither calm nor lucid. He refused to recognize the appointment, seized the estates of Canterbury, and defied the formidable Innocent III. The Pope placed an interdict upon England. All church services were suspended. In an age of faith an interdict was a powerful weapon. At once John retaliated. He ordered all barons to renew their homage. He seized the lands of the regular and secular clergy who obeyed the interdict. Then, in November, 1209, Innocent III excommunicated the king. The fearful sentence cut John off from the services and sacraments of the church and damned his soul if he died before the curse was removed.

John was not cowed. He continued to despoil the church and the Jews. He used his loot to buy mercenaries. His tyranny increased. Violence begets violence. In the government and the courts maladministration grew. On every class the king's minions made exorbitant demands. The tale is squalid.

Recent scholarship has shown that we may have to revise our conclusions about the alleged deposition of King John as related by Roger of Wendover. Whether or not Innocent III in fact deposed King John and thus released his subjects from their allegiance, it is certainly true that the Pope gave the kingdom of England to Philip Augustus of France. The clutching fingers of Philip were long and powerful. Confronted with this new peril John surrendered to Innocent III in the spring of 1213. He accepted Langton as archbishop of Canterbury. He promised, among other things, to restore all church property and to compensate all the people he had despoiled.

He made over his kingdom of England and Ireland to the papacy and received it back as a fief, for which he agreed to pay a tribute of 1,000 marks a year. For a long time this humiliation was to gall and haunt Englishmen.

Thus John lost Normandy and was beaten in his long and bilious battle with the old warrior Innocent III. He had won some skirmishes but he had lost the war. And now several irreconcilable barons of his own land were to inflict a third defeat upon him. John was to be compelled to accept and seal Magna Carta, a document prepared by men who were well aware of the precedent established by the Coronation Charter issued by Henry I in 1100.

MAGNA CARTA

In the early thirteenth century the income of England was growing and John could not tap it by any legal means. His royal expenses were increasing by the month and he could not press them down. Again and again the hard and calculating king tried new, ingenious, and often unscrupulous methods to raise money. On every hand signs of opposition to his policies multiplied. John had raised an army to defend England against Philip Augustus of France. Now, his quarrel with the Pope settled, he wanted to strike at France on the Continent. His barons, still claiming that under feudal law they were not required to serve outside of England, refused to go to wage war across the Channel. John sailed with mercenary troops. In July, 1214, he and his European allies were defeated in the battle of Bouvines. In September he reached England with the remnants of a glum army and a badly wounded policy. At once he demanded a scutage to pay for the disastrous campaign. It was then that a group of barons, some of them John's personal enemies, prepared for open conflict. The years of sniping were over. The issue was soon to be squarely joined.

In January, 1215, the hostile barons, still determined to check the royal violations of feudal custom and preserve their own skins in the doing, presented several demands. John, adamant and wily, asked his nobles to wait for an answer until Easter. He hoped to find support in the interval. That hope was vain. The royal power crumbled like a rope of sand.

This was no sudden storm, no minor squabble. The barons, called by Roger of Wendover "the chief promoters of this pestilence," sent to the king the formal *diffidatio* which the feudal law required a vassal to send his lord if he proposed to depart from trust and loyalty and make war. The Cistercian chronicler Ralph of Coggeshall tells us how several barons "distrusted their king and withheld their allegiance from him. Having seized Northampton, they assailed certain castles of the king and boldly carried off booty." Soon they moved into London on a quiet Sunday. It was May 17, 1215.

On June 15, the king met a number of his barons at Runnymede beside the Thames between London and Windsor. There, in a bitter hour, he agreed to a provisional list of baronial demands. In a few days the details of a final surrender were settled. The result was the sixty-three clauses of Magna Carta, a document put in the legally binding form of a land conveyance grant or warranty deed.

Any king must depend upon the nation for instruments to exercise his royal functions. Even in the Middle Ages the magnates and the lesser landowners and townsmen had a degree of self-government under the law—hence the title of a scholarly volume by Professor A. B. White: *Self-Government at the King's Command.* Now some of these men were not prepared to be effective instruments through which the king's functions could be exercised. They believed that the king was no longer the mainspring of their government. They feared that he would continue to violate what they conceived to be their property rights, and property rights have been fruitful sources of discord both before and after 1215. These barons were also certain that John would keep on breaching the barriers of the feudal law unless they stopped him by force.

It must not be concluded that all the barons opposed John. There were only about 45 rebel barons holding 39 baronies out of a total of 197. About the same number actively supported the king. As Professor Sidney Painter has shown conclusively, most barons stayed out of the struggle.[2] The idea, so long and widely held, that a united baronage with unanimous voice defeated King John is simply untrue. "The leaders of the rebellious barons were the king's personal enemies bent on revenge and on recovering and protecting what they thought were their individual feudal (or private) property contractual rights." True, Archbishop Langton had broader concepts than the meager ones of the aristocratic baronage. As Professor Painter has wisely remarked, the barons had "sufficient good sense and political acumen to accept Langton's ideas." The power and ability of Stephen Langton have come to be more fully appreciated only in the light of the scholar-

---

[2] See Sidney Painter, *The Reign of King John,* Chapter VIII.

ship of recent years. The makers of Magna Carta, and posterity after them, owed much to Langton, the king's first baron, the Pope's delegate, the primate of all England, a great landlord.[3]

The barons were not interested in proclaiming abstract principles. Magna Carta simply redressed wrongs. The significant thing is that the wrongs were substantially those of all bad governments in any age and the principles of redress have changed but little through the centuries. Each clause was addressed to a specific problem, written in direct and simple language, prepared by practical men who knew what they were about.

Let us now examine the important terms of the settlement.[4] John was forced to yield on many fronts. The church, said the charter, was to have "its rights entire and its liberties inviolate." This phrase meant, above all, that the king should no longer interfere with the election of bishops and abbots (Clause 1). There was to be no more overriding of feudal law by force or chicanery in the collection of aids and reliefs (Clauses 2, 12, 43). John also agreed to stop plundering fiefs that fell under his wardship (Clauses 3–6) and to protect widowed heiresses (Clauses 7, 8). No scutage or aid was to be levied except those explicitly provided by feudal law unless the great council had given its consent (Clauses 12, 14). Merchants were to be defended (Clause 41). Abuses of the forest laws and all "bad customs" were to be ended (Clauses 44, 47, 48).

Several officials were to be dismissed and all mercenaries were to be sent home (Clauses 50, 51). All hostages and charters seized by John were to be returned immediately (Clause 49). The claims of London and other towns to liberties and customs granted in earlier reigns were protected (Clause 13). Specific provisions were made to control the activities of royal officials within and without the courts (Clauses 18–20, 24, 28, 30, 38, 45), the treatment of debtors (Clauses 9, 26), bridge service (Clause 23). It was clear that the makers of Magna Carta wanted to stop the growth of Angevin "bureaucratic justice."

In Chapter V were explained some aspects of the origin of the Court of Common Pleas and the court soon to be called the Court of

---

[3] See *Acta Stephani Langton, Cantuariensis Archiepiscopi A.D. 1207–1228*, collected, transcribed, and edited by Kathleen Major, Oxford University Press, 1950.
[4] The significant clauses of the original Magna Carta and the later reissues are printed in *Sources of English Constitutional History*, ed. Carl Stephenson and F. G. Marcham, pp. 115–126.

King's Bench. The Court of Common Pleas had to do with the recovery of debts and the recovery of lands. These cases—hence the name of the court—were called "common pleas." The court that was to become King's Bench at first had to do with breaches of the king's peace and with crimes and wrongs of every sort. These cases, "pleas of the crown," were at first supposed to be heard before the king in person (*coram rege*) and therefore such cases followed the king wherever war, administration, or holidays might call him. A third court, the Court of Exchequer, was concerned with the royal revenue in cases earlier described. By the end of the reign of Edward I (1272–1307) there had clearly emerged three superior courts of common law. At first each possessed a distinct jurisdiction but later all came to have concurrently a complete common law jurisdiction. Several features of the growth of these courts will be described later. Reference to them at this point has been made because Clause 17 of Magna Carta was of considerable importance in the development of the Court of Common Pleas.

Clause 17 fixed in the law the already customary practice of holding common pleas at Westminster and marks a definite stage in the cleavage of the Court of Common Pleas and the *coram rege* court that is on its way to becoming the Court of King's Bench. This Clause 17 is very precise. It says: "Common pleas shall not follow our court but shall be held in some definite place." There were several reasons for this decision. For instance, we know from the *coram rege* rolls that many litigants objected to the *coram rege* jurisdiction. By the fourteenth century Clause 17 was widely held to mean that the judges of the Court of King's Bench had no authority to hold pleas in land cases because land cases were included in "common pleas" and thus were not to follow the king and his court on their travels. The same clause was also held to forbid trials of common pleas in the Court of Exchequer. So it was that Clause 17 of Magna Carta aided in the differentiation of the common law courts.

Several other clauses referred to the law and the law courts. "To no one will we sell, to no one will we deny or delay right or justice," ran the famous Clause 40. "No freeman shall be captured or imprisoned or disseised or outlawed or exiled or in any way destroyed, nor will we go against him or send against him, except by the lawful judgments of his peers and by the law of the land," stated the celebrated Clause 39 about which historians have engaged in so much controversy, speculation and scholarship.

Although many lawyers and historians later believed and said that Clauses 39 and 40 guaranteed trial by jury and the right of habeas corpus they in fact did nothing of the kind. Nevertheless, here is the beginning of one significant chapter in the growth of the idea of "due process of law," so important in the history of the British Commonwealth and Empire and the United States.

Clause 34 declared that no baron or other freeholder was to lose jurisdiction over his men as a result of the issue of the royal writ *praecipe*: "Henceforth the writ called praecipe shall not be issued for any one concerning any tenement whereby a freeman may lose his court." Here was another aspect of the baronial attempt to check the expansion of the royal courts and the royal justice.[5]

The barons knew that John must be restrained by the threat of coercion into keeping his promises. What sanctions should be available to enforce the Charter? Under the provisions of Clause 61 the barons were to elect twenty-five of their number to whom complaints could be made about any violations of the agreement between king and barons. Any four barons could call the king's attention to such transgressions, and if no remedial steps were taken within forty days, the four barons were to report the delinquency of the king to the committee of twenty-five. "And those twenty-five barons, together with the community of the entire country, shall distress and injure us in all ways possible . . . until they secure redress according to their own decision . . . and when redress has been made they shall be as obedient to us as they were before." The humiliated John also promised to make his subjects swear obedience to the mandates of the twenty-five barons.

In 1215 the barons could find no constitutional method of checking the king. Hence they adopted the clumsy expedient of legalizing the general right of insurrection and civil war. It was a crude way of protecting Magna Carta; but in 1215 nobody could think of any other effective method of doing it. In any event, the meaning and intent of the barons was clear enough. They were determined to enforce upon the king what they considered to be the essential principles of the law of their day.

Most nineteenth century historians believed and declared that Magna Carta was a golden milepost on the road to national liberty.

---

[5] See Naomi D. Hubbard's complete discussion of the actual use made of the writ *praecipe* before and after Magna Carta in *Studies in Medieval History Presented to Frederick Maurice Powicke*, edited by R. W. Hunt, W. A. Pantin and R. W. Southern, 1949.

They were right about some things, very wrong about others. Magna Carta was reissued in 1216 and again in 1217 and 1225, each time with many revisions. Under succeeding kings it was frequently confirmed, as in the famous Confirmation of the Charters of 1297. The new arrangement of 1225 was the form usually used in these later reissues and confirmations. In the rolls of Parliament there are recorded 17 confirmations for the reign of Edward III (1327–1377), 12 for the reign of Richard II (1377–1399), 6 for Henry IV (1399–1413), and 2 for Henry V (1413–1422). There are also statutory confirmations not listed in the rolls of Parliament. Each confirmation by a monarch after the rise of Parliament was paid for by a Parliamentary grant. After the feudal "gracious aid" had become a Parliamentary tax on movables Parliament usually made grants of tax income to the king on certain conditions such as the confirmation of charters, the issuing of new ordinances, and the redress of specific grievances.

In the fourteenth century Parliament recognized the binding force of Magna Carta and often tried in its enactments to add elements to the Charter that were not there before. "This theoretical sanctity and this practical insecurity of the Charter," wrote Professor F. W. Maitland, "was part of the perennial medieval problem of law enforcement." In medieval England, of course, no one enactment produced final results. Professor C. H. McIlwain has further remarked that a Parliament in the fourteenth and fifteenth century began its business by re-enacting or affirming "the whole body of the fundamental law, including statutes of the king's predecessors." [6]

At this point, however, it is desirable to point out that the theses of those who stress the predominantly judicial character of the medieval Parliament and the companion concepts of fundamental law have not stood without challenge. In the seventeenth century Francis Bacon and Sir Edward Coke held that Magna Carta was an unalterable part of the fundamental law, despite the fact that Coke himself, and others too, forged documents about "the growth and glosses of the idea of Magna Carta" as weapons of the Puritan-Parliamentary party. Several modern scholars have remarked that the idea of the Charter as fundamental law squares ill with the theory of Parliamentary sovereignty. Professor T. F. T. Plucknett has also shown that "in practice the fourteenth century lawyers did not treat the Charter as unalterable fundamental law." The whole question is admirably dealt

---

6 See C. H. McIlwain in *Magna Carta Commemoration Essays,* p. 141.

with in Professor Faith Thompson's *Magna Carta: Its Role in the Making of the English Constitution, 1300–1629.*

In 1215 Magna Carta was a feudal document and a feudal record. It contained almost no new law and asserted no new liberties. It was really a rather conservative product of baronial labors. Yet Magna Carta is more than a purely feudal document. One of the most significant facts the student should remember is that Magna Carta became a symbol and a precedent because it contained the idea that there were certain things a king might not do. The concept of royal responsibility was carried over to the modern state. Long after almost everything else in feudalism had fallen into ruins, the contract principle continued to relate the sovereign to his subjects and became a part of the origin of limited monarchy.

In Magna Carta it is clear that the grant is not only to the tenants-in-chief but to all English freemen. "The rights of the freemen against the king," says Professor Sidney Painter, "were made as sacred as those of a vassal against his lord. Thus the feudal concept of a system of law that governed the relations between lord and vassals was carried over into the realm of non-feudal relationships." The principle that John was bound by what the barons considered a feudal contract became expanded into the broader idea that in some directions any king is bound by law. He must respect the rights of his subjects, although these "rights" were not easily defined. If the king violates these laws and rights, said the expanded principle, he may be compelled by law to observe them.

The concept of kingship implicit in many clauses of Magna Carta had never before been so sharply asserted. Throughout the next century, and far beyond it, the opponents of prerogative power repeatedly strove to defend and expand the basic idea that the monarch was not unfettered and unbridled. They insisted that the king was bound by law, limited by a contractual relationship that he could not destroy through any unilateral action. This concept, about which barons and freemen continued to be vehement and obstinate, provided an adequate reason for conflict in succeeding centuries.

King John had no intention of observing Magna Carta if he could escape his pledges. It is clear that many barons did not look upon the charter agreement as anything but a frail truce. The northern nobles prepared for war against their king. John sent abroad for mercenaries and asked the Pope to pronounce the agreement invalid. Innocent III wanted John to go on a Crusade and had no desire to have the strength of his vassal king sapped by recalcitrant and factious barons. In August, 1215, he declared Magna Carta to be unjust, unlawful and void. Philip Augustus sent the barons siege guns. In October, 1215, civil war broke out. Fear and hatred once more darkened England's skies. Several barons offered the English throne to Louis, son of Philip Augustus. French forces flowed across the Channel. When Innocent III died in July, 1216, even the future support of Rome for the king's cause was uncertain.

In October, 1216, John lost much of his baggage and treasure when his forces were caught by the quicksands and rushing tide of the sea arm called the Wash. A few days later John died at Newark. His last enemy had conquered.

CHANCERY AND WARDROBE

In Chapter V it was explained how the Treasurer went "out of court" before the Chancellor did; how the charter, patent, and close rolls appeared; and how the nature of the Exchequer was gradually altered. Reference was also made to the fact that the Chancery became fully separated from the Exchequer in Richard I's reign. From these events others followed. During the disturbed years before and after Magna Carta several silent changes were occurring in the structure and function of administration and government.

Let us first consider the Chancery. Between 1234 and 1238 the Chancery was given permanent headquarters at Westminster. The Chancellor, however, still continued to accompany the court about on its travels. Not until early in Edward III's reign (1327–1377) did the Chancellor cease to follow the court and hence we really cannot say that the Chancery went "out of court" until the middle of the fourteenth century. Of course, many staffmen of Chancery stayed at Westminster even before the permanent office was established in the 1230's. In John's reign these officials usually kept the Great Seal of the sovereign at Westminster while John wandered over his realm. John, always suspicious, was troubled by the possibility of misuse of the Great Seal. Hence he used a new instrument, called the Privy Seal, to authenticate documents. This royal seal was usually in charge of the Controller of the Wardrobe, the keeper of the duplicate rolls of the royal correspondence.

In 1311 a group of the barons rebelling against Edward II were to force the keeper of the Privy Seal out of the royal Wardrobe. The barons took this step because they wanted to prevent the king from using the Privy Seal to circumvent their wishes and obtain obedience to his will. Hence the barons made the Keeper of the Privy Seal responsible to Parliament. Although this proved to be only a temporary arrangement the Privy Seal never returned to the full control of the king. It came to be used by several branches of the government. Then, of course, the kings of the fourteenth century used new devices, among which was the personal royal signet ring, to authenticate documents. Later it became customary for the king to sign many royal orders with his own hand and this was called the sign manual. By the fifteenth century the sign manual became a warrant to the Keeper of the Privy Seal to authorize the Chancellor to affix the Great Seal to a document of major importance. Documents of lesser importance were usually issued under the sign manual or the Privy Seal. This long and complex process, here so briefly described, was thus given unexpected momentum by the wary John's desire, early in the thirteenth century, to use the Privy Seal. "He trusted no man, and no man trusted him."

A further change of interest in this period is the slowly altering status of the royal Wardrobe. The Wardrobe had its origin in Anglo-Saxon days when the Chamberlain was called the Keeper of the Wardrobe and was in charge of the royal garments, the armor, the king's treasure, and anything else that happened to be stowed away for safekeeping in the Wardrobe. The Chamberlain and his staff transported the Wardrobe wherever the king travelled. Soon these officials became responsible for the custody of bows and arrows and other battle gear. As these things could not be easily carted around England they were stored in the Tower of London. One section of Wardrobe clerks, called the Privy Wardrobe, kept custody of these military supplies. A separate staff guarded surplus jewels, money, plate, and other valuables in the crypt of Westminster Abbey. This royal treasure was kept by the monks of the Westminster chapter house until some rascals among them tried to steal it in 1303. Then the royal treasures were moved to the Tower of London where they still remain. In 1318, the barons, who were then challenging the authority of Edward II, succeeded in taking the Wardrobe out of the king's control and placing it under the effective authority of the Exchequer.

It may be that in recent years a few historians have forgiven King John too completely for what he did when he lived. Lord Acton once remarked: "The strong man with the dagger is followed by the weak man with the sponge." However these things may be, it is sufficient here to note that Magna Carta was sealed and challenged, that King John was dead and unhonored. In October, 1216, his nine-year-old son was crowned Henry III at Gloucester in the presence of four bishops and a few barons. England was on the threshold of many decades of ferment, misrule, and civil war. Among the events of a troubled century was the slow growth of the English Parliament. This is one of the capital facts of modern civilization. The next chapter traces the first steps towards the creation of a permanent and national assembly that would one day represent the mind and will of the British people.

CHAPTER VIII

The Rise of Parliament

HENRY III: CROWN VERSUS BARONS

ONE of the most remarkable features of Magna Carta was its essentially conservative character. The barons did not make any serious or sustained attempt to alter the machinery of government established by the monarchy in the past. True, restrictions were placed on the crown. The expansion of royal justice was temporarily impeded until the king's lawyers found technical means of wriggling out of some of the binding clauses of the Charter. Then there continued once again the diversion of jurisdiction in land disputes from feudal to royal courts. The right of rebellion was legalized because that was the best method the barons could find to make the king obey the law and refrain from infringing the clauses of the Charter. Nevertheless, these and other provisions were not calculated to damage or disturb the mechanism of government. The structure of government at the accession of Henry III was essentially that of his grandfather Henry II. It had survived many storms and was destined to sail unscathed through more.

No sensible man can say what might have happened to the course of history if King John had not died within sixteen months of the drama at Runnymede. His son, Henry III, was a minor and that fact was of great importance. Between 1216 and 1227 England was ruled by a regency and regencies seldom brought advantage and order in the Middle Ages.

The men who carried on the government in the new circumstances were necessarily members of the baronage. The thankless office of regent was first held by the able, honest, blunt, and respected William Marshal, Earl of Pembroke. As soon as Marshal took control he set out with his usual energy to restore order. He made several administrative, financial, and legislative reforms to conciliate the disaffected and strengthen the disjointed royalist party. By September, 1217, the French, defeated on land and sea, were forced to make peace. But Marshal did not long enjoy the sweets and achievements of power. He died in 1219 and with his death his authority was divided.

Marshal himself committed the young king to the care of the papal legate Pandulph. Opposed to Pandulph was the powerful Justiciar, Hubert de Burgh, a soldier turned priest for preferment, slow at the gospel but quick at politics. A second enemy of Pandulph was the crafty Peter des Roches, the Poitevin Bishop of Winchester, tutor of the king, leader of the foreigners who had come to the court from Poitou. In such circumstances, the machinery of the regency inevitably became weak and disrupted. Stephen Langton, archbishop of Canterbury, bitterly opposed the attempts of Pandulph to wield the full authority of regent. The policies of Hubert de Burgh, the Justiciar, continued to rouse the anger of several English magnates. The Justiciar, for instance, insisted that the barons who had unlawfully seized or fraudulently taken over lands, castles and sheriffdoms should hand them back to their rightful owners. The barons who defied Hubert's authority were punished. Stephen Langton helped with bell, book and candle to check those who resisted the demands of the regency wielding authority in the king's name. The Earl of Chester, for example, was compelled to disgorge three castles and three sheriffdoms at one time. Baronial cliques were apparently prevented from organized rebellion by their own suspicions and rivalries and by the steady vigilance of the Justiciar and his allies.

We cannot enter here into' the details of the struggles of rival interests after 1216. Indeed, there are several aspects of the whole scene that need further research and study. Professor F. M. Powicke, for example, is convinced that "the evidence available to us does not confirm the traditional view of Henry's minority as a struggle between the justiciar and the bishop."[1] For our purposes the important fact is simply this: there began to emerge during the minority of King Henry III a series of conflicts premonitory of signal dislocation to come.

---

[1] F. M. Powicke, *King Henry III and the Lord Edward: the Community of the Realm in the Thirteenth Century*, vol. i, p. 75.

In 1227 the council formally declared Henry III free from all the restrictions imposed upon him during his minority. Henry was devout, artistic, refined, a patron of art and letters. Morally, he was feeble. He was vain and capricious, a poor judge of men. He was weak, extravagant, easily bullied, and impractical. He planned a great campaign in France and it collapsed, mainly because of his gross mismanagement. He fought about papal taxation and national policy with his Justiciar, Hubert de Burgh. To the anger of many Englishmen Henry encouraged and protected Peter des Roches and the foreign parasites who came over from Poitou, hungry for place and plunder. In 1234 a baronial league, supported by revolting Welshmen, forced Henry to pack the Poitevins back home. This event is usually left unstressed in comments about the reign of Henry III but it should certainly be remarked that the crisis of 1233–1234 helped to establish effectively some of the principles of Magna Carta and was therefore an important prelude to the later Provisions of Oxford.

Henry also tried an experiment in personal rule. He tried, to an increasing extent, to get along without baronial advisers. He sought to evade baronial control of policy by drawing upon the skill of household officers and using them for many purposes of government. Thus the Crown undercut the power of the Chancellor, the Treasurer, and other heads of departments who were often under baronial influence. For example, Henry lifted the royal Wardrobe of the household to such importance that it became a rival of both Exchequer and Chancery. The contest between the household offices and those gone out of court was now exacerbated. These steps to support the royal will were not illegal but they were very unwise. Henry really was not and apparently did not desire to be an absolute ruler. However, when he took the measures described above, the unfortunate king soon found that he had little support except that given him by his own household officials and that was not enough to ensure victory in a crisis. Professor S. B. Chrimes bluntly states a fact: "Henry was not equal to his heritage; he could not make the machine work for the general advantage."

In the midst of fumbling activity the capricious Henry took another step. In 1236 he married Eleanor of Provence. The splendid ceremony lowered the level of the Exchequer still more. Then the relatives and compatriots of the new queen descended from across the Channel. They obtained titles and spoils and power. English barons complained that they were being treated like lackeys in their own land. The domain of the Crown continued to be reduced by improvident grants. By 1254 the royal debts of Henry III stood at about £235,000, many times his annual income. Foreign churchmen were drawing out of England about £47,000 annually, a sum greater than the regular royal revenue.

In 1254 the uncautious Henry, so deficient in political sense, agreed to accept the Pope's offer to confer the empty honor of the disputed crown of Sicily upon Edmund of Lancaster, Henry's second son. The Pope claimed that as suzerain of Sicily he could dispose of the crown. True, he was not in possession of Sicily and was, in fact, fighting the occupant of the throne. If Henry III wanted the prize for his son he might have it, provided that he could conquer Sicily and would pay £90,000 to compensate the Pope for the expenses already incurred. It was a silly enterprise and in 1255 the great council and the clergy both refused to grant any money. Soon there were more disturbances in Wales. The abortive campaign of 1257 resulted in an inglorious retreat by Henry from the borderlands. The tide of baronial indignation mounted.

In April, 1258, the great council refused to help Henry III pay an installment due on the £90,000 he owed the Pope. The barons insisted that they intended to end the excesses of the royal administration. The king, they declared, must dismiss the aliens and sanction the appointment of a committee that would have complete control over the Exchequer and full power to reform the government. Henry III, too alarmed to resist, agreed to these demands. Royal power, as often in the feudal age, now gave way to baronial oligarchy. A committee of twenty-four barons was appointed to submit a report to the great council.

THE PROVISIONS OF OXFORD

Simon de Montfort, Earl of Leicester, led the rebelling barons. He had been a counsellor of Henry III, governor of Gascony, a leader in a Crusade in the Holy Land. He had married the king's sister. After a series of quarrels with Henry, de Montfort became active in the movement for reform. It was he who had helped prepare the "articles of complaint" submitted to the council in June, 1258. Simon de Montfort must not be looked upon as a radical, a constitutionalist, or "the introducer of a democratic element into English government." Despite the kindly words written by some historians about de Montfort it seems that he was really an arrogant Frenchman. "He was full of hatred," wrote Professor F. M. Powicke, "against the men who ruled at court. He was willing to head a faction and became an autocrat in order to maintain a scheme of government which he had devised and which he believed to be best."

The baronage, temporarily united in the great council, agreed upon the Provisions of Oxford, a series of articles that in fact put the kingship into commission. Several committees were appointed and all were responsible, not to the king, but to the great council acting in the name of the king. The monarch who had attempted to stave off baronial influence had been forced into unconditional surrender. All important administrative officials, such as the Chancellor, Justiciar and Treasurer, were to be appointed by and be responsible to the barons. The sheriffs were likewise under the control of the council. In many respects, then, the royal prerogative was to rest in the hands of the barons.[2]

"For the common good of the whole kingdom," fifteen magnates, including nine from the barons' party led by de Montfort, were to act as a standing supervisory organ of the government, a permanent council. "And they shall have the power of advising the king in good faith concerning the government of the kingdom and concerning all matters that pertain to the king or the kingdom; and of amending and redressing everything they shall consider in need of amendment or redress." The king's ministers were responsible to the committee of fifteen. A second body of twelve, representing the great council, was ordered to meet with the fifteen barons three times a year to consult and join with them in exercising the functions of the great council; the great council itself might be called at any hour. Thirty-four additional barons were appointed to consider the problems of aid to the king. To all these things Henry III submitted—for a time.

The actual operation of the Provisions of Oxford was not successful. The barons wrangled among themselves. Some agreed that no reforms should affect their own relations with their tenants. Others, including de Montfort, insisted that the welfare of all classes, including the lesser feudatories, should be considered. In 1259 the Provisions of Westminster finally contained a list of reluctant concessions and supplementary reforms of particular value to the sub-vassal class. For

2 See Carl Stephenson and F. G. Marcham, *Sources of English Constitutional History*, Records of the Baronial Crisis (1258–66), pp. 142–149. The attention of the student is particularly directed to the introduction of Section IV, pp. 127 ff.

example, private law reforms in local affairs decreased the judicial powers of landlords; they were deprived of half their suitors.

In 1261 Pope Alexander VI was persuaded to absolve Henry III from his oath to obey the Provisions of Oxford. Henry said he would deal with the "few malicious schemers" and gathered foreign mercenaries. He dismissed the committee of fifteen. Early in 1264 the saintly Louis IX of France agreed to arbitrate the quarrel between Henry III and his barons. In the famous Mise of Amiens, Louis decided in favor of Henry III. The result of the French king's decision was civil war in England.

Simon de Montfort was himself probably the greatest soldier in England. At the battle of Lewes, fought in May, 1264, he defeated and captured Henry III and his son Prince Edward. Then a new baronial council of nine replaced the old council of fifteen. Aware of the weakness and dissension always to be found in baronial ranks de Montfort set out to bid for wider support. He sought the adherence of the country knights and the burgesses of the towns. To the famous meeting of the great council summoned in the king's name in 1265 came two knights from each shire and two burgesses from every city and borough that supported the baronial cause. Only the twenty-three magnates who backed de Montfort were called to this packed and partisan meeting of the great council, a meeting that was really a party convention. Instead of a royal despotism England was now faced with the threat of a revolutionary dictatorship.

The actions of de Montfort drove several alarmed barons over to the royal camp. The deserting nobles could not accept what they considered impetuous and radical reform. In May, 1265, Prince Edward escaped from his captors and joined his father's rising forces. In August, 1265, the rebelling barons lost the three-hour battle of Evesham. Simon de Montfort fell, stabbed in the back.

The king's appointees went back to their jobs. By 1267 the last flames of revolt were extinguished. Once again the tradition of baronial opposition to the crown had been renewed. Another chapter in the background and idea of limited monarchy had been added to the accumulating precedents. The events of 1265 were signposts. Only slowly did the evolution of Parliament permit the representation of interests other than those of the barons, of the desires of those of lower birth and lesser substance. It was fortunate that England's next king was to be Prince Edward, who had learned much from de Montfort. Prince Edward, who became Edward I, was "one of those people whom revolutions teach." He came to the throne in 1272. Londoners rioted outside the court as Henry III lay dying at Westminster.

Both parties to the struggle between crown and barons had learned some new things about the art and craft of administration. There had also emerged a real constitutional conflict. A number of crucial facts pointed to an impending change in the nature of the central authority, a basic and significant alteration in the scheme of government. Shrewd eyes looking backwards over the centuries can now be sure that the feudal organization of the state was not healthy in the thirteenth century. When feudalism was no longer necessary to hold the state together it began slowly to wither. The detective historian can now see that there was a vague beginning of a "national" consciousness in the reign of Henry III, the slow dawn of a new idea: the state exists for the separate classes of the corporate medieval community. Secondly, the medieval concept of kingship was changing. The changes were slow, subtle, often almost imperceptible. Nevertheless, they were effective and sure. For instance, the idea of the king as lord of all vassals with the power to use his kingdom as he pleased was dying. England was no longer regarded by all men as the king's lordship, his barony. Magna Carta showed that the sovereign must not be permitted to invade the rights belonging to the barons under feudal law. Later decades moved this concept over to a new ground and expanded its application to cover the relationship of the government to the governed.

There was no theory uttered by the articulate barons of the days of John and Henry III. Their problems, as they saw them, were immediate and practical. There were specific abuses and precise complaints. What were the interests of the king? How did they conflict with the interests of the barons? What was to be done with Magna Carta? How could the magnates, those loyal Englishmen, compel the foreigners, those leeching favorites of the king, to go home to France and Italy? What could be done about the financial exactions of the papacy? How could the kings be coerced into keeping their promises? How could they be stopped from a scandalous waste of the income of the state? It was to questions of this kind that the barons sought answers. The answers they found were to produce results that neither the kings, the barons, nor anybody else foresaw.

It was in these years that the assembly called Parliament entered upon its long and unique journey to supremacy in the state. Our eyes and attention must now turn to that institution, one of the strong links in the great chain of the progress of western civilization.

IDEAS AND SCHOLARS

Today "Parliament" is the name given to the supreme legislature of the kingdom of Great Britain and Northern Ireland. Many of the legislative bodies of the world are modelled upon this famous institution. In the assembly called Parliament sit the lords spiritual (archbishops and bishops) and the lords temporal, constituting the House of Lords, and the representatives of the counties and boroughs, constituting the House of Commons. These two houses with the king or queen form the modern Parliament. The Crown, pre-eminent in rank and dignity, is still the legal source of all parliamentary authority. The House of Lords is distinguished by peculiar privileges, dignities and jurisdictions. So, too, is the House of Commons. The latter, for instance, has the undisputed right of originating the imposition of all taxes and of granting supplies for the service of the state. It also has the right to determine all matters regarding the election of its members. Its privileges, designed to protect its independence and authority, are great and numerous.

Early in its history the word "parliament" came to mean an assembly of persons in which discussion occurred. It was often given to the councils of medieval kings to indicate their deliberative functions. They were holding, in the word used by Matthew Paris, a *colloquium*. They were treating of "the business of the king and his kingdom." In the thirteenth century, quite unconscious of their future power, the commons from the community of the realm took their places in the great council of the king. By 1300 Parliament had assumed substantially its present structure of king, lords and commons.

It is neither convenient nor feasible to try to set forth in this chapter all of the difficulties and confusions revealed by the careful scholarship of learned students of the history of Parliament. The tale is complex. The plot is often obscure. That which at first seems simple is often shown to be an enigma. The jungle of problems the professors once thought well and fully answered still plague and puzzle the experts today.

Seventy-five years ago the revered Bishop Stubbs finished the three volumes of his *Constitutional History of England*. Stubbs looked upon Parliament as the pivotal instrument of progress in the thirteenth and fourteenth centuries. He knew what the medieval events foreshadowed. He knew what the institution of Parliament was to become. Hence he failed to heed, as Professor Geoffrey Templeman has remarked, "the necessity for interpreting the early history of Parliament in medieval terms and in the light of medieval conditions."

The views held by Bishop Stubbs and other students of his generation have been radically modified in recent years. Following in the footsteps of Professors F. W. Maitland and T. F. Tout, modern scholars of distinction have made systematic studies of the vast and complicated judicial and administrative organization of the king's government. They have discovered that Parliament, far from dominating the medieval scene, was but an appendage of a massive governmental mechanism of councils and courts, each with its elaborate and formal procedures. They have discovered many other facts, but the tasks are far from done. In 1951 the English houses of Parliament sponsored new and long-range plans for the writing and publication of a history of Parliament. The scope and importance of the scheme is indicated by the fact that central offices for the administration of the project were established at the Institute of Historical Research at London and Professors F. M. Stenton, J. G. Edwards, L. B. Namier, J. E. Neale and T. F. T. Plucknett were appointed as an editorial board.[3]

Many authorities are not in agreement about the meaning and significance of what has been discovered so far. The student should be aware that what he concludes about the evolution of Parliament will largely depend upon what books or articles he reads and what he hears in the classroom. To avoid leaving him without chart and compass the following paragraphs describe a few of the main positions held by some reputable scholars in the past fifty years.

Professor F. W. Maitland, for example, stressed, in his introduction to the *Memoranda de Parliamento* (1893), the importance of the king's council in the Parliament of 1305. He concluded that the early Parliaments were occasional enlarged sessions of the council. Professor C. H. McIlwain, in the *High Court of Parliament and Its Supremacy* (1910), stated his conclusion that the early Parliaments were mainly judicial bodies and that medieval "legislation" was the result of activities essentially judicial in character. In 1920 Professor A. F. Pollard's *Evolution of Parliament* stated with coherence and skill

---

[3] This project is not to be confused with the International Commission for the History of Representative and Parliamentary Institutions established in 1933 by the International Committee of Historical Sciences.

some of the conclusions of both Maitland and McIlwain. When Professor Pollard went beyond the pages of published scholarship on this subject he was frequently in error and his book must be approached with caution. Minefields await the unwary reader.

During the past thirty years several scholars have built upon the foundations laid by Stubbs, Maitland, and McIlwain. Among these are Professors H. G. Richardson and G. O. Sayles. Their research has satisfied them that Parliament was not deliberately created by anybody. They are convinced that "at every stage in its early growth Parliament's functions determined its composition and organization." In the beginning, in the opinion of Richardson and Sayles, the major task of Parliament was to remedy grievances and evils, especially those created by local misgovernment. Parliament dispensed, as a court, "the highest kind of justice." Most of Parliament's early normal business, assert these two scholars, arose as a direct result of petitions presented to the council in Parliament and these petitions were the vague beginnings of bills and acts of Parliament. Richardson and Sayles regard Parliament as existing in established and definite form by 1272, the year of the accession of Edward I.

A number of scholars have found themselves in deep disagreement with Professors Richardson and Sayles. Professor G. L. Haskins has said that during Edward I's reign "in their capacities as representatives and individuals the knights and burgesses presented very few petitions to Parliament." In her *Medieval Representation and Consent* Miss M. V. Clarke was deeply concerned, as the title of her book suggests, with the doctrines of consent and the ideas of representation brought into the workings of Parliament through the examples and activities of the church. Professor Bertie Wilkinson, too, has been particularly interested in the traditions of cooperation between king and subjects in the business of government. He has insisted that Parliament was essentially political in its origin, because there the magnates and lesser men representing the whole state met to consider the affairs of the realm. Parliament, asserts Professor Wilkinson, was never the occasional enlarged session of a powerful council that Professor Maitland once held it to be. Council and Parliament, in the judgment of Wilkinson, were functionally separate. The council's duties were mainly advisory. Parliament's judicial functions were secondary. The primary task of Parliament, Professor Wilkinson repeatedly maintains, was to carry out its part in the medieval tradition of government by consent and cooperation. The views of Miss

Clarke and Professor Wilkinson are thus clearly and sharply in opposition to the conclusions of Professors Maitland, McIlwain, Richardson and Sayles (who themselves do not agree) about the early functions and structure of Parliament.

Professors F. M. Powicke and T. F. T. Plucknett agree with Professor F. W. Maitland that Parliament grew up about the council. They do, however, dispute the contentions of Professors Richardson and Sayles that Parliament was an established institution in the late thirteenth century. They insist that Parliament was fragile, indistinct, dependent, still in a formative stage until the third or fourth decade of the fourteenth century. Nor does Powicke feel that the transaction of judicial business is a special mark of Parliament. He calls attention to the known fact that the name "Parliament" was given to different kinds of sessions, some of them having but little to do with judicial matters. Further, he notes that problems of finance, justice, and general policy were all heaped together in the business of Parliament. He concludes that whatever was feasible, whatever was convenient, was done in Parliament without thought for theory or principle. Professor Plucknett stresses the rising body of Parliament's legislative activity by the early fourteenth century and remarks a steady decline of its judicial business. These scholars are only a few of those trained and cautious men who have examined the old ground with startling results.

Enough has now been written here to show the reader how lively and intense are the modern controversies and conjectures about the origin and growth of Parliament. The student who wishes to read further will find several selected references in the bibliography at the end of this book.[4] As he reads, he must remember, as Professor Richard A. Newhall has so well remarked, that the men of the thirteenth century sensed the idea of "the community of the realm" much less clearly than the historians who live and write today.

PRELUDE TO PARLIAMENT

In tracing the early growth of Parliament we discover that there were important examples of the idea of representation—we must not exaggerate the significance of the phrase—at a very early hour in the history of England. Perhaps the most significant illustrations are to

---

[4] Highly recommended is the essay "Some Recent Advance in English Constitutional History" in G. T. Lapsley's *Crown, Community, and Parliament in the Middle Ages*, edited by H. M. Cam and G. Barraclough (1951).

be found in the history of the county courts. It will be recalled that once all freemen were required to attend the shire assemblies. Later only a part of the total number of the freemen attended regularly, usually those from specifically designated land holdings. Those who came to the court spoke for all the county. It will also be remembered that whenever the itinerant justices came around to the full meetings of the shire courts in Henry II's day they found each vill represented by the reeve and four other reputable men and each borough by twelve sober and respectable burgesses. Likewise, when a presentment jury accused suspected criminals the members were, in a vague way, representing the neighborhood. Now, of course, these local activities are far from representation in a modern sense. Nevertheless, scholars have recently done much research and writing on the genesis of the idea of representation in the local devices and immemorial practices of the ancient neighborhoods. Their studies have brought an abundant, if somewhat confusing harvest.

Another source from which the modern idea of representation was undoubtedly derived was the church and the canon law. The canon law formed an important part of the life and background of medieval Englishmen and the Roman legal system substantially influenced the development of several concepts of government. Professor Gaines Post and other scholars have recently shown conclusively some of the ways in which the church contributed to the emergence in a secular world of the twin ideas of representation and action by representative bodies through the community of the realm. For instance, the procedure of summons to church councils, as in 1226, has been shown to be of considerable consequence in the history of representation and taxation. The idea of representation can be traced also to such organizations as the Dominican Order, as well as to the Convocations of the church.

It was quite natural that the idea of representation evident in local and church activities should not be limited to those spheres. Indeed, local representatives had certainly been called to appear before Richard I and probably before his predecessors. In the 1190's four lawful knights from a shire were required to come in person to the king's court to report and appeal any cases of a false judgment of a shire court. By the early thirteenth century it was quite customary for the king to order knights of the shire to come up to Westminster to give whatever information the crown required and to speak and report for the whole county. These knights, so active in county affairs, were now helping the sheriffs and other royal officials to bridge the gap between court and country, to widen the lines of communication. They were, in fact, the predecessors of the elected members of Parliament of a later generation.

The fact must be stressed that whenever the knights came to the king's court they came to report a decision of a local body. They were not required and not expected to settle or debate questions undecided when they were chosen. This kind of action seemed to the men of the early thirteenth century to be a usual and normal thing.

Shortly after he came to the throne, King John, for his particular purposes, was summoning spokesmen from all of the shires at once. The practice continued. In 1213, a year of grave difficulties, he wrote to the sheriff of Oxford: "We command you that all the knights of your bailiwick who have been summoned to be with us at Oxford, fifteen days after All Saints Day, you cause to come with their arms, likewise the barons, but without arms; and you are to cause to come to us there at the same time four discreet men of your county, to speak with us about the affairs of our kingdom." In 1227 Henry III ordered the sheriff of Cumberland to see to it that four of "the more lawful and discreet knights" were elected in the county court to come down to Westminster "for the purpose of there showing the complaints, if they have any, against you in regard to the article in the charter of liberties granted to them."

In 1254, Henry III, deep in the military and financial mires of Gascony, found it imperative to get more money rapidly. The regency in England, acting in Henry's name, tried to raise an aid. In order to bring pressure upon the great council to grant this aid it was agreed that an attempt would be made to obtain the consent of the counties to the projected grant in advance of the council meeting. The sheriffs were asked to explain the great needs of the king at special meetings of the shire courts. The courts were to come to a decision about the aid and elected knights were to report it officially to the great council. The counties were to elect four knights, said the writs of 1254, so that "they may arrange what kind of aid they wish to furnish us in so great need." "And you yourselves," the regents told the sheriffs, "are diligently to set forth to the knights . . . our necessity and our so urgent business, and you are effectively to induce them to furnish us an adequate aid at the present time." The Archbishop of Canterbury was also directed to summon the lower clergy to persuade them to grant a liberal aid. Discreet clergymen were to report the decision to the great council in the same way as the knights of the shires.

During the Barons' War each side saw the advantage of obtaining wider bases of political support by recruiting members of the class of knights and burgesses, those men of good position and solid income. In 1261, for instance, one group of barons called three knights from each shire to meet them at St. Albans. Henry III then ordered the knights to come instead to him at Westminster. In June, 1264, Simon de Montfort, victor of the battle of Lewes, summoned in the name of the king four knights from each shire. Earlier in this chapter we saw that de Montfort issued, again for the king, the writs of December, 1264, calling the famous Parliament of 1265. "Whereas, after the grave peril of the disorders recently experienced in our kingdom, Edward, our dearest first-born son, was delivered as a hostage to assure and strengthen the peace of our kingdom; and whereas, now that the aforesaid disorders have—thank God!—been quieted, we must hold a deliberation . . . to establish and consolidate full assurance of peace and tranquillity . . ." therefore Henry commanded, on the grounds of "faith and love," two "lawful, upright, and discreet knights" to come from each county and two burgesses from each borough, "setting aside every excuse and leaving all other business." For the first time in English history men from the rural and urban elements in the upper middle class were summoned to attend the same enlarged session of the great council.

Thus Parliament began. For reasons of administrative expedience and financial necessity the knights and burgesses, elected by their neighbors, were summoned by royal command to "treat upon those matters" in which the king was interested. At first they were usually called to facilitate the collection of aids and to help the crown centralize administration more effectively. Parliament still continued to be the high court, the king's court. The royal prerogative loomed above the passive commoners who sat and stood as petitioners and servants, their grievances redressed only to the extent that it pleased king and magnates to soothe and solve.[5]

---

[5] For a lucid and brilliant discussion of the shaping of the doctrine of corporate consent see Professor S. K. Mitchell's *Taxation in Medieval England*, edited in 1951 by Professor Sidney Painter. In the thirteenth century there still persisted the ancient concept of the "gracious aid" granted by the individual tenants-in-chief to the king in the form, for instance, of a carucage or a tax on movables or revenues. Nevertheless, "the practical effect of a grant by the great council was to make the decision binding on all holders of

These first assemblies, meeting for so short a time and so infrequently, nevertheless produced at the outset measures and discussions of a very illuminating sort. Parliament slowly began to create and impose, like any organism discharging its function, the law by which it lived. Expediency and custom merged and precedents and principles multiplied. Slowly, very slowly, the activities which today we most associate with Parliament began to move into the foreground.

EDWARD I AND PARLIAMENT

Edward I came to the throne in 1272; he died in 1307. This king was one of the strongest of England's medieval monarchs. He was a man of sense and action, efficient, hard-working, and thorough. In Edward's day the kingdom was not to be wounded by baronial strife. In the England ruled by Edward I there was no disorganized demolition or calculated mayhem. The results of Edward's constructive achievements in legislation and administration have flowed through the centuries to the present day. In the next chapter are described the shrewd activities of Edward in expanding the scope and efficiency of law and administration. In this chapter we must examine the changes in the growth of Parliament that occurred under his strong hand.

There has never been anything fixed or static about the English constitution. Problems of government may not greatly alter from generation to generation but solutions to them vary and they perhaps vary more when there are few theories and conventions to trammel and confine with dogma and intolerance. Edward I stood so close to the beginning of Parliament that there were no lawyers or professors to protest his experiments on the ground that he was violating laws or breaking precedents.

To understand the significance of Edward I's successful experiments and repairs we must remember the importance of the great council, the king's central *magnum concilium,* in the beginnings and growth of Parliament. The council was the parent of the common law courts and the possessor of all jurisdiction not sloughed off and given to those law courts. It still remained the highest court in the land, the king's court, the "high court of Parliament." Many cases, either within or without the cognizance of the courts of common law,

---

the type of property being taxed." Such a development in the field of taxation and finance procedure was of significance in the subsequent growth of the pattern and powers of Parliament, especially after the House of Commons became a body separate from the House of Lords.

were tried before it. Difficult problems were often sent up to the council by the common law courts. Appeals from the decisions of the itinerant justices or from the Court of Common Pleas were settled in the council sitting as a court. Because of its residual jurisdiction its tasks were manifold.

It is also wise to stress again the fact that the council was the most important administrative body in the kingdom, particularly in its reduced form as a small council which, as we have seen, was already beginning to separate into what are now the various departments of government. The council was also the body most competent to advise and consult with the king. It was inevitable that the functions of the council should grow as the burdens of royal administration increased. The king in his council had a higher legal, political, and moral authority than the king alone. When the full council met mainly for judicial purposes it was usually called a Parliament in the reign of Edward I. Sometimes the smaller permanent council alone sat in the Parliament. Further, the council sometimes settled cases when Parliament was not in session at all. Finally, the sessions of the council to deal with petitions for the remedying of grievances and injustices were usually called Parliaments. Insistence upon the necessity of understanding facts such as these cannot easily be too strong or too prolonged. In Edward's day there was no such thing as a "normal" Parliament.

Let us now broaden our explanations and look closely at a series of facts stated in more detail. First, it is important to remember that almost everything depended upon the will and initiative of the crown. Royal ability and zeal, and sometimes the lack of them, have exercised a very great deal of influence in English history. It is quite clear that Edward I, like Henry II, usually showed a quick eye and a solid judgment. In certain circumstances, as he could see, it was often less awkward to call knights and burgesses to Parliament than it was to do business through itinerant justices or other royal agents in the local communities. It was manifestly desirable to get the support of middle class men for any royal programs involving taxation and aids. It was sometimes useful to have their advice on other aspects of government. The particular motives and desires of the king were mixed and varied according to the needs and circumstances of the hour. What is politic today may not be practical tomorrow. That is the reason why most modern scholars discern no consistent pattern, no serried ranks of closely packed precedents in the summoning of Parliament. Some nineteenth century historians, with their rich dyes of imagination, made many explanations and theories. We have been unmaking them ever since.

To Edward's first Parliament in 1275 came four knights from each county and six or four burgesses from each borough. In 1282 Edward tried to raise money for a war in Wales by separate negotiation with the counties and boroughs. When he failed in this he summoned four knights from each of the five northern counties and two men from each city and borough in that area to meet with him at York. Representatives of the counties and boroughs of the rest of England were called to meet at Nottingham. Another assembly, similar in character, met at Shrewsbury in 1283. Royal writs summoned two knights from each of twenty-two towns. In 1290 and in 1294 there were two similar assemblies. These details are sufficient to show the reader that the period was indeed filled with different ways of doing things. At the same time it will be seen that the practice of associating the representatives of the local communities with the lords in the great council was becoming more common. Parliament was slowly emerging as the usual instrument for the transaction of important national business. The middle class knights and moneyed burgesses from the organized communities of the rural shire and the urban borough were being consulted by the king on matters of policy important to the realm.

We must be cautious. If we assume too much about the tangled skeins of any age we invite disaster. Stern and demanding are the traditions of sound scholarship. Thus we are bound to add that there is a less favorable side to the picture of middle class participation in Edward's Parliaments than the previous paragraph might perhaps suggest. Indeed, the powers and spheres of action of the middle class spokesmen were in Edward's reign still narrow, still circumscribed. Only the council received petitions and dealt with them. Their answers are recorded in the long rolls of Parliament. Only the council was concerned with the judicial tasks which formed a large part of the early work of Parliament. The king, as we have seen, consulted the knights and burgesses about proposed taxation programs, about the state of public opinion in their local areas, sometimes about the drafting of ordinances. When that was done, the knights and burgesses usually went home, leaving the king and his magnates in the council to accept or reject their advice. Only slowly did the prescriptive customs of feudal principles cease to dominate the practice of politics.

In these years public policy was steadily expanding its scope. Commerce and trade swelled in every port and borough. The demands of the royal administration, of justice and police, grew apace. These new enterprises cost money. No longer could the king "live of his own." Whatever austerities and stringencies might be imposed upon the king's government the fact still remained that the crown obtained too little income from the royal demesne, from feudal incidents swelled by court fees, fines, occasional tallage or scutage levies. So it was that new sources of income had to be found and tapped. For instance, the more extensive use of customs duties eased the royal needs. This was particularly true after 1275, when Parliament granted Edward, as a part of his regular permanent revenue, specified export duties on wool and leather hides "for the use of our said lord the king." Import duties of two shillings were also levied on each tun, or cask, of foreign wine and each pound of merchandise. Such duties were soon called "tunnage and poundage."

In addition to the hereditary revenues and certain specified customs duties Edward I requested and received nine separate subsidy grants from Parliament of a total value of about £450,000. These grants were in the form of direct taxes, similar to the Saladin tithe which Henry II had imposed (1188) on all individuals who were not going on the Crusade. Such levies were usually in the form of percentage taxes on movable goods, a uniform levy on the personal property of all classes. The feudal lords and burgesses in Parliament normally granted "a tenth and a fifteenth," or ten per cent from the townsmen and about seven per cent from the landowners. The churchmen made their own separate grants or "free gifts." This granting of money was important; it was part of the national revenue; and it was done by a national assembly gradually inching towards a greater power.

In 1295 Edward I summoned the gathering, later called the Model Parliament, the like of which England had not seen before. This assembly included the great council, representatives of shires and towns, the heads of cathedral chapters of the church, the archdeacons, one procurator for the clergy of each cathedral and two for the clergy of each diocese. The cathedral and parish clergy soon preferred to attend their own purely ecclesiastical assemblies, the convocations of Canterbury and York. They wanted to deal with the crown separately, and they did so. The clergy continued to tax themselves in convocation until 1664, when they decided at last to be taxed by Parliament. Thus the lower clergy withdrew from Parliament in the 1330's and failed to become an important element in what was one day to be the sovereign power in England.

The Model Parliament was called in 1295 to deal with "certain arduous affairs touching us and our kingdom" and "to consider the said affairs and to give us your counsel." Edward I was at war with France and a series of disasters had imperilled England. He wanted money grants to wage war, and he wanted them from all classes of his subjects. The barons and knights gave Edward a tax of an eleventh on their goods; the burgesses granted a seventh; the clergy granted a tenth.

The Model Parliament was a step, and a long one, in the line of precedent and practice that gradually established the custom of consulting the middle class in Parliament. But nothing was determined, nothing rendered necessary. Indeed, twelve of the twenty Parliaments called after 1295 by Edward I contained no representatives of the counties or towns. Only three followed the model of 1295. It is always wise to remember that Parliament, in its final structure, was not the result of careful planning or deliberate organization but rather the result of time, chance, and constant compromise.

In 1297 Edward I needed more money for military operations in France and Scotland. Many barons were angered at the successive tax levies. The clergy had been ordered by Boniface VIII to refuse payment of taxes without papal permission. The merchants were furious at Edward's placing of an irregular exaction, or maltote, on their export wool; his levy amounted to a forty shilling tax on each sack of wool. At a Parliament held at Salisbury there were violent scenes.

When Edward had been absent on the Continent Parliament had forced the reissuance of Magna Carta, the Charter of the Forests and other concessions earlier made by the Crown. The liberties guaranteed in the past were "to be observed without impairment in all their particulars." In November, 1297, at Ghent, Edward reluctantly accepted the "Confirmation of the Charters" (*Confirmatio Cartarum*). In doing so he agreed, under Clause 6 of the document, that in the future he would not levy "aids, taxes, and prises except by the common assent of the whole kingdom and for the common benefit of the same kingdom, saving the ancient aids and prises due and accustomed." Historians are not in agreement as to whether the words "aids, taxes, and prises" (prises being requisitions or customs charges) meant non-feudal taxes of the type levied by Edward I before 1297.

Nor do they agree that "the common assent of the whole kingdom" necessarily meant the approval of a representative body such as a Parliament in which non-noble knights and townsmen participated. The weight of learned opinion today inclines to accept the view that Clauses 6 and 7 of the Confirmation of the Charters really did promise to the knights and burgesses in Parliament at least a share in controlling the amount and incidence of non-feudal taxes levied upon personal property. If this learned opinion is correct, then it follows that representatives of the middle class—if Edward and his successors strictly kept the pledge—must be summoned to all Parliaments where any extraordinary or non-feudal taxation proposals were to be discussed. Of course, we know that the promises were not strictly observed and so we have no stream of unbroken precedent. And yet there is no doubt that here is a significant step towards the later control of the purse by Parliament. This control, limited though it may have been in some respects, was to provide a power that Parliament frequently used to persuade the king to grant concessions. One reason for the later extension of the legal power and the political liberties and privileges of Parliament was that Parliament grasped the power of the purse. As we shall see, the positive and negative poles of constitutional development were to be concession, or redress of grievances, on the one hand and the granting of supply on the other. Through the centuries the king was to press for more than his normal income. Parliament was to press for more than its normal powers. "Born of the irresistible will of the king," Professor S. B. Chrimes wrote recently of Parliament, "it came in time to express the irresistible will of the people."

It was significant that the middle class spokesmen, primed in their local communities, might present petitions. By means of this right they were gradually able to take part in the making of law. The knights and burgesses could petition the king, with or without the support of the great barons of the council, for a redress of general or specific grievances. If the petition was accepted by the king, the council might prepare for the enactment into law of the measures proposed in the petition. In this manner the representative elements in Parliament could work with the king and his council.

As the years passed, the judicial character of Parliament altered, although the House of Lords remains today the highest court in the United Kingdom. With the decline of judicial and administrative functions there was more than a corresponding increase in the legislative functions. Parliament was to become primarily a maker of laws, a representative assembly with broad powers of legislation. In Edward I's reign this development was still in the future, but the conditions for its growth had been created. In some of the most crucial chapters of human history there has been no violence or blood, no drama. The origin and rise of Parliament is one of them.

CHAPTER IX

Edward the First:

law and constitution

THEMES AND PROBLEMS

How could a feudal kingdom be ruled efficiently when the rights and duties of neither king nor nobles had been precisely defined? That was a problem of importance to Edward I as it was to all monarchs in the Middle Ages. The previous chapter has described some of the methods used by Edward I to extend and improve his government in the years when the beginnings of a money economy were already threatening the bases and pillars of feudalism. In this chapter we will be mainly concerned with three themes: (1) the structure and practice of the royal courts; (2) the major writs issuing from those tribunals; (3) the statutes relating to the land, to baronial franchises, to the church, and to royal administration throughout the island. In these developments, as in the rise of Parliament, there can be clearly seen across the centuries the initiative and power of Edward I. Wrote Bishop Stubbs: "The improvement of the laws, the definite organization of government, the definite arrangement of rights and jurisdictions, the definite elaboration of all departments, which mark the reign and make it the fit conclusion of a period of growth in all these matters, were undoubtedly promoted, if not originated, by the personal action of the king." [1]

THE KING AND THE COURTS

Specialization of functions in the twelfth century resulted in the gradual separation of the Exchequer from the *curia regis*. The Ex-

---

[1] Excellent selections from the mass of documents relating to these subjects are to be found in Carl Stephenson and F. G. Marcham, Sources of English Constitutional History, pp. 161–187. Students are again advised to consult this volume, examining with special attention the statutes and the excerpts from the *de banco* rolls, assize rolls, exchequer plea rolls, coroners' rolls, *coram rege* rolls, parliament rolls, and manorial court rolls.

chequer slowly emerged to assume a dual role as a collection agency and as a court. In 1234 Henry III appointed several royal clerks as special "barons" (here the word "barons" means only "king's men") to the Upper Exchequer, the accounts division earlier described. In the next year the plea rolls of the Exchequer began. Late in his reign Edward I appointed one of the clerks as "chief baron." This official was usually a lawyer rather than an accountant. The duties of all the Upper Exchequer officials became a mixture of the judicial and the administrative. When the Exchequer functioned as a court it was of course mainly concerned with fiscal disputes arising out of the collection of revenues by the dread Exchequer of Account. Here the procedure was speedy and effective, a custom that has since continued in the modern methods of collecting government income.

The limits of the jurisdiction of the Exchequer court varied considerably, especially when the limits of what had been inherited by the Exchequer from the parent *curia regis* were vague. In fact, the Exchequer for a time even entertained petitions for reliefs and remedies outside the common law. Suits were sometimes heard in the Exchequer that properly belonged in the Court of Common Pleas. Several decrees and statutes of Edward I's reign and the later ordinances of 1311 entirely deprived the Exchequer of the right to hear common pleas. Thereafter the activities of the court decreased until ways were found to circumvent the laws that restricted its operations. Some of the necessary remedies, from the Exchequer's point of view, became available in the fourteenth century. What happened then to the Exchequer in its judicial capacity is described in the next chapter.

A second court, the Court of Common Pleas, has been briefly mentioned earlier. The reader will remember the comments in Chapter V about recent interpretations of the fact that in 1178 Henry II ordered five men from the royal household to sit permanently at Westminster "to hear the complaints of the realm and do justice" in cases not covered by Exchequer jurisdiction and in those not of sufficient importance to be considered by the whole *curia regis*. These men, as we have observed, had mainly to do with the recovery of debts and the recovery of lands, the trial of cases between private citizens, the common pleas. Finally, as we have also noted, Clause 17 of Magna Carta said: "Common pleas shall not follow our court but shall be held in some definite place." The reasons for that clause and its importance in the differentiation of the common law courts have been emphasized in Chapter VII. In the latter part of the reign of Henry II and again during the minority of Henry III the common pleas jurisdiction merged once more completely into the *curia regis*. Fortunately this condition did not long prevail. About 1234 the stationary "court of the bench," the Court of Common Pleas, began to keep its own records in the *de banco* (bench) rolls. Thus the records of this court were finally separated from the rolls of the court that was viewed as being held in the presence of the king himself (*coram rege ipso*). In 1272 a Chief Justice was appointed for the central Court of Common Pleas. At first the justices in this court were royal administrative clerks. After about 1300, however, there were very few judges who were not men trained and skilled in the law.

For six hundred years (until 1875) the Court of Common Pleas remained essentially unchanged. Its jurisdiction covered the older forms of action relating to land, the real actions, together with such other actions as covenant, detinue, and debt. By the old writ of *pone* the Court of Common Pleas could order cases transferred to it from the local inferior courts. Throughout later centuries there were protracted rivalries and disputes about duties and jurisdiction between the Court of Common Pleas and the other great law courts of England. More business meant more money. Some of these struggles will be referred to later.

A third court, the Court of King's (or Queen's) Bench, also began to emerge more clearly from the parent body of the *curia regis* in the thirteenth century. Its origin can best be explained by reminding the reader that the judges doing justice in the presence of the king—they were deemed to be in the king's presence even though he might in fact be far away—were partly operating within the judicial body of the *curia regis*. This *coram rege* group thus exercised an undefined residual jurisdiction. It was these judges who set right the errors of inferior courts and who heard particularly difficult or important cases and settled the knotty legal problems arising from them. We have also seen that these men naturally judged many cases involving the king, the pleas of the Crown. Their activities through the years marked a steady development in the early history of the Court of King's Bench.

In 1268 a significant step occurred in the growth of this third central common law body: a chief justice was appointed. Despite events such as these, the cleavage between the *curia regis* and the Court of King's Bench did not become complete and final until about 1400. In the interval the court remained closely linked to the council proper.

Henry IV (1399–1413) was the last monarch to sit as a judge in it.

The actual power of the Court of King's Bench was very great. From its nature as a royal court so intimately connected with prerogative functions and pleas of the Crown its jurisdiction was at once civil and criminal, original and appellate. By issuing prerogative writs it could correct and control all the lesser courts of England. Indeed, it could check and limit any court, large or small, except Chancery.

Three ways in which this jurisdiction was exercised may be illustrated here. There was, for instance, the King's Bench use of the writ of *certiorari*. This writ could be utilized to bring the records of any case before the Court of King's Bench. Let us suppose that King's Bench doubted that an accused person was having a fair trial in Newcastle or concluded that several points of law were too difficult to be handled at Doncaster. A *certiorari* writ would be issued, ordering that a full report of the proceedings be brought before the justices of the Court of King's Bench. If the judges there were satisfied with the conduct of the case they might send it back to the court from which they had summoned the records. If they found some aspects of the records unsatisfactory they might cause the case to be heard in King's Bench.

A second writ used by the Court of King's Bench was the writ of error. In the court procedure of the Middle Ages there was no provision for the retrial of any case that had once been heard. The only way to re-open a case was to assert that there had been "a false judgment by a false judge" or an error in the records. If a higher court decided to examine these alleged errors the result was the same as if there had existed a method of appeal. Thus, by issuing a writ of error, the Court of King's Bench was able to extend its jurisdiction both in cases affecting the Crown and in civil cases.

A third writ used to control and limit the jurisdiction of other courts was the writ of prohibition. This was a prerogative writ. It simply forbade an inferior court to continue proceedings on the ground that the case in question was outside the jurisdiction of that inferior court. On the other hand, the writ *mandamus* ordered an inferior court to perform the functions that should have been carried out.

The shaping hand of Edward I can be discerned in all of these stages of growth in the three courts of common law. Edward I, like Henry II, was a practical king. It is therefore not surprising that he sought and found a way of adequately meshing the central common law courts with the system of itinerant justices. Magna Carta had provided that assizes were to be held four times a year in every county (Clauses 18, 19) and John had agreed in the Charter to send two commissioners to take each provincial assize. John did not live to keep or break his promise and Henry III was content to issue hundreds of special commissions without establishing regular assize circuits staffed by permanent justices. Edward I showed neither the character nor the methods of his father. He and his aides carefully set up a number of judicial circuits upon each of which two judges were to travel regularly.

To these arrangements Edward I added another. In 1285 the Statute of Westminster II stated that for all pleas begun in the central royal courts writs were to be directed to the local sheriffs commanding them to assemble jurymen to report to Westminster on a certain day unless before (*nisi prius*) that date "two sworn justices" of assize had come into their county and had taken the verdict of the jurymen. If the justices had come into the county and had obtained the decision of fact from the jury they were to report it to Westminster. The report would then be placed on the central court rolls as if the case had in fact been heard during one of the four terms of the central court at Westminster. Usually the writ summoning the jurymen was issued at least a year in advance of the day appointed for their appearance in London. The obvious effect of this Second Statute of Westminster was to make royal justice as easily available in the assize courts as it was at Westminster itself. At the same time, the extension of royal justice helped to hasten the decline of the local courts, a process accelerated by a series of statutes to be discussed later in this chapter.

The thirteenth century was an age of wide experiment and growth in all the major areas of government, law, and administration. In these pages we have not yet reached the years marked by the conflict of the three great courts of common law among themselves and with the Crown and Chancery. We are still far from the Civil War between king and Parliament in the seventeenth century. The reign of Edward I is a time of building and of preparation. We have noted the singular advance in the growth of Parliament and the new forms and powers assumed by the courts of common law. It now is desirable to look closely at further developments in the nature and efficiency of the writ system used by the courts of the king.

WRITS AND CASES

The original writs steadily multiplied from the reign of Edward I. The writs of *certiorari* and *mandamus*, the writs of error and prohibition, these and others arose to add their powers to the courts of the king and their remedies to the king's subjects. Meanwhile the older forms of action, such as the possessory assizes, continued and expanded. The strength and effectiveness of entry, covenant, debt, detinue, *pone*, and replevin remained unimpaired for a time.

It has been shown that the speedy and effective writ of trespass was the most important of all personal writs. Hence it is not surprising that courts and suitors tried to enlarge the action of trespass to cover as many cases as possible. The tale of the expansion of trespass is long, fascinating and complex. By the fourteenth century the action of trespass had grown to cover almost all torts and some contracts. One of the reasons for its swift extension lies in the thirteenth century and it lies in the rise of a procedure known as "action on the case."

The Provisions of Oxford had stated the objections of the barons to the increase in the number and kind of writs issued by Chancery. It was quite natural that they should have objected because the royal writs were steadily decreasing the jurisdiction and income of the baronial courts. The document usually called the Second Statute of Westminster (1285) not only set up the *nisi prius* system but it also said that a new writ might be issued by Chancery when an existing writ did not exactly fit the facts stated by the plaintiff but where those facts were similar, or *in like case* (*in consimili casu*), to those already in an existing writ. Sir William Holdsworth and other famous scholars have held that the procedure called "action on the case" was dependent upon the Statute of Westminster II, which authorized "action in like case." Other scholars, including Professor T. F. T. Plucknett, do not agree. In any event, as the Register of Writs shows, after the statute was passed by Parliament, the courts and the lawyers devised new sets of fictions, a devious and circuitous development of the law.

It is clear that many older writs could be used for new purposes by an "action on the case" procedure. In the area of trespass development, a plaintiff might allege that almost any kind of personal injury was trespass, because it was similar (*in like case, in consimili casu*) to trespass. Chancery would then issue the old writ of trespass to cover what was really a new kind of action. This kind of writ was called "trespass on the case," or sometimes simply "case." The true cause of action would usually be hidden by a screen of fictions of fact, fictions of process, or fictions of reasoning, so that the writ of trespass on the case could be used. This writ, of course, allowed a plaintiff to recover civil damages in what had earlier been solely criminal actions. It also permitted the use of arrest, a process formerly restricted to pleas of the Crown, cases involving crimes.

The idea and practice of trespass on the case could obviously be extended in several directions. The fertile writ of trespass has many important progeny. At this point it may be remarked that the law of contract grew partly out of the law of trespass through the action of deceit because deceit actions gave remedies for breaches of agreements. A student in a college of liberal arts need not remember this comment but he will have cause to recall it if he enters a college of law. There he will also learn much more about the motive power and tensile strength of legal fictions. He must never be impatient with the legal fictions described in this and other books. If it were not for these fictions the existing form of law would indeed be a sad one. In medieval practice there is no room for the abstract speculations of the later days of jurisprudence. Medieval actions are actions devised for specific purposes. Today, for instance, our modern courts place much emphasis upon the importance of "intention" or the lack of it in criminal and civil actions. This concept is modern. The medieval justice, were there one sitting with us now, would find our verbal searches for definitions of intention certainly confusing and probably unintelligible.

One variety of the advancing forms of trespass on the case was devised to cover broken contracts. The province of contract operations was one that paid the courts well. Chancery and the church courts were satisfied in the fat days before the courts of common law evolved procedures to deal with agreements or contracts not under seal, sometimes including such relationships as those between surgeon and patient, lender and borrower, seller and buyer, master and servant. In the years when men were moving, in Sir Henry Sumner Maine's famous phrase, "from status to contract" people and courts began to seek remedies for breaches of relationships such as those listed above. Thus trespass on the case was extended by the writ of *assumpsit*. Courts began to say that although there might be no sealed contract yet certain relationships were similar to (the familiar phrase: *in like case*) contracts. For instance, if a blacksmith drove a nail into a horse's foot, if a surgeon punctured a patient's diaphragm, if a bricklayer used poor mortar in building a tower, then surely the doers of these deeds were liable for damages, whether or not there was a sealed contract.

The courts said that in a case such as any of these the defendant had "taken upon himself" (*assumpsit super se*) to do certain things. If he did them badly (misfeasance) then he should be made to pay. Later, by the middle of the fifteenth century, the judges were allowing the flexible writ *assumpsit* to issue when the defendant had done nothing (nonfeasance) to carry out his undertaking. It should be made clear, however, that in these later days the judges usually refused to allow the writ to issue in cases of nonfeasance unless the plaintiff had paid something to bind the bargain. So arose the flexible and comprehensive doctrine of "valuable consideration," the theory of the simple contract, so important in our law of contracts today and so superior to the old insistence upon sealed or "nominate" contracts. *Nuda pacta* (bare agreements) will not be enforced. There must be a consideration involved and a liability thus accepted.

A further illustration of the extension of trespass on the case is in the area of property law. A form of action called trover, based on the idea of damages caused to the plaintiff by a loss of possession, was developed from the fifteenth to the eighteenth century to cover most of the field of wrongs to chattels. In this action the plaintiff alleged a loss of property by himself, a fictitious finding (trover) by the defendant, and an attempt by the defendant to convert the property to his own use. This wrong is now called conversion. Its foundation is in the alleged wrongful disposition of the property of the plaintiff by the defendant. As a result of the appearance of trover most of the older forms of action, especially detinue, were largely superseded. In some cases, indeed, trover became an alternative to replevin.

These events were of great importance in the growth of the English legal system. Any arrest in evolution would have had harsh consequences for a nation expanding in economic and political strength. That the common law courts came upon the principle of the flexible action on the case was indeed fortunate. Here, of course, we have succinctly described only a few of the results of this discovery. Many readers of this book are on the threshold of studies in schools of law. There the nature and significance of case developments will be examined with diligence and care. The student will find, for example, that actions of case contributed much to the law covering several torts such as Nuisance, Defamation, Seduction, and Deceit or Fraud.

ROYAL LAW AND LOCAL COURTS

The massive reputation of Edward I rests upon many foundations. The important enactments of his reign were numerous and their character was varied. When we look at the laws made during the years of his rule we find that few were the result of royal ordinances in council. Most of them were enacted with the assent of the great council or of full Parliaments. Such pieces of legislation, intended to be permanent, were beginning to be called statutes. The word was still vague, being generally used to describe any very formal statement of law. Statutes of the realm, or acts of Parliament, were soon to be considered superior to common law and custom. They were to be the law of all the land.

Edward I was aided in making a large body of legislation by several professional lawyers and other expert aides. To carry the laws into execution he needed a more efficient administration. So it was that many dullards and loafers were dismissed. From such places as the Wardrobe, the Chancery, and the Exchequer Edward chose able and loyal servants for promotion to higher administrative ranks. Many of these men were not of noble birth. They were men of the middle class. Because the civil service was to them a career they became increasingly loyal to a king to whom they owed their jobs and who rewarded work and merit.

Among the changes wrought by Edward I in the judicial system stand clearly the results of his challenge to the local courts. From the days of Henry II the royal courts had steadily expanded the scope of their jurisdiction and the volume of their business. This advance had obviously been accomplished by the invasion of many functions previously performed by the shire courts, the hundred courts, and the seigniorial courts. Where outright seizure had not occurred, many local or baronial powers had been eaten away by a protracted process of nibbling, especially by ingenious extensions of the common law by shrewd royal judges. There are several striking examples of this kind of expansion of royal court power by judicial decision. One of the most famous arises from the clauses of the Statute of Gloucester of 1278.

The Statute of Gloucester expressly provided that no person should have a personal action writ from Chancery unless the property involved was worth at least forty shillings. This provision obviously meant that no such case could be heard in the king's courts when the amount at stake was less than forty shillings. One of the purposes of this apparently simple rule was to reduce the pressure upon royal courts by keeping minor cases off the docket. Royal judges used a mixture of imagination and legal logic to interpret this provision as meaning that personal actions could not be brought in any local court if they involved amounts *greater* than forty shillings. This was a fairly substantial amount in the thirteenth century but as money values dwindled forty shillings became a small sum indeed. Thus the work of the local courts decreased. Meanwhile, too, the sheriff's tourn, a royal court of record, absorbed most of the criminal work of the hundred court. As England moved into the fourteenth century the once great authority of the shire and hundred courts was shrinking to a petty civil and criminal jurisdiction.

Edward I recognized that an effective government must be centralized as much as possible. As in his father's reign, the centripetal tendencies of feudalism had resulted in many evils when feudal barons got out of hand. In 1274 Edward ordered itinerant justices to ask juries throughout each hundred in England about baronial exemptions and "liberties" possibly prejudicial to royal authority and the execution of justice. The material collected by these commissioners was embodied in the Hundred Rolls in a report like the fiscal statements of Domesday Book.

The Statute of Gloucester of 1278, in addition to stating the "forty shilling rule" described above, also required all barons to show by what authority (*quo warranto*) they held private courts and enjoyed several privileges. Edward hoped to stop the nobles from exercising feudal rights for which they could not show a royal warrant, grant, or charter. Armed with the information gathered by the commissioners who had investigated and made their reports, the justices set out on their *quo warranto* inquiry. They were ready to challenge the claims of everybody whose right to jurisdiction might be open to doubt. Apparently jurisdiction by prescription was now to be ended. Where no express grant of a franchise could be shown, the presumption was that the claimant had usurped the powers he was exercising because peace and justice belonged to the Crown and to nobody else. Pollock and Maitland succinctly state the heart of the matter: "Time does not run against the king."

The royal justices aroused much resentment among those lords who saw their privileges imperilled. In many cases old established baronial franchises rested upon no known charter foundation but only upon the fact that the rights had been held for a long time—"whereof the memory of man runneth not to the contrary." Edward I finally agreed, in the Second and Third Statutes of Gloucester (1290), that the uninterrupted possession of privileges and other franchise exemptions from

1189–1190, the first year of Richard I's reign, should be deemed conclusive and constitute a title. Thus the limit of English legal memory was fixed, and remains, at 1189–1190.

Despite this compromise, the franchise courts, as distinct from the feudal courts of right, gradually withered away. Nevertheless, so gradual was this decline that recognition was made of special powers vested in some local magnates in England in the County Councils Acts of 1846 and 1848.

The feudal courts of right also declined. The honor courts, those held by the lords over their own feudatories, had never been strong because the scattered holdings of the mesne lords made attendance by the rear vassals inconvenient. Moreover, since the days of Henry II they had been buffeted by the royal blows of *praecipe* and weakened because they could not offer the royal method of trial by jury. Ordeal and compurgation had to be used in the honor jurisdictions. It was not surprising that almost all free tenants brought their cases into royal courts.

In 1259 the baronial government had finally yielded to the pressures of the mesne tenants or rear vassals, the lesser knights and the small landholders, and had issued the document called the Provisions of Westminster. The subtenants had asked, among other things, that the lords' court rights should be defined and limited. The lesser knights and their fellows did not want to be obliged to attend the lords' courts. They did not want their chattels attached by the lord in order to compel them to appear in his court in cases involving their freehold lands. On the other hand, they did want exemptions from penalties for alleged false judgments. These, and other abuses such as the occasional illegal use of juries by seigniorial courts, were presumably corrected and ended by the Provisions of Westminster. Many of the reforms were incorporated in the Statute of Marlborough of 1267. By measures such as these the baronial courts were being weakened from below at the same time as the royal courts were pressing upon them from above.

The Statute of Marlborough also declared that any lord who insisted upon trying the case of a vassal in his own feudal court must first show a clear and express stipulation or prescription from the king or by custom going back beyond the technical limits of legal memory. It also provided that no mesne tenant should be compelled to attend court (the duty of attendance: suit of court) if it could not be shown that he had performed his duty as a suitor during the previous thirty-nine years. This decision really meant that "no freeholder could be distrained to appear in the lord's court without the king's writ."

There were, of course, many other reasons for the decline of the honor courts. For instance, there was no appeal from an honor court to a royal court, through the method of a writ of error or otherwise. This fact meant that honor courts could never develop an intermediate jurisdiction between the inferior manorial courts (or the courts leet) on the one hand and the royal courts on the other. Secondly, as changes in the criminal law occurred and new names and new definitions were given to old crimes the barons found that they no longer had powers of jurisdiction because the new names did not appear in the original description of their rights. In other areas, as we have seen, new writs provided new remedies that only the royal courts could give. Thirdly, the flow of criminal jurisdiction to royal courts was hastened by the very nature of the definition of a felony in England, today the basis of English criminal law. A felony originally meant a failure to do a feudal duty and therefore an offense against a feudal lord. Because every man took an oath of direct allegiance to his king a felony was an offense against the king, the sovereign lord, as well as against the immediate feudal master. Hence there grew the broadening empire of royal jurisdiction over those important pleas of the Crown.

Thus twilight slowly began to fall upon the franchise and honor courts. The customary manorial courts, those feudal tribunals with jurisdiction over the unfree tenants, continued for some time to resist royal encroachment. The manorial stewards, trained or advised by lawyers trained in the common law, heard many pleas. Only in the latter part of the fifteenth century did the manorial courts begin to decline. There are several reasons for this fairly long survival. One reason is this: for centuries the manorial tribunals were courts of first and last instance. No appellate jurisdiction was exercised by the royal courts until the late fifteenth century when both the common law courts and Chancery began to intrude to see that right was done. Later, in the seventeenth century, the prerogative courts of Star Chamber and Requests also intervened.

So it happened that by frontal assaults and flank attacks the persistent Edward I progressively narrowed the scope of private jurisdiction. The encroachments of royal justice left once powerful courts conquered and silent, or nearly so.

Still another development, unheralded then and sometimes unremarked today, was the altering of the structure of England's common law. When the royal courts took jurisdiction over feudal problems they decided those problems by the rules of feudal law. Therefore a section of feudal law became a part of common law. A large portion of the salvaged feudal law of course concerned real property. Hence it was that this element became such an important part of the common law. That is one reason why such a large area of the real property law of the British lands and the United States remains essentially feudal today. When Justice Felix Frankfurter referred not long ago to the "unwitty diversities of the law of real property" he was stating a fact that has plagued and perturbed generations of judges, lawyers, and students.

LAW AND ADMINISTRATION

A further phase of Edward I's legislation was calculated to reform and consolidate both law and legal procedure. The first Statute of Westminster, passed in 1275, contained fifty-one clauses and was almost a code in itself. It declared that right was to be done to all, without respect of persons. It said that elections were to be free and no man was to disturb them by "force, malice, or menace." Echoes of Magna Carta were clear: there were to be no abuses of wardships, irregular demands for feudal aids, or excessive amercements. The law of wreck, the Provisions of Oxford, the functions assigned to the coroners by Richard I—these were some of the subjects dealt with in the First Statute of Westminster. Further evidence of the methods and activities of Edward I is shown by the Statute of Winchester (1285). This law stated that because "robberies, murders, and arsons be more often used than they have been heretofore" penalties were to be imposed on individuals who protected or concealed criminals. Parliament re-enacted the Assize of Arms (1181), with its provisions that every man should keep armor and weapons proper to his status in society and be ready to join in the "hue and cry" for suspected criminals. The old ideas about watch and ward, about local military and police protection, stand forth in almost every clause. The gates of towns were to be closed at night. The people dwelling in each county were to be answerable for robberies and damages done within their borders. Hedges and underbrush along the highway apt to shelter lurking highwaymen were to be cut. These were the main provisions of the Statute of Winchester.

The search for collective security, for order, for efficient organization, continued steadily. If we now turn to the Articles of 1300 (*Ar-*

ticuli Super Cartas), well towards the end of Edward's reign, we see that there was no relaxation of the efforts to increase the social stability of the state and the general observance of the law. The Articles contained twenty clauses that supplemented the Great Charter and the Charter of the Forests. Commissioners were appointed to look into all cases where the charters had been infringed. The operation of the jury system was to be closely examined. The administration of the forests was to be more carefully regulated. Certain abuses in the practices of royal officers and in the system of purveyance (the providing of goods or services for the crown by pre-emption or impressment) were remedied, so far as law could do it. Finally, it was ordered that "no common pleas shall henceforth be held in the Exchequer, contrary to the form of the Great Charter. On the other hand, the king orders that the Chancery and the justices of his bench shall follow him, so that he may always have near him certain men expert in the law, who, whenever the need arises, will know how rightfully to despatch all such business as may come before the court." Measures such as these show that the pace of the effective separation of powers in the great courts of law was not slackened, even under the shadows of the wars with France and Scotland.

In addition to a large body of legislation dealing with the reform of law and administration there were other constructive measures calculated to encourage and strengthen certain groups of men within the state. In 1283, for instance, the Statute of Merchants (*De Mercatoribus*) provided that a man might be legally imprisoned for debt. This law, of course, was particularly pleasing to the rising merchant class. The statute said that the movable goods of a debtor, or even his land, might be sold by the mayor and clerk of London, York, or Bristol in order to satisfy legitimate demands of creditors.

There is still another class of activity. We must briefly look at the land of Wales. If all of Edward's aims were to be attained or even approximated it was essential that Wales, always a turbulent land, should be subdued. The sinister history of the borderlands, those pools of misery, is a tale of violence and massacre, raids and reprisals. The persistent and prolonged campaigns of Edward I in the borderlands, in Wales, and in Scotland too, were a serious and powerful manifestation of his will to conquer and his determination to organize. Let the recalcitrant Welsh and the Scotsmen do their worst. Edward used strategy and armies and terror and guile. Checkmated often, he never admitted defeat.

This book is obviously not the place to enlarge upon the pathetic and bitter chapters in Welsh and Scottish affairs, upon ramshackle policies and scant and impotent remedies. We are dealing with another problem. It is enough to remark that after Edward I defeated the Welsh for the second time (1282) he built a girdle of castles in northern Wales, an insurance against rebellion. Merchants flooded up the valleys and one aspect of English civilization at last broke upon the Celtic settlements. In 1284 the Statute of Wales, or Rhuddlan, provided that with the exception of certain specified Welsh laws and customs, English law was to prevail in the newly annexed areas of the native principality of Wales. A special judicial system and six sheriffdoms were created.

Not all Welshmen quietly accepted this settlement. Another strong revolt occurred in 1294. In the strongholds of the marcher lands there was little change. The local barons continued to rule their lands as private jurisdictions, subject to the king only in the sense that he was their feudal lord. They fought among themselves and slew and pillaged at will. Henry VIII (1509–1547) was to end their chronic disorders by incorporating all Wales into England in 1536. Several marcher lords that he found undesirable were executed. The violence of remoter times was spent. The field of battle was replaced by press and Parliament as the forum of debate and dispute.

LAW, LAND AND LAWYERS

Professor Bertha Putnam once wrote that it was sometimes desirable "to stress legal intelligibility rather than palaeological accuracy" in writing about medieval laws and law courts. The professor who travels with celerity and skill through the land legislation of the thirteenth century knows what a difficult task it is in a classroom or a textbook to be both clear and accurate about his subject. The body of matter-of-fact knowledge with which we are here concerned is massive and complex.

One of the most important of Edward I's land laws was contained in the enactment of 1285 usually called the Second Statute of Westminster. The second clause of this document begins with the words *"De donis conditionalibus"* (Concerning conditional gifts) and it is by these words that this piece of legislation is almost invariably described.

The *De donis* law resulted from the concern and fear of landholders lest their lands be alienated and their estates be broken up by careless or incompetent heirs. Many barons had been distressed and angered by the attempts of the royal courts to permit the free alienation of land. The barons, for their part, naturally attempted to attach conditions to the disposition of the fee simple holdings of their families. It was quite natural that most prominent landlords wanted to find some way of ensuring that their wide fields would remain in the possession of their descendants. They did not want their heirs to leave or lose the land that to them meant wealth and power.

The economic side of feudalism was becoming increasingly important in the thirteenth century and the military and political aspects of it were diminishing in meaning and value. All landlords wanted to keep the economic income from a feudal tenure system. Any transfer of property was unwelcome if it reduced the income from such feudal sources as reliefs, escheats and wardship.

These are the main reasons why the barons demanded, and the king consented to, the important *De donis* clause in the so-called Statute of Westminster II. *De donis* provided specifically that land granted to a man "and the heirs of his body" must descend according to the order (*formam*) stated in the original charter (male or female, in the limiting "words of procreation"). The grantee could not alienate the land in a manner that would injure or destroy the interests of his heirs. If, at any time, there was a failure in the line of descent and thus no direct issue appeared, the land would escheat or revert to the heirs of the donor or grantor.

Such estates came to be called estates or fees tail because they were limited by the line of descent specified in the original charter and would thus be carved or cut short (*taillé*) by a failure of issue. Technically, *De donis* only forbade alienation by the first grantee and thus the first heir should have been free to dispose of the estate in fee simple fashion, as the interest was disposed of in fee conditional cases, a subject discussed in Chapter III. But in 1307 the royal courts held that the law was intended to control the estate down to the fourth degree (great grandchild). Later the principle of perpetual entail was established. Professor Edward Jenks once called *De donis conditionalibus* "a monument of colossal family pride and feudal arrogance." Professor Bertie Wilkinson says: "It is hard to see in it anything but the solicitude of a feudal monarch for his greater lords."

If a man held an estate upon any other than a fee simple basis it is clear that he did not possess all the rights in the land. In the case of a fee tail, for instance, the holder's living and lawfully begotten heir had an obvious interest and right in the estate—the right of succeeding to it. This interest is called a "remainder" because it was a right in the property that would remain (abide) for him when the holder died. Secondly, the fee tail was also limited, as remarked earlier, by the fact that if the line of holders died out then the estate would revert to the line of the original donor or grantor. Thus the heirs of the original donor were reversioners. Thirdly, the original charter may have named an alternative line to hold the land if the first line failed of issue at any time. Thus, if a parcel of land was entailed by A "to B and the heirs of his body and then to C and the heirs of his body," C and his heirs would be alternative remaindermen so long as B and his heirs lived and held the land. Together with B's son while B lived and the heirs of the original donor, C and his heirs would be holders of "estates in expectancy" as opposed to B himself, the holder of an "estate in possession." These "estates in expectancy" were considered to be real property. Under the law the holders of them had several quite definite rights as against the man who was actually holding the fee tail. For example, they might stop the latter from destroying too many trees or otherwise harming the property.

A further characteristic of "estates in expectancy" and remainders must now be mentioned. Let us suppose that an estate is granted to M for life and is entailed so that only M's male heirs may come into possession. If M then dies at any time his son is ready to come into possession at once, "vesting his possession as soon as the prior estate determined." Under these conditions it is said that M's son has a "vested remainder." Let us now suppose that an original charter says that M has the estate for life and by the same instrument says that M's son will inherit provided that he goes on a Crusade to the Holy Land. Under these terms M's son does not get the estate until he satisfies the stipulated conditions. When the contingency has been fulfilled then, and only then, does the estate vest in possession. Under these conditions it is said that M's son has a "contingent remainder" during the time before the provisions of the charter are met and he obtains the estate. Common law lawyers were frequently inclined to dispute the validity of contingent remainders because they felt that the basic concepts of seisin were challenged by the practice. Lawyers and justices also argued about the uncertainties of contingencies and the illegality of the conditions sometimes established by the grantors. The judges, of course, were anxious to avoid creating entails that could never be broken (unbarrable) because the stated limitations were such that an act necessary to break them was either physically impossible or obviously illegal. After a long and complex history through six centuries, the problem of contingent remainders in the law was dealt with in several complex pieces of legislation, particularly in the Real Property Act of 1845 and the Contingent Remainders Act of 1877. In 1925 the Law of Property Act marked the final abolition of contingent remainders.

Under the practice of entail, in the thirteenth century and later, not even a spendthrift or a black sheep could alienate so much as a single acre. The estates, said the great landowners, must be kept intact. The successive heirs had only a life holding. The *De donis* clause of the Second Statute of Westminster was one reason for the maintenance of large estates in England through several centuries. Not until 1925 was the creation of new entails prohibited. For six hundred years the practice of the entail system in family settlements of freehold land was an important part of the property law, a significant strand in the social and economic fabric of England.

The Crown, for reasons that have been explained, was opposed to the creation of undying entails or perpetuities. Was it socially desirable, quite apart from the problem of royal income, for the first holders of land grants to control estates through centuries of time, through altered circumstances and new societies? Kings and royal judges thought not. They worked together to evade the intents and purposes of the irksome *De donis* and other statutes against free alienation. We cannot here describe all of the various legal contrivances for breaking entails devised by the judges and lawyers. A few examples of the most commonly used operations will be sufficient to show what was happening in this important sector of English legal history. The first process we must look at is one form of the collusive action called "common recovery," an application invented from the complex law of warranty.

Let us begin by stating that A holds an estate tail. He wants to sell that land, to alienate it in fee simple to B. In these circumstances, A and B agree to start a collusive suit, an action to try title. Now follow the successive steps of the action agreed upon. First: B pays A for the land. Second: B enters suit against A. Third: A says that he obtained the land and the title to it from a third party, a man named C. A accordingly "vouches C to warranty" (*i.e.*, C is now a party to the suit because he has "warranted" the title to the land to be good) and when C acknowledges the grant and the responsibility of defense the next phase of the suit begins. Fourth: C then fails to answer the suit in court (the third party is usually a propertyless fellow who is paid to act his part).

Fifth: the court gives judgment against the defaulting C and awards the land in fee simple to B. The entail is thus broken (barred) by a court order. B's title is derived from a court judgment, not from the original settlement creating the entail. B has bought the land and now has it. C has been paid for his services. A, who wanted the entail destroyed, sees it ended and the cash for the land in his pocket. Everybody is satisfied but the various remaindermen, whose legitimate interest in estates tail was described earlier. When the remaindermen go to complain in court they are told that they must take action against C, the third party, the voucher to warranty. But where is C? Perhaps he cannot be found. Even if he is located, fishing down by the river, what can the remaindermen do? C has nothing to be sued for. If the remaindermen did get judgment against him, they could not collect. B and A selected C for that very reason. There is no blood in a stone.

It is easy to see why this process, first used about 1340, became so popular that it was called "common" recovery, probably after the judges finally approved its use in Tolcarns' Case in 1472. More involved forms of recovery, sometimes with a "double voucher" and more straw men, became quite usual in the sixteenth century. The opinions of many were expressed by Sir James Dyer, Chief Justice of the Court of Common Pleas in the days of Elizabeth I: "He is not worthy to be of the profession of the law who durst speak against common recoveries, which are the sinews of assurances of inheritances and founded upon great reason and authority."

The use of such devices as common recovery to evade the provisions of *De donis* and other statutes marked but one phase of the struggle about perpetuities. It was a long road to the year 1833, when the conveyancing processes of fines and recoveries were both abolished. Later chapters will also show how the battle over "springing uses" went on through many decades in the sphere of substantive law.

We turn now to another important land law of the reign of Edward I: the Statute of Westminster III of 1290. Before we examine the provisions of this law it is necessary to recall some of the principles of subinfeudation described in earlier chapters. Under the customary practice of subinfeudation the grantor enfeoffed the grantee to hold of the grantor as feudal lord. Hence, if the Crown granted some manors to A, then A could alienate to B so that B became a tenant of A and not of the Crown. In such a grant the services B would owe to A would often be different, and often more onerous, than those owed by A to the Crown for the same parcel of land.

In the Third Statute of Westminster there was one section which took its name from the opening words: *Quia emptores* (Because purchasers). This section of Westminster III provided that there should be no further subinfeudation, no future purchases of land subject to the condition that the buyers become rear vassals, mesne tenants, subtenants of the sellers. The new *Quia emptores* said that an individual should be entirely free to transfer at his pleasure and without restriction the most complete rights in a piece of land, the full fee simple interest. Thus the seller was to lose all his feudal rights over the land. The new purchaser was to be feudally responsible to the lord of the seller in exactly the same way and with exactly the same services as the seller had been. If, after the passage of *Quia emptores*, W, holding land from X, transferred a part of that land to Y, then Y would hold the land from X, not from W. The old feudal pyramid of subinfeudation, the multiplying of subtenants down and down the pyramidal structure, was checked.

Before 1290 the English kings had often tried to safeguard themselves against the loss of services and incidents resulting from subinfeudation. For instance, they forbade their tenants-in-chief to alienate any land without royal permission. That permission was not granted unless the king was certain that the tenant-in-chief still kept enough land to pay all the services he owed the Crown. No medieval king viewed with calmness the prospect of having his feudal services and revenues impaired or drained away by subinfeudation. By the late thirteenth century the great magnates themselves were strongly inclined to oppose the further extension of subinfeudation with its attendant dangers—the threat of sharp declines in revenues, the family problems if too many acres of the broad estates were allowed to slip into the hands of strangers. *Quia emptores* was enacted, not in opposition to, but largely at the behest and with the support of many of the magnates.

One slow result of *Quia emptores* was a great increase in the number of tenants who held land directly of the crown. Intermediate lords sometimes had no heirs. Sometimes they were found guilty of felony or treason. In all such cases the land escheated to the overlord or was forfeited to the king. Thus the importance of the tenurial principle was decreased as the seigniory of all freehold lands held in fee simple tended to become concentrated in the Crown. The earlier feudal conception of organization was thus undermined by the gradual extinction of mesne tenures. As Professor G. P. Cuttino has remarked: "The consequence of the removal of restraints on alienation was to make land for the first time a marketable commodity in the full sense, and thus finally to destroy the rigidity of the feudal organization." The modern principle, of course, is the rule that any condition against alienation in the grant of a fee simple is without legal meaning and hence void.

EDWARD I AND THE CHURCH

Troublesome still was the problem of the church, so rich in its lands and so strong in its jurisdiction. Controversies between church and state in the Middle Ages shifted into various themes but the central focus was always the same: the problem of power.

In the long struggle between the opposed powers of church and state the reign of Edward I does not form a chapter as violent as that of William II, Henry I, Henry II, or John. The papal demands, so precisely formulated by Innocent III, that militant Pope and excellent canon law lawyer, were not relaxed in the thirteenth century. When Henry III was king the privileges and power of the clergy in England had grown steadily stronger. Edward I was also a devout son of the church. He was anxious to avoid open struggles with the papacy. He knew that the loss of papal friendship had always proved costly to his predecessors. He also knew how the taxes imposed upon the clergy swelled the royal exchequer. Thus reasons of profit, policy and religion combined to persuade Edward I to maintain friendly relations with the church.

Nevertheless, as king of England, Edward wanted no papal claims to press wedges into his temporal jurisdiction. He was as determined to block clerical invasions of what he regarded as his proper sphere of authority as he was to check the baronial claims to excessive strength. It is not surprising that several chapters of his legislation were quite unpopular in Rome.

One aspect of the power struggle was the question of the jurisdiction of the church courts, a cause of dispute since the days of William I. In the thirteenth century the secular authorities still watched and limited the ecclesiastical tribunals as they had in times past. The king's judges warded off the challenge of the church in several ways. One was by issuing writs of prohibition forbidding the church courts to proceed with cases over which the secular courts claimed jurisdiction. By the late thirteenth century this procedure was not sufficient to halt the gradual encroachment of the ecclesiastical tribunals in matters whose cognizance belonged to the Crown.

In 1285 Edward I supplemented the device of the writs of prohibition by a new writ called, from its opening words, *Circumspecte agatis* (Act cautiously). First used in a case involving the bishop and clergy of Norwich, the writ stated the duties of the ecclesiastical courts and defined the boundaries between temporal and spiritual jurisdictions. Like the earlier ordinance of William I it reserved to the courts Christian all cases that were purely spiritual matters (*qua mere sunt spiritualia*) such as those involving adultery, perjury, assaults upon clergymen, defamation, tithes, and the like. Thus the writ *Circumspecte agatis* was one of many medieval attempts to define the limits of ecclesiastical jurisdiction sharply and narrowly.

Edward I also refused to permit the collection of several new clerical taxes that Rome proposed to levy. He made it clear that he would not allow any papal interference in the election of bishops. This firm policy of the king roused no open opposition in Rome until the election of Boniface VIII in 1294. Boniface VIII, arrogant and learned in the canon law, was vehement and vigorous in pressing extreme papal claims. When Edward I and Philip IV of France were battling over the possession of certain lands in France, Boniface VIII ordered both of them to submit their dispute to him for arbitration. When they refused to do so, Boniface issued in 1296 the famous bull *Clericis laicos* which forbade the clergy to pay taxes or make gifts to laymen without papal consent. Boniface VIII insisted upon complete immunity of the clergy from taxation by the state. The bull asserted that the Pope intended "utterly to repudiate this so horrible abuse of the secular power."

The clergy of England, heavily hit by Edward's recent taxes, hastened to obey Boniface VIII. In 1296 they refused to accede to a royal demand for a tax of a fifth of the assessed value of their revenues and movable property. Edward then outlawed the clergy, placing them outside the protection of the lay law. In 1301 Boniface issued the bull *Ausculta filii*, reasserting the papal power over kings and kingdoms. In 1302 he continued his offensive with the bull *Unam sanctam*, declaring that the Pope was the supreme authority on earth in spiritual and temporal matters. It was all to no avail. The aged Boniface finally relented and permitted churchmen to make "gifts" to the secular rulers in lieu of taxes. In the midst of the controversy Boniface was seized by the agents of Philip IV of France. Although he was soon freed, he died a month later, doubtless in part from anger, shame and shock.

In England most of the clergy paid the tax of a fifth Edward demanded. Those who failed to do so saw their goods confiscated. When

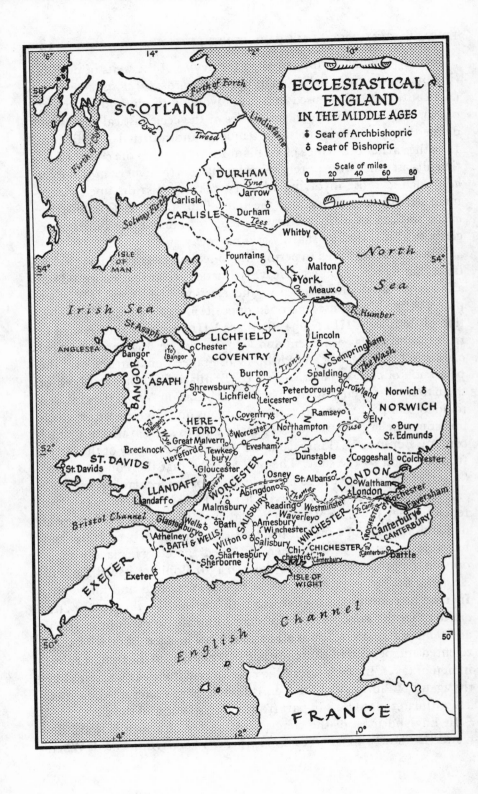

ECCLESIASTICAL
ENGLAND
IN THE MIDDLE AGES

Seat of Archbishopric
Seat of Bishopric

Scale of miles
0   20   40   60   80

SCOTLAND

Firth of Forth

Lindisfarne

Clyde

Tweed

North
Sea

DURHAM
Tyne
Jarrow

Carlisle

CARLISLE
Solway Firth

Durham
Tees

Whitby

ISLE
OF
MAN

Fountains

YORK

Malton

York
Ouse
Meaux

Irish Sea

Humber

St. Asaph

ANGLESEA

Bangor

To
Bangor

LICHFIELD
&
COVENTRY

Chester

Lincoln

Sempringham

The Wash

BANGOR

ASAPH

Shrewsbury
Lichfield

Burton

Spalding

Crowland

LINCOLN

Norwich

NORWICH

Peterborough
Leicester

To
Bangor

HERE-
FORD

Coventry

Worcester

Northampton

Ramsey

Ely

Bury
St. Edmunds

Ouse

Wye

Brecknock

Great Malvern
Hereford
Tewkes-
bury
Gloucester

Evesham

Dunstable

Coggeshall

Colchester

ST. DAVIDS

St. Davids

LLANDAFF

Llandaff

WORCESTER

Osney
Abingdon

St. Albans

Waltham

LONDON

London

Rochester

Faversham

Severn

Malmsbury

Reading

Thames

Westminster

To Cant.

Bristol Channel

Glastonbury
Wells
Athelney
BATH & WELLS

Bath

SALISBURY

Amesbury

Winchester

ROCHESTER

Canterbury

CANTERBURY

Wilton
Salisbury

WINCHESTER

Chi-
chester

CHICHESTER

To
Canterbury

Battle

EXETER

Exeter

Shaftesbury

Sherborne

ISLE OF
WIGHT

To
Canterbury

English   Channel

FRANCE

Clement V became Pope in 1305 relations between England and Rome improved. Edward permitted the papacy to increase its revenues by the collection of a new tax from the English clergy. This tax, called annates, was the full return from the first year's occupancy of any ecclesiastical office. It was to be paid by all clergymen appointed to benefices in the British Isles. Clement V, for his part, quashed the offending decrees of Boniface VIII and ordered the English clergy to pay Edward I a tax of a tenth for seven years.

In 1307 the Parliament of Carlisle, angered by the fiscal policy of the church, petitioned Edward to stop the flow of annates and other new papal taxes to Rome. The Statute of Carlisle, enacted in that year, was intended to prevent the drain of English gold to Rome through the channel of clerical exactions. It forbade the payment of tallage on monastic property and rendered illegal certain other levies responsible for the movement of large sums of money to Italy. After the Parliament was dissolved, Edward I, always anxious to cooperate with the papal power when it was to his advantage, ordered the gathering of the annates. At the same time, he upheld the Parliamentary prohibition regarding the collection of any other payments not previously made to Rome.

The Statute of Carlisle is mainly important as a precedent upon which was based the later acts of Provisors and Praemunire and a whole series of anti-papal laws of considerable importance in the long history of the relations between England and Rome. The Pope was soon to go into "captivity" at Avignon in the south of France. The Hundred Years' War was approaching. In such circumstances, many Englishmen were not likely to respect or hearken to a papacy that could be considered a French institution.

Meanwhile, both king and barons were troubled by the fact that large amounts of land had passed under ecclesiastical control. The possessions of the church, said the Hildebrandine tradition, were sacred. They were not to be touched by lay hands, even those of a king. Through the centuries many men had left fat acres to the wealthy church, some of them in the hope that such gifts would pave the way to paradise. Land acquired by the church seldom lapsed back into the hands of the king. The church was a great corporation. It was never under age, so the king got no profit from wardships. It never committed felonies, so the king got no income from those great pleas of the Crown. It never married, so the king had no profit there. It never died, and thus no feudal casualties brought gain to the royal treasury.

No acres were ever escheated, no fields ever lost. The clenched hand of the church was often as strong and unrelaxed as that of a dead man, stiff in rigor mortis. Hence ecclesiastical tenure, frankalmoign or otherwise, was often called mortmain.

In 1279 Parliament enacted the Statute of Mortmain (*De viris religiosis*). This statute was enacted to prevent future transfers of property to the church without royal permission. The Statute of Mortmain is, in form, a royal instruction to the justices. It was hoped, of course, that the new law would help to protect the income of lay landlords, including the king, by stopping the alienation of more land to the church. Such alienation, as we have noted, always meant consequent loss to the lay lord of the incidents of feudal tenure. The Statute of Mortmain pointed out that despite earlier prohibitions in 1217 and 1259 "men of religion have nevertheless entered upon the fiefs of others as well as their own—by appropriating them, buying them, and sometimes receiving them through gifts of other men—whereby the services which are owed from such fiefs, and which were originally established for the defence of the kingdom, are wrongfully withheld and the principal lords do lose their escheats." The statute then ordained that "no man of religion or any other whatsoever shall buy or sell lands or tenements, or under any colour of donation, lease, or other title of any sort shall receive them from anyone, or presume artfully and craftily to appropriate them in any way whatsoever, whereby land and tenements of this sort may somehow come into mortmain."

The intent of the Statute of Mortmain soon came to be widely evaded. For political and other powerful reasons, kings sometimes granted licenses permitting the alienation of land to the church. There also grew into use the legal procedure of common recovery, with the devices and fictions described earlier in this chapter. Confronted by the ingenuity of the lawyers and the connivance of the judges the Statute of Mortmain could not succeed in its purpose. The church was thus able to have the benefit and use of many new grants and gifts.

Another method of defeating the Statute of Mortmain, as well as all other statutes against the free alienation of land, was the system of "uses," whereby land was granted not to religious houses or other parts of the church directly, but nominally to other men who permitted the church to use that land. In law the land was owned by Smith, but in practice the use and enjoyment belonged to the church. The subject of the growth of the concept and practice of the expedient of "uses" in English law is so important that it demands separate treatment in a subsequent chapter. Too late did a new Statute of Mortmain—enacted under Richard II (1391)—prohibit the employment of "uses," those predecessors of the modern trust. Even Henry VIII, as will be described later, had much difficulty with his Statute of Uses of 1536.

The swift development of legal fictions often evaded or effectively throttled pieces of legislation. If, for instance, land was brought into the possession of the church under the pretense of purchasing it as a burial ground, who could prove the intention was to circumvent the law? In cases such as this, the common law, which provided so many remedies, would not go beyond or behind the documentary evidence.

In 1307 Edward I died in the midst of an attempt to invade and subdue Scotland. Edward II was a hollow counterfeit of his mighty father. His reign was short and his fate tragic. We now turn to the fourteenth century, an age of war and rebellion and social unrest.

CHAPTER X

Barons, Courts, and Parliament

THE BARONS: TRIUMPH AND DISASTER

THREE kings ruled in England in the fourteenth century: Edward II (1307–1327), Edward III (1327–1377), and Richard II (1377–1399). Their reigns were disturbed by domestic broils and foreign battles. The period under review in this chapter was the century when the Hundred Years' War with France brought a harvest of victory to England at Sluys, Crécy and Poitiers. This was the century that also brought defeat in the darkness of the desperate years when Edward III was old and dying and, later, when Richard II was king and England's energy and exchequer were low. This was the century of the Black Death of 1349, of the Peasants' Revolt of 1381, of new quarrels with the church, of rising trade and commerce, of John Wycliffe and Geoffrey Chaucer, of the Revolution of 1399.

Edward II was thoroughly weak, manifestly unable to grasp and hold the reins of power. The restless baronage, remembering their golden hours when Henry III was king, were anxious to extend their strength once more. To baronial ambition was added annoyance as Edward II dismissed several of his father's ministers and replaced them by personal favorites, men whom the barons regarded as objectionable upstarts devoid of political knowledge or skill. After many quarrels with the king the barons came to Parliament in 1310 with armed retainers and compelled Edward II to submit to their control. This event, this decline once more into conflict, marks the first phase of the constant agitation for the reform of the royal administration characteristic of the fourteenth century.

A reform commission of twenty-one lay and ecclesiastical magnates, the "Lords Ordainers," forced Edward to accept their rules for the

188

improvement of the household and government. The "ordinances of London," completed in 1310 and confirmed by Parliament in 1311, were reminiscent of the Provisions of Oxford that had humiliated Henry III in 1258. Forty-one clauses of the Ordinances of 1311 declared that "through bad and deceitful counsel our lord the king and all his men have everywhere been dishonoured and his crown in many ways has been debased and ruined." Edward II's favorites, many of them aliens, were to be dismissed: "We ordain that all the evil counsellors shall be put out and utterly removed." The way would thus be opened for "fit persons," such as the barons, to advise the king. The "counsel and assent" of the baronage in Parliament was to be obtained before any major appointments in household or administration were made by Edward II.

These Ordinances of 1311 also stated that "the customs of the kingdom shall be received and kept by men of the kingdom and not by aliens." Edward II was not permitted "to go out of the kingdom or to undertake an act of war against anyone without the common assent of his baronage and that in Parliament." Other clauses, sometimes written in trenchant phrases, further limited the royal power in numerous ways. The whole body of the ordinances, said the final document, confirmed and sealed by the king, was to be "maintained and observed" and sent into every county of England "to be published, held, and strictly kept, as well within franchises as without."

In this phase of baronial rebellion all might have turned out as the barons had planned but for two facts, ominous for them. In the first place, the new "Lords Ordainers" were as greedy and incompetent as Edward II's bosom friends had been. Successful government always means steady attention to business and this the "Lords Ordainers" were not prepared to give. Secondly, Edward II used trained, competent, and loyal members of his permanent household, so greatly strengthened under Edward I, to circumvent and outwit the barons set about him. These assistants, alarmed at baronial intrusions, handled the specialized business of government to the king's advantage —and their own. Fools or scoundrels, in rank far over the heads of civil servants, could never carry on the king's government well. That was a task for experts.

Thus the aristocratic committee of barons proved unable to use effectively the power they had wrested from the king. They showed their lack of concern for the national welfare by refusing to help Edward II against the Scots; the result was the battle of Bannockburn.

Taxes rose. Internal disorders multiplied. Scotsmen raided northern England. Meanwhile the barons continued to be divided among themselves as they wrestled and scrambled for the profitable powers they had seized from the king's hands. They made the same disastrous mistakes that had helped to shatter their cause in the days of Henry III.

In 1322 Edward II, seeking revenge, struck swiftly and defeated the barons in a bold and brief campaign. A Parliament held at York revoked the Ordinances of 1311, declaring that for the future they had lost "all title, force, virtue, and effect." The halting baronial experiment in coercion had failed. Several barons were hanged or exiled. In no chapter of English history has it proved wise to put the crown into commission. The Statute of York that repealed the Ordinances of 1311 asserted that by those decrees "the royal power of our lord the king was wrongfully limited in many respects to the injury of his royal lordship and contrary to the estate of the crown." Finally—and this is especially important—the Statute of York declared that "matters which are to be determined with regard to the estate of our lord the king and of his heirs, or with regard to the estate of the kingdom and of the people, shall be considered, granted, and established in Parliament by our lord the king and with the consent of the prelates, earls, and barons, and of the community of the kingdom, as has been accustomed in times past."

Several modern scholars have spent much time and thought in debate upon the meaning and significance of this passage in the Statute of York.[1] A perusal of their interpretations will show that they are in precarious disagreement. Their assumptions and arguments about the use of the word "community" or "commonalty" cannot be dealt with here if this text is to keep a reasonable degree of perspective and proportion. Nevertheless, it should be noted that in the Statute of York, whatever the precise meanings of some phrases may be, there is indisputable evidence that the political importance of Parliament, and especially of the knights and burgesses in it, was becoming more clearly recognized. It is not accidental that representative men of "the community of the kingdom" were more and more regularly summoned to sessions of Parliament. In another context in this chapter we shall see what important things "the commons" were to achieve.

The barons were now defeated, jealous and impotent. Hence they

---

[1] See the works listed in the selected bibliography for Chapter X at the end of this volume.

welcomed a chance to plot with Isabella, Edward II's disaffected queen, and several exiled nobles. Many Englishmen, weary of Edward's misrule, joined the forces that landed in England in 1326 to fight the king. The jackals whom Edward's bounty had fed ran away. He was captured on the Welsh coast. Pressed by the lords of Parliament, Edward abdicated in favor of his son and before the end of 1327 he was murdered. The way of a weakling is sometimes harder than that of a scoundrel.

The Articles of Accusation against Edward II did not really allege that the grounds of his deposition were what we would call constitutional. Edward's contemporaries knew, and historians know, that the reasons for his ousting were mainly personal. Edward was lazy, incompetent, occupied with dark vices, "giving himself up to unseemly works and occupations, neglecting to satisfy the needs of his realm." Indolence and incompetence are always a danger to the state. The forced abdications of Richard II in 1399 and James II in 1688 were historically much more significant than that of Edward II. The main importance of Edward's removal is that it provided a precedent—and precedents are valuable.

Some historians have held that the baronial opposition in the reign of Edward II endeavored to subject the king to the rule of law, to preach and practice the basic meaning of the principles of Magna Carta. On the other hand, there are strong grounds for examining the documents and insisting that the barons were less concerned with the omnipotence of law than they were with the state of their own fortunes. The results of baronial activities, whatever the full intentions behind them, were valuable for several reasons, one of which was that Englishmen were not given an opportunity to forget the principle that a king who broke the law should be resisted. Precedent and policy often go hand in hand. For the third time within a hundred years the barons had tried the experiment of putting the government into the hands of a group of nobles. For a third time they had failed. They were able to attempt these weighty and dangerous gambles because they succeeded, for a time, in controlling John, Henry III and Edward II. But their schemes were unworkable, their methods were bad, and their rivalries split their unity and drained their energies.

If England had had a succession of strong kings in the thirteenth and fourteenth centuries the barons probably would not have tried by violence to impair the power of the Crown and increase their own. If they had never rebelled, much might have been lost. As Professor

A. B. White wisely wrote: "With reference to the establishment of limited monarchy, it was hardly an unmixed evil that Edward I was not followed by kings as great as himself." A long tradition of strong, effective, and centralized monarchy probably could not have paved the road to a democratic system of government.

Edward III (1327–1377) was energetic and popular, especially among the nobles. The long conflicts between royal and baronial policies almost disappeared. Edward's main interest was in war, the sport of kings. During his reign he moved into battle against Scotland. With France he began the Hundred Years' War. That formidable conflict lasted intermittently until the middle of the fifteenth century. Through these long years many important pages of constitutional and legal history were being penned at home. In the tale of the growth of the English constitution the fourteenth century is mainly important for the swift rise of parliamentary institutions, particularly the appearance of a bicameral legislature and a series of restraining controls of the Crown successfully developed by Parliament. To the study of these events we now turn.

PARLIAMENT: ROADS TO POWER

Throughout the fourteenth century the word "Parliament" meant a special meeting of the king and those summoned to counsel him, including the lords spiritual and temporal, some permanent royal advisers and servants of the household, and the knights and burgesses of the counties and boroughs. Thus it is impossible, in writing about this period, to make any separation between what might be called Parliamentary affairs on the one hand and the affairs of the Crown and council on the other. The absence of any separation of powers in medieval government can be illustrated in many ways. Professor Bertha Putnam, for instance, has recently shown how Sir William Shareshull (Chief Justice of the Court of King's Bench 1350–1361) was active in council, active in Parliament, active in making laws, active in enforcing them, active in experimenting with the new local officials soon to be called "justices of the peace." It is especially important to note these minglings of many affairs in numerous organs of government, administration, and law because otherwise it would be easy to misunderstand a short and simple statement saying, quite accurately, that most Parliaments in the fourteenth century lasted only a few days or weeks. Of course, there were frequent meetings—in 1328 there were four Parliaments and in 1340 there were three. Parliaments were called in almost every year of Edward III's reign. A precedent, valuable for the future, was being established. Nevertheless, the mere fact of a Parliament assembling at a certain time is but one aspect of the growth of that institution. Many shaping and dynamic forces were active in the fourteenth century at times when there were no Parliaments meeting at all. Indeed, the procedure of keeping the same Parliament in existence for a long period and calling it from time to time into sessions was probably not invented until the reign of Richard II, who "packed" his Parliaments and wanted to hold on to a friendly body once he had it.

Parliament rolls, statutes and ordinances, the best sources for the constitutional history of the fourteenth century, show many significant developments. In many respects the thirteenth century Parliament had been a vague and formless body. Early fourteenth century changes in the organization and functions of Parliament were not to contemporaries prophetic of major changes. The members of the council, and they alone, heard pleas and provided, when they so desired, redress and remedy for the hardships of individuals or classes. The knights and burgesses were still, as it were, suitors at court, men in an inferior position.

In the Easter Parliament of 1341 the prelates and magnates were ordered to meet in the White Chamber in the oldest section of the Palace of Westminster. Slowly the council in Parliament was to become the House of Lords in a bicameral legislative system. This event gradually happened when the council group in Parliament came to be composed only of a fixed hereditary element of lay lords and ecclesiastical lords (archbishops, bishops, and certain abbots) and the royal officials of the council disappeared from Parliament and took no part in its work. In the later Middle Ages the House of Lords contained about a hundred men—two archbishops, nineteen bishops, thirty or forty abbots, and about forty temporal peers.

It was also in the Parliament of 1341 that about two hundred knights and burgesses were ordered to meet in the Painted Chamber in Westminster Hall. In later years these men still met in full sessions with the lords spiritual and temporal. After these opening meetings the lords and "the Commons" usually separated to debate and decide most questions among themselves, especially those set before the full Parliament in the king's speech at the beginning of the meetings. Thus began the House of Commons. In 1352, 1376, 1377, and 1384 the Commons met in the chapter house of Westminster Abbey. In the early fifteenth century they sat in the refectory of the Abbey. From 1547 to 1834 they met in St. Stephen's Chapel in Westminster Palace.

The knights and burgesses had their own clerk. They soon elected a Speaker, often a royal nominee, to speak for them in the full sessions of the Parliament chamber. The Speakership became an important institution in later centuries. Presiding over the House of Commons, it is today the Speaker's duty to maintain the dignity of the House; to ensure free and courteous debate; with indisputable impartiality to apply and interpret the formidable body of precedent that now constitutes Parliamentary law.

The first increase in the power of Parliament in the fourteenth century came through the mounting control of finance. The costs of the Hundred Years' War were so great that Edward III (1327–1377) was compelled to ask Parliament for large and numerous grants of money. From his own estates and feudal dues he obtained annually about £50,000, a third of his income. The rest came to him from direct and indirect taxes. The Commons sometimes seized the chance to demand concessions from the king in return for money grants. They had experimented with that procedure a few times earlier in the century. For example, on two occasions in Edward II's reign the Commons had asked for a redress of grievances before they granted taxes on personal property. In each case the substance of their petition was approved and enacted into statutes by the king and the lords.

By the later years of Edward III's reign it was becoming quite customary to attach conditions to money grants. To obtain the one the king had to grant the other. Here was the beginning of the modern system of Parliamentary appropriations. Parliamentary committees were sometimes set up to audit the royal accounts. There were frequent complaints about Crown expenditures. Parliament often insisted that money granted should be spent for certain specific purposes, and no others. In the Parliament of 1376, for instance, a knight of the south country asserted that "all we have given to the war for a long time we have lost because it has been badly wasted and falsely expended."

Despite these facts, it is not wise or accurate to say that Parliament had secured control over finance by the end of the fourteenth century. Indeed, one modern student has claimed that even the grants made to the Crown were held to be no more than the "revenues" of the king's high court, that Parliamentary taxation was considered to be "a profit of the king's Court of Parliament to which he was entitled in the same way as to the fines of, say, the Court of King's Bench." It is, of course, necessary to remark at this point that several scholars with special knowledge and the highest critical perception are in deep disagreement about the problems of the medieval purse strings and the hands that held them. For our purposes it is enough to say that before 1400 Parliament's command and authority in the field of finance was advancing but was far from complete.

The second main extension of Parliamentary power was in the field of legislation. The king and council wanted order. The judges wanted clarification of the laws. The men of the middle classes and those on the lower rungs of the ladder wanted various reforms and rightings of wrongs. There were, as always, local rivalries, class fissures, government abuses, jobbery and corruption to be inquired into by shrewd royal agents and corrected by men in Parliament and council deemed to be honest and wise. "Nearly every interest in medieval society left its trace on the enactments of Parliament and council." Professor G. L. Haskins, commenting upon Professor Helen M. Cam's *The Legislators of Medieval England,* wrote this: "She describes the legislative activity of medieval England as 'a joint stock enterprise' and comments pointedly on the importance of such combined endeavors on the part of many sorts and conditions of men in creating a consciousness of national welfare which was to find expression in the Parliamentary activity of the modern period."

The House of Commons had no right of initiative except by starting the process of legislation through common petitions, as distinct from the petitions of individuals, to the king and his council. It was many years before the Commons' expressed desires almost automatically became statute law. In the fourteenth century the king and his council sometimes altered petitions before they were enacted and enrolled as statutes. Sometimes they refused to accept them at all. This was a problem of considerable importance in the fourteenth century. There were others, too. For instance, as Professor G. L. Haskins has noted: "So late as 1389, it was necessary for the Commons to petition that the Chancellor and council should make no ordinances conflicting with the common law after a session of Parliament had been dismissed."

This quotation shows that there was still another difficulty: the king and his council might make ordinances and proclamations which were as much laws as statutes. Probably in the fourteenth century no man was radical enough to think that the method of legislation by king and council should be eliminated and replaced by the new system of Parliamentary petition procedure. Only very slowly was it tacitly agreed that ordinances were to be considered temporary measures. Statutes, on the other hand, were part of the permanent law of the land. At the end of the century the vexed problems of legislative dominance were not fully solved. It remained for the next age to develop new pressures, privileges, and procedures.

At this point it should be remarked, as Professor T. F. Tout pointed out long ago, that all medieval laws were declarations of blended ideals. Nobody, even in the royal administration, looked upon them as measures to be enforced in detail and in all cases. Then, too, the king himself frequently circumvented or disabled the statute law, and even the royal ordinances, by using his prerogative dispensing power to permit individuals or groups to do things forbidden by the law. Further, there was always the fact that the power of a legislative enactment ultimately depended upon its effective enforcement by informed and approving local officials and local lords. If these men did not cooperate with the central authorities then it mattered little what stern words stood upon the rolls of Parliament. Thus the significance of early legislation was reduced, both directly and indirectly, by the raw realities of the medieval world. All modern scholars know that the presence of a statute does not prove that it was enforced. For conclusive evidence of action or apathy they must make cautious exploration and criticism in scores of places further afield.

So it was that Parliament gradually strengthened its position with respect to national finance and legislation. It also made a series of lesser gains in a third field by frequently seeking to influence the policy of the government. There were two main ways in which this could be done. In the first place, Parliament could refuse money grants and thus force the king, through his financial dependence, to yield to their wishes. Secondly, there was the weapon of impeachment, a process very effective because it meant a direct accusation and arraignment of an individual for misconduct. In the later Middle Ages impeachment was useful in controlling the king and his ministers, particularly because it involved less danger of revolution and civil war than the methods of armed baronial opposition. As a result of the use of the impeachment device a minister of the Crown could be held directly responsible to Parliament for his official acts. A charge against a king's minister would not be liable to provoke a civil war, whereas a charge against the king himself was always dangerous. Hence the principle: a king can do no wrong; but his ministers can.

The impeachment process led to a criminal trial. The House of

Lords has always kept several of the functions of the old great council. It was, and still is, the highest court of law in the land. The House of Commons, by acting as a grand or accusing jury, could present ministers or other servants of the king before the House of Lords for trials for serious offenses, such as treason or felony. If the upper house found the accused guilty of the charges against him the penalty might be death. The consequences of giving bad advice or obeying bad orders might well make the royal servants walk warily. In such risky circumstances irresponsible or arbitrary rulers might expect to have difficulty in finding able and loyal ministers. The House of Commons in the "Good Parliament" of 1376 impeached Richard Lyons, a merchant and customs officer, together with others who had used their government offices for illegal purposes.

By such slow processes the privileges and powers of Parliament grew more numerous. In the fifteenth century, at least until 1460, the authority of Parliament steadily expanded. The foundations laid by the generations of men who lived in medieval England were solid and strong. They had to be, for they were destined to support the mighty structure of Parliament in the modern age.

LABORERS AND CHURCHMEN

In the summer of 1348 England was struck by a virulent plague that had swept along the trade routes to Europe from some mysterious fountainhead of disease in the East. The Black Death, as it was called, rolled from the west of England and leaped into London during the winter. Through the filthy medieval streets of the larger towns the deadly infection raced unhindered. In some English villages nearly all the inhabitants died. The manor rolls, episcopal registers, and parish and borough records tell a frightful story. Full statistics are, of course, not available for the fourteenth century, but sober estimates set the mortality at from twenty-five to twenty-eight per cent of the total population of England.

The social and economic results were immediate and important. It is true that the Black Death merely hastened changes it was formerly thought to have originated; but the speed at which those changes occurred after 1350 gave tremendous impetus to the decline of feudalism, to servile emancipation, and to the whole tide of economic and social discontent among the lower classes. The smaller society that survived the Black Death was upset. Agriculture, trade, government, religion, administration, all were disrupted. When the labor supply decreased it was inevitable that hired rural and town workers in England should demand and receive higher wages. The villeins who had survived the plague insisted upon their freedom. They did not want to do any more compulsory labor. They wanted wages. The tenants replacing those who had died demanded easier terms from their landlords. The income of the landlords went down as their overhead costs went up.

Could the tottering manorial system be supported by an act of Parliament? The landowners attempted to put back the clock by passing the Statute of Laborers in 1351, a law based on an ordinance made by the king and his council in 1349. The statute of 1351 explained that the ordinance of 1349 had been passed "to curb the malice of servants who after the pestilence were idle and unwilling to serve without securing excessive wages." Despite the law, continued the statute, "to suit their ease and their selfish desires" these servants "refrain from serving the lords or other men unless they receive double or triple that which they were accustomed to have—to the great danger of the lords and the impoverishment of all men of the said commons." All workmen were ordered to accept the wage rate customary before the plague. Employers who paid higher wages were to be fined. Workers who accepted them were to be imprisoned. Prices were to be held stable. If prices did not rise, workers did not need higher wages.

Enactment was one thing. Enforcement was another. In 1357 and 1360 further statutes were passed to control wages and to stop the price rise. Despite the language of the laws many workers simply refused to accept lower wages. They knew that masters and landlords had to have help. They knew that the demands of the valuable laborers would be met, no matter what the statutes might say. They were right. The landlords yielded—all but the most recalcitrant. When many lords of the manors found that they could not work their own demesnes they leased their lands for money rents to tenant farmers. They were becoming "landlords" of the modern type. To a greater extent than ever before the lords began to commute the feudal services required of villeins into straight money payments. The villeins, too, were becoming rural wage earners. Cash was everywhere replacing kind and physical services in the manorial economy. Thus the basis of the feudal manorial system was being rapidly destroyed. During the later part of the century the social malaise mounted.

Laborers were unhappy with their lot. They wanted higher wages,

Medieval England

Scale ▭▭▭▭ Miles

A manly man to be an Abbot able

The Franklins dispensed hospitality in their manor houses

The Black Death snatches his little Pearl from a heartbroken father

known for mystery and morality plays

Miracle Play

Piers plowmans vision

Peasant revolt started here

Monk copying Manuscript

Chaucer administers the Royal Estate in Somerset as Reve.

"with many a tempest has his beard been shake.

Joan of Arc burned as a witch

in hope of standing in his ladys grace

Carlisle
Newcastle
Durham
Fountains Abbey
York
Beverly
Bangor
Chester
Lincoln
Lichfield
Norwich
Guildwas Abbey
Coventry
Peterborough
Cambridge
Bury St Edmunds
St. Davids
Hereford
Gloucester
Oxford
St. Albans
London
Tintern Abbey
Malmesbury
harrow
Westminster
Tabard Inn
Canterbury
Bath
Wells
Salisbury
Winchester
Chichester
Canterbury pilgrims
Exeter
Ottery St. M.
Dorchester Abbey
Ramsey Ab.
MAGDA LAYNE
PIRAB
CHAUCER
FLANDERS

lower rents, better working and living conditions. Those who had fought in France knew that an arrow could bring down a gentleman as well as a peasant. These things were the prelude of an approaching storm when England entered upon a period of military and economic disaster after 1369. In 1381 came the Peasants' Revolt, the first uprising of the submerged classes in England on a large scale, their first fumbling attempt to act for themselves. "When Adam delved and Eve span, Who was then the gentleman?" The rebellion was crushed in a strong and cruel reaction. Nevertheless, by the fifteenth century most of the peasantry were free wage earners, yeomen farmers, sailors on the sea, or soldiers in foreign wars.

Thus it was that in these long years the economic, social, and political causes working towards the disappearance of villeinage and serfdom rolled on their relentless way. The feudal system was slowly disintegrating. Meanwhile, the merchants and knights were increasing in wealth and importance. Their power in Parliament grew apace. For example, the watching townsmen forced Edward III and Richard II to abandon almost completely the earlier practice of granting special privileges to foreign merchants. The influence of the commons, particularly the new capitalist class, was also made evident in the number of steps taken by king and Parliament to regulate commerce in the interest of English traders. The Navigation Act of 1381 required Englishmen to use English ships to export or import goods. True, the statute was not enforceable because there were too few English ships. Nevertheless, Parliament approved its provisions and there was no doubt about the prevailing climate of opinion.

In Parliament merchants and other business men from the boroughs loudly complained about things they did not like. They found fault with the king's account books. They repeatedly called attention to the need of governing the royal household with "good moderation of expenses." They did not want to see so much money spent outside of England. The export of bullion was curtailed so that there would be more cash in circulation at home. These restless activities show something of the temper of the age.

The crevices and crannies of official documents do not reveal all the reasons why Parliament passed a Statute of Laborers or what happened when the axe was first put to the roots of feudalism. The reader who would sense and see these things must look beyond the formal records to the sources of what is usually called social history. Deplorable results follow a prolonged and lonely concern with the language of statutes and case decisions if no study is made of other aspects of society. Successful scholarship derives its hue and shape from its sensitive awareness to the ebb and flow of many men and motives. The riddles and answers of human history are not all listed in the domestic and foreign state papers. The fourteenth century, so filled with unrest, provides rich sources of poems, sermons, tracts, and dialogues to light the path of the inquiring student beyond the limits set by the rolls of courts and Parliament.

The important directional thrusts of history are usually not confined to one state. In these troubled years the sense of medieval unity was slowly departing all over Europe. In England, even as the fabric of feudalism was being torn, the anti-papal and anti-clerical sentiment rose to new levels, especially after the Popes took up their long residence at Avignon. This feeling was increased still more when two Popes, each denouncing the other, divided the church (1378–1415). English opposition to papal authority and papal taxation, always an important factor in the relations of church and state, became steadily more vehement and effective.

The anti-papal temper of the age was evident in the enactments of Parliament. In 1343 Parliament forbade anyone to bring letters from Avignon that might be prejudicial to the interests or rights of the king. In 1351 the first Statute of Provisors, extended in 1390, was designed to prevent the Pope from giving any English benefices to his followers. The act declared that any persons accepting papal appointments to English benefices should be imprisoned until they paid fines and had surrendered their newly acquired holdings. The Statutes of Provisors apparently had small effect because they were laxly enforced.

In 1353, as a result of "clamours and grievous complaints," the first Statute of Praemunire, reissued and strengthened in 1365 and 1393, forbade appeals from the English courts to the Pope's courts in cases "of which the cognizance pertains to the court of our lord the king." The new law stated that judgments given in the king's court were "being impeached in the court of another." One of the results, in the words of the statute, was "the undoing and annulment of the common law of the said kingdom at all times customary." The Statute of Praemunire established a process for dealing with people who were charged with appealing to the Pope or with like offenses. Accused individuals were to be summoned "before the king and his council, or in his chancery, or before the king's justices in their courts . . . there to answer to the king in proper person regarding the contempt involved."

This statute of 1353 said that if the accused did not appear for trial at the proper time then "they and their procurators, attorneys, executors, notaries, and supporters" were to be subject to the penalty of outlawry and the forfeiture of goods. The later statutes of Praemunire (1365 and 1393) provided severe penalties when the accused was found guilty of such dealings with the papacy as were forbidden by law.

The laws of Provisors and Praemunire stand as clear expressions of the anti-papal feeling in the fourteenth century. They stand also as an indication of something else that is sometimes overlooked and should be explained. King, council, and courts wanted to keep their exclusive control of land over which they had assumed jurisdiction. The attempt of the papal court to extend its powers over borderline cases about the right of presentation to benefices (some of them endowed by the king himself), its continuous efforts to broaden church jurisdiction in scores of ways, these were the things the laws of Provisors and Praemunire were designed to stop. Writs of prohibition could be issued to block the activities of church courts in England but such a writ could not run against the Pope. Thus Parliament enacted the Provisors and Praemunire statutes in which the lawmakers did not deny the papal jurisdiction but only insisted that it stay confined to what the king and his Englishmen considered to be its proper province.

In 1366 Edward III refused the Pope's demand for the 1,000 marks of annual tribute King John had promised to pay earlier in the century. England was then about thirty years in arrears; after 1366 she paid no more. Meanwhile, too, the anti-papal pens of men like William of Ockham and John Wycliffe were bitter and busy. The church replied in kind and declared that heretics should be "cast into the outer darkness wherein is weeping and gnashing of teeth, where the fire is not quenched, nor shall the worm of conscience die."

THE REVOLUTION OF 1399

Edward III died in 1377 and Richard II, son of the Black Prince, came to the throne. Richard was only eleven years old and because he was a minor England was ruled by a regency. Parliament tried, in these years of social and economic discontent, to control the government of the regency. Under Parliament's watchful guidance some of the council members did try to manage national affairs adequately. They attempted to stop the maladministration of England's armies abroad. Their efforts were unsuccessful because of their own incompetence and their factional disputes.

When Richard was seventeen years old he began to gather about him several men who were willing to aid the impetuous youth in his plans to curb or end the control of Parliament in governmental affairs. Some of these associates of the young king also wanted to reduce the power of the great nobles. Some desired to make an immediate peace with France.

Against Richard and his ministers stood several jealous barons, including one of Richard's uncles. These men were turbulent, unscrupulous, itching for power. In 1385 Richard stubbornly refused to yield to Parliament's request that he dismiss several of his ministers. At the same time there were long and ugly disputes with the House of Commons about the expenses of the royal household. From a confusing welter of events into which we need not enter here, there finally emerged a heavy defeat for Richard II and his supporters. The so-called "Merciless Parliament" of 1388 ordered the execution of many of the king's friends, including the Lord Chief Justice, the mayor of London, and even Richard's harmless tutor. Even moderate members of Parliament wanted to see effective control established over the restless king.

Richard II was compelled, for a time, to submit to the control of Parliament and the unquiet ambition of the few prominent lords who had triumphed over him, the "Lords Appellant" led by the unscrupulous Duke of Gloucester, Richard's uncle. After these men had ruled for a year Richard II suddenly declared that he would take the reins of government into his own hands. He asserted that he would govern in harmony with the advice of Parliament. Thus he defied the gang of men who had set themselves about him and his defiance was successful.

For eight years Richard ruled well. Then, suddenly, in 1397, the period of order and quietness ended. The king burst the bonds tied about him by Parliament and turned to revenge himself upon those lords who had slain his friends nine years before. His vengeance was complete. The last of his enemies was punished. A Parliament packed with Richard's supporters voted him a life income and set up a committee of eighteen submissive creatures of the king to exercise several Parliamentary powers. New treason laws expanded the definition of treason and wrapped it up in such ambiguous language that any opposition to the king might be called treason. Law after law was broken by the royal commands. Richard recklessly interfered with the courts of law and justice. No man's life or property was safe. Richard was king indeed.

Early in 1399 the banished Henry Bolingbroke, the wily and unscrupulous Duke of Lancaster and heir of John of Gaunt, landed in England to claim the Lancastrian estates that Richard II had arbitrarily seized. Thousands of Englishmen flocked to serve under Henry's banners. Richard II, who had earlier been lured to Ireland, returned home too late. His troops melted away. He made every possible mistake at the crisis. Helpless, he surrendered and abdicated.

Richard II had apparently aimed at making himself an absolute monarch. The result was revolution and the establishment of the Lancastrian dynasty. The Parliament of 1399 accepted Richard's abdication and a commission was appointed to draw up the final document of deposition. "The statements of his crimes and defaults were notoriously sufficient for deposing the same king," said the Parliament roll of 1399, "considering also his own confession with regard to his incompetence." Richard was denounced above all because he had broken the fundamental laws of England. He was formally charged with the crime of having declared the laws to be "in his own heart." Edward II had been deposed because he governed too little, Richard II because he tried to govern too much.

Almost all the happenings in the reign of Richard II are intricate and ill-reported. The contemporary evidence about the revolution of 1399 is tainted and partisan. A modern student has shown, for example, that on three points the official Parliament roll has distorted or suppressed the truth. Despite the obscuring fogs of prevarication and ignorance that have drifted over more than five centuries of time there is no doubt about the importance of the swift revolution of 1399. Richard II was perhaps the last truly medieval king of England. He was certainly the last king to rule by strict hereditary right. In 1327 Parliament had deposed Edward II. In 1399 Parliament not only deposed Richard II but chose his successor. When Parliament selected the cheerless Henry, Duke of Lancaster, as king it passed over far better hereditary claims. Henry could not show the dimmest pretense of hereditary right. He was king by the fact of conquest.

The Lancastrians are usually said to have ruled by Parliamentary title. However, as Professor Gaillard Lapsley has conclusively shown, that title was a frail one because no legal Parliament existed at the time that Henry assumed the crown.[2] The first Lancastrian "could have had a complete and technically correct Parliamentary title and

---

[2] G. T. Lapsley, "The Parliamentary Title of Henry IV," *English Historical Review,* XLIX (1934). See the selections from the Parliament Rolls in Carl Stephenson and F. G. Marcham, *Sources of English Constitutional History,* pp. 250–257.

his supporters intended that the revolution should be accomplished in that way." But the throne was seized by the swords of Henry's men amidst the applause of the populace and Henry IV's legal title was left far from complete. Probably no man in 1399 was ready to ask indiscreet questions about deficiencies of title. When all things are said, the most important fact that the events of 1399 proclaimed was that Henry IV and his successors were to rule only if they heeded the limitations imposed upon them by Parliament and the laws of England. A king who consistently failed to satisfy Parliament could not long expect to keep his crown.

BRACTON AND THE YEAR BOOKS

Whenever the modern scholar studies the world of the Middle Ages he is profoundly aware of the medieval concern with the nature and meaning of the law. In the thirteenth and fourteenth centuries the study of Roman law flourished at Oxford. English students went to Bologna to study under Azo, "lord of all the lords of law." Many men were learned in both Roman and English common law. The kings had able legal minds about the throne.

One of the most famous of medieval textbooks is one probably written by the jurist Henry de Bracton and called *Tractatus de Legibus et Consuetudinibus Angliae (A Treatise about the Laws and Customs of England)*. This study was of great significance both in the study of jurisprudence and in the actual development of English law.

Bracton was well qualified to write about the substance and operation of the laws and customs of England because he was both Dean of Exeter and a royal justice. He travelled on the assize circuit or sat at Westminster from about 1245 until his death in 1267. During these twenty years he collected a large number of distinctive rules and precedents from the decisions of two judges. Fortunately the clear and precise *Note Book* Bracton made has been saved from the disasters of damp and time.

Despite the fact that Bracton was a churchman he showed quite clearly that he was loyal to the law administered by the courts of his king. His famous *Treatise* was divided into two parts. The first was a rather long scientific discussion and exposition of certain broad principles of the law. The unfinished second section carefully described, explained, and summarized how different writs were prepared and issued and what happened in the court procedures. Bracton was clear, precise, learned. His work has well merited the description of a famous

scholar who called it "the crown and flower of medieval jurisprudence."

Several smaller works were written during the thirteenth and fourteenth centuries, partly because the lawyers and judges realized the
importance of Bracton and the usefulness of books such as his in the
law courts. Professor G. E. Woodbine selected and published in 1910
Four Fourteenth Century Law Tracts with an admirable introduction.
Most of the lesser contemporary works were written in the Anglo-
Norman vernacular. One of them, called Britton, was composed in the
form of a code. Most of the others were concerned almost solely with
procedure. This is not to be smiled upon, for handbooks about practical procedure were always useful to judges and lawyers in the Middle
Ages.

In the next chapter will be discussed the rise of the four great law
schools of England: Lincoln's Inn, the Inner Temple, the Middle
Temple, and Gray's Inn. "Taught law is tough law," said F. W. Maitland and these schools, the Inns of Court, had a decisive influence in
hardening and toughening English law. In the law schools were used
the Year Books, so called because there was one for each regnal year.
These volumes began in 1292, at an hour when Edward I had appointed commissioners to investigate the increasing divorce between
law and learning. They appeared with almost unbroken regularity
until 1536 and then they stopped abruptly.[3]

The Year Books were anonymous law reports written in French.
The pages are filled with precise and clear discussions and comments
made by prominent judges and lawyers about points of law and bases of
judgments in actual cases tried before the royal justices either at Westminster or on circuit. Each volume shows a watchful eye for the flexible application of vital and expanding legal principles, the careful
handling of the jewels of precedent, the meticulous use of competent
logic, the creative power of the legal fraternity as they reasoned upon
the mass of records, the rules, the precedents, the "judge-made law,"
which were the tap roots of future growth.

It is quite true that "the custom of the realm was often in large
measure the custom of the courts." The Year Books were written by
lawyers for lawyers. They remain today the most important source of
our knowledge of the medieval common law. From legal principles and
judicial precedents the common law justices continued to derive the

---

[3] An excellent general description of the Year Books is in F. W. Maitland, *Year Books of
Edward II,* vol. i, pp. ix–xx (Selden Society, vol. xvii).

rules of law to apply to new combinations of circumstances. A judge today will only follow a "binding" authority when it is a correct statement of the law. Through the pages of the great Year Books, especially those of the fourteenth century, all students move with amazement and reverence. The motto of the Selden Society's edition of selected Year Books is a quotation from Roger North: "He (Sergeant Maynard) had such a relish of the old year-books that he carried one in his coach to divert him in travel, and he said he chose it before any comedy."

In the latter part of the fifteenth century the once powerful and constant Year Books began to become slipshod and broken. Legal French showed a steady deterioration for several centuries, a decline that can be easily illustrated by a brief quotation from a curious report about a Salisbury assize. The report stated that Chief Justice Richardson "fuit assault per prisoner la condemne pur felony; que prius son condemnation ject un brickbat a le dit justice que narrowly mist."

After the Year Books came to an end in the sixteenth century there appeared several Abridgements. A series of "private reports" continued to be published until the nineteenth century, such as those of Dyer, Plowden, Yelverton, Coke, Hobart, Jenkins, Vaughan and Douglas. After 1865 the semi-official Law Reports appeared regularly. These Reports superseded the earlier private publications prepared by judges and lawyers and others.

CHANCERY AND EQUITY

Thus it was that in the fourteenth century Parliament was moving towards new thresholds of power and men learned in the law were writing about the nature and purpose of their precedents, writs and actions. Meanwhile significant adjustments were being made in the complex and tough judicial mechanism. One of the most important of these changes was the growth of the court of Chancery.

Several prerogative powers form essential parts of kingship. The king, for instance, must possess the power to give mercy and justice to his subjects. In earlier centuries, as in our own, it was the king's duty to help the poor and defenseless. He, and he alone, had the right to remedy all wrongs, to judge with justice the pleas *ad misericordiam,* the appeals to his mercy. Much of this authority was exercised through the king's council. It became one of the functions of the council to provide just remedies where the courts of common law erred or where no adequate solutions were provided by those courts.

The rules of the common law, so inelastic and so formal, could not easily be stretched or bent to bring about justice. Common law courts could only give a fixed form of judgment. They could not always provide relief where sense and justice made it obviously necessary. A man might lose a case if he chose the wrong writ. There were other difficulties. For instance, after the rise of the trying jury it was clear that the jurymen, chosen to decide the facts in a case, often found it hard to follow a complex series of arguments or "pleadings." For a long time a witness who stood to gain or lose by a decision or who was a party to an action was forbidden to give evidence. Such rules often kept out of court the evidence of everybody who knew anything about the facts in the case.

Nevertheless, as was suggested in the latter part of Chapter VI, it is easy to stress too strongly the adherence to forms and rules in the common law courts. Procedure developed by pleadings and "plaint" as well as by writs. As Professor T. F. T. Plucknett has also shown, the judges in the thirteenth and fourteenth centuries did use wide discretionary powers, and judicial discretion may bring justice. Judges in the common law courts sometimes made exceptions, even in the teeth of the common law. They did, on occasion, sturdily refuse to apply statutes and insisted on abrogating the legal rules. Professor Bertha Putnam and Professor Faith Thompson have also noted the fact that many justices were less well informed about the text of the law than later generations have supposed. As Professor Putnam has remarked: "It would be most interesting if one could say with certainty what copy of the statutes the court used—whether the statute roll, close roll, patent roll, or one of the semi-official registers now preserved at the Exchequer or whether they had a copy for their own use—but as to this there is no evidence. It would seem that the court had not always a text at hand." In any event, there is evidence of "equity" long before any need of a separate court was felt. "Relief against penalties" appeared in practice very early.

Much of the power of the council to deal with problems of moulding relief in particular cases gradually passed into the hands of the Chancellor. It was the Chancellor who issued the numerous writs and thus he knew what remedies could be obtained at common law. Because the Chancellor was usually a churchman (as in earlier days, still the "keeper of the king's conscience") he was expected to know what was moral and right as well as what was legal. There were always wrongs to be mitigated and evils to be avoided. So the Chancellors slowly developed equity as the praetors did in ancient Rome.

What is equity? In its beginnings in England it was the extraordinary justice administered by the king's Chancellor to enlarge, supplant, or override the common law system where that system had become too narrow and rigid in its scope. Equity was later to be built into a legal body of rules and doctrines designed to supplement and aid the common law. The basic idea of equity was, and remains, the application of a moral governing principle to a body of circumstances in order to reach a judgment that was in accord with Christian conscience and Roman natural law, a settlement that showed the common denominators of humanity, justice, and mercy.

In the sixteenth century Christopher St. Germain denounced what F. W. Maitland once called "the excessive veneration for prescriptive formulae of the common law courts." He wrote in his famous dialogue *Doctor and Student* (1523): "Conscience never resisteth the law nor addeth to it, but only when the law is directly in itself against the law of God or the law of reason." The snares of formalism, that eighth deadly sin, must sometimes be cut in the interests of the laws of God and of reason, which together mean equity. This is the corrective function of equity. This is the moderating, moral ideal and power that the Anglo-Saxons called "mildening law." If a student looks at W. P. Baildon's edition of *Select Cases in Chancery 1364–1471* he will see how frequently his eyes encounter the words "good faith," "reason," "conscience and law," "law and right," "reason and good faith." The common law demanded certainty throughout its broad kingdom. Equity, on the other hand, demanded justice in individual cases.

Professor F. W. Maitland once remarked: "We ought to think of equity as a supplementary law, a sort of appendix added to our code." Or, again, "Equity had come not to destroy the law but to fulfill it." Finally, in the words of Lord Ellesmere, famous Chancellor of the seventeenth century: "Equity remedies the law, wherein the law is defective because of its generality." New substantive law was created as existing individual rights were extended by the remedial and merciful measures of equity. Sir Henry Sumner Maine once said, in a famous dictum, that the agencies of the growth of the law are three: legislation, fictions and equity.

Chancery moved at a very slow pace towards complete bifurcation from the council. Only by gradual steps did it develop its own procedural methods. As the decades passed, fewer members of the council attended Chancery meetings. In 1349 an ordinance of Edward III gave the Chancellor general authority to grant relief on all matters having to do with the wide "prerogative of grace." This royal decision made it possible for the Chancellor to act without a preliminary writ or order from the king. Historians do not know precisely when the Chancellor began to act independently. There is really no definite date at which the scholar can say: "In this year Chancery was entirely separated from the council." One historian believes the final cleavage occurred during the reign of Richard II (1377–1399). We do know that in 1377 the Chancellor heard a petition addressed to him alone and dismissed it himself—so far as we are aware he did not consult the council. But one swallow does not make a summer. Several scholars are certain that it is unwise to see a full separation before about 1474 when there is no doubt that the Chancellor was dealing independently with wrongs against conscience and thus extending his equitable jurisdiction.

When Chancery had quite clearly developed a court jurisdiction separate from the council in the fifteenth century the Chancellor was aided by twelve assistants called Masters in Chancery. These men had to know both common law and Roman civil law. They heard cases in a corner of the great hall at Westminster Palace. They made recommendations to the Chancellor for his final decision. They assisted the council in diverse ways. Sometimes they acted as the king's secretaries. Until 1833 they were all appointed by the Chancellor. The chief of these assistants and deputy of the Chancellor was the Master of the Rolls, originally the keeper of the records. There were also six superior clerks, whose job was to prepare and check original writs and Chancery bills. Their duties became important as the tide of business swelled and in later days they were to be partly responsible for the cost, complexity, abuse, and delay in Chancery that plagued England until the nineteenth century. As Chancery slowly extended its jurisdiction and consolidated its power it became more and more a court where only the wealthy could go.

Where there had once existed only legal remedies there slowly grew a duality of law and equity. Legal and equitable doctrines and remedies moved side by side. The doctrines of equity came to supplement the law of property when problems of trusts arose. They altered the structure of the law of contracts by introducing the idea of equity as to specific performance, which is the technical term used to describe the ordering of a defendant to carry out his promise in a breach of contract case. The modern rules for specific performance were not developed until the eighteenth century. These doctrines of equity even extended the laws of torts and such things as the common law of mortgages by the equitable procedures relating to redemption. They also made possible other supplementary remedies by developing mandatory and prohibitory equitable operations such as those relating to specific restitutions, injunctions, the obligations of principal and surety and the like.

The growth of what Professor A. B. White aptly called "the upstart jurisdiction" of Chancery was not, of course, viewed with approval by the common law courts. The battle between the two was historic and it lasted for a long time. Common law lawyers did not like to see their fees decrease as the work of Chancery grew in scope. One of the earliest disputes occurred in 1483 when two judges of the common law courts agreed that if Chancery put two men in prison for failing to stop their actions at common law then the common law judges would loose the prisoners on application by a writ of *habeas corpus*. This writ of *habeas corpus* played an important part in the quarrels relating to Chancery jurisdiction even before its great constitutional importance following the Habeas Corpus Act of 1679. So too, of course, did the writ of prohibition. Not until the late seventeenth century, aided by the new social conditions, did the protracted battle between Chancery and the common law courts abate. Accommodation and reconciliation came very slowly.

The Chancellor, technically the instrument of the royal will, disregarded many of the procedures of the common law courts. Chancery used no juries. The evidence usually consisted of written affidavits and examinations under oath by a procedure called "discovery." No original writs were issued. Instead Chancery issued a judicial summons commanding the person or persons accused to appear under penalty (*sub poena*) to answer the "matters within contained," *i.e.* the bill or petition of the plaintiff. Upon the appearance of the parties concerned the Chancellor or his aides conducted an examination and studied the written affidavits. The defendant, in a procedure apparently borrowed from the canon law, was required to answer on oath the charges brought against him. At the end of the session the court of Chancery, judge of both law and facts, decided upon an "equitable" settlement and ordered the individuals before the court to do some things and to refrain from doing others.

Early in the seventeenth century the courts of Common Pleas and King's Bench were both issuing writs of prohibition against Chancery. James I (1603–1625) decreed, on the advice of a commission headed by Sir Francis Bacon, that when the rules of common law and equity conflicted then the rules of equity must prevail. "When a judgment is obtained by oppression, wrong, and a hard conscience," said the king, "the Chancellor will frustrate it and set it aside." Writs of prohibition could no longer run against Chancery. James I, of course, always supported Chancery because it was most favorable to his prerogative claims.

The reader can easily understand how the slow rise of equity principles and procedures, so flexible before the hardening processes of the eighteenth and nineteenth centuries, proved constantly annoying to the common law courts, so dedicated to the ways of formality, fixity, and order. It was inevitable that they should resent encroachment upon their jurisdiction. "Equity is a roguish thing," said John Selden in the seventeenth century. "For law we have a measure, but equity is according to the conscience of the Chancellor." In the eighteenth century, Lord Mansfield, Chief Justice of the Court of King's Bench, incorporated into common law many results of equity decisions. He once remarked that he never liked the law so much as when it resembled equity.

One striking fact which must now be dealt with is the part played by Chancery in the development of what we call "uses." It was almost at the twilight of the Middle Ages that the policy and procedure of "uses" came into wide practice. The results were incalculable.

THE PROBLEM OF USES

A use is usually a passive trust, originally a trust of land. It is the equitable right given to a person or persons to enjoy the rents and profits of property although the legal title and possession are vested in someone else in trust for a beneficiary. One party has the legal right to the land while another has the use of it. Thus property may be nominally given to A to hold for the use of B. Because A has a moral obligation to hold that property to the advantage of B, the courts have always maintained a direct and immediate interest in the administration of such trusts. Today the doctrine of uses is applied in wide areas for a vast range of purposes.

The origins of uses and the laws of trusts is very obscure. Uses are found in early Teutonic law (treuhand) and there are several of them in England by the twelfth century. Men going on the Crusades often put their property in the hands of relatives or friends to hold to the use, or in behalf of, minor children. In all such cases the keen eye of the Chancellor watched to see that no harm was done to the interests of the true owners. Equity will always go beyond the documents. In the case of uses it protected the beneficial interest enforceable in equity.

We have earlier observed the growth of devices to defeat statutes against the free alienation of land and the complex rules of entail. By the thirteenth and the fourteenth centuries the methods of common recovery and like procedures were supplemented by the rapid and extensive growth of the practice of uses. Although uses could only exist in the case of an estate in fee simple there was still ample room for the employment of them. There were naturally many men in England who wanted to avoid the heavy incidents of tenure, such as relief and wardship. Moreover, under feudal law land could not be willed but had to pass to the heirs by the rules of feudalism. In these circumstances A conveyed land to B to use for A. A might also say that he wanted the income from the property after his death to go to his younger children who would inherit no land from A under the feudal law. The system of uses was also employed sometimes to defraud creditors. A statute of 1377 was designed to stop the application of a use for such dishonest purposes.

Medieval kings inevitably resented this legal evasion of feudal responsibilities. What was more their own than the dues and incidents of tenure incidental to their feudal overlordship? Uses destroyed the royal feudal income. Nevertheless, how could the Crown effectively and squarely confront the whole issue when the whole procedure was legal enough and the large landowners dominated politics?

After the passage of the Statute of Mortmain (1279) the device of uses was also employed to turn lands over to the church. A would transfer a parcel of land to B and B, as the trustee, would carry out the wishes of A and give the income from the land to the church. Common law courts would not look beyond the fact that B held the legal title. But the Chancellor, a churchman, made certain that B did in fact what he had agreed to do. It was a problem of morals, a question of conscience, the proper province of equity.

A statute was designed in 1392 to prevent evasions of the Statute of Mortmain by prohibiting conveyances to the use of corporations. This statute, and others later, could not be enforced. Until the sixteenth century, with no major let or hindrance, the practice of equitable uses continued. It remained for Henry VIII, who needed all the income he could get, to attempt a solution to remedy the difficulties of the crown. This he did in the famous and formidable Statute of Uses of 1536.

Meanwhile there continued to grow and flourish new kinds of old evasions. Outstanding among these were "springing" uses and "shifting" uses, complex and dazzling operations executed by subtle lawyers and sympathetic judges. About these things more will be said shortly.

OTHER COURTS AND OTHER CAUSES

There was a second court that emerged from the king's council to administer a system of justice not ruled by the common law and close to the civilian doctrines of Rome. This was the Court of Admiralty. In years of mounting foreign and coastal sea trade it became impossible for the port town courts to cope effectively with cases increasing in number and complexity. About the middle of the fourteenth century the Court of Admiralty, under the jurisdiction of the Lord Admiral, then a member of the council, separated from the parent body. In the beginning its jurisdiction was largely a disciplinary one over the royal fleet and a criminal one extending over all ships and men engaged in activities forbidden by the Code of Oléron. Soon, however, Admiralty jurisdiction, enforcing the rights of the Crown on the sea, was broadened to include certain civil cases. Among these were such things as Crown prize claims (especially in cases of enemy goods and ships), flotsam and jetsam and salvage problems, shippers' contracts, quarrels on the high seas and on ships in river estuaries or channels (*i.e.*, in the waters downstream from the first bridge over a river; under the law the events in all such cases were deemed to have occurred in the London district of Cheapside). In the reigns of Richard II (1377–1399) and Henry VIII (1509–1547) Admiralty criminal jurisdiction was carefully restricted. On the other hand, its civil jurisdiction was gradually enlarged by Parliamentary statute and royal dispensation.

The common law courts naturally attacked Admiralty as soon as it appeared outside the council. These attacks continued until the eighteenth century. In the early seventeenth century, for instance, Sir Edward Coke, Chief Justice of the Court of Common Pleas (1606–1613) and Chief Justice of the Court of King's Bench (1613–1616), denounced both Chancery and Admiralty. As a result of the pressure of the common law courts the civil jurisdiction of Admiralty was markedly reduced. Nevertheless, the common law courts never succeeded in dealing with the law merchant, despite Lord Mansfield's incorporation of some law merchant into common law in the eighteenth century. In the nineteenth century, as will be later explained, many areas of jurisdiction were given back to the Court of Admiralty which is now a special division of the High Court of Justice (see Chapter XX). Today Admiralty law, like the merchant law and the law of wills and personal property, shows many signs that it originated far from the main sources of English common law and close to the fountains of Rome.

Admiralty law was a segment of the ancient law merchant, a body of law observed in most European countries during the Middle Ages and administered in the courts merchant and the pie powder courts of the fairs and boroughs earlier described. The most important merchant courts were in the seaport and staple towns—in medieval England the name "staple" meant a designated town where certain goods were to be bought and sold, a steady market. Thus England's Calais was the "staple" port through which all wool had to come to be sold, the mart for European buyers. In 1297 Edward I established certain "staple" ports within England so that the royal revenue taxes could be collected more easily. Specified "staple" commodities, such as wool, hides and tin, moved through these "staple" ports. Hence it was necessary to have commercial law courts in such strategic places. These tribunals were particularly concerned, of course, with cases of debt, contract, trespass, shipping disputes and the like. They had no juries, no jurisdiction in felonies or freeholds. The purpose of the courts merchant in the ports, as the similar pie powder courts, was to give quick and effective justice. If there was denial or delay an appeal might be made to the Chancellor. These summary jurisdiction merchant courts were held frequently—"from day to day, from hour to hour, from tide to tide." A staple town court usually included the following members: the mayor, two constables, and two merchants (one from the north of England, one from the south). If aliens were directly involved in a case then it was usual to add two foreign merchants to the court.

Magna Carta had guaranteed foreign merchants freedom of movement to and from England and permission to establish residence if they wished (Clause 41). It was quite natural that several members of the English merchant and craft guilds, confronted by alien competition, were displeased. The boroughs with franchise rights (also guaranteed once more by Magna Carta and by numerous charter confirmations later) sometimes restricted foreign traders. On the other hand, English kings were usually willing to grant concessions to foreigners provided payment was made for the privileges obtained. Sometimes royal grants gave foreign merchants rights in wholesale trade, rights of residence, rights of special court treatment. The Statute of Staples of 1353, for instance, permitted certain foreigners to carry on a wholesale trade in a specified list of staple towns and gave them precisely stated privileges in each staple town merchant court.[4]

Such was the status of the Court of Admiralty and the merchant tribunals in the fourteenth century. Meanwhile new developments occurred in the Court of Exchequer.

When the character and functions of the Exchequer Court were examined in earlier chapters considerable stress was placed upon the fact that the operations of that court were effective and rapid. It was natural that private creditors wanted to use a tribunal with such swift remedies. In the fourteenth century, when the common law courts entered a long struggle among themselves as rivals for jurisdiction and profit, these private creditors, for a fee, were permitted to employ the royal instruments of justice. Because affairs of debt usually provided a lucrative business the barons of the Exchequer were glad to make whatever legal adjustments were necessary to bring such cases into their courts. There was one major difficulty. In previous chapters it was explained that several laws forbade the Court of Exchequer to hear common pleas. How could this formidable obstacle be overcome?

Let us never underestimate the skills of our ancestors. A very large part of our legal history is the history of "fictions" in the law. The barons of the Exchequer agreed that if a private creditor wished to use the process and resources of their court to collect his debt he could use the writ of *Quo Minus* and it was first used for this purpose in 1345.

Under the writ of *Quo Minus*, the creditor alleged that he, the plaintiff, was indebted to the Crown. He further alleged that he was in financial difficulties because he could not collect the debt owed him by the defendant, by reason of which he was the less (*quo minus*) able to pay the king. A case like this obviously touched the revenue interests of the Crown. Hence it could be heard in the Exchequer Court and the decision could be executed by Exchequer methods. This plea, however genuine in some cases, was capable of extension by fiction, a fiction that could not be formally denied (traversed) in the courts.

During the next two centuries the power and jurisdiction of the Exchequer Court steadily grew. By the last quarter of the sixteenth century all barons of the Exchequer were both lawyers and sergeants-

---

4 For a discussion of guilds, trade, finance in the thirteenth and fourteenth centuries see Goldwin Smith, *A History of England*, a companion volume in the Scribner's Historical Series, pp. 93–98, 153–155.

at-law (the select inner circle of experienced members of the profession, whose training and functions will be explained in the following chapter). After 1579 these skilled men went on circuit with the other judges of the common law courts. So it was that the judicial business of the Exchequer Court was still further increased and it continued to function effectively until it was absorbed into the High Court of Justice in 1873. Today the primary task of the Court of Exchequer, now merged with the Court of Queen's Bench (by Order-in-Council, 1881), is to decide questions between the Crown and the taxpayer, and the Crown and its accountants.

The Court of King's Bench in the Middle Ages always claimed a supervisory power over the royal courts. Disputes between the Court of Exchequer and the Court of King's Bench were frequent in the fourteenth century and in 1357 Edward III (1327–1377) established a special court to hear and judge complaints of error in process, including record, made in the Court of Exchequer. This court was headed by the Chancellor and the Treasurer and contained some justices. It is usually called the Court of Exchequer Chamber. According to Sir Edward Coke and some modern authorities there were really three additional Courts of Exchequer Chamber: (1) a court that heard cases in equity for the Exchequer Court; (2) a court to consider questions of error made in the Court of King's Bench when Parliament (the House of Lords) was not in session; this court consisted of the justices of the Common Pleas and the barons of the Exchequer or any six of them; (3) a consultative tribunal of rather indefinite composition containing all the judges of England (the barons of the Exchequer joined the justices of the other courts in 1579). The task of this body was to deal with particularly difficult cases. It did not render decisions but merely advised the major courts. Hence it was not a court in a strictly technical sense. The learned opinion of the majority upon any issue of pure law was taken as binding upon the court from which the knotty problem had been referred (adjourned) in the first place. What else could be expected when this Exchequer Chamber contained the best judicial minds of the age?

In 1830 a new Court of Exchequer Chamber was created to replace the four courts listed above. This body assumed most of the functions previously exercised by the four courts. It heard appeals from all the common law tribunals. Appeal from this court was, of course, still possible to the House of Lords, always the final appellate court. In 1873 the Supreme Court of Judicature Act abolished the Court of Exchequer Chamber and that court's tasks were performed in another way and by a reformed judicial system to be described in Chapter XX.

We have now seen how Chancery, Admiralty, Exchequer, and the Exchequer Chamber made progress in seeking power and order in their affairs during the fourteenth century. Meanwhile, as we have also noted, numerous rivalries arose among all the courts. The pressures and probings and detours continued to produce the kinds of evasions and fictions earlier described in such processes as *quo minus,* ejectment, trespass on the case, and common recovery. The judges in each of the separate law courts understood quite well the dangers of demobilizing forces or leaving soft spots in their defenses. The Court of King's Bench, for instance, knew that the Court of Common Pleas would seize any opportunity to encroach upon the jurisdiction of King's Bench. Justices in Common Pleas, for their part, kept watch and ward on their ramparts and annexed whatever legal territory they could claim. The devices of attack and defense multiplied. Appropriate fictions, those imagined facts apparently quite unbridled by reality, were steadily invented by shrewd judges and lawyers, proud feudal barons in the empire of the law.

The rise and use of two typical fictions not hitherto described may be briefly mentioned here. The first appeared in the fifteenth century as an effective operation developed by the judges of King's Bench. It involved two steps in procedure. The first step was called the Bill of Middlesex and the second the writ of *Latitat.*

For many reasons the jurisdiction of the Court of King's Bench was steadily extended through several centuries. The action of trespass on the case, for instance, helped greatly to expand the province of King's Bench activity. As the King's Bench reached into more areas of civil jurisdiction it was aided by the established idea that a court had jurisdiction over any case involving either officials of that court or prisoners in its power. If, therefore, a man could somehow be brought into the custody of the Warden of the King's Bench Prison (Marshalsea) then any civil action (except, of course, real property actions) could become triable in King's Bench. The first problem was clearly this: how could King's Bench legally get custody of a defendant when he was somewhere else?

The necessary seizure and imprisonment was brought about by a procedure called the Bill of Middlesex, an order from King's Bench to the sheriff of Middlesex to arrest the defendant on the fictitious charge of trespass *vi et armis et contra pacem domini regis* and to put him in the Marshalsea. As soon as the named individual was seized on the basis of his alleged trespass and put in the King's Bench Prison then, of course, the principle that King's Bench had jurisdiction in all cases where the defendant was in the custody of the Warden began to operate. Hence any civil action could begin.

If the defendant did not reside in Middlesex or could not be found there, then the Bill of Middlesex was followed by a writ called *Latitat* sent to the sheriff of the county where it was believed that the suspect "lurks and runs about" ("latitat et discurrit"). The writ ordered the sheriff to seize the man and turn him over to King's Bench. As soon as this was done and bail was given then the allegation of trespass was dropped and the court turned to the real cause of the action. In time, as usual, both the alleged trespass and the bail became no more than fictions.

It is not surprising that the rival Court of Common Pleas insisted that the Court of King's Bench was guilty of unprovoked robbery and aggression, however legal the procedure of Middlesex and *Latitat* might be. When a statute (1662) provided that no cause might be tried unless it was clearly stated in a writ then the King's Bench merely added to the allegation of trespass a second clause (the "ac etiam" clause) setting forth the real and proper cause of action. This fictitious proceeding continued until all such forms of fictions were abolished by the Uniformity of Process Act of 1832. Litigants, of course, usually preferred the King's Bench process to that of Common Pleas because it was simple, effective, and far less costly. Advantages of process were seldom overlooked by suitors.

A second typical fiction evolved during the centuries of struggle among the law courts grew out of the old writ *Quare Clausum Fregit* ("whereas he has broken the enclosure," *i.e.*, smashed the fence or levelled the hedge). This writ was a writ of trespass and hence a plea of the Crown. For a long time, however, it had been used by the Court of Common Pleas because it concerned land rights. During the reign of Charles II (1660–1685) Chief Justice North of the Court of Common Pleas saw that it would be advantageous to issue the *Quare Clausum* writ containing the customary allegation of trespass plus a second clause stating the true cause of action. This device was obviously similar to the "ac etiam" clause added to the Middlesex and *Latitat* procedure of King's Bench. As soon as the defendant appeared before the justice in Common Pleas the "broken close" charge was dropped and the court proceeded to try the true cause of action. This fiction was also abolished by the Uniformity of Process Act in 1832.

It would be quite incorrect for the reader to assume that all the major changes upon the judicial stage were to be seen in the great central law courts. In the local scenes of the boroughs and counties numerous alterations, some of them important and useful, were occurring. A complete description would involve a mass of details that would obscure the main lines of development which this chapter is attempting to trace. One essential thing to remember is that few parts of a national life ever stay still while others move along. Hence in both the central and local arenas were presented new characters and new events in the fourteenth century. One of the most significant of these was the appearance in the rural areas of the country gentlemen who were called "justices of the peace." In scores of ways through many centuries these men helped the central Crown officials in the government of England.

It was natural that the central authorities should ask local men of ability and substance to aid in judicial business and administration and keep watchful eyes upon the sheriffs. Some knights of the shire had been appointed in the twelfth century to help keep the peace and this custom was continued. Early in the fourteenth century (1327) men called "conservators," or custodians, of the peace were used to perform a miscellaneous collection of duties such as receiving indictments of suspected criminals, quelling riots, and, in certain cases after 1328, to act as trial judges and to punish offenders. About 1350 these men began to be called "justices of the peace." Soon, especially after the local labor problems brought by the Black Death of 1349, their tasks increased. They were on their way to becoming, in a phrase made famous by F. W. Maitland, "judicial beasts of burden."

There were several statutes in the fourteenth century setting forth the duties and responsibilities of these local servants of the Crown. Statutes of 1360 and 1361 provided for the appointment by commissions of several local amateur justices in each county. Their duties were clearly and carefully specified. The courts held by them have met four times a year since the fourteenth century. In later days these tribunals came to be called Quarter Sessions. When the courts were not in session the justices of the peace continued to perform their numerous judicial tasks and the varied duties involved in local administration. They dealt with minor offenders in cases where no juries were needed. They prowled and probed and reported to the central government and they carried out the orders that flowed down to them.

The functions of the Quarter Sessions courts have often been defined and changed by statute. For instance, difficult cases were usually held for the assize judges to deal with. The Quarter Sessions Act of 1842 stated that the justices of the peace were not to hear certain cases, such as those involving treason or murder. By the Criminal Justice Administration Act of 1914 the Quarter Sessions were given an appellate jurisdiction from the summary courts called petty sessions. Justices of the peace never possessed any civil jurisdiction.

From these comments it can be seen that the local institution of the justice of the peace became vigorous and strong in the counties. Several aspects of the later work of these justices will be described in the appropriate chapters below. Watched and guided from Westminster, they tried cases involving the disturbance of the peace. They had some control over wages and prices, weights and measures, the supply of agricultural laborers, apprenticeships. They heard complaints about the sheriffs, the mayors, the bailiffs, the high constables of the hundreds, the petty constables of the parish.[5] In the Tudor period (1485–1603) the power of these voluntary and unpaid servants stood at its height. Burdened with multifarious tasks and "stacks of statutes," they discharged their wide duties with ability. Usually respectable, well versed in local business, these magistrates of the gentry class became the instruments of the Crown's trust, the pillars and pivots of local government.

The results of the changes discussed in this chapter were often not sharply evident in the century that followed. The fourteenth century was a vigorous age. The fifteenth century was in many respects barren and sterile, a distracted hundred years of foreign and domestic warfare, a tale of faction, conspiracy and violence. Nevertheless, there were a few bright chapters. Among these were the continued progress of the middle class and new phases of constitutional and legal advance. Meanwhile, in the bloody and convulsive Wars of the Roses, feudalism was to fall on its own sword. The surviving barons, touched by doubt and weakened by battle, could not hold back the trampling power of a new age. Medieval England, its values now so dim and frayed, was slowly dying.

---

[5] See *Proceedings before the Justices of the Peace in the Fourteenth and Fifteenth Centuries, Edward III to Richard III*, ed. by Bertha H. Putnam (1938).

CHAPTER XI

The Fifteenth Century:
precedent and privilege

PARADOX AND CONTRAST

WHEN the student turns to the fifteenth century he may not see very clearly. The distance is great. Even contemporaries saw much confusion and ambiguity in the pulsing activities of their age. But if a long and careful look is given to the falling world of feudalism the student will find several specific facts that point to definite conclusions. He will see, by the fitful light, that the fifteenth century was an age of throbbing action and clashing ideas. New skills appeared. New ranges of challenging thought gleamed beyond the foothills. New ideas rose and soared. Worlds changing into something brave and different usually believe that they can outgrow their benighted past. Often impervious to advice, goaded by ambition or power, reckless of good and evil, they accelerate their pace towards the unknown. Such a time was the fifteenth century. The Middle Ages were not nearly so sleepy and static as many individuals think. The late Professor Eileen Power said they looked to her as lively as an ant-heap.

The years of the Wars of the Roses were very lively indeed. So exciting and dramatic were the nobles' feuds that contemporaries then and historians later often stressed far too much the importance of violence in the tales of the fifteenth century. It is true, of course, that the Wars of the Roses brought one phase of the death agonies of feudalism. But it is also true that we shall get a false picture of the fifteenth century if we see it merely as "futile, bloody, and immoral" and the cockpit of contending disasters. Not all of the barons were coroneted brigands. Many were not shocking fellows at all—they were scholars and gentlemen. Not all Englishmen, great and little, were active in hacking down their fellows. Many paid scant attention to the tides of battle. To them the things that mattered most were the rains and the harvests, the begetting of children, the mingled hopes and fears about their individual tomorrows. The deeds of violent or evil men may be recorded in the annals of the fifteenth century or in the modern newspaper headlines. Nevertheless, neither the baron's sword nor the hangman's noose has marked the progress of man as well as the philosopher's pen or the old man harrowing clods in the dusk.

The nobles of England had birth and influence and land—that significant medieval symbol and tool of power. At the same time, one happy event of the fifteenth century was the real increase in the prosperity of the mass of the people. Domestic trade and industry advanced. Many new winds were blowing. England was in the midst of a transition from a feudal to a bourgeois society. The structure of classes, as Professor Sylvia Thrupp has remarked, was "not nearly so clear as we should like it to be." Social groups were not sharply set apart. There were no high fences between them. It is important to remember this partial fluidity lest our attention be distracted too much by the blood and fire of the years when the majesty of feudalism was shrinking. A fact of great importance in the changing face of England is, then, the steady progress of lesser men through the welter of disharmony brought by dynastic wars. When the strong Tudors (1485–1603) came to harness and command, the foundations of a new age had already been laid.

It is true that the fifteenth century brought blood and death to England. There were social changes dangerous to the existing order. There were undermining speculations and rebellious voices. The transactions of Parliament and the administration of Crown and courts were enfeebled. But—this is a fact of overwhelming significance—they were not destroyed. Justice was often perverted and defied. *Inter arma leges silent.* But the principles of English law were not shaken off and forgotten. The decisions of the battlefield did not ultimately prevail over the voices of the court room and council chamber.

In this volume it is not possible to linger and watch such fascinating things as the extraordinary gambles, intrigues, and struggles of the Wars of the Roses, the tides of trade and commerce, prose and poetry. From the rich chapters of the later Middle Ages we must select those paragraphs that have most to do with the decisive phases of the growth of law and government.

As we gaze back over the salient features of the fifteenth century landscape we see that the gulf between that age and our own is deep and wide. Nevertheless, in the midst of blurring overtones and cross-currents we can see some mingled signs that we are approaching the end of the Middle Ages, that broad avenue into the modern era. In those days and ours the fusing principles of continuity and erosion are constantly at work. All the ages of English history have contributed something to the constitution and to the theory and practice of the law.

THREE LANCASTRIAN KINGS

Henry IV, first of the Lancastrian rulers, reigned in England from 1399 to 1413. He was followed by Henry V (1413–1422) and Henry VI (1422–1461).

Force and fraud had established the Lancastrian dynasty and the direct royal line was excluded from the throne until its claims were later acquired and asserted by the Yorkists. But the foes of Henry IV did not accept their defeat tamely. There was the constant danger of counter revolutions. Englishmen who had upset one government could upset another. It was no simple matter to quell disaffection. There were several rebellions in the first nine years of Henry IV's reign. The crown that the energetic Henry IV had wrested from Richard II did not rest easily upon his head.

Against his enemies Henry IV sought the support of Parliament and the church. He was dependent upon that support. Parliaments could be courted or packed or bribed. Usually Henry IV courted them. To persuade the church to champion his cause Henry IV used different tactics. It was no accident that in 1401 a statute usually called the *De Haeretico Comburendo* provided for the burning of Lollards and other heretics. The clergy had long sought such legislation. Strategic and popular measures, together with moderate policies in most things, won Henry the cautious confidence of Parliament and church.

Meanwhile a series of victories on the battlefield strengthened Henry IV's hold upon the crown. Lancastrian forces defeated Richard II's half brothers, the Welsh insurgent Owen Glendower, the powerful northern Percy family and their Cheshire archers. After "Harry Percy's spur was cold" there were other rebellions. These, too, were crushed. Scotland was defeated. France made peace. Heretics had been burned and traitors hanged. The Lancastrian throne seemed at last secure.

The arduous demands of war and business were not the only heavy cares of Henry IV. His council was torn by personal and factional strife. His son was no aid or comfort. Harassed and unloved, Henry IV suffered for about five years from an illness popularly believed to be leprosy. In 1413 he died. The throne passed to Henry V, a hard and intense man who soon decided to renew the Hundred Years' War against France.

In August, 1415, Henry V invaded France. In October he captured Harfleur and won the famous battle of Agincourt. In 1417 he mounted an offensive again. By the terms of the Treaty of Troyes—an Anglo-French settlement signed in 1420—Henry V agreed to marry the daughter of the king of France. The treaty also provided that on the death of the French king, Charles VII, the throne of France should go to Henry of England.

Later in the century, France was saved from final defeat by the peculiar fortune and genius of Joan of Arc, an illiterate peasant girl who roused her countrymen to courage and her befuddled king to conquest. In the end only Calais remained of all the English possessions in France.

Henry V died of dysentery in 1422 at the age of thirty-five. His son and heir Henry VI was an infant. During the king's minority the country was ruled by a regent, the Duke of Gloucester, brother of Henry V. Gloucester was unsteady, unpredictable, bellicose. He battled with his councillors and squabbled with his family. The quarrels became bitter. Factions arose. The nation moved to the edge of civil war. Law and order were temporarily shattered. Bands of brigands and other malefactors roamed the roads and forests. Justice staggered before unbridled and often conscienceless power, violence, and corruption. Great lords gathered armies of liveried retainers, overawed the sheriffs, plundered their weaker neighbors and fought among themselves. Disillusionment paralyzed those who had the task of maintaining law and order upon the established principles. Such was the disordered and menacing state of affairs that prevailed when Joan of Arc and her armies were bringing disaster to British arms in France.

In 1437 Henry VI was declared of age. Weak and gentle, Henry was a king who did not belong in his time. He yielded and fell back before the demands of too many of the self-seeking barons and relatives. Then he married Margaret of Anjou and the scene changed. The new queen was a vixen, able, ruthless and dominating. She plotted with one group of nobles against another. The financial situation was desperate. Confusion and maladministration brought disaffection and distrust. Jack Cade led a famous rebellion in 1450. The manifesto of the rebels demanded the dismissal of incompetent and possibly disloyal ministers; a reform of the royal government; the end of widespread interference with justice and the packing of the House of Commons by the great lords backed by their private armies of liveried servants; the protection of real and personal property against greedy and powerful robbers. Cade's revolt failed, but the suppression of it brought no tide of peace, no final settlement.

In August, 1453, Henry VI went insane. Richard, Duke of York, was appointed regent. Richard was a moderate man, filled with cautious ambition. He was powerful and popular. He had a personal history in war and peace that commended him to Englishmen. With a double descent from Edward III Richard had a strong claim to the throne. True, he made no attempt to supplant Henry VI but he was certainly hopeful of succeeding him. Many of his followers were quite prepared to plot and fight to place Richard upon the throne.

The hostility of Yorkists and Lancastrians was heightened by two events. In October, 1453, a son was born to Henry VI and Margaret of Anjou, thus excluding Richard from the succession to the throne if the Lancastrian claim of 1399 continued to prevail. Then, in 1454, Henry VI unexpectedly recovered his sanity and his clever and vindictive wife now determined to dispose of the Yorkists as quickly as possible. She restored several of her favorites to power and completely excluded Richard and his followers from the government. The queen held a council "to provide for the safety of the king's person against his enemies." In 1455 Richard took arms, declaring that he did so to protect the Yorkists. He made no open claim to the throne, although his adherents were asserting that the Lancastrians were no longer capable of governing England.

Thus began the intermittent civil and dynastic war later called the Wars of the Roses. Most of the mass of the English people viewed the outcome with indifference. Many nobles shifted sides from time to time. There were no principles to fight for, none to desert. The instability of conviction in the fifteenth century is evident on every hand. Throughout the war the weight of the burdens fell upon the nobles. Their numbers were greatly reduced by battle casualties and savage executions. "The Wars of the Roses were a bleeding operation performed by the nobility upon their own body."

It is unnecessary here to describe the tide of conflict as the Lancastrians and Yorkists conspired and killed. Late in March, 1461, two armies met at Towton, near York. A bloody and savage battle brought a decisive victory to the Yorkists. Thousands of Lancastrians never rose from the battlefield. Many Lancastrian nobles who had survived the slaughter were beheaded later. Henry VI, his queen, and his young son fled to Scotland. Edward, son of Richard, Duke of York, went to London. There he was crowned Edward IV in 1461. For sixty-two years Englishmen had lived under three Lancastrians. For the next twenty-four years they were to be ruled by the victorious Yorkists.

THREE YORKIST KINGS

Edward IV, first of the Yorkists, was shrewd, handsome, coarse and cruel. He had a remarkable gift for cultivating popularity, especially among the rising commercial classes. It was unfortunate that his main interests did not lie in government and administration. The big, sensual Edward preferred eating, drinking, and numerous love affairs. That is one reason why the disruptive power of the feudal lords remained uncrushed.

The strong Richard Neville, Earl of Warwick and Salisbury, the famous "kingmaker," had helped to put his cousin Edward upon the throne. Soon, however, Warwick and Edward IV quarrelled. Warwick allied himself with the Lancastrians, overthrew Edward IV, and was in turn defeated and slain. Soon Henry VI's queen, Margaret of Anjou, that French termagant, was captured. Her son, Prince Edward, was slain. The demented Henry VI, long a prisoner, was murdered in the Tower. It was stated that he had died "of pure displeasure and melancholy." The direct line of the Lancastrians was thus ended. Edward IV and the Yorkists were triumphant, unchallenged, and safe. But the structure of the medieval community was breaking down.

Edward now brought quiet and security to an England long troubled by intestine broils and distracted by conspiracy. He encouraged commerce. He improved the administration of justice. If he had not spent much time in the pursuit of voluptuous and distracting pleasures the latter part of his reign might have shown more fruitful results.

In 1483 Edward IV died suddenly, probably worn out by dissolute living. With his death at the age of forty-one the crown passed to his son Edward, a child twelve years old. It was a depressing prospect that faced England. Edward's unscrupulous uncle Richard, Duke of Gloucester, forced the council to declare him regent and protector. He then secured custody of Edward V and his younger brother the Duke of York. Claiming that these sons of Edward IV were illegitimate Richard packed Parliament with his supporters and had himself declared king. In July, 1483, he was crowned king as Richard III.

There appears to be no doubt that Edward V and his brother were murdered in the Tower and that the pitiless Richard III was responsible. Even in a callous and bloody age the vicious murder of the two princes by an uncle who had them in his trust shocked the nation. Much as men dreaded the renewal of civil war many determined to fight Richard. Many Yorkists joined the Lancastrians in formidable rebellions against the villainous king.

The nearest male representative of the house of Lancaster was Henry Tudor, Earl of Richmond. Numerous enemies of Richard III hurried to join Henry Tudor. Many unhappy Yorkists were doubtless soothed by Henry's proposed marriage to Elizabeth of York, Edward IV's eldest daughter.

On August 22, 1485, the armies of Henry Tudor met the forces of Richard III at Bosworth Field in Leicestershire. In the battle many of Richard's soldiers deserted. Several barons craftily wavered and then betrayed their king. In the midst of treason Richard fought manfully and was slain. The Wars of the Roses were ended. But the memory of that dark disaster and the accompanying breakdowns of government did not easily die.

Henry Tudor, by the fortunes of battle and by act of Parliament, was now to become Henry VII. Richard III was dead. Feudal anarchy had wrecked itself in England's time of troubles. The ranks of the old nobility were thinned. The magnates hitherto responsible for much of the chronic disorder and grave injustice were now no longer possessed of the perverted power that made them odious to the people. These barons might still claim to be "the natural leaders of society," but in the sixteenth century the pivotal strength in England came to rest in the linked authority of Crown and Parliament. The stronger force was then the monarchy and the Tudors kept it so. In the seventeenth century, that confused age of the Stuarts, the balance of strength was to move again. It shifted then to the side of Parliament and there it has since remained. The nemesis that fell upon Richard of York at Bosworth Field had consequences massive and unforeseen.

It has often been emphasized that the struggle between the king and lords for effective power in the fifteenth century led to a state of government once called by Professor G. B. Adams "startlingly and prematurely modern." As we carefully consider the total scene, however, we are once again reminded that one of the gravest problems of the constitutional historian is how to reconcile the known facts with the theories. The historian must be wary of generalizations, especially when he draws them from regions of mist in the far past. There are yawning gaps between modern constitutional practices in England and those of the fifteenth century. What actually happened was that in Parliament there gradually grew new methods of limiting the Crown, new ways of controlling taxation and influencing high policy and legislation. In the government of the realm, as Professor S. B. Chrimes has remarked, "expedients repeated become habits, and habits become customs, and customs can change the law." Repetition, habit, custom —these are important words in the Middle Ages.

Although the fifteenth century was the golden age of the magnates in the king's council and the House of Lords, the middle classes—and thus the House of Commons—were rising steadily in power. In the next century the Commons were to be a major pillar of Tudor government. When the old and overmighty aristocracy was enfeebled in the Wars of the Roses the road was open for the Tudor monarchy, so strongly supported by a new nobility "cutting across feudal ties"— the phrase is Professor J. E. A. Jolliffe's. The Tudors were also constantly aided by the knights and burgesses, prosperous and safe.

Many things that happened in the Parliament of the sixteenth century were obviously made possible, and sometimes made as inevitable as human events can be, by the development of Parliament in the Lancastrian and Yorkist age. We must now turn to consider the changing conditions in government and administration in these years of uncertainty within the state.

THE PATTERN OF PARLIAMENT 1399–1485

We have seen that there have been several ideas and notions about the essential character of Parliament in the years of its early growth. There was, and there remains, the emphasis of some historians upon the idea that Parliament derived its first qualities from the fact that it began as the *curia regis,* the high court of justice of his majesty the king, a tool created by the king's prerogative, an organ that might advise but not command. From the fact that Parliament was a great court, it is held, grew the roots of its legal powers.

Among several divergent ideas there appeared a second: Parliament was an assembly composed of the three estates of the realm, a body possessing a bundle of powers derived from the natural orders and ranks of society as well as from the fact that the members made up the high court of the king. From these twin sources of authority—the prerogative power of the Crown and the natural power of the estates or communities of the realm—Parliament could claim its place and function in the state.

A third point of view is this: Parliament could claim its place and function in the state without any reference to the fact that it was a king's court at all. Apart from any attributes it might have as a court it was a representative assembly. As Professor S. B. Chrimes once said: "The Commons grasped the notion that they were come to Parliament to represent not merely a number of local communities but an estate: the commons of all the realm. . . . From this it is only a step to the idea of an act of Parliament deriving its force less from the fact that it had the sanction of the king . . . and more from the fact that every man in England was party and therefore privy to it." [1]

It is doubtful whether the disagreements of constitutional historians upon several aspects of the history of Parliament will be easily settled. About certain bodies of fact, however, there can be no dispute. Very significant chapters occurred in the tale of Parliament in the fifteenth century. Most important of these was the steady expansion of Parliament's place and strength in the machinery of government.

When Henry IV obtained the throne the House of Commons expressed the wish that Henry should be "in as great royal liberty as his progenitors were before him." Nevertheless, Henry's "great royal liberty" was less than he could have wished because he found it imperative to hold the good will of Parliament and to hold the good will of Parliament he had to yield sometimes, to compromise, to make concessions. The impecunious Henry was frequently compelled to ask Parliament for money to finance his wars. When the members of Parliament, aware of their strong position, began to demand more privileges and power Henry IV was compelled to retreat and submit. All of the Lancastrians were too weak to raise any money by extra-parliamentary methods. Henry V depended upon Parliament for money to fight the Hundred Years' War. When Henry was absent in France his council and administrative officers often sought Parliamentary approval for their actions. Henry VI was a minor when he came

---

[1] Various scholarly opinions about the origins of the structure of Parliament have been described in Chapter VIII. There has also been much discussion, as suggested above, about the nature and origin of the powers of Parliament and the rise of the idea of "representation" in medieval assemblies. The idea of the "full power" (*plena potestas*) of the English parliamentary representatives is not easily fused with several other concepts sturdily held by competent authorities. Because all of the learned arguments obviously cannot be mentioned or examined here the writer has diffidently stated, as succinctly and simply as possible, those conclusions that seem to him most valid in the light of existing evidence.

to the throne; he was pathological in his instability when he became of age; then he had alternate spells of lucidity and madness. In these circumstances it was not surprising that the powers of Parliament expanded. It would have been surprising if they had not. The contributions of the fifteenth century to constitutional theory and practice were by no means negligible. In the seventeenth century and later, of course, these contributions were often emphasized as formative thrusts and precedents beyond the decent limits of accuracy and proportion. Fortunately modern scholarship has done much to redress the balance of the old.[2]

Before the costs of litigation in Parliament had swollen to a startling size scores of petitions for royal grace and favor had been submitted to Parliament as the high court of the Crown. But by the fifteenth century almost all such cases in equity were dealt with by the Court of Chancery. On the one hand, this fact helped to decrease the need for long sessions of Parliament. On the other hand, the decline of Parliamentary activities that were clearly and essentially judicial helped to stress something else. It underlined the idea that Parliament was responsible for many things besides handling petitions and judicial affairs. As the Commons shared in more state business, they seemed to be assuming the rights and duties of what both Professor Helen M. Cam and Professor G. L. Haskins have called "a joint stock enterprise," an enterprise in which Crown, Lords, and Commons labored together.

One gain of Parliament was in the realm of finance. Late in the fourteenth century the practice of the separate taxation of each estate by its own representatives had come to an end, except in the case of the clergy. The Commons, as distinct from the Lords, kept control of the right to originate and grant taxation. In 1395 the grant to the king was made "by the commons with the advice and assent of the lords." In 1407 the king agreed that he would listen to reports about money grants only "by the mouth of the Speaker of the Commons." The right of the Commons to originate taxation was a customary right, not one stated in a statute. Nevertheless, the custom that grants of money should originate with the Commons was not easily shaken. In

---

[2] See Carl Stephenson and F. G. Marcham, *Sources of English Constitutional History* for selections from the Parliament Rolls for the Parliaments of 1401, 1404, 1406, 1407, 1414, 1422, 1427, 1429, 1439, 1451, 1455 and 1483 (pp. 257–273). For the period 1399–1483 see also in the same volume selections from important statutes and Privy Council, Chancery, and Borough Records (pp. 273–295).

1407, for example, Henry IV failed when he tried to proceed first through the House of Lords. The Commons refused to accept such "a great prejudice and derogation of their liberties."

Parliament also extended its power in the control of government expenditures and the earmarking of appropriations of supply for particular purposes. The chronic insolvency of the Lancastrians was of concern to everybody who had anything to do with the operations of the government. Almost always it was stated that general taxes granted to the king were for national defense; a part of the custom on wool was to be for the maintenance of Calais; the tunnage and poundage tax, by this time normally granted to the king for life, was to be spent for such specific purposes as the navy and "the safeguarding of the sea and in no other way." The normal royal income was, as usual, to be used for the expenses of the royal household. In 1406 Parliament asked permission to audit the royal accounts. Henry IV replied that sovereigns did not render accounts. Despite these words, in November, 1407, the accounts were laid before Parliament by the Chancellor who said: "that with regard to all these matters, the same chancellor had already accounted to them . . . firstly orally and then in writing, by means of a schedule . . . [explaining] how and in what manner the said tenth and fifteenth as well as the subsidy and the tunnage and poundage, had been spent."

Before 1460 Parliament met frequently and hence the corporate feeling of the Commons was increased. The members were greatly concerned about such privileges of the House of Commons as freedom of debate, freedom of the members, to a certain extent, from arrest for themselves and their retainers. If the members of Parliament, with their wide interests in the affairs of the kingdom, were denied freedom to speak without fear of reprisal, then they could not be independent of the king. If they were to be punished by the king for saying or doing things displeasing to him, then they could not check arbitrary government. Freedom of speech was a right fundamental to the power of Parliament, for without it Parliament might have no power at all.

The case of Thomas Haxey in 1397 had shown the importance of guarding against royal interference. Haxey, though not a member of Parliament, had prepared a petition that the Commons had adopted and presented to the king. Richard II had imprisoned him for writing the petition. Before Henry IV had come to the throne Haxey had been released, probably because he was in holy orders. In 1399 the House of Lords approved a petition from Haxey for a reversal of the judgment against him. Later in the year the Commons repeated the petition and again the House of Lords approved; this was equivalent to an action by the whole Parliament. Haxey was cleared of all shadow. In this case, at least, an important principle had been successfully defended: the king must not attempt to coerce Parliament by the arbitrary arrest or imprisonment of its members or its agents.

In 1400 the Speaker of the House of Commons said that certain members of Parliament had been in the habit of making reports to the king about matters on the agenda of the Commons, "before the same had been described and agreed upon among the said commons by which the king might be incensed against them or some of them." The Speaker asked the king to take no notice of such reports and to exert no royal pressure as a result of them. Henry acknowledged the right of the Commons to debate freely and promised not to listen to unauthorized accounts of their activities.

In 1407 Henry IV proclaimed that the Lords and Commons might "commune among themselves in this present Parliament and in every other in time to come, in the absence of the king, of the estate of the realm and of the remedy necessary for the same." Four years earlier, Henry IV had formally recognized the privilege of members of Parliament from arrest on civil process during a session of Parliament and in going to or returning from one. This privilege was regulated and extended during the reign of Henry VII (1485–1509). Thus the bulwarks against royal influence in Parliament were being strengthened and the precedents were being created for assertions of Parliamentary privilege. On several occasions, however, the House of Commons could not maintain its claims of privileges. In 1451, for instance, Thomas Yong, the member for Bristol, was imprisoned by the king and Commons for proposing that the Duke of York should be declared heir to the throne. Thereupon the Duke of York compelled the release of Yong and forced the council to compensate him. In 1453 the Duke also ordered the arrest of Thomas Thorp, the Speaker of the House of Commons. Despite the angry protests of the Commons Thorp stayed in prison.

Thus it was that before 1460 Parliament had broadened its powers in the area of finance, taxation, freedom of debate and freedom from arrest. There were other advances. As its strength grew under the watchful eyes of the knights, burgesses, and lawyers the problem of regulating representation increased. The House of Commons usually contained about 200 burgesses and about 75 knights from the shires.

In the Middle Ages few men were deeply concerned about the qualifications of burgesses or the manner in which they were elected. The county representatives were "knights of the shire" or gentlemen born. In the late fourteenth and early fifteenth century, however, there had been much interference in elections. Parliaments had often been packed as a result of the activities of the kings and the nobles. Several men had been elected in the counties who were not in fact knights of the shire. In the county courts were still held the local elections for members of Parliament. But in the fifteenth century the county court was not the sturdy body it once had been. Many of its functions had been turned over to the justices of the peace and the Quarter Sessions. The freeholders were no longer required to attend personally the monthly sessions of the court. In these circumstances it was not difficult for powerful sheriffs to manipulate and falsify election returns. Fear of the mighty doubtless hushed many local complaints.

Several steps were taken to check the defects and misdeeds of the sheriffs. For example, it was required that mayors, bailiffs and sheriffs must make their election returns by sworn indentures, certified by some of the voters. For each false return a sheriff was to be fined £100. Persons aggrieved in fraudulent elections were given new legal remedies. Several acts of Parliament tried to regulate elections, to insist on certain qualifications for representatives, to get competent men to stand for election and go to Parliament. In 1445 a statute formally required all those elected from the counties to be gentlemen born. It further provided that all members should reside in the locality they represented, an enactment designed to check the sheriffs from reporting their own nominees, often from outside the county, as winners in the election. (This was an active and thorny question—there were similar laws passed in 1413 and 1430.) "The knights of the shire for the Parliament . . . shall be notable knights of the same counties for the which they shall be so chosen, or otherwise such notable esquires, gentlemen of birth of the same counties, as shall be able to be knights." Finally, the act of 1445 provided that all the electors must be resident and hold qualifying freeholds in the counties in which they voted.

In 1429 it was provided by statute, later extended in 1432, that the right to vote in the counties should be limited. The statute recited the reasons for the decision: "in many counties the elections of knights of the shires . . . have of late been carried out by too great and excessive a number of people dwelling within those same counties of which the larger part have been people of little substance or of no worth, each pretending to have the same voice in such elections as the most worthy knights or squires." Accordingly the new law provided that only the famous "forty shilling freeholder" class could henceforth be electors in the counties. In this new and noted disfranchising law is the first statement in English history of election as a political right. The electors after 1429 were to be residents of the county, "whereof every one of them shall have free tenement to the value of forty shillings by the year at the least above all charges." For four hundred years all men who had incomes of less than forty shillings—in 1429 equal to the purchasing power of about £40 today—were denied the vote in the counties.

One reason for the statute was declared to be the "homicides, riots and assaults" at county elections held in the public county court sessions. Another reason was that the limitation of the franchise reduced the interference of kings and nobles in the elections. Hitherto the county members had been returned to Parliament by all who were freemen and above. The nobles had been using their numerous servants to swing elections. After the new statute this evil was ended. A man who owned enough freehold land to yield a clear profit of forty shillings a year was a moderately wealthy man in the Middle Ages. The general body of the freemen suitors in the county court no longer had the vote. These acts of 1429 and 1432 governed the franchise in the counties until the Reform Bill of 1832. No change was made in the system of election in the boroughs. They maintained their numerous and differing procedures until the nineteenth century.

Meanwhile the frequency of Parliaments before 1460 increased the experience of many members of the Commons in the conduct of business and speeded the rise of efficient forms of procedure. More and more the petitioning activities of the Commons increased. These were the normal methods of bringing about redress of grievances or changes in the law. At the same time, the House of Commons broadened its share in legislation. In 1414 the Commons claimed, quite without historical justification, that no statute had ever been made without its assent. It was able to secure a definite royal pledge that statutes based on Parliamentary petitions should not contain "either additions or subtractions which in any particular or particulars change the meaning and intent" of the petitions. Under Henry VI bills began to be substituted for petitions: the bill contained the statute asked for in exactly the form in which it was to be approved. Thus the king or his servants could not make changes in drafting the statute because it was already drafted in the bill. The important point is this: the consent of the Commons in legislation became more and more necessary. The increasing consequence of the Commons is shown, for instance, in the fact that it was asked to approve the Treaty of Troyes with France in 1420. Later in the century a court held that no enactment could be called a statute unless the Commons had agreed to it.

Despite these remarks regarding the House of Commons it must be remembered that the resources of government were still medieval. The magnates of England remained the political and social leaders. They were the great ones of the kingdom. The strength of aristocratic factions was sharply evident in both Parliament and royal administration. Powerful and often unscrupulous, the barons frequently controlled or influenced Parliamentary elections. They battled the Lancastrian kings over the composition of the council.

Parliament was able, in a spasmodic way, to control the royal council and household fairly effectively before 1460. We may also note that several officials of the royal household were dismissed during Henry IV's reign at the instance of the Commons. Both the household officials and the members of "the great and continual council" were named in Parliament. In the fifteenth century, of course, there was no constitutional way in which these royal servants could be made responsible to Parliament. In 1406 the council was almost entirely reconstituted and "the wisest lords of the realm" were "to have the supervision of everything that should be done for the good government of the kingdom." All important documents issued by the king were to be approved by the council. For a time the council remained almost completely under the control of Parliament. However, when we read the phrase "under the control of Parliament" we must remember that one wing of Parliament was the house of the magnates of England, the lords spiritual and temporal. They stood everywhere and their power was great. No Lancastrian king was strong enough to use such royal instruments as the Privy Seal or the Wardrobe in the royal household (as Edward II had done) to defeat baronial attempts to control policy and administration.

When Henry V came to the throne Parliament lost some of its power over the council. The absence of Henry overseas left a large part of his executive power in the hands of the council members although the council, as noted earlier, did frequently seek Parliamentary sanction for its actions. During the minority of Henry VI the whole royal prerogative was in the hands of an oligarchic council. That baronial group looked after themselves very well. (In the years 1437–1439, for instance, they spent less than £10 on the king's ships.) At other times, in hours of intimidations or public or private war, such as the years when the Earl of Suffolk dominated Henry VI, the council was almost powerless. After Suffolk was impeached in 1450 and fled into the hands of his murderers, neither council nor Parliament could maintain control. In the middle of the century the council was merely the instrument of shifting baronial policies and the battleground of feuding noble factions. These were years of fantastically bad government.

When Edward IV gradually asserted his authority after 1461 he was aided by many forces. The middle and lower classes of England wanted peace and stability under a strong king. Merchants wanted encouragement of trade, the recovery of the lost domain of the sea. The humble men of the rural areas and the shopkeepers and artisans of the towns wanted an end to the habits of lawlessness and the defiance, decay, and perversion of justice. What could be done to strengthen the enfeebled local governments, to weaken the menacing strength of the local lords, those proud robber barons with their badges, liveries, tokens and private armies of retainers? Why should the king's justices and the sheriffs be compelled to gesture but feebly in local disputes and then sink to silence in the presence of the great lords? Why should the king's men be unable to repress disorder, corruption, riots, routs and unlawful assemblies? Why should empanelled juries be browbeaten and intimidated? The remedy for such ills could be found, surely, in the revival of the power of the monarchy. Edward IV seemed to promise precisely that.

The new king had supplies of money denied to his predecessors. The acres of the Yorkist estates were broad. The lands seized from the Lancastrians were not small. An early Parliament granted Edward tunnage and poundage and several other customs grants for life. From his wealthy subjects the king collected forced gifts called benevolences. He gathered heavy fines from his courts. He made considerable profit from his activities as a trader. In 1475 he agreed to withdraw from a war with France in return for a cash payment of 75,000 crowns and a promise of 50,000 more.

In the light of facts such as these it is not surprising that the Parliamentary power of the purse was almost without meaning. In his reign of twenty-two years Edward IV summoned only six Parliaments. Crown bills, based upon no previous petition of the Commons, became more usual in Edward IV's reign than they had ever been before. These facts are briefly mentioned to remind the reader how very much the position of the House of Commons in the scheme of things was determined by the power and prestige, or the weakness, of the Crown.

It was upon the council, not upon Parliament, that Edward IV depended for service and efficiency. He wanted a rehabilitation of government, an instillation of energy into administration. The Tudors who followed after him were to view the council as the real organ of actual government acting for a stronger monarch. Such an instrument the council of the Tudors remained until the death of Elizabeth in 1603. Under Edward IV the council was the servant of the king and Parliament had no control over its composition. Edward eliminated many nobles from the council and increased the number of trained and expert administrative officials. The administrative and judicial functions of the council increased as it became the normal instrument for executing the king's commands. Prerogative courts, such as the famous Court of Star Chamber (the council, or a part of it, sitting in its judicial capacity), handled many cases and often supplemented the legislation of Parliament. As Miss C. L. Scofield has remarked: "The Star Chamber not only expounded the laws, but even made laws." Meanwhile, too, the civil jurisdiction of the council was almost completely surrendered to the Chancery Court, with its vast legal and administrative resources.

The royal household became more active as the monarchy became strong again. These comments are hints of events in the next century. Had Edward IV been more interested in government and administration a solid bridge to the Tudor age might have been built. The Yorkists might then have shared in the dividends of praise that posterity has freely given the Tudor sovereigns.

At the end of the fifteenth century Parliament had not yet expanded in the sunshine of its strength. With few exceptions, the precedents set in the days of Henry IV and in brief later moments were to remain largely forgotten until the seventeenth century. It was to be two hundred years before the modern Cabinet system made the royal ministers responsible to Parliament. The methods by which that responsibility was obtained were not to be impeachment, bills of attainder, or the uncertain machinery of the Lancastrian and Yorkist age.

THE LEGAL PROFESSION

In the Middle Ages, as in the twentieth century, suspected or known criminals were taken into custody by the process called arrest. Sheriffs, constables and other agents of the Crown could command any of the king's subjects to aid in the seizure and control of criminals. Loosely defined, a "crime" was, and is now, "any act or omission forbidden by the law and punishable upon conviction." Such acts or omissions are often classified under several kinds of headings, such as treasons, felonies and misdemeanors. In Britain and the British realms a crime is an offense against the king or queen, the state, the public.

We have already seen how various steps were taken through the centuries to compel the appearance of defendants in court. If, for instance, a fugitive could not be apprehended he was asked for in five county courts. If he was not then made available he might be placed beyond the protection of the law. In the early Middle Ages the property of an "outlaw" was legally forfeited. His life might be taken by anyone. Later only the sheriff had authority to slay an outlaw and he was required to have a warrant before he set about his task.

The process of arrest was steadily extended in practice to several kinds of civil cases, as in various actions of trespass, the procedure of the Bill of Middlesex, the writ *Latitat,* and the like. Of course, in real property cases there were various devices used to persuade defendants to come to court. These included, as we have seen, the taking of pledges, the attachment of chattels, the direct summons of the sheriff, even the award of property to the plaintiff in certain suits in right. Despite these procedures, both real and personal actions were often delayed for years by the ingenious and immoral uses of devices of process. The reader will remember, for example, how vexed and confused was the problem of the essoins often involved in writs of right operations (Chapter VI).

Once a defendant came to court there began to operate the complex rules of pleading. Accused criminals were not permitted to have legal advice and assistance until the nineteenth century. Before that time judges were often quite generous in allowing these alleged wrongdoers to concoct numerous technical pleas, some of them worthy of the most notorious shyster lawyers of the modern era. In civil cases the defendant could admit his fault or he could oppose the plaintiff's claim (count). If he took the latter course, the defendant could enter a plea or demurrer (objection), saying: (1) that the plaintiff was quite correct in his statement of the facts and (2) that those facts were not sufficient to constitute any legal basis for the action begun by the plaintiff. Then the plaintiff had to enter a reply, a "joinder in demurrer," and thus an issue of law was raised before the court.

There were numerous kinds of pleas a defendant might make. He might assert that no date had been pleaded; that defects or errors in form had occurred; that the court had no jurisdiction; that the defendant was a minor; that the parties named in the writ were not the parties that should have been named. If any of these pleas proved successful the whole action collapsed.

The defendant had still other roads he might choose to follow. He could, for instance, make a "plea in bar," answering the charge directly. He might do this by what is called a "traverse" or by a plea in "confession and avoidance." A "traverse" was, and is, a formal denial of the allegation of fact made by the opposite party. By using a "traverse" the defendant thus put the plaintiff's declarations in issue to be decided by the judge or jury.

If a defendant used a plea in "confession and avoidance" with its complex rules and numerous niceties he first admitted the facts alleged by the plaintiff. Then he introduced new facts designed to nullify the legal effects of the plaintiff's assertions. If this happened, the plaintiff replied with a demurrer, or traverse, or confession and avoidance and a kind of complicated legal chess game began. It must be remembered that in the Middle Ages all pleas had to be formally disputed and thus put in issue in the court before they could be tried. Much expert legal learning, fine and precise technical skill, prolix argument, long delays, and heavy hardships are to be found in the records of these pleadings long ago. Today, of course, many of these complex maneuvers are unnecessary because all material statements of fact in any case are deemed to have been denied and are thus automatically put in issue in the court.

It is not possible for most of us to understand all of the fine distinctions involved in the precise techniques of the prolix pleading that appeared in the later Middle Ages. As Professor S. B. Chrimes has gently remarked: "Acts of advocacy were often more ingenious than ingenuous then as they are now." Nevertheless, it is quite possible to realize that the development of methods and procedures of pleading had several remarkable results and implications. At the risk of attempting to digest too vast an amount of information into brief statements it may be said that the effects of the potent rules emerging in the courts revealed themselves in many ways. Expert pleaders defined more sharply the causes of action. Because this was so, the body of both substantive and adjective law grew larger and more solid. In the case of substantive law many broad general principles were extended and bulwarked by the logical and detailed application of the new rules. The growth of adjective law was accelerated by the decay of older forms of action in all the fields of remedies at common law. These were increasingly replaced by actions of trespass and its offshoots. Thus there was the inevitable appearance of more uniformity of procedure in the frequent and common forms of trespass action and the elaborate fictions based upon them.

Our attention must also fall on other changes that slowly invaded the courts. One of these resulted from a condition of affairs that any layman in any age can easily comprehend. In the first place, when a case opened in a court several assertions of fact were made—the allegations upon which the writ was issued to start action. Secondly, the lawyers pleaded and maneuvered and traversed and confessed and avoided before the jurymen, who were probably often confused by the un-wearied wrangle and unintelligible chatter. But there did at last come an hour when the laymen on the jury had to decide upon a question of fact. They had to say "Yes" or "No."

In order to define issues with skill and clarity before they came to court, to save time, to decrease the confusions of jurymen, there gradu-ally began to appear written pleadings in the fifteenth century. Writ-ten pleadings had many advantages. They were drawn up carefully out of court. They were exchanged by all parties to an action, with copies to the judges. They were easily cited. They helped the development and authority of case law and also aided the formulation of legal princi-ples. By the early sixteenth century, as the Year Books show, the com-mon law courts were using to an increasing extent the system of writ-ten pleadings long employed by Chancery and the prerogative Court of Star Chamber.

The common law courts also began to use written evidence more frequently. Indeed, the common law established quite early the princi-ple of evidence that a document takes precedence over oral testimony. The word "evidence," of course, must be used carefully in any sen-tences about the courts and the law of the Middle Ages. The English law of evidence does not really begin to assume its modern form until the latter part of the seventeenth century. At that time the judge in a common law court ceased to have any discretionary power in deciding what constituted evidence and the same rules of evidence began and continued to apply in all courts and causes. The core question, the essential problem, is always this: did the alleged event occur or did it not? The jury decides upon the questions of fact. The judge knows the answers of the law. (*Ad quaestionem juris non respondent juratores; ad quaestionem facti non respondent judices.*) [3]

Judges, clerks, and many other royal officials played their parts in all these developments. They were steadily aided, of course, by the men of the legal profession, those adept and quick individuals who made their livings by helping, for a price, the laymen who found themselves in the courts of the king, sometimes helplessly entangled in the meshes of the law. In Norman days there were apparently some busy amateurs around the king's courts. The reader needs no further comments about the casual bystander who gives advice to all who will pause and listen. It seems that about 1100 a man was permitted by the courts to have a pleader, often a churchman, speak for him in the court. This pleader had to know quite a bit about substantive law, especially as it grew more complicated. He had to be well informed about procedure or he might easily lose his cases and his clients.

By the thirteenth century we see several men, most of them lay pleaders, who can properly be called professionals, men really skilled in the practice of the law. These men are usually called barristers because they appear at the bar (the dividing barrier) of the courts. The barrister still takes the part in the court that his client would have to take if he conducted his own case. The barrister speaks to the judge and jury in the trial. He questions and cross-questions the witnesses. He argues and contends with his learned opponents. He submits his case to the court. He is not an official of the court but simply an individual qualified to speak for clients before a court and to give them advice on legal affairs.

A visitor today at the courts by Chancery Lane and Fleet Street may sit quietly in the gallery and determine by observing such things as the cut of the gowns and the depressions in the wigs the ranks of the men on the floor of the court below. Of all these the barristers stand at the highest level in the profession. They are the men who have been "called to the bar" and given the title of barrister-at-law. The right of granting these privileges is held by the Inns of Court, four powerful, self-governing bodies whose history and functions are to be described shortly.

For several centuries a selected group of distinguished barristers

---

[3] Especially valuable to students interested in these subjects is Margaret Hastings, *The Court of Common Pleas in Fifteenth Century England: A Study of Legal Administration and Procedure* (1947). Miss Hastings has examined and interpreted with scholarly caution and bridled imagination a mass of unpublished legal records. Her monograph is an admirable example of modern scholarship in a field too little explored.

was chosen, after at least sixteen years of service, by the Justices of the Court of Common Pleas to be sergeants-at-law. These sergeants obtained a monopoly of the most important and lucrative cases and from their ranks judges were usually appointed. They were the aristocracy of the barristers. They had their own lodgings in Old Sergeants' Inn in Chancery Lane. They had the right to wear a small white silk cap called a coif (hence the phrase "take silk") which they did not doff even when talking to the king.

Since the sixteenth century a small number of the barristers have been known as King's or Queen's Counsel, appointed by royal letters patent on the advice of the Lord Chancellor. These men replaced the earlier sergeants-at-law whose title and office were abolished in 1877. They receive higher fees than the ordinary barristers. They sit "within the bar" on the front benches in the courts. They wear silk instead of "stuff" gowns.

Below the aristocracy of the barristers stand the attorneys. In Charles II's reign (1660–1685) an attorney was once called "an immaterial person of an inferior character." During the early centuries the business of an attorney was mainly to be an agent for his clients. For instance, the burden of "suit of court" in the feudal system was often an annoying business for an individual who held land of several lords. An attorney could lighten that load by agreeing to appear in the feudal courts as an agent for a tenant, provided the tenant paid a fee for the service. This procedure was accelerated by the Crusades because a Crusader busy in the Holy Land could not appear in the feudal courts. Therefore his agents, or attorneys, appeared for him. Some men retained attorneys to prepare legal papers and to do numerous other routine legal jobs. By the end of the fourteenth century the common law courts listed on their rolls the names of those men who were approved as agents or attorneys. The courts have always maintained rather strict control of the attorneys and their profession. Hence the rule that an attorney is not only an agent of his client but also a court official. If an attorney does not behave himself and is guilty, say, of malpractice he may be "struck off the roll" of the court. If that happens, he is in the same position as a "disbarred" barrister—he no longer has a profession.

The group of men usually called solicitors first appeared in the sixteenth century to "solicit" the causes of suitors who had cases delayed in Chancery. Side by side with these solicitors of the Court of Chancery were the proctors or procurators of the old ecclesiastical jurisdictions, men who were agents or attorneys in the spiritual courts. There were also the scriveners, the high class copyists or stationers who drew up contracts. In the eighteenth century the proctors and scriveners were technically merged with the solicitors and placed under the jurisdiction of the Law Society. Today all members of the legal profession other than barristers are under the control of the Law Society which has specific powers granted by Parliament. The Society, for instance, sets the examinations for entrance to the profession, prescribes the periods of apprenticeship under articles of clerkship, and the conditions of attendance at designated schools for legal education. It is the task of the solicitor to carry through the early phases of litigation and he usually deals directly with the barrister's clients. He may also advise the public in non-litigious matters, such as settling estates and preparing various legal papers. He may, on occasion, argue cases in inferior legal tribunals such as the Quarter Sessions or the county courts.

THE INNS OF COURT

It was quite natural that a king like Edward I should be concerned about the skill and deeds of the nation's servants in the law courts. The status of the legal profession rose appreciably during his reign. Professional opinion helped to frame the great statutes with which the name of Edward I is forever associated. Wherever a law was insufficient or a remedy defective there the men of the law could suggest precise statutory supplements. Edward I usually knew what he was about. The power of the massed ranks of the legal profession was vividly shown by the fact that they brought about an investigation into the conduct of all the judges of the common law courts before Parliament in 1289. Two judges alone were "faithful found among the faithless." The rest were dismissed or fined.

As the power of the profession increased, so also did its means and methods of education. In 1292 a commission of Edward I said that students "apt and eager" should be kept near the courts of law at Westminster. Before the suppression of the Knights Templar in England in 1312, students of the law were laboring with their masters in the neighborhood of the Temple and probably about 1327 they began to occupy the Temple buildings on the boundary of the City of London. Their quarters included the Inner Temple and, later, the Middle Temple. That part of the Temple outside the control of the corporation of the City of London was never occupied by the lawyers and hence there is no Outer Temple.

Besides the Inner and Middle Temple there soon appeared two other voluntary Inns of Court. The first was Lincoln's Inn, so named because it was earlier the town house of the Earl of Lincoln. The second was Gray's Inn, named from the Lords Gray of Wilton and occupied by the law scholars about 1365. In the nineteenth century, Charles Dickens—then a clerk in the Gray's Inn chambers—described the famous legal citadel as "a Sahara Desert of the law" and "one of the most depressing institutions in brick and mortar known to the children of men." Dickens's grumpy comments were similar to those of the reformer William Cobbett, who found his months as a quill-driver in 1783 "totally unattended with pleasure." Cobbett, of course, was not easily satisfied with anything. It was indeed true, however, that by the nineteenth century the pastoral serenity of an earlier age had passed. Even in the seventeenth century something, at least, of the earlier charm had remained. The ubiquitous Samuel Pepys found no drabness at Gray's Inn and, later still, Charles Lamb remarked upon the "altogether reverend and law-breathing" aspect of the gardens and South Square.

In addition to these four large Inns of Court there were ten smaller Inns of Chancery, preparatory schools where students studied original writs issued out of Chancery. These Inns of Chancery were later completely abandoned to the attorneys and no barristers were trained there. In the reign of Mary Tudor (1553–1558) all solicitors and attorneys were excluded from the Inns of Court. For the past three centuries only students preparing to be barristers have been in residence there.

In each of the Inns of Court the senior and most famous barristers became benchers, so named because at dinner they sat on a bench behind the high table at one end of the hall. A committee of benchers were the governors of the Inn, concerned with administration, education, and discipline. They were the "masters of the bench" and, among other great privileges, theirs was the exclusive power of changing the student, or "inner" barrister, into an "outer" barrister. This was done by a formal "call" to the bar as a result of which an individual might practice law in his chambers or at the bar of a court of law. This "call," this admission to full membership in an Inn, became the one and only qualification necessary to practice law in England. If an Inn ejected a barrister he was "disbarred" and thus lost his professional status.

The students or apprentices in the Inns of Court, the "universities of the common law," were required to attend the court sessions during term time. Under the supervision of the older men, they argued moot cases before a bencher and two barristers sitting as judges. Competent barristers of the Inn delivered exhaustive and learned lectures. Often these lectures were upon a section of a statute or a whole statute. Such "readings" meticulously analyzed the subject and explained its importance to the common law. Famous readings, for example, were those of Thomas Littleton on *De donis,* James Dyer on the Statute of Wills, Sir Edward Coke on the Statute of Fines, Sir Francis Bacon on the Statute of Uses.

There were also frequent discussions of difficult cases. The students studied the Year Books, the statutes, Glanville, Fleta, Britton, and other authorities. Usually a young man was called to the bar after about six years of study. When masters and students lived and moved together in the corporate life provided by the Inns of Court the shrewd eyes of the masters could tell when the student was ready to become an "utter" or "outer" barrister.

Sir John Fortescue said that in the Inns of Court every virtue was learned and every vice was banished. It may have been so.

FORTESCUE AND LITTLETON

In fifteenth century England there were two judges who won special fame for their writings in the field of law and political philosophy. The first of these was Sir John Fortescue, a soldier, statesman, and lawyer (c. 1394–c. 1476). Fortescue became Governor of Lincoln's Inn in 1425 and was Chief Justice of the Court of King's Bench from 1442 to 1461. At the time of Jack Cade's rebellion (1450) Fortescue was apparently quite unpopular in certain quarters. A contemporary wrote: "The Chief Justice hath waited to be assaulted all this sevennight nightly in his house but nothing come, as yet, the more pity." During the Wars of the Roses Sir John was an active supporter of Henry VI and the Lancastrians. Attainted of treason by the first Parliament of Edward IV (1461) he went into exile. In 1471 Fortescue submitted to Edward IV and was pardoned. He then served in the council of the king until his death about 1476.

Fortescue was a consummate master of the common law. Between 1468 and 1470 he wrote the *De Laudibus Legum Angliae.* This book, written in the form of a dialogue, skillfully described the English law, the courts, the jury system, and the Inns of Court. In this remarkable description and defense of the laws of England Fortescue cogently argued that statute law was wise because it was based on the consent of the whole kingdom. It provided the people with justice and "for want of justice the human race would have torn itself to pieces in mutual slaughter."

In the English political system, called by Fortescue a *dominium politicum et regale*, the king was not an absolute monarch. "The king makes not the laws, nor imposes subsidies without the consent of the three estates of the realm." Even judges, though commanded by the king, were bound by oath not to render decisions against the law of the land. It was far otherwise in France, as Fortescue frequently insisted, because there the civil law and the Roman principles were diligently followed; there the king was absolute. The English Fortescue disliked both the French and their system of law and government and he lost no opportunity to say so. The English lawyers of the seventeenth century, as well as opponents of the civil law in all later centuries, inherited and employed the principles of Fortescue. The *De Laudibus* was not printed until the reign of Henry VIII. It was then published three times later in the sixteenth century and three times in the eighteenth.

In the *De Laudibus* and the later *Monarchia* or *Governance of England* (not printed until 1714) Fortescue also analyzed some of the faults, as he saw them, of the English method of government and put forward some concrete proposals for reform. Fortescue wanted a strong executive such as that later developed by the Tudors. "The law, not Parliament," asserted Fortescue, "should limit royal absolutism." This idea occurred in all of Fortescue's works. He once proposed, for example, that the royal council should prepare legislation for Parliament. In later years propagandists for the cause of Parliament against the king used Fortescue's theory of the distinction between *jus regale* and *jus politicum et regale* for their own purposes. In doing so, they badly warped Fortescue's ideas. Apparently they conveniently overlooked his comments about the subordinate position of Parliament and his plans for conciliar reform. Fortescue, like Sir Edward Coke later, would have been as much opposed to the absolutism of Parliament as to the absolutism of the king.

A second writer of importance was the great lawyer and judge Sir Thomas Littleton (c. 1407–1481). Littleton was a Worcestershire man who was probably a member of the Middle Temple. After 1445 he apparently practiced in Chancery. About 1453 he became a justice of assize on the northern circuit and under Edward IV, probably in 1466, he became a judge of the Court of Common Pleas. He died in 1481 and was buried in Worcester Cathedral.

Sir Thomas Littleton is deservedly famous as the author of the classic treatise on estates and real property law usually called the *Tenures*. The volume is a full summary of the common law in the field of real property as it stood in the fifteenth century. First printed in 1481 the *Tenures* passed through more than seventy editions by the seventeenth century. The book was originally written in "law French"—a mixture of English and Norman French phrases used in writing upon legal subjects after the popularity of Latin declined. The *Tenures* was issued in an English translation early in the sixteenth century. "Law French" lingered in writings about law until its use was finally forbidden in 1650. A statute of 1363 had declared that oral proceedings in the courts of England must be in English rather than French, a language "which was much unknown in the realm."

The *Tenures* was the first textbook about the English law of property. Littleton carefully examined, digested, and scientifically classified the intricate laws relating to the rights of men over land. He used the Year Books, the long rolls of many courts, the masses of case decisions. The result has made his name forever famous among the students of the laws of England.

Sir Thomas Littleton wrote the three books of the *Tenures* in the form of a series of letters to his son, a student at Cambridge. In the first book there were several clear definitions and accurate statements about the characteristics of different kinds of tenancy in Littleton's day, such as the fee simple—always the largest interest in land known to the law—and fee tail, copyhold, the various tenancies at will, and the like. Statements of principle were almost invariably accompanied by illustrations. The second book carefully explained the law of tenures and rents and the duties and rights of lords and tenants. The third and final book set forth the various methods by which rights over real property could be obtained or terminated. Except in the section on "Releases" there is but slight reference to equitable interests in land. Littleton was obviously less interested in the numerous problems of equity than he was in the nature and function of the complex webs of common law touching real property.

RETROSPECT

In recent chapters the narrative has stressed the leading and formative ideas and themes of constitutional and legal development in the later Middle Ages. These were hard times, times of gigantic effort, of mingled justice and beauty, of ruthlessness and evil. They were times of concrete achievement. Looking back from the Here and Now in the time scale we can see that the creative vitality displayed by these medieval centuries was indeed remarkable. During the four hundred years between the conquest of the Norman William I and the Welshman Henry VII many pages were written in the long tale of the evolution of the English courts and constitutions. What was inscribed in those pages is eloquent evidence of the competence and good fortune of medieval man.

We have seen how this challenging period was marked by the emergence of the great courts and the legal system, by the bright, slow dawn of Parliament. Before the shaping thrust of complex forces the thoughts and actions of Englishmen increasingly dealt with their collective life and destiny. From faint and faltering beginnings there grew the dynamic principles and orderly institutions that have been regularly exported to many lands. The astonishing and permanent things that rose hugely from the medieval centuries are among the most important creations of mankind. The British law and the British legislative system still stimulate the admiration of free men everywhere. At one end of a time curve we see the shame of the *curia regis* that collapsed in the diminutive and divided England of Stephen's reign. Eight centuries later stands the pride of an Imperial Parliament that passed the Statute of Westminster of 1931.

As the past flows into the present the river of time is sometimes broken by rapids and cataracts. Today may become the tomorrow of human history in the midst of war and revolution, pestilence and famine. Often, too, the events that are not heralded by guns and meteors change and jar the face of the whole world. This is merely saying that the important events of history do not always wait upon the making of war and peace or upon the rise and fall of kings and queens. Nevertheless, there are still "key" dates, the years and hours of high significance in human affairs. One of these critical crests was 1485. This was the year when Henry VII, first of the Tudors, ascended with firm step an unstable throne.

When Henry VII won the crown of England in 1485 an age was

dying. The world of the Middle Ages was about to merge gradually into what we call the modern era. A new period of growth, of transition, of revolutionary change and adventure, of unified national achievement, was at hand. The winds of the Renaissance spirit were sweeping lightly over the English Channel. The vast and varied Tudor world that we salute across the centuries reveals a quickening tempo of change, a momentum that came to stay.

CHAPTER XII

The Early Tudors:

a new imperium

KINGS, QUEENS, AND PEOPLE

As we move by the milestones of the years of the Tudor age (1485–1603) we see that the strength of the feudal nobles was diminished. The sway of the Roman Catholic Church in England was ended. The astonishing magnificence of the Renaissance spread its many-splendored colors through an era of power and versatility. The country gentry and the merchants of the middle class grasped new tools of wealth and influence. Markets across distant seas called to English traders. The ships of English adventurers furrowed many waters. It was an acquisitive and superstitious age, at once ruthless and noble. Men were cruel to heretics and traitors, "witches" and imbeciles. Fallen courtiers, rebels, and old priests were marked for execution and carried in the Tyburn cart that climbed the heavy hill of Holborn. The Tudor century was filled with violent contrasts, kaleidoscopic shiftings of tumultuous patterns. The generations who won such success in these years were crowded with personality, talent and force. And these, too, were qualities possessed by the Tudor monarchs, all except one—and he was a little boy.

In the sixteenth century a masterful and rejuvenated monarchy helped England towards the power and unity of a united nation, a modern state. The early Tudors were Henry VII (1485–1509) and Henry VIII (1509–1547) and this chapter is about the legal and constitutional developments that took place when these two remarkable men were sovereigns.

Historians sometimes call the period from 1485 to 1603 "The Tudor Despotism." This title, like so many others bestowed upon periods in history, is convenient but not quite accurate. It is true that the rulers of the Tudor dynasty were usually powerful and often autocratic. If they had been soft and pliable the English nation would probably have suffered worse disasters than the bloodshed and general disruption of the Wars of the Roses. But the Tudors were not soft and pliable. Nor were they tyrants. Did they consider their wills superior to the laws of England? No. Did they ever coerce or compel Parliament to do what it did not want to do? No. Did they ever defy the laws? No. They might sometimes evade or pervert those laws, but they never defied them. True, they did extend their prerogative powers. At the same time, they usually depended upon the cooperation of their people in making their rule effective. When there was innovation they tried to legalize it by Parliamentary statute. Usually, too, they tried to cite precedents. Such is not the practice of despots.

In these days, the practice and doctrines of absolutism were far more prevalent on the Continent than in Britain. Alien ideas of the Roman law were not widely received in England, although some Roman law principles did have a strong influence, especially in the new prerogative courts to be described later. The common law was certainly not in a flourishing condition in the sixteenth century. Nevertheless, as Sir Edward Coke shrewdly remarked later, it was "tough." The strong and efficient machine of the Tudor system was based upon the monarchs, the Parliament, and the law. The alliance between Parliament and the law courts was very important. It was to be still more important in the next century.

Nobody was concerned about the definition or location of "sovereignty" in Tudor England. It remained for the Stuarts to get troubled about such things and thus spill the essence of Tudor statecraft in the dust. The real "despotism" in Tudor days was mainly that of public opinion, which always played a major part in keeping England in "a bridle of good order." Of course, the phrase "public opinion" does not mean today what it meant in the sixteenth century. The era of Henry VIII and Elizabeth was an aristocratic age, far from any theory or practice of equality. "The heavens themselves," wrote William Shakespeare, "the planets and this centre, Observe degree, priority, and place." The Tudor ideals of order and harmony, the links of a great chain of being, the inherent sinfulness of disorder and rebellion, all these are stressed in diverse places through many years. The Tudors were always very successful in uniting the twin principles of royal authority and popular consent. This practice, of course, operates very well so long as there is a quiet understanding that neither of the two principles will be pressed to extremity. Probably the most important achievement of the Tudor monarchs was that they gave England more order and peace than she had known for a century.

The vigorous Tudor government was essentially government by a king or queen in conformity with the rules of the game. Royal acts were always carried out within the proper limits of the authority that belonged to the monarch. True, the power invoked might sometimes be very personal and discretionary but no man could deny that it was inside the proper province of the prerogative. It must be emphasized again that there was a body of rules of statute and common law that provided a part of the legal framework within which a monarch was required to move. The basis of the state was not arbitrary will. It was law.[1]

HENRY VII: DISEASE AND REMEDY

Henry VII, victor of Bosworth Field, was a cautious, cold, inscrutable, Machiavellian individual, a man of tenacious purpose and creative energy. On November 7, 1485, Parliament passed an Act of Succession formally recognizing Henry as the holder of the crown he had won by arms. "In avoiding all ambiguities and questions" it was declared that the inheritance of the Crown should "be, rest, remain, and abide in the most royal person of our now sovereign lord, King Henry VII." To strengthen a frail hereditary claim Henry married Elizabeth of York, eldest daughter of Edward IV and possessed of the best Yorkist claim to the throne. Throughout the first years of his reign he met and crushed several challenges from rival claimants. The throne must be made secure.

To strengthen the Tudor position by marriage and by smashing rebellions was obviously not enough. The laws of treason were expanded. The control over Ireland was broadened (Poyning's Law, 1494). A statute concerning justices of the peace (1489) declared that the king's laws were not duly executed, "wherefore his subjects be grievously hurt and out of surety of their bodies and goods, to his great displeasure." This law provided heavy penalties for any justices of the peace who failed to discharge their duties well. "In the corrupted currents of this world," wrote Shakespeare later, "Offence's gilded hand may shove by justice . . . but 'tis not so above." Henry VII wished it were not so in England.

---

[1] Many relevant documents for the whole Tudor period are printed in Carl Stephenson and F. G. Marcham, *Sources of English Constitutional History*, Section VII, pp. 296–401.

Throughout the years of his rule Henry tried to obtain popular support. He saw that the future of himself and his dynasty depended upon whether he could bring peace and prosperity to his subjects, especially to the farmers and the merchants. Agriculture and commerce flourish best when there is no internal disorder and no foreign war. Under Henry VII Navigation Acts protected commerce. The royal income from customs duties increased from about £32,000 a year in 1485 to about £42,000 in 1509. Henry's navy became very powerful. He built a great naval base at Portsmouth. His shipyards made fine cargo vessels. He found and maintained markets for English cloth. Henry "could not endure to see trade sick." Commerce was also helped by the making of trade treaties with Flanders, Denmark, and other lands. Government control over the craft guilds was increased. The domestic manufacturing system was aided in several respects. Henry VII was a shrewd business man. What his biographer Francis Bacon called "the considerations of plenty and the considerations of power" were always important to Henry VII.

One of the great centers of disturbance and threats to peace was the nobility. Henry determined to use every possible agency to curb the powerful nobles who had caused such disorder among high and low. "Rebellion had become a habit, treason an occupation." The primary objects of the pertinacious Henry VII were peace, order, and the restoration and expansion of the actualities of power. The administration of the law must be strengthened through the common law courts and through special prerogative bodies. Intrigue, lawlessness, and conspiracy must yield to the royal strength.

Men of the middle class strongly approved when Henry VII moved against the "overmighty nobles" to force them to keep the law and the peace. The magnates who had rejoiced so long in the strength of military feudalism now reluctantly bowed before the strong king. In his first Parliament, Henry compelled the lords to take an oath that they would not maintain large bands of liveried men who might be used as servants one day and soldiers or robbers the next. In 1504 an act of Parliament referred to earlier legislation against the practice of liveries and maintenance and provided that "no person, of whatever degree or condition he be, . . . shall privily or openly give any livery or sign or retain any person, other than such as he giveth household wages unto without fraud or colour."

There were other remedial measures. A series of acts provided for the punishing of jurors who returned false verdicts. Townships that failed to discover and arrest murderers were fined heavily. Coroners who neglected to hold inquests were also punished. Such steps were important. More important still was Henry's effective use of the royal prerogative. Henry was prepared to strain the resources of the Crown for purposes that seemed to him to be desirable. Let us now see what he did and how he did it.

Nathaniel Bacon once said: "Henry VII taught the people to dance more often and better to the tune of prerogative than all his predecessors had done." This statement, so nearly accurate, tells much about the change under Henry VII from "the lack of governance and politic rule" in the fifteenth century to the effective "new monarchy" of the Tudors. Henry VII, always ready to do what policy required, saw clearly that weakness in the Crown had been a source of great evils: internal strife and the acute decline of law and order; palsy and corruption in the administrative body; overweening and refractory magnates defying the king, sending their private armies to maraud and murder. To Henry VII it was obvious that the spacious and ill-defined net of the prerogative could be cast widely by a strong and determined king. The potentialities of that prerogative were tremendous. After 1485 "the customary bounds within which the prerogative had operated were left behind . . . they were widened to admit much that was new within what in form was old."

A major cause of Crown weakness had always been the lack of money. Henry VII raised revenue by every means he could find and use. "That king thrives best who has money in his purse." For example, in 1492 Henry accepted as an immediate payment about £180,000 and an annual pension of about £12,000 from Charles VIII of France in return for Henry's withdrawal from a war neither monarch wanted to fight. Most of Henry's income came, of course, from internal revenue sources. The methods he employed to collect it were usually clear, simple, and quite ruthless.

Henry VII at once proceeded, for instance, to search out and enforce his traditional rights as feudal overlord. These included the collection of much gold and silver and services. Obsolete or obsolescent clauses in old laws and arrangements were discovered, revived, and made the foundations of numerous new departures, all directed towards the end of expanding royal revenues. Crown lands alienated during the Wars of the Roses were taken back. Many other acres were seized by the king. If a man thus dispossessed wanted to recover the lands in question the only legal processes available to him were cumbersome and slow. Crown lands were more effectively administered. Between 1491 and 1504 the income from Crown lands increased about sevenfold. The total Exchequer income tripled in Henry's reign. Huge fines and forfeitures were collected from rebels who failed. Prerogative wardship rights were expanded. Benevolences were levied upon the weakened nobles. "The benevolent mind of the rich sort was searched out and by their open gifts the king would measure and search their benevolent hearts and loving minds so that he who gave most should be judged his most loyal friend and he who gave little be esteemed according to his gift."

Special agents helped reform the royal revenue apparatus and collected forced loans and benevolences. The rich could always be fleeced. If a noble lived well he was informed that he could surely afford to make a gift to the king. If he lived poorly he was told that he must be saving enough to do the same thing. By such means the king ceaselessly enlarged the contents of his purse and the spheres of his activity. As early as 1490 the crown accounts were balanced. Henry VII was one of the most efficient of the many business men who have sat upon the English throne. Henry was aided, of course, by his superlative avarice and his rugged will.

As Professor Samuel E. Thorne and others have pointed out Henry VII usually stayed within the law.[2] Nevertheless, Henry could and did evade the spirit of the law by "maneuvers and circumventions, subterfuges, subtleties." The economic claws of the great must be clipped. Rival sovereignties must be wiped out. The royal authority, so diffused in the fifteenth century, must be concentrated. Henry VII was a king who could do these things. "What he minded, that he compassed," wrote Francis Bacon.

One of the most effective uses of the royal power can be seen in the rejuvenation of the Court of Star Chamber, a prerogative court. So important was this body in English legal and constitutional history that it is imperative that we examine it carefully. Nowhere does the enigmatic Henry reveal himself and his purposes more clearly than in his use of this court. "Kings have long arms," says an Italian proverb, "and many have eyes and ears."

The king's council, with its many combined judicial, administrative, and deliberative functions, had thrown off the great courts of law in the twelfth century and the equitable jurisdiction of Chancery later.

---

[2] See Samuel E. Thorne (ed.), *Prerogativa Regis* (1949).

Meanwhile the Crown continued to possess its indefinite supreme jurisdiction exercised through the council. After Parliament appeared in the thirteenth century the king's council became a body distinct from the spiritual and temporal magnates in the House of Lords. When Edward III was king (1327–1377), the Chancellor, the Treasurer, the justices and some other members of the council began to exercise jurisdiction as a prerogative court supplementary to the ordinary courts of common law and equity. Persons summoned before it were called by the privy seal of the king. The name "Court of Star Chamber" may have been derived from the stars studding the ceiling of the old chamber (*camera stellata*) at Westminster where this royal court usually met. Many facts about the name and origin of the Court of Star Chamber are obscure.

In 1487 an act of Parliament altered the machinery for the extraordinary and stringent jurisdiction of the council exercised through the Star Chamber. The act provided that a specified group of seven members of the council should decide certain cases: the Chancellor, the Treasurer, the Keeper of the Privy Seal, or two of them, "calling to them a bishop and a temporal lord of the king's most honorable council and the two chief justices of the king's bench and common pleas . . . or other two justices in their absence." It is sometimes believed that the act of 1487 set up or established the Court of Star Chamber. As a matter of historical fact, no statute ever did this. We have seen that some members of the council had been acting as a prerogative court for more than a hundred years before 1487. The act of 1487 simply gave new life and strength to Star Chamber by stating its composition and powers more precisely. It was not until after the early development of the Privy Council following 1526 that Star Chamber came to be thought of as a separate court, quite distinct from the council.

The statute of 1487 gave the Court of Star Chamber authority "to punish divers misdemeanours." It said: "The king, our sovereign lord, remembereth how, by unlawful maintenances, giving of divers signs and tokens . . . untrue demeaning of sheriffs . . . by taking of money by juries, by great riots and unlawful assemblies, the policy and good rule of this realm is almost subdued . . . to the increase of murders, robberies, perjuries, and unsureties of all men living, and losses of their lands and goods, to the great displeasure of Almighty God." Men who were summoned before Star Chamber, said the statute, and found "defective," were to be punished "after their demerits . . . in like manner and form as they should and ought to be punished if they were thereof convict after the due order of the law. . . ."

The vague jurisdiction of the Court of Star Chamber was thus made more than supplementary under the statute of 1487. In certain cases its jurisdiction superseded that of the ordinary courts. This was particularly true in cases that were counted too serious or important to be dealt with by the common law courts. It was clear that the common law courts might not be strong enough to handle some problems and some offenders. The Court of Star Chamber was not weak. It could stop proud lawbreakers from causing turbulence and trampling upon the rights of the king or his subjects. It could reach out and punish powerful offenders. It was, after all, the instrument of the king's prerogative. Sir Thomas Smith, that great Elizabethan, once said that the purpose of Star Chamber was "to bridle such noblemen or gentlemen who would offer wrong by force to any manner of men."

The Court of Star Chamber was in fact an elastic law unto itself. It took notice of felony, forgery, fraud, libel and slander, murder, perjury, treason, various kinds of disputes between men of prestige and power, between English and foreign merchants. In practice its jurisdiction was almost unlimited. "All offences may be examined here if the king wills." There was no jury. Even the greatest lord could not bribe or frighten the judges. The court did not depend upon the common law. As has been explained, its authority and procedural methods were ultimately derived from the deep fountain of the royal prerogative. As Professor F. W. Maitland once succinctly observed: "The common law was not lusty in the sixteenth century." An accused individual might be summoned by writ or Privy Seal to appear before the Star Chamber court on the basis of rumors alone. Often he did not see the witnesses against him. He was not permitted to cross-examine. He might be tortured. He might be sentenced to any kind of punishment (imprisonment, fine, branding, mutilation, etc.) except death or the loss of his freehold property. So it was that the Court of Star Chamber could be used to strike at the most powerful lords and evildoers in England. Those accused of such crimes as livery and maintenance, bribery, overawing the common law courts, and "undue demeaning of sheriffs" had short shrift before it. For example, the proud Earl of Oxford paraded six hundred liveried retainers to honor his king. He was astounded when the Court of Star Chamber fined him £10,000 for violating the statute against the practice of liveries and maintenance. As used by Henry VII the Court of Star Chamber swiftly put the fear of the law into the turbulent nobles and brought them to heel.

The Court of Star Chamber was an important and valuable body at the end of the Wars of the Roses. During the Tudor age it was an admirable and efficient instrument for bringing order and respect for law out of turbulence. Under the Stuarts, when there was no "harmony of powers," the Star Chamber was to become a vicious instrument of tyranny.

A second prerogative court was set up by Henry VII in 1493. This was the Court of Requests, a companion court to Star Chamber, a court for civil causes. It was originally a standing committee of the council established to hear the pleas of poor suitors who claimed that they had not obtained justice in the common law courts as a result of such things as corruption, bribery, and the intimidation of the jurymen. Here tenants appealed against their landlords. Here the copyholders sought to stay enclosures. Here the widow asked aid for herself and her son.

The Court of Requests might be called a minor court of equity. Despite the fact that it was really an equity court, it did not use the Great Seal of Chancery. To do that was costly and administratively awkward. Instead, the Privy Seal was used and the Lord Privy Seal presided at the court sessions. Like Chancery and Star Chamber, the Court of Requests used no juries. It was, after all, a prerogative court. Again, like Chancery and Star Chamber, it naturally collided with, and was strongly opposed by, the common law courts. In Henry VIII's reign (1509–1547) Thomas Wolsey shaped its structure more completely and later still there were two Masters of Requests presiding over a busy court. Until the great Civil War of the next century the common law courts issued writs of prohibition against proceedings in the Court of Requests, but to no avail. Sir Edward Coke insisted that the Court of Requests had not "any power by commission, by statute, or by common law." Shortly after the Court of Star Chamber was abolished by the Long Parliament in 1641, the Court of Requests was also wiped away. The jurisdiction of Star Chamber and Requests was never revived.

It was obviously easier to bring the stern blessings of Henry VII's rule to the central and settled areas than it was to the marches of Wales and the lands of the North. So it was that in the North from about 1490 and in the Welsh borderlands from about 1500 there slowly emerged two councils called the King's Council of the North Parts and the Council of the Marches of Wales. These regional bodies performed nearly all the functions carried on by the parent council at Westminster. By the famous order of Henry VIII in 1545 the Archbishop of York was confirmed in his post as Lord President of the Council of the North and, with the aid of sixteen councillors, was to exercise wide powers.

Meanwhile the Tudor privy council, with relentless law and logic, proceeded to strengthen still further the coherence of the state. It soon gave signs of what it was to become under Henry VIII and Elizabeth: a mighty, energetic, incorruptible, arbitrary, ruthless instrument of the royal will, a flexible organ of government. The council concerned itself with scores of matters, great and minute. Questions of high policy mingled with the petty problems of obscure citizens. Council and Star Chamber served the Tudors, and England, with tireless zeal. "I will make a star-chamber matter of it," shouted Justice Shallow to the Welsh parson. "If he were twenty Sir John Falstaffs, he shall not abuse Robert Shallow, esquire. . . . The council shall hear of it." [3]

Parliament did not move in the foreground when Henry VII was king. It was used, of course, for the necessary business of finance and legislation. Most of the time it stayed in the background. The important body was the council. Henry VI held twenty-two Parliaments in thirty-nine years. Edward IV called seven in twenty-two years. Henry VII also called seven docile Parliaments in his reign, six of them before 1497. From these assemblies he asked only five grants of direct taxes. Despite this temporary near-eclipse of Parliament there was no diminution of its essential rights. These were now too sturdily rooted to be easily killed by axe or drought. In the next reign the power of king in Parliament was to grow greater than it had ever been before.

As the old aristocracy declined in numbers and power Henry VII turned for support and assistance to the solid and more easily controlled middle classes. Many men of the "new nobility," destined to be outstanding statesmen or rascals of the Tudor era, were drawn from the ranks of the country gentry or the city men of business. Henry VII and his successors also drew heavily upon the ranks of established

---

[3] The diversity of council activities is revealed by the regulations, letters, reports, and minutes quoted in Carl Stephenson and F. G. Marcham, *Sources of English Constitutional History*, pp. 331–337. Records of typical cases in Star Chamber are given in the same volume, pp. 337–344.

lawyers and experienced civil servants to aid them in national and local administration. Several of these lawyers were unsavory, sophisticated shysters. They valued their necks and their other interests and hence they were loyal servants of the crown. The Tudors wished to see few members of the old nobility in positions of power. From the middle classes Henry VII showed his skill in choosing competent advisers and servants. Into the royal council came many sinewy middle class men whose loyalty to the crown was increased by the fact that they held their positions solely as the result of the royal will and not from any blood titles. From the middle classes were recruited the famous Yeomen of the Guard, the bodyguard of the sovereign. At the same time Henry VII began the revival of the medieval paternalism towards the humble workers, the poor, and the sick in the state. There were many strong bases to a "popular despotism."

In 1509 Henry VII died, a lonely, soured figure, surrounded by men he could command but seldom trust. He had amassed a fortune of nearly £2,000,000, a remarkable achievement. Those who had challenged his right to the throne were dead. His nobility was subservient. His Parliaments were submissive. The reign of this calculating and unamiable king had brought relative security, peace and prosperity.

The continuity that is the dominant characteristic of the development of English government had been maintained. The institutions, unprotected by fundamental or organic laws, had survived the Wars of the Roses and had been strengthened under Henry VII. They still possessed, as they possess today, several inherent attributes bespeaking their medieval origin; but the purposes for which they were increasingly used we can rightly call "modern." In England continuity has never meant rigidity and lack of change. The legacies from the Middle Ages have been ceaselessly moulded and sometimes logically merged with new organs of government. By flexibility, by adaptation, by modification, by subtle understanding, by addition—and sometimes by subtraction and atrophy—the constitution has altered from century to century. Englishmen have never uprooted or denied their long traditions. In the English constitution, as a meteor phrase of John Stuart Mill has said so well, "the centuries have given one another rendezvous."

HENRY VIII: CHURCH AND STATE

The handsome and lusty Henry VIII had unusual gifts of personality and brains. He was a magnificent athlete, a musician, a poet, the living example of the Renaissance ideal of the versatile man. To his court came scholars from all over Europe to nourish and spread the spirit of the Renaissance. Henry soon added to the popularity so freely given him when he ascended the throne. The personal element in monarchy was still very strong. It is true that feudal political arrangements were ceasing. Nevertheless, ideas lagged behind practice and political sentiment remained largely feudal in the sixteenth century. The practice of government had not ceased to be personal and Henry kept it so. For example, under Henry the royal council could go for days without the touch of the royal hand; but that was only because Henry VIII permitted it. "His car of state might be allowed to run of its own momentum because he knew that its controls would instantly respond to the slightest inclination of the royal person." Every minister drew his power from one source: the king's favor. Church and state, metropolis and province, politics and economics, all the varied workings of national life were watched over by the royal council and behind the council stood the colossus of the king. "We will that none of our servants shall belong to any other person but to us," said Henry VIII.

After Henry VIII's canny father died, a new era of restless diplomacy began. Henry was anxious to shine in European affairs. As a result he became involved in a complex game of intrigue with such hoary chessmasters as Maximilian, Holy Roman Emperor, and Ferdinand VII of Spain. Henry led and sent armies to Europe. He fought the Scotsmen. He helped to upset the balance of power in Europe. After Charles V of Spain beat the French at Pavia in 1525 the value of England's alliance was reduced to little or nothing. Charles V was master of Europe. Gorgeous diplomacy and ineffective wars cost money and brought no glory to Henry VIII or to England.

Meanwhile there were brewing the storms at home that were to bring the Reformation Parliament (1529–1536) and the final departure of England from the fold of Rome. We cannot be occupied here with the problems involved in the "divorce" of Henry VIII and Catherine of Aragon, the perils of the succession, the massive obstacles that stood in the way of delay. Nor can we examine the vexed question of Henry VIII's motives in destroying papal supremacy in England. But we must, as students of legal and constitutional history, look once again at the relations of the church and state before the days of Henry VIII and the Reformation Parliament. Secondly, we can examine precisely what Henry VIII and Parliament accomplished by statutory enactments after 1529. Thirdly, we can consider the results of these events in the pattern of the subsequent relations of church and state.

Before the Reformation Europe was Christendom. The medieval ideas of unity, order, hierarchy, and religion prevailed in the oneness of all Christian Europe. The seamless web of the Church Universal had not yet been torn asunder. In each nation the church and state were looked upon as different aspects of the same society. Every man, except Jews or wandering Moslem merchants, was a member of a state and a son of the church, a Christian. Both church and state possessed its head, its laws, its machinery, its area of power. The visible church could not be independent of the state. The state could not then get along without the church pervading every aspect of life with its holy influence. True, there had been major disputes in Europe and in England about the precise borders and provinces of power. Readers will remember the sporadic dislocations, especially during the reigns of William II, John, Henry II, Edward I, Henry III. Various statutes, such as the statutes of Provisors of 1351 and 1390 and those of Praemunire in 1353 and 1393, betokened the level of the anti-papal, anti-clerical, and anti-Italian feeling in England. We have seen how closely interwoven with the government and administration of England were the lives of her faithful churchmen. We have also frequently noted the extensive jurisdiction of the ecclesiastical courts and the disputes arising from that fact.

In 1527 the armies of Charles V, Holy Roman Emperor, sacked Rome. Pope Clement VII was a prisoner of Charles. And Catherine of Aragon, Henry VIII's queen, was the aunt of the Emperor Charles V. It was not reasonable to expect that Henry would obtain a favorable hearing when he asked for an annulment of his marriage at the papal court. It was difficult for Pope Clement VII to say that an Emperor's aunt had been living in sin for eighteen years, especially when the soldiers of Charles streamed about the streets of Rome. Embassy after embassy sent by Henry to the papal court returned with the same reply. Henry was entangled in a jurisdiction that admitted no superior. The attractions of Anne Boleyn joined with the demands of conscience and imperious egotism to speed Henry onwards.

There were also the old questions of royal and papal jurisdiction. There was the growing English nationalism, coming to be more sharply personified by the king, particularly when opposed to the internationalism of the church and the papacy standing against the dual allegiance demanded of the clergy. When Henry declared that "England is an Empire" he was speaking the language of a defender of the sovereignty of a modern nation state. Englishmen, in this age of rising nation states, were increasingly aware of their separateness from other nations. Their emotions were becoming more and more attached to the king and to England. "Can the papal court, a foreign tribunal, stand between England and the maintenance of the Tudor succession? Catherine of Aragon cannot give Henry VIII a male child. Perhaps Anne Boleyn can produce a prince." Englishmen turned less and less to Rome. The emotions that linked them to Rome or to the Christendom of the Holy Roman Empire had never been national ones and the fires of nationalism were now burning brightly. At the same time England was naturalizing the medieval ideas about harmony, order and unity.

Henry VIII was theologically orthodox. Many sincere and orthodox churchmen in England, like Erasmus, Sir Thomas More, Hugh Latimer, and John Colet, pleaded for reform in their beloved church. They wanted to stop the evils in a church headed by such freeliving, warlike, and pagan popes as the Borgia Alexander VI, Julius II, and Leo X. They wanted to end the decline of the mendicant orders, the profligacy of the higher churchmen, the degeneracy of the monasteries, the abuses of benefit of clergy, the corruption of ecclesiastical courts. A large body of pamphlet literature arose. There was popular objection and complaint to the endowed wealth of a church enriched by generations of Catholic piety and to the burdens of church taxation. In the wake of these sincere reformers and objectors within the church there came a flood of new men, men from Europe, men preaching the Protestant doctrines of Martin Luther.

In 1529 the strong-willed Henry VIII called Parliament. He hoped that the state of opinion would result in a Parliament sufficiently opposed to papal power in England to support the royal demands upon Clement VII. Henry knew how many Englishmen resented the authority and the exactions of the Pope. He also knew that the majority of those in the propertied classes would not shrink from plundering the churchmen, a wealthy and unpopular minority.

Where it was possible and convenient Henry VIII used the royal influence to gain supporters in Parliament. Nevertheless, he did not pack or browbeat that assembly. Charges of servility, packing, or terror have frequently been made, and they remain unproved. Parliament concentrated and expressed with the forms and sanctions of law the accumulated feeling of a resentful nation. Slowly Parliament came to stand for the ousting of an alien authority, the cause of insular independence, the anti-Roman idea of the subjection of the church in England to national control. When the Parliament met in November, 1529, the members "began to commune of their griefs wherewith the spirituality had before time grievously oppressed them."

Early in its sessions enactments of Parliament prohibited non-residence of clergy and other obvious abuses. Clement VII wrote to Henry, "admonishing him in all benevolence and threatening excommunication." In 1531, Henry VIII, by a broad interpretation of the law, accused the whole clergy of violating the acts of Praemunire (1353, 1393) because they had recognized Thomas Wolsey as papal legate. The clergy, quite alarmed, voted in Convocation to purchase pardon by paying a contribution of £100,000. They were also forced to acknowledge Henry VIII to be their "especial protector, single and supreme lord, and, as far as the law of Christ allows, even Supreme Head, of the church and clergy of England." The spirit of resistance was draining out of the men of the cloth.

Early in 1532, act after act was passed demolishing church authorities, cutting sinews of control, and giving the king effective power over the clergy and ecclesiastical law. Among these was the Act in Conditional Restraint of Annates. This law stopped new incumbents of benefices from paying their first year's revenues to the Pope. These payments, called annates, were said to have totalled £2,000,000 in gold between 1485 and 1532. The restraint was at first declared to be "conditional" because if Clement VII agreed to meet Henry VIII's wishes the payment of annates might possibly be permitted again.

In 1533 an act of Parliament forbade appeals to Rome: "Where, by divers sundry old authentic histories and chronicles it is manifestly declared and expressed that this realm of England is an empire . . . governed by one supreme head and king . . . and inconveniences and dangers . . . have risen and sprung by reasons of appeals sued out of this realm to the see of Rome . . . the king's highness . . . doth therefore . . . by the assent of the lords spiritual and temporal and the commons . . . enact, establish, and ordain . . . that all causes [here follows the defining list] shall be from henceforth heard and definitely adjudged and determined within the king's jurisdiction and authority and not elsewhere." In 1534 Parliament passed an Act for the Submission of the Clergy, an Act Concerning Ecclesiastical Appointments and Absolute Restraint of Annates, an Act Concerning Peter's Pence and Dispensations.

In January, 1533, Henry VIII had married Anne Boleyn. In April, 1533, Thomas Cranmer, archbishop of Canterbury, announced that Henry's marriage to Catherine of Aragon had never been valid. In September, the Princess Elizabeth was born. The English ambassador was recalled from Rome. In 1534 the First Act of Succession—"an act for the establishment of the king's succession"—provided that the children born to Henry VIII and Queen Anne should be direct heirs to the throne and that anybody who by "writing, print, deed, or act" did "any thing or things to the prejudice, slander, disturbance or derogation of the said lawful matrimony . . . for every such offence shall be judged high traitors" and as such doomed to execution. Any subject who made an oral statement slandering the marriage or the children born of it was guilty of "misprision of treason" or criminal contempt.

All that had gone before was crowned in 1534 by the Act of Supremacy, the coping stone of a safe and prudential reformation. This famous act declared that "the king, our sovereign lord, his heirs and successors, kings of this realm, shall be taken, accepted, and reputed the only supreme head on earth of the Church of England . . . to the pleasure of Almighty God, the increase of virtue in Christ's religion, and for the conservation of the peace, unity, and tranquillity of this realm." The authority of the Crown was now supreme over all persons and causes. The issues between the rival powers of church and state were at last settled. The legal breach with the See Apostolic was complete.

A national Parliament had placed itself by the side of the nation's king. To all the steps taken by Henry VIII the Reformation Parliament gave legislative form and sanction. The church was annexed to the state. Henry VIII was head of the state and head of the English national church. Parliament and Convocation were now in a similar relationship to the Crown.

In 1536 the lesser monasteries were dissolved by act of Parliament and their property given to Henry VIII. In 1539 the Six Articles Act was passed and in the same year the greater monasteries were dissolved. It is probable that about one-sixth of all the land in England passed into the king's hands. Twenty-eight abbots dropped out of the House of Lords in one year. Soon it was difficult to believe that the mitred abbots and greater priors had once been in a majority in the House of Lords. Of all the lords spiritual only the archbishops and bishops now remained. Henry VIII gave away or sold the larger part of the monastic lands. Within a few years he had made 1,600 grants of property

LONDON Scale 500 feet

RENAIS-SANCE ENGLAND 100 Scale of Miles

Martin Frobisher seeks a route to India 1576

GABRIEL MICHAEL

The nobles remodel their castles with windows and gardens where once were loopholes and moats

Elizabeth visits the Earl of Leicester

Dublin University

Caxton's successor pours books from his printing press in Westminster

England rings with songs and merrymaking

HARDWICK HALL

Shrewsbury school

KENILWORTH CASTLE

Morris dancers

Shakespeare's birthplace at Stratford on Avon

WARWICK CASTLE

Rugby

FOTHERINGAY CASTLE

here was executed Mary Stuart

King's College

Cambridge Univ.

PEMBROKE CASTLE

BERKELEY CASTLE

OXFORD UNIV.

Magdalene College

Eton

Harrow

WINDSOR CASTLE

LONDON

Elizabeth orders Bibles placed for public reading in churches

DEVON

Drake circumnavigates the earth and brings back to Plymouth millions in gold

Cabot sailing for America in 1497

SALISBURY CASTLE

Winchester School

Charterhouse school

ARUNDEL CASTLE

DOVER

to Calais

Defeat of the Armada 1588

Fortune Theatre

E. Raisz

valued at £800,000. The church was indeed the junior partner of the state. The power of the Crown was tremendously increased. The propertied classes who shared in the plunder from the church were now more firmly bound to the house of Tudor and the repudiation of papal supremacy.

The Reformation Parliament was the first Parliament in history to sit for a long period (1529–1536). It met for the last time on July 18, 1536. The Speaker compared Henry VIII to the sun dispelling all noxious vapors and ripening all things good and necessary. Henry refused to accept the compliment and ascribed all the glory to God.

PARLIAMENT AND COURTS

Fifty-six years old, irascible, ill, and suspicious, Henry VIII still at the end commanded the loyalty of his nation and his ministers of state. The interests of the Crown most certainly, in the days of the early Tudors, became closely identified with those of Englishmen. It is true that the acts of Henry VIII were often arbitrary, cruel, unjust and selfish. Yet they touched but few men and those that the king harmed were usually not loved in England. With steady energy Henry VIII tried to make his subjects devoted to him. He created and courted public opinion and brought almost every major question to the floor of Parliament. He magnified Parliament for his own ends. He increased the constituencies by incorporating Wales and Chester into the Parliamentary system and by creating several new boroughs in England. In this practice he was followed later by his daughter Elizabeth I. There were 298 seats in the Commons in 1509 and 467 in 1603, the year of Elizabeth's death.

Both Henry VIII and Elizabeth I usually refrained from "packing" or bullying Parliaments. There are scant signs of robbery, jobbery, or bribery by any of the Tudors. It is, of course, true that Henry VIII and Elizabeth I naturally liked to see members elected who would favor royal policies but neither monarch was prepared to browbeat or bribe to obtain cowed and pliant supporters. Meanwhile the competence and self-consciousness of Parliament increased. Henry VIII did not mean to encourage the independence of Parliament and would have been quite startled if anyone had suggested that his methods were preparing for the day when Parliament would be a very independent body indeed. Henry merely tried to see that in all the great affairs of his reign and realm the Englishmen who sat in Parliament said the same thing as their king.

It is sometimes said that "the authoritarian tendencies of the Tudor monarchs were largely a continuation of the methods of their predecessors." If this sentence stands alone it has little meaning or accuracy. To it must be added some of the statements of the previous paragraph and a reminder that during the Middle Ages in England the king had not been supreme and only occasionally "authoritarian"—the power of the church, the law, and the magnates was never negligible.

In Henry VIII's day political writers taught that non-resistance was essential for the security of the state. "Encomiums in praise of kingship," wrote Professor Franklin Le Van Baumer a few years ago, "and a doctrine of sovereignty sufficiently vague—rather than precise analyses of the actual power wielded by the king—became the order of the day." What Professor Baumer aptly called "the Henrician cult of authority" can be, and has been, carefully documented. Always it "typified English nationalism as against the internationalism of the papacy and the Catholic Church." [4] William Tyndale and others claimed that "the king is, in this world, without law, and may at his lust do right or wrong, and shall give accounts but to God only." Throughout the Tudor period the inherent sinfulness of rebellion is often stressed in pamphlet, pulpit and book. The functional ideal of society in sixteenth century political literature was almost inevitably discussed in terms of degree and of rank, of Edmund Dudley's "due order by grace," or in words about the paramount importance of duty, honor and loyalty.

Tudor government was thus far more than a brutal dictatorship born of fear and based upon force. True, reason of state was sometimes above the letter of the law. Public interest, real or alleged, towered above the rights of the subject. But the main pillar of Tudor government was the consent and cooperation of crown and subjects. The Tudor monarchs never monopolized, in a personal sense, the power of the system they controlled. They used and nourished the council and its offshoots. They used Parliament. They ordered and encouraged the development of local administration and government. Of these things more will be said later.

By the sixteenth century Parliament was quite clearly considered a representative assembly of the three estates of the realm. King, lords and commons together possessed greater power and dignity than any

---

[4] Franklin Le Van Baumer, *The Early Tudor Theory of Kingship* (1940), p. 86. The quotations from this volume are made with the permission of Professor Baumer and the Yale University Press.

one of them alone, even the king. The attitude of many Englishmen—
it is a familiar view now, but it was new then—was stated in a famous
speech by Henry VIII to Parliament: "We be informed by our judges
that at no time do we stand so highly in our estate royal as in the time
of Parliament, wherein we as head and you as members are conjoined
and knit together in one body politic" (1543).

We cannot here consider all of the shifting winds of doctrine or the
details of emerging principles about the position and power of Crown
and Parliament. Henry VIII called very few Parliaments in the early
years of his reign, partly because his mighty servant Thomas Wolsey
disliked them. None were summoned between 1515 and 1522. There
were only nine assembled during the thirty-eight years of Henry's
reign. Nevertheless, as we have seen, the robust Henry VIII used Parliaments for what he deemed the good purposes of the state. As any
case book of Tudor documents will show, Henry VIII aided the development and definitions of such privileges of Parliament as freedom
of speech and freedom from arrest during sessions of Parliament. The
whole Reformation, as we have also seen, was undertaken by the
Crown and by Parliament. What was done was achieved by statute, and
statutes were made in Parliament. Kings as yet had few fears of the
men who came down from the counties and boroughs to Westminster.

Parliament was a useful ally of the crown, an excellent instrument.
Henry VIII instructed his agents at Rome in 1532 to inform Pope
Clement VII that "debate in our Parliament is free, and it is not
possible for us to interfere in their discussions about any matter, and
forsooth they decide as they think fit according to what they deem to
be the profit or otherwise of the state." We do not know whether or not
the Pope accepted these assurances as statements of matters of fact. We
do know that Henry VIII, like all the Tudors, availed himself of Parliament when he had a use for it. When he wanted the support of
statutes Henry turned to Parliament. When he had no need of Parliament to forge legislative weapons he usually ignored it.

A second point should now be stated and stressed. Henry VIII kept
and used the prerogative courts of Star Chamber and Requests, the
Council of Wales and the Council of the North. To these potent executive instruments he added other judicial offshoots of the council: the
Court of High Commission, the Court of Augmentations, and the
Court of Wards and Liveries. Two of these courts, High Commission
and Augmentations, grew out of the separation of the English church
from Rome. The task of the Court of High Commission was to main-

tain the compromise Church of England against all assaults of her enemies. "Wherever there is a creed," as Professor Alfred North Whitehead once remarked, "there is a heretic round the corner or in his grave." In Tudor and Stuart England there were really several "commission courts," of which the High Commission was one. This was so because royal commissions for ecclesiastical causes were issued to groups of the laity and clergy in each province and diocese of the church to aid in enforcing ecclesiastical law. Because the commission of the province of Canterbury was most important, it was called the Court of High Commission. The activities of this court veered and varied under different monarchs and public opinions. Always, however, its wide jurisdiction enabled it to control and punish those whose doings seemed to threaten the established settlement and who merited appropriate discipline.

Until its abolition in 1641 the Court of High Commission interfered, enforced, and prodded. It was the duty of its zealous members "to visit, reform, redress, order, correct, and amend within this our realm of England all . . . errors, heresies, crimes, abuses, offences, contempts, and enormities spiritual and ecclesiastical . . . to the pleasure of Almighty God, the increase of virtue and the conservation of the peace and unity of this our realm. . . ." [5]

The Court of Augmentations was another sub-unit of the council established to meet a particular need. It dealt, like an Exchequer Court, with specific cases connected with the ecclesiastical revenue by which Henry VIII was augmenting his income after the separation from Rome. A third prerogative court, the Court of Wards and Liveries, was created in 1541 for the purpose of enforcing effectively the collection of incidents of military tenure for the benefit of the Crown. These land levies—the best word to describe them is extortions—were ruthlessly gathered in. They included, of course, the usual incidents of homage, wardship, and marriage. Henry VIII also continued practices like the old distraint of knighthood by which he compelled men possessing a certain amount of property to accept knighthood, at a price. Henry, as might be expected, sold compulsory knighthoods at bargain rates. In 1656 the Court of Wards and Liveries was abolished under the Commonwealth and military tenure was changed into free socage. Feudal wardship, homage, marriage, livery, primer seisin, and

---

[5] For selected documents relating to these courts see Carl Stephenson and F. G. Marcham, *Sources of English Constitutional History*, pp. 321–323, 384–387. See also W. C. Richardson, *Tudor Chamber Administration 1485–1547* (1952).

other incidents were ended. After Charles II returned from exile in 1660 this abolition was confirmed by the Statute for the Abolition of Military Tenures.

Meanwhile Henry VIII strengthened and extended the power of the Council of the North and the Council of Wales. He temporarily added another regional council for efficiency's sake: the Council of the West (1540–1550). It is sometimes said or suggested that these councils, especially the Council of the North, were *ad hoc* creations of Henry VIII to meet the disturbances incident to the Reformation in England. This is simply not true. The regional conciliar remedies for distance and dislocation were older than Henry VIII and they were based upon very ancient practices in march organization and march law.[6]

THE PROBLEM OF USES

The Tudor sovereigns shared with their royal predecessors a strong and active dislike of the multiplication of equitable uses, those strange legal devices by which one party had a legal right to land while another had the use of it. The system of uses had two major advantages for those who had the use of land under the arrangement: (1) they obtained the use and profit of the land and escaped the responsibilities of ownership and (2) under common law it was impossible to will land and the use system provided a way in which an individual could determine who should have the use of his land after him.[7] These uses, as we have seen, often impaired the revenues of the Crown by making possible the evasion of such things as the feudal obligations of wardship and marriage. Henry VIII and his fellow monarchs could not, of course, foresee the contribution of the Chancellor's equitable jurisdiction to the emergence of the modern law of trusts. They were probably not very deeply concerned about the perversions and frauds visited by their subjects upon one another through the employment of the tortuous ways of use procedures. What they did know and what they did care about was that the operation of this very complicated branch of English property law deprived them of the incidents of tenure and similar incomes that once swelled the royal revenue. Should

---

[6] Some students may wish to read a superbly written article first published by Professor Gaillard Lapsley in 1900 under the title "The Problem of the North." This essay has recently been reprinted in *Crown, Community and Parliament in the Later Middle Ages* (1951).

[7] See W. S. Holdsworth, *History of English Law*, IV, pp. 449–473.

not the dues resulting from his feudal superiority be indeed the monarch's own?

In 1536 Parliament enacted a famous Statute of Uses under the watchful and guiding eyes and hands of an aroused Henry VIII. In the difficult task of framing the bill the king was aided by the lawyers and judges of the common law courts. These common law men were especially energetic in this business because they disliked their strong rival, the equally jealous Chancery court. To them the Statute of Uses seemed an excellent way of reducing the strength and dignity of Chancery. Henry VIII was also helped by the fact that many large landowners who had long supported the use arrangements so advantageous to them were either dead, dying, or enfeebled. The march of the royal prerogative following the Wars of the Roses put Henry VIII in a strong position to do what previous rulers lacked the power or the nerve to try. So it was that in 1536 Henry squarely confronted the problem and his Parliament passed the Statute of Uses.

The Statute of 1536 did not abolish uses or prevent the continuance of trusts of land. It said, first, that "divers and sundry imaginations, subtle inventions, and practices have been used whereby the hereditaments of this realm have been conveyed from one to another by fraudulent feoffments, fines, recoveries, and other assurances craftily made to secret uses." It said, second, that "the king's highness or any other of his subjects of this realm shall not in any wise hereafter . . . be deceived, damaged, or hurt by reason of such trusts, uses, or confidences." It said, third, that in nearly all future cases of use arrangements the seisin, or possession, of any legal estate of freehold would be vested in the beneficiary (*cestui qui use*). Before 1536 the man who held the legal title to some freehold land "to the use, trust, or confidence" of somebody else could be compelled by Chancery to carry out the exact terms of the arrangement. The person or persons who got the income from the land or who had the "beneficial interest" in it thus had to depend upon Chancery to protect and enforce their rights. After 1536 the individuals who used and profited from the "honours, castles, manors, lands, tenements, rents, services, reversions, remainders, or other hereditaments" would henceforth be judged the legal owners. Thus large numbers of uses were in fact turned into legal ownerships. The Statute of Uses meant, for instance, that if lands were being held in trust for a minor, that minor would henceforth have the legal estate in those lands.

The Crown found very satisfactory one immediate result of the operation of the Statute of Uses. After 1536 the beneficiaries of any feoffment, conveyance, or the like—now the legal owners of estates "to all intents, constructions, and purposes in the law"—were immediately subject to all the liabilities and disabilities of legal ownership. The king got his incidents of tenure and anything else he could lay his royal hands upon. The common law courts and lawyers had driven a lance into Chancery. Their business rapidly increased and they were probably not displeased.

The statute of 1536 in fact destroyed what had been a system of willing land. Let us suppose that the last will and testament of John Miller established a use arrangement with his brother as trustee and his minor son as beneficiary, the terms of the arrangement to take effect at the hour of John Miller's death. Before 1536, as was explained earlier, the brother would have held the estate in fee simple but Chancery would have compelled him to hold it for the benefit or use of the minor son. After 1536 the son would become immediately seised of the whole estate when his father died. The uncle would get and take nothing, even though the son had never been near the land. To repeat this important fact: after 1536 the son became the legal owner instead of a person having a beneficial interest enforceable in equity.

Earlier all uses declared in a feoffor's will had been scrupulously protected by Chancery. Now this method of devising lands was in large part wiped away by the Statute of Uses. In the opinion of Sir Francis Bacon and Sir Edward Coke the Statute of Uses "abolished all devises except those that would have been good at common law as conveyances." [8]

In 1540, before a mounting outcry against the Statute of Uses, Henry VIII and Parliament passed the Statute of Wills. This act permitted individuals to dispose by will of two-thirds of any lands held in military tenure and all lands held by socage tenure, provided that the Crown was adequately compensated for any loss of feudal income. A Statute of Enrollments, passed at the same time, declared that no sales of estates of freehold or inheritance would be held valid unless they were made in writing under seal and enrolled in a royal court of record. This statute was rather loosely drawn and was frequently evaded by men who did not want the records of their business operations immediately available for public scrutiny.

---

[8] For a detailed discussion of the Statute of Uses see F. Pollock, *The Land Laws*, pp. 97–106.

These statutes brought many interesting results in their train. Let us look first at the developments in a process called "lease and release." In the Middle Ages landlords had sometimes, for a price, given title to land to their tenants by the "lease and release" procedure. By this method a piece of freehold land was first leased to the tenant. Shortly after the tenant entered upon the land the landlord gave him a deed to it, completely releasing him from the lease or other responsibilities. When the Statute of Uses was passed this procedure of lease and entry and release was rendered unnecessary because, after 1536, the moment the tenant had obtained a formal lease his landlord was deemed to hold the land involved "to the use" of his tenant for the term of years specified in the lease. Under the provisions of the Statute of Uses these interests of the tenant vested in him completely and thus he had actual possession. It was then easily possible by a simple deed or grant for the landlord to release his full rights to the tenant provided that the tenant paid the landlord's asking price for the land thus disposed of.

The landlord's rights or "interest" consisted in the "return" of the property when the lease expired. This interest is called a "reversion." Therefore, when the landlord surrendered in a deed his "interest" or "freehold reversion" he was really giving up, for a price, all his rights and claims. Usually, in these arrangements, the lease was made for a year and the release was dated the day after. The Statute of Enrollments, it will be recalled, applied only to freehold interests. The tenant, in the device of "lease and release," had only a leasehold interest.

This rather confusing transfer device came to be the usual form of conveyance until 1841. Then it was provided that a simple statutory release would suffice without the formality of a bargain and the sale of a lease. At this point the student should perhaps be reminded that all lease estates had their origin in the personal writs of covenant (see Chapter VI). The action of covenant required a seal. Hence leases were required to be under seal if the lessees were to be able to possess any remedies in an action at law. The famous Statute of Frauds of 1677, designed to clarify the law of contracts, required all short-term leases (less than three years) to be in writing if they were to be enforceable in the courts. Formal deeds were required by the Real Property Act of 1845 and by the Law of Property Acts of 1922 and 1925.

The reader knows that many judges and lawyers in Chancery were interested in the welfare of their own tribunal and opposed to the common law courts. It was now their task to break or slip out of the bonds placed upon them by the Statute of Uses and some of the subsequent pieces of legislation. The student may be helped towards an understanding of the nature of the changes effected by the muttering men of Chancery if a few specific illustrations are given of their intense activities as they tried to find or make holes in the Statute of Uses.

If this were a book mainly concerned with the development of property law it would be possible to handle and elaborate upon many topics in that vast land. For our purposes the important question must be this: What could the landed families and their Chancery lawyers do beyond what they had been able to achieve in the fifteenth century? To their undoubted delight they found that they were able to do a very great deal indeed.

Despite the strong assertions of the common law lawyers the Statute of Uses did not in fact entirely abolish uses—fortunately for the modern law of trusts. It soon became obvious that there were several cases that the Statute of Uses did not cover at all. This discovery gave the Chancery lawyers their opportunity to rally and fight once more. So it was that the long battle about perpetuities entered a new phase.

There now arose an extension of a system that came to be called "springing uses." It required only a simple procedure to create a "springing" use once the idea occurred to some fertile minds three hundred years ago. The basic pattern was this: (1) let a use be created in a freehold estate—this estate at the beginning must have no remainders carrying future interests—to take effect in the future; (2) the use is to take effect when, and only when, a specified heir is born *provided that* upon reaching the age of twenty-one that heir holds the land as a use for his heir, and so on.

In this system, one use obviously sprang out of another and hence the descriptive words "springing uses" fit the events effectively. Once a seisin was conferred upon the original grantee (the seisinee to uses) of an estate in freehold to take effect in the future the succeeding steps were inevitable because a second use automatically sprang from the first, a third from the second, a fourth from the third. Let us say, for instance, that a grant is made to Smith for the use of Smith's son when the latter becomes twenty-one years old. Under the terms of the original grant, when Smith's son does become twenty-one he has the use of the land until his son, in turn, becomes of age, and so on. There were, of course, several kinds of springing uses, but the one described here is the most common form.

All of this may seem very complicated to the reader. Still more technical was a system called "shifting uses." The basic idea was this: it is possible to limit an estate in fee simple through the long future by deciding upon and stating certain future events that alone would alter the passage of land from son to son. For instance, a grant might be made to Harding and his heirs to the use of Brown and his heirs but if any Brown should ever marry one of the Miller family then the land should go to the use of Bateman and his heirs. So long as no Brown married a Miller then the Browns would have the estate in fee simple. But if one day a Brown did marry a Miller then the Batemans would take the legal estate in fee simple and the Browns would have nothing.

It is perhaps fortunate that students in law schools today seldom find it necessary to labor with problems of "uses upon uses." The long fear of perpetuities on the part of the Crown and the common law judges resulted in resistance to the executory limitations of springing and shifting uses and other like devices. Late in the Tudor age the common law courts said that if a future limitation (the "when Smith's son becomes twenty-one" kind of limitation) could be construed by a court as a legally destructible remainder then it must be considered as being one. Some common law judges also said that the same kind of rule (thus providing for the destruction of shifting and springing uses) should be applied to all future interests.

When the common law courts tried to make future interests destructible then Chancery began to give relief in equity. The Chancery court, for a time, was victorious when it ruled that indestructible future interests could be created by wills or conveyances (executory devises). Meanwhile, too, transactions called trusts, similar to the older uses, began to appear and multiply in the seventeenth century. The modern classification of trust principles is still Lord Chancellor Nottingham's famous decision in Cook v. Fountain in 1676.

In 1682 Nottingham laid down the rule that an executory devise, such as a will, starting a springing use chain of future interests was not valid unless the date at which those interests would vest (be ended, determined, become destructible) was not too far in the future. In 1832 the courts held that no estate could be inalienable for longer than twenty-one years plus a life. The modern rule against perpetuities also prohibits the creation of any contingent interest for a period longer than twenty-one years plus a life. The reader will see how similar this provision is to the ninety-nine year limits in various phases of the laws of the United States.

In Great Britain there continued to be pressure to keep the large estates intact. This has often been accomplished by a complicated process called "the strict family settlement" by which the father holds the family lands in a trust. Primogeniture is not yet destroyed in England. Nor are the great estates entirely wiped away, despite the heavy succession duties and recent pieces of legislation. One of these new laws, for instance, has changed the law of intestacy. That law provides that if a person dies intestate his real property shall be divided in the same way as his personal property: equally among his heirs. As will be explained later, the Property Acts of 1925 effected a considerable tidying up of the litter of several centuries.

A SUMMING-UP

In January, 1547, Henry VIII died. Men still debate about Henry's political genius and monstrous iniquity. For good or ill the actions of the second Tudor were always on a grand scale. Whatever may be said about his morals and his sins, the fact still stands that Henry VIII consolidated the Tudor power and strengthened England as a nation state.

Henry VIII's heir was a little boy. The shocks and upheavals that followed the death of Henry are themselves evidence of his force and his power. Many of these events have only a fleeting and fragmentary effect on English constitutional and legal developments and we need not deal with them here. Others are mainly political passages, likewise of minor consequence for our purposes in this book. Still other events are inert things, of significance to those men who shaped or participated or died in them, but of no consequence in the long growth of England.

In this chapter about the early Tudors we have not been concerned with the dramatic aspects of the remarkable events of the reigns of Henry VII and Henry VIII. These are ably discussed in several texts easily available to the student. Our major business has been with something else: what happened in the first part of the sixteenth century that was most significant and most permanent in the legal and constitutional history of England? Briefly stated, we noted these things: (1) a strong and determined monarchy, with able servants in courts and councils, helped England towards the coherence and power of a modern state; (2) the royal prerogative was stretched and massaged to become at once more supple and stronger than it had been for centuries; (3) the unique qualities of the "popular despotism" contributed to a peculiar and delicate harmony of spirit that anticipated the age of Elizabeth I; (4) peace, security, and reasonable prosperity replaced the giddy years of the previous century; (5) in a body of legislation of massive importance the nation's church was given a new head: the Crown; (6) the lawyers of England, with their usual skill and ingenuity, wrote some significant chapters in property law, especially after the passage of the Statute of Uses in 1536.

Not all of the achievements of these years are to be counted on the credit side of the ledger of Englishmen. Many tales of human affairs make a history of crimes and follies. Nevertheless, in all ages, as in our own, there are places where we can rightly say that we can see mankind inching forward. When Henry VIII died it seemed that England might suffer a relapse into the fever of the Wars of the Roses. There were several years of national imbalance under Edward VI (1547–1553) and Mary (1553–1558). Englishmen—and they were not alone—disputed and fought about roads to salvation. In 1539 the Statute of the Six Articles had carried the brief title: "An act abolishing diversity of opinions." But even Henry VIII was not able to abolish diversity of opinions in his realm. Nor was Edward VI, or Mary, or Elizabeth I, or any monarch or legislature on earth. Indeed, one characteristic of the sixteenth century was that it fitted men more and more completely with heresies and orthodoxies.

CHAPTER XIII

Elizabeth the First:
the Vital balance

ROADS TO SALVATION

THE iron hand of Henry VIII had held many forces in control. Now England felt the grip of that hand no more. Edward VI was a lad only nine years old in 1547 and his kingdom was badly governed by a regency of sixteen men. Englishmen soon saw the flames of rebellion licking at the foundations of the state. Through court and castle spread the slow poison of intrigue. Within the council of regency were knots of men divided by doctrinal hatreds, by jealousies, by conflicting interests. The Duke of Somerset was Lord Protector and head of the council. Only a strong man could have curbed the conspiracies of councillors greedy for profit and power. Somerset was not strong. He was plagued by doubts. He vacillated. To be weak invited disaster.

With the approval of Edward VI Somerset proceeded to secure the passage of laws pointing towards Protestantism. The Six Articles Act of Henry VIII's reign was repealed. Various enactments against heresy were wiped away. Protestant preachers came in from the Continent to explain their reformed religions. In 1549 the First Act of Uniformity ordered a new Prayer Book to be used in all churches. This book contained the beautiful liturgy prepared by Thomas Cranmer. The Prayer Book and ritual stood as a compromise between the extremes of both Protestantism and Roman Catholicism. All who did not like compromise, evasion and obscurity protested, often with violence. The Second Statute of Uniformity (1552) did little to placate the Roman Catholics because it moved England, so far as law could do it, closer to Protestantism. It altered the services again. It abandoned five sacraments. It denied transubstantiation. It asserted the doctrine of justification by faith.

280

Meanwhile Somerset and his pro-Protestant oligarchy proceeded to carry further the confiscation of church property. Council members, eager for plunder, "gorged themselves with manors." Priceless treasures of medieval art were knocked down, torn, or burned. The desecration and the excesses of Protestant mobs alienated many who had hitherto been lukewarm. Squabbles and skirmishes multiplied.

During these tragic years there occurred a profound economic disturbance. World markets and trade routes were being changed. Trade centers were shifting. The medieval structure of industry was everywhere weakened. The gold and silver from the New World caused the value of currency to depreciate. Commodity prices inevitably rose. Wage disturbances grew worse. At the same time the hardships of rural England were increased by the enclosure by great landlords of many open fields and much common land to provide broad ranges for sheep and to grow wheat. Almost everywhere there was robbery, pressure and fraud.

Somerset fell from power and was executed as a result of the plots and power of the self-seeking and dishonest Duke of Northumberland. When Edward VI died, Northumberland tried to place Lady Jane Grey upon the throne. He failed in his scheme and went to his death on the scaffold. Mary, the daughter of Henry VIII and Catherine of Aragon, now ascended the throne as the rightful queen. In the confusion of Edward VI's reign there had been no chapters of importance in legal and constitutional history.

Nor were there to be any significant developments when Mary ruled. Before she came to the throne her life had been one of neglect and humiliation. Despite the fact that she was only thirty-seven years old, Mary was a worn and bitter woman in 1553. Her spirit was harsh and warped by brooding over her mother's religion and her mother's wrongs. She was unattractive and obstinate. She was determined to bring Englishmen back to Roman Catholicism. It had been her refuge and her consolation. To her it was the true way, the only way that could save the souls of her people. Her attachment to the church of Rome was honest and passionate.

Mary took swift steps. The leading Protestant bishops were deprived of their sees. Several were imprisoned and some were burned at the stakes of Smithfield. Roman Catholics were placed in positions of power. Mary's first Parliament passed the First Statute of Repeal in 1553. The act restored Catholic doctrine and service as they had stood at the end of the reign of Henry VIII. The members of this Parliament, however, refused to overthrow the Act of Supremacy and to restore papal authority.

At this point Mary alarmed England by marrying Philip II, king of Spain. Popular fears whispered that England might become a Spanish province. There were three rebellions. A second Parliament refused to repeal the Act of Supremacy. A third Parliament, carefully packed, did repeal the Act of Supremacy (1555) after obtaining assurance that the Pope would not insist upon the return of church lands. The old heresy acts were revived and the burning and persecution of heretics continued and increased.

These steps did not weaken Protestantism. Many Englishmen were alienated from the queen's beloved church. To Mary it was a tragedy. So, too, was her unhappy marriage to Philip II of Spain and her loss of Calais in a conflict with France. The life of Mary Tudor, who was not ignoble, was a dark and bitter tale.

Mary's last enemy was a tumor. In November, 1558, the unfortunate queen was asked by her council to recognize as her successor Elizabeth, daughter of Henry VIII and Anne Boleyn. Mary did so, requesting pathetically that Elizabeth retain the Roman Catholic religion. Would this daughter of Anne Boleyn undo and ruin all of Mary's work? Would Elizabeth solve the problems of a new age? Would the third and last of Henry VIII's children succeed where the other two had failed?

The years of Edward VI and Mary contributed but little of permanent value to the English law and constitution. We now approach the reign of Elizabeth I. The harvest is better there.

ELIZABETH I AND THE CHURCH OF ENGLAND

Elizabeth I ascended the throne in 1558 according to the provisions of Henry VIII's will and by virtue of good fortune. Her early life had been filled with intrigue and dangers. In Mary's reign Elizabeth had been close to execution. The hard school of experience had made her wise, subtle, sceptical, a queen with a peculiar political genius. Above all, her nature was essentially cautious and practical. She was well aware of what she could and could not do. Like her father before her, she craved power; and she knew that power rested upon popular approval. Subtle but irresistible shifts in the balance of economic and political strength were slowly leaving the monarchy with its rights in theory intact but without the resources to put the theory into full practice unless the responsible part of the people approved. If there was to be any absolutism it was to be absolutism by consent.

The popularity won for the Tudors by Henry VIII had been largely dissipated in the reigns of Edward VI and Mary. When Elizabeth I came to the throne the nation supported her because the alternative was civil war. Most men saw the evils that would result if the nation should again be violently divided upon the question of religion. England's prestige abroad had fallen. Misgovernment had produced discontent. Economic dislocation had pressed heavily on the poorer classes.

Tactful and shrewd, with increasing knowledge of men and affairs, Elizabeth I paid careful heed to public opinion and often helped to create the kind of opinion she wanted. It had been the habit of Henry VIII to stoop to conquer. It was also the habit of his daughter. As her reign progressed, Elizabeth I became a symbol for the nation. Throughout the forty-five years of her reign Elizabeth never lost sight of the fact that man is a political and patriotic animal. The words of her speeches to Parliament rolled over England. "And though you have had, and may have many princes more mighty and wise sitting in this state, yet you never had, or shall have, any that will be more careful and loving."

Elizabeth I worked hard. She might be capricious, petulant and vain, but these qualities had small place in state affairs. Politics was a hard and ruthless business. The tools of a successful monarch must be temperance, caution, good sense, a calm and critical intelligence. Most of these abilities Elizabeth showed when there was need for them. In all her great affairs she was aided, like her father and grandfather, by the fact that she was able to gather about her council table a group of able men. Such a queen and such councillors heralded a new order in the making of modern England.

In dealing with the vital question of religion Elizabeth moved circumspectly. The Roman Catholics waited and hoped. In the first public document of the new reign an "et cetera" was placed at the end of the royal titles where Henry VIII and Edward VI had written "Supreme Head of the Church." At first Elizabeth attended mass, maintained her ambassador at Rome, refused to permit changes in the service. The new queen wanted to avoid the hostility of Rome until her hold upon the throne was reasonably secure and Englishmen had become accustomed to her authority. Mary, Queen of Scots, great granddaughter of Henry VII, was a dangerous Roman Catholic candidate for the English throne. Her husband was the French king, Francis II. France backed Mary's claim and French power in Scotland was strong. If Pope Paul IV declared his opposition to Elizabeth I there would be trouble with the Roman Catholics in England and there might be war with France and Scotland. Elizabeth was fighting for time and she fought with consummate skill.

England's astute queen made haste slowly. Many Protestants who had fled to Europe during Mary's reign were allowed to return. When Parliament assembled in January, 1559, the council placed before the members a series of measures designed to establish the English church on a broad middle ground of doctrine and practice. The new state faith was to be a fiat religion, to which all must publicly conform.

The Marian laws that had brought England back into the Roman fold were repealed. The Second Act of Supremacy (1559) revived the acts of Henry VIII that had brought about the separation of the English church from Rome. This act also abolished once again the papal power in England. All church and state officials were required to take an oath that the queen was "the only supreme governor of this realm . . . as well in all spiritual or ecclesiastical things or causes as temporal." They were further required to deny the spiritual jurisdiction of any "foreign prince, person, prelate, state, or potentate" and to "utterly renounce and forsake all foreign jurisdictions, powers, superiorities and authorities." Persons refusing to take this oath were debarred from all church and state offices.

The famous compromise settlement had other important chapters. An Act of Uniformity of 1559 imposed uniformity of religious service under penalties. It enjoined the use of the Prayer Book of Edward VI (1552) in all churches. Alterations were made to provide a form of service acceptable to as many Englishmen as possible. Doctrinally much scope was left for varying shades of belief. Precise doctrinal definition was carefully avoided. The Prayer Book was a masterpiece of ambiguity where ambiguity seemed necessary. Roman Catholic and Protestant doctrines were merged together in a chameleon communion service that could mean different things to different individuals. The completely contradictory words of Zwingli, the Swiss Protestant reformer, and the mass book on the sacrament were neatly compressed into one sentence.

Conciliation was the pivot of Elizabeth's whole ecclesiastical policy in the early years of her reign. Later, in 1571, the Thirty-Nine Articles stated the final doctrines of the Church of England. This revision purged the Forty-two Articles of Edward VI of their extreme Protestant elements. The Thirty-Nine Articles kept the traditional Catholic element in the faith of the Church of England and at the same time stressed the areas of kinship with the teachings of the Protestant Reformation. Elizabeth and her advisers also made certain that the continuity of the Anglican Church was protected by an unbroken line of bishops in the apostolic succession.

Elizabeth I and her advisers wanted to preserve a convenient peace in the church. They did not want to set England agog with spiritual excitement, always social dynamite, an enemy to concord. They hoped that their compromise settlement, tempered later by successive doses of toleration, would meet the wishes of a majority of Elizabeth's subjects. To "open windows into men's souls" was not their intention. They demanded only external conformity. They did not insist upon unity of hearts or convictions. Few governments were less swayed by purely religious motives.

Both Roman Catholics and the Puritans—demanding further Protestant reforms—opposed the Anglican compromise. The result was a famous series of attacks, plots and pamphlets. Elizabeth's government passed several repressive acts against "seditious sectaries" and other disloyal persons. In 1571 Parliament altered the laws of treason and prohibited bulls from Rome. This law was passed in reply to Pius V's bull of 1570 declaring Elizabeth a usurper and freeing her subjects from their allegiance. In 1593 Parliament passed an "act against Papists." Offensives occurred on several fronts. When Mary, Queen of Scots, fled from Scotland to safety in Elizabeth's realm she became the center of several Roman Catholic plots. In 1587 she was executed. Philip II of Spain sent a mighty armada against England in 1588. That great fleet was defeated by the guns of England's seadogs and the winds of the narrow seas. When the Puritans preached and protested too vehemently Parliament passed "an act to retain the queen's subjects in obedience" (1593) providing for the imprisonment of all offenders until they should conform. Many Puritans found themselves the victims of the Court of High Commission. Some were put to death. Some fled overseas. Others remained in England to prepare a formidable challenge for the successors of Elizabeth I. In the sixteenth and seventeenth centuries the vitality of the embattled forces of religion can be seen on every hand. The terrible wars of religion bear testimony to the fact that ideas about the nature of God and the destiny of man were among the most potent forces in the world.

All sorts and conditions of men were affected by the Elizabethan settlement. This famous compromise has never been undone or warped. The Church of England and the Episcopal Church of the United States have not departed from the basic tenets of the Thirty-Nine Articles. Nor is it an accident that in the Order For Morning Prayer it is stated that "the last two Collects shall never alter." The one Collect is for Peace and the other is for Grace. To the clergy of the sixteenth century Peace and Grace were consummations devoutly to be wished.

When we turn our eyes from the problems of church and state we find that the Tudor currents of change are everywhere strong and continuous. One salient aspect of change in the growth of the constitution is to be seen in the remarkable alteration in the royal council. Let us look now at what happened to that important part of government when Elizabeth I was queen.

CROWN AND COUNCIL

Henry VII, the first architect of the Tudor system, made his dynasty and his government secure by using any tools he could find. The result, as we have seen, was a curious amalgam of the medieval and the modern. Henry wanted efficient and inexpensive government. To gain his ends, he twisted and stretched the law. He hurried the decay of the feudal aristocracy but he revived the feudal revenues to reduce his need for asking Parliament for money. He built a vigorous civil service to help him collect revenue and keep order. He left a full treasury to Henry VIII. Henry VII, first of the Tudors, was richest of them all. When he died in 1509 the government was strong and centralized.

And yet the so-called absolutism of Henry VII and all the Tudors was hedged in by the conditions we have noted: the common law, with its long memory; the ancient rights of Parliament, so carefully guarded; the lack of royal machinery in the shires to make the Crown's will effective if the local gentry stood opposed to it; the lack of sufficient non-Parliamentary income to carry on government adequately—the shortage of hard cash. The absolutism of the Tudors was limited absolutism.

Henry VIII spent the capital his father had left him and seized, by what was really an act of state, the capital of the church. His ally in the mass operation was Parliament and Parliament always, in the end, obtained its price: a greater share in government. Before Henry VIII died, and while Edward VI and Mary lived, a great wave of inflation swept over Europe. The confiscated wealth of the church went in the same way as the hoards of Henry VII. When Elizabeth I came to the throne her state was divided; it was threatened by invasion from abroad; and it was bankrupt.

Because these things were so it is not surprising that the shrewd Elizabeth I dealt with the problem of the church as she did. Nor is it surprising that she relied, more and more, upon the hard and efficient members of her council as the principal instruments of her policy. Both the composition and the functions of the council depended upon the royal will and the royal strength. Elizabeth I had plenty of both. Like her father before her Elizabeth used her council regularly in the details of administration and in settling major policy problems. Policy had always, or nearly always, been made in the council. Elizabeth's reign is the last blaze of council power. Soon policy is to be made in Parliament and in Parliament alone.

Henry VIII usually had about 16 individuals in his council. Under Edward VI there were 12 to 16. Under Mary there were approximately 40 and under Elizabeth I from 12 to 18. The monarch in Parliament was of course the main authority in the state. But Parliaments came and went. "The council was always in being, always at work, always vigilant and active."

In the Tudor age the term "privy council" was used very frequently to describe the part of the council that was in regular attendance upon the monarch and usually busy with problems of administration, legislation, taxation and the like. In 1526 the regulations for the council of Henry VIII stated that in order to have matters of justice and complaints and "other great occasions . . . the better ordered and with his grace more rapidly debated, digested, and resolved from time to time . . . it is ordered and appointed by his highness that a good number of honourable, virtuous, sad, wise, expert, and discreet persons of his council shall give their attendance upon his most royal person, whose names hereafter follow. . . ." There were thus two rings of councillors. Some were in the Privy Council and some were not.

Most of the judicial business was in the hands of the council members and others who sat in the prerogative courts like Star Chamber, Requests, Wards and Liveries and High Commission. In these years, of course, the functions of all parts of the council were steadily broadened. There were problems concerned with public order, foreign affairs, defense, local government, and so on. Meanwhile, too, the committee system became highly developed. Committees are always important cogs in the machinery of successful government.

A glance at the Privy Council records for this period will show a broad range of activities. For instance, the members of the Privy Council bombarded Lord Wharton with inquiries as to what damage was done by the raids of the Scots. They asked the lord warden of the Cinque Ports to see to it that Sir John Baker was a knight of the shire in the next Parliament—later they advised the sheriff of Kent to "use things in such sort as the shire may have free election." They investigated clothiers' prices, the coal industry in Newcastle. They allowed Thomas Galiard "to transport beyond the seas 200,000 pairs of old shoes."

The letters of council and the committees of council to the sheriffs, the lords lieutenant and the justices of the peace would fill many volumes. They asked for reports and they issued instructions. They wanted to know if Agnes Mondaye practiced witchcraft. Two men were accused of robbing a widow and the council members authorized the lieutenant of the Tower of London to use the rack "for the better bolting out of the truth of this matter." The council called John Hawkins through the judges of the Admiralty to explain why he was fitting out a ship to go into Spanish trading areas. They wanted to know why the people of Maidenhead had not pursued a thief through the thickets after hue and cry had been raised. They sent a letter to the vice-Chancellors of Oxford and Cambridge forbidding plays or interludes within five miles of the universities because such public performances might poison "the fountains from which learning and education doth flow." [1]

The Lord Chancellor and the Lord Keeper of the Great Seal were equal in rank, the senior officers of the council. The chief of state finance was the Lord Treasurer. The other important members were the Lord Privy Seal, the Lord President of the Privy Council, and the King's Secretary, soon to be called the Secretary of State. The Secretary was increasingly important as an officer of the realm. It is from his office that all the modern officials bearing that title today in the United Kingdom and the Commonwealth are descended. In the sixteenth century the Secretary was usually the chief minister of the Crown. It was inevitable that men of subtle intellects and resolute wills like Thomas Cromwell, Francis Walsingham, and William Cecil (Lord Burghley) should have expanded the scope and strength of their office. They were professional administrators, loyal servants of the monarch and the

---

[1] For further illustrations of the multifarious activities of the council in every part of the governmental system see Carl Stephenson and F. G. Marcham, *Sources of English Constitutional History*, pp. 331–336, 376–383.

state. The volume of business was so heavy that after 1539 there usually were two principal Secretaries appointed. Slowly the processes and structure of government and administration were beginning to resemble those of the modern state.

The members of the council were also members of the House of Lords or the House of Commons. They were thus able to exert much influence in both houses. Later in this chapter some further comments will be made about the degree and extent of the power of the council in the House of Commons. It is also important to stress a second fact: the original power of the king's council to make or "discover" laws had never been lost or surrendered and there was a marked increase in royal proclamations (the forerunners of the modern Orders-in-Council) in the Tudor age. This extension of government by council did not meet with strong opposition when the Tudors ruled. After the Stuarts came the facts were otherwise.

In the twentieth century the procedure of Orders-in-Council (for which the Cabinet is today responsible) is not frequently used in the United Kingdom or the other realms of the Commonwealth except in national emergencies. When a state of war exists, for instance, speed is imperative. The need is met by the executive power of the Crown in council. The council can move more rapidly than Parliament and move rapidly it does. An enemy state, for example, will find all of its assets and those of its nationals in a British state blocked and controlled by the Custodian of Enemy Property almost immediately upon the outbreak of war. The police and intelligence agents and the economic warfare divisions begin at once to take an official interest in the suspect and watch lists. Those engaged in trading with the enemy are hunted and bagged. In the early stages of hostilities much of this is made possible by the swift decisions of the council. So far has it travelled since the eleventh century.

CROWN AND PARLIAMENT

In the Middle Ages kings considered that they possessed their kingdoms as hereditary overlords. Henry I's writs, for instance, spoke of his realm as though it were a feudal honor. The sovereign was always "dominus" as well as "rex." A medieval monarch usually looked upon himself as being personally responsible for the government of the state and officials of the royal administration as being answerable to him alone. Always, of course, the authority of medieval kings was curbed by the sovereignty of law and history. Here was the ark of the medieval constitutional covenant. The monarch who ignored the sanctions of legality did so at his peril. The king must govern responsibly.

When the barons agreed with the king on policy, all went well. When they did not, all went badly. If the barons could not get along with the king they could not get along without him. The recurrent crises of 1215, 1233, 1258, and 1297 showed how baronial reform movements degenerated. It was fortunate that Parliament slowly emerged as an institution and the representative principle was introduced. Then checks were provided upon royal power on the one hand and tendencies to baronial anarchy on the other. As the conception and the structure of the state gradually became less feudal and more national, a broadly based Parliament grew in power, bringing into focus the unity of the kingdom in king, lords and commons. The many in Parliament were soon to be more important than the aristocratic few in the king's council.

We find ourselves in the midst of a remarkable transition in constitutional history during the Tudor age. The trends evident in the reign of Henry VIII continued during the rule of Elizabeth I. To them are added new turnings that suggest, quite forcibly, the beginning of new problems of government. One of those problems was to arise in the next century as the result of varying ideas about the place of Parliament, the power of the king, and the freedom of the subject. Many Englishmen have agreed with the English philosopher T. H. Green that "the term of freedom should not be used to express anything but a social and political relation of one man to other men."

The long evolution of Parliament must always be seen in perspective. Sometimes ideas fade and institutions rot and crumble. Always they alter, for good or ill. There is nothing made by man that is immutable. Continuity and change are the twin "laws" of history.

For the House of Commons the reign of Elizabeth was a period of assimilation and of apprenticeship. When the men of Parliament debated and fought the Stuarts and Royalists in the next century they did not battle without basic training in procedure and principles, strategy and tactics. Students of constitutional history are usually requested by professors to read Professor Wallace Notestein's *The Winning of the Initiative by the House of Commons*. In this deservedly famous essay Professor Notestein has explained how the House of Commons, growing to maturity, slowly grasped new reins of power in the early seventeenth century. The Commons were able to do this, as Professor J. E. Neale and others have shown, because their level of competence rose very appreciably under Elizabeth I, the last and greatest of the Tudors. The tale of this unwitting increase of ability and power is told in a rich harvest of records: in the journals and rough notes of the Clerk of the Commons, in diaries, in letters and pamphlets.[2]

The greatest Parliamentarian of the reign was the queen herself. "Sure she did play well her tables," wrote Sir John Harington, "to gain obedience thus without constraint." Elizabeth I was well aware of the greatness of her position as the keystone of the arch of government. She was also aware that the House of Commons "out of a reverent regard" would be unwilling to pursue policies and adopt attitudes "offending the Queen's Majesty very much." If, as happened on occasion, they meddled with matters of state or ventured to discuss the prerogative, Elizabeth, as a contemporary remarked, "left no doubting whose daughter she was." Sometimes, too, the House of Commons itself took stern measures against members who seemed to speak out of turn. For instance, when Peter Wentworth began a famous speech in 1576 and remarked that "None is without fault, no not even our noble Queen," the Commons stopped him and sent him to the Tower, his speech unfinished. It was a consequence he had foreseen: "My own fearful conceit did say unto me that this speech would carry me unto the place whither I now shall go."

When Parliament met in 1563 the Commons gathered in the shadow of a great anxiety. Elizabeth had fallen ill of the smallpox and a fear swept over England that with the death of Elizabeth the years of Tudor quiet and surety would be ended by a long struggle for a throne to which there were no Tudor heirs. The House of Commons at once petitioned the queen to marry. About the question a large pamphlet literature arose.

To petitions and pamphlets the queen had one answer: "It is unfitting and unmeet for you to require them that may command . . . or to frame my will to your fantasy." In the Parliament of 1571 the queen announced to the Commons her high displeasure with "those audacious, arrogant and presumptuous men, who, contrary to their

---

[2] Professor Notestein's essay is published in *Proceedings of the British Academy*, 1924. See also J. E. Neale, *Elizabeth I and Her Parliaments 1559–1581* (1953). Several relevant documents about proceedings in Parliament are in Carl Stephenson and F. G. Marcham, *Sources of English Constitutional History*, pp. 358–375.

duty and place that they be called unto, . . . are concerned with matters neither pertaining to them, nor within the capacity of their understanding."

Students should never be persuaded to believe that no opposition to the queen ever appeared. It is true that there were no ugly or sustained quarrels. Nevertheless, on such questions as religion, Elizabeth's marriage, the succession to the throne and the grants of monopolies there were sharp divisions of opinion. A small, vocal and radical group did utter arguments opposed to those of Elizabeth I. Some of these men went to prison. Despite this fact, they did speak, and what they said had its important effect. It must not be concluded that the battles between the Stuarts and Parliament blew up suddenly out of a vacuum. In human affairs such things do not happen.

It is very easy, and very dangerous, to confine oneself to quoting Richard Hooker and other doughty champions of the harmonious and decently reasonable middle way dedicated to the principle of law and degree and duty. The fact is that the close and continued study and admiration of the blazing age of Elizabeth has made inevitable the discovery of numerous contrasts between the rule of the Tudors and the Stuarts. These contrasts have been so frequently made and multiplied that the shaping spirit of the historian's imagination threatens at once to create and to destroy: to create a Tudor Utopia that never existed; to destroy, in part at least, our ability to sense the temper of the last decades of the sixteenth century. Obvious and vexatious abuses had their places in the Tudor strong monarchy. A study of the literature of complaint in sixteenth-century England casts some shadows over the familiar picture of a nation filled with harmony and peace and founded in power and stability. The whirlwind that the Stuarts could not ride was not entirely of their own making. Not too much should be made of the conclusions of the Whig historians.

Nevertheless, Tudor rulers like Henry VIII and Elizabeth I were usually able to curb and to control, always using their own methods. In 1592 the Lord Keeper spoke to the Commons in the name of the queen: "For liberty of speech her majesty commandeth me to tell you, that to say yea or nay to bills, God forbid that any man should be restrained or afraid to answer according to his best liking, with some short declaration of his reason therein, and therein to have a free voice, which is the very true liberty of the House, not as some suppose to speak there of all causes as him listeth, and to frame a form of religion, or a state of government as to their idle brains shall seem meetest. She sayeth no king, fit for his state, will suffer such absurdities."

It is also an illuminating comment on Tudor statecraft to say that Elizabeth I's reproofs to Parliament were usually mingled with conciliation. Part of a subsidy might be remitted or monopolies cancelled. Often the Commons were soothed by sentences that made them for the moment forget the royal reprimand. "I will never . . . conclude anything that shall be prejudicial to the realm." "Far above all earthly treasures, I esteem my people's love." The banner of harmony cannot be pulled down in the midst of royal words like these. It was not easy to forget the words of Elizabeth I in Parliament, in council, or before her Englishmen at Tilbury in an hour when the Spanish Armada was sweeping towards her land and theirs.

The interests of Elizabeth I were served, as we have seen, by an able and devoted group of councillors in the House of Commons. Their influence carried much weight. They were able always to guide and frequently to dictate the policies and attitudes of the House. The canny Cecils "sate near the chair," together with Sir Francis Walsingham who thought "the proper position of Parliament was to secure the interests of the Crown." Sir Francis Bacon also had his place, secure until later in the possession of honor and power.

To the direct and skillful intervention of the queen's prerogative and the pervasive influence of the council may be added the importance of the Speaker of the House of Commons. His position and prestige assisted further in preventing the growth of a strongly organized opposition to the Crown. He was always nominated by the council. He was indeed an important link between the queen and her Parliament. It was he who recognized those who desired to speak from the floor of the House. He determined the course of business and what subjects were to be discussed.

From these brief suggestions of influence and prerogative in the House of Commons it will be concluded that there was no perceptible increase in the authority of the lower house during the reign of Elizabeth I. There was neither increase in authority nor any change in form. The stirrings that occurred were developments in a manner certainly unintended, and perhaps unobserved, by the queen and her council. Two things happened. In the first place, there was a distinct growth of self-consciousness, the self-consciousness of a corporate body. Secondly, there was an increase of enthusiasm and interest sharpened by experience in Parliamentary procedure and practice. There was no idea of constitutional advantage in the movements of the House of Commons during the reign of Elizabeth. And yet heightened interest and increased experience prepared the way for a generation of men who knew not fear of the royal prerogative and were not coerced by the dread of a sovereign's wrath.

The numerous ferments and agitations that marked the coming of the Renaissance to England were concomitant with an increased interest in political affairs. Professor R. H. Tawney, Professor Conyers Read and others have taught us that a new upper middle class had arisen. The younger members of this expanding gentry group had gained at the universities more than an education in the classics. By association with other students of this upper middle class they had become aware of a feeling of unity and understanding and sympathy. With this class-consciousness fully awakened young men turned to literature, to religion and to politics. The sense of unity filtered beyond the immediate circles of university students and graduates to become, in this powerful middle class, a significant force in thought and action throughout the nation. No longer was attendance at the House of Commons a duty—it became a privilege. The gentry, the country gentlemen, not only represented the counties but many boroughs as well. Prominent and able men, leading lawyers and merchants, were often keen to serve without demand or hope for payment.

When young men of the middle class went to Parliament they felt themselves bound to many of their fellows by friendship, common experience at the universities, social or family connections and the possession of wealth. Many diligent justices of the peace took to Westminster their "private and local wisdom." Men who had little experience in state questions, whose sole connection with London had been through the medium of occasional letters, sought eagerly the "coyners of news" and the opinions, experiences and prejudices of the other members of the House of Commons. Thus it was that a slow change in the composition of the lower chamber of Parliament brought a new interest, a deep enthusiasm, and an earnest desire for experience in politics and statecraft. In 1601 Sir Robert Cecil was "glad to see the Parliament so full, which towards the end used to grow thin." It is also important to note that many members were returned for several Parliaments. In 1566, for instance, there were few new representatives and the House was proud to declare that it met as a body with the experience of a session behind it.

Members often came to the Commons eager to participate in debate, to deliver speeches carefully prepared and to circulate manuscript copies among their friends. The larger number of members strove to speak "modestly and wisely and truly," in a manner worthy of themselves and of the approbation of the House. The queen and the councillors commanded and suggested and trained the members in the methods of debate and the procedures of legislation. Professor A. V. Dicey once said: "Our parliamentary procedure is nothing but a mass of conventional law."

Before each session the warning of the queen was presented to the House. She disliked "Contentious Reasonings and Disputations, and all sophistical, captious, and frivolous arguments . . . , utter Enemies to all Concord and Unity, the very marks that you are now to shoot at." Councillors who sat in the House of Commons were always ready to check those whom they found "fit to be bridled" and the lesson of a rebuke from the lips of a Bacon or a Cecil was not soon forgotten. It was meet and fit that gravity, judgment, and decorum should characterize the great business of a court of Parliament.

With increasing care and courtesy in debate there were formulated in the House of Commons new modes of procedure and practice. The committee system, for instance, was still further developed and expanded. Such calculated changes were accompanied by a heightened watchfulness to safeguard precedent and privilege through the preparation of parliamentary journals. These journals were to be of high importance under the Stuarts in the consolidation of many new or disputed powers.

Most of those who came as representatives to Westminster shared with all England a devotion to the person of Elizabeth I. So well did Elizabeth understand the temper of the House, so carefully were her speeches phrased and her policies exhibited, that there seldom prevailed, despite the radical voices of a few men, anything other than confidence between the queen and the people. Thus it was that Peter Wentworth, though he spoke with the accents of the great Puritan constitutionalists of the next century, found his temper and untamable tongue greeted with amazement rather than understanding and sympathy by most members of the Commons. With the death of Elizabeth I the old idea of the extent and character of the prerogative vanished. The unkingly James Stuart could command neither the affection nor the loyalty of a people accustomed to Elizabeth Tudor.

Sir Thomas Smith, the Elizabethan author of the *Commonwealth* of England (*De Republica Anglorum*, 1589), insisted that the whole power of the state was present when the monarch led the army or was present in Parliament. We have seen how recourse to the authority of the Crown in Parliament was a basic characteristic of Tudor rule. In the opinion of Sir Thomas, every Englishman, high and low, was "intended" (understood) to be present in Parliament. "And the consent of the Parliament is taken to be every man's consent." Any student who reads this famous book—students cannot easily do better than study the actual documents—will note that Sir Thomas Smith pays no attention to the contrasting powers of Elizabeth I and her Parliaments. He says nothing about "the divine right of kings" or the "law of nature." He is only concerned with explaining the nature and functions of "the High Court of Parliament" as contrasted with the other courts of England. The description of the procedures of the House of Commons, although perhaps inferior to William Lambarde's work, is one of the most interesting parts of Sir Thomas Smith's book from the point of view of the historians who study the constitutional history of the Tudor century. Sir Thomas fights no cause but contents himself with describing institutions and techniques as he sees them.

Richard Hooker's *Laws of Ecclesiastical Polity* was the prose masterpiece of the age. Hooker's organic hierarchical idea of the nature of a good state and a good individual was based on the theology of the Anglican church. A constitutional monarchy, he declared, was "the most sweet rule of kingly government." Law, he asserted, was "the very soul of a politic body." The seat of law "is in the bosom of God whose voice is the harmony of the world." To law all things in heaven and earth must do homage, for law is "the mother of their peace and joy." In the unity of prelacy and monarchy, twin preservers of public tranquillity, Hooker saw the happiness and stability of England. In almost every page of Hooker's great work there was an insistence upon the importance of continuity in the corporate life of church and state, an emphasis upon the idea of patience and compromise in all aspects of political and religious life.

And yet, even as Sir Thomas Smith and Richard Hooker were writing, the Tudor "system" was moving towards its end. Despite the words of many Whig historians, the dislocations of the next age are not to be attributed solely to Stuart malevolence or ineptitude. True history cannot be compressed into such formulas, however neat they may be. Had Elizabeth I lived a decade longer she might not have found her great political skill sufficient to cope successfully with restless and ambitious men in an increasingly independent Parliament. She knew that even in the sweet language of admiration so often heard in the Commons there were often hidden the tough fibers of Puritanism. Elizabeth also knew that the Puritans would never stop at conquering the church. They would try to subdue the state.

How many Englishmen could then have foreseen what was to happen so soon after the death of Elizabeth? Nobody could know the tasks that were shortly to confront Parliament and the courts of common law. The important fact is this: the discerning eye of the historian perceives that Parliament was trained and ready to act. As soon as a rift occurred between Crown and gentry there was certain to be trouble. A king who neglected or battled with the gentry faced the threat of disaster. Such a king was James I.

COUNTY AND PARISH: PILLARS OF POWER

Men of the solid gentry class were used to an increasing extent to carry on the extensive business of local government. The respectable propertied gentry men, recognized leaders in their communities, were thus called to perform the public duties once discharged by the feudal lords in the long days before the decline and fall of the old feudalism.

The local gentry usually had social prestige. They had economic and political power. They were energetic and they worked hard. They served England and the Tudors well. There were times, of course, when the demands of the Crown and the law clashed with the interests of the gentry. When that happened, the Crown's local servants did not carry out their duties with celerity and skill. They often looked the other way and virtually ignored the commands of the central government at Westminster. As Professor Conyers Read has rightly observed, "their concept of the welfare state was a class concept." [3]

One of the secrets of the amazing success of the Tudors and their chief servants was their capacity for taking pains. In the care and attention given to local concerns and local administration they took very great pains indeed. No longer were the sheriffs the great agents of the Crown in the counties. No longer were they greeted by the gentleman's calculated smile or the yokel's stare. Their power, once so great,

---

[3] The student is advised to read Professor Conyers Read's essay "Tudor Economic Policy" in *The Making of English History*, edited by Professors R. L. Schuyler and H. Ausubel (1952). Many interesting and valuable documents about local affairs, including judicial records, are printed in Carl Stephenson and F. G. Marcham, *Sources of English Constitutional History*, pp. 390–399. The student is also referred to the speech of the Lord Keeper on the administration of justice (1559) in the same volume, pp. 361–363.

had become tainted and enfeebled by the encroachments of the royal justices, by their own rivalries and corruptions. The bailiffs, too, found themselves with diminished powers, and for the same reasons. Whom could the Tudors trust? They turned to the new lords lieutenant of the counties (first mentioned in an act of 1550), responsible for the appointment of the mustering masters and the training of the shire militias and for the keeping of good order. The Tudors also turned to the justices of the peace, those men of the gentry class, those royal servants derived from the "conservators of the peace" described in earlier chapters.

The widely quoted statute of 1489 had provided heavy penalties for justices of the peace who did not perform their duties well from the crossroads to the courts. About twenty justices served in each shire. One of them had to be present at every session of the quarter sessions courts. They were technically appointed by the Lord Chancellor and were under the presidency, in each county, of the Keeper of the Rolls (*Custos Rotulorum*). They were not paid for their labors. As they were men of substance and prestige they needed no money. Because they were landed men, these unpaid amateurs could usually be relied upon to be conservative and careful. They knew their neighbors and they understood the nature and needs of their communities.

The best contemporary description of the duties of the justices of the peace occurs in the speech of the Lord Keeper in 1559 on the administration of justice. "How can the uncareful man that maketh no account of any of the common causes of his country but respecteth only his private matters and commodities, become a just and diligent searcher out, follower, and corrector of felonies, murders, and suchlike common enemies to the commonwealth?" Under the queen's commission the justices were to "do equal right to the poor and to the rich after your cunning, wit, and power, and after the laws and customs of the realm and the statutes thereof made." They were, among other things, to hand in the incomes from fines and forfeitures, "without any concealment and embezzling."

There were many other specific jobs to be done. With some aid from the coroners—the importance of the office of the coroner was declining in importance in the sixteenth century—the justices of the peace carried out a large number of judicial, police, and administrative tasks. Their judicial and administrative duties steadily mounted in volume and importance. Under their "stacks of statutes" their powers became very extensive. They were the judges in the local courts. They directed the administration of the poor laws and appointed overseers of the poor. They licensed inns and beggars. They forced the physically fit to choose between going to work and going to jail. They had some control over weights and measures. They determined local wages and prices. They supervised the building and maintenance of public works. They had broad powers of control over roads, bridges, hospitals, sewers and prisons. They could fine a man for failure to attend church. They could make and enforce rules in time of plague. They enforced the laws against the Puritans and Roman Catholics. They usually appointed the surveyors, the overseers and the petty constables of the parish. Even the coroners, who were elected officials, walked warily in the presence of the watchful justices. All the local royal officials, except the lords lieutenant of the counties, were in fact responsible to the justices of the peace. The justices of the peace, for their part, were ultimately responsible to the Privy Council of the queen.

Within the county still stood the hundred. It remained a financial unit where taxes were collected by the petty constables appointed and assigned to this task by the assize justices. The hundred was also a military unit where the muster masters collected militia forces. The hundred courts, as we have seen, had few functions left by the sixteenth century.

After the hundreds declined and the manors decayed many of their functions were taken over by the parish, the local unit of the church. When the church came under royal control, the parish meeting, the assembly of the parishioners, began to be responsible for many routine secular and ecclesiastical tasks. Some officers, such as the wardens, sextons, beadles and clerks, were elected in a vestry meeting. The main task of the wardens was to act as trustees of church property, to keep it in repair, and to levy taxes for its support. Other officers of the parish were appointed by the central government, such as the overseers of the highways whose duty it was to supervise the parishioners in six days' work a year on the local roads and bridges.

These sentences are sufficient to show the rising importance of the parish as an instrument of administration in Tudor England. Throughout the century, as has been noted earlier, there was a steady elaboration of local government, a steady shifting of many tasks and burdens to the localities. Professor Mildred Campbell has recently shown that in the unpaid offices of the parish the yeomen—the freeholders of common rank—were becoming increasingly important. Their responsibility and position trained them towards habits of individual initiative and judgment long before England approached democracy. Yeoman power in local government rose like the gentry power after the defeudalizing of local government began in the reign of Edward III. The parish made its appearance as a civil unit after the Reformation and poor relief became more a civil than a religious function. Then the yeomen became more active in quarter and petty court sessions in regard to cases involving paupers, often the cause of bitter inter-parish quarrels.

Towards the end of the reign of Elizabeth I the parish was formally given the task of administering the poor laws. Earlier, under the Beggars Act of 1536 (supplemented in 1576), there had been merely a rather general provision that local units of government should "succour, find, and keep all and every of the same poor people by way of voluntary and charitable alms" and set the "sturdy vagabonds and beggars" to work. Under the clauses of the Poor Relief Act of 1598 (extended in 1601) the churchwardens of every parish and a specified number of householders were to be called overseers of the poor and were to be responsible to two justices of the peace. These overseers were given authority to erect houses of refuge for the "impotent poor," to help the poor with money or goods, to provide raw materials to set the poor to work, to place the poor children out as apprentices, to collect taxes or "poor rates" at a level set by the parishioners, or the churchwardens and constables, or the justices of the peace in general or quarter sessions. They were also to "do and execute all other things . . . as to them shall seem convenient."

HARMONY AND DISCORD

The success of the government of Henry VIII and Elizabeth I was largely a personal triumph. These Tudors fingered the pulse of public opinion, or at least of the opinion that counted. They frequently helped to create the kind of sentiment they wished to have. They "tuned the pulpits." They spread rewards judiciously. They chose able servants. They avoided excessive taxation. Possessing unique political talents, ruthless and shrewd, Henry VIII and Elizabeth I moved through the critical decades that marked the great transition from the medieval to the modern world. Never had the tide of loyalty run more strongly than in Elizabeth's later days. England was prosperous and England was strong.

Despite these facts, new pens and voices were soon to give strong challenge to the Tudor ideals of harmony and order, to Tudor ways and values. Restless men moved towards ideas that were to shape and alter the whole concept of a man's relation to his prince, his church, and his fellows. Shakespeare might write of the "ancient service of the antique world, Which sweats for meed, not for promotion." The generation that followed him contained many men whose values, confused and disruptive, were far different. Within and without the little island girt by its silver sea strange questions were asked. The varying answers that were given, often with loud voices and clenched fists, were not calculated to contribute to harmony, order, or "the unity and married calm of states."

In March, 1603, when she was seventy years old, Elizabeth I died. Post horses carried the news northwards to Edinburgh, where James VI of Scotland was waiting to hear that he had inherited the throne of England. James VI was the great-grandson of Margaret, sister of Henry VIII, and son of Mary, Queen of Scots. When he was proclaimed James I of England the union of the two royal houses of England and Scotland was at last accomplished.

James I had to cope with new men and new ideas in a world he never made. Tactless, gauche and garrulous, he began his eventful reign, quite unaware that he was the captive of an age filled with tragic dilemmas. James I was confident that he, at least, understood the forces surging over his kingdom. He did not. Neither did anyone else. "On every subject," said Plato in *Phaedrus,* "there is but one mode of beginning for those who would deliberate well. They must know what the thing is on which they are deliberating, or else of necessity go astray."

CHAPTER XIV

Crossroads of Power:

prerogative and Parliament

THE TURNING TIDES

Did authority in the state of England derive from the king or from Parliament? Was a full partnership in the business of government possible? Were the monarchs and their prerogatives within and under the common law of the nation? Or were they outside and above it? These questions had not often been asked. They had never been answered. The attempt by Englishmen to do both in the seventeenth century is the reason why Professor S. B. Chrimes has called the period the Heroic Age in English constitutional history.

The events and ideas of the unstable Stuart age are usually told in the language and tones of the Whig historians. The reputation of the Cavaliers has been darkened by the odium of some of their contemporaries and by the fact that Charles I (1625–1649) was defeated and executed. Nothing succeeds like success. Historians, human beings as they are, have usually been mainly concerned with the causes that have succeeded. They have perhaps not been sufficiently occupied with studying the hopes that never came true, the crusades and causes that did not quite come off.

Marching under the banners of Thomas Babington Macaulay, the Whig historians have explained the conflicts of the Stuart reigns almost solely in terms of a clash between absolutism and the rights of the people. These explanations are not quite true. It should be remembered, for instance, that the Parliamentarians stood forth as champions of established law. At the beginning, they were no innovators. Not until the Leveller days of the mid-seventeenth century was liberty declared to be a war aim—and to the Levellers "liberty" meant many things. It should also be remembered that the leaders of

Parliament were often the ones guilty of aggression under the early Stuarts. It was often they who attacked the citadel of monarchy. James I and Charles I seldom sallied out to mount offensives. It was the men of Parliament who shattered the ministers of the Stuarts: Sir Giles Mompesson, Sir Francis Bacon, Lionel Cranfield (first Earl of Middlesex), Thomas Wentworth (the Earl of Strafford), Archbishop Laud. It was the Parliament men who starved James I and Charles I of money and compelled the Stuarts to resort to monopolies, wardships, distraint of knighthood, excessive import levies and the like to hold their creditors at bay. These things are briefly mentioned here so that the student may be aware that much more may be said for the Stuart kings and causes than is suggested in the orthodox Whig interpretations.

In the early decades of the Stuart age the basic harmony between the Crown, the courts of common law and Parliament collapsed. The reason for the breakdown was mainly this: James I and Charles I interpreted the English system of law and government quite differently from the way in which it was viewed by many members of the House of Commons and most members of the common law courts. The Crown based its case on one body of premises, one set of values. The common law lawyers and Parliamentarians found an entirely different collection of values and tools of logic to confound the arguments of the two Stuart kings and their followers. The kings and their men, in turn, appealed from the precedents cited by their opponents by quoting the letter of the law. If they could not do that, they usually succeeded in getting interpretations favorable to their position. The important point is this: between the Crown on the one hand and the courts of common law and Parliament on the other there emerged a sharp struggle of principles that were incompatible, of ideas and values that were completely opposed. The result was an alignment of parties and forces that led to the Civil War. Each side moved with doctrinaire obstinacy. Each was unprepared to consider gradual adjustments of their ideas looking towards compromise. Each side gave intolerant and exclusive regard to the elements in the constitution that suited its purpose.

JAMES I: FACTS AND FORMULAS

James I (1603–1625) was unaware that a new nobility and a new middle class, with immense economic power, represented a great shift in the balance of English society. The men of that class wanted more political power, and from their places in Parliament they were prepared to reach out and grasp it. In these endeavors they were aided by several circumstances. For instance, into the great council Elizabeth had made there came dissension and weakness. Personnel deteriorated. Fissures widened. The power and prestige of the council declined. There were no pilots to steer a course favorable to the king. In the midst of centrifugal and disintegrating forces an inept king and an anaemic council could not control the House of Commons. The decrease of council influence effectively aided the growth of an organized and cooperating opposition. The rise of favorites about the court contributed still further to executive indecision and paralysis. The problem of the decreasing financial resources of the Crown burst upon the Stuarts in the very years that the expenses of government were mounting. In return for grants of money by Parliament the king had to promise to make concessions, to reduce grievances. "Every shekel that he doth receive Doth cost a limb of his prerogative." Was the royal prerogative to be considered something divisible, pieces of which might be marketed, traded, peddled, sold?

There were other complicating factors. Among the chief interests of James I was the royal prerogative power. He had clear theoretical ideas about monarchy. The books and essays of this "Solomon of kingcraft" contained several learned expositions of that theme. "He could criticize a theory, but he could not judge a man." James I believed in what is usually described as "the divine right of kings." According to this theory, a king was appointed by God and responsible only to Him. His subjects might not resist the king's commands, for resistance was a sin. The people were a "headless multitude" who owed active obedience to the king who conferred organization, at God's command, upon the nation. Under such a theory the king, as deputy of God, was above Parliament, above the laws of England, above the people. It was his duty to see to the welfare of his subjects, for God would one day hold him accountable for his stewardship. But beyond that point he had no responsibility. Whatever privileges Parliament possessed, the law courts possessed, or any individual possessed, were theirs by grace of the king, and were not held by any right. It was clear that when quarrels arose between the king and his subjects there would be heavy trouble.

The hammering vehemence of Puritan dissatisfaction with the Anglican Church demanded a careful and shrewd royal policy. The various Puritan groups—the "Broad Church" element, the Presbyterians, the Independents and the like—cannot be defined with precision and brevity. It must suffice here to say that the term "Puritan" is usually applied to those Protestants within and without the Church of England who wanted less ritual, more relief from ceremonies. Some wanted to re-cast episcopacy and build a doctrinal bridge over to Presbyterianism. Others wanted nothing to do with state religion. These Independents were opposed both to Anglican and Presbyterian doctrines. Added to such bodies of dissent were numerous smaller sects. Across the centuries still crackle the imagery and insults of these Puritans attacking the Church of England.

At the Hampton Court Conference of 1604 James I moved into conflict with the Puritans. He feared, among other things, that the growth of Puritanism might spread a democratic temper in the state. "If you aim at a Scottish presbytery," he exclaimed, "it agreeth as well with a monarchy as God with the devil. . . . I thus apply it . . . no bishop, no king. . . . If this be all your party hath to say I will make them conform, or else will harry them out of the land." Thus James I antagonized the formidable Puritan groups. Every year their numbers increased. God revealed himself in many ways.

Soon James I began to dispute with leaders in the courts of common law and in Parliament. As conflicts in these spheres increased in number and violence the nation became alarmed.

THE COURTS OF COMMON LAW

From the common law courts James I and Charles I encountered strong resistance. One of the greatest foes of the Stuart concept of sovereignty was Sir Edward Coke, famous author of the *Institutes*, Chief Justice of the Court of Common Pleas, later Chief Justice of the Court of King's Bench (1613) and, later still, a member of Parliament (1621). Coke and his supporters among the judges and lawyers insisted that the common law controlled the province of the royal prerogative power. They asserted that the rights of both king and Parliament were derived from and defined by precedent. They were usually determined to enforce these views quite sturdily. Coke himself was an obstinate fighter. To him the peculiar wisdom of the common law determined the goods and liberties of the people. The wisdom of the king, asserted Coke, could not do that. The king, Coke held, was legally limited by the common law. The law was greater than the Crown. Coke's attempts to curb the prerogative really meant that he was challenging the right of the king to alter the tough common law at his royal pleasure. There were several rough encounters, in one of which Coke fell "flat on all fours" as James I threatened to strike him, "looking and speaking fiercely with bended fist."

Several judicial cases are of special interest. In 1606 John Bate, an English merchant trading with the East, refused to pay on some currants a duty of five shillings a hundredweight imposed by James I in addition to the import levy established by Parliament. Bate was brought to trial before the Court of Exchequer. The court upheld the legality of the king's duties, arguing that impositions on foreign goods and all foreign relations were matters of state and belonged in the province of the king's "absolute" power ("The king's power is double, ordinary and absolute"). Because the king must have revenues, said Chief Baron Fleming and Baron Clark, he must and can take them when he has need to do so. In such affairs, the king governed by his "absolute," indisputable, private prerogative and this might not be disputed in the courts. The "ordinary" prerogative, on the other hand, was subject to the courts' rulings.

Said Baron Clark: "And the revenue of the crown is the very essential part of the crown; and he who rendeth that from the king pulleth also the crown from his head, for it cannot be separated from the crown. And such great prerogatives of the crown, without which it cannot be, ought not to be disputed, and in these cases of prerogative the judgment shall not be according to the rules of the common law, but according to the precedents of this court. . . ." Said Chief Baron Fleming: "The absolute power of the king is not that which is converted or executed to private use, to the benefit of any particular person, but is only that which is applied to the general benefit of the people. . . . To prove the power of the king by precedents may easily be done. . . . Wherefore I think the king ought to have judgment." To these propositions, of course, there were many objections. How far might the king go in imposing duties? Was it to be left "to the wisdom of the king, who guideth all under God by his wisdom"? How large and how permanent did this unparliamentary revenue seem likely to become, especially when Lord Treasurer Salisbury prepared the royal Book of Rates? The ruling of the judges might be technically sound enough but it was obviously pregnant with danger. And why did the judges of the Exchequer Court have to echo so clearly the king's own political ideas?

A second problem of importance appeared in Calvin's Case or the

Case of the *Postnati* (1608). Here the judges also upheld the arguments of the Crown. This case began with an assize of *novel disseisin* brought by the guardians of Robert Calvin, a Scottish minor. The plaintiffs claimed that a London freehold in the possession of two Englishmen in fact belonged to Calvin. The defendants asserted that they were not bound to join the action because Calvin was an alien born in Scotland in 1606. Under English law an alien could not own land in England because land carried with it political duties which an alien could not perform. The plaintiffs said that Calvin had been born under the allegiance of James VI of Scotland after his accession to the English throne as James I. Therefore, asserted the plaintiffs, because Calvin was born after (*postnatus*) the beginning of James I's reign he bore allegiance to the same king as the English. Hence he could bring suit in an English court to get possession of English lands. The defense said that James VI and James I were essentially two separate kings holding two separate offices. Such important problems of common law and equity were involved that the case was transferred to the Court of Exchequer Chamber and there heard by all the judges of the central courts. James I, of course, was anxious to have English rights secured for his Scottish subjects.

The Court of Exchequer Chamber held, in the words of Lord Chancellor Ellesmere, that allegiance belonged to the person of the king and not to the legal office. The major reports were given by Sir Edward Coke and the Lord Chancellor. Said Coke: "Whosoever are born under one natural ligeance and obedience due by the law of nature to one sovereign are natural-born subjects. . . . Whoever is born within the king's power or protection is no alien. . . . Whatsoever is due by the law or constitution of man may be altered, but natural ligeance or obedience to the sovereign cannot be altered. . . . Lastly, whosoever at his birth cannot be an alien to the king of England cannot be an alien to any of his subjects of England." Lord Chancellor Ellesmere considered the defendants' assertion that James VI and James I were separate legal entities to be unwise: "This is a dangerous distinction between the king and the crown, and between the king and the kingdom. . . . Upon this subtle and dangerous distinction of faith and allegiance due the king and . . . due the crown and the kingdom . . . there follow too many gross and foul absurdities. . . . Robert Calvin, and all the *postnati* in Scotland are in reason and by the common law of England natural-born subjects . . . of the king of England, and enabled to purchase and have freehold and inheritance of lands in England and to bring real actions for the same in England. . . ."

A third judicial question arose in Bonham's Case. The problem before the court came from the following circumstances. Henry VIII had granted a monopoly of medical practice in London to the members of the College of Physicians and men licensed by them. This grant was confirmed by an act of Parliament. When Bonham, holding a medical degree from Cambridge, came to London he was refused permission to practice. Bonham then proceeded to treat the sick and to charge fees. He was imprisoned and fined by the London College of Physicians. Bonham retaliated by starting an action for false arrest and imprisonment against the College. The case came before Sir Edward Coke, then Chief Justice of the Court of King's Bench.

Coke's famous decision upheld the contention of Bonham. Coke declared that "when an act of Parliament is against common right and reason, or repugnant, or impossible to be performed, the common law will control it, and adjudge such an act to be void." The Chief Justice was thus saying that there were principles of the fundamental common law which were superior to both king and Parliament. He cited four precedents, of which Professor T. F. T. Plucknett has said "There was at least one clear and incontestable precedent in his favor."

Does this mean that common law had a higher sanction than statute law? The attitude was common enough but "the cases in which judges actually announced that a statute could be invalid for infringing any other portion of the common law than that which guaranteed the integrity of the existing governmental structure are few." [1] Coke's proposition that a statute was void if it conflicted with natural law was one of the five ostensible reasons for which he was later removed from the bench. Coke's exaltation of the common law was too strong. His opinion in Bonham's Case could not be maintained, although Chief Justice Holt did accept it in City of London *v.* Wood (1701).

Sir Edward Coke's decision in Bonham's Case is one of several that showed his idea of the position of the courts in the constitution. The orthodox interpretation of Bonham's Case is that Coke stated the doctrine of judicial review—later so important to the United States—

---

[1] F. D. Wormuth, *The Royal Prerogative 1603–1649*, p. 64. (The permission given by Professor Wormuth to quote this and other passages is gratefully acknowledged.) See also T. F. T. Plucknett, "Bonham's Case and Judicial Review," *Harvard Law Review*, XL, 30.

which maintains the principle that acts of the executive and legislative branches of government might be reviewed by the judges and overthrown if the courts found those acts in contravention of a higher law. This interpretation has been challenged by several authorities. Professor F. D. Wormuth, for example, has pointed out that Coke was really denying the right of the College of Physicians to be a judge in its own case against Bonham and if Coke's dictum is taken to apply *only to this or similar situations* the limitation upon the legislative power is one of procedural due process, not substantive due process.[2] There may be no reference to the constitutional question consciously raised. It is probable, indeed, that Coke's appeals to a higher law were often seen more clearly by later commentators than by Coke himself. James Otis was apparently well aware of this danger when he was deriving from Bonham's Case his famous arguments against writs of assistance in the Revolutionary Era of American history.

It may be argued that the power Parliament possessed after the Revolution of 1688 was more similar to what James I was claiming than to what Coke asserted. In the early seventeenth century all men edged along a road they did not know. In the end, the supremacy of Parliament was won. Therefore the idea of a fundamental law broke off short in England. In the American colonies that idea was taken up in the eighteenth century. It seems that the governmental structure of the United States, including the system of judicial review, would have been more intelligible to Sir Edward Coke than the idea of the sovereignty of Parliament.

There were several other judicial problems and cases of consequence in the reign of James I. For instance, Sir Edward Coke frequently directed a jealous and jaundiced eye towards the rival Chancery and the prerogative courts. He weakened the church courts by ruling that they had no right to imprison individuals charged with adultery. He also laid down the principle that if the common law courts provided a remedy the ecclesiastical tribunals should not have jurisdiction. Sir Edward Coke was always anxious to preserve and extend the jurisdiction of the common law courts. One way of doing

---

[2] See Professor F. D. Wormuth's comments in *The Origins of Modern Constitutionalism*, Chapter XXI: "Double Majesty and Judicial Review," pp. 207 ff., and in *The Royal Prerogative 1603–1649*, p. 63. See also S. E. Thorne, "The Constitution and the Courts: Re-examination of the Famous Case of Dr. Bonham," in *The Constitution Reconsidered*, ed. by Professor Conyers Read (1938). Despite the wide and erudite discussions of the meaning and implications of the decision in Bonham's Case there remain several complex issues as yet unresolved.

this was to multiply the writs of prohibition issuing out of the Court of King's Bench on matters of disputed jurisdiction.

Church officials frequently complained that the ecclesiastical courts were being unjustly bombarded by these writs of prohibition. In Fuller's Case (1607) the issue was raised directly. Fuller was a Puritan lawyer who insulted the Court of High Commission, whereupon he was locked up. Fuller thereupon appealed to the Court of King's Bench for a writ of prohibition, asserting that the Court of High Commission had no right to imprison for contempt. The writ was issued and the case was referred to the Court of Exchequer Chamber. When Archbishop Bancroft appealed directly to the king Sir Edward Coke intervened. Coke's reports of his interview with James I are perhaps unduly dramatic. Nevertheless, the issue was clearly stated: "The king in his own person cannot adjudge any case, either criminal . . . or betwixt party and party . . . ; but this ought to be determined and adjudged in some court of justice according to the law and custom of England . . . his majesty was not learned in the laws of his realm of England, and causes which concern the life or inheritance or goods or fortunes of his subjects are not to be decided by natural reason, but by the artificial reason and judgment of law—which law is an art which requires long study and experience before that a man can attain to the cognizance of it. . . ." In the end the king agreed with the judges of Exchequer Chamber that King's Bench should continue to issue writs of prohibition, although with discrimination and sound sense.

In the Case of Proclamations (1610) Sir Edward Coke and his fellow justices took issue with the Lord Chancellor who said that "every precedent had first a commencement and that he would advise the judges to maintain the power and prerogative of the king, and in cases in which there is no authority and precedent to leave the king to order in it, according to his wisdom and for the good of his subjects." Sir Edward and his colleagues decided "that the king by his proclamation cannot create any offence that was not an offence before; for then he may alter the law of the land by his proclamation. . . . For, if he may create an offence where none is, upon that ensues fine and imprisonment. Also the law of England is divided into three parts: common law, statute law, and custom. But the king's proclamation is none of them. . . . Also it was resolved that the king hath no prerogative but that which the law of the land allows him." In the specific case at issue Sir Edward ruled that a man could not be brought to trial for building a house in a particular spot in defiance of a royal proclama-

tion. Coke said simply that a royal proclamation was not a law. Therefore the man before the court had not been charged with a legal offense.
The effect of the Case of Proclamations was virtually to destroy the
legal grounds upon which the authority of proclamations had been
deemed to rest.

Sir Edward Coke was also involved in Peacham's Case (1615).
Peacham was a Somerset preacher with radical Puritan leanings. When
he was dismissed from his parish because he allegedly made libellous
remarks about his bishop, a search of his study disclosed notes, probably for a sermon, about the possible death of the king. There were
also written comments about dubious activities at the royal court.
James I insisted that Peacham be tried on a charge of treason. But
were these notes to be considered "overt acts" under the law of treason?
The king privately questioned the judges who were eligible for appointment to the western circuit in order to select men who would
find against Peacham. Coke insisted that the judges must be consulted
in a body, never one by one. Here, for once, precedent was against
Sir Edward and James I had his way. Peacham was tried and convicted.

One other case of high importance was the occasion of further dispute before Sir Edward Coke was dismissed from the Court of King's
Bench. This was the Case of Commendams (Neile's Case, 1616). Neile
was a clergyman who was appointed Bishop of Coventry and Lichfield
in 1614. He obtained the king's permission to hold two other ecclesiastical livings temporarily (in commendam). There were two objections
to holding livings in this way. In the first place, canon law stated that
no bishop should have any position involving pastoral duties. Secondly, these livings were technically advowsons and their owners were
actually deprived of their right of appointment by the fact that Neile
occupied and profited from them.

The owners of one of the advowsons sued Neile in the Court of
Common Pleas for interfering with their rights. The case came before
Sir Edward Coke and the other judges in the Court of Exchequer
Chamber. At this point Sir Francis Bacon, the attorney general, summoned the judges before the king. James I wanted to have a delay in
the case in order to survey the whole problem before a decision was
reached by the Exchequer Court. The real question was this: Did
James I have a right to present Neile, or anybody else, to a church
living on a temporary appointment, in commendam?

When the summons from the king came before Exchequer Chamber, Sir Edward Coke apparently persuaded his fellow judges that the

order of Sir Francis Bacon was illegal because all judges were bound by their oaths to delay no case. Sir Edward was not alone in feeling that if proceedings were halted then the king would bring such heavy arguments and pressure to bear upon the court that the judges would find it expedient to decide in favor of Neile, the defendant. The summons of the attorney general was therefore ignored and the Exchequer Chamber continued to hear arguments for and against *commendams*.

James I at once ordered the twelve judges to appear before him in the council. He then compelled them to listen to his arguments. They were asked a question: "Whether if, at any time in a case depending before the judges which his majesty conceived to concern him either in power or profit, and therefore required to consult with them and that they should stay proceedings in the meantime, they ought not to stay accordingly?" Eleven judges agreed that they would halt proceedings and acknowledged it to be their duty to do so. The twelfth judge was Sir Edward Coke and he said "that when that case should be, he would do what should be fit for a judge to do." All the judges but Coke yielded to James.

Shortly afterwards the council, at the request of the king, began proceedings against Sir Edward Coke. He was charged with failing to pay an installment on a debt owed to Sir Christopher Hatton, with "speeches of high contempt, uttered as he sat in the seat of justice, touching the overthrow of the common law," with failing to give a satisfactory answer "to excuse his uncivil and indiscreet carriage before his majesty. . . ." Coke was suspended from the council and the summer circuit of assize and ordered to review his "book of reports, wherein (as his majesty is informed) there be many exorbitant and extravagant opinions set down and published for positive and good law."

Sir Edward Coke refused to alter the sections of his manuscript that seemed adversely critical of the royal prerogative. In November, 1616, he was dismissed from all offices under the Crown. No judge obtained the immortal fame that belongs to Coke. Few proved to be as recalcitrant as he. Some, indeed, were selfish and nerveless. Many of them really ceased to interpret the law and became civil servants instead. Hence most of the later judicial decisions were found in favor of James I and Charles I. Nevertheless, the voice of Coke was not stilled. His acute defense of the common law provided an arsenal of ideas for the men of Parliament as they battled with the first two Stuarts. Coke himself was soon elected to Parliament and he was not idle there. His legal writings were studied long after the head of Charles I had rolled.

Professor Frederick William Maitland once believed that in the sixteenth century England nearly moved to a "reception" of the Roman law. This event had occurred in France and elsewhere. It was a natural result of the Renaissance. Roman law has always proved to be of great value in the establishment of a tyranny. (*Quod principi placet legis habet vigorem*—what the ruler wills has the force of law.) In England the dangers of conciliar justice must have seemed great and immediate as men looked upon Chancery, upon the council and its offshoots: the prerogative courts of Star Chamber, High Commission, Requests, the Council of the North and the Council of Wales. The perils of the native common law were in fact considerable, although the degree of the danger has perhaps been stressed overmuch. In any event, the challenge of Rome—if it can properly be called that—was defeated. The tough common law showed an extraordinary renaissance. The sons of the Inns of Court were triumphant. "In the hands of Coke," a contemporary scholar has written, "the common law forged the axe which beheaded Charles I." Although this statement may not be sufficiently cautious it still underlines the important truth that Sir Edward Coke was a most redoubtable champion of the common law.

KING *VERSUS* PARLIAMENT

James I abandoned the Tudor precaution of ensuring the election to Parliament of a goodly number of privy councillors and royal officials. This is one reason why his first Parliament was not at all subservient. James found that the members of the assembly of 1604 were quite unprepared to yield to the idea of divine right. A strong party championed Parliamentary rights. Controversy exploded almost at once.

Early in the first session two questions of Parliamentary privilege arose. The first was the case of Thomas Shirley, arrested for a private debt. Because he was a member of Parliament for Sussex he claimed freedom from arrest. The king accepted the decision of the House of Commons upholding Shirley's contention. The second case was that of Sir Francis Goodwin. Goodwin was returned as a knight from Buckinghamshire, but he had earlier been outlawed in the process of a civil suit and the royal proclamation summoning Parliament had barred such candidates. Accordingly, a writ of election was refused by Chancery. In a new election the defeated candidate, Sir John

Fortescue, a privy councillor, was elected. When Parliament assembled it insisted that by precedent it had the right to rule in election disputes. The members agreed that Goodwin was legally elected and returned.

James I not only denied that the first election was valid but declared that he was not bound by the precedents set by his predecessors. He informed the Commons that "since they derived all matters of privilege from him, and by his grant, he expected they should not be turned against him." After a long dispute, James granted the right of the House of Commons to be a court of record and judge of returns of its own members. He suggested that the elections of both Goodwin and Fortescue should be declared void and a new election held. This proposal was accepted by the Commons. James, of course, did not abandon his position that all the privileges of the Commons resulted from an act of grace on his part.

When the Commons began to debate some reforms of the Church of England James proceeded to rebuke them. Such matters, he asserted, were beyond their proper province. This message of the king was clearly an interference with freedom of speech. The active pressure of Puritan zeal was sufficient to have forced a demand for liberty of discussion even if there had not been defenders of the Commons to draw up a program and to assert their traditional rights, and more. Meanwhile, the members had been elaborating Parliamentary procedure and marshalling legal precedents for their privileges and powers. They now prepared a cogent statement called the Apology of the Commons which was presented to James on June 20, 1604.

This document spoke of "the ancient rights of the subjects of this realm" and stated that "our privileges and liberties are our right and due inheritance, no less than our very lands and goods." The Apology raised again the disputed points in the Goodwin Case. The privileges of the Commons, it declared, are held by right: "They cannot be withheld from us, denied, or impaired, but with apparent wrong to the whole state of the realm." By reason of the "misinformation" earlier received by James I "not only privileges but the whole freedom of the parliament and realm have from time to time upon all occasions, been mainly hewed at." The Apology referred to the "troubles, distrusts and jealousy" that had arisen. It reminded James that the Commons contained "the whole flower and power" of the kingdom, "the sole persons of the higher nobility being excepted." It asked that James "receive public information from your Commons in Parliament" rather than private misinformation. It stated that "the voice of the

people in things of their knowledge is said to be as the voice of God."
Finally, it declared: "What cause we your poor Commons have to
watch over our privileges is manifest to all men. The prerogatives of
princes may easily and do daily grow. The privileges of the subject
are for the most part at an everlasting stand. They may be by good
providence and care preserved, but being once lost are not recovered
but with much disquiet." When James prorogued Parliament late in
1604 he sarcastically referred to the Commons as "my masters of the
Lower House."

Meanwhile the costs of government were mounting. Elizabeth I had
left a debt of about £300,000, a large sum in those days. James I was
himself extravagant and his court favorites apparently looted at will.
Crown revenues, especially from land sales and rents, were decreasing.
Hence James sought to increase royal revenue by other means. Monopolies were widely sold. Earlier in this chapter we have seen how James
got into a dispute upon Bate's Case and the collection of import duties.
The royal Book of Rates (1608) contained still more impositions. Were
the arguments of the Exchequer Court judges to be accepted by the
House of Commons? If so, it was clear that Parliament would have no
legal control of this arbitrary taxation.

In 1610 the Commons objected to numerous schemes adopted by
James I to increase the royal income, particularly the collection of
feudal dues and the use of purveyance; the first was a practice almost
obsolete and the second, the right of the king to buy provisions for
the royal household at a value fixed by royal appraisal, was especially
offensive. When the Commons began to discuss the royal power to
levy impositions, James forbade them to continue. The Commons
thereupon refused and announced that they would proceed to "a full
examination" of the king's alleged prerogative powers regarding taxation. Weary of haggling, irked at the delay in granting money, and
annoyed at new discussions about the Puritans, James dissolved Parliament early in 1611.

In 1614 the financial position of the Crown was so precarious that
James was again compelled to resort to Parliament for taxes. He hoped
that this "Parliament of love" could be persuaded to vote him plenty
of money. He was soon disillusioned. The rising tides of public anger
sent scores of hostile members to the new House of Commons. They
were in no mood to grant supplies. At once they turned to grievances.
Not a single bill was passed during two months of debate about the
king's prerogative, about impositions, about a speech of the Bishop

of Lincoln in the House of Lords charging the Commons with sedition. "The Commons growing insolent . . . the king sent them word he would dissolve them unless they attended at once to his wants . . . the house being more like a cockpit than a council." On June 1, 1614 James dissolved this so-called Addled Parliament which had refused to vote him a penny. After the dissolution four members of Parliament were arrested and sent to prison at the king's command.

During these years, and later, James I had other difficulties. He had always been addicted to favorites and these men, especially the Scotsman Robert Carr and George Villiers, the Duke of Buckingham, were irresponsible and incompetent. Public annoyance mounted. Meanwhile, too, the successive failures of James I in foreign affairs angered a proud people. In 1621 there was a prospect of war with Spain. Because he could obtain money in no other way James called Parliament once again.

The new Parliament of 1621 wanted precise explanations about war plans. They insisted upon information regarding the proposed marriage between Prince Charles, the son of James, and the Spanish Infanta. They made a small grant to the king and then began to debate their grievances. Led by Sir Edward Coke, they denounced the excessive granting of monopolies, particularly to royal favorites. Coke brought about the impeachment of the Lord Chancellor, Francis Bacon, before the House of Lords. Bacon was one of the chief defenders of the royal prerogative and when he was convicted of taking bribes from suitors at court (there were twenty-three charges) a strong pillar of the king was removed. The weapon of impeachment, unused since the fourteenth century, was now, it seemed, to be employed by Parliament against royal officials and favorites who could not otherwise be reached.

In vain James I, in a letter to the House of Commons, noted that the members must not talk about foreign affairs or insult the Spanish ambassador. They had ventured to "argue and debate publicly of the matters far above their reach or capacity, tending to our high dishonor and breach of prerogative royal." James commanded that "none therein shall presume henceforth to meddle with anything concerning our government or deep matters of state." The king added that he thought himself "very free and able to punish any man's misdemeanours in Parliament, as well during their sitting as after." This was the way, surely, to deal with the distrusted opposition.

The House of Commons at once demanded an explanation. It was unsatisfactory. Thereupon the Great Protestation was prepared and inserted in the Journal of the House of Commons. It declared that the Commons' privileges were "the ancient and undoubted birthright and inheritance of the subjects of England." James ripped the Great Protestation from the pages of the Journal. ("King James in council with his own hand rent out this protestation.") He then dissolved Parliament.

Obviously James I could not wage war with Spain. He had no army, no supplies. In 1623 Prince Charles and Buckingham went to Madrid to view the Infanta. Both were annoyed at their reception and returned to England hot for war. The public rejoiced. James now proceeded to call Parliament again. This assembly granted him some supplies, impeached the pro-Spanish councillor the Earl of Middlesex and passed a bill declaring monopolies "altogether contrary to the laws of this realm."

In 1625 James I died. In his reign, as described earlier, the influence of the council steadily slackened and the campaign against the Crown gathered momentum and strength. Committees of the House of Commons increased the scope and importance of their activities. Parliamentary procedure improved greatly. Able members of the Commons waged skillful battles, widely publicized, against the assertions of the royal prerogative. The liberties and privileges of Parliament were defended by shrewd, courageous and dangerous men, well trained in Parliamentary tactics, skilled in oratory, swift in logic. Meanwhile the Puritan attacks on the bishops grew more violent and bitter. The abuses of benevolences, monopolies and impositions took their place beside the other causes of reform urged by the House of Commons. Less dramatic and less easily described was the simple fact that the Crown was drawing away from large numbers of people throughout the land. The bonds that meant so much in the years of the Tudors were perceptibly loosening. This James I did not see amid his quarrels about liberties, prerogatives, taxation, and all the rest. He was tragically unaware of the currents of social, political, and economic forces, the flood of which no king could stay.

So it was that Charles I entered upon his dubious heritage. James I had been politically unwise, tactless, obstinate, often guilty of gabbling indecorum. Charles I was dignified, conscientious, unimaginative, incapable of learning wisdom from experience. England soon discovered that the new king believed in divine right, as he had been taught to do. He was, he felt, the anointed of the Lord, bound in honor to defend the prerogatives of the Crown, even though his own life be forfeit. The danger signals were flying. The phase of decision was now at hand.

CHARLES I: THE GATHERING STORM

The opposition and misgivings that darkened the reign of James I continued in the early years of the reign of his son. When a new Parliament met late in 1625 the Puritan members were strongly hostile to the Anglicanism of Charles. They were also suspicious of the Duke of Buckingham, so lacking in capacity, and the French Henrietta Maria, the Roman Catholic queen. Hence they refused to vote adequate funds to Charles to wage a war against Spain. They immediately made it clear that they intended to debate foreign affairs and religious reforms and they were taking no chances upon Charles dissolving Parliament as soon as he had money. Instead of granting tunnage and poundage duties to the new king for life, in accordance with custom, the Commons gave them for one year only. In fact, Charles did not get this income at all because he later dissolved Parliament before the House of Lords had passed the bill.

The second Parliament (February to June, 1626) was at once concerned with two costly and badly led expeditions undertaken by the Duke of Buckingham, the one against Spain, the second to help Louis XIII of France subdue his rebellious Huguenot subjects at La Rochelle. The truculent Commons again refused to grant supplies. One of their leaders, the belligerent Sir John Eliot, declared: "Our honour is ruined, our ships are sunk, our men perished, not by the enemy, not by chance, but by those we trust."

"Remember," said Charles I, "that Parliaments are altogether in my power for their calling, sitting, and dissolution; and therefore, as I find the fruits of them to be good or evil they are to continue or not to be." Despite such threats from the king the debate went on. Finally, the Commons began impeachment proceedings against the Duke of Buckingham, charging him with corruption and maladministration. To save Buckingham, Charles dissolved Parliament.

The problem of money supply was urgent. More cash Charles I had to have. He now pawned the crown jewels and mortgaged Crown lands. He sought to obtain tunnage and poundage by royal ordinance. When nothing was forthcoming he attempted a forced loan in 1627. This was in effect taxation without Parliamentary sanction. Charles arbitrarily imprisoned several men who refused to contribute to his cause. A wall of resistance seemed to rise up everywhere.

Among those imprisoned were five knights, who at once sued for writs of habeas corpus from the Court of King's Bench on the ground that they had not been charged with any specific offense. The writs were granted by the court but the Warden of the Fleet Prison refused to release the prisoners. He declared that he was acting on a warrant from two members of the Privy Council ordering the knights to be held "by special order of his majesty." The prisoners, upon being informed that they were not bailable, asserted that the ancient rights of the subject, set forth in Chapter 39 of Magna Carta, were at stake. Freedom from arbitrary arrest was a basic English liberty. In the Case of the Five Knights (or Darnel's Case) Chief Justice Hyde was evasive and weak. He based his decision upon a judgment of 1591 and upon considerations of public and private (the fear of dismissal) policy. "If no cause of the commitment be expressed," he said, "it is to be presumed to be a matter of state which we cannot take notice of." The five knights were not released. The constitutional question whether Charles I could imprison his subjects without showing cause was, for the time, left unsettled.

Meanwhile, England's war with Spain broadened into a war with France. The Duke of Buckingham was mainly responsible for another military fiasco. He led a bungled expedition to relieve La Rochelle and came home defeated. Amidst debt, defeat, and disorder Charles I, with great reluctance, summoned his third Parliament to get money to meet "the common danger."

In March, 1628, that new and suspicious Parliament assembled. Twenty-seven members had earlier been imprisoned for refusal to pay the forced loan demanded by the king. Charles I had raised enemies abroad and increased them at home. When he demanded money from the Commons and insisted, quite rightly, that he desperately needed it, the Commons paid no attention. Instead of making even a small grant they turned with vigor to condemn and protest. Carefully advised by Sir Edward Coke they decided to put their major grievances in a forceful and clear Petition of Right, which was read three times in each House. This document carefully cited precedents and asked Charles to cease actions "not warrantable by the laws and practices of this realm." The members of Parliament did "humbly pray your most excellent majesty that no man hereafter be compelled to make or yield any gift, loan, benevolence, or such like charge without common consent by act of parliament." They also asked that no one should be "confined, or otherwise molested or disquieted concerning the same, or for refusal thereof"; that no one should be arbitrarily imprisoned for any reason. The petitioners further requested the king to stop the compulsory billeting of soldiers and sailors in the houses of the people "against the laws and customs of this realm." They asked that punishment by martial law should cease "lest . . . your majesty's subjects be destroyed or put to death, contrary to the laws and statutes of this realm." Such were the main aspects of the petition submitted to the king for "the safety and comfort" of his people.

Charles I reluctantly agreed to consent to the Petition of Right. At first his answer was ambiguous: "the king willeth that right be done according to the laws and customs of the realm, that the statute be put in due execution, that his subjects may have no cause to complain of any wrongs or oppressions, contrary to their just rights and liberties, to the preservation whereof he holds himself as well obliged as of his prerogative." The Commons felt that this reply left Charles free to act upon his own interpretation of the law. Both the Lords and the Commons finally obtained the king's answer in words usually used in assenting to a private bill: *"Soit droit fait come est desiré."*

The Petition of Right was therefore not a statute and there is some doubt as to whether the procedure followed actually gave this famous document any precise force in a legal sense. In fact, of course, its main provisions were enacted in statute form later in the century. Its principles, as well as others, were not really won until the physical power of two revolutions made them more acceptable to the Crown. The historical and constitutional meaning of the Petition of Right stands in line with the more important Magna Carta of 1215 and the Bill of Rights of 1689. Its immediate practical value was not great. It stated principles and precedents and it became a precedent itself in the long assertions of the powers of Parliament and the supremacy of law in England.

After Charles I granted the Petition of Right the Commons voted him money. Then, still belligerent, they turned to censure preachers who had exalted the royal prerogative, to argue over impositions, to threaten Buckingham. The king forbade them to attack his ministers, on whom he wanted "no scandal or aspersion." The result was another storm. One member of the Commons declared: "We sit as men daunted. Let us put on the spirit of Englishmen and speak to purpose." A second said: "If we must not speak of ministers, what must we do?" So the Commons continued to debate their grievances about Buckingham. They also discussed with heat the king's insistence that tunnage and poundage, an indirect tax, was not covered by the Petition of Right; that his promise to impose no levies without Parliamentary grant applied only to direct taxes; that the judicial decision in Bate's Case gave legal authority for the royal levying of all kinds of indirect taxes. On June 26, 1628, Charles prorogued Parliament. "It may seem strange that I come so suddenly to end this session. Wherefore, before I give my assent to the bills I will tell you the cause; though I must avow that I owe an account of my actions to none but to God alone. A while ago the House of Commons gave me a remonstrance—how acceptable every man may judge. And for the merit of it, I will not now call that in question; for I am sure no wise man can justify it. Now, since I am certainly informed that a second remonstrance is preparing for me, to take away my profit of tunnage and poundage—one of the chief maintenances of the crown—by alleging that I have given away my right thereof by my answer to your petition, this is so prejudicial unto me that I am forced to end this session some few hours before I meant it, being willing not to receive any more remonstrances to which I must give a harsh answer." Many Englishmen felt, and not for the first time, that the king was simply being petty and dishonest. It was always difficult for Charles to accommodate his conduct to the facts.

One grievance was soon removed when the Duke of Buckingham was murdered by a malcontent lieutenant. Charles I was overcome with grief. There was national rejoicing. Thus the problem of Buckingham was settled. Soon, however, other grievances surged to the forefront of the national scene. When a second session of Parliament met in 1629 numerous Puritans plunged into bitter objections to a royal proclamation ordering literal acceptance of the Thirty-Nine Articles by all laymen. There was no doubting the fact that William Laud, soon to be Archbishop of Canterbury, and the Anglicans who strongly supported the royal prerogative were steadily expanding their power and dictating the religious policy of the government. It was natural that the Puritans, within and without the Commons, should feel that these Anglicans were going to bring in "popery and Arminianism" and poison the sweet waters of the faith. (Arminius was a Dutch divine who denied Calvin's doctrine of particular election and limited atonement.) Therefore they began with their usual vehemence to denounce Laudian Anglicanism, insisting that they would not allow the religion of England to be changed in any way opposed to their wishes.

There seemed no way to halt Parliament's attacks on royal ecclesiastical policy and the claim of the king to tunnage and poundage except by the familiar weapon of dissolution. Charles at first ordered a short adjournment, then a longer one. The obstreperous House of Commons, anxious to get its opinions on record, voted against adjourning. When Speaker Finch tried to comply with the royal order (the Sergeant-at-Arms had been sent to seize the mace, the symbol of the House's authority) he was seized and held in his chair. The doors were locked. With the House thus technically in session three resolutions were swiftly passed. They were: (1) Whoever imported innovations in religion or favored popery or Arminianism should be considered capital enemies of the kingdom; (2) Whoever advised the collection of tunnage or poundage without Parliamentary consent should also be considered "a capital enemy to the kingdom and commonwealth"; (3) Whoever voluntarily paid tunnage and poundage thus levied should be considered a traitor to the liberties of the land. After these resolutions were passed the Commons voted their own adjournment. The doors were unlocked and the royal messengers admitted. From a political point of view this action was probably reckless and ill-advised; it went beyond the point favored by the moderates. The Commons, declared Charles I, had been attempting "to exert an universal, overswaying power which belongs only to me, and not to them." Parliament was dissolved on March 10, 1629. It was not to meet again for eleven years. Charles I decided that he "abhorred the very name of Parliament." He would govern "by those means God put into my hands." He would not again be embroiled in degrading hostilities.

There can never be a division of spheres of interest when one side is bent all the time on expansion and the other side is determined to resist. The Puritan leaders, at least, were anxious to slice away what Charles I considered integral and indivisible parts of the prerogative. The king was obstinate in his decision to keep inviolable the powers that, in his honest belief, God had given to him.

THE "ELEVEN YEAR TYRANNY"

The impoverished Charles I continued his levies of tunnage and poundage. He revived such obsolete customs as the compulsory distraint of knighthood and the forest fines based upon Henry II's Assize of the Forest of 1184. He expanded his extensive sale of monopolies: soap, fisheries, the vintners' company, etc.—the revenue for Charles was about £30,000 a year. He collected feudal dues wherever he could.

There now arose the question of ship money. In earlier centuries this had been a levy imposed in times of national emergency on the port towns of England by which these ports were asked to provide ships for the navy. The collection of ship money by Charles I was not the use of an archaic device, as is often supposed. Writs for the collection of it had been issued in 1626 and 1627 when England was in a really critical situation. The money Charles I collected was not used to strengthen his financial position; it did go to the building and equipment of ships. Writs were again issued for a levy in 1634. In 1635 the system was extended to all the counties of England and Wales; quotas of ships were demanded from every community, urban and rural. This general levy was defended by Charles I on the plausible grounds that the inland counties were protected by the royal navy as well as the outer. Although the money was again actually spent on ships, the collection of it at a time when there was no emergency needed stronger justification than the king provided. Many declared that ship money had become in fact a tax levied without a Parliamentary grant, violating the Petition of Right. The opposition of the propertied classes, who dominated Parliament and local government, was not, of course, entirely innocent of self-interest. Men with property pay taxes. Constitutional scruples and religious zeal were not solely responsible for the disputes described in these chapters.

Charles I addressed a letter to his judges "which, we doubt not, are well studied and informed in the right of our sovereignty." He asked them two questions: May the king compel his subjects to contribute ship money in a national emergency? May not the king decide when an emergency exists? The judges replied in the affirmative to each question and the collection went ahead. Many declined to pay. In 1637 a test case was made when John Hampden of Buckinghamshire, a cousin of Oliver Cromwell, refused to pay twenty shillings assessed upon his land in accordance with the king's writ. Hampden was summoned before the Court of Exchequer Chamber where judgment was finally given against him by a vote of seven to five. On every front, it seemed, the determined Charles I had been victorious.

Meanwhile the religious issues between the Anglicans, led by Archbishop Laud, and the Puritans became steadily more bitter. The various phases of the tumultuous controversy need not concern us here. Laud, with his demonic energy and with the support of the king's personal government, tried to make a single ecclesiastical system prevail throughout England. All must be reduced to uniformity. All publications must be strictly censored. Local compounds of heresy and indifference must be wiped away. To the Puritans a man could settle his accounts with God by personal efforts. He needed no loving ritual, no fine music, no allegedly papistical tendencies. The Laudian policy antagonized important social groups, especially those of power and rank in an expanding commercial and industrial society touched by the new dynamic faiths from across the Channel. These men were often convinced that their material gains in this world were given them by God because He approved of individuals who were diligent in their business. As the Court of Star Chamber persecuted the Puritans and inflicted heavy penalties strong tides began to run against the Anglicans. Laud was driving the moderates over into the ranks of the opponents of his ecclesiastical policy. At the same time, Laud's master, the king, continued to alienate the moderates who might have supported the royal cause in matters of government. The support of the men who stand in the middle of the way is always important.

The proposal of Archbishop Laud and Charles I to impose the Anglican episcopal system in Scotland was stark insanity. Laud prepared a liturgy similar to the English Prayer Book to be used in all Scottish churches. He decided that bishops should rule the Scottish Kirk. The result was widespread revolt, tumult, riots and a forest of claymores. A woman in Edinburgh threw a stool at the Bishop which nearly hit the Dean. The Scotsmen raised an army and dared Charles to fight. The words of James I echoed over the moors: "No bishop, no king."

Charles I now recalled from his post in Ireland the able Sir Thomas Wentworth, military proconsul and political engineer. Charles made Wentworth the Earl of Strafford and asked his advice. It was Strafford's judgment that the king should call Parliament. He argued that the Scots were rebelling and the English nation, long anti-Scottish, would support the king.

Strafford miscalculated. His hopes were vain. When Parliament met on April 13, 1640, it was not gravely concerned about the menace of the covenanted and undutiful Scotsmen and the national emergency. It began to debate the grievances, one by one, of the past eleven years. At last, on May 5, 1640, Charles dissolved this brief and barren assembly, aptly called the Short Parliament. It had lasted for five weeks. "Some cunning and ill-affected men," said the king, "have been the cause of this misunderstanding." For the last time he put his leading opponents in prison. Charles I did not see that the sense of national wrong was now deep and wide. John Pym, the great Somerset squire, observed amidst the popular disturbance: "Things must go worse before they go better." He was right. England stood on the edge of war.

We may pause at this point to weigh the significance of the revolutionary developments in the decades before armed conflict burst upon England. We have seen how the solid gentry had risen to increased power in the state and how the king's council had declined to the rim of impotence. The House of Commons, now holding the initiative in legislation, had steadily made a series of demands based, as they claimed, on law and precedent. The intractable Sir Edward Coke and the courts of common law had set forth the law as they had found it to be. The Anglican Church, torn by dissent within and attacked by hostile forces without, zealously attempted to impose the Laudian uniformity, "the beauty of holiness," upon most recalcitrant Puritan material. A serious scrutiny also shows that the economic, social, and political facts of the face of England were combining to make the position of the Stuart monarchs untenable. Their rearguard actions were admirable but the supply lines were breaking down. The Crown's need for money is a part of every chapter of the dramatic tale. All of these discords and convulsions imperilled the whole fabric of government and administration.

From the days of Jean Bodin to the days of John Austin, political theorists, jurists, and philosophers have sought to locate sovereignty. It must lie somewhere in every state. The first half of the seventeenth century confronted many critical questions: If the king's power was absolute how could there be any rights against him? If his prerogative was limited, who placed the limits upon it and who would determine the extent of those curbs? *Quis custodes custodiet?* Was the king's discretionary power derived from and limited by the law or not? Could it be abridged by an act of Parliament? Were the common law courts to vacate jurisdiction in any cases where the royal prerogative was involved, in the areas that James I called "transcendent matters"? Indeed, could Parliament interfere with or control the royal prerogative in any legitimate way? Did the privileges and liberties claimed by Parliament belong to it by right or as the result of a royal act of grace?

Questions such as these show the tragic dilemma of Englishmen in the years before the Civil War. Their first proposed solutions were to be republicanism, egalitarian democracy, the ideas of government by the saints and other fantasies. The sword has never been a good political primer.

CHAPTER XV

Civil War
and Common Weal

THE TWILIGHT OF PEACE

THE king stood at bay. Was it futile to fight? Was it sensible to capitulate? Was it wise to flee? Was it wiser still, in these hours of rupture, to seek a compromise? These questions may occur to the modern reader. They would have been without meaning to Charles I. What divine right ruler could degrade himself and his cause by surrendering the prerogatives he believed bestowed upon him by God? Charles had been unable to persuade and so he had been driven to coerce. When he had turned to demand he found that many of his subjects had refused to obey. They had grappled with the Lord's anointed. They had tried, in the eyes of Charles I, to besmirch and deface the sacred prerogative. They had hacked their way to the foot of the throne. Such, indeed, was the view of the king. On the other hand, the case against the Crown was very strong. Remedies and redress must be found, surely, for the bitter dissatisfactions in church and state.

We must be careful not to suggest more than the facts support. Even as broad rifts were widening in society there still remained great areas of common sympathies and understanding among Englishmen. In *The Crisis of the Constitution* Miss Margaret Judson has carefully documented this aspect of political thought in the first half of the seventeenth century. The long and intensive studies of Professor Willson H. Coates have led him to this conclusion: "At least up to the latter part of 1641 parliamentarians not only believed in monarchy but recognized areas of government where the king was not limited by human institutions; royalists at the same time admitted inviolable rights of the subject and found the rule of law compatible with their exaltation of the king. The ideal of both parliamentarians and royal-

326

ists was a balanced polity, and parliament, regarded neither as a sovereign body nor as a creature of the king, was where harmony between king and people was achieved." [1]

In the Short Parliament, John Pym, long a Parliament man, had said: "a Parliament is that to the Commonwealth, which the soul is to the body. . . . It behooves us therefore to keep the faculty of that soul from distemper." But the Short Parliament had become filled with distemper and the angry members had been sent home. Then Charles I tried desperately and in vain to borrow money from the London merchants. Nor were the kings of France and Spain, the banks of Genoa or the Pope prepared to lend gold or silver. Thereupon the king seized pepper from the warehouse of the East India Company and bullion from the London goldsmiths. All the king's efforts to get money and military equipment failed. The Scots invaded England's northern counties and occupied Durham. After Charles I made peace with them they insisted upon staying in England until the peace was ratified by Parliament. They also demanded that the English government pay their expenses at a rate of £850 a day. When Charles I summoned a great council of peers they could give him no advice but to call Parliament "to buy the Scots out of England."

On November 3, 1640, the famous Long Parliament assembled. It was not to be finally dissolved until March 16, 1660. The mood of this Parliament was black and tempers were swiftly roused. Under the leadership of John Pym and John Hampden the House of Commons struck first at the royal advisers, the instruments of government. The Earl of Strafford was summoned to London. ("I am tomorrow to London with more dangers beset, I believe, than ever man went out of Yorkshire.") Archbishop Laud was arrested. Strafford was accused of subverting "the fundamental laws," of "exercising tyrannical and exorbitant power." When it was clear that Strafford would never be found guilty of high treason by the judicial process of impeachment before the House of Lords, the Commons turned to condemn him to death by an act of attainder by which no proof of guilt needed to be offered. Such an act simply condemned the accused to death. The bill passed the Commons. The House of Lords yielded and also passed it, alarmed by the howls and threats of the London mobs. Charles I,

---

[1] Willson H. Coates, in a review of Miss Margaret Judson's *The Crisis of the Constitution: an Essay in Constitutional and Political Thought in England 1603–1645* (1949), *The American Historical Review* XL, No. 4 (July, 1950), p. 887. The quotation is made with the permission of Professor Coates.

pleading the danger to his family and his throne, signed a bill condemning his servant to execution. On May 12, 1641, about 200,000 people saw Strafford die. Four years later, too brave to flee, Archbishop Laud followed Strafford to the block.

Meanwhile Parliament turned to consider other grievances. It swiftly undertook legislation designed to make arbitrary government impossible in the future. To protect itself against a possible "untimely adjourning, proroguing, or dissolving" by the king it passed an act stating that it could not be dissolved without its own consent. A second piece of legislation "for the preventing of inconveniences happening by the long intermission of parliaments" was the new Triennial Act. This law provided that Parliament was to assemble once in every three years whether or not it had been summoned by the king.

Other acts swept away the prerogative courts of Star Chamber, High Commission, and Requests. The Council of the North and the Council of Wales were also abolished. Ship money and other arbitrary levies were forbidden. "The said charge imposed upon the subject for the providing and furnishing of ships commonly called ship money . . . and the said writs . . . and the said judgment given against the said John Hampden, were and are contrary to and against the laws and statutes of this realm, the right of property, the liberty of the subjects, former resolutions in Parliament, and the Petition of Right made in the third year of the reign of his majesty that now is." Other acts defined forests and forest laws, ended the ancient abuse of forest fines and abolished fines for distraint of knighthood.

There remained the question of religion. On this issue John Pym and his associates could find or forge no unity. Was the system of Laudian Anglicanism to be destroyed? If so, what would be put in its place? Some thoroughly radical Puritans prepared a "Root and Branch" bill designed to wipe out episcopacy completely and to remodel the church on Presbyterian lines. Opposed to them were the conservatives and moderates who did not want a Presbyterian system, who denounced much tampering with the Prayer Book. They only wished to purge the church of some Laudian innovations, nothing more. They were vehemently opposed to any change in Anglican church structure and organization. Debates grew violent. The salvation of souls was at stake. The minds and spirits of honest and sincere men were divided. Here was ferment and turmoil and a dangerous political crisis.

It was clear that the defenders of the existing church could not permit their opponents to seize executive power or to gather and control an army. In the middle of the disputes Parliament adjourned for six months. Riotous disturbances and strange, fanatical religious cults sprang up throughout the country. Moderates began to shrink from the visible evidences of a disordered state and to become still more conservative. Meanwhile, the Roman Catholic Irish rebelled to redress their manifold wrongs. Thousands of Protestant Ulsterites were slain or driven from their homes and lands.

When the Parliament met again in October, 1641, the angry Commons wanted to crush the Irish rebels at once. At the same time they hesitated to put an army under the command of Charles I. The king might use that army to scatter the members of Parliament. John Pym and the radicals, for their part, wanted to have the control of the army in the hands of ministers approved by the Commons. But such a step, surely, would make Parliament superior to the king. Pym and his associates argued that an even balance in government between Parliament and Crown would never be achieved and maintained. It was necessary, they asserted, to go a step further and make Parliament superior. On the other hand, many conservatives and moderates, frequently touched by an anti-Puritan spirit, consented only to support a reduction of the royal power so that the king would be equal to Parliament. Beyond that point they would not go.

Both England and Parliament were now divided in mind and spirit. Most Episcopalians were Royalists and most Puritans were Parliamentarians. Nevertheless, the total of those who were undecided, who did not know precisely where they stood, was large. In these circumstances the issues became more sharply defined when the Pym group took the revolutionary road towards Parliamentary government, declaring that it was the only practical thing to do. They accordingly prepared the Grand Remonstrance in November, 1641. This famous document of the Puritan anti-Royalist group recited acts of Charles I and his servants that had been offensive. It set forth what had been done to remedy national grievances. It also advanced new demands. For example, it proposed that the king should use only ministers "such as Parliament may have cause to confide in." It asked him to curtail the powers of the bishops and to end "oppressions in religion."

This Grand Remonstrance was passed in the House of Commons by a majority of only eleven. Charles I now had the support of a strong group in the Commons and a majority in the House of Lords. Many moderate men were saying that enough had been demanded of

Charles. Others were asserting that the king stood for what was lawful against an increasingly revolutionary assembly of radicals who wanted a whirlwind of disturbance that would wreck both the monarchy and the church and prepare the way for their own rise to power. It seemed that no compromise was possible. The House of Commons was sharply and bitterly divided. Rumors, charges and counter-charges raced through the streets and corridors of Westminster.

At this moment Charles I made a serious tactical blunder. On May 4, 1642, the king came down to the chapel of St. Stephen's where the Commons sat. With him were 400 swordsmen. His purpose was to arrest Pym, Hampden, and three other leaders because, Charles said, they were trying "to subvert the fundamental laws." They were also charged with "inviting the Scots to invade the kingdom of England, and with raising tumults in order to compel Parliament to aid them in their treacherous designs." By his renewed appeal to force, Charles threw away the support of those who might otherwise have followed him. Warned of the king's coming the five members had fled by the river. Charles asked where they were. The Speaker of the Commons replied that he had "neither eyes to see nor tongue to speak in this place but as this house shall direct me." The king had failed. Moreover, by invading the House of Commons he had again violated their privileges.

Early in 1642 Henrietta Maria left for France. Shortly afterwards Charles went to York. Meanwhile the Irish rebellion still continued. To crush it Parliament proposed to call out the militia. Would Charles use these forces against Parliament? Because the Commons thought he might, a Militia Bill was introduced which took the control of the militia forces out of the king's hands and gave Parliament power to appoint all militia commanders. When Charles refused to agree to this transfer of command, the Commons proceeded to turn their bill into an Ordinance of the Houses. The Ordinance referred to "this time of imminent danger" and "the bloody counsels of Papists and other ill-affected persons."

This procedure of Parliament departed from the conventions and forms of the constitution as they stood in the early seventeenth century. The Militia Ordinance was in fact saying that sovereignty belonged to and was exercised by Parliament. It said that if Charles I, called king and sovereign, did not approve of a bill Parliament could call it an ordinance and thus make it a law. On May 22, 1642, the king ordered the people by royal proclamation to disobey the ordinance of Parliament. If they should obey it, "we will then call them in due time to a strict account and proceed legally against them as violators of the laws and disturbers of the peace of this kingdom." On the same day both houses of Parliament declared that the ordinance must be obeyed.

In June, 1642, Parliament asked Charles to accept a new document, the Nineteen Propositions, "as the most necessarily effectual means, through God's blessing, of removing those jealousies and differences which have unhappily fallen betwixt you and your people." By the terms of the Nineteen Propositions the privy councillors, the principal officers and judges of the state, the tutors of the king's children, all were to be appointed only with the approval of Parliament. The king was asked to put the royal forts and castles under Parliament's control; to dismiss his military forces; to take away the votes of all Roman Catholic peers; to promise that his children would not conclude any marriage not approved by Parliament; to enforce the laws against Jesuits, priests and Popish recusants.

Such were the major demands of the Nineteen Propositions. They set out a new constitution under which Parliament would be supreme and Charles I would be a puppet. It is doubtful if Parliament really hoped that Charles would agree to the harsh terms of this document. It was an ultimatum, the ultimatum of men who were now ready to go to war.

Charles I refused to accept the Nineteen Propositions. Parliament at once appointed a Committee of Safety, declared Charles to be the aggressor, ordered the enlistment of 10,000 men for active service. On August 22, 1642, in the summer green near Nottingham, Charles raised the royal standard on a hill. Two governments were to join battle within a single state. The Civil War had begun.

THE KING'S ENEMIES

The center of political, social, and economic gravity had moved to the gentry class. "The heirs of the feudal past," in the words of Professor R. H. Tawney, "no longer held the keys to the future." Those keys were tightly grasped by the moneyed men of the middle classes who wanted greater political power. Yet when these things are said there remains the fact that the Civil War was not solely a cleavage between classes. It is absurd to explain such things as war and peace entirely by economic determinism or in terms of economic status and the pride of the pocketbook.[2]

Many men of the country gentry fought for Charles I side by side with the poorer townsmen. Many who disliked episcopacy fought for Charles because they opposed the extreme pretensions of Parliament. Several refused to desert the king because they thought it a dishonorable thing to do. Classes and families were shot through with disunity. Geographical areas were split. On both sides most men entered the war with reluctance and sadness, for they were fighting no foreign foe but Englishmen.

We cannot here concern ourselves with the tale of campaigns and battles. It lies outside our purpose to trace in detail the violent partisanship and revolutionary changes that had but little permanent effect on England's legal and constitutional history. Of some interest to the student may be such practical measures as the Solemn League and Covenant (1643), a treaty concluded between Parliament and the Scotsmen to bring the latter effectively into the struggle against Charles I. As a result of this agreement a joint executive Committee of Both Kingdoms was established to prosecute the war. Of interest also is the Self-Denying Ordinance (1644) passed by Parliament to end the reign of lukewarm and incompetent commanders. This document required all members of Parliament to resign their army commands. Those whom the military authorities wanted back again were reappointed; the others were not. This procedure avoided vicious bickering and recrimination about who should retire and why.

In February, 1648, the New Model Army was created by Oliver Cromwell, who had remained a member of Parliament, and his colleagues "for a more speedy, vigorous, and effective prosecution of the war." This force became an efficient and formidable fighting machine under strict discipline. It performed its tasks, fearing God and keeping its powder dry. The religious fervor of the Puritans in the New Model Army united with its training and discipline to wreak havoc on the Royalists. In the spring of 1646 Charles I surrendered to the Scots.

Amid the seething confusion of sects and parties, of battling ideas and stormy creeds, Parliament had apparently triumphed over the

---

[2] See, for instance, William Schenk, *The Concern for Social Justice in the Puritan Revolution* (1949) and "A Democratic Tercentenary," *The Hibbert Journal*, XLVI (1947). Protesting against a frequent tendency to stress unduly the economic forces in history Dr. Schenk contended that the Puritan Revolution must also be carefully viewed in its religious and social context.

king. What was to be done with the victory? What new arrangements should be made in church and state? From 1642 onwards there had been strong signs that the only bond holding various groups together was a common opposition to Charles I. When the war had begun, Parliament had divided. Some had gone to the king's standards; some to the army of Parliament; and a few had just gone home. Those of the Long Parliament who were united against Charles had rapidly disagreed about other things. In 1646 they were still divided.

The religious problem was most explosive. All men remaining in Parliament generally opposed episcopacy. The majority, Presbyterian in sympathy, wanted a Presbyterian state church. But would the Presbyterians, asked many men, be any less intolerant than the Roman Catholics or the Anglicans ("New presbyter is but old priest writ large")? The followers of John Knox were surely as rigid in their views as Archbishop Laud's adherents. And there were thousands of Anglicans in England, increasing thousands of Independents, uncounted sons of other sects in all the counties. What of them? Would the Presbyterians ever incline to toleration for them? The Parliamentary party, within and without Parliament, was bitterly split. The Independents, of course, hated presbyters as much as they hated bishops. And the army, winning victories for Parliament, contained thousands of these Independents as well as representatives of most other sects. It was politically wise to heed the army.

When Parliament had accepted the Solemn League and Covenant in 1643 it had practically agreed to set up a Presbyterian Church in England. After Charles I surrendered to the Scots in 1646 this Parliament calmly went ahead with its Presbyterian projects. It presented the Propositions of Newcastle to Charles demanding the establishment of a Presbyterian Church in England; the control of the army and navy by Parliament for twenty years; the enforcement of the anti-Catholic penal laws. Charles I, of course, was devoted to the Anglican Church. His character was such that he tried to play the Independents against the Presbyterians. It was a dangerous game. Charles hesitated, parleyed, and temporized. Then the Scottish Covenanters, angered by his opposition to Presbyterians, gave him up to Parliament.

With Charles I in their hands Parliament passed bills establishing a Presbyterian church system. It insisted, as William Laud had done, on a uniform religion throughout England. It persecuted and it bludgeoned. Early in 1647, the New Model Army, already infuriated by the denial of religious liberty, was ordered by Parliament to disband. No provision was made for paying the soldiers' back wages. This was a risky thing for Parliament to do. The soldiers of the New Model Army did not go home. Calculations of justice and safety said otherwise.

Parliament now sought to join forces with the king and the Royalists. It offered to restore Charles I with his authority unimpaired if he would establish a Presbyterian Church in England for only three years. At this point the army kidnapped Charles, thus making it clear that there could be no Royalist-Presbyterian arrangement directed against the Independents or anybody else.

DEMOCRATIC IDEAS

Stated in pamphlet after pamphlet in the decade after 1640 were a series of radical doctrines, social, economic, and political. Especially had democratic political ideas been developing in the rank and file of the army. Through the long months of war the common soldiers had been debating their policies and attitudes. Having found much wrong in the country they began to talk about ways of setting things right. In doing so it was natural that they should find agreeable answers in the radical proposals of the Levellers.

These Levellers were mostly Independents, standing for laissez-faire in religion, stressing the individual freedom of the believer. Hence they opposed a national church and they believed in relatively independent and self-sufficient congregations. They wanted to conduct their own form of worship without authority from ecclesiastical powers or civil magistrates. A democratic set of concepts such as these, arising mainly from the ideas of Christian liberty and equality, easily became political in their direction and consequence. Many men in the Puritan parties were first interested in the Christian and then in the natural man. Thus numerous Independents, within and without the army, found themselves politically democratic Levellers. Lord Lindsay recently remarked: "The fundamental ideas of democracy, if divorced from the religious context in which they belong, become cheap and shallow and easy of reputation." [3]

Many soldiers, artisans, small tradesmen and farmers were united as Levellers because they were interested in maintaining human rights, the rights of Englishmen as persons. Behind legal rights of property and station they saw natural rights and natural justice. Political equal-

[3] See A. S. P. Woodhouse, *Puritanism and Liberty* (1938, 1950).

ity, they declared, should have no economic implications. Parliament should represent the people, not property. "Sovereignty lies only with the people and Parliament governs only by their consent." Thus came into prominence the Leveller ideas of the inalienable rights of the individual, of law having authority by the "consent of the people," of universal manhood suffrage, of the origin of government in an original compact and, finally, of the idea that the powers of government should be limited by a fundamental law emanating from the people. "The laws of the land are only valid when they are a statement of higher laws." Throughout all the later period of the Civil War runs the pervasive influence of the Levellers, weakening reverence for social distinction and dignity of office.

When the officers of the army were confronted with these ideas of the common soldiers they could not approve. It was impossible for them to agree with the famous words of a Leveller that "the poorest he that is in England" should rank with "the greatest he." One of the leaders of the officers was the austere Henry Ireton, Cromwell's son-in-law and in many respects Cromwell's mentor—"Cromwell only shot the bolts that were hammered in Ireton's forge." Ireton debated brilliantly at Putney and elsewhere with the Leveller leaders. This Nottingham squire had been wounded and taken prisoner at Naseby. He had "fought like a lion" and escaped. When Parliament had offered to settle £2,000 a year in land upon him after the battle of Worcester Ireton refused it: "I should be more content to see you doing the service of the nation than so liberal in disposing of the public treasure." Ireton died in 1651 at the early age of forty while serving as Cromwell's deputy in Ireland. It is said that he died because, even though desperately ill, he refused to neglect his public business.

Henry Ireton was obviously a man of conviction and courage. He honestly and strongly believed mankind was corrupt and likely to remain so. He thought that the Leveller doctrines logically led to communism and anarchy. "All the main thing that I speak for is because I would have an eye to property." In his judgment, the soldiers of Parliament had fought a civil war to reform or purify the existing constitution that had been broken by the king. The purpose of the state, as Ireton saw it, was to keep the peace and defend property. Only those should possess a vote who had "a permanent fixed interest in the kingdom . . . that is, the persons in whom all land lies, and those in corporations in whom all trading lies." To Ireton, "the people of England" meant the landowners and the merchants. He believed that a state not based on property must be ruled by the poor and the result would be anarchy.

The Levellers, of course, could not agree with this conclusion. One said: "We have engaged in this kingdom and ventured our lives, and it was all for this: to recover our birthrights and privileges as Englishmen; and by the arguments urged there is none. . . . It seems now, except a man hath a fixed estate in this kingdom, he hath no right in this kingdom. I wonder we were so much deceived." The Leveller ideas did not, apparently, seize upon the argument that if the existing distribution of property must always determine the composition of Parliament and the nature of government then there would be little space for change or political progress.

Oliver Cromwell persuaded the army to offer the king a final settlement. This was done in the long and detailed document called the Heads of the Proposals (1647), generally believed to have been composed by Henry Ireton. This document would have permitted the restoration of the monarchy and the House of Lords with their powers essentially the same as before the war. Charles I was asked to agree to the dissolution of the Long Parliament and the election of a new one. In the future a Parliament was to be called every two years. Each Parliament was to sit at least three months "unless adjourned or dissolved by their own consent." The Heads of the Proposals also asked that plans be developed to ensure "more perfection of equality" in the distribution of seats in Parliament, a broader franchise, "freedom in the election, order in the proceeding thereto, and certainty in the returns." The document also requested religious toleration except for Anglicans and Roman Catholics; the redress of a number of other grievances regarding forest laws, monopolies, excise taxes, and the like. Finally, it was proposed that Parliament assume control of the army and the great offices of state for ten years.

Had Charles I accepted these terms the royal power would have been reined and checked; it would not have been essentially changed. From the king's point of view, however, there could be no sharing or diminution of the prerogative royal. He rejected the Heads of the Proposals.

The soldiers now did what Oliver Cromwell had earlier tried to prevent them from doing. Suspicious of their officers, who represented different class interests, and distrustful of Charles I, they drew up their own proposals for dealing with the menace, as they saw it, of Charles I's absolutist government. As a basis for discussion, they decided to prepare their draft of a constitution. They called this document, filled with the ideas of the Levellers, the Agreement of the People (1649). It was strongly buttressed by Puritan theology and the Independent church order. As Professor A. S. P. Woodhouse has carefully shown, this Agreement everywhere "concentrated on the shaping of a perfect civil constitution."

The Agreement of the People abolished the monarchy and the House of Lords. Government was to be in the hands of a single-chamber Parliament elected by universal manhood suffrage, with the provision that those who had supported Charles I in the war might not vote or be elected to Parliament for seven years. Religious toleration was to be given to all men. The democratic form of government set forth in the Agreement was limited by an exact and written statement of a bill of rights setting forth certain fundamental liberties, based on the laws of reason and nature, of which the subject could never be deprived. Among those inalienable rights was private property, founded in the laws of nature and guaranteed by God. One power withheld from the Parliament provided for in the Agreement was the power to level estates. It is a mistake to think that the Levellers attacked the institution of private property.

At first the soldiers hoped for a referendum on the merits of their draft constitution. It must be accepted or rejected by the "sovereign people." They were finally persuaded to temper their document and then to submit it to Parliament instead of holding a popular plebiscite. Ireton called it "political moonshine." Parliament, of course, would have nothing of what most members considered the chimeras of wild and revolutionary spirits.

The Agreement of the People, stating so many of the Leveller theories, grew out of the religious ideas of the Independents and the old concept of a constitution as a statement of fundamental law. Here was evolved the idea of a written constitution with paramount laws limiting the powers of government. This constitution, as all law, was to be enforceable through the courts. Here, too, appears sharply and vividly the idea that there are individual, inalienable rights possessed by all men. Mankind has been endowed by the Creator with rights such as those later more precisely defined as life, liberty, and the pursuit of happiness. And, finally, there appears the idea of the overwhelming sovereignty of the people. The Leveller and Independent ideas of democracy in seventeenth century England united with the angry and robust voice of Sir Edward Coke to exert a profound influence on later democratic institutional development in the United States. Some of these consequences flowed directly, as in the case of Independent colonists and their descendants. Others were channelled through the works of such men as John Locke and the French philosophers to Thomas Jefferson and his contemporaries who were concerned with the state and dignity of man.

THE FALL OF THE MONARCHY

In November, 1647, Charles I escaped. He was recaptured. Then he negotiated with the Scots and finally agreed to establish Presbyterianism in England for three years. As a result of this royal bargain the Scots invaded England to help Charles I put himself in a position to keep his agreement. Early in 1648 Oliver Cromwell met the leaders of the New Model Army and the soldiers went to war again. The second Civil War lasted only a few weeks before the Scots were defeated. Meanwhile Charles had been negotiating with the House of Commons. The Independents wanted an absolute Parliament no more than they wanted an absolute king. Cromwell returned to London and on December 6, 1648, he stationed Colonel Pride and some musketeers at the door of Westminster Hall. They prevented about a hundred Presbyterians from entering and haled about fifty more off to prison. When "Pride's Purge" was over, only ninety members were left to form the so-called "Rump" of the Long Parliament. They were all Independents, representing the army. The galling knot of Presbyterian opposition had been cut by the sword of Cromwell.

On January 6, 1649, the ninety men of the "Rump," despite the opposition of a dozen peers left in the House of Lords, passed an "act" creating a High Court of Justice "for the trying and judging of Charles Stuart, king of England." Charles I, this prolix document declared, "hath had a wicked design totally to subvert the ancient and fundamental laws and liberties of this nation and in their place to introduce an arbitrary and tyrannical government . . . he hath prosecuted it with fire and sword, levied and maintained a cruel war in the land against the Parliament and the kingdom." Charles was to be tried for these crimes, and for treason against the people of England.

Could the charge of treason legally be brought against the king? Under the new theory of popular sovereignty such a procedure might have been theoretically arguable had the "Rump" represented a sizeable portion of the people. Legally, however, Charles could not be tried for treason. He was still the king, and treason against himself the king could not commit. The court was illegal. Charles I told the members so.

The outcome of the trial was never in doubt. To put the king to death seemed the expedient thing to do. It was, in the words Oliver Cromwell is supposed to have used, "cruel necessity." On January 30, 1649, with the winter sun shining upon him, Charles I was executed in front of his palace at Whitehall. He died nobly, in the manner of a king. The nation was stunned. Even some of the regicides were temporarily appalled at what they had done. In the moment of his death Charles prepared the way for the failure of his foes.

Now there was no turning back for the makers of revolution. The Presbyterians had brought Charles I to the steps of the scaffold. The Independents had cut off his head. The sword had won the war and had executed the king. The sword, then, was to maintain the new republic. It did so, for eleven years.

Before the eleven years were gone Oliver Cromwell was dead and so was Henry Ireton. After Charles II was restored to the throne in 1660 the House of Commons voted that the bodies of Cromwell and Ireton should be drawn on a hurdle to Tyburn, hung up in their coffins there and afterwards be interred beneath the gallows. Thus the dust of Cromwell and Ireton has long since mingled with the drain pipes of the Edgware Road.

THE COMMONWEALTH

A hundred years ago Thomas Babington Macaulay wrote these words about the victorious army and the Independents: "In the act of enslaving their country they had deceived themselves with the belief they were emancipating her." This is a hard and harsh sentence; but it is just. For eleven years England was to be governed without a monarchy by a minority of men trying to answer discontent by oppression. Successive governments collapsed and successive schemes failed. Fires built by zeal blazed and guttered out.

After the execution of Charles I the only stable element remaining was the army. Oliver Cromwell was its Captain-General. Early in 1649 the Rump Parliament, dominated by the army, passed an act "for abolishing the kingly office in England, Ireland, and the dominions thereunto belonging." It proclaimed the devitalized House of Lords at an end. It passed a new Treasons Act providing that it was high treason to say that the government was "tyrannical, usurped, or unlawful" or that the Commons were not "the supreme authority in this nation." It was also high treason to "plot, contrive, or endeavour to stir up or raise force" against the government. England was declared to be "a commonwealth and free state." The executive power of the new Commonwealth was fixed in a council of state whose members were to be appointed annually by Parliament. The council of state at first numbered forty-one individuals; about thirty of them were members of the Rump Parliament. "A most happy way is made for this nation, if God see it good, to return to its just and ancient right of being governed by its own representatives or national meetings in council."

Freedom of public worship and toleration was granted to all except Anglicans, Roman Catholics and Unitarians. On a new Great Seal these words were inscribed: "In the First Year of Freedom by God's Blessing Restored." But there was no freedom. The new republic was a thinly veiled military despotism in which the generals were aided by a godly oligarchy. "The tragedy of Oliver Cromwell was that he was never able to find a constitutional basis for his government."

The men of the army had acted in the name of the people. Now they found active champions of democracy against them, the people themselves generally hostile. Even the army was not wholly satisfied. The army's Levellers, for instance, could not approve of recent events. When the Leveller leader John Lilburne denounced the government as a tyranny and usurpation he was brought to trial on the charge of treason. When he was acquitted by a jury and later freed by the Rump the soldiers beat their drums and blew their trumpets. Cromwell shouted in anger to the Speaker of the Rump: "I tell you, Sir, you have no other way to deal with these men but to break them or they will break you." England was held together by force and force alone. The opponents of the officers of the New Model Army and the Independent saints were so divided among themselves that the fall of the Rump and the army would have resulted in anarchy. Only Oliver Cromwell, the army, and the Rump could defend the Commonwealth and give it temporary stability.

The tasks facing the new regime were heavy and hard. Domestic discontent was heightened by economic problems. High taxation and unemployment pressed upon the people. Imperial and foreign problems brought war with the Scots, with the Irish, with the Dutch. State expenditures rose. The financial measures of the Rump Parliament were often harsh and unsound. When it found that it could not borrow sufficient funds it resorted to the renewed sale of church and

Crown lands. It also sold the seized property of the Royalists. It increased the collection of fines through the courts and its interference in the judicial sphere became steadily more obnoxious.

Meanwhile the size of the navy was doubled. England's commercial power was slowly revived. The famous Navigation Act of 1651, aimed at the Dutch, was passed for "the increase of shipping and encouragement of the navigation of this nation." It provided that no goods from Asia, Africa, or America should be imported into England, Ireland, or the English colonies except in English or colonial ships "whereof the masters and mariners are also for the most part of them of the people of this commonwealth." No goods from Europe were to be imported into England or the English colonies except in British ships, the majority of the crews in each case being British. To this rule there was added one exception: goods might be shipped to England or her colonies in vessels belonging to an exporting European country provided that the cargoes were produced in the country from which they were exported. The Navigation Act of 1651 was thus designed to give England and her colonies a larger share of the carrying trade, to help English shipping and increase the number of English seamen.

The soldiers disliked the war that was being waged with Holland. They demanded reforms in the church. They were weary of the repressive, arbitrary, and frequently ill-advised acts of the Rump. The unpopularity of the Commonwealth administration among the civilian population was patent everywhere. Cromwell and his cohorts were discovering that it was harder to build a structure of civil government than it was to tear it down. Cromwell, of course, tried to reduce the rising frictions and to compromise because he saw that the Rump alone prevented open military rule. But several of the political leaders attempted to push through a bill providing that no member should be elected to the next Parliament who was not approved by the Rump. At this point the angry Cromwell summoned musketeers and went to disperse the remnants of the Long Parliament. "Your hour is come," he informed the Rump. "The Lord hath done with you . . . I will put an end to your prating. You should give place to better men. You are no Parliament!" The musketeers drove out the members and the doors were locked. Open force had settled one question.

Could there now be a free election? The army publicly declared they wanted one. Nevertheless, all were aware that a freely elected Parliament would probably restore the monarchy and probably end toleration for the Independents. The army, largely composed of Independents, knew that a free election was impossible. Popular sovereignty would have overthrown the Puritan government. Cromwell and the army leaders finally decided to adopt the idea of rule by an aristocracy of "godly" men. They asked the Independent congregations to submit nominations; from this list the army officers chose men "faithful, fearing God and hating covetousness." This nominated Parliament, later called the Barebone Parliament after one of its members, Praise-God Barebone, contained 140 members. It met in July, 1653, and soon demonstrated the impracticality of rule by a well-meaning assembly innocent of skill. The members were pious men, better men than the crafty jugglers of the Rump; but they had too many ideas about reform.

During the Cromwellian regime almost all existing institutions were put on trial. Extremists in religion carried their emotions and ideas into the realm of government and the sphere of political theory. Often, too, cautious and sober men shared the feeling of discontent and supported demands for change. In these circumstances, it was inevitable that the Barebone Parliament should carry on a long agitation for the reform of the laws of England. Especially obnoxious were the severe criminal laws, the slow court of Chancery, the expense involved in appeals to the law, the lawyers and the judges. Some noisy groups wanted to repeal all human law, to summon the people of England from the wilderness of sin and establish the rule of God. Others wanted to remove all traces of Norman elements in the law. In 1650 a Parliamentary committee report on law reform was presented to the House of Commons. A second committee sent up another report in 1652. After July, 1653, the Barebone Parliament argued and discussed. There were few among them who understood the technical complexities of the problems. Later, in 1656, Cromwell appointed another committee, also containing a number of well-meaning but helpless amateurs. Despite several minor reforms the movement for large-scale alterations in the law failed completely. In the years of passion and turmoil it was perhaps fortunate that the dedicated reformers were not successful. A period of disturbance seldom provides the atmosphere necessary for calm and unhurried judgment. Honest zeal is never an adequate substitute for precise knowledge and careful consideration.

"Nothing was in the hearts of these men," said Cromwell, "but overturn, overturn." The debates, it seemed, were interminable. The plans for reform, it was certain, were dangerous. So alarmed were the moderates in the assembly that in December, 1653, they carried a vote in a scattered house (while most of the radicals were away at prayer) bringing the Barebone Parliament to an end. Another experiment had failed. "I am more troubled now," Cromwell had said, "with the fool than with the knave."

THE PROTECTORATE

After the failure of the Barebone assembly in 1653 it was decided to jettison the idea of the supremacy of Parliament. The army officers drew up a new and ingenious written constitution, called the Instrument of Government. This document of forty-two paragraphs followed, in many respects, the lines of the historic constitution. It is the first written constitution put into operation by a great state. By its terms, some of which were derived from the Heads of the Proposals, there was to be a Lord Protector, chosen for life; a council of state, containing civilian and military members; a Parliament (containing 460 members, of which 60 were to be sent from Ireland and Scotland) elected by limited suffrage every three years. The council of state was apparently designed to check and balance the Protector—he could not, for instance, make war or peace or approve ordinances without its advice. The Instrument of Government stated that the Parliament could pass a measure over the Protector's veto by a simple majority vote. The Protector was given revenues to provide for an army of 30,000 men, a navy, and the expenses of civil administration and government (£200,000). There was to be religious liberty for all but those who believed in "popery or prelacy" or practiced "blasphemy or licentiousness."

Constituencies were remodelled. A revised county franchise was established, providing that the right to vote was to be held only by those possessing at least £200 real or personal property (instead of the freehold of forty shillings). It was obviously intended that those classes should be represented whose interests were supposedly attached to a republican form of government. Certainly the men elected to Parliament under such a franchise would be conservative, not strongly democratic or Leveller in sympathy.

The first Lord Protector was to be Oliver Cromwell. Despite the terms of the Instrument the actual power of government was in his hands. Backed by the army, Cromwell was really the dictator of England. He tried to bring peace, but he had to carry a sword. The saint would have to be a warrior saint. How else could order be maintained?

As Professor Francis D. Wormuth has remarked, the main problem was not one of constitutional checks or balances between agencies in a government system. "It was an opposition of military interests to civilian interests, and these two were flatly incompatible."

The first Parliament to be summoned under the Instrument of Government met on September 3, 1654. In the first session the distracted condition of England was clearly revealed. There was no united opinion. Much of England was Royalist. The Puritans were irreconcilably divided among themselves. Cromwell at once purged his Parliament of almost a hundred members. He wanted conservative Puritans and that is what he got. Nevertheless, the new Parliament was far from pliable. It immediately objected to several powers of the Protector. Claiming that it represented the nation as against the army, Parliament declared itself opposed to religious toleration. It wanted to take over control of the army and the navy, the election to the Protectorship and the council of state.

In vain Oliver Cromwell defended the "fundamentals" of the Instrument of Government. In vain he reminded the Parliament that it was not a constituent assembly, that the Instrument was not flexible or subject to amendment. This Parliament was making the same bid for power that the Long Parliament had made. It wanted to end the despotism of a military junto. Cromwell, on the other hand, wanted to stop the factions from bringing anarchy and intolerance. "I am as much for government by consent as any man," he said, "but where will you find that consent?" To maintain order, to stop the ceaseless challenge to the Instrument, to keep religious toleration, to prevent an "irresponsible assembly" from becoming the prey of bitter parties, the Protector waved the sword and the members of Parliament went home in January, 1655. Cromwell, like Robespierre, found it hard to establish a republic of virtue. He also found, like James I and Charles I, that to govern with a refractory Parliament was difficult.

Meanwhile Cavalier and Leveller conspiracies threatened. Many judges resigned rather than enforce ordinances issued under the Instrument of Government. England was divided into twelve districts, in each of which a major-general enforced his stern will and the moral "blue laws." All merry England felt the grim constraints of godly zeal. At the same time, Cromwell moved into war with Spain. Puritan nationalism reached its peak when Roman Catholics were the enemy.

Domestic trade slumped. Foreign trade was hampered. A commercial depression threatened and war taxes rose. The government needed still more money.

Cromwell called another Parliament in September, 1656. This Parliament, from which about a hundred "undesirable elements" had been excluded, tried still another experiment. It prepared the Humble Petition and Advice, a new constitution that would have had Cromwell as king with power to nominate his successor. It also proposed to create a second chamber consisting of members nominated by Cromwell for life. This chamber was not to be called the House of Lords but rather the "other house." A large fixed revenue was to be authorized. The principles of religious toleration were to be slightly extended.

Cromwell refused the crown. He accepted the rest of the Humble Petition and Advice. Forty members of the Commons were appointed to the "other house." Presbyterians and republicans were admitted to the Commons from which they had earlier been excluded. At once "these tumultuous and popular spirits" began to plot with Royalists and Levellers to oust Cromwell. The Commons violently attacked the "other house" and the constitution under which they sat. All was built on shifting sands. Cromwell angrily dismissed his last Parliament. He had moved far along the same road the Stuarts had travelled before him. "I think it high time that an end be put to your sitting, and I do dissolve this Parliament. And let God judge between you and me." This dissolution occurred on February 4, 1658. Seven months later Oliver Cromwell died.

With the strong hand of Cromwell gone there came confusion and anarchy. The new Lord Protector was Cromwell's son Richard, a weak man. He called a Parliament that quarrelled with the army. The army officers then forced Richard to dissolve Parliament. When that was done, they began to dispute among themselves.

The nation was weary of military rule. In the turmoil of these dark days the Royalists, the business men, and the landed Parliamentarians stood against the army, the challenge of the sects, and levelling radicalism. The old Rump Parliament assembled at Westminster. Richard Cromwell went to France. General Monk, the commander of occupation forces in Scotland, marched to London in February, 1660. Allying himself with the fearful landowners and business men, Monk declared for a "free Parliament."

In March the restored Long Parliament dissolved itself. An election was held. The new Convention Parliament prepared for the restoration of the monarchy. The son of Charles I, it seemed, provided a visible means of salvation for a nation distracted by unhappy and ineffective experiments. "An heroic age raises questions, but it takes a sensible age to solve them."

CHAPTER XVI

Charles the Second
and James the Second:
political arithmetic

A DYNASTY RESTORED

"Ask for the old paths, where is the good way, and walk therein, and ye shall find rest for your souls," said the poet and prophet Jeremiah. "Tampering is the useless vice of restless and unstable minds," said Edmund Burke. These quotations well describe the mood and mind of many Englishmen as they turned away from the tampering and ineffective experiments of the Commonwealth and Protectorate and sought the familiar signposts along the old paths.

The events of 1660 not only ended the arbitrary rule of the civilian and military groups that dominated the eleven years of the interregnum. They also restored the old institutions of government, the legislative and fiscal authority of Parliament, and the executive power of the monarchy.

The new king was Charles II (1660–1685). Many descriptions have been penned of this king who came back from exile over the water to take his heritage. Charles II has not suffered from a lack of biographers. Most of those who have written about him have not, however, been inhibited by deep knowledge of the historical evidence. The drama of the period has attracted the shaping imagination of the novelist, the poet and the dilettante. Too frequently lacking has been the caution of the professional historian. A few years ago Professor Clyde L. Grose remarked very wisely that "the convincing biographer who would portray Charles as a great and good king must have consummate literary skill and a general blindness as to facts." [1]

---

[1] Clyde L. Grose, "Charles the Second of England," *The American Historical Review,* XLIII (1938).

There is no doubt that Charles II possessed a character marked by indolence and flexible principles. Fortunately for his safety and his throne, he showed unusual gifts of intelligence, tact and intuition. Charles was astute, subtle, calculating, wary, adaptable, cynical, patient. Because this was so, and because he did not want "to go on his travels again," Charles II did not persist in any attempt to overstep the limits that divided the possible from the impossible. The insight of the king—together with his skill in compromise and dissimulation—undoubtedly forestalled and prevented much trouble. The shrewdness did fail sometimes—as in the case of the secret Treaty of Dover—but Charles always managed to draw back or leap aside in time to avoid disaster. He often maintained his ascendancy by his wits and his wits alone. His unadaptable successor's misfortunes were in part the results of errors of judgment of which Charles II was not guilty. "There is only one thing worse than a crime," said Talleyrand later, "and that is a blunder."

Englishmen summoned Charles II to the throne without requiring him to make any promises, commitments, or constitutional guarantees. No allusion was made to the issues of the Civil War. No reference was made to the vexed question of the proper relationship between king and Parliament. Charles II was not asked to admit the supremacy of Parliament, to say that he was bound by the common law or the wishes of his people. The Convention Parliament only stated that "according to the ancient and fundamental laws of this kingdom the government is, and ought to be, by Kings, Lords, and Commons" and it invited Charles II "to return and take the government of the kingdom into his hands."

Nevertheless, nothing could cancel out the preceding twenty years. Recent events had been inscribed for all to see and remember. The realities of power were different from what they had been before the Civil War. It has been well remarked that 1660 marked "a restoration of Parliament, even more than a restoration of the king." Despite superficial appearances, the year 1660 did not mark a return to the status quo. All of the restrictions imposed upon the crown before 1642 still stood unchallenged and unchanged. Such things as ship money, benevolences, and forced loans were illegal and they remained so. The king could not legislate or tax outside of Parliament. At the same time, the strength of the common law was maintained and extended. For instance, the prestige of the Court of Admiralty declined and it lost several provinces of jurisdiction. The prerogative courts had been abolished and consequently the common law courts annexed large blocs of the territory once controlled by such bodies as the courts of Star Chamber and High Commission and the councils of Wales and the North. When we say, therefore, that the king could not do justice outside the existing system we mean that the jurisdiction of first instance lay under the sole control of the superior courts of Westminster.[2]

Because the king's council had been stripped of most of its judicial powers it was no longer possible to carry on the Tudor ideal of a carefully formulated public policy depending mainly for its success upon royal and conciliar authority. Henceforth the common law courts would decide cases and problems upon the basis of statute and common law. These courts alone would settle legal questions about the relationships between the government and the governed.

An excellent example of the importance of these changes can be seen in the altered activities and powers of local government authorities. Before the Civil War these officials had been swiftly responsible to the royal council, as in the age of the Tudors. After the Civil War they turned to the common law courts to find out what the letter of the law said about their duties. The result was an increased independence in local administration. The local justices of the peace, those men of the propertied class, acted more and more on their own initiative and in their own interest. They became more irresponsible, less heedful of the national welfare than in the days when the royal council watched and the crown punished them for their iniquities and omissions.

These facts, and others, show that there had been an essential change in the balance of power in the constitution. Parliament alone could levy taxes. Parliament could refuse and control supply. Parliament could bring royal advisers to account by the ancient device of impeachment, a valuable tool because it enabled Parliament to attack royal policy without starting rebellion or war. As Professor G. M. Trevelyan has said: "The Civil War had reversed the relation between Whitehall and Westminster; the members now feared nothing from the Court, but courtiers feared much from Parliament."

It is therefore clear that after 1660 Parliament and the common law

---

[2] There were several disputes about jurisdiction in this period. For a protracted argument about original complaints and writs of error between the House of Lords and the House of Commons see the documents on Skinner *v.* the East India Company (1668–1670) in Carl Stephenson and F. G. Marcham, *Sources of English Constitutional History*, pp. 561–563.

courts could often destroy, demolish or check the programs and schemes of the monarch. Nevertheless, it could not effectively determine or manage policy in any positive sense. No method had been yet devised to secure the responsibility of the king and his ministers to Parliament. The constitutional devices of the Cabinet system or ministerial responsibility were not developed until the next century. On the one hand, it was clear that government could not be carried on against the wishes of the classes represented in Parliament. On the other hand, it was not clear which constitutional power, the executive or the legislative, had the larger say. Certainly neither king nor Parliament could legislate alone. The Treasons Act of 1661 specifically stated that it was treason to say "that both houses of Parliament or either house of Parliament have or hath a legislative power without the king, or any other words to the same effect." Until the location of final authority was determined the jostling and bickering that marked the latter seventeenth century were inevitable.

The Convention Parliament was swiftly legalized in 1660—legally it had not earlier been a Parliament because the election had been held without the authority of writs issued by the king. This assembly immediately returned crown and church lands to their original owners. Such an action struck heavily at many Puritans who had purchased church land. The army was paid and disbanded; only three foot regiments were kept. A regular annual income of £1,200,000, made up of the port duties added to hereditary excise, was granted to the king; this was to be raised by taxes. However, as the promised revenue was never forthcoming Charles II still had to ask Parliament frequently for more money. The lords spiritual, shut out of the House of Lords by the Exclusion Act of 1642, were brought back to their ancient places in Parliament (1661). The Convention Parliament also declared that the reign of Charles II had legally begun in January, 1649, on the execution of Charles I. All acts passed by Parliament between 1642 and 1660 that had not received the royal assent had no force de jure. Hence, as described earlier, almost all the great reforms carried through by the Long Parliament in 1641 were left unchanged.

Other measures carried into law by the Convention Parliament included an act for erecting and establishing a post office and a new Navigation Act extending still further government control of the carrying trade to and from English ports and applying especially to the colonies in America. An Act Abolishing Feudal Tenures provided, as indicated by the long form of its title, for the "taking away of the court of wards and liveries, and tenures *in capite* and by knight's service, and purveyance, and for setting a revenue upon his majesty in lieu thereof." This enactment was obviously welcome to the landed classes whose representatives guided it through Parliament. Among other acts of progressive legislation in Charles II's Parliaments were those amending the poor laws (1661) and repealing the penalty of burning for those found guilty of heresy (1678).

On December 29, 1660, the Convention Parliament was dissolved. A new Parliament was elected and met in May, 1661. This assembly was the so-called Cavalier Parliament, filled with young men, Cavalier and Anglican, men who enthusiastically believed in peace and order and ranged themselves behind the church and the king. These individuals represented the conservative interests of the landed gentry who wanted some compensation for the lean years after 1649. The Cavalier Parliament has been aptly described as being more royalist than the king and more Anglican than the bishops. This fact, of course, is one major reason why Charles II did not dissolve it for eighteen years—he was able to keep it in being for this long period because the Triennial Act of 1641 was repealed in 1664. The Presbyterians and other Puritan elements almost disappeared from the House of Commons. John Milton and many another Puritan were for a time "with darkness and with dangers compassed round."

THE RESTORATION OF THE CHURCH

The king and the constitution had been restored. So also was the Anglican Church. The royalist Cavalier Parliament, so pleasing to Charles II, contained nearly all Anglicans, zealous for church and king. They brought with them no hope of compromise with the Presbyterians or any other Dissenters, no plan of "comprehension." Against them the fifty Presbyterian members stood bravely but in vain. The Anglicans were animated by a thoroughgoing detestation of every species of religious opposition. Like the Puritan revolutionaries before them, they were prepared to persecute those who refused to believe as they did. The idea and practice of religious toleration, so precious to democratic states today, grew slowly in the hearts and hands of Christian men.

By order of Parliament, the Solemn League and Covenant was burned by the public hangman. In 1662 a Licensing Act required the printing trade to prevent "the frequent abuses in printing seditious, treasonable, and unlicensed books and pamphlets" which many "evil-disposed" persons had printed and sold "to the high dishonor of Almighty God."

The Anglican inclinations of the Cavalier Parliament led to a strong and coherent program of legislation. One of the leaders of the Cavalier group was Sir Edward Hyde, Earl of Clarendon and Lord Chancellor. The name of this chief minister was unjustly attached to the new religious settlement: it is usually called the Clarendon Code. Hence the name of Clarendon is still odious to the Dissenters. The persecuting acts of this Code decreed and enjoined conformity. They ended toleration and imposed, for a time, a narrow Anglicanism upon the nation.

The Cavalier Parliament struck first at the political strength of the Nonconformists in local government and administration. The severe Corporation Act (1661)—"an act for the well governing and regulating of corporations"—placed the boroughs under Anglican control. All municipal officers were required to renounce the Solemn League and Covenant, to take the oaths of allegiance, supremacy, and nonresistance, and to take communion according to the rites of the Church of England within a year of their election. Thus Dissenters of all sects were banished from political office in the boroughs.

In 1662 a new Act of Uniformity required every minister in the Anglican Church to obtain episcopal ordination and to give his unfeigned consent and assent to everything contained in the Book of Common Prayer. The use of the Prayer Book, now so modified that no Presbyterian could accept it, was enjoined in all public worship. This was done because "great mischiefs and inconveniences during the times of the late unhappy troubles have arisen and grown and many people have been led into factions and schisms, to the great decay and scandal of the reformed religion of the Church of England and to the hazard of many souls." Nearly 2,000 rectors and vicars, a fifth of the whole body of the clergy, were forced to resign from their parishes. The loss to the Church of England was irreparable. Many valuable elements were to stand until the present day outside the pale of Anglicanism.

Severe penalties were visited upon those who refused to conform and stayed outside the Anglican Church. For instance, under the Quaker Act of 1662 more than 5,000 Quakers were imprisoned. The Conventicle Act of 1664 made punishable by fine, transportation or imprisonment all those who attended meetings or "conventicles" of more than five persons, other than members of any one household, for "any exercise of religion in other manner than is allowed by the liturgy or practice of the Church of England." The Five Mile Act of 1665 ordered Nonconformist ministers who had been driven out of their parishes by the Act of Uniformity to swear that they held it unlawful to resist the king and that they would not "endeavour any alteration of government in church and state." Those who had refused to take these oaths were forbidden to go within five miles of any borough or of any parish where they had earlier preached so that they would not "distil the poisonous principles of schism and rebellion into the hearts of his majesty's subjects, to the great danger of the church and kingdom."

Thus dissent was punished by ecclesiastical and political disabilities. The execution of the enactments was to be carried out by the justices of the peace. Many of these gentlemen were glad to harass the Puritans who had once plagued them. Often, of course, the Puritan gentry took the unheroic course of conforming publicly to Anglicanism because they wanted to keep their political and social position. Among the middle and lower classes persecution did not break or end dissent. Until the end of the century the annals of Englishmen are filled with chapters of violent and bitter drama. Events showed that reasonable peace could not be gained by the dangerous imposition of one state church upon the people. It slowly became clear that Englishmen could not be dragooned along a single road to God. The alternative was the granting of freedom to all religions provided that their methods were not too explosive or fanatical. The time of toleration was not to be long delayed.

CHARLES II: POLICY AND POWER

Behind the idleness and frivolity of the court of Charles II there were several dark designs. These went forward through the troubles of the Dutch war, the plague and the great fire of London. One of the objects of Charles II was to secure for Roman Catholicism at least the status of legal equality with all other religions. This statement does not mean that Charles had steadily settled plans. His one resolve was to stay on the throne. Such a king would not quarrel about power, religion, or anything else if the results seemed to promise danger. Nevertheless, one of the king's deliberate intentions was to do what he could to enable those who were not Anglicans, especially the Roman Catholics, to move and worship freely.

Charles II was aided by the fact that the Earl of Clarendon, the Lord

Chancellor, was forced out of power and into exile by an ill-informed and unjust Parliament that blamed him for many things: the king's Catholic marriage, disasters in the Dutch war, the religious persecutions, even the plague and the fire. When Clarendon fell, the king renewed the custom of consulting with an inner circle of ministers. The size of the royal council had been increased in 1660 and at times contained fifty members. Hence it was obviously too large for the effective conduct of daily business. Charles II therefore chose a small group of men to help him. The members of this group were not responsible to or dependent upon Parliament in any way. They were sometimes called by the sinister word "Cabal" and were a step towards the later Cabinet. It so happened that the initials of the five ministers closest to Charles after Clarendon's fall in fact spelled out the word "Cabal." Two were Roman Catholic and three were Protestant. They were agreed on only one thing: religious toleration, to which Parliament was opposed. None was Anglican. These men planned to end the Anglican monopoly and to restore toleration for Dissenters. The Protestant members of the Cabal may not have known that Charles II intended to use toleration for Dissenters as a wedge to bring toleration for Roman Catholics.

In June, 1670, Charles II and Louis XIV of France agreed upon certain significant terms in the secret Treaty of Dover. With the aid of French gold and French arms Charles hoped one day to establish both absolute government and Roman Catholicism in England. In the discreditable Treaty of Dover, known to only four of his Roman Catholic aides, Charles agreed to support France against Holland in return for an annual pension to keep him independent of Parliament, and with arms and men when Charles wanted them. In 1672 Louis XIV invaded Holland, and England supported him by moving into the third Anglo-Dutch war. On the eve of hostilities, Charles II issued a Declaration of Indulgence ordering that "all manner of penal laws on matters ecclesiastical against whatsoever sort of nonconformists or recusants" should be suspended. This was the king's way of keeping the promise of the Treaty of Dover.

As early as 1662 Charles had made his first attempt to find out whether the royal prerogative could be used to grant relief to Dissenters. He intended, he said, to persuade Parliament to "enable us to exercise with more universal satisfaction that power of dispensing which we conceive to be inherent in us." In other words, Charles was probing to find out if a loyal Cavalier Parliament would agree that he had the prerogative power to dispense with existing statutes if he considered circumstances warranted such action. In 1662 Charles was obliged to drop whatever plans he may have had. Parliament could not be persuaded to agree with him.

The Declaration of Indulgence of 1672 was not submitted to Parliament at all. Charles simply relied upon the royal prerogative as he professed to understand it: "we think ourselves obliged to make use of that supreme power in ecclesiastical matters which is not only inherent in us but hath been declared and recognized to be so by several statutes and acts of Parliament. . . . We do declare . . . our will and pleasure to be that the execution of all and all manner of penal laws in matters ecclesiastical against whatsoever sort of nonconformists or recusants be immediately suspended, and they are hereby suspended."

The Dissenters refused to have any toleration that was also extended to Roman Catholics. Public panic about the dangers of Roman Catholicism arose again. In the public mind the Roman Catholics were associated vaguely with power and with fire; the ancient and unmuted antipathy to Rome rolled strongly through the counties and boroughs. Especially was the court suspect. James, the Duke of York, was an avowed Roman Catholic. He commanded the English fleets. Many of the officers of the army were believed to be Roman Catholics. The union of England and France against Protestant Holland was unpopular among the people.

In dismay, anger and distrust the firmly anti-Catholic Parliament assembled after an interval of three years. Were the war and the Declaration of Indulgence parts of a plot to establish Roman Catholicism and royal tyranny? The House of Commons resolved that "penal statutes in matters ecclesiastical cannot be suspended but by act of Parliament" and refused to grant supplies until the Declaration was withdrawn. Charles thereupon abandoned it, insisting that he meant no harm.

A Test Act was rapidly passed through an angered and frightened Parliament in 1673. This law excluded from civil or military office all who refused to take the sacraments according to the rites of the Church of England, or who refused to deny transubstantiation or who refused to swear the oaths of allegiance and supremacy. Thus all Roman Catholics would be excluded from office under the Crown. The king and his advisers were doubtless startled at the storm that thundered over the land. After Charles II gave his assent to the Test Act the Duke of York had to resign his office of Lord High Admiral. The Roman Catholic Clifford resigned as Lord Treasurer. Hundreds of other Roman Catholics followed. In 1678 a parliamentary Test Act imposed the same conditions as the law of 1673 upon all members of Parliament. Catholic peers had to surrender their seats in the House of Lords. Charles II never forgot the lesson of the failure of his plans. His brother James II never learned it.

POLITICS AND ADMINISTRATION

In the latter part of the reign of Charles II there were formed the two historic political groups called Whigs and Tories. Although there were to be many changes before these two elements became political parties in the modern sense, the beginning of that long development was at hand. The Tories, taking their name from the insulting epithet once bestowed upon Irish bandits, were led by Thomas Osborne, Earl of Danby. They were the court party, a party based on the old Cavalier principles of devotion to the royal prerogative and the Church of England. These Tory principles were particularly popular among the rural gentry and the clergy. Close links were forged between the Cavalier gentry and the Anglican clergy, between bishops and lay lords, squires and parsons. These men stood for the vested landed interests, the consolidated values of monopoly, privilege and power. Here, too, were the lay and spiritual leaders of victorious and intolerant Anglicanism.

Opposed to the Tories stood the Country Party led by Anthony Ashley Cooper, the nimble and diligent Earl of Shaftesbury. The men of this group, soon to be called Whigs—a nickname once given to covenanted Scotsmen who murdered bishops—were liberals who crept out of the shadows to meet at the Green Ribbon Club in Chancery Lane. They distributed propaganda. They sent out missionaries. They built bonfires and held street parades. They believed in toleration for Protestant Dissenters. They asserted the indestructible Roundhead idea of Parliamentary supremacy and the liberty of the subject. Their appeal was strong among middle class Dissenters, the commercial classes, and even certain groups of nobles. Through Shaftesbury and the Whigs many political traditions of the Puritans and Parliamentarians were given new life and strength. The Whigs stood against the Tory ascendancy. They challenged the Crown. They nursed and cherished opposition to Catholicism. They defended contractual notions of property. Between them and the Tories a great gulf was fixed.

The Whigs and Tories grew in strength at an important hour in the history of Parliament. It was a time when the steady weakening of the royal council had left the Crown without adequate defenses in the Commons. We have seen that because the council was too large and unwieldy for the efficient despatch of business Charles II had relied for advice and assistance on small groups of ministers. Under pressure from Parliament the Earl of Clarendon fell and fled. The Cabal was wrecked. Charles knew that if he did not dismiss unpopular ministers they would be impeached. The legislative branch of government could still curb the executive by the cumbersome weapon of impeachment. It also possessed, of course, the useful control of financial appropriations.

If a monarch did not want his policies and his ministers overthrown he must then have skilled support in Parliament. Thus it was of great advantage to Charles II to have the Earl of Danby and the Tories so zealous of his cause and their own. Through Danby and his followers Charles II was able, for a time, to obtain and hold a wavering control in Parliament. Danby, tainted by the pervasive depravity of his age, was a competent tactician and strategist. He could maneuver and trick and corrupt. He was also an able financier. He used lavish bribery— in an organized way—and judicious distribution of patronage to get and hold support for his king, his Tories and himself. So long as the Tories were able to keep the Whigs at bay in the complicated battleground of politics all would be well with their cause and their king. If they failed to defend themselves against Shaftesbury and his followers, their prospects would be grim indeed. In these days, politics were full of poison, violent, crude. Meanwhile, as the royal council grew enfeebled, the Parliament became still more aggressive and strong.[3]

Less dramatic than the events in the political arena were the changes in the central administrative system. As the effective power of the total Privy Council declined, the activities of its various committees increased. Several of these committees had existed since the Middle

---

[3] The power of the Commons in Parliament was steadily increased by several events. Convocation ceased to tax itself and surrendered that right to Parliament. The House of Lords as a court of law no longer claimed original jurisdiction (although it did enforce its claim to hear appeals from Chancery). The Lords unsuccessfully asserted the right to amend money bills—this precedent was of importance in the controversy of 1909 over the Lloyd George budget. See Carl Stephenson and F. G. Marcham, *Sources of English Constitutional History:* "On the Right of the Lords to Amend Money Bills" (1671), (1678), pp. 563–567, 572; the case of Shirley *v.* Fagg (1675), pp. 569–572.

Ages. In the Tudor period there were sometimes four, five, or six. Throughout the Stuart reigns there were more committees and more jobs for them to do. Each group had special administrative responsibilities. The first duty of all officials in committees or departments was to serve the king. The functions of this executive power actually came to be exercised more and more by these committees and less and less by the full Privy Council.

The activities of the committees of the Privy Council, the immediate forerunners of several modern ministries or departments, were especially important in the fields of foreign affairs, public complaints and grievances, the armed services of the state, and trade, commerce and plantations. This last committee had widely ranging tasks. It was "by his majesty appointed, constituted, and authorized by commission under the great seal as a standing committee to inquire into and certify all things tending to the advancement of trade and commerce. . . ." Another separate committee of council on trade and plantations was set up in 1675 under the direct control of the Privy Council. It was in committees such as these that there developed expert administrative officers, the predecessors of the higher civil servants who serve the modern chiefs of departments, the ministers of Queen Elizabeth II. It was also in these days that new divisions of administration were added to the famous offices that first appeared in Norman and Angevin times.

There were further developments. In 1640, for instance, the Secretaries of State, whose functions have been earlier described, divided a part of their tasks. One looked after diplomatic matters involving the Baltic region. The other became responsible for the Mediterranean area. This is the reason two Departments appeared: the Northern and Southern Departments. Later, in 1782, one of the Secretaries became the Secretary of State for Foreign Affairs and the other, responsible for colonial and home affairs, was called the Home Secretary. Still later a new office of Secretary of State for the Colonies was created.

Several alterations were made in the Admiralty. When James, Duke of York was Lord High Admiral (1660–1672) he had under him a naval board (of which the famous Samuel Pepys was the clerk) and a board of ordnance. These boards were particularly successful under Clarendon's administration. After the Catholic Duke of York was compelled to resign under the terms of the Test Act a committee or commission of three (later five) men, called the Lords of the Admiralty, was established under the chairmanship of the First Lord. Since the early eighteenth century the Admiralty has been almost continuously in commission.

WRITS AND CASES

In 1679 Parliament passed the Habeas Corpus Amendment Act, rightly entitled "An act for the better securing of the liberty of the subject and for the prevention of imprisonment beyond the seas." The writ of *habeas corpus,* whereby a prisoner could demand that he be speedily brought to trial, had been a well established and frequently used legal device since the early Middle Ages. The common law courts began to use it in the fifteenth century to check the jurisdiction of Chancery. In the sixteenth century *habeas corpus* became a valuable weapon in the attempts to curb the expanding claims of the prerogative courts, such as Star Chamber and High Commission. Nevertheless, particularly when political prisoners were involved, several ways had been found to evade *habeas corpus*—James Harrington, for example, had been taken out of the Tower of London and put upon an island where the writ did not run. The whole procedure needed clarification and sharp definition.

The act of 1679 tried to block the loopholes so dangerous to the liberty of the subjects of the king. The executive was shorn of several powers that might be used to support arbitrary government. Officers were required to bring all persons committed or restrained to the courts before whom the *habeas corpus* writ was returnable within a specified number of days from the issuance of the writ. The officials were then to certify the "true causes" of the detainer or imprisonment. Judges to whom application for the writ was made were required to issue it except in certain specified cases. The number of tribunals that could issue the writ was increased. Means were provided by which a prisoner might obtain a writ of *habeas corpus* during the vacation of a court. To forestall devices such as those used in the case of James Harrington, mentioned earlier, it was "further enacted . . . that no subject of this realm . . . shall or may be sent prisoner into Scotland, Ireland, Jersey, Guernsey, Tangier, or into any parts . . . beyond the seas . . . and that every such imprisonment is hereby enacted and adjudged to be illegal."

The writ of *habeas corpus* still remains a famous remedy against illegal imprisonment, an integral part and support of the rule of law. Today the perfected process of *habeas corpus* is clear and simple, speedy and effective. Any individual asserting that he is wrongfully held in custody may make application directly or through another person to a judge for a writ or a "rule nisi." This document, as in earlier days, directs the person or persons holding an individual to bring him before the court immediately "together with the day and cause of his detainer. . . ." If a prisoner is found to be held under a legal warrant he is either remanded to custody (he must then be put on trial without undue delay) or freed on bail. If he is not legally held he must be immediately released. If any court has ordered his release there is no appeal against that decision.

One of many cases illustrative of the effective way in which the writ of *habeas corpus* may operate occurred in 1923. The Home Secretary, ostensibly acting under a regulation arising from the Defense of the Realm Act, ordered a man named O'Brien to be arrested and deported to the Irish Free State on the basis of an allegation that O'Brien was plotting against the state. O'Brien got a writ of *habeas corpus* from the Court of Appeals directed to the Home Secretary. As O'Brien was not then in the custody of the Home Secretary the court gave the latter one week to obey the writ. The House of Lords rejected the Home Secretary's appeal and O'Brien was freed. An Act of Indemnity was speeded through Parliament compensating O'Brien. If such an act had not been passed, O'Brien would have been free to sue the Home Secretary in a civil case and prosecute him in a criminal case for illegal imprisonment.

Under the restored Stuarts there were several judicial cases of interest. One that should certainly be mentioned here is Bushell's Case. In 1670 Edward Bushell and eleven other jurymen acquitted several persons accused of riotous assembly (including William Penn). This acquittal was in outright defiance of the judge's instructions. Because of their insubordination Bushell and the other jurors were fined by the Recorder of London and, in default of payment, were imprisoned. The legality of this imprisonment was challenged before the Court of King's Bench as a result of *habeas corpus* proceedings. The judgment of Chief Justice Vaughan, who discharged the prisoners, was precise, cogent and a famous precedent.

Chief Justice Vaughan said: "The verdict of a jury and the evidence of a witness are very different things, in the truth and falsehood of them: a witness swears to what he has heard and seen . . . to what hath fallen under his senses. But a juryman swears to what he can infer and conclude from the testimony of such witnesses by the act and force of his understanding . . . the jury cannot follow the judge's instructions, for 'A man cannot see by another's eye, nor hear by another's ear' . . . the jury, and not the judge, resolve and find what the fact is. . . .

"No case can be offered . . . that ever a jury was punished by fine and imprisonment by the judge for not finding according to their evidence. . . . Sure this latter age did not first discover that the verdicts of juries were many times not according to the judge's opinion and liking. But the reasons are, I conceive, most clear that the judges could not nor can fine and imprison the jury in such cases. . . ."

CHARLES II: THE LAST PHASE

In the late 1670's the Earl of Shaftesbury and the Whigs had a chance to advance their political cause. One of the pillars of the Whig party was the widespread fear and dislike of Roman Catholicism. Shaftesbury fanned the popular distrust and alarm. "Popery is breaking in upon us like a flood!" He cried out against "popishly infected persons" in high places. He spread the frightening truth that Charles II had an army of 20,000 men and thousands of pounds given him by Louis XIV.

Amid the general clamor an irresponsible man named Titus Oates used his fertile and febrile brain to invent colossal lies. He told of a Jesuit plot to murder the king, seize the government, and set up the Roman Catholic Church in England. Wild and monstrous stories spread. Parliamentary committees were appointed to investigate. As a result of public hysteria about 2,000 Catholics were sent to prison. Five Catholic peers were locked up. Every Catholic was ordered to leave London. Such were some of the consequences of the tales purveyed by Oates and others of his ilk.

In 1679 it was proved that the Tory leader Danby had signed a despatch pressing for a cash payment by Louis XIV to Charles II. Although Danby had acted on the king's order he was impeached. In the midst of a series of curious and melodramatic events Charles II dissolved the Cavalier Parliament. In the panic election that followed, Shaftesbury and his Whigs were victorious. Charles II had only thirty supporters in the new House of Commons. By destroying the Cavalier Parliament the king had temporarily saved Danby but he was now faced by the Whigs. They immediately sent the unfortunate Danby to the Tower for five years. They forced Charles to send James, Duke of York, into exile and to disband a part of the army. The king also appointed a new Privy Council containing Shaftesbury and other leaders of the Whig opposition to the Tories and the court. "They have put a set of men about me," Charles is said to have remarked, "but they shall know nothing."

The new Parliament now introduced a bill to exclude the Catholic James, Duke of York, from the throne. In the prevailing state of opinion it seemed almost certain that the Whigs, with their power in the Commons and the country, could compel the Lords and the king to accept their Exclusion Bill. It passed its second reading in the Commons by a majority of 79 votes. Charles II therefore prorogued and later dissolved this Parliament, determined that the Exclusion Bill should not be passed. The Whigs were thwarted again.

In the years between 1660 and 1679 it had become increasingly clear that it was impossible to maintain a balanced and regulated relationship between the authority of Parliament in legislation and finance and the authority of the Crown in policy and administration. During these years, the Cavalier Parliament had steadily assaulted the royal prerogative. It had broadened its control over Crown supply, expenditure, and auditing. It had even tried to intervene in diplomatic matters. It had used the machinery of impeachment to hurl down the king's minister. It had formally refused to admit that Charles II had any dispensing power in ecclesiastical matters. It had passed statutes to the effect that only Anglicans were to be officials under the Crown.

Charles II had maneuvered skillfully to take advantage of the animosities flaming among Whigs and Tories as these two inchoate political parties battled in court and country. In a large measure Charles had been successful. Now he was determined to stop the passage of the Exclusion Bill. Between 1679 and 1681 he summoned three Parliaments—the last one was held at Oxford, away from the menace of Shaftesbury's London mobs. In each of these assemblies the Exclusion Bill was vehemently debated. Each time Charles dissolved Parliament to save his brother.

Charles II was soon aided by several circumstances. In the first place, the Tory party, out of power, slowly became more unified and consolidated than it had ever been before. Secondly, the Whigs began to quarrel among themselves. Not all of them agreed that the Duke of York should be excluded from the throne. Some Whigs were quite prepared to have James as king provided that Parliament precisely limited his powers by statute. Thirdly, the Earl of Shaftesbury proposed that the Duke of Monmouth, illegitimate son of Charles II, be recognized as heir to the throne. Most of his Whigs would not support him. Even those who favored the Exclusion Bill wanted the throne to go to the next in line after James: James's Protestant daughter Mary, wife of William of Orange. The fissures in the Whig party widened. There was now no concerted opposition to the king and the Tories. Meanwhile, Charles II was strengthening his position still further. Louis XIV was subsidizing him again and he was relatively independent of Parliament. Popular excitement about the Popish plot was dying down. The Whigs were growing unpopular. They had overreached themselves. Many Englishmen feared that Whig policies might provoke an outbreak of civil war. The "Whig frenzy" was collapsing. The Tory spirit drooped no more. It revived. The loyal children of the Cavaliers roused themselves to seek revenge.

Asserting that Shaftesbury had conspired to assassinate him and to raise a rebellion in support of the Duke of Monmouth, Charles II tried to have the Whig chieftain convicted in the courts. Although Shaftesbury was acquitted, he feared for his life. He fled to Holland and there he died quite suddenly of natural causes. Meanwhile the Whig leaders were tried for their alleged parts in the fabricated Rye House plots. Lord Russell and Algernon Sydney were condemned by packed Tory juries and died by the headsman's axe. The Earl of Essex cut his throat in the Tower. The Duke of Monmouth, never a brave man, fled terror-stricken over the sea. Charles II saw to it that Tories moved in to control many borough and county governments from which the Whigs were ousted. By devious manipulations the Whig party was now shattered and dispersed, for a time. The revenge of the king and the Tories seemed complete. They were everywhere victorious. The ancient liberties of Englishmen seemed again in jeopardy. Nevertheless, the new power of Charles was based on the support of the Anglican Tories. If a royal attempt were ever made to raise the Roman Catholics and depress the Anglicans, then Tory support would be withdrawn.

On February 6, 1685, Charles II died. He had tried, for a quarter of a century, to subvert the Restoration. He had chafed under a system that had not restored the prerogative courts, that had made him financially dependent upon Parliament except when Louis XIV supplied him with money. The new king was James II, the Duke of York, whom the Exclusion Bill would have proscribed.

JAMES II: THE NEW DESPOTISM

Despite the fact that Charles II wanted an absolutist regime and the restoration of Roman Catholicism he consciously avoided going beyond the edge of safety. True, he sapped the strength of the Restoration arrangements but he made no direct onslaught upon them. With James II it was otherwise. He had no tact, no political sense. He tried to use his suspending and dispensing powers to direct a frontal assault upon the Restoration settlement. He had learned nothing from the experiences of the earlier Stuarts. He attempted to bring Roman Catholicism swiftly into the state. He attempted to put himself above Parliament. He attempted to trample upon the law. So the Whigs joined with the Tories and together they put James II outside. Let us see how they made a second revolution to protect what they had won in the first.[4]

The first Parliament of James II (May, 1685), strongly Tory and passionately loyal, granted him £400,000. When the Duke of Monmouth rebelled in July, 1685, he was captured and executed. A thousand Englishmen were hanged, fined, scourged or exiled. This victory seems to have hastened James's decision to bring England back to Rome. He was obviously secure upon his throne. What was there to fear? The Tories were not then alarmed about either the Whigs or their king. Monmouth was gone and for the Whigs and Dissenters there was nobody to support but Mary, the elder Protestant daughter of James and her husband, William of Orange. Anglicans thought that James would treat his religion as a private matter. James thought that the Anglicans would favor Roman Catholicism because they hated Protestant Nonconformists. Both were mistaken.

James II increased the army and placed 13,000 men in a camp on Hounslow Heath to threaten, if need be, London and Parliament. It was James's folly to think that he could erect a royal and Catholic despotism upon a military basis. Meanwhile, too, Roman Catholics were placed in several key positions. When the members of Parliament met again in November, 1685, they wanted the army reduced, the Catholics removed from important offices. James II, for his part, insisted that the Test Act must be repealed. Both Lords and Commons refused. James thereupon promptly prorogued and later dissolved Parliament. It did not meet again in his brief reign.

---

[4] The origin and significance of these events are brilliantly described by Professor G. M. Trevelyan in *The English Revolution 1688–1689* (1938).

The new king proceeded swiftly along the road to his own ruin. He defied the law and appointed Roman Catholics to the Privy Council. He established an arbitrary court of ecclesiastical commission similar to the earlier Court of High Commission: this body suspended anti-Catholic bishops. Catholic chapels were opened in London. The Jesuits began a school in the Savoy. James forced Roman Catholics into the faculty and administration of Oxford and Cambridge. He heeded no storm warnings as the antagonism to the royal will and the alarm at the royal deeds rumbled over England.[5]

A test case about the appointment of Roman Catholics as officers in the army was pre-arranged after James II had packed the Court of King's Bench with judges favorable to him. Sir Edward Hales, a Catholic colonel in the royal forces, had been indicted and convicted at the Rochester assizes for failure to take the oaths of allegiance and supremacy prescribed by the Test Act. Arthur Godden then brought suit, under the provisions of the act, for the sum of £500 forfeited by Hales. In the Court of King's Bench Hales pleaded that he had letters patent from the king dispensing with the oaths required by the law. Chief Justice Herbert delivered the judgment of the court that James II did possess the power to dispense with the law. The judges in the packed court voted eleven to one in favor of the contentions of the king. They said: "(1) that the kings of England are sovereign princes; (2) that the laws of England are the king's laws; (3) that therefore 'tis an inseparable prerogative in the kings of England to dispense with penal laws in particular cases and upon particular necessary reasons; (4) that of those reasons and those necessities, the king himself is sole judge; and then, which is consequent upon all, (5) that this is not a trust invested in, or granted to, the king by the people, but the ancient remains of the sovereign power and prerogative of the kings of England; which never yet was taken from them, nor can be." This language, so reminiscent of the packed courts of James I and Charles I, was strong enough. But a single court decision does not stop a revolution.

In 1687, James II, blind to the probable consequences of his policy, issued a Declaration of Indulgence, modelled on that issued by Charles II in 1672 but swiftly withdrawn. This document granted freedom of worship to all Protestant Dissenters and Roman Catholics and abolished all religious tests for office. In April, 1688, James issued a

---

[5] See Charles F. Mullett, "Religion, Politics, and Oaths in the Glorious Revolution," *The Review of Politics*, X (1948).

second Declaration of Indulgence and soon ordered all bishops to have copies of the declaration distributed through their dioceses where it was to be read publicly on two successive Sundays. It was read in only four churches in London. The action of the king confronted many Anglican clergymen with a major problem: they believed in the doctrine of non-resistance and so found it difficult to resist the king's order to read the declaration. On the other hand, to read it was to support the king's threat to the established Anglican Church. Meanwhile, six diocesan bishops, together with Sancroft, Archbishop of Canterbury, petitioned James and protested that the declaration was illegal: "Your petitioners therefore most humbly and earnestly beseech your majesty that you will be graciously pleased not to insist upon their distributing and reading your majesty's said declaration."

James II, asserting that the petition was a "standard of rebellion," sent the petitioners to the Tower, prosecuted them for seditious libel after their petition was circulated in print. Amid fierce public demonstrations the bishops appeared at the bar of the Court of King's Bench. It was a confused and unusual case. There were many judicial questions, including the privileges of the bishops as lords of Parliament, the proper place to present petitions, the suspending powers of the king under the prerogative. The judges were divided on questions of law: two against the Crown, two for it. To the jury Justice Powell declared: "Truly I cannot see, for my part, anything of sedition, or any other crime, fixed upon these reverent fathers, my lords the bishops. For, gentlemen, to make it a libel, it must be false, it must be malicious and it must tend to sedition. As to the falsehood, I see nothing that is offered by the king's counsel, nor anything as to the malice. . . . I can see no difference, nor know of one in law, between the king's power to dispense with laws ecclesiastical and his power to dispense with any other laws whatsoever. If this be at once allowed of, there will need no Parliament; all the legislature will be in the king—which is a thing worth considering, and I leave the issue to God and your conscience." On July 30, 1688, the jury found the bishops not guilty.

Meanwhile, on July 1, the queen, the Italian Mary of Modena, gave birth to a son. The heir to the throne was now a Roman Catholic. The prospect of Catholic rule in England induced the chief Whig and Tory leaders to act without delay. They had long been in communication with William of Orange, husband of Mary, Protestant daughter of James II by his first wife. On July 30, the day of the bishops' acquittal, four prominent Whigs and three Tories despatched a formal invitation to William to come with an army to England to aid in the restoration of English liberties and the delivery of the realm from absolutism. The Tory doctrine of non-resistance was laid on the shelf. The royal resort to naked force left no doubt of the king's goal or the nation's answer. King James stood alone in his realm. The Tory Danby soon led a rising in the north. Everywhere men hastened to serve under the banners of rebellion. There was to be no Roman Catholic despotism similar to that of Louis XIV in France.

THE REVOLUTION OF 1688

On November 5, 1688, William of Orange reached England with the aid of a "Protestant wind." He landed in Devon and marched unopposed to London. The royal army of James II disintegrated, especially after John Churchill, its commander, joined William. The country gentlemen also deserted the king. In early December James II fled to France to find refuge at the court of Louis XIV. That he might leave anarchy behind him he burned the writs for the new Parliament, wrote an order for the dissolving of the army, threw the Great Seal of England into the Thames. He never saw England again. James II possessed the obstinacy of his father but not the courage.

With the flight of James, England was left without a lawful government. The House of Lords, always the heirs of the "common council of the realm" of ancient days, all who had sat in the Commons during the reign of Charles II, and the aldermen and councillors of London met in an informal assembly to decide what steps should be taken to create a legal government in the leaderless state. This group, finally deciding upon a focus of policy, asked William to take over a provisional government and to issue letters to the borough and county electors requesting them to elect representatives to a Convention. This Convention was not, of course, a legal Parliament. It was, however, the best answer that could swiftly be found to the sullen problems. The members of the Convention met on January 22, 1689. Shortly thereafter Whigs and Tories mingled their scruples and principles in the famous resolution that James II, "having endeavored to subvert the constitution of the kingdom by breaking the original contract between king and people, and having, by the advice of Jesuits and other wicked persons, violated the fundamental laws and withdrawn himself out of the kingdom, has abdicated the government and the throne is hereby vacant."

Early in the Convention there were many opinions about what

should be done. It was especially embarrassing to the Tories to be compelled to agree upon a policy of resistance to an anointed king and to jettison their doctrines of divine right. They were uneasily aware that it was flatly contrary to their philosophy to accept the Whig ideas of contract, religious toleration, and the superiority of Parliament. Were these Tories going to get themselves into an enchanted quagmire of contradiction? What else could they do? What valid guides, in such an imbroglio, could be found?

The Tories, so urgently pressed, first proposed a regency in the name of James II. Then they held out for Mary as sole sovereign, the successor by hereditary right (except for the young Roman Catholic son born to James II in 1688). But Mary refused to reign alone. William told Danby that he did not intend to be prince consort, merely his wife's gentleman usher. So William and Mary were proclaimed joint sovereigns in February, 1689, after they had accepted a Declaration of Rights which later became the Bill of Rights. The actual administration was to rest with William alone. William and Mary were clearly rulers by act of Parliament. Only a small group of Tories, henceforth called Jacobites, clung to the divine right principle. About 400 Anglican clergymen, called Nonjurors, refused to take the oath of allegiance to William and Mary. All the rest of the Tories and Anglicans bowed with ill grace to the blunt demands of inexorable circumstance.

The Convention was now legally converted into the first Parliament of William and Mary. One of the early acts of this body was to change the Declaration of Rights, which had accompanied the transfer of the crown to the new rulers, into the Bill of Rights. There must be no doubt, no ambiguity about the conditions under which the Crown had passed to the new rulers. The Bill of Rights, in the tradition of Magna Carta and the Petition of Right, specifically listed most of the arbitrary acts of which the Stuarts had been guilty and declared them all contrary to the laws of England. "The pretended power of suspending laws or the execution of laws by regal authority without consent of parliament is illegal . . . the commission for erecting the late court of commissioners for ecclesiastical causes and all other commissions and courts of like nature are illegal and pernicious . . . levying money for or to the use of the crown by pretence of prerogative without grant of parliament, for longer time or in other manner than the same is or shall be granted, is illegal . . . it is the right of the subject to petition the king . . . for redress of all grievances and for the mending, strengthening, and preserving of the laws parliaments ought to be held frequently."

This long and exact document also provided for freedom of speech in Parliament; for fair jury trial; for the ending of excessive bail and unduly heavy fines. No standing army was to be maintained in time of peace without the consent of Parliament. The Crown was settled on William and Mary and their heirs. If there were no heirs, the succession rights were to pass to Anne, Mary's sister, and then to her children. The famous Bill of Rights added a number of clauses to the original Declaration, notably providing that no Roman Catholic, or anyone married to a Roman Catholic, should ever succeed to the throne of England. "It hath been found by experience that it is inconsistent with the safety and welfare of this Protestant kingdom to be governed by a popish prince or by any king or queen marrying a papist."

By these events the power of Parliament and the liberty of the subject were at last secured. In later days they were to be challenged, but never successfully and never for long. The essential constitutional principles of limited monarchy, often enunciated earlier, were finally established by the Bill of Rights. The "glorious revolution" marked the end of the long struggle that had begun with James I. The rule of the nobles, the country gentry, and the merchant classes who sat in Parliament seemed now assured.

This Bloodless Revolution brought in its train further important legislative enactments bulwarking the Bill of Rights. The Toleration Act of 1689 allowed all but Roman Catholics and Unitarians to worship in their own way. Nonconformists were still legally excluded from participation in municipal or national government. Soon, however, Dissenters began to hold government positions when they practiced "occasional conformity," which meant taking the Anglican sacrament once a year. Annual indemnity acts also helped to nullify the effects of the Test and Corporation Acts. The latter were not formally repealed until 1828. In 1689, however, the Toleration Act was viewed as a great charter of religious liberty.

The Bill of Rights forbade the maintenance of a standing army in time of peace without the consent of Parliament. A supplementary statute called a Mutiny Act permitted the raising of an army and the use of martial law for a period of six months. Since 1689 Mutiny Acts, now called Army Acts, have been regularly passed, usually at yearly intervals, to enable the Crown to keep the British Army in being with the consent of Parliament. A new Triennial Act of 1694 provided that elections must be held at least once every three years. The Treasons Act of 1696 protected the accused in treason trials by requiring that he must be permitted to see a true copy of the whole indictment at least five days before his trial; that he should have legal council, learned in the law; and that nobody should be indicted or tried for treason but by the testimony of "two lawful witnesses." Censorship acts and licensing rules giving the Crown authority over the press were allowed to lapse.

The last important part of the Revolution arrangements was the Act of Settlement of 1701, passed to make legally clear the nature of the succession, to guard against the restoration of the old Stuart line, and to make a series of specific rules upon other matters shortly to be described. After Mary died (1694) without issue the heir to the throne upon the death of William (1701) was Mary's sister Anne. By 1700 the last of Anne's thirteen children had died and this event meant that the direct Protestant line of the Stuarts would end with the passing of Anne. The Act of Settlement declared that Anne should succeed William and that if she died without direct heirs the throne should pass to the Electress Sophia of Hanover and her issue. Sophia was the daughter of James's daughter Elizabeth and Frederick the Elector Palatine. The succession of the Hanoverians thus seemed assured.

The Act of Settlement also explicitly confirmed the action of Parliament in the Danby Case (1679) earlier described in this chapter. It provided that the king's pardon under the Great Seal would not be a bar to an impeachment by Parliament. By another important provision judges were to hold office during good behavior instead of at the king's pleasure. They were to be removed or have their salary altered only upon an address by both houses of Parliament as a result of charges of misconduct proved in Parliament. The Act of Settlement further provided that the sovereign must be a member of the Church of England; that if he were a foreigner England was not obligated to defend his foreign possessions; that he might not leave England without the permission of Parliament. A new rule declared that "all matters and things relating to the well governing of this kingdom, which are properly cognizable in the privy council by the laws and customs of this realm shall be transacted there, and all resolutions taken thereupon shall be signed by such of the privy council as shall advise and consent to the same." Among other things, this meant that future monarchs must not evade the control of the Privy Council by transacting business through other channels. By 1706, however, the fear of secret or confidential committees was ended and this section of the Act of Settlement was repealed in the interests of simple efficiency. Finally, the Act of Settlement provided that "no person who has an office or other place of profit under the king or receives a pension from the crown shall be capable of serving as a member of the House of Commons." This clause in the Act of Settlement was extended in the Place Act of 1707.

With the passage of the Act of Settlement the mixed and clever legislative arrangements following the conservative and sensible revolution of 1688 were complete. For all practical purposes the nation had grasped sovereignty. The Coronation Oath Act of 1689 provided for the following question and answer. "The archbishop or bishop shall say: 'Will you solemnly promise and swear to govern the people of this kingdom of England and the dominions thereto belonging according to the statutes in Parliament agreed on and the laws and customs of the same?' The king and queen shall say: 'I solemnly promise so to do.' "

England now stood on the threshold of the brilliant and prosperous eighteenth century. We cannot trace here the remarkable growth of capital and industry, the great figures of art and literature, the thrusts of energy in colonial expansion, the foreign wars, the strengthening sinews of trade and commerce, the emergence of Britain as the foremost of European powers. Our concern is with constitutional and legal history.

In recent chapters we have seen the fundamental importance of the legal and constitutional struggles and crises of the Stuart age. We have noted the essential elements in the statutes following the Revolution of 1688. It is clear that the sanctions underlying kingship by divine right were destroyed. The so-called sacred, indefeasible, and absolute powers of the monarch were at an end. The law of the land, the enshrined will of the community, was apparently supreme.

The ebb and flow of events such as those described in these chapters inevitably leave large consequences on the shore. They pose problems. Among the questions confronting Englishmen in the early eighteenth century were these: "How can we find peaceful methods to make effective in practice the responsibility of the king's ministers to Parliament? Must we always have recourse to impeachment and bills of attainder?" The answer found by Englishmen is probably their greatest contribution to the science of government.

CHAPTER XVII

Growth of the Cabinet System: ends and means

THE BALANCE OF POWER

THE aftermath of the Revolution of 1688 began a new chapter in the constitutional and legal history of England. At last the long struggle between absolute and limited monarchy was settled. The old disputes between the prerogative courts and the courts of common law had been answered by events. Circumstances alter cases and they alter ideas too. The circumstances resulting from the seventeenth century simply made many ideas obsolete and many interpretations of the constitution untenable. The Stuart theories of the nature of the constitution were never seriously considered or soberly uttered again except by lonely Jacobites or by scholars intent upon understanding the minds and hearts of the protagonists in the struggles of the Stuart age. The main problem of the new world after 1688, as suggested at the end of the previous chapter, was that of finding ways and means to make the settlement of the Revolution effective in the operations of legislation, administration and law.

If we look carefully at the British structure of government after the Revolution settlement we see that there had been a significant change from the days of the strong executive in the Tudor period. After 1688, no single differentiated part of the government was superior to any other. The powers of the government were divided among the parts and those parts were in delicate equipoise. The executive authority, as limited by law, remained in the Crown. The House of Lords had co-equal legislative power with the Commons, except in financial matters. It still held its supreme appellate jurisdiction in civil cases. The House of Commons had full control over finance. It had freedom of speech, freedom from arrest, and the like. The great courts of common law moved unchallenged in their broad lands. Such divisions of power, such checks and balances, are in themselves excellent only if the various parts of government are closely and harmoniously coordinated. Only then can the total machinery function effectively. The disruption of 1689 solved several problems but not this one: what devices could be found to guarantee that the Crown and Parliament—the executive and legislative branches of government—would work together, most of the time, in reasonable harmony?

One obvious result of the victories of Parliaments and courts had been to define the nature of the royal prerogative much more precisely than it had ever been defined before. The reader will have noted, however, that the sentences of definition were usually written in the negative. The use of certain prerogatives was proscribed: the king might not do this; the king might not do that. He might not do such things as suspend the laws, levy taxes, use the dispensing power without the consent of Parliament. After 1701, the judges were independent of the Crown. In brief, it had become increasingly clear what the king might not do. It was often less clear what powers were still properly within the monarch's sphere of action.

There was left intact a large part of the royal prerogative. The king had the powers of veto and mercy. He created peers. He made peace and war. What was very important, he was still expected to frame and shape policy. To aid him in this task he possessed and used the prerogative and privilege of choosing his own ministers. The king might use "influence"—such as pressure, sinecures, pensions and bribes—to gain and control his men and his ends. He might be guided by his likes and dislikes or his memories of service or treachery on the part of his royal servants. His ministers were indeed his ministers.

And yet the king found it necessary to work in and through Parliament. In the Parliament were parties, cliques, and factions of men, prowling and hunting for office in packs. From which group or groups was the king to select his ministers, for what purpose, and with what results? How could his ministers be successful in policy if they were opposed by a majority of the members of Parliament?

If a majority in Parliament stood adamantly against the king and his ministers they could always bring a deadlock by refusing supplies or impeaching the royal servants. The king, for his part, could follow in the steps of an earlier Stuart or a Cromwell and dissolve Parliament. Such a state of affairs was obviously undesirable. "The king's government must go on" and it must go on within the machinery of the established constitution. To harmonize the policies of Crown and Parliament, the executive and legislative branches of government, there slowly developed the practice of ministerial responsibility that we call the Cabinet system.

LOYAL GOVERNMENT AND LOYAL OPPOSITION

Before we examine the slow and irregular steps by which this admirable Cabinet machinery was constructed it seems desirable to state and explain, as succinctly as possible, the essential principles of Cabinet government today. A compass is of no value unless you know where you are. It serves no purpose unless you know where you wish to go. Let us first see where England has arrived in the growth of the practical and elastic Cabinet system—a system that has been adopted by more than fifty other lands. Then we can more easily understand and appreciate the problems and the answers, so efficient and sensible, that have emerged in the last two hundred and fifty years.

A French writer once remarked: "The English have left the different parts of their constitution just where the waves of history have deposited them." We begin with the Privy Council, the lineal descendant of the old king's council. Today that Privy Council, sitting as a whole, has only a few formal duties to perform. True, when it issues Orders-in-Council they have the force of law. But the Orders are only issued under the legal authority of parliamentary statutes or the royal prerogative and the ministers of the Cabinet must always be responsible for initiating them. The actual powers of the total Privy Council, once so formidable, have gradually withered. At the same time, the committees of that council have important tasks. The Judicial Committee of the Privy Council, for instance, is the final court of appeal from the courts—with some exceptions—of the Commonwealth and Empire. Technically the modern Cabinet is still a committee of the Privy Council holding numerous powers of the Crown in commission and carrying on almost all the public business of the Crown except the judicial business properly belonging to the courts. The word "Cabinet," however, is unknown to the laws of England although "Ministers of the Crown" are paid specified salaries since the Minister of the Crown Act of 1937. The office of Prime Minister is but slightly known to the law—it is mentioned in only three acts of Parliament, all of them in the twentieth century.

The members of the Cabinet, this committee of privy councillors, exercise the political and executive power of the Crown in the name of the monarch. The Cabinet, consisting of Her Majesty's servants who are ministers of the Crown, forms the directing and deciding forces in government. Queen Elizabeth II herself takes no part in politics. She utters no political statements. The Crown stands above creeds or parties. To phrase the position of the Crown in another way: today the queen must have the same politics as the majority in the House of Commons.

In modern times, most of the ministers of the Cabinet are members of the House of Commons. There are but few from the Lords. The Minister of the Crown Act of 1937 permits fifteen of the usual Cabinet posts to be held in the Commons. The ministers, whether from Lords or Commons, are chosen from that political party which has a majority in the lower chamber. Although in form selected by the sovereign, the Prime Minister is the leader of the largest party in the Commons (except in cases of coalition or cooperative governments). Because the office of Prime Minister is not legally an office at all, the Prime Minister has no right to sit in the Cabinet unless he does hold some office that has legal status. Since 1937 he must be First Lord of the Treasury. He may, of course, also hold other portfolios. Within the Cabinet he holds a position of undisputed ascendancy because in practice be is the directing chief of the government. He may ask for the resignation of any colleague. He has the power of appointment to many offices of government, including the highest posts in the civil service. He is the leader of the House of Commons. He controls the agenda at Cabinet meetings and he presides over these meetings. He may recommend a dissolution of Parliament. He may himself resign and thus end the whole government.

In recent years this great power has increased. Much depends, of course, upon the personal attributes of the man who is Prime Minister. Sir Winston Churchill, for example, expanded the strength of the forces in 10 Downing Street. Some of his predecessors, on the other hand, have increased neither the power nor the prestige of that famous post.

It is also the Prime Minister who determines the composition of the Cabinet, a body that usually consists of between twenty and twenty-four members. The most important of these are the Lord Chancellor, the Chancellor of the Exchequer, the Secretaries of State for Foreign Affairs, Home Affairs, Commonwealth Relations, War, Air, the Colonies, Scotland, the First Lord of the Admiralty, the Minister of Defense, the President of the Board of Trade, the Ministers of

Agriculture and Fisheries, Education, Health, Labour, National Service, and Transport. There are some ministers who are seldom, or never, members of the Cabinet. These include such men as the Minister of Pensions, of Overseas Trade, and the Law Officers of the Crown. Whether of Cabinet rank or not, all ministers resign when the Cabinet falls.

In matters of government today the sovereign acts only upon the advice of the Cabinet. The members of it are her constitutional advisers responsible to Parliament. They are always bound in practice to answer questions and defend their decisions before that shrewd legislative body. Individually, then, the Cabinet members are heads of great departments of state. Collectively, they formulate the policy of the government and defend it in Parliament. Thus they form the indispensable bridge joining the executive and legislative organs of government.

Each member of the Cabinet, as remarked earlier, is individually responsible for a department of government. At the same time, he shares a collective responsibility for the work of all of his colleagues. Cabinet responsibility is one, united and indivisible. "As a general rule," wrote Viscount Morley, "every important piece of departmental policy is taken to commit the entire Cabinet, and its members stand or fall together. The Chancellor of the Exchequer may be driven from office by a bad dispatch from the Foreign Office and an excellent Home Secretary may suffer from the blunders of a stupid Minister of War." [1] By an adverse vote on any major issue the Cabinet can be driven from office. It must do all it possibly can to keep its majority in the Commons. Waiting to take office are the men of the "shadow Cabinet," the opponents of the government who are called Her Majesty's Most Loyal Opposition. The leader of that opposition is paid a salary of £2,000 a year by the state because of the dignity attaching to his position and his political responsibilities.

It follows from these remarks that if a member of the Cabinet does not agree with the policy of the majority of his colleagues he must decide what to do next. If he stays in the Cabinet he must publicly support the policy decisions of his government. If he cannot support the policy agreed upon by his colleagues he must resign, as Mr. Anthony Eden resigned from the government of Mr. Neville Chamberlain. The Cabinet speaks as a unit to Parliament and it gives advice

---

[1] John, Viscount Morley, *Life of Sir Robert Walpole* (1889), p. 155.

as a unit to the Crown. The doctrine of collective responsibility is essential if mutual confidence, without which Cabinet government cannot easily succeed, is to exist.

These pared and pruned paragraphs may suggest that Cabinet government is a simple institution. On the contrary, it is an intricate mosaic of precedents, usages, and subtle niceties. The conventions of the constitution, too numerous and complex to be traced and described in detail here, are indispensable to the successful functioning of the British governmental machinery.[2]

The motive power in the English government today is the Cabinet and its various important committees. Here general policy is discussed and decided. The wisdom or folly of policy decisions is what ultimately sustains or breaks a government. Although it is said, quite rightly, that the Cabinet is constitutionally responsible to Parliament, we also recognize the paradox that the Cabinet, particularly a strong Cabinet, in fact dominates Parliament most of the time. The members of the Cabinet, as we know, are the leaders of the party that possesses the majority in the House of Commons. That party is held together by principles, by loyalties, by platforms, by interests, and by all the irreducible facts of the political scene. A member on the back benches really needs no party Whip to warn him of the consequences of carelessness or insubordination—he knows the procedures of local and national political committees and caucuses. If he wishes to be returned to Parliament in the next election he will walk warily. Cabinet government means party government.

The modern Cabinet system was painfully built by the labors and experiments of more than two hundred years of history. Today, as we are aware, the Cabinet practices are the keystone in the arch of the British method of responsible and democratic government. In the last century Walter Bagehot wrote: "The efficient secret of the English Constitution may be described as the close union and nearly complete fusion of the executive and legislative powers." He was quite correct. How did this happy event come to pass?

THE CABINET: GENESIS AND GROWTH

The brilliant work of the late Professor E. R. Turner and other scholars upon many difficult problems and ambiguities of the early

---

2 The best account of the Cabinet system is contained in W. I. Jennings, *Cabinet Government* (1936). For documents of value on the subjects discussed in this chapter see Carl Stephenson and F. G. Marcham, *Sources of English Constitutional History*, pp. 612–654.

history of the Cabinet is indicated in the bibliography at the end of this book. There are still many disputed points, such as the precise steps in the idea and acceptance of the name and office of the Prime Minister, the approximate date of the appearance of a Cabinet that really framed policy, the growth of the concept of collective and individual responsibility. To these questions no easy and certain answers have been found, as the reader of the books and articles listed in the bibliography will soon discover. Much more detailed research needs to be undertaken before adequate conclusions can be obtained.

In the sixteenth and seventeenth centuries, as we have seen, a large part of the work of the Privy Council was in fact done by committees. Under the Stuarts the Privy Council itself grew awkwardly large. Because this was so, the committees did more work than ever before. It was almost inevitable that these committees would include regular and important members of the Privy Council. Some time before 1693 the strong members of the Privy Council gathered together to form the Committee of the Privy Council. This was a standing committee, outranking the temporary committees of privy councillors and soon to dominate the Privy Council itself. On occasion, this standing committee seems almost to be merged with the Cabinet Council of the king's confidential advisers. After 1688 there remained three consultative bodies under the Crown: the Privy Council, an increasingly formal body declining in importance and power; the Committee of the Council; and the Cabinet Council.

The Committee of the Council, formally sanctioned in 1714 and 1727, has been called "the work-a-day aspect of the Privy Council." It was concerned with such conciliar business as matters regarding the Channel Islands, the plantations, and Irish bills. Sometimes contemporaries, as scholars working in the field well know, confused this Committee with the Cabinet Council and with the Privy Council. All we need remark here is that the Cabinet Council usually determined policy; the Committee of the Council usually performed important administrative work; the Privy Council itself formally expressed and recorded the final royal decisions. This comment is undoubtedly too neat and tidy; but for our purposes it must serve.

When William III, never a popular king, came to the English throne in 1689 he had little interest in England, except as an aid in the main object of his life, which was to defeat Louis XIV. To accomplish that end he must have efficiency in government. To obtain efficiency he must have Parliamentary support. When William discovered the jarring factions and treacheries within the Whig and Tory parties he refused to recognize party at all and made up his government of Whigs and Tories combined. Hence men of both groups appeared in the Privy Council, the Cabinet Council and the Committee of the Council.

The Tories began to oppose the war and carried out a policy of obstruction. The Whig Earl of Sunderland, resolutely supporting the war, advised William to dismiss (1694) the last of the Tories from office and to form a ministry of Whigs, depending upon the support of the Whig majority in the House of Commons. Sunderland and the Whigs, of course, were simply seeking a monopoly of office. William was slowly persuaded to follow Sunderland's advice. Shortly afterwards, however, the Tories obtained a majority in the election and William was forced to appoint a number of Tory ministers.

In 1695 the Whigs were again returned with a majority in the Commons. William, most deeply concerned with the progress of the war, replaced all the Tory ministers with powerful Whig leaders of the so-called "junto." These men were closely united in thought and action and possessed considerable administrative talent. After peace with France was signed in 1697 the interparty war went on, a war of intrigue and calumny. The Tories came into power in 1698 and immediately reduced the army and navy. There were so many disputes with the king that the hitherto redoubtable William III threatened to leave England forever. In all these events, the important law was expediency. William's advisers, his ministers, were still his servants. He was not responsible to Parliament and neither were they.

It will be remembered that the third section of the Act of Settlement attempted to place and fix executive responsibility solely in the hands of the Privy Council. It was provided that "all matters relating to the well governing of this kingdom which are properly cognizable in the privy council by the laws and customs of this realm shall be transacted there. . . ." Under this provision in the Act of Settlement the king's ministers in the Privy Council were required to sign the measures they supported and thus their responsibility could easily be proved by the evidence of their signatures. The object of this clause was mainly to prevent the king from moving in policy matters through channels other than the Privy Council. The secrecy of many of the means and ends of kings such as Charles II and James II had frequently troubled Parliament as in the case of the Cabal and other inner councils.

This Parliamentary attempt to limit the executive responsibility to the Privy Council was a failure, as it was bound to be. Among other facts, it was too late to try to put such executive power into the hands of the Privy Council. The real decisions were taken by the smaller groups of ministers in the Cabinet Council and sometimes in the Committee of the Privy Council. The Privy Council itself—let us repeat this salient fact—was becoming an increasingly formal body. In any event, the limiting clause was repealed in 1706 because there was less fear of secret committees and because the attempted controls were simply unworkable. At the same time, another clause of the Act of Settlement was wiped away because its enforcement was not practicable. This was the section that made any man incapable of sitting in the House of Commons if he held "an office or place of profit under the king" or received a pension from the Crown. If this latter clause had not been repealed the ministers of the Crown would have been ineligible to become members of the Commons. After 1706 it was provided that the principal officers of state might sit in the House of Commons if they stood for re-election after being appointed to office. If either of these two provisions of the Act of Settlement had remained in force the Cabinet obviously could not have developed into its present form.

The processes here described were not the result of anything but a combination of accident and expediency. There was no deliberate intention of making the royal ministers in the Cabinet Council or anywhere else directly responsible in the modern Cabinet sense. This practice and this idea were to come much later. In William's reign most devices were haphazard. Expediency ruled his councils and his methods.

In 1701 Queen Anne came to the throne. She was to reign until 1714. The years of her rule were filled with the War of the Spanish Succession abroad and with bitter political battles at home. There were no spurts in the development of the Cabinet in her reign but a steady growth of tendencies and practices pointing towards the ultimate solution of a difficult problem. The "lords of the Cabinet Council" had come to stay. This group, a rather informal gathering of important ministers, met at least weekly in the presence of the queen and decided most major questions of policy. More and more, the Privy Council was limited to the formal transaction of routine business. As the impulses of Queen Anne, so strongly inclined to the Tory and Anglican view of all things, frequently overrode her reason, her ministers often talked over questions before they met her. When her advisers took a united stand Anne seldom refused to yield. She could not be bullied; but she could be persuaded. Here, perhaps, is the germ of the later custom that the Cabinet must be publicly unanimous.

Soon after Anne came to the throne she dismissed several of the Whig ministers. The Tory Duke of Marlborough, England's great soldier, was a favorite of the queen. His brilliant wife, the imperious termagant Sarah, was soon the queen's inseparable companion. Sidney Godolphin, a moderate Tory, became Lord Treasurer and head of the ministry. The chief policy of Tories like Godolphin and Marlborough was to carry on the war against France and Spain and to keep down the convulsions of party politics. For a time, the extreme Tories in Parliament were willing to go along with Marlborough and Godolphin in fighting the war, partly because they themselves were so busy battling the Whigs. Soon, however, conflicts about the conduct of the war divided the Tory party. The extreme Tories were gradually dropped from the ministry and moderate ones were taken in, such as Robert Harley, later the Earl of Oxford, and Henry St. John, later Viscount Bolingbroke.

Harley and St. John were the two outstanding Tory figures in the reign of Queen Anne. Stolid and clerkish, "Robin" Harley was famous for his gifts of conciliation and for the fact that he was a most skillful Parliamentarian. Always involved in petty intrigues he failed lamentably as a party leader. The queen soon complained that "he neglected all business; that he was seldom to be understood; that when he did explain himself, she could not rely on the truth of what he said." Harley's associate was the elastic and knavish adventurer Henry St. John, who was to provide the Tory party with a new philosophy and English history with many scandalous tales.

In the election of 1705 the Whigs obtained a majority in the Commons. Marlborough and Godolphin turned to the Whigs for support in the war. Despite the remonstrances of Queen Anne, many Tories in the government were replaced by Whigs. Harley and St. John were forced to resign. By 1708 the ministry was in fact composed entirely of Whigs supporting Marlborough and Godolphin. The Whig junto prospered.

Meanwhile the protracted war inevitably brought public dissatisfaction and muttered questions. Were the Whigs deliberately prolonging the war? And meanwhile, too, the Duchess of Marlborough fell from the queen's favor. Into her place came Abigail Masham, cousin of

Robert Harley. "The fortunes of Europe have been changed by the insolence of one waiting woman and the cunning of another." Harley and his associates began to tunnel under the government. Backstairs schemes and subterranean plots developed.

In 1709 the High Church Dr. Sacheverell preached an inflammatory sermon in St. Paul's on the dangers of toleration and the duties of non-resistance to the Crown. Sacheverell denounced Godolphin as an enemy of the church. He violently condemned Whigs and Dissenters. When the Whig government impeached Sacheverell for apparently questioning the legality of the Revolution of 1688 the storm began. London mobs disturbed the streets. Sacheverell was hailed as a martyr. Forty thousand copies of his polemical sermon were printed. Houses were wrecked and the chapels of Dissenters were often burned. Pamphlets rained over the country. Then the House of Lords reached its decision on the impeachment trial. Sacheverell was found guilty by a vote of 69 to 52. He was forbidden to preach for three years.

The queen at once dismissed Godolphin and the Whigs. In the general election that followed the Tories were returned to power by a large majority. Queen Anne had her beloved Tories about her once more. Robert Harley (now the Earl of Oxford) and Henry St. John (now Viscount Bolingbroke) replaced Marlborough and Godolphin in favor and in power. The Tories stayed in control until the death of Anne in 1714.

Queen Anne always exercised her royal prerogative of appointment and dismissal without any reference to the situation in the House of Commons. Every time she dismissed a ministry it was at an hour when that ministry controlled a majority in the Commons. Every election that followed a dismissal gave the new ministry a majority. In Anne's day, a single minister's office might be quite insecure even if his party did possess a majority in the Commons. Piecemeal changes were frequent. There were often mixed ministries. Thus the Cabinet Council was a shifting body with little coherence. There was no precision of form, no clear definitions of relations among the members of the ministry. There were many plots, many private conferences, many diverse political opinions, even among men belonging to the same party groups. A restricted "inner" group of varying size and composition usually decided major policies. Nobody then perceived the relationships that we see so clearly today: the policy of the government can be realized efficiently only if the Cabinet is always chosen from the party that has a majority in the House of Commons.

Nevertheless, there is no doubt that the embryonic Cabinet was becoming more responsible for carrying out the legislative program of the government. An illustration of this fact is seen in the last exercise of the royal veto in 1707. If the Cabinet functions successfully, then a veto is not needed. If it fails, then a new Cabinet is clearly necessary. Such is the logic of the situation. "The royal veto is literally as dead as Queen Anne."

In 1712 Queen Anne created twelve Tory peers to make the majority of the House of Lords of the same party as that of the majority of the House of Commons. The Whig-controlled Lords had been blocking too many bills sent up by the Tory-controlled Commons and deadlock threatened. Because what happened in the lower representative House was deemed more important than what happened in the upper hereditary House, Queen Anne created the Tory peers. It is also true, of course, that Anne's personal interest in the political fortunes of the Tories played its part in her decision.

At the end of the reign of Queen Anne we can note these major facts: (1) the Cabinet, or Cabinet Council, had replaced the Privy Council as a body of advice and direction in the planning and execution of state policy; (2) the Cabinet was no longer regarded as a cabal or junto secretly created by royal prerogative power and potentially dangerous to the rights and liberties of Parliament and Englishmen; (3) the sovereign was present and active at the Cabinet meetings; (4) there was no firm, formal, and regular organization of the Cabinet and it shifted in membership steadily; (5) the real work, especially on crucial problems, was actually done—often with speed and secrecy—by a small group of ministers. This restricted circle was not an integrated organization composed solely of the principal ministers of state. It was a varying group and its composition depended upon such considerations as the nature of the questions to be studied, the wishes of the monarch, and the personal relationships of the ministers.

THE CABINET: THE SECOND PHASE

Professor D. L. Keir has called the period from 1714 to 1782 "the Classical Age of the Constitution." He has repeatedly stressed the substantial, secure, prosperous, and stable aspects of life and society as the pendulum swung away from the fervors and emotions of the seventeenth century. Certainly the accession of George I in 1714 marked an early chapter in an era of tranquillity, moderation, balance, self-confidence and, on frequent occasions, of enlightenment. It may be that we have not looked carefully enough at these facts in our study of the growth of the English constitution in the eighteenth century. Perhaps we render less than justice to that age because we have been taught, as our fathers were taught, to fix our attention upon the darker aspects of robbery, jobbery, snobbery and corruption within and without an unreformed House of Commons.

In 1714 George I (1714–1727) came to the throne under the provisions of the Act of Settlement. He seldom attended Cabinet meetings after 1717. It is often said that George I almost ceased his attendance because he did not understand English. But he did speak French and he did converse with Walpole in Latin. It has recently been suggested that George I in fact withdrew from the Cabinet Council because he was not interested in the discussions but rather in the proposals of his ministers. George II occasionally presided at Cabinet meetings; George III presided at least twice. The important points are these: when the king was absent, one of his ministers presided and the reports of the meetings had to be submitted to the monarch by his advising ministers. "It thus made possible both a Prime Minister and a Cabinet minute-book."

George I saw that the Whigs had brought him from his beloved Germany for political and religious reasons. It seemed to the new king that the Whigs alone could hold the house of Hanover safely upon the throne. It was therefore not surprising that he immediately appointed a Whig Cabinet. An election in 1715 gave the Whigs a substantial majority in the House of Commons; they already had a majority in the House of Lords. The new Cabinet of George I contained fifteen members. As usual, there was a small and rather secret group of "effective" ministers (as opposed to the "honorific" or "nominal" ministers whom Lady Cowper called "the Mob of the Cabinet" in 1720). The small inner group—sometimes called the *conciliabulum* —contained, of course, the five chief ministers (the First Lord of the Treasury, the Lord Chancellor as leader in the House of Lords, the two Secretaries of State and the Lord President of the Privy Council) and anybody else these ministers or the king invited.

Modern scholars, particularly Professor Wolfgang Michael, have shown that George I played a far more active part in politics and policy than the conclusions of nineteenth century historians led us to believe. Sometimes, indeed, certain famous Whig historians suffered from a convenient amnesia and quoted facts that they found most convenient for their purposes and ignored the others. The result was a rubble of myth and misunderstanding that is only now being cleared away by contemporary scholars. It must always be remembered that in the early eighteenth century the ministers were more closely related to the king than to one another. They were the king's servants rather than colleagues in the modern sense of a united ministry. Hence it is quite unjust to condemn the Hanoverian kings for failing to do what nobody in their own age expected them to do. Modern ideas about Cabinet government or about anything else must not be projected into the past.

It is impossible to state when the private meetings of the "effective" ministers became official in the eighteenth century. Much learned controversy upon the subject has developed in recent years. We can certainly say that by 1745 there is no doubt that formal recognition was given to the small, interior, confidential, and "efficient" Cabinet group ("the lords of confidence") as distinct from the large, exterior, more unwieldy, nominal, honorific Cabinet Council. More and more, the inner Cabinet became what Henry Pelham called in 1741 "the active part of the administration." The next chapter will show how time and utility slowly joined to make the "inner Cabinet" the "effective" Cabinet and the main constitutional executive organ, the body from which the modern Cabinet is lineally descended. Meanwhile, likewise at a slow pace, the nominal Cabinet Council began to disappear.

As the reader's eye passes over these sentences he will realize that the history of the origin and evolution of the Cabinet is much more complex than it is sometimes made to appear. There are no fixed patterns, few certain dates. We are concerned with something tentative, elastic, pragmatic, protean. Only gradually did the Cabinet develop and move towards its present proved and permanent place. Political usage, far more than legal forms, determined the flow of events.

SIR ROBERT WALPOLE

Much has been written and said about the position of Sir Robert Walpole, often called England's first Prime Minister. What actual evidence do we possess of his work and his status?

Walpole was well fitted to be a squire and a member of Parliament in the eighteenth century. He was a hale, lusty, coarse-grained and sensual materialist, interested in hunting, the game of politics, the pleasures of the bottle. At the same time, he was a master of debate, a superb manager of men, and possessed of a sagacious business sense. Holding a low view of human nature, Walpole believed that most men had their prices. By unscrupulous patronage, by bribery, by interest pressures of all kinds, and by hard work he managed and controlled his own Whig party and often inveigled some Tories into supporting him, for a price. He wanted to maintain the internal equilibrium of the nation. He wanted to keep the Hanoverians on the throne. He wanted peace and prosperity. He wanted to let sleeping dogs lie, to provoke no disputes, no public fuss. "I am no reformer," he once said.

In 1721 Sir Robert Walpole was summoned to salvage what he could from the financial disaster called the South Sea Bubble. Had he not warned the crazed speculators that they would reap the whirlwind? Was he not widely believed to possess the shrewdest financial mind in England? Thus Walpole came to take charge of the Exchequer and to save the Whig party. His measures were sound and bold. For twenty-two years he was to be the leading minister of two kings. After 1721, Walpole held the office of First Lord of the Treasury. It soon became a precedent that the First Lord of the Treasury should lead the ministry, mainly because the man in that position controlled much of the royal patronage. Walpole also remained Chancellor of the Exchequer. He soon came to be called the Prime Minister, although the title was repudiated by him and widely denounced as suggesting a flavor of arbitrary government.

The fact should be stressed—it is often forgotten—that Walpole "did not, as his insecure position on George II's accession shows, enjoy any tenure independent of royal favor." [3] But he did keep that royal favor. He obtained the affection of George I. He gathered and held the esteem of George II's adroit wife, Caroline of Anspach. If more royal approval were needed Walpole got it by adding £100,000 to the revenue provided for the private use of George II (1727–1760). Secondly, Walpole had the strength of his own personality, the power of his own cynical shrewdness, the skill of his own methods, ruthless and hard. For instance, when some of the ministers did not support him in the famous Excise Bill struggle of 1733 Walpole forced their removal from office. Thirdly, he led the Whig party and he saw to it that the Whigs held a majority for more than twenty years. Fourthly, his personality and administrative skill placed him first among the ministers in his Cabinet. In brief, Walpole superbly met the demands placed upon a directing minister in the eighteenth century: he satisfied his king and he kept the majority of the votes in the House of Commons by

---

[3] D. L. Keir, *Constitutional History of Modern Britain, 1485–1937*, p. 332.

persuasion, patronage, management and corruption. Much as a later day may condemn the systematic use of such instruments and methods, called "influence" in the eighteenth century, they were then used and accepted as a part of the political conventions, the necessary lubricants of the machinery of the state.

There was something else. We have remarked that Walpole was the king's minister, the king's servant dependent upon royal favor. It should be noted further that Walpole did not choose his own colleagues; they were chosen for him by George I or George II. When Walpole left office in 1742 he did not carry his fellow ministers with him; they were responsible to the king and not to Walpole or to the House of Commons. These statements are made here because it seems that too much has sometimes been claimed for the reign of Walpole as "the first modern Prime Minister," which fact and caution tell us he was not. His main achievements, some of which have been briefly mentioned earlier, included the accidental one of serving as a link, for the first time in British history, between the Commons, where he was a minister and member, and the inner circles of the royal court, where he was an executive minister. The weight of the task of explaining and defending executive policy fell heavily upon Walpole because most of his colleagues in the ministry were members of the House of Lords and hence incapable of appearing in the Commons.

Walpole had many talented and venomous opponents. As one result of England's entry into the conflict of Jenkins' Ear in 1739 and the later War of the Austrian Succession, Walpole's popularity and power declined. He had sturdily opposed the war. He wanted to resign; but George II demurred. When the war did not go well for England Walpole was unjustly charged with thwarting and starving the British war effort. The elections of 1741 went against the Whigs supporting Walpole, and his majority in the Commons dwindled to three or four. He fought hard against the many enemies his long monopoly of power had made. In the end they beat him by one vote on an election petition. This was on January 28, 1742. Three days later Walpole resigned, thus doing much to establish the principle that he who cannot command a majority in the House of Commons should make way for one who can.

After the prudent and practical Walpole was gone, there was a swift succession of ministries. Between 1742 and the death of George II in 1760 there were five separate governments.

Some historians have seen in the confused years between 1742 and

1760 a number of events that they consider to be crests and watersheds in the development of the modern Cabinet system. On the other hand, it may perhaps be held that there are to be clearly perceived only a few general tendencies. Speculations are frequently interesting. However, if they are tied to the known and solid evidence by frail and tenuous threads they do not properly belong in the province of the historian. W. Ralph Inge ("the Gloomy Dean") once remarked in an essay that "a journey through the unreal is an unreal journey and leads nowhere."

The "general tendencies" to which reference was made in the previous paragraph may be briefly described. During the period 1742–1760 the king's power to create and maintain ministries was clearly declining, partly because strong leaders were becoming more willing and able to state and fight for the terms upon which they would accept office. If the king made Cabinets in which the leading Parliamentary figures were not included then those men could make it almost impossible for the Cabinets to carry on. The ministers were also beginning to move away from the king and to draw closer to Parliament and one another.

These, then, are the directional thrusts in the evolution of the Cabinet that are clearly perceptible in the early and middle years of the eighteenth century. The remainder of this chapter is concerned with two other topics: significant acts of Parliament and important judicial cases in the years before the accession of George III.

WILLIAM III TO GEORGE III: LAWS AND JUDGES

At least four pieces of legislation passed by Parliament in the early eighteenth century are of immediate interest to the student of constitutional and legal history. They are the Act of Union with Scotland (1707), the Riot Act (1715), the Septennial Act (1716), and the Irish Parliament Act (1719).

Despite considerable loyalty to the ancient Scottish house of Stuart, many Scotsmen recognized that the Calvinist William III would look kindly upon Presbyterianism. Accordingly, a Convention held at Edinburgh in 1689 prepared a "Claim of Right" similar to the English Declaration of Right and offered the crown to William and Mary under terms which included recognition of the Presbyterian Church as the state church of the nation. The offer was accepted.

Within a few years a trade war developed between English and Scottish interests. The Scots wanted to increase their foreign trade and to establish colonies overseas. When Scottish merchants in London tried to form trading companies they were blocked by the hostile English Parliament and the monopoly-gorged East India Company. The English were also ready to make great efforts to keep the Scotsmen out of all foreign markets. Meanwhile, Scotland's Darien Company lost thousands of pounds in a disastrous scheme to found a settlement on the isthmus of Darien (Panama).

As Anglo-Scottish disputes increased about the succession to the Scottish throne it was decided to negotiate about the possibility of uniting the two nations in a mutually satisfactory political and economic arrangement. After long debate the English and Scottish commissioners reached agreement. In the summer of 1707 "an act for the union of the two kingdoms of England and Scotland" was passed. England and Scotland were to be "united into one kingdom by the name of Great Britain." The Scottish Parliament came to an end. Scotland was given a representation of sixteen peers in the House of Lords and forty-five members in the House of Commons. Scotland also assumed a small part of the public debt. It kept unchanged all its own institutions, such as the law courts and the Presbyterian Church. It received the right of full free trade with England and the colonies and henceforth shared in English enterprise throughout the world. The economic and political agreements under the Act of Union were a good bargain for both countries. England no longer had an enemy on her northern border. Scotland began to prosper and to make a massive contribution to the national and imperial life of the new Great Britain.

A second significant act of Parliament was the Riot Act of 1715. This statute was made at a time when Englishmen were decidedly restive. It was widely felt that George I was subordinating the interests of England to his beloved Hanover. Riots and other disturbances against the king and his German loyalties became so frequent that the Whig government passed the Riot Act, "for preventing tumults and riotous assemblies and for the more speedy and effectual punishing of the rioters." This famous enactment is still on the statute books. It states that "any persons to the number of twelve or more, being unlawfully, riotously, and tumultuously assembled together to the disturbance of the public peace" may be ordered "to disperse themselves and peaceably to depart to their habitations or to their lawful business." The command to disperse may be given by a justice of the peace, a sheriff, a mayor, or certain other specified officers. One of these officers "shall, among the said rioters or as near to them as he can safely come, with a loud voice command or cause to be commanded silence to be while proclamation is making." Then the officer is required to make, quite loudly, the brief proclamation set forth in the Riot Act. This proclamation orders all persons, in the name of the sovereign, "immediately to disperse themselves and peaceably to depart to their habitations or to their lawful business. . . ." Under the terms of the act, if the assembly has not broken up within an hour all individuals remaining become thereby guilty of a felony. If any of the rioters "shall happen to be killed, maimed, or hurt . . . by reason of their resisting the persons . . . dispersing, seizing, or apprehending . . ." the officers inflicting such injuries "shall be free, discharged, and indemnified . . . of, for, or concerning the killing, maiming, or hurting of any such person or persons. . . ."

The country became still more restless. To the Whigs it seemed that the carnival of corruption and riot accompanying a general election might be dangerous. In 1716 Parliament passed the Septennial Act to take the place of the Triennial Act, thus extending the life of Parliament from three years to seven. The Septennial Act remained in force until the Parliament Act of 1911.

Finally, a dark phase of Anglo-Irish relations was marked by the passage of the Irish Parliament Act of 1719, an act reminiscent of the harsh Poyning's law (1494). After William III had defeated the forces of James II in Ireland at the Boyne neither the northern Irish Protestants nor the southern Roman Catholics moved towards peace. The Irish Catholics kept up the war until 1696. A series of cruel acts were passed against them. Roman Catholics were excluded from the Irish Parliament. They were forbidden to sit on juries, on town councils, to serve in the army or to teach in Irish schools. No Roman Catholic was allowed to buy land. When a Catholic landowner died, his estate had to be divided among all of his children. Restrictions were placed on the Irish woolen trade. Another bitter chapter was being written in the tragic history of Ireland.

It was against this background that the Irish Parliament Act was passed in 1719. The important provisions contained in the law were carefully prepared "for the better securing the dependency of Ireland upon the crown of Great Britain." They were designed, among other things, to stop the Irish House of Lords from altering the decisions of the royal courts of justice in Ireland. The law declared that "the said kingdom of Ireland hath been, is, and of right ought to be subordinate unto and dependent upon the imperial crown of Great Britain, as being inseparably united and annexed thereunto; and that the king's majesty, by and with the advice and consent of the lords spiritual and temporal, and commons in Parliament assembled, had, hath, and of right ought to have full power and authority to make laws and statutes of sufficient force and validity to bind the people and kingdom of Ireland. . . . that the house of lords of Ireland have not nor of right ought to have any jurisdiction to judge of, affirm, or reverse any judgment, sentence, or decree, given or made in any court within the said kingdom; and that all proceedings before the said house of lords upon any such judgment, sentence, or decree are and are hereby declared to be utterly null and void to all intents and purposes whatsoever."

The position of Ireland, it seemed, was clear. Ireland was to continue to be dependent upon and subordinate to Great Britain. If the members of the Parliament of 1719 could have foreseen the events of the next two centuries they would certainly have doubted the efficacy of their legislation. But they could not pull back the veil of the future. What they did in 1719 seemed to them to be the gospel of wisdom. They were not the last legislators whose conclusions have been confounded by later events.

In this famous and relatively stable age of peaceful advance and retreat the courts of law continued to move through the long decades with their measured and ordered routine, their dignified and relentless pace. In the next chapter there will appear several passages about the legal history of the age of the Hanoverians. At this point we are concerned with one theme of high significance, a task and a problem that appear as a constant thread in the history of democratic states. The task is always the same: the execution of those laws upon which the liberty of the subject depends. The problem is always the same: precisely what does the voice of the law say about guilt or innocence, right or wrong, in a particular set of circumstances?

In a Parliamentary election at Aylesbury in 1700 a cobbler named Matthew Ashby was one of the Whigs excluded from voting by the Tory mayor of Aylesbury and some constables acting as returning officers of the borough. Ashby claimed that he had a right to vote in choosing a burgess for his borough because he had burgage tenure. He brought action at the assizes against White (the mayor) and the constables. This was an action on the case because the law was asserted to have conferred a definite right to vote. The decision at the assizes was in favor of the plaintiff Ashby. Later, the Court of Queen's Bench reversed that decision, asserting that the case was one of Parliamentary privilege and therefore outside the jurisdiction of the common law courts. Three judges of Queen's Bench held (1703) that the Commons alone had authority to adjudicate on the qualifications of voters and therefore decided for the defendants.

From this opinion the famous Chief Justice Holt dissented. He insisted that the Commons had jurisdiction only when there was a case of a disputed election to be settled. Because there was no dispute in the election at Aylesbury there was no question, in Holt's judgment, of Parliamentary privilege at all. It was incumbent upon the court to protect Ashby. "I think the action well maintainable," said Holt, "that the plaintiff had a right to vote and that, in consequence thereof, the law gives him a remedy if he is obstructed; and this action is the proper remedy. . . . It is a vain thing to imagine there should be right without a remedy; for want of right and want of remedy are convertibles. If a statute gives a right, the common law will give remedy to maintain it; and wherever there is injury, it imports a damage. . . . the law consists, not in particular instances, but in the reason that rules them; and if, where a man is injured in one sort of right, he has a good action, why should he not have it in another?"

On a writ of error the judgment of the Court of Queen's Bench was reversed by the House of Lords. Thus Holt's opinion was upheld.

The case of Ashby v. White provoked resolutions from the House of Commons asserting that Matthew Ashby became guilty of a breach of the privileges of the House of Commons when he "commenced and prosecuted an action at the common law." On the other hand, the House of Lords declared that the House of Commons, by its resolution, was clearly "assuming a power to control the law, to hinder the course of justice, and subject the property of Englishmen to the arbitrary votes of the house of commons." The formal resolution of the House of Lords also declared that any individual deprived of his right to vote did have a remedy in the common law courts. To assert otherwise "is destructible of the property of the subject, against the freedom of elections, and manifestly tends to encourage corruption and partiality in officers who are to name returns to Parliament, and to subject the freeholders and other electors to their arbitrary will and pleasure."

Thus the judgment of the House of Lords supported the case and cause of Ashby. Shortly afterwards a second test case arose: the Queen v. Paty and Others. Several burgesses of Aylesbury proceeded to sue the constables who had excluded them from voting. The Commons, many of whose members had been aided by bribery and intimidation in the elections, committed the plaintiffs to Newgate Prison for breach of privilege (1704). By a writ of *habeas corpus* the prisoners were brought before the Court of Queen's Bench but that court refused to free them. Once again Chief Justice Holt stated his dissenting opinion: "When the House of Commons exceed their legal bounds and authority, their acts are wrongful and cannot be justified more than the acts of private men. There is no question but that their authority is from the law and, as it is circumscribed, so may it be exceeded. If we should say they are judge of their privilege and their own authority, and nobody else, that would make their privileges as they would have them. In such case, if there be a wrongful imprisonment by the House of Commons, what court shall deliver the party? Shall we then say that there is no redress, and that we are not able to execute the laws on which the liberty of the subject depends?"

The case of the Queen *v.* Paty and Others finally went to the House of Lords. When Parliament was prorogued in 1705 the dispute between the two houses was dropped. Fortunately for the prisoners the House of Lords had freed them before the prorogation. Unresolved, of course, was the legal problem as to whether any writ of error lay upon a judgment given solely on a writ of *habeas corpus* by the Court of Queen's Bench.

THE CABINET AGAIN

There have been three themes in this chapter: the early stages of Cabinet growth; the causes and nature of significant legislation; the points at issue and the legal decisions in some typical judicial cases. Many strands, old and new, were being woven into the fabric of the national life in the early eighteenth century.

Subjects such as these were manifestly important in English constitutional and legal history. Of special significance, of course, were the slow experiments in government and administration that pointed towards the modern Cabinet method of making the executive branch of government responsible to the legislative. Such events were of primary significance because they shaped and strengthened the human lines of communication without which societies and states could not continue to exist.

The reader must not conclude that the comments about the Cabinet in this and other chapters are complete and final. Numerous monographs yet remain to be written about the evolution of the Cabinet before all the dark places are thoroughly illuminated. Today it is necessary for the scholar to make so many reservations and postulates that they sometimes dominate the scene. One of the tasks of the historian is to keep his critical spirit active and alive. Where caution fails, scholarship is changed into opinion and error. That is the reason why reputable modern historians are frequently not prepared to make more than tentative suggestions with respect to several aspects of Cabinet development.

The casual evolution of the Cabinet may seem untidy to the modern student living in a world made efficient by organized science. Nevertheless, it should be remembered that the important affairs of men are often less neatly arranged than a modern business executive or a professor of history might wish. It is demonstrably true that many signal achievements of human beings have resulted from apparently directionless effort in the midst of plaguing muddle and thwarting discord. Across the slopes of time we can read and hear the words and voices of men asking, often desperately and in baffled darkness, the questions born of frustration and tension: "How can we find something that will work? How can we pump the water from the mine? How can we control the king? How can we reach the silks and spiceries of the East? How can we discover what is happening in the sub-atomic universe?" It is not surprising that modern students of ideas and institutions sometimes wonder how contending forces ever reached equilibrium.

In the years after the flight of James II the men, who were destined to make the early Cabinet system, walked with a halting tread towards their substantial achievements. The slow progress along tortuous pathways did not come to an end in 1760, the year that George III ascended the throne. Cabinet power, challenged by many opposing forces, hesitantly increased its scope and effective authority during the years when George III was king.

CHAPTER XVIII

Courts and Cabinets:
the politics of power

ELECTIONS AND INFLUENCE

EIGHTEENTH century England was ruled by the aristocracy and the landed gentry. Those who possessed land had political power. The lords and the gentry designated most of the members of Parliament and shamelessly influenced elections by bribery, pressures, and many other corrupt practices. Complicated systems of bargaining and blackmail prevailed.

In the middle of the century 51 peers and 45 commoners made or effectively influenced the return of nearly 200 members of Parliament. The Duke of Norfolk controlled 11 seats; Sir James Lowther, 9; Lord Darlington, 7. About 75 interrelated families really governed the House of Commons. In some cases, the great landowners owned whole boroughs. Thus they had the right to choose the representatives of those "pocket" boroughs, so called because the landowners carried the nominations in their pockets. In other cases, the population of the boroughs was so small that it was easy for a wealthy landowner to manage the elections—hence the descriptive words "rotten" boroughs.

There had been no redistribution of seats in Parliament since the early seventeenth century. No new boroughs had been made after 1667. Because the population had been largely concentrated in southern and eastern England when boroughs were being created in the period from the Middle Ages to the seventeenth century, these areas contained 115 out of the 203 boroughs. Borough members of Parliament were more numerous than county members; 203 boroughs returned 483 members; 40 counties returned 82 members. One quarter of all the members of the House of Commons came from the area covered by the counties of Cornwall, Devon, Dorset, Somerset, and Wiltshire.

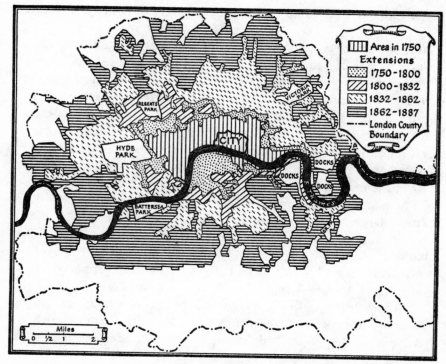

LONDON: THE GROWTH OF A CITY

The Lincolnshire borough of Dunwich was falling into the North Sea, but it sent two members to Parliament. A deserted meadow and an ancient wall also sent two members to Westminster. On the other hand, the cities of Manchester, Leeds and Birmingham sent no members at all, although the population of Manchester was about 130,000 and of Leeds and Birmingham about 80,000 each. The corresponding disparity in county representation can be seen in the fact that populous Yorkshire sent two members to Parliament; but so also did the tiny shire of Rutland.

The franchise requirements were haphazard and narrow. In the counties the franchise was granted only to individuals with freehold property worth forty shillings annually. This rule had been declared by statute in 1430. Leaseholders, copyholders, tenants-at-will, and cotters had no vote. In the boroughs the most chaotic and diverse conditions prevailed. Sometimes there was no voting at all. In some boroughs the right to vote was given to all who paid local taxes; in others only to the hereditary "freemen." In still others, the vote was given only to individuals who owned or occupied certain houses. The whole political structure was shot through with corruption. Voters were widely bribed. Traffic in seats was considered quite in order and was certainly normal. A seat in the House of Commons could usually be bought for £7,000 or £8,000. When elections were contested they were often bitter and costly. After the Septennial Bill was passed in 1716 and Parliaments were to last for seven instead of three years men were willing to spend even more. The polls were kept open for fifteen days and hence the expenses of electioneering were higher than they would have been in a shorter voting period.

After the eccentric Duke of Newcastle became Secretary of State in 1724 he began the building of a powerful political machine. He kept political power for forty years by gold and corruption. He loved the game of politics. In playing it he spent three-fourths of his ducal fortune.

The world of authority indeed belonged to men of property. When pressure groups were formed, family connections were almost as important as political ties. The importance of patronage, family connection, and "influence" in eighteenth century politics cannot easily be overstressed. The political life of the state was not determined by enfranchised masses. There were approximately 160,000 voters in the latter part of the eighteenth century and through direct patronage and other persuasive and lubricating instruments the king's court obtained the majorities it needed to support government policy. Its patronage resources were considerable: honors here, pensions there, sinecures all about. In 1779 George III wrote to John Robinson, Secretary of the Treasury: "Certainly the times are not so virtuous that persons will labour for the public without reward." [1]

From these remarks it follows that there was nothing approaching a modern party system in the eighteenth century. There were the party names of Whig and Tory but often there was little more. True, it did happen that the distinctions and controversies between the High Church groups and the Low Church and Dissenting elements were often strong and bitter in local areas. In court and Parliament, how-

---

[1] Quoted in Herbert Butterfield's *George III, Lord North, and the People 1779–1780*, p. 195 n. (1949). The royal "influence" was indeed considerable. Because the word "influence" will appear frequently in this chapter it should be explained that, as it was used in the eighteenth century, the word meant the various methods by which the king and his ministers could persuade a majority of the members of Parliament to vote for government measures. Royal "influence" never meant royal prerogative power. It was used to describe the appeal, usually successful, to men hungry with ambition or greed or both.

ever, these differences were not of vital political importance. The chief lines of demarcation in Parliament were not based on political party principles at all.

There were really three groups at Westminster. The first included those who were usually in positions of power and influence, the "placemen," the steady followers of the court. The second group comprised the country gentlemen who were independent and hence, under the iron laws of oligarchy, very seldom in the pivotal points of power. The third group included all the various rival elements struggling for office, authority, and income. These shifting bands stood between the independent country gentlemen on the one hand and the court's "placemen" on the other. It was they who caused the most excitement in the political history of the latter eighteenth century. Led by professional politicians, battling and tough and often dishonest, the factions jostled for place and profit. As Sir Lewis Namier has remarked, these men were "focusing upon themselves the attention of the public and of history." [2]

It has already been said that the three main groups in Parliament were not political parties. They were cliques and pressure groups bound together by such things as ambition, personal affection, family relationship, and common political or personal animosities. The research of Sir Lewis Namier has led him to conclude that in the year 1761 the result of not one election was determined by party. Not until the latter part of the nineteenth century when the systems of influence and aristocratic control had largely collapsed did there really arise an urgent need for modern party systems and programs, principles, disciplines, and organized prejudices. Public opinion—shaped to an increasing degree by the press and the platform—slowly began to replace first the Crown and then the aristocracy as the directing power in the political life of Britain. The transition from royal to Parliamentary government was a gradual and silent process and it actually happened much later than is sometimes believed. The principles came early. The practice came late.

GEORGE III: PATTERNS OF GOVERNMENT

George II died in October, 1760, and his grandson, George III (1760–1820), succeeded to the throne. The history of this new king's reign is often written in the style of a political pamphlet. Disputes are

---

[2] The quotation is from the Romanes Lecture for 1952: "Monarchy and the Party System." Sir Lewis knows more about this subject than anyone.

multiplied and only a few historians in England and America have avoided capital blunders of fact and interpretation. Generations of professors have uncritically reproduced the tales invented by Horace Walpole and others. For example, it is now certain that "a break, clean and final, occurred between the king and Lord Bute in August, 1766." Lord North was not Bute's nominee. The legend that George III's letters to Bute have perished is not true; they have been printed and published by Professor Romney Sedgwick.[3]

The oft-repeated tale that George III was brought up on Bolingbroke's *The Idea of a Patriot King* is also inaccurate. There never was any historical evidence for several of our Whig convictions about the character and policy of George III. "In his own time," writes Professor Sedgwick, "George III was accused by his opponents of attempting to subvert the system of government established by the Revolution. By subsequent historians this charge was translated into that of attempting to subvert the system of responsible government. Thus by a double distortion he has been represented as having endeavoured to imitate the Stuarts when he ought to have anticipated Queen Victoria." Or, again: "In reality George III carried on, to the best of his more than limited ability, the system of government which he had inherited from his predecessors."

The king who came to the throne in 1760 did possess several undesirable qualities. He was a bundle of complexes. He was arbitrary, petty, obstinate, and inept. Compromise was a word he uttered with reluctance. He worked hard to fulfill the duties of kingship as he understood them. His mistakes and his tragic fate resulted from ill-directed ability, from obtuse stubbornness, from a set of perverted ideas, and from the incompetence of several futile, pompous and unimaginative ministers. Many of those ministers, contrary to the frequent assumption, did possess some qualities well above the ordinary; it was unfortunate that they were seldom employed in the service of the state.

George III was not bound to accept the advice of his ministers. True, they were chosen to give him adequate advice. But they held office during his pleasure. The majority in the House of Commons was made and held largely by Crown patronage. The effective ministers of the smaller Cabinet were only responsible to George III and to the courts, including the House of Lords before which they might be impeached.

---

[3] See L. B. Namier, *Avenues of History*, p. 118 (1952); Romney Sedgwick (ed.), *Letters from George III to Lord Bute 1756–1766* (1949).

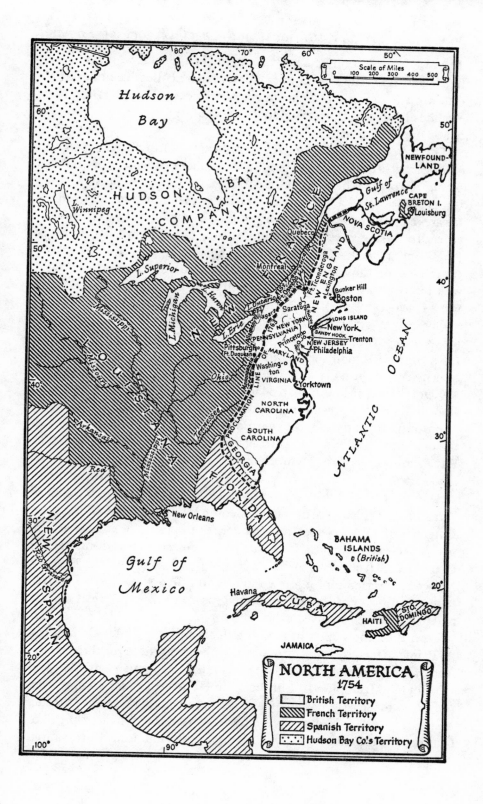

NORTH AMERICA
1754

British Territory
French Territory
Spanish Territory
Hudson Bay Co.'s Territory

They were not responsible to Parliament. The idea, as well as the practice, was simply alien to the age. Nor was there collective or corporate Cabinet responsibility. That idea was not accepted until after 1827. Responsibility was thus individual and legal. It was not collective and it was not Parliamentary.

The ministries of George III were usually formed by agreements among groups and "connections" in Parliament provided that nobody offensive to the king was selected. The royal wishes must be met. George III wanted a body of administrative servants that he liked. So far as we know, he attended and presided over Cabinet meetings only twice. In the six years before the ministry of William Pitt the Elder (1766–1768) George III did send henchmen to spy, and sometimes to try to control, the executive for him. Later there was less direct royal interference with the executive body. Later still, as we shall see, there was a distinct decline of royal "influence."

George III preferred to be his own chief minister. He wanted, so far as was possible, to "manage" the House of Commons. He tried, for a time with high success, to do this through his ministers. These crown servants usually aided the royal cause, and their own, by the judicious distribution of patronage. In the early part of the reign of George III such a procedure was not possible because the Whigs were in power in the famous war government of the Duke of Newcastle and the masterful William Pitt. During this period of the Seven Years' War Pitt's genius helped to produce the military victories abroad and Newcastle's political power, money, and skill gathered and held the necessary votes in the House of Commons. For some time the services of Pitt and the Whigs were necessary. George III did place his friend Lord· Bute, a Scottish Tory sporting grandee, in the inner or effective Cabinet as Secretary of State. Bute saw and reported all to his master. In October, 1761, Pitt was forced to resign. Lord Bute and the Duke of Newcastle carried on for a few months and then Newcastle departed, lonely and bitter as his friends looted his crumbling political empire and fled to serve new masters.

Lord Bute thereupon headed the third ministry under George III. As Prime Minister, Lord Bute was mainly responsible for the negotiation of the Treaty of Paris (1763) that ended the Seven Years' War and left England friendless in Europe. The House of Commons approved the treaty for several reasons. Chief among them, perhaps, was the fact that Lord Bute paid cash for numerous votes. The "golden pills" of George III were a useful vaccine against opposition. Lord Bute wanted to pull down from the political heavens the constellations of Whig oligarchs and he succeeded, for a time.

The king used royal revenue to buy seats in Parliament as well as votes. George III also scrutinized the lists of voters in Parliament and saw to it that rewards and punishments were distributed accordingly. It was a rather serious setback when Lord Bute became the target of a venomous newspaper campaign. Bute was widely detested for his part in the negotiation of the Treaty of Paris. Wincing under a barrage of unruly insults and harassed by several public disturbances, Bute resigned.

A new ministry was then formed under the leadership of George Grenville. This government lasted until 1765. Not until 1770 was George III able to dispense with makeshift ministries. Then, at last, he found it possible to obtain and hold steadily in power an effective ministry under the Tory Lord North. It should be noted, however, that a modern scholar has found no trace of "any political project more sinister than the vague idea, common to all oppositions of the period, that a 'reformation in government' was needed, with a view to 'purging out corruption' and combatting the 'venality of the age.' " The malevolent intentions so often ascribed to George III by the Whig historians seem not to be there. On the other hand, his ineptness, rashness, and obstinacy, so often confused with evil purposes, stand forth clearly to the end.

In 1765 George Grenville gave way to Lord Rockingham, a sensible and second-rate Whig. When Rockingham refused to yield to several wishes of the king the Whig majority in the Commons dwindled. In 1766 William Pitt, mighty leader in the Seven Years' War, agreed to form a non-party ministry. The result was a heterogeneous combination, "a diversified mosaic, a tessellated pavement without cement." Pitt seemed to think that he could control both George III and his colleagues. But he was gouty, old and ill and the king worked steadily against him. When he went to the House of Lords as Earl of Chatham Pitt's influence in the Commons further declined. His Cabinet got into difficulties for arbitrarily using an Order-in-Council to prohibit the export of grain; it was defeated on a money bill; it was divided on the question as to whether conciliation or coercion should be used in America. Amidst this confusion and disorganization Pitt collapsed and retired, a sick lion. For two years (1768–1770) the Duke of Grafton stayed the head of a weak and divided ministry.

In January, 1770, George III at last rid himself of the Whigs and put

Frederick, Lord North at the head of the government. The able and submissive Lord North was to remain in office for twelve years. The exact role of Lord North in the king's system of government and in the years of the decline of the first British Empire has yet to be determined by competent historians. In later days Lord North insisted that the actions of George III were misunderstood. It may be so. Certainly more evidence is necessary before any final conclusion can be reached. In any event, there is no doubt that Lord North yielded to the wishes of his king. George III, after ten years of hope and planning amidst unstable and disunited ministries, had at last obtained a subservient Cabinet, a pliable majority in a House of Commons where nearly two hundred members held office under the crown. The ousted and hostile Whigs, with their many factions, were no longer a formidable threat. Sometimes, indeed, their internal battles were so violent that they were not a threat at all. Meanwhile, Lord North, despite his strong conviction that the policy towards the American colonies was mistaken, still stayed in office. He was the servant of the king and he remained loyal.

The grievances and events that brought revolution in America are beyond the scope of this volume. The unfortunate steps in colonial policy, the unhappy procedures of administration, the passage of such pieces of legislation as the Stamp Act (1765), the Declaratory Act (1766) and Townshend's Revenue Acts (1767) are chapters of first importance in the political and economic history of the western world. The Declaratory Act, for instance, set forth for the first time the constitutional status of colonial possessions in legal terms. So far as the constitutional and legal history of England is concerned, however, the actual loss of an empire was not of major consequence.

Nevertheless, there were several events and attitudes in England that flowed immediately from the failures of George III, Lord North and his Tory colleagues. After 1778 popular clamor for a speedy end to the war rose steadily. Many Englishmen continued to insist that they supported the colonies. They asserted that the designs of the obstinate and maladroit government must be thwarted. "Magnanimity in politics," said Edmund Burke, "is not seldom the truest wisdom." "A great empire and little minds go ill together." Upon George III there fell an increasing public condemnation for his share in the conduct of affairs. Demands for a reform of Parliament had multiplied. A debate in the House of Commons about Lord North's government in 1779 revealed a bitterness of temper reminiscent of the Stuart age. References were made to the "most calamitous and disgraceful effects" of Lord North's administration. "If anything can prevent the consummation of public ruin, it can only be by new counsels and new counsellors without further loss of time."

In 1780 George Dunning's famous resolutions declared "that the influence of the crown has increased, is increasing, and ought to be diminished." [4] The Commons carried Dunning's resolution by a vote of 232 to 215. Was what Dunning called a "most corrupt and unconstitutional influence" now to be diminished?

In March, 1782, Lord North resigned. He had wanted to resign in 1779. George III talked of abdicating and going to Hanover. Yorktown had ended many things. George III was now compelled to accept a Whig ministry under Lord Rockingham, and soon another one under Lord Shelburne (1782–1783). Late in 1783 the Whig Charles James Fox, who had been forced out of the Rockingham ministry, shocked the nation by forming an unexpected alliance with the Tory Lord North against whom he had shot his venomous shafts for so many years. George III was astounded by the "desertion" of North and the triumph of Fox, whom he hated. The Fox-North union, said the king, was "the most unprincipled coalition the annals of this or any other nation can equal." In the eyes of the king, North was an ungrateful traitor. Fox, the leader of the detested Whigs, had corrupted the Prince of Wales. But Fox and North stood together and defeated Shelburne. The king determined to have his revenge.

His chance came soon. Through the House of Commons Fox passed a bill to extend government control over the East India Company. George III called the bill "a monster of graft and iniquity," which it was not. In December, 1783, he authorized Earl Temple to make the statement among the peers that "whoever voted for the India Bill was not only not his friend, but would be considered his enemy." The House of Lords rejected the bill.

A motion was at once passed in the Commons protesting that "to report any opinion or pretended opinion of his majesty upon any bill or other proceeding depending in either house of parliament, with a view to influence the votes of its members, is a high crime and misdemeanor derogatory to the honor of the Crown, a breach of the fundamental

---

[4] Extracts from the Commons' debates on Dunning's resolutions are printed in Carl Stephenson and F. G. Marcham, *Sources of English Constitutional History,* pp. 690 ff. Important documents for the period 1760–1810 are to be found in the same volume, Section XII, pp. 657–718. The student should be aware that the word "influence" in the Dunning resolutions is used in its eighteenth century sense, earlier explained. "Influence" must not be considered synonymous with power.

privileges of Parliament, and subversive to the constitution of this country." George III paid no attention. He at once dismissed Fox and North. He then called young William Pitt, the second son of the deceased Pitt the Elder, Earl of Chatham, to form a Cabinet. The precocious Pitt was only twenty-five years old, the leader of a reviving Tory party. "A kingdom trusted to a schoolboy's care," laughed his political foes. But Pitt fought the experienced and wily politicians until he judged the hour ripe for an election. In the election of 1784 the supporters of Fox and North lost seat after seat. Pitt came back into power with a working majority. George III, who preferred the Tory Pitt to the hated Whigs, also found that Pitt would usually have his way, even against the king.

A new era was opening for England. Pitt's first ministry was to last for seventeen years. In the development of the Cabinet and the constitution this was an important event. More important still was what happened within the next few decades.

CROWN AND CABINET: CHANCE AND CHANGE

It is easy to oversimplify the slow alterations in England that resulted in the decline of the "influence of the Crown" in the political arena. Nineteenth century writers frequently pointed to 1832, the year of the first Reform Bill, as a time when royal influence was measurably reduced. Others repeatedly called attention to the Rockingham economic reforms, to such things as the Place Act (1782), and to the fact that Pitt the Younger used no court patronage. In their judgment, the demise of "the old system" came to an end about the time of the resignation of North in 1782 or Pitt's assumption of office in 1784. Recent research, particularly the distinguished work of Professor Archibald S. Foord, has made necessary several new conclusions and interpretations. The decline of court "influence" began long before 1832, although not with the ministry of Pitt in 1784. It began for reasons hitherto unsuspected or, at least, unproved. Now there remains no doubt that most of the earlier orthodox descriptions and judgments are inaccurate and invalid.[5]

There was, of course, wide objection in the eighteenth century to the crown's use of pensions, peerages, and places to obtain and hold majorities in Parliament favorable to the king. Dunning's resolutions

---

[5] See A. S. Foord, "The Waning of 'The Influence of the Crown,'" *English Historical Review* LXII (1947), pp. 484–507.

were merely the sharp utterance of the opinion held by many men and their fathers before them. Nevertheless, "the king's business" had to be done in Parliament. Practical ministers of the Crown saw in the judicious use of patronage and threats the sole methods by which they could be reasonably assured of carrying through "the king's business" and staying in office themselves. Nobody, or almost nobody, really thought it necessary or desirable to destroy the Crown's "influence" altogether—even Dunning limited himself to saying that it "ought to be diminished." At the same time, it seemed clear that George III was exercising, directly and indirectly, far too great a "fund of influence with which nobody else could compete."

Despite the repeated statements that Pitt the Younger was master of his king after 1784 the facts are otherwise. The conclusion that reforms and legislation immediately after 1782 checked the Crown influence does not alter the fact that George III's baits of persuasion gave Pitt a majority in the election of 1784. On the other hand, there is no doubt that the royal system of creating and nursing majorities in the House of Commons had virtually ended some time before the Reform Bill of 1832. Thus "the influence of the Crown" did not cease in the early 1780's or in 1832. It steadily diminished in the fifty years between the coming of William Pitt and the coming of William IV. Successive droughts reduced the flood of patronage to a trickle. The durable scholarship of Professor A. S. Foord and others has made it quite clear when, how, and why the gradual reduction of "the king's interest" occurred. It was an important event in English constitutional history.

Not all of the reasons for the diminution of Crown influence can be stated here. Most important was the simple fact that the supply of funds formerly available for government distribution was gradually reduced. In the eighteenth century Parliament had no control over expenditure. Nor was there a sharp distinction between public property and the private property of the king. The ministry could use for political purposes without account or challenge the moneys from such sources as the civil list and the Crown's hereditary revenues. In 1780 the House of Commons resolved "that it is competent to this house to examine into and to correct abuses in the expenditure of the civil list revenues, as well as in every other branch of the public revenue, whenever it shall seem expedient to the wisdom of this house to do so." A commission of public accounts was appointed in 1785 to examine the whole financial system. In the same year five commissions were appointed to audit all public accounts. Burke's Place Act (1782) was entitled "an act for better securing the freedom of election of members to serve in Parliament by disabling certain officers employed in the collection or management of his majesty's revenues from giving their votes at such elections." This act also divided all charges against the civil list into eight classes. A separate departmental budget was allotted to each. Every department was placed under a royal official who was responsible for the authorization of all expenditures. In all departments accounts were to be audited. Even the hereditary revenues of the Crown slowly came under governmental control. Only the privy purse remained under the full regulation of the sovereign. Long before 1832 the monarch and his ministers had lost control of public funds for political purposes.

There were further restrictions. The Bribery Act of 1809 made it virtually impossible for the Crown or the ministers to use bribery as a political instrument in the boroughs and counties. In 1812 Sir Robert Peel and Lord Liverpool agreed that it was wrong to promise the creation of two peerages in return for the delivery to the government of seven seats in the Commons. By 1820, or thereabouts, the Tory government was granting far fewer honors for political reasons than had earlier been the case. Various controls were established to stop the ministers of the Crown from using government contracts to obtain votes or other "interests" in elections.

Pitt the Younger began the policy of encouraging government loans from all reputable firms after the issuance of a public notice of an intended loan. This new policy was far different from the earlier private arrangements among the politicians and their friends in the financial world. There were also several attempts to remove Crown lands from politics by curtailing their use for political purposes—as in the control of leases and the like. The functionless sinecure offices were reduced in number. For instance, Burke's Place Act, mentioned earlier, abolished 134 offices in Household and Treasury. Professor A. S. Foord, whose research and writing have made possible the writing of these pages, has pointed out that in 1795 William Pitt abolished 765 unnecessary revenue offices. Legislation and custom united to destroy the patronage, "placemen," and "influence" system as it prevailed before 1783. Indeed, by 1812, in the words of Professor Keith Feiling, the "old cement of patronage was more than half gone." This was an emphatic and important trend.

It was indeed a trend, nothing more. The pace of change in the period between the 1780's and 1832 was not that of a rapid revolution.

There were numerous quiet forces, many pieces of legislation, administrative reforms, subtle alterations in public values and attitudes. Political parties in opposition saw and took opportunities to curb the power of their opponents. The heavy costs of long years of war made retrenchment and economy imperative. To be successful, any kind of "influence" must rest mainly upon money, and money for such purposes was not to be had in the age of the French Revolution and the Napoleonic Wars. Meanwhile, too, the rise of the press and the platform helped to bring both monarch and ministers closer to the bar of public scrutiny and judgment.

In summary, then, the Crown was gradually losing control of policy. The link of "influence" between the monarchy and the Commons was being broken. Although the Crown was still in politics, effective power was slowly passing to the Cabinet. At the same time, the Cabinet was extending its authority over the civil service. Meanwhile, year by year, the ministers of the king were increasingly responsible to the House of Commons. Within the Commons the Whigs and Tories were moving more rapidly towards a closer integration of their group organizations and a clearer definition of their principles. Modern party government was still several decades in the future but the foundations for it were being laid.

Through all these years the House of Commons remained still unreformed. To bring responsible party government, to place the Crown beyond politics, to destroy completely the political power of royal patronage were the tasks of the following century. The first step towards these achievements was the reform of Parliament and the extension of the electoral franchise. To the dramatic first episodes in the movement for Parliamentary reform we turn in the next chapter.

THE WILKES CASE

As successive chapters of the development of the Cabinet were being recorded in the pages of English history other events of importance occurred. One of these was the case of the famous struggle between the government and John Wilkes. The first phases of this protracted struggle happened during the Grenville ministry (1763–1765).

John Wilkes, the son of a wealthy distiller, was a member of Parliament and the publisher of a journal called the *North Briton*. He used his paper to denounce the unpopular Treaty of Paris of 1763. In No. 45 of the *North Briton* he wrote an insolent and anonymous comment on the king's speech and the peace arrangements, asserting that George

III had given "the sanction of his sacred name to the most odious measures and to the most unjustifiable public declarations from a throne ever renowned for truth, honour, and unsullified virtue."

George III insisted on the prosecution of Wilkes and the Cabinet acceded to his demand. A "general warrant," so called because it did not specify the person to be arrested or the property to be seized, was issued by the Secretary of State against "the authors, printers, and publishers" of the *North Briton*. Under this warrant John Wilkes and forty-five other persons were arrested. After Wilkes had been imprisoned in the Tower of London his house was searched and some papers were removed. Wilkes claimed that the general warrant was "illegal and ridiculous." He asserted that as a member of the House of Commons he was exempt from arrest except on charges of treason, felony, or breach of the peace.

Chief Justice Pratt decided that a general warrant was a practice "in itself illegal, and contrary to the fundamental principles of the constitution." When the Crown lawyers argued that the act was one "of state necessity" Chief Justice Pratt replied that "public policy" was not an argument "in a court of law." Wilkes was released under a writ of *habeas corpus*. In 1765, Chief Justice Pratt, then Lord Camden, rendered a decision in the case of Entick *v.* Carrington that ended the use of general warrants for all time. "If it is the law, it will be found in our books. If it is not to be found there, it is not the law. . . . The silence of the books is an authority against the defendant and the plaintiff must have judgment." As a result of this judgment Wilkes collected heavy damages in 1769.

Because the Cabinet controlled a majority in the House of Commons the Commons voted that Parliamentary privilege did not extend "to the case of writing and publishing seditious libels," ordered No. 45 of the *North Briton* to be burned by the public hangman and expelled Wilkes from Parliament. Wilkes was seriously wounded by a crack shot who forced a duel upon him. He was popular among the people but he had few friends in the upper levels of society. Faced by danger and filled with fear, Wilkes fled to France. When he did not return to face the main charge of libel filed against him by the government he was outlawed by the Court of King's Bench.

George III had won a costly victory. The arbitrary methods used by the government to suppress freedom of speech had roused London. Members of Parliament were mobbed. The cry "Wilkes and Liberty!" rolled over England. Six years later the failure of the prosecution against the mysterious "Junius" for his *Letter to the King* established the right of the press to criticize the king himself.

Wilkes stayed abroad for three years and then returned to England. He stood as a candidate for Parliament from Middlesex and was elected. The government dropped the outlawry declaration but sentenced Wilkes to twenty-two months in prison on the libel charge. George III wrote to the Duke of Grafton, then Prime Minister: "I think it highly expedient to apprise you that the expulsion of Mr. Wilkes appears to be essential and must be effected." Parliament thereupon put Mr. Wilkes outside as an undesirable libeller.

Tracts and placards appeared in the streets. Wilkes became the hero of the cause of liberty and the symbol of opposition to the Crown. He was again elected to Parliament. The Commons quite illegally resolved that "Mr. Wilkes, having been in this session of Parliament expelled this House, was and is incapable of being elected as a member to serve in the present Parliament." In a third election Wilkes was elected by a four-to-one majority. The Commons declared that his opponent, a man named Luttrell, "ought to have been returned."

Wilkes had become a martyr. Mobs shouted his name and his glories. He himself was a scoundrel, but he became a champion of popular rights. Clubs and societies, such as the Supporters of the Bill of Rights Society, were formed to promote the cause of Parliamentary reform. But George III was obstinate. He had beaten Wilkes again. Reckless of results, he failed to see that a radical spirit was rising. The legal battles of Wilkes had confirmed important freedoms, as in the case of general warrants. His unsuccessful attempts to stay in Parliament had stressed the unrepresentative character of the House of Commons and its dependence upon the Crown. Wilkes had shown the dangers to personal liberty inherent in the existing system. He had helped in the development of the growth of the idea of public meetings, new methods of agitation, and deliberate organization of individuals for concerted action. The episodes in which John Wilkes was involved were warnings of the challenges to kings and ministers that were soon to come over the hills of the future.

ACTS OF PARLIAMENT

Before 1776 Parliament had approved a series of ill-advised measures in colonial policy. It had thus given further impetus to forces that were slowly breaking apart the first British Empire. Such pieces of legislation as the Stamp Act, the Declaratory Act, and Townshend's

Revenue Acts are important milestones in the last stretches of the history of the thirteen colonies. Upon the constitutional and legal history of England, as earlier remarked, they had little effect. There were, however, two other acts of Parliament of later consequence both to America and Great Britain.

These two statutes were the Quebec Act of 1774 and the Canada Act of 1791. They dealt with problems in the lands that had passed from France to England under the terms of the Treaty of Paris of 1763. The Quebec Act gave offense to the thirteen colonies because it extended the boundaries of Quebec southwest to the Ohio and west to the Mississippi. The new law thus cut off the lands claimed by Massachusetts, Connecticut, New York and Virginia. The French Canadians were allowed to "have, hold, and enjoy the free exercise of their Roman Catholic religion." They were also to retain their French civil law. "And whereas the certainty and lenity of the criminal law of England and the benefits and advantages resulting from the use of it have been sensibly felt by the inhabitants from an experience of more than nine years" the Quebec Act provided that English criminal law should be maintained. To Puritan New England the concessions to French Roman Catholics were especially offensive. Nevertheless, the Quebec Act helped to keep Quebec, the fourteenth colony, in allegiance to Britain while the other thirteen rebelled. If there had been no Quebec Act the loss of Quebec, the "catastrophe shocking to think of" that Governor Murray once described, might have come to pass. Thus the Quebec Act was a step of no small consequence in the history of England and Canada.

In 1791 the Canada Act divided Quebec into two British provinces north of the Great Lakes and the St. Lawrence: Upper Canada, largely English, now the province of Ontario; and Lower Canada, mainly French, now the province of Quebec. Each was given a legislative assembly. The road towards responsible self-government stretched ahead for sixty years. The lands to the north of the Great Lakes and the forty-ninth parallel were to remain within the Empire. The wisdom that dictated the passage of the Quebec Act and the Canada Act helped to make possible the continued allegiance of Canada.

It was far otherwise in Ireland. During the long and fateful struggle between Britain and Napoleon Bonaparte the volcano of the Irish problem erupted violently. "England's difficulty is Ireland's opportunity." Earlier in the century Ireland was discontented and ill-governed; but there were no major disturbances. It was true that many of the cruel statutes against the Catholics were not harshly enforced in an age of reason. The Irish were able to develop new commercial activities and to increase their income by smuggling. Nevertheless, in Ireland the Roman Catholic was excluded from political office—no Roman Catholic might vote or sit in Parliament. The Test Act also kept the Ulster Presbyterians from taking part in the government. Thus the majority of Irishmen had no political rights and few economic ones. They were ruled by a few Anglican families. Even the Irish Parliament in Dublin, unrepresentative as it was, was dependent upon England because it could pass no legislation without the approval of the English government.

The moderate Irish Protestant Henry Grattan, a landowner and a statesman of vision, led an Irish national revival during the American War for Independence. A fearful English Parliament was then persuaded to wipe away many obnoxious restrictions on Irish trade. In 1783 Parliament repealed Poyning's Law, which had originally been enacted in 1494 by the Irish Parliament, not the English. This law had made the Irish Parliament subordinate to the Privy Council in London. The Irish Appeals Act of 1783 was "an act for removing and preventing all doubts which may have arisen or might arise concerning the exclusive rights of the Parliament and courts of Ireland in matters of legislation and judicature." It said that the final validity of the acts of Ireland's Parliament and the decisions of Ireland's courts "shall be and it is hereby declared to be established and ascertained forever, and shall at no time hereafter be questioned or questionable." Thus Ireland received a considerable degree of legislative independence. No longer did the acts of the Irish Parliament have to be "certified into England." Soon the penal code was modified and the Roman Catholics were given the vote (1793); but they were not permitted to sit in the Irish Parliament.

With the outbreak of the French Revolution the clouds darkened. The Society of United Irishmen corresponded with French republicans who promised to help them. Radical Irish leaders like Wolfe Tone preached violence and outrage. An ugly civil war broke out as Orangemen and Catholics battled passionately about the ancient questions of religion. A Roman Catholic revolt of 1798, inadequately supported by the French, was swiftly crushed by British forces.

Against this background of violence and doubt William Pitt proposed a legislative union between the English and Irish Parliaments, similar to that which had been made between England and Scotland in 1707. Pitt promised that if the Irish agreed to send representatives to Westminster instead of to Dublin the Irish Catholics would be given full political rights and the laws against them would be repealed. This proposal of Catholic Emancipation helped to carry the bill for the legislative union through the Irish Parliament. The separate Dublin Parliament ceased to exist on January 1, 1801 when the Act of Union came into effect. After that date Ireland was represented at Westminster by 100 members in the House of Commons and 28 peers and 4 bishops in the House of Lords. There was to be full free trade between the two countries. The kingdom of Great Britain, formed in 1707, became the United Kingdom of Great Britain and Ireland.

The solution of the Act of Union might have been made real and workable had the Roman Catholics been emancipated or enfranchised. The intermittently insane George III obstinately refused to give the Irish Catholics their political freedom because he claimed that in doing so he would violate his coronation oath. Pitt worked in vain to convince the king of the practical wisdom of removing the disabilities of the Roman Catholics. George III's anti-Catholic prejudices were too deeply rooted—he threatened to go completely mad if the Catholics were enfranchised. Pitt felt that he had given his promise to the Irish and must see the measure through Parliament or, as a matter of honor, surrender his office. In 1801 he resigned. In Ireland a disillusioned people prepared to travel a long road of conflict and misunderstanding.

The enactments relating to Canada and Ireland were accompanied by a series of acts of an entirely different kind. So long as the French Revolution had stayed in its moderate phase many Englishmen looked upon it with sympathy or at least with tolerance. But when it moved into excesses of violence and confiscation the English reaction was swift and strong. When Edmund Burke published his famous *Reflections on the French Revolution* (1790) the conservative elements became fearful of the molten lava of Jacobinism. The result was a long suppression of the movement for Parliamentary reform, a pervasive suspicion of all opinions that might be described as liberal or radical or Jacobin. Those who were not suspects were suspected of being suspects. Suspicion, that most deadly of political plagues, swept over England.

In 1793 France declared war upon England. In 1794 the "Act Suspending Habeas Corpus in Certain Cases" was passed. It was declared to be "an act to empower his majesty to secure and detain such persons as his majesty shall suspect are conspiring against his person and government." It asserted that "a traitorous and detestable conspiracy has been formed for subverting the existing laws and constitution and for introducing the system of anarchy and confusion which has so fatally prevailed in France." It provided, as its title indicates, for the temporary suspension of *habeas corpus*. A Treasonable and Seditious Practices Act was passed in 1795. In the same year a Seditious Assemblies Act forbade meetings "of any description of persons exceeding the number of fifty . . . for the purpose of or on the pretext of considering of or preparing a petition . . . for alteration of matters established in church or state" unless specific notice was given to the authorities by at least seven householders. A new Treasons Act was passed. Restrictions were placed upon the press and upon societies and associations. In numerous instances justice retreated before public hysteria and widespread unreason. Not for the last time did the hard impact of anger and conflict bring sad results.

During these years of fear and danger Parliament embarked upon a program of legislation in the field of social and economic affairs. In 1795 a Poor Relief Act provided that "under certain circumstances of temporary illness or distress" the parish overseers or guardians of the poor might give direct relief to the "industrious poor" in their own houses, a procedure that had not been possible under "the inconvenient and oppressive" provisions of a statute of 1722. In 1800 a Cotton Industry Arbitration Act provided for the arbitration of disputes between masters and workmen "engaged in the cotton manufacture in that part of Great Britain called England." In the same year, a Combination Act declared that any agreements or contracts among workmen or other persons "for obtaining an advance of wages . . . , or for lessening or altering their . . . usual hours . . . of working, or for decreasing the quality of work, or for preventing or hindering any person . . . from employing whomsoever he . . . shall think proper to employ . . . shall be . . . illegal, null, and void." Journeymen and other persons were also forbidden to stop an unemployed worker from taking a job or to "decoy, persuade, solicit, intimidate, influence, or prevail on any journeyman . . . or other person" to quit his work. Men convicted of these offenses were to be sent to jail for two or three months. Persons attending meetings for purposes such as those described here, or soliciting or paying money to aid such causes, were liable to heavy penalties. On the other hand, by the terms of this Combination Act of 1800, "all contracts . . . made or to be made by or between any masters or other persons for reducing the wages of workmen, or for adding to or altering the usual hours . . . of working, or for increasing the quantity of work . . . are hereby declared to be illegal, null, and void."

In 1802 a Factory Act was passed "for the preservation of the health and morals of apprentices and others employed in cotton and other mills." Detailed regulations were made for the provision of clean and well ventilated quarters for the apprentices. No apprentice, said the act, should be compelled to work more than twelve hours a day. Provisions were made for training in reading, writing, and arithmetic and for education in religion. Inspectors were appointed to inspect the mills and factories and to file reports with the justices of the peace in the quarter sessions courts.

These were some of the attempts made by Parliament at the end of the eighteenth century to solve a few of the problems resulting from the economic revolution. Many of the enactments were evaded or defied. The voices of the Christians and other humanitarians were persuasive and loud but their hands were not yet powerful. It remained for the nineteenth century to take further measures to ease the pain of man's inhumanity to man. Meanwhile, the gap between the ideal and the actual remained wide, even among the enlightened sons of the Age of Reason. In William Blake's *Marriage of Heaven and Hell* it is fitting that Hell should be a type factory.

THE LAW AND THE LAWYERS

Of Lord Hardwicke, Lord Chancellor from 1737 to 1756, a contemporary said: "Touch but a cobweb of Westminster Hall, and the old spider of the law is out upon you with all his younger vermin at his heels." The eighteenth century was a conservative and relatively static period, a time of great judges but not of major reforms in the law and the legal system. Changes in the cumbersome legal procedures were few. Even moderate reform proposals were defeated in Parliament. The obsolete and the absurd were retained despite numerous objections. So far as the courts and the laws were concerned, these were the quiet years before Jeremy Bentham and the philosophical radicals roused the land with their vehement voices and their insistent pens.

The modern student of procedure will find of interest the fact that in 1733, despite wide opposition from the judges, the court records began to be prepared in English rather than Latin. The original declarations and all subsequent pleadings entered in the court rolls became literal translations of the Latin forms. In 1772 it was provided in an act of Parliament that any person refusing to plead to a criminal charge and standing mute in court should be deemed to have pleaded not guilty. Thus was finally ended the long tale of the institution of *peine forte et dure,* a practice that played such an inglorious part in the growth of the jury system and brought death to many obstinate men.

Throughout this period the Inns of Court declined from their once high estate. The advance of legal education was obstructed by the indolence and lethargy of teacher and student. Readers discharged their duties in a perfunctory fashion. Conscientious and industrious students usually attached themselves to older lawyers and learned what they could in the law chambers and the courts.

Despite the somnolence of the Inns of Court there appeared several judges and lawyers who wrote books about the law. A number of Abridgments were published in which attempts were made to state the law under alphabetical headings. When such a method was used it was obviously impossible to set forth the principle of any division of the law in a logical fashion. The famous three volumes of *Equity Reports,* usually called Atkyns, suffered from this defect. A few workers in the Abridgment field did show more skill and promise. One of these was Charles Viner, who published a twenty-three volume revision of an *Abridgment* issued in 1668 by Henry Rolle, Chief Justice of the Court of King's Bench. Viner also provided an endowment for the famous Vinerian professorship of English Law at Oxford University. Before this time the English universities had taught only canon and civil law. The introduction of studies in the field of English law was particularly important at a time when the influence of civil law was increasing in England. For instance, Lord Camden, Lord Hardwicke, and Lord Talbot all held the office of Lord Chancellor and each was a systematic student and exponent of civil law.

In the past four centuries England has been fortunate in possessing many outstanding legal scholars and jurists. The sixteenth century saw the work of such men as Sir James Dyer, Sir Anthony Fitzherbert, Edmund Plowden, John Rastell. The Stuart age is famous for Thomas Ashe, Sir Francis Bacon, Sir Edward Coke, John Cowell, John Selden, Sir Henry Spelman. Probably the most famous of the seventeenth century writers was the pious, independent and diligent Sir Matthew Hale (1609–1676). An Oxford man, Hale wanted to be a soldier but went to Lincoln's Inn instead. He was called to the bar in 1637, the year of the famous Ship Money cases. Throughout the Civil War Sir Matthew Hale safely and honestly steered a middle course. In 1653 he became a judge in the Court of Common Pleas. In 1655 he was a member of Parliament. In 1660 Charles II made him chief baron of the Exchequer and later Chief Justice of the Court of King's Bench. The sagacious Hale was a learned man, a hard worker, and an excellent writer in law, religion, philosophy, and science. His systematic *Pleas of the Crown*, first edited in 1730, became a standard treatise in criminal law. The incomplete *History of the Common Law* has also been held in high regard for nearly three hundred years. All of Hale's printed works—some manuscripts are still unpublished—first appeared in the eighteenth century.

Many standard textbooks were also published between 1700 and 1800: Fearne's *Contingent Remainders,* Foster's *Common Law,* Gilbert's *Uses* and *History and Practice of the Exchequer,* Hawkins' *Pleas of the Crown,* Preston's *Estates,* Sanders's *Uses.* The most comprehensive survey of the contemporary legal system was the *Commentaries* of Sir William Blackstone (1723–1780). Blackstone had been a student at Oxford and the Middle Temple. In 1746 he was called to the bar and in 1750 he became a doctor of civil law. In 1758 he became Vinerian Professor of English Law at Oxford. Jeremy Bentham described Blackstone's lectures as being "cold, reserved, and wary, exhibiting a fixed pride." Later Blackstone became a member of Parliament, "where amidst the rage of contending parties, a man of moderation must expect to meet with no quarter from any side." Between 1765 and 1769 the four books of Blackstone's Oxford lectures were published under the title *Commentaries on the Laws of England.* For a long time this famous work was the main support of legal instruction in the law schools of England and the United States.

The themes of the *Commentaries* may be summarized thus: "The objects of law are rights and wrongs. Rights are either rights of persons or rights of things. Wrongs are either public or private." Under these subject headings the four books of the *Commentaries* were written. In almost every page of the *Commentaries* Blackstone showed his complacency and his conservatism. He believed firmly in the law of nature of the eighteenth century. He was a sturdy defender of the existing order. Jeremy Bentham, as usual, was angered by Blackstone's attitude in the *Commentaries* and on the bench. He considered Blackstone "the enemy of all reform and the unscrupulous champion of every form of professional chicanery." Despite the objections that may be raised to Blackstone's position and attitude the *Commentaries* was a milestone in the history of the law. Written in clear and simple English it marks the complete abandonment of French and Latin as the exclusive language of the legal profession. In some respects, indeed, the *Commentaries* is less a legal treatise than an intelligible handbook of the law for laymen. This is one reason why generations of men have perused it with profit. "Lawyers know life practically," said Dr. Samuel Johnson. "A bookish man should always have lawyers to converse with. They have what he wants."

The name of William Murray, first Earl of Mansfield (1705–1793), stands high on the list of the great jurists of England. After completing his studies at Westminster School, Oxford, and Lincoln's Inn he was called to the bar in 1730. He soon appeared in behalf of the city of Edinburgh when it was threatened with disenfranchisement. In 1737 he won an immense reputation for a single speech at a jury trial. He then became successively solicitor-general (1742), attorney-general (1754) and Chief Justice of the Court of King's Bench (1756–1788). His varied and brilliant achievements can only be touched upon briefly here. At one time, for instance, Mansfield was Speaker of the House of Lords when the Great Seal was in commission. He was a member of the Cabinet for fifteen years.

It is of the first importance to note that Lord Mansfield helped to extend and transform the existing principles of the law. He aided in moulding the laws of shipping, commerce, insurance. It was Lord Mansfield who tried to introduce into the common law—with a clear head and passionate pen—some of the flexible principles of Chancery (though equity was even then beginning to harden). In this endeavor Mansfield was not entirely successful. There was to be no fusion of the substantive law of equity and the common law if the common law judges and lawyers could prevent it.

Lord Mansfield did succeed in persuading the common law courts to use some of the convenient and sensible principles of the law merchant in cases involving men of the trading and financial world. As commerce developed it was clear that the common law was inadequate to deal with the cases and customs that arose. No principles had been derived in the cases that had occurred. "Mansfield found the law in this chaotic state and left it in a form that was almost equivalent to a code." He has always been rightly regarded as the major founder of English mercantile law. He could not, of course, convince his fellow judges that the civil law was the foundation of jurisprudence. They could not approve what one called the "loose notions" frequently expressed by their eminent colleague.

There were further reasons for Lord Mansfield's fame. He helped to expand the common law action of *assumpsit* "until it enforced a recovery upon almost every kind of pecuniary obligation." He amplified the laws of evidence. He always protected the rights of conscience. He conducted the cases over which he presided with consummate ability, passionless polish, fairness and propriety. It was he who supported Lord Camden's decision against general warrants and reversed the outlawry of John Wilkes. It was he who freed the slave in Somersett's Case (1772) and gave the decision on points of law in Campbell *v.* Hall (1774).

There were some objections to Lord Mansfield's decisions in the trials of libel involving Junius and Horne Tooke and, later, in the case of the Dean of St. Asaph on the ground that Mansfield was supporting arbitrary power. In the latter case, Mansfield uttered several paragraphs about jury trial that all students should read and remember.[6]

The objections to Mansfield's decisions in the cases mentioned were not well founded. He was supported by precedents and the great majority of judges and lawyers agreed with him. It is important to remember that no bill of exception was ever tendered to any of Lord Mansfield's rulings. Only two of his judgments were reversed.

DECAY AND CHANGE

In 1800 George III hastened the resignation of William Pitt and delayed the coming of Catholic emancipation for nearly thirty years. The new Tory Prime Minister was Henry Addington, later Lord Sidmouth, a mediocre man handicapped by lack of ability and imagination. Pitt came back into office in 1804. After Pitt died in 1806 three governments held office before 1812: Lord Grenville and Charles James Fox (1806–1807); the Duke of Portland (1807–1809); Spencer Perceval (1809–1812). Then came the long reign of Lord Liverpool (1812–1827). Meanwhile, in 1810, George III went permanently mad.

The tale of these shifting ministries contains few pages of importance for the student of legal and constitutional history. What mattered most in these years was the fact that several new forces were

---

[6] These statements of Lord Mansfield are printed in Carl Stephenson and F. G. Marcham, *Sources of English Constitutional History*, pp. 713–715. Excerpts from other decisions of Lord Mansfield are to be found in the same volume, pp. 710–713.

rising, prophetic of future conflict. One of these was the demand for Parliamentary reform.

Even before the French Revolution began or the heavy hand of Napoleon fell upon Europe there had been strong pressure in England for a reform of Parliament. William Pitt had led a debate upon the question in 1770. Parliament had rejected reform bills in 1776 and 1780. In 1782 William Pitt again urged Parliament to undertake an investigation of the inequitable distribution of votes and seats. Another reform bill was rejected in 1785.

When the French Revolution came it was inevitable that the conservative ruling classes would set their faces still more firmly against any proposals for change. New plans failed in 1790, 1792, 1793 and 1797. The alarm of the ruling classes increased with the pace and pressure of war with France. Soon came the ugly repressive legislation described earlier in this chapter. So it was that the French Revolution and the age of Napoleon helped to retard the reform of Parliament for several decades. The legislators of Parliament, alarmed by unreason, suspended *habeas corpus,* passed such harsh measures as the Treasonable and Seditious Practices Act and the Seditious Assemblies Act. There was now no chance to agitate for reform. The counter-revolutionary tide was in full flood. So far as the government was concerned the gospel of reform meant the same thing as a call to revolution.

Meanwhile the currents of economic change increased the urban population. The means of communication were improved and extended. Clubs and societies multiplied. Men and women talked about their angers and their hopes. Orators and agitators harangued for numerous causes, always hampered by the law, the police, and the lurking government spies. Pamphlets, broadsheets, and newspapers spread fact and fiction. Through the long years of war and reactionary fear a new public opinion was being shaped. The thrusting strength of novel aims and strange desires shot through the spirits and minds of men who worked in the factories or fled from the landlord.

The next chapter is about three subjects: the reform of Parliament —the first in four hundred years; the changes in the law and the legal machinery; and the tide of reform legislation that changed the destiny of every Englishman.

CHAPTER XIX

Reform and Democracy:
the price of progress

REPRESSION AND REFORM

THE years of the French Revolution and the triumphs of Napoleon had brought no victory of reason and the laws of nature, no dividends of felicity, no Heavenly City in this world. Weary after twenty years of war, Europe wanted peace and security. When the Congress of Vienna ended its labors in June, 1815, there seemed reason to believe that peace and security had been achieved. Napoleon was a prisoner on St. Helena. A new map of Europe had been shaped. Steps had been taken to ensure conservative stability against the dangers of liberalism and destructive revolution.

England was now the foremost power in the world. As unchallenged mistress of the seas she controlled the water lanes of trade. Her colonies had steadily increased in number and importance. No foreign competitor was yet able to threaten her industrial and commercial supremacy. Her position seemed impregnable.

Despite the advantageous situation of England in 1815 so far as the world beyond her shores was concerned the scene at home was neither calm nor satisfactory. It was difficult to transform the economy of a nation that had been at war for twenty years into a peacetime system. The various economic dislocations—the fall in foreign trade, the currency inflation, the bad harvests, the industrial collapses—were inevitably matched by social disturbances. Such was the shadowed landscape of 1815. During the next three years the darkness of a great depression spread over all England. More grain crops failed. Factories closed. Poverty, disease, dirt, ignorance, and a widespread feeling of disillusionment and frustration united to produce bitter complaints and violence.

The Tory government of Lord Liverpool (1812–1827) took only a few steps calculated to do some good. To protect the farmers from the competition of foreign grain the Corn Law of 1815 was passed and the duty on grain was raised to prohibitive heights. The price of grain spiralled and the landowners were satisfied with what their Tory government had done for them. The price of a loaf of bread increased to more than a shilling at a time when the usual wage of the farm laborer was about eight shillings a week. To please the middle classes the income tax was abolished in 1817. Two weeks later the Bank of England resumed payment in specie; this action resulted in a healthy deflation of the currency and made a minor contribution to economic recovery.

Here the Tory government of Lord Liverpool stopped. It was natural that the English landed aristocracy should not welcome new ideas or the prospect of change in a state of society that had given them power and prosperity. They were angered by any challenge to order, discipline, or to their monopoly of power. They had been frightened by the excesses of the French Revolution and still thought it possible that Jacobinism or some radical plague equally unpleasant could come to England. When economic maladjustments pressed upon the country after 1815 the Tory Cabinet under Lord Liverpool had no important remedial or ameliorative measures of legislation to offer. No major steps were taken to deal with a mounting economic crisis or to attempt by legislative means to cushion the impact of the disruptive forces at work in England. When popular dissatisfaction brought widespread disturbances the answer of the Tories was repression, not relief. Against that repression rose riots and sabotage. Pamphlets denounced the men whom the writers considered to be the makers of low wages and unemployment. The prose of Jeremy Bentham and William Cobbett united with the poetry of Shelley to spread the gospel of dissent. Demands for reform pierced the thick walls of the solid country houses of the aristocrats and echoed in the corridors of the House of Commons.

The reformers were of many kinds. At least they did agree upon two things: their opposition to the power of the aristocracy and their desire to reform Parliament. It was felt that once Parliamentary reform was accomplished many other reforms would swiftly follow. The apostles of Wilberforce would see slavery abolished. Sir James Mackintosh would see the criminal code amended. Francis Place would speed the departure of the iniquitous Combination Acts. Such was the hope, such the dream.

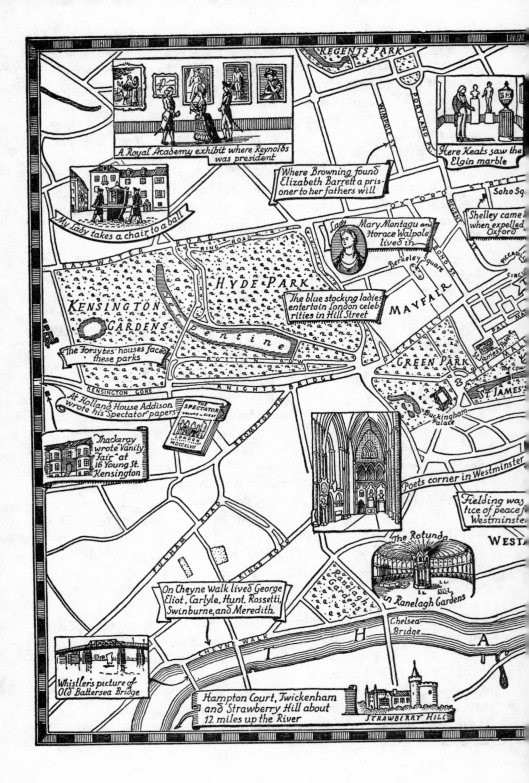

A Royal Academy exhibit where Reynolds was president

Where Browning found Elizabeth Barrett a prisoner to her fathers will

Here Keats saw the Elgin marble

Soho Sq.

Shelley came when expelled Oxford

My Lady takes a chair to a ball

Lady Mary Montagu and Horace Walpole lived in

Berkeley Square

HYDE PARK

RING ROAD

BAYSWATER ROAD

KENSINGTON GARDENS

The blue stocking ladies entertain London celebrities in Hill Street

MAYFAIR

PICCADILLY

Pentine

The Forsytes' houses faced these parks

ROTTEN ROW

GREEN PARK

KENSINGTON GORE

KNIGHTS BRIDGE

St. James's

THE COW

ST JAMES'

At Holland House Addison wrote his 'Spectator' papers

THE SPECTATOR
VOLUME the FIRST

LONDON
MDCCXLVII

Buckingham Palace

Thackeray wrote "Vanity Fair" at 16 Young St. Kensington

BROMPTON RD

Poets corner in Westminster

Fielding was tice of peace f Westminster

WEST

The Rotunda

WESTA

On Cheyne Walk lived George Eliot, Carlyle, Hunt, Rossetti, Swinburne, and Meredith.

Ranelagh Gardens

in Ranelagh Gardens

Chelsea Bridge

CHEYNE WALK

H

A

Whistler's picture of Old Battersea Bridge

Hampton Court, Twickenham and Strawberry Hill about 12 miles up the River

STRAWBERRY HILL

REGENTS PARK

WIMPOLE ST

PORTLAND PL

OXFORD STREET

REGENT ST

BOND ST

FULHAM ROAD

KINGS ROAD

Will's Coffee House

Greys Inn

here Johnson wrote his Dictionary

Cheshire Cheese haunt of Johnson, Dickens etc.

East India House

here worked Lamb

British Museum

Lincolns Inn

HOLBORN

Old Bailey

NEWGATE

Fleet Prison

St. Paul's

Guildhall

GRUB ST

BISHOPSGATE

Old Curiosity Shop

FLEET ST.

CHEAPSIDE

WATLING ST.

THREADNEEDLE

LOMBARD ST.

ALDGATE

Jonathan's

The Temple

Bow Bells Church

Boars Head Tavern

DRURY LANE

Covent Garden

MAIDEN LANE

STRAND

Savoy Theatre

Billingsgate Market

CESTER SQUARE

THEATRES

ICAR S.

ING CROSS

WHITEHALL

Old Scotland Yard

EMBANKMENT

VICTORIA

R   I   V   E   R

London Bridge

Tabard Inn

Burke pleads the American cause in Parliament

BLACK FRIARS ROAD

Marshalsea prison where Dickens' father was confined for debt, and here Mr. McCawber suffered likewise

Houses of Parliament

LAMBETH

Bethlehem Hospital (Bedlam)

GREAT DOVER STREET

Blackheath infested by highwaymen

to Dover-Calais-France

The Lamb

Blake engraved his songs in Lambeth

Vauxhall Gardens

Eighteenth and Nineteenth Century

LONDON

0   ¼   ½

Mile

Only the main streets are shown

E. Raisz

For many years the movement for the reform of Parliament had been guided by rather moderate and quiet men working through peaceful channels such as the Hampden Club or the numerous "corresponding" societies. It has earlier been explained that William Pitt the Younger had some quite progressive ideas about the necessity of changing the system of representation in the House of Commons. In 1776 John Wilkes had proposed a re-allocation of seats more in accordance with the distribution of population. In 1780 the Duke of Richmond had submitted a plan for equal districts and universal suffrage. A decade later, as the reader is well aware, the coming of the French Revolution and the war with Napoleon gave a strong setback to the movement for Parliamentary reform.

When the war ended in 1815 forces long held in check were released. The idea of reform was embraced by radical organizers of mass action and it became merged in the confused flood of agitation and violence resulting from economic grievances. Because the working class began to call for a "radical" reform of Parliament many of the middle class confused moderate ideas of reform with extreme projects of violence. For a time they took alarm and stood aside from the reformers, meanwhile continuing to denounce the Liverpool Cabinet for its reactionary policy.

The policy of the Liverpool Cabinet was indeed reactionary. The police broke up a meeting at Spa Fields near London. The leaders of a small army of unemployed workers, called the Blanketeers, were arrested and their plan to march on London collapsed. In 1819 eleven individuals were killed and about five hundred injured in the famous "Peterloo Massacre" near Manchester. This sad event occurred when the local magistrates of Manchester, filled with prejudice and panic, ordered the cavalry to charge upon an orderly and unarmed crowd that had gathered to hear a speech about Parliamentary reform.

Repressive legislation mounted in volume and severity. To cope with the uneasy temper of these years the Tory government again suspended the Habeas Corpus Act. There followed a series of so-called "liberticide acts." The Seditious Meetings Act, for instance, extended the provisions of the act of 1795 earlier described. The new measure required all public meetings to be licensed by magistrates. The Cambridge University debating society was closed. Government spies watched the activities of reformers to see if they attended unlicensed meetings, a treasonable offense. The repressive Six Acts showed how frightened and furious reactionaries could stubbornly defend themselves and their interests. The first of the Six Acts was an Act for the Prevention of Unauthorized Military Training, a desirable measure which has never been repealed. A new Seditious Meetings Act made any assembly of more than fifty people illegal; this act was in force until 1824. The Newspaper Stamp Duties Act included a fourpenny stamp tax on all periodical publications whether they were newspapers or not. It was hoped that this law would make it difficult for the poor to obtain pamphlets or papers of any kind and impossible for most of the radical press to carry on under the increased cost of publication. In 1836 the tax was reduced to one penny and entirely removed twenty years later. Other acts in this illiberal series gave magistrates power to search private houses for arms, and made more embracing and stringent the laws regarding blasphemous and seditious libels.

Among all who sympathized with the reform movement, there was indignation and deep concern. To the historian it is clear that the blunder of the "Peterloo Massacre" marked the height of the Tory reaction. The sympathy that flashed through England was not confined to the workers and to the popular pamphlets lamenting the martyrs. It touched men in the middle classes, the merchants and the mill owners; students at the universities; even some younger Tories who could not sympathize overmuch with men of the lower classes but who disapproved of killing or wounding them. For several years the memory of Peterloo was an important political fact.

The Six Acts did little or nothing to improve the total situation. The Tories used force to defend their policy and their incompetence. Extremists among the workers replied in kind. In February, 1820, a gang of about twenty homicidal radicals plotted to murder the Cabinet. The plotters were discovered, arrested and executed. This event was called the Cato Street Conspiracy. The immediate result of the frustrated assassination plan was to discredit the reformers and to stir up the old doubts about them. The moderate reform elements found themselves shadowed by the plots of the extremists of Cato Street.

Violent and extreme doctrines became less attractive after returns from crops and trade increased in the years following 1820. Unemployment declined and wages slowly rose. Both Whigs and Tories became aware of those reformers who sought to achieve a reform of Parliament by peaceful means. Within the Tory group friction grew between the extreme Tories such as Liverpool, Castlereagh, Eldon, Sidmouth and Wellington, and the younger and more liberal Tories such as George Canning, Sir Robert Peel and William Huskisson. This internal stress was more than merely the result of differences within a political party regarding general problems of principles or action. It was a part of the important story of the mounting struggle between the landowning aristocrats and the middle class industrialists, merchants, and professional men. This struggle began long before the 1820's and in some respects is not ended yet. Only the first long chapter was to be concluded in 1832 when the franchise was obtained by the middle class.

In the early nineteenth century both the Whigs and the Tories contained two groups shading into each other: the ultra-conservatives or reactionaries, and the liberals. More and more the real division in England came to be between conservatism and liberalism. The conservative groups in each of the two parties had more in common with each other than with the left wing elements of their own parties. The conservatives usually included the landowning aristocrats and gentry who wanted as little change and as few new ideas as possible. The liberal groups usually included those who were sympathetic to the middle class point of view and who understood much more of the meaning of the economic revolution in industry and agriculture than the old-line Tories and Whigs.

The coming of a new liberal Toryism as an effective political instrument really began with the suicide of Lord Castlereagh in 1822. Castlereagh was widely unpopular. The Tory government now had a further chance to save itself from the consequences of its weakness and its folly. So long as Castlereagh lived, the grip of the extremely reactionary Tories had been slipping only gradually. Now that he had gone, the liberal Tories were more optimistic about the future of their party and themselves.

One of the important steps in the needed reconstruction of the Cabinet was the return—as the Secretary of State for Foreign Affairs—of the brilliant and ambitious George Canning. Canning was noted for his liberal tendencies and his energetic opposition to the reactionary right wing. By his side stood two able Tories. The one was Sir Robert Peel, who always put his principles before the dictates of Toryism. The other was William Huskisson, President of the Board of Trade. It was an able triumvirate of Tory reformers. They were responsible for immediate and decisive changes in government policy. George Canning brought a more liberal foreign policy. William Huskisson brought freer trade. Sir Robert Peel brought law reform. After 1822 the old, inelastic Toryism was compelled to yield on many fronts. The road was open for a series of moderate and progressive reforms.

With several of these reforms we can have little concern here because they lie beyond the limits of our main themes. It is sufficient to say that William Huskisson proclaimed and carried out a complete revision of tariff theory and practice. He abolished many restrictions and steadily carried England towards free trade. He and Canning overturned the foundation of the old British colonial and commercial system by making important changes in the Navigation Acts and negotiating reciprocity treaties with other nations. In 1825 a sliding, or price thermometer, scale of tariffs on foreign grain was substituted for the rigid Corn Laws of 1815 and earlier; this act was changed and slightly improved in 1828. In 1825 the Combination Acts, passed by Pitt's administration in 1799 and 1800, were repealed. Canning helped to lead England out of the reactionary Quadruple Alliance. He aided the Latin American revolutions against Spain with British skill, arms and money. He was active in consultation as the United States forged the general statement of principles known as the "Monroe Doctrine." He helped to make it politically possible for Greece to win independence from Turkey.[1]

In 1827 Lord Liverpool died and was succeeded as Prime Minister by George Canning. Eldon and Wellington would not serve under a liberal Tory and at once resigned from the Cabinet. Canning thereupon turned to include some Whigs in the ministry. It was unfortunate that Canning died five months after taking office. The incapable Lord Goderich then tried to carry on and failed. In 1828 the Duke of Wellington became Prime Minister. He immediately dropped the Whigs from the Cabinet and carried on for two years despite the added difficulties brought by the resignation of the saddened liberal Tories.

The narrow, ultra-Tory Cabinet of Wellington was faced by the pressing question of the religious inequalities in England and the civil disabilities imposed on various Protestant dissenting groups. Since the reign of Charles II the Test and Corporation Acts had forbidden Nonconformists to hold national and municipal offices. In practice, as was earlier explained, a yearly Indemnity Bill had been passed to exempt non-Anglican Protestant office-holders from the necessity of

---

[1] Extracts from the most important pieces of legislation discussed in this chapter are printed in Carl Stephenson and F. G. Marcham, *Sources of English Constitutional History*, pp. 676 ff.

taking the oath to conform to the religion of the Church of England. It was therefore not difficult to secure the passage of a bill introduced in 1828 by the Whig Lord John Russell to repeal the Test and Corporation Acts. This action merely recognized a state of affairs already existing. The Anglican Church monopoly was not in fact seriously challenged.

More important in its implications was the explosive issue of Catholic emancipation facing the weakened Cabinet of Wellington. Roman Catholics in England and Ireland were still refused admission to Parliament, to the law courts, and to the universities. It will be remembered that before the passage of the Act of Union in 1801 the Irish had been given cause by William Pitt to hope that these and other grave restrictions upon the Roman Catholics would be repealed. After George III had refused to agree to any change and Pitt had resigned, the Irish Catholics were left where they had been before. Not until 1823 did an organized movement for Roman Catholic emancipation called the Catholic Association arise in Ireland under the leadership of Daniel O'Connell.

In 1828 the expected trial of strength between the Irish Catholics and the Wellington government was finally joined. In County Clare Daniel O'Connell was elected to Parliament. Because he was a Roman Catholic the new member was forbidden to take his seat in the House of Commons. The issue was clear: either the law must be changed or O'Connell would be expelled from Parliament and there would be a general rebellion in Ireland.

After long debate the Cabinet agreed to undertake the task of releasing the Irish Catholics from the civil disabilities imposed upon them. The Tories in Parliament, outraged by this capitulation, this granting of a concession extorted by the Irish, were gradually bludgeoned into line by the Iron Duke. The Oxford dons, the high and dry squires, and many Anglican parsons loosed a torrent of invective. The old cry of "No Popery" was heard in the streets again. It was true that the Wellington Cabinet had abandoned one of the sacred laws of the Tory party but they had done so because they had become convinced that only by granting Catholic emancipation could the shameful tragedy of civil war in Ireland—and possibly a Whig government at Westminster—be avoided.

After the languid fears of George IV had been overcome Parliament reluctantly accepted Catholic emancipation. The Roman Catholic Emancipation Act of 1829 provided, among other freedoms, that any persons professing the Roman Catholic religion might sit and vote in either house of Parliament upon taking an oath of allegiance to the Crown. The required oath included the following declaration: "I do swear that I will defend to the utmost of my power the settlement of property within this realm as established by the laws. . . . And I do solemnly swear that I will never exercise any privilege to which I am or may become entitled, to disturb or weaken the Protestant religion or Protestant government in the United Kingdom."

This surrender to Roman Catholic demands was in part cushioned by a new law requiring voters in Ireland to possess £10 freeholds. Nearly 200,000 forty shilling freeholders were thus disfranchised. The Catholic Association was suppressed. The government also took a petty revenge by snubbing and insulting O'Connell, who remarked bitterly that the smile of Peel was like "the silver plate on a coffin." Nevertheless, no currents of ill-will could alter the fact that Roman Catholic emancipation had been granted. A new precedent had been established; an important breach with the past had been made.

This event also helped to sweep away the old Tory party. In driving the Roman Catholic Emancipation Bill through Parliament Wellington not only alienated many of the liberal Tories still more but added to his enemies the High Tories led by Lord Eldon. All these stood together and prepared to pull Wellington down even if it meant putting the Whigs into office. The long eclipse of the Whigs was soon to be ended.

Two subjects must now be considered before we turn to the dramatic events that led to the passage of the Reform Bill of 1832. The first is the changing nature of the Cabinet in the early years of the nineteenth century. The second is the story of reforms in the law and the legal machinery of the state.

KING AND CABINET

Despite the growing power and cohesion of the Cabinet George IV (1820–1830) selected and appointed several ministers himself. In 1821 he refused to admit George Canning to the Cabinet. He once remarked to Lord Sidmouth "that it was time to determine whether the Ministers were the servants of the King or the servants of Lord Liverpool." Only the later rise of strong and organized political parties ended the Crown's practice of choosing ministers. It is strange that the legend persisted so long of "constitutional government" under George II and Sir Robert Walpole. It is also strange that George III could be soberly accused of acting in an "unconstitutional" fashion when he claimed the right of choosing his own ministers.

George IV insisted that certain men be appointed and others be excluded. Sometimes, however, the king did not have his way because the ministers stood together against him and he was not prepared to dismiss them all. On occasion, too, individuals simply refused to take office. In 1822, for instance, George IV offered Sir Robert Peel the Chancellorship of the Exchequer and the leadership of the House of Commons but Peel "begged to decline saying a word on the subject." In 1827, after Lord Liverpool's death, it was the king who decided that George Canning should be the next Prime Minister. He deeply resented Peel's refusal to serve under Canning. After Canning's death, when Peel was the logical choice to be Prime Minister, George IV turned instead to Lord Goderich. The king's candidate for the Chancellorship of the Exchequer, a mediocrity named Herries, was opposed by a majority vote of the Cabinet; but the king insisted and Herries was appointed.[2]

It must be remarked that for more than a century the executive had found it possible to carry on "the king's business" only because it was able, with royal aid, to influence, to manage, to control the House of Commons. Many men who opposed the Reform Bill of 1832 did so because they saw that a reform of the Commons would undermine, and probably upset, the whole foundation of management and influence upon which a successful ministry had hitherto depended. As we shall see, these opponents of the reform of Parliament were quite right in one sense: Parliamentary reform meant that the Crown had lost a large part of the control it had previously exercised in the House of Commons. As the conditions of political life changed "the monarchy ceased to be the pivot of politics and became a rallying point; there was scope for a different kind of personal monarchy in which the symbols of the office were to develop freely."

It was also true that the growing tendency towards cohesion in the Cabinet resulted, among other things, in more Cabinet initiative. Secondly, the increasing inclination of men of property and influence to abandon their cliques and to move into increasingly powerful Whig and Tory groups limited the scope of the royal choice of ministers. These groups were not parties in any modern sense but they were be-

---

[2] See A. Aspinall, *The Grand Cabinet 1800–1837* (1942).

coming more unified than they had ever been before. There were fewer cliques, fewer fragmented elements, fewer small and scattered personal followings and factions. Thirdly, new forces had been unleashed by the economic revolution and numerous other tempests of change in the eighteenth century: complete and accurate reporting of events in Parliament; rapid transmittal of news; independent newspapers; clubs, societies, platform speakers; humanitarian enterprises; educational advances; more employers and workers increasing the population swarms of the great cities.

Here, indeed, were the makings of a new age and a new society. That amorphous, elusive, and mighty power that is called public opinion was slowly being formed. Before the nineteenth century nothing that can be called the opinion of the public—the yeoman, aristocrat, merchant, thief—ever appeared except in hours of crisis. Public opinion emerged in England as a dynamic force at the dawn of the age of progress. The political, economic and social channels for its expression gradually increased. The sum of it all is this: public opinion slowly replaced the Crown as the directing force in British politics. How this happened is a large part of the total tale of the nineteenth century.

LAW REFORM

Other developments equally remarkable were occurring elsewhere upon the national scene. One of the most significant of these was the movement for reform in the laws and the legal system.

Sir James Mackintosh, Sir Samuel Romilly and other able advocates of criminal law reform had long urged a careful and sane revision of the criminal code. The whole system of criminal law was cumbersome and honeycombed with injustice. Nothing had been done because successive Cabinets had not chosen to do anything. Time and circumstances through the centuries had accumulated much criminal law and, for those who violated it, provision for drastic punishment. In the early nineteenth century the statute books were disgraced by a large number of laws providing many penalties for offenses once serious, later trivial.

For instance, the game laws set forth the harsh punishment to be inflicted on poachers who took partridges, rabbits, or pheasants from the estates of the wealthy landowners; a law of 1816 stated that even the possession of a net for catching rabbits was punishable by transportation for seven years, in such cases usually to the convict settlements of Australia. Over two hundred so-called crimes were punishable by death. It was a capital offense to steal fish or five shillings' worth of goods from a shop. The theft of a cow or a sheep was less dangerous. That crime was punishable only by transportation.

Many draconic penalties were so far from fitting the crimes that juries frequently refused to convict men charged with lesser offenses. In 1819, for example, of 14,000 individuals committed for trial only 9,500 were convicted. The inevitable result was an increase in crime because the chances of being punished had so markedly decreased. In the midst of man-made hunger and poverty a repressive penal code was not enough to curb the violent and reckless habits born of hatred and despair.

Sir Robert Peel, who succeeded the reactionary Lord Sidmouth as Home Secretary in 1822, began his work by consulting Jeremy Bentham (1748–1832) about law reform. Bentham and the Utilitarians believed that the foundation of values and morals was the principle of utility, defined as "the greatest happiness of the greatest number." They had long been insisting that any law, institution, or custom was to be judged by the answers that could be given to the question: "What is the use of it?" If anything could not be proved "useful" it should, they asserted, be reformed or discarded. The Utilitarians agreed that there could be no rational basis for defending proved abuses or evils on the ground of tradition or of natural law. Law, they insisted, should be the instrument of social welfare; the end of all law and all institutions is the happiness of the many rather than the few. Such ideas of Jeremy Bentham, often roughly translated, permeated very large areas of English thought and feeling.

In the field of law, Bentham naturally attempted to test the conclusions of the judges and the clauses of the statutes by the rules of expediency or utility, the needs and the wants of men. He had formulated some of his principles in *A Fragment on Government* (1776) and the *Principles of Morals and Legislation* (1789). Later, in the *Rationale of Judicial Evidence* (1827), Bentham attacked the separate jurisdictions of law and equity, the technical common law procedures, the mysterious incantations of the learned lawyers in the courts. On every hand rose the voices of the followers of Bentham demanding practical reforms, the redress of wrongs and the extension of rights. Why were the methods of pleading in the law courts so complicated? Why were they not made simple? Why should the courts not be made more easily accessible? Why were legal remedies so slow and so costly? [3]

In his labors for the reform of the law Sir Robert Peel obtained the steady aid and advice of Jeremy Bentham. He was also helped by the sagacious Sir James Mackintosh. Sir Samuel Romilly, who had long wished to alter the penal code, had committed suicide in 1818 and his services were not available to Peel. The new Home Secretary had need of all the help he could summon because he had many strong opponents. Lord Eldon, for example, stood as a formidable obstacle to reform before and after he was so savagely pilloried in Shelley's *Masque of Anarchy*. Lord Chancellor Eldon looked upon the abolition of rotten boroughs as the invasion of vested property rights. He opposed all changes in the law of property. He stood squarely against the abolition of the death penalty for larceny. He feared that any reforms in the common law courts might lead somehow to encroachments upon Chancery and equity jurisdiction. In later days he considered the railway engine a dangerous innovation. He sturdily opposed any proposals for changes in Chancery, a court renowned through centuries for its slow and expensive procedures, so clogged with ritual. In justice to Lord Eldon it should also be said that in his long tenure of office as Lord Chancellor (1801–1827) he did much to lay the foundations of modern equity. His decisions, which fill thirty-two volumes, are distinguished for their learning and their judgment. Lord Eldon's professional reputation was deservedly high.

Within a few years Sir Robert Peel and his supporters had secured the passage of five statutes abolishing the death penalty for over a hundred offenses. Nearly three hundred acts providing harsh punishments for minor crimes and misdemeanors were removed from the law books. The result was a steady decrease in crime. Reason and humanity demanded this kind of legislation. However, despite steady progress, it was some time before all the barbarous enormities were excised from the criminal code. As late as 1837 a workman was sentenced to trans-

---

[3] We cannot pause here to discuss in detail the heavy impact of Benthamite doctrines and practices upon the nineteenth century society. Because so many of the great reforms of this period depended to a large extent upon the Utilitarians it is suggested that the student read widely about their ideas, methods, and achievements. A brilliant and provocative essay about one important aspect of the subject is Professor J. Bartlet Brebner's "Laissez Faire and State Intervention in Nineteenth Century Britain," first published in *The Journal of Economic History, Supplement*, VIII (1948) and reprinted in the *Making of English History* (1952) edited by Professors R. L. Schuyler and Herman Ausubel, pp. 501–511.

portation for life for stealing a Bible and Prayer Book from a local church. In 1838 three men received the same sentence at the Monmouthshire assizes for stealing a colt.

Sir Robert Peel was also successful in stopping the use of government spies among the workers. He ended the foolish public prosecution of the radical agitators and the press. In the Gaol Act of 1823 provisions were made for greater cleanliness and sanitation in the prisons of England; it was also recommended that the prison authorities regularly employ chaplains and schoolmasters. The laws concerning juries were consolidated. In 1829 Peel established the metropolitan police force in the growing London district. It was his idea that an efficient police system would do more to curb crime than the multiplication of capital felonies by statute law. Within the next quarter century Peel's plan was adopted throughout England. Efficient and impartial, the London civilian police—often called "Bobbies" or "Peelers" after Sir Robert—were soon widely respected. These police could deal with London mobs; and all the mobs knew it. The metropolitan police force and similar police units elsewhere in England brought a decrease in crime, a greater respect for the law, and more ordered liberty.

The strong movement for legal reform resulted in a series of changes in the operation of the common law. The Uniformity of Process Act of 1832 provided that all personal forms of action were to be opened by the use of a common form of writ on which the nature of the action was to be indicated. The purpose of this legislation was to erase anomalies brought about by numerous fictions and to coordinate, as the title of the act suggests, more of the functions and methods of the common law courts. The Real Property Limitation Act (1833) abolished all real actions except Ejection, which then became the usual action for the recovery of land. The Civil Procedure Act of 1833 made provision for the appointment of a committee of judges to reform the complicated rules of procedure. Unfortunately, the long labors of a conscientious committee brought forth only a few minor changes. Later, however (1852–1860), there were several procedural reforms of consequence. For instance, these reforms made provision for the use of equitable defenses and remedies in common law courts. The Prescription Act (1832), The Inheritance Act (1833), the Wills Act (1837), the Law of Property Act (1845), the Law of Property Amendment Act (1859) and several other statutes provided for greater simplicity and efficiency in making titles to land firm and clear.

In 1846 the County Courts Act established new civil courts for about five hundred districts with fifty-nine circuits. These courts, called county courts, were at first formed to deal with small civil actions involving sums of money under £20. The new county courts were the successors of the Courts of Requests earlier set up to hear causes not exceeding forty shillings. Thus cheap and swift judicial settlements were available to all who had small civil cases. Where the amount involved was over £5 a jury of five men might be used. Because of the increasing popularity of these local courts they were later permitted—under the County Courts Acts passed between 1888 and 1934—to hear cases in torts and contracts involving sums up to £200 and in equity up to £500.

These statutory county courts still form the most important body of England's inferior tribunals. Only a few old local jurisdictions, such as the Liverpool Court of Passage and the palatine courts of Chester, Durham, and Lancaster, continue to survive today. Now, as a hundred years ago, the Chancellor appoints selected barristers to be county court judges on the circuits. In the modern county courts these judges administer both common law and equity (since 1868). In some areas they have almost unlimited jurisdiction except, of course, that they never handle cases involving difficult legal problems, such as those that often arise in actions involving such things as libel, slander and seduction. In about forty courts they exercise Admiralty jurisdiction. In some courts, too, they possess bankruptcy jurisdiction. In several areas, the judges act as arbitrators in workmen's compensation cases.

In 1857 the Court of Probate Act established a Court of Probate to deal with the probate of wills and the appointment of executors. In the same year, the Matrimonial Causes Act gave a new Court of Matrimonial Causes power to deal with divorce cases. This secular court could grant separations and, in cases of proved adultery, final divorce. By these two acts of Parliament the ecclesiastical courts lost their ancient jurisdiction over probate and divorce cases.

During the first half of the nineteenth century there were also several reforms in the system of equity as administered by the Court of Chancery. In the previous two centuries, as was described earlier, there had been a steady hardening of equity procedure. In the seventeenth century, the increased tendency to ritual and formalism had been accelerated by Lord Nottingham, who introduced into equity a rather large body of known principles derived from precedents established in equity cases. In the eighteenth century, Lord Hardwicke and some other Chancellors helped to fix and cement the famous principle that "Equity follows the law," by which they meant that equity would follow the common law whenever no equitable principle had been established by the case law precedent of previous decisions in equity. By the nineteenth century, equity had become almost as inelastic and reactionary as the common law. There were also seams of corruption in Chancery. Rampant abuses plagued both court and suitors. Clogged and complicated machinery brought the long delays that Charles Dickens denounced and mocked in *Bleak House*. Every student should read the famous case of Jarndyce *v.* Jarndyce. It was once said that anybody who started a suit in Chancery would not live to see the end of it.

Gradually the Court of Chancery was reformed. A Chancery Commission was appointed in 1825. This commission suggested no radical reforms but even small remedial measures were a welcome change after long decades of inaction and somnolence. In 1833 the Chancery Regulation Act provided that every suit should commence with a writ instead of a subpoena. This change, for reasons too complicated to discuss here, loosened many strangling technicalities. In 1843 the laws of evidence were changed to permit interested witnesses to testify, instead of being compelled to use the old methods of commissions, affidavits, and interrogations.

There were also several internal reorganizations in the Chancery Court. In 1831, for instance, a separate Bankruptcy Court was set up. In 1851 a Court of Appeal in Chancery was established, intermediate between Chancery and the House of Lords. In the Chancery Amendment Acts (1852, 1858) several procedures and offices that had contributed to the long delays of proceedings in Chancery were abolished. Certain privileges formerly belonging to the common law courts were now also given to Chancery, such as the right to award damages and to try issues of fact by jury. The Trustee Relief Acts (1850, 1852) substantially altered the laws relating to trustees. There have been three later Trustee Acts: 1888, 1893, 1925.

A thorough description and analysis of the various legal reforms in the early nineteenth century is clearly impossible here. The name of every statute mentioned, however, demonstrates the attention that was being given by the courts and the government to the increasingly urgent problems of the legal machinery of England. The various difficulties, techniques, and interlocking interests of the courts became a matter of sharp concern. It was increasingly obvious that the years of dallying and hesitation must be ended. Full and expert investigations, assessments and decisions were imperative. Piecemeal reform of the legal system was not enough. Too many judges and commissions, some of them obstinate in their incapacity, had not come to grips with basic problems, especially those of competing jurisdictions and a multiplicity of courts. Time had dribbled away. So it was that the stage was being prepared for the Judicature Act of 1873 that was to demolish forever so much of the old court machinery. This piece of legislation, described in the next chapter, was a statute that was overdue and necessary. Fortunately for modern England, it was also an act of common sense and vision.

THE REFORM BILL OF 1832

Meanwhile the demands for political reform continued. The High Tories of Wellington's ministry did not intend to retreat before the rising clamor when they came to power in 1828. True, they repealed the Test and Corporation Acts and passed the Roman Catholic Emancipation Act. Nevertheless, on the subject of Parliamentary reform they were adamant. In that area they were not prepared to undertake anything more than a few sedative compromises. In 1828, for example, the Cabinet decided against giving any representation in Parliament to Birmingham and Manchester.

Professor G. M. Trevelyan has remarked that if the Tories had really wished to keep inviolable the sacred rotten boroughs and the aristocratic constitution they should have stopped the Industrial Revolution, locked up George Stephenson, and hanged James Watt. Once they had failed to take these rather drastic steps they were merely fighting rearguard actions, postponing the day of their surrender to the forces of the new order. Scientific invention, "the blind titan that makes and moves the world," had decided the final answer. The Tories did not know it, but the society that had protected and nourished them was gone forever.

The recalcitrant attitude of the Tories, so honest and sincere in their opposition to major political reforms, had slowly roused the moribund Whigs. Earlier the Whigs had not embraced the reform cause, partly because it was both a radical and a working-class movement after 1815. The Whigs and the middle class industrialists did not want to become associated with any dubious crusade like that. By 1830, however, as bad crops and bad times brought economic blight to England, the prospects altered. Recruits and volunteers in the regiments prepared to fight for the reform of Parliament multiplied swiftly. In 1830 Thomas Attwood founded the Birmingham Political Union, an association of both middle and working classes, to agitate for the reform of Parliament. Middle-class men and working-class men united to oppose the "rotten" boroughs and the boroughmongers. Earl Grey and his Whig colleagues at last realized the needs of the nation before most of the Tories did—there were, of course, a few "reforming" Tories. So it was that the rejuvenated Whigs probably saved themselves and their party from disaster and oblivion. It is Professor G. M. Trevelyan's judgment that their Reform Bill also saved England "from revolution and civil strife."

It should now be said that the reformers in England were not united in knowing precisely what they desired when they demanded a reform of Parliament. Some wanted household suffrage; some wanted socialism; others wanted a currency reform; still others felt only that a dose of social equality was needed to temper the gentlemanly tradition; and some knew only what they did not want. Despite the wide divergence of opinion among the reformers, their "constant and active pressure from without" upon Cabinet and Parliament was a constructive historical force. Hence it follows that any explanation of political or economic reform conceived largely in terms of the men in Parliament and Cabinet is inadequate.

In the previous chapter it was made clear that Parliament was in fact quite unrepresentative in 1830. The operation of the franchise was irregular and restricted. Corruption and bribery had not greatly decreased from the high level of the eighteenth century, although direct patronage had declined. The system of representation, flagrantly unfair, was based upon a population distribution and a national economy that belonged to an age long past.[4]

When George IV died in 1830 a new Parliament was necessary on the accession of his brother, William IV (1830–1837). In the election of August, 1830, the Whigs supported moderate Parliamentary reforms, such as the abolition of the "rotten" boroughs and the exten-

---

[4] There is an excellent essay about fourteenth to eighteenth century enclosures entitled "The Deserted Villages of Leicestershire" in W. G. Hoskins, *Essays in Leicestershire History* (1950). Of particular interest are the descriptions of the depopulation of several villages by medieval plagues, especially in the fourteenth century. Between 1450 and 1600 sixty Leicestershire villages and hamlets were swallowed up by enclosures, one-sixth of the medieval total of 370. The first phases of the problem of the long redistribution of England's population faced at last in 1832 was already in process 400 years before.

sion of the franchise, not to the workers but to the propertied middle class. For the first time reform became an issue between the Whigs and the Tories. Meanwhile, in July, 1830, the French overthrew the reactionary Bourbon Charles X and put the bourgeois Louis Philippe on the throne of France. This July revolution, unlike many French experiments, was neither long nor bloody. The English middle classes took note.

Before Parliament met in November, 1830, the strength of the Whigs and Tories was not known. Many members of Parliament were still joined together in groups, cliques, and compacts. These men were not necessarily loyal supporters of either party or, as remarked in some detail earlier, united by a set of political principles in which they were all agreed. Hence the Duke of Wellington could be certain of commanding a majority in Parliament only by taking certain steps, politically wise in the circumstances. If Wellington had given some better answer to the advocates of reform than the usual sophistries of chartered right, he might then have rallied sufficient support to weather the attacks upon his ministry. But he failed to do so. The Whigs, for their part, had already adopted moderate reform as a policy. They had also done much to reconstruct their party. They were dangerous political opponents.

Wellington had reversed George Canning's liberal policy in Greece. He did not approve the Belgian revolution of 1830. He did not like the tricolor back in France. In brief, he did not propose to adopt a liberal foreign policy. In the matter of Parliamentary reform he took the offensive. He declared that the existing British system of government was the most perfect ever devised by the hand of man. He was convinced that the Parliament answered "all the good purposes of legislation, and this to a greater degree than any legislature has ever answered in any country whatever." Within two weeks every liberal reforming group in the House of Commons came together to support Earl Grey and the Whigs. The High Tories, who hated Wellington for betraying them on Roman Catholic emancipation, girded themselves to vote against him. On a minor civil list question the Wellington government was defeated, and resigned.

The composite, strange, and aristocratic Cabinet created by Earl Grey contained some troublesome Radical Whigs, some moderate men like Grey himself, and several reforming Tories. They were able men, representing the fused power of all shades of advanced and liberal opinion. "It was more than a new Cabinet, it was a new party, a party of Whigs and former Tories brought together to reform Parliament."

In March, 1831, the Whig Reform Bill was introduced in the House of Commons amidst an outburst of popular enthusiasm. It was a bold and unexpected proposal, much more a departure from the existing system than the earlier cautious program planned in Whig meetings.

The debate on the first reading in the Commons took seven nights. On the morning of March 10 the bill passed its first reading without a division. The vote on the second reading came on March 23. "It was like seeing Caesar stabbed in the Senate-house or seeing Oliver take the mace from the table, a sight to be seen only once, and never to be forgotten." The bill was carried by a majority of only one. After considerable difficulty in the Commons and a defeat in Committee Earl Grey recommended the dissolution of Parliament. "Your Majesty's confidential servants have arrived at the painful conclusion that there is no reasonable hope of the ultimate success of the Reform Bill in the present House of Commons." In the election campaign the slogan of the reformers was "The Bill, the Whole Bill, and nothing but the Bill." On September 22 the new House of Commons carried the bill by a majority of 109. On October 7 the House of Lords rejected it by a majority of 41.

An explosion of popular anger swept through the country. A mob at Bristol controlled the city for three days, looting and burning at will. The jails at Derby were opened and the prisoners loosed. The castle of the Duke of Nottingham was gutted by fire. In many areas social order almost gave way to anarchy. The windows in the residence of the Duke of Wellington were smashed. A run on the Bank of England began: "To get the Duke, go for gold." Public opinion was really the decisive element in the situation.

Meanwhile the bill, with slight changes, was passed again by the House of Commons in the third reading of March 26, 1832. The House of Lords wanted to amend and mutilate the bill. "The Bill once passed," said the Tory John Croker, "good night to the Monarchy, the Lords, and the Church." At this point the Cabinet decided to recommend to William IV the creation of fifty or sixty new Whig peers to force the bill through the House of Lords. This device had not been used since the days of Queen Anne. William IV found the large number of peerages proposed a "fearful" prospect and refused to agree. The Cabinet thereupon resigned. On May 10, 1832, the king sent for the Duke of Wellington; but in this famous crisis of "the days of May" the Duke could not form a government. Five days later Earl Grey's

Cabinet was back in control—as a matter of fact, they had never technically vacated office at all. The king gave his effective royal guarantee that he would create enough Whig peers to pass the Reform Bill "unimpaired in its principles and in its essential provisions." In the face of the threat of a deluge of new Whig peers a sufficient number of Tory lords absented themselves to give the Whigs a majority in the House of Lords. On June 7, 1832, the Reform Act at last took its place among the statutes.

This famous Reform Act did not equalize electoral districts. It did deprive many inconsiderable places of the right of returning members to Parliament. By schedule A it disfranchised fifty-six boroughs with less than two thousand inhabitants. By Schedule B it took away one member each from thirty boroughs having less than four thousand inhabitants. There were other reductions in representation. From the seats that thus became available for redistribution two each were given to forty-three urban areas; large, well-populated counties were given additional representatives. Scotland obtained eight more members, Ireland five. Thus the reform in the representative system was considerable.

The worst evils in the narrow franchise controls were also removed. In the boroughs the franchise was extended to all occupiers of property with an income value of £10 a year, subject to certain residence requirements and the payment of local taxes. Nearly all the old anomalous qualifications for the borough franchise were eliminated. In the counties, the famous forty-shilling freeholder, residing on his freehold, kept the right to vote. Holders of long-term leases (sixty years or more) and copyholders paying £10 annual rent were admitted to the franchise. So also were the short-term leaseholders and tenants-at-will who paid at least £50 annual rent. Finally, the Reform Act helped to decrease election evils by reducing the voting period from fifteen days to two; by providing for a more adequate list of legally qualified voters; and by limiting election expenses.

Thomas Babington Macaulay, that famous Whig, had declared to the House of Commons: "The voice of great events is proclaiming to us, reform that you may preserve. Renew the youth of the state. Save property, divided against itself." The Reform Act of 1832 meant that the monopoly power of the aristocracy was badly damaged, but not destroyed. It also meant that an alliance had been forged between the middle classes and the Whig aristocracy. About one-half of the propertied middle class was enfranchised, but none of the working class. In the following decades the shift from landed aristocratic control to control by the commercial and industrial classes continued steadily. Land accounted for 66 per cent of the economic interests represented in the House of Commons in 1832. By 1865 land accounted for only 44 per cent and industrial and commercial interests for 56 per cent. Meanwhile the laboring classes found that the upper middle class and the aristocracy were united, as men of property, in making common cause against the pressure of working class movements and demands. Property was no longer divided against itself.

Earl Grey stated that in passing the Reform Bill he intended to "stand by his order" and defend the interests of the nobility and the landlord class. If the Duke of Wellington and the old Tories had prevailed, there would have been no compromise or concession and the result might well have been violent revolution. By compromise and cooperation, especially with men of the middle class, Earl Grey did save for the aristocracy some, at least, of the power it could never have held if barricades had gone up in the streets. In that sense, he was able to "stand by his order" more effectively, in the long pull, than Wellington and the die-hards could ever have done. It was an excellent thing for England that the Whig voices of Charles James Fox and the Yorkshire Reformers were never completely muffled, even by the roar of the cannon and the tumbril wheels of France.

THE REFORM BILL: THE NEW HISTORY

Generations of students have learned that the year 1832 stands on the landscape of English history like a castle on a hill, taking its place alongside such dates as 1066, 1215, 1485, and 1688. Our fathers before us have been taught that in 1832 the "age of democracy" began with the famous changes in the English representative system and the widening of the franchise to include the middle classes.

Twentieth century historians seem to delight in demolishing familiar landmarks and ideas. Mr. Norman Gash, for instance, a very able demolition expert indeed, has recently shown conclusively that there was no intention of taking any steps towards democracy in 1832. He has also shown that the aristocratic society continued, long after 1832, to be bulwarked by property and influence—the influence of employers upon workers, customers upon shopkeepers, landlords upon tenants, clergymen upon congregations, brewers upon the owners of pubs, lords and gentry upon the lesser folk everywhere. In the considered judgment of several contemporary scholars aristocratic society held preponderant power in the political world until the passage of the Reform Bill of 1867 and the giving of the vote to the urban artisans. The careful reappraisal of Mr. Gash and others has also proved that patronage was collapsing before 1832 to a greater degree than was previously thought possible or probable. It is therefore certain that the decline of patronage, often said to be the result of the famous Whig legislation of 1832, in fact had little to do with either the Reform Bill or the year 1832.[5]

The Reform Bill of 1832 left in existence many evils and anomalies it is usually said to have cut away. Some pocket boroughs survived. Property and influence remained, for a long time, more important than principle or party. Elections stayed violent and steeped in corruption. Seats were still bought and sold. "Changes had been made," states Mr. Gash, "but they were modifications and not revolutions in the previous order." True, many rotten and pocket boroughs were banished; the Old Sarums and the Gattons were no more. Nevertheless, between them and the New Manchesters "lay a wide and almost untouched field where the eccentricities and contrasts of the old system continued to flourish."

The growth of party systems was effectively held in check until the latter half of the century partly because the interests of communities were fairly fixed interests. The vote was not given by an impartial unattached electorate upon national interests or upon what party leaders decided were national issues. The votes were given by men who saw through the glasses of their community, past and present. Among other important facts is this: so expensive were election campaigns that more than half the seats were uncontested as a result of local constituency compromises. Thus no party leaders could easily change any shifts of opinion into votes and seats in the House of Commons. In such circumstances the party leaders were weak. How could they be otherwise when so many members of the Commons knew that what had elected them was no voice or power in London but the support of their own folk in their own ridings? In those days the fixed smiles of a party executive or the harangues and handclasps of an honest organizer were usually of little account. For the "men of party" the delayed hours of triumph were to begin when "the reformed system"

[5] See Norman Gash, *Politics in the Age of Peel* (1953).

of 1832 began to be reformed again after 1865. Then it was possible for party machines to function effectively and central organizations to send groping tentacles into remote hamlets.

The constitutional historian may soon expect more sifting of evidence upon such controversial issues as the effects of the great reform bills of the nineteenth century and the growth of party government. It is probable, indeed, that a substantial part of our interpretations of the nineteenth century techniques and structures of politics will be completely revolutionized. Constitutional theories and legal machinery do not always sufficiently explain the complexities of what a wise contemporary historian has called "the unceasing conflicts between ideal ends and imperfect means."

TIDES OF CHANGE 1832–1850

The popular attitude of the hour was questioning, reforming, humanitarian. Vigorous and able royal commissioners were appointed to investigate and report to the Whig Cabinets of Earl Grey (1830–1834) and Lord Melbourne (1835–1841). Popular agitation continued apace. Philosophers and planners like Jeremy Bentham, John Stuart Mill and Robert Owen were supported by many people who had no general theory of the aims and purposes of government. These individuals knew only that they were repelled by the unhappy results, as they saw them, of laissez-faire. The appeals of popular pamphlets and the revelations of Parliamentary reports united with the protests of the agitators to influence the House of Commons. Famous writers such as Thomas Arnold, Thomas Carlyle, Charles Dickens and Mrs. Gaskell appealed to the Christian and decent humanitarian instincts and sentiments of the English people. Christian Socialists, such as Charles Kingsley, attempted, with some success, to apply Christian ethics to the reform of the state. Leagues and societies, including the great Mechanics' Institutes, were founded for numerous causes and purposes. These voluntary associations spread through society as arteries of public discussion. By propaganda and dissemination of facts they helped the growth of adult education and aided the rise of a more alert and informed public opinion. These were the years of the appearance of Owenism, of the Oxford Movement, the Chartist disturbances, the Utilitarian doctrines, the strong agitation for the repeal of the Corn Laws, the coming of a tide of reform legislation the like of which England had not seen before.

In 1833 slavery was abolished in the British Empire. In the same year a famous Factory Act was passed by Parliament. This act placed limits upon the hours of labor to be required of children in most of the textile (except silk) factories. It also provided for such things as medical examinations for children employed in these factories, improved sanitary conditions, and government inspection of the factory conditions. Such legislation as the Mines Act of 1842 and the Ten Hours Act of 1847 helped to transform the working conditions of the industrial laborers of England. In 1834 the Poor Law Amendment Act provided that no relief was to be given to able-bodied men unless they entered government workhouses where life was not attractive. The act also reorganized the administration of relief. Control was placed in the hands of three Poor Law Commissioners for England and Wales. These Commissioners, later called the Poor Law Board, were to become the Local Government Board in 1871; the Local Government Board became the Ministry of Health in 1919. The drastic but effective surgery of the workhouse system established a new series of rules "for the amendment and better administration of the laws relating to the poor in England and Wales."

The Grey Ministry was also responsible for the passage of the Municipal Corporations Act of 1835. A royal commission revealed that the control of most municipal governments was actually in the hands of small local rings and family compacts. In an unrepresentative and inefficient system corruption and jobbery of all kinds were rampant. Officials often used and manipulated municipal property to their advantage. Large salaries, banquets, and bribes absorbed tax money. The Municipal Corporations Act abolished the charters of a number of small boroughs. In all remaining boroughs there was established a uniform type of town council to be elected by male taxpayers who had been resident within seven miles of the borough for at least seven years prior to the election. To ensure a continuity of experience in each council a system of rotation was established. Two-thirds of the council was to serve for three years, one-third retiring each year. The mayor of each borough was to be elected annually by the council. The council was also to appoint the town clerk and all other officials. Finally, the council was to make such by-laws "as to them shall seem meet for the good rule and governance of the borough." The Municipal Corporations Act still remains the basis of the English municipal government system, though later legislation has expanded the duties and the powers of the borough councils. Thus local government was reformed in the towns and cities. Many anomalies and evils that had endured untouched for centuries were wiped away. There was no reform in the counties until 1888.

Lord Grey was succeeded by Lord Melbourne as Prime Minister and leader of the Whigs. There was no confidence or harmony between William IV and his Whig Cabinet. When Melbourne feared that his government might break up or founder on the rock of the Irish Church question he informed the king. At once William IV dismissed the Whigs whom he so strongly disliked and called upon Sir Robert Peel, the Tory leader, to form a government. William IV was the last English ruler to dismiss a government without the direct advice of the Prime Minister. When Peel was commissioned by William IV to form a ministry he had the support of not more than one quarter of the House of Commons. He did not expect to stay in office long. True, in the election of 1835 the strength of the Tories increased from 150 to 232; but they lacked a clear majority, even with the additional support of about forty renegade Whigs. Sir Robert Peel had no opportunity to do more than proclaim in the famous Tamworth Manifesto that the Tories had ceased to be a party of reaction and henceforth would support the cause of moderate progress at a gentle pace. Within a few months Peel resigned and the Whig Lord Melbourne carried on a government until 1841. In that year a general election gave Peel and the Tories a clear majority. As a matter of fact, Peel had held a majority in the Commons since 1839 but he had refused to take office unless the young Queen Victoria (1837–1901) dismissed the Whig ladies of the bedchamber. This the queen declined to do, insisting that they did not serve her as political appointees. In 1841, however, Peel carried a resolution in the House of Commons that it was "at variance with the spirit of the Constitution for a minority to continue in office without the confidence of the House." Victoria could not keep Sir Robert Peel out of office any longer. This incident is usually cited, and rightly, to illustrate the decline of royal influence in politics between the days of George III and his granddaughter Victoria.

Meanwhile the eyes of many Englishmen were turned to the urgent problems of the colonies. The second British Empire continued to grow without settled pattern and often without intention. In Australia, India and Africa the power of England advanced. The missionary societies expanded their activities. The Bible, the flag, the gunboat and the trader moved on their relentless ways. At home the problems of emigration and colonization were made more intelligible by a group of men usually called the "colonial reformers" or "the theorists of

1830." These men were at once reformers, idealists, empire builders, and sometimes sound business men. The writings and activities of these individuals infused a new spirit into public and government consideration of colonization, emigration, administrative reform, imperial expansion, and the forms of colonial government.

In 1837 a Canadian challenge to the outworn colonial system rolled across the Atlantic when two rebellions broke out in Upper and Lower Canada (now the provinces of Ontario and Quebec). The Canadians demanded responsible government, by which they meant that Canadian ministers responsible to Canadian legislative assemblies should have executive authority. The Governor-General in Canada, as the representative of the Crown, should have a position similar to that of the monarch in England. He should reign, so to speak, but not rule. His Canadian Cabinet should rule. Such was the position of the Canadians.

The Whig Cabinet sent to Canada as high commissioner the brilliant and radical Lord Durham. In his famous *Report on the Affairs of British North America* of January 31, 1839, Lord Durham made two important recommendations. The first proposal was that Upper and Lower Canada should be united—Lord Durham hoped that the French-Canadians and the English in these provinces would merge into one people and would cease to be "two nations warring in the bosom of a single state." The second major suggestion of the *Report* was that complete self-government should be granted in all matters that were the sole concern of the Canadian colonies.

In the Union Act of July 23, 1840, the provinces of Upper and Lower Canada were joined together but the hope of Lord Durham that the French and English would happily merge and mingle remained unfulfilled. The principle of responsible government was established by Lord Elgin's simple act of signing the Rebellion Losses Bill in 1849. This bill provided for the financial compensation of those who had suffered damage in the rebellion of 1837. It was opposed alike by the British government and by the Canadian Tories. Nevertheless, it passed the legislative assembly by a large majority. When Lord Elgin signed the bill a significant step towards responsible government had been taken; the precedent was established. Later in the nineteenth century the Canadians progressively obtained more control of their fiscal and foreign affairs in the gradual extension of self-government into new areas. In Canada, Australia, New Zealand, and South Africa the foundations were slowly laid for the development of the autonomous communities which today form the British Commonwealth of Nations.

In the midst of this spate of reform activity and legislation the Chartist movement, demanding more freedom and power for the workers, rose and fell. Sir Robert Peel was converted by the logic of facts and proposed the repeal of the Corn Laws. By taking this step, Sir Robert wrecked his political career, split the Tory party, and kept it out of any long spell of power for nearly thirty years. The landlords, leaders of the protectionist Tory defenders of the Corn Laws, felt that Peel had betrayed them. They joined with the Whigs and the Irish members to force Peel out of office.

Thus the Whigs came into power under Lord John Russell in 1846. They carried on the policy of free trade, repealing the Navigation Acts in 1849. They passed the first Public Health Act of 1848. This act was largely due to the energetic efforts of Edwin Chadwick, a famous humanitarian reformer, in behalf of the "cellar population" of England. The government, said Chadwick, must wage ceaseless war against poverty, disease and dirt. Chadwick's Public Health Act was the first step in a long series of reforms. It marked the beginning of governmental concern with the health of the nation. Far away were the days of laissez-faire. Lip-service was still paid to the principle of non-interference by the state but in practice, as Lord Tennyson phrased it, "the individual withers and the state is more and more."

For several years after 1850 the divergent and battling groups within the Whig and Tory parties usually prevented the passage of important domestic legislation. Thus the middle years of the nineteenth century were almost barren so far as major reforms were concerned. Cabinets rose and fell. Between 1846 and 1868 there were eight different ministries. It was fortunate for England that from the fluctuating factions of these troubled and zealous years the two strong and homogeneous Liberal and Conservative parties were slowly to emerge.

CHAPTER XX

The
Victorian Age

THE CRAFT OF POLITICS 1850-1875

MANY snags and muddles in national and international politics arise from the fact that politicians and statesmen can never start from the beginning in any problem or in any debate. They always have different things to gain or protect. Political history seldom reveals any consistent patterns of rigorous logic and clear thought, precise formulations and strict deductions. On the contrary, the political drama is played by human beings like ourselves who have the deep infirmities as well as the strengths of their characters and their causes. Some of them wrangle and push as they grope or run towards their goals. The tactics of other men often reveal military ingenuity and acumen of a high order. Sometimes, too, political arguments display considerable technical skill in inventiveness. Meanwhile, rhetorical phrases leap and fall. Dark intuitions shuffle by. Strategy, skilled and unskilled, is made in the smoke and the shadows. Men of high moral principles find themselves allied with machine politicians whose ideals, if not innocent, are clearly seen through their half-shut eyes. Some men upon the political stage plod slowly and surely, refusing to make any compromise, even with common sense. Others are sure that they can travel fast and gloriously by restless and exhilarating shortcuts. These things, and many more, are the atoms and elements with which any adequate analysis of politicians and politics must begin and terminate.

Many paragraphs have been written about political history, about political science and government in our democratic societies. It is indeed strange that so little has been written or said about the role of the professional politicians. Their position in society has been gradually changing, but their nature and character, their skills and methods,

449

are of steady importance. This subject merits closer scrutiny by students of history, government and sociology.

The third quarter of the nineteenth century was a lively period in the unrolling English scene. England moved along a broad road to roaring prosperity. Wages rose, employment grew more regular, trades unions and cooperatives increased in number and size. Swiftly paced political events led to the emergence of new philosophies, new men, and new organizations. At long last political parties in the modern sense were slowly shaped. The constituency caucus was created and it has never been abandoned. The caucus, then and now, moulded party methods and programs and purposes. The dawn of the age of mass organizations was at hand. The whole technique and content of politics was slowly altered. Industrialism and education helped to create a new electorate. New means of communication, together with old means adapted to new ends, were devised to press and persuade the public. No longer were the instruments of persuasion carelessly tooled or haphazardly used. The works of the press and the platform became more scientific. The manipulating hands of the party organizers were seldom idle. The calculating brains of the professional politicians chose the gambits and plotted the checkmates. This aspect of the middle years of Victoria's reign is too frequently neglected. Indeed, the written history of the whole Victorian age has had almost nothing to do with the organic growth of political parties. It is also the least explored period of English constitutional history.

PALMERSTON, DISRAELI AND GLADSTONE

After Sir Robert Peel and the Tories were defeated in 1846 Lord John Russell and the Whigs took office and clung precariously to power until 1852. What brought the final collapse of Whig control was a quarrel between Lord John Russell and his masterful and ebullient foreign minister, Lord Palmerston.

The whole career of Lord Palmerston is of particular interest to the student of diplomatic history. At the same time, certain aspects of that career are of consequence to the student of developments in constitutional practice and policy. Confident in his knowledge of foreign affairs, assured of his steady popularity among the English people, careless of the opinions of his colleagues, Palmerston often behaved as though he could do as he pleased without consulting anybody. Lord John repeatedly warned him that he must consult the queen and the

Cabinet on matters of policy. It seemed to Russell, and to others, that Palmerston's diplomatic methods were dangerous. His deeds were certainly alarming.

In 1847 Palmerston, on his own initiative, advised the Italian rulers to avert revolution by making reforms. In 1848, without telling the Cabinet, he authorized the Woolwich Arsenal to supply the rebelling Sicilians with arms. He instructed the British ambassador in Vienna to inform the Austrians of the "disgust" their repressive vengeance against the liberals had excited in England. He instructed the British ambassador in Madrid to tell Queen Isabella of Spain that England did not like her illiberal domestic policies. As the Spanish queen felt that the internal affairs of Spain should not be England's business, she forthwith dismissed the ambassador.

In 1851 Lord Palmerston risked war and offended both Russia and France by sending a British fleet to force Greece to compensate Don Pacifico, a Gibraltar Jew, for damages inflicted upon his property by a Greek mob in Athens. Although Palmerston won a vote of confidence in the House of Commons, Queen Victoria and Lord John Russell concluded that Palmerston must at last be removed. It was clear, of course, that if the apparently incorrigible minister should be forced out of the Cabinet then the Whig government would probably fall, so great was Palmerston's personal power outside the House of Commons. Therefore Victoria and her Prime Minister waited. Meanwhile, the queen sent a formal memorandum demanding that the Foreign Secretary let her know precisely what he proposed to do before he acted "in order that the Queen may know as distinctly *to what* she has given her Royal sanction." The queen also insisted that Palmerston's despatches be submitted to her before they were sent off and not arbitrarily altered after she had approved them.

In December, 1851, Palmerston made a mistake which cost him his post. Louis Napoleon had carried out a carefully planned coup d'état and had overthrown the Second French Republic. Palmerston, who had never liked republicans, was delighted. Without waiting to ascertain the wishes of Queen Victoria or the Cabinet he indiscreetly expressed his approbation to the French ambassador at an hour when the British government had decided, for the time being, to follow a policy of strict neutrality. "The real question now," said Lord John Russell, "was whether the Secretary of State was entitled, on his own authority, to write a dispatch as the organ of the Queen's Government in which his colleagues had never concurred and to which the Queen had never given her royal sanction." Palmerston was dismissed. Two months later he brought about the defeat of the Russell government.

The Tories under Lord Derby and Benjamin Disraeli now took office. Disraeli, shrewd Tory leader in the House of Commons, announced that his party would abandon the policy of tariff protection. Thus quietly ended the dispute that had divided the Tories in 1846. Would the Peelites who had followed Sir Robert Peel into the wilderness in 1846 now return to the Tory party? There were many reasons why this was impossible. One reason, simply stated, was this: the Peelites as a group were moving towards the Whigs and away from the Toryism to which they had given full allegiance before 1846. The old Tory party was dead. The new Conservative party, to which Derby and Disraeli were to contribute so much, was not yet born.

In December, 1852, after about nine months of power, the first Derby-Disraeli government was defeated and resigned. Because no party had a majority in the Commons a coalition party was formed under the leadership of Lord Aberdeen, a veteran Scottish Whig peer. There were soon disputes. Meanwhile Aberdeen and his divided Cabinet were drifting towards the Crimean War. The period of the great peace (1815–1854) soon ended. In March, 1854, England and France moved into conflict with Russia.

The Aberdeen government could not survive the attacks made upon it when the tale of its incompetence and maladministration in the Crimean War was revealed to the public. The Cabinet fell in January, 1855, and Queen Victoria was forced to accept Palmerston, in whom the people had confidence. Palmerston's Cabinet was a coalition of Whigs and Peelites. Partly because of Palmerston's reforming zeal and skill the war soon turned in favor of the allies. International peace came with the Treaty of Paris in 1856.

But there was no political peace in England. The road of party politics was still winding and rocky. The Peelites left Palmerston's ministry in 1857 and a motion of censure was passed upon the government in the Commons. In the ensuing election Palmerston won a majority of eighty-five, the largest held by any government for several years. However, it is important to note that this majority was not a party one. It was Palmerston's personal following that had been increased, nothing more. A personal majority can melt away. Palmerston's did. In 1858 he was defeated and resigned. Derby and Disraeli formed their second ministry. It held office for about a year. Then Lord Palmerston returned, bringing into his Cabinet the Peelite William Ewart Gladstone.

The Peelites and the Whigs were ending their long trek towards the goal of a new Liberal party. When Gladstone joined Palmerston the Peelites really ceased to exist as a separate element in the House of Commons. Party lines were beginning to harden, more and more. Palmerston stayed in power until 1865. He has been described as "the last of the Whigs." When he died, his successor was William Ewart Gladstone. Gladstone was the real leader and champion of the new Liberal party, although the titular head was Lord John Russell. The Liberals were opposed by the new Conservative party. The real leader of that party was Benjamin Disraeli, although the nominal head was Lord Derby.

So it was that after a succession of unstable governments in a political world uneasy and divided there came a new era. Through the dull, dark, locust years after 1846 Benjamin Disraeli had worked patiently with Lord Derby and others to rebuild the shattered Tory party. Now, in 1865, as Disraeli faced his rival Gladstone across the House of Commons, a new Conservative party was slowly growing stronger to match the strength and stature of the Liberals. As masters of politics and statecraft Disraeli and Gladstone were to hammer out and squarely fashion coherent policies and principles. Party lines became more tightly drawn every year and political vagabonds were sorted out and sent packing home.

When Lord Palmerston died in 1865 Lord John Russell formed a ministry that held power until it was overturned by a sudden squall in June, 1866. Lord Derby and Disraeli then came into office again and stayed there until 1868. In that year Gladstone formed the first and greatest of his four Liberal ministries (1868-1874). In 1874 Benjamin Disraeli defeated Gladstone and there followed (1874-1880) a series of brilliant and important events in the history of the Conservative party and of England.

Such is a scaffolding of fact and chronology in the political history of the period 1850-1875. Meanwhile three events were occurring of high consequence in the legal and constitutional history of England. The first event was the extension of the franchise to certain classes of the city workers. The second was a number of sweeping reform measures in the machinery of the state, the church, the army, the schools, and colonial administration. The third was a general reconstruction of the procedure and organization of the courts.

REFORM AND THE NEW SOCIETY

The Russell ministry that came to power in 1866 was faced with difficult problems. The reversal of Palmerston's foreign policy was complete and swift. A cold attitude of non-intervention abroad succeeded the full-blooded warmth of Palmerston's coursing frontal assaults. This change of strategy and tactics caused grave concern in some quarters. There was a serious Fenian conspiracy in Ireland, a cattle plague in England, a Negro rising in Jamaica. Overshadowing these questions there was the mounting pressure for Parliamentary reform.

After Chartism collapsed in 1848 there had been little agitation for a greater extension of the franchise. Lord John Russell, always prone to entertain reform ideas, had three times put forward a bill: in 1851 to his Cabinet, which opposed him; in 1852 to the House of Commons, which defeated him before the bill was passed; in 1853 to his colleagues in the Aberdeen coalition and later to Parliament, where tepid enthusiasm forced him to drop it. In 1859 Disraeli had proposed a bill to extend the suffrage in the rural areas where the Conservatives were strong. Russell claimed it did not go far enough because the vote should be given to the city workers who would vote for the Liberals. After the Conservatives were defeated, Russell advanced his fourth bill. Widespread indifference within and outside Parliament again persuaded him to withdraw his proposals.

In 1866 Gladstone introduced a bill to extend the franchise to certain classes of city workers. This bill was of course opposed by the Conservatives. It was also denounced by some rebels within the Liberal party who were more Whig than Liberal. Their leader, the imprudent Robert Lowe, said that he did not trust the moral and intellectual competence of the working classes. Lowe claimed the bill was revolutionary and dangerous because it would lead to the dread end, as he saw it, of pure democracy. The followers of Lowe were a rather talentless and wavering group, but they stood together long enough to aid the Conservatives in smashing Russell's bill. Russell resigned but Gladstone felt that the Liberals could not long remain out of office. "You cannot fight against the future; time is on our side."

When the third Derby-Disraeli government had been patched together it found itself faced by the fact that the former apathy towards Parliamentary reform had gone. Parliament and people were "very hot for reform without delay." The adroit Disraeli at once decided to make capital for the Conservative party out of the reform tumult. Aware that the Conservatives were still associated in the public mind with Tory reaction, Disraeli wanted to show that his party did not in fact distrust the people; that there could be an association between the aristocracy and the workers; that the Conservatives had an historical title to deal with reform. In brief, the narrow Tory policies of Lord Liverpool and his successors were to be discarded, and for them substituted the broad and comprehensive program of what was to be called "Tory democracy."

Disraeli introduced a new reform proposal, declaring that the Conservatives wished to establish the character and functions of the House of Commons "on a broad popular basis" and to undertake a prudent and practical redistribution of seats in the House of Commons. To do all this was not easy. As Disraeli said: "I had to prepare the mind of the country, and to educate—if it be not arrogant to use such a word—to educate our party."

The more conservative groups in both parties wanted no reform. So Disraeli withdrew his first bill and put forward a second, designed to appeal to all liberal and radical elements, regardless of party. In its final form the bill went far beyond anything proposed before. The old High Tories grumbled, but finally came to heel. Amidst national excitement the bill passed into law. Earlier Lord Derby had said the Conservatives were "making a great experiment and taking a leap in the dark." Gladstone, his followers divided by dissensions and plots, denounced the "diabolical cleverness of Dizzy" and his "revolting cynicism." The splenetic Thomas Carlyle denounced the reform bill as "shooting Niagara" and compared the people of England to "mesmerized, somnambulant cattle." Robert Lowe commented: "We must now at least educate our masters."

The Representation of the People Act of 1867 added over 1,000,000 new voters to the lists. It brought almost universal manhood suffrage to the boroughs of England. In the boroughs the act enfranchised two classes of adult males: (1) those who for at least a year had been inhabitant occupiers, as owners or tenants, of dwelling houses on which the poor rates had been paid; (2) those who for at least a year had occupied, as sole tenants, unfurnished lodgings worth £10 annually. Likewise two classes of adult males were admitted to the franchise in the counties: (1) those who were property owners or long-term renters (sixty years or more) of lands or tenements of an annual value of at least £5; (2) those who were occupiers of lands or tenements of an annual ratable value of £12 or more. Finally, there was a small redistribution of seats. Towns with populations of less than 10,000 were allowed only one member of Parliament instead of two; a few boroughs were disfranchised. This change gave twenty-five new seats to the counties and nineteen to the towns and cities.

An important result of this act of 1867 was that the "respectable" artisans and the other small householders, who formed the largest part of the English working class, now had the vote. The rural county laborers were not yet enfranchised; their turn was to come in 1884. Meanwhile the rule of the middle classes, which had begun so brightly in 1832, seemed now at an end.

In its short term of office the Derby-Disraeli ministry also passed the British North America Act of 1867. This act created a Dominion of Canada, a federal union with the British parliamentary system of government. In this union the provinces were specifically given fifteen powers in addition to their exclusive control over purely provincial matters. All other powers, twenty-nine of which were listed, remained with the Dominion government. To the Canadian fathers of Confederation it seemed that the American Civil War might not have happened had the residual powers in the United States been vested in the federal government rather than in the separate states. In 1867 the new Dominion consisted of four provinces: Nova Scotia, New Brunswick, Quebec and Ontario. British Columbia and Manitoba joined in 1871; Prince Edward Island, in 1873; Alberta and Saskatchewan, in 1905; Newfoundland, in 1949.

In 1868 Lord Derby retired and Disraeli became Prime Minister in name as well as in fact. Meanwhile Gladstone and the Liberals had recovered from the shock tactics of the Conservatives in the political reform battle. Gladstone now challenged Disraeli upon an old problem: British policy in Ireland. There repression had been unsuccessful. Bitter Irishmen burned and murdered. From behind Irish hedges the snipers' bullets hummed. Gladstone felt that his mission was to pacify Ireland. This could never be done, he asserted, by violence and coercion. He proclaimed a policy of sweeping Irish reform. On that issue he defeated the Conservatives in the House of Commons. On that issue he fought the election of 1868. The householders that Disraeli had enfranchised voted for Gladstone. Under the new impulse for reform the constant Liberal assaults on outworn institutions and vested interests gathered momentum. Victorian England began to doubt still more the value of the legacies of laissez-faire. Again and again the state intervened to promote social welfare. Energy and conscience increased their scope and area.

Gladstone's first ministry disestablished and disendowed the Anglican Church of Ireland, thus dissolving its connection with the state and putting it upon a voluntary basis. In 1870 Gladstone's Irish Land Act compelled the landlord to pay compensation to a tenant evicted through no fault of his own. But the purpose of this act was never fully realized because it gave Irish tenants no protection against increased rents.

Probably the greatest achievement of Gladstone's first ministry was the passage of the Education Act of 1870. Before 1870 there was no system of education in England providing for the masses of the people. The new Education Act created a national system of elementary education. A national system of secondary education came in 1902. The step of 1870 meant that the working classes no longer had to rely on the voluntary Anglican and Nonconformist church schools, with their religious bias, or the private schools, some of which were like Charles Dickens' Dotheboys Hall. Before 1870 more than 2,000,000 children of school age were not attending school at all. By the act of 1870 the local school boards were authorized to build and maintain schools where voluntary schools were not already in existence and answering community needs. Expenses were to be met by national grants, local taxes, and children's fees. Not until 1891 was elementary school education free in England. Each school board might require attendance of all children between five and thirteen years of age; but not until 1880 was such attendance made compulsory by an act of Parliament.

In 1870 male illiteracy was nearly 20 per cent; at the turn of the century it had fallen to less than 2 per cent. Only slowly, however, was there acceptance of the idea that an opportunity to acquire an education should be available to the sons of nobles, millionaires, and paupers alike.

Gladstone's first ministry passed a number of other reform measures of importance. It boldly opened almost all posts in the civil service to competitive examination and thus helped to form a public-spirited class of permanent administrative servants who would remain at their posts, aloof from politics, while governments rose and fell. In the army, too, significant reforms were achieved. It was decided that the system by which army officers bought their commissions should be ended. Promotion, it was widely felt, should depend on merit. To this Liberal measure there was strong opposition, particularly in the House of Lords where many peers had bought, or intended to buy, army careers for their younger sons. Although the Lords defeated the ministry's bill, Queen Victoria abolished the purchase of commissions by issuing a royal warrant.

There were still other reforms. In 1869 imprisonment for debt was abolished. In 1871 the religious tests which had kept Nonconformists out of Oxford and Cambridge were removed. Steps were taken to increase facilities for the education of women. In 1872 the Australian secret ballot replaced open voting. This was especially useful because it protected the newly enfranchised city workers from undue influence or intimidation by their employers.

Liberal domestic policy brought mounting unpopularity—somebody is usually hurt or annoyed by any reform. When the number of reforms is large any government must think about the practical political consequences of losing too many votes, however desirable from a national point of view the projected reforms may be. So it was with William Ewart Gladstone. As he progressed, the mordant words of Disraeli followed him. The country was weary of the deluge of reform measures. It was particularly impatient with Gladstone's handling of foreign affairs, with his retreats, hesitations, and apparently weak surrenders. The British lion, it seemed, roared no longer. The apparently inept and spineless handling of external affairs told heavily against the Liberals.

Disraeli waited for the Liberal oaks to go down with a resounding crash. He wanted a national election where the Liberals, he believed, would be soundly trounced. Then the Conservatives could return with a large majority and a solid triumph.

Soon the English harvest failed. Foreign trade declined and a business depression began. In January, 1874, the Liberal Cabinet asked for a dissolution and got it. The victory of Benjamin Disraeli and the Conservatives, so long awaited, was at hand.

THE LAW COURTS OF ENGLAND

Liberty, contract and property were three very important words in the nineteenth century. Jeremy Bentham and the utilitarians stated that the freedom of the individual in society should be strengthened and extended. Said they: so long as A does not make himself a nuisance to B he should be left free to pursue his own self-interest. Several other philosophies, theories and attitudes supported the view that the government existed primarily to protect property and to enforce contracts. It was asserted that a minimum of interference by the government was essential for the well-being of the state and the individual.

In the latter part of the nineteenth century there were only a few voices declaring that the laws of England were unsatisfactory. Did those laws not ensure natural liberty and freedom of contract? Did they not protect property? On the other hand, there were many who denounced the machinery of the legal system as creaking and inefficient. They insisted that the administration of justice was clogged and halting. What was urgently needed, in their judgment, was a radical systematization and consolidation of the whole body of arrangements by which the law was made available to the citizen. There must be an end to the multiplicity of costly courts. There must be an end to competing jurisdictions.

Lord Nottingham (1621–1682) and Lord Hardwicke (1690–1764) had done much to fix firmly the rules of equity and by the nineteenth century the judges in Chancery followed precedents as strictly as their brethren in the common law courts. Thus two sets of tribunals in England were empowered to deal with the same matters and were compelled to proceed in many cases on entirely different principles. Often Chancery intervened in cases in the common law courts to prevent suitors claiming rights recognized by the common law as valid but deemed unjust by Chancery. In many cases it was not clear whether Chancery or a common law court was the proper tribunal to carry through an action. Sometimes a suitor found that he had fought a protracted and expensive case in the wrong court. Lord Westbury once remarked sarcastically that in the English judicial system one court was set up to do injustice and another to stop it.

The minor and partial reforms of the early nineteenth century were mainly procedural and few lawyers or laymen were satisfied with inadequate, piecemeal reforms. Fortunately, the Judicature Act of 1873, which took effect in 1875, provided an effective answer to most adverse criticisms. This famous piece of legislation began a general reconstruction of the procedure and organization of the central courts. A Supreme Court of Judicature was created, containing two divisions: the High Court of Justice and the Court of Appeal. The High Court of Justice was formed to include the jurisdictions of the three great courts of common law, together with Chancery, the Courts for Probate, Admiralty and Matrimonial Causes (based on the civil law), the Court of Common Pleas at Lancaster, the Court of Pleas at Durham, the ancient courts erected by the commissioners of Gaol Delivery, Oyer and Terminer and Assize.

The new High Court was originally separated into five divisions: the Chancery Division, the Probate, Divorce, and Admiralty Division, the Common Pleas Division, the Exchequer Division and the Queen's Bench Division. In 1880, the Common Pleas Division and the Exchequer Division were merged into the Queen's Bench Division. Hence, from 1880 until the present day, the High Court of Justice has consisted of three divisions: Chancery, Queen's Bench and the division of Admiralty, Probate, and Divorce. The absorption of the latter division into the High Court of Justice virtually ended the distinction between the civilians, or doctors of the civil law, and the common law lawyers. The first major step in this direction, of course, was taken in

BRITISH COURTS OF LAW

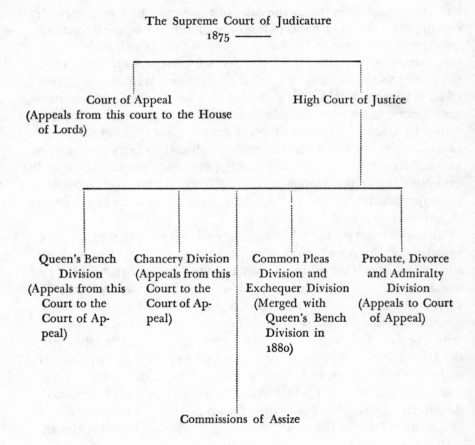

The Supreme Court of Judicature
1875 ———

Court of Appeal
(Appeals from this court to the House of Lords)

High Court of Justice

Queen's Bench Division
(Appeals from this Court to the Court of Appeal)

Chancery Division
(Appeals from this Court to the Court of Appeal)

Common Pleas Division and Exchequer Division
(Merged with Queen's Bench Division in 1880)

Probate, Divorce and Admiralty Division
(Appeals to Court of Appeal)

Commissions of Assize

1857 when the secular courts took over the jurisdiction formerly held by the ecclesiastical courts in questions of probate and matrimonial causes.

Under the Judicature Act it was provided that the judges of any one division might serve in another. Common law and equity were to be administered concurrently in all divisions. The twenty-fifth section of the act declared that where there was "variance or conflict between the rules of equity and the rules of the common law with reference to the same matter the rules of equity shall prevail." In a general sense, the "fusion of law and equity" was full and complete. A single judge was to try both questions of law and questions of fact when no jury was used.

Several alterations were made in the common law in order to bring it more completely into harmony with equity. On the other hand, the Judicature Act of 1873 provided that the Chancery Division should try actions with oral evidence instead of affidavits, thus bringing the Chancery proceedings more into line with those of common law courts. Because this method of trial was new to the judges and lawyers in Chancery two additional judges were appointed in 1877 and 1879 to expedite Chancery proceedings.

These statements are sufficient to show how the Judicature Act of 1873, the later Judicature Acts that were passed until 1910, and other supplementary laws provided for the complete amalgamation of competing jurisdictions and ended the scandal of rival tribunals. The Court of Admiralty, for instance, recovered several areas of jurisdiction earlier taken away in the struggle with the common law courts. The new legislation simplified procedure, removed many anomalies, helped speed the administration of justice, and made it less expensive. Here, at last, was created one set of omnicompetent courts with no competing jurisdictions. As Lord Cairns remarked of Chancery, "The court is not now a court of equity, but a court of complete jurisdiction." Henceforth, in the words of Lord Bowen, "It is not possible for an honest litigant in Her Majesty's Supreme Court to be defeated by any mere technicality, any slip, any mistaken step, in his litigation."

In civil cases the High Court of Justice has formed, since 1873, one superior court with universal jurisdiction in cases of first instance, *i.e.* before whom cases come for a first hearing. Several members of the Queen's Bench Division still travel about on circuits or assizes. Usually two justices travel together: one tries criminal cases and the other tries civil or *nisi prius* cases.

No judge of the Supreme Court of Judicature may be removed except as the result of a direct and formal address to the Crown by both Houses of Parliament. Thus is maintained the principle stated in the Act of Settlement (1701) that judges are to be appointed to hold office during good behavior ("that . . . judges' commissions be made *quam diu se bene gesserint*"). The salaries of judges are determined by Parliament. They may take no part in political affairs. They may not be members of Parliament.

Above the new High Court of Justice it was necessary to erect a Court of Appeal. The general rule of law today is that there may be at least one appeal allowed to a higher court from the decision of every court of first instance, always on questions of law and usually on questions of fact. The Court of Appeal was therefore created mainly to hear appeals from the High Court of Justice. The framers of this section of the Judicature Act were considerably aided by the fact that the processes of appealing had been widely amended—especially the faulty writ of error procedures—by the Common Law Procedure Acts between 1852 and 1860. They were to be further amended, as described below, by the Criminal Appeal Act of 1907.

After 1875 the Court of Appeal took over the jurisdiction of the Court of Exchequer Chamber, the Court of Appeal in Chancery, certain of the functions of the Judicial Committee of the Privy Council, the Court of Appeal from Lancaster, the Court of the Lord Warden of the Stannaries (the ancient mining courts of Devon and Cornwall earlier described). There are several *ex officio* judges—who seldom act —headed by the Lord Chancellor. In addition, there are the "working judges," the five Lords Justice of Appeal. The Court of Appeal does not concern itself with reviewing questions of fact—it accepts the facts as the court of first instance decided upon them. It hears no evidence. It has no juries. It considers questions of law and law alone. Technically, therefore, there can be no appeal from a jury's decision in the High Court of Justice upon a question of fact. Nevertheless, as is also the case in lower courts, application for a new trial can be made by asserting that the presiding judge failed to direct the jury correctly or that the evidence before the trial jury made necessary a verdict other than the one given. If the application for a new trial is found to be frivolous, the applicants are dealt with severely.

Before 1907 there were no appeals possible in criminal cases. Sometimes, of course, a man who had been summarily convicted in petty sessions despite his plea of innocence would have his case heard again at quarter sessions courts. The Criminal Appeal Act of 1907 completely opened the road in criminal cases to an absolute right of appeal on questions of law and a limited one on questions of fact. Since 1907 the Court of Criminal Appeal, which contains at least three judges of the Court of Queen's Bench, hears appeals. On points of law the Attorney-General may give permission by certificate for appeal to the House of Lords.

Beyond the Court of Appeal still lies the House of Lords, the highest court in the English judicial system. In order to strengthen that House in exercising its appellate jurisdiction provision was made by the Appellate Jurisdiction Act, 1876, for the Crown to appoint Lords of Appeal in Ordinary—at first two, now nine. These men are eminent specialists, learned in the law. They are paid specified salaries by the government and are members of the House of Lords for life. Their dignities do not descend to their sons. Today the Lords who are not lawyers or judges take no part in the judicial work of the Lords. Technically, of course, there is no legal way of stopping a peer if he insists upon sitting in the House of Lords when it is acting as a court—that is his undoubted right as a peer. But by convention the peers who have not held judicial office at some time or other simply do not take part in deciding issues of law.

Below the House of Lords, the Court of Appeal, and the High Court of Justice stand the local inferior courts of criminal jurisdiction. These various courts parallel the statutory county courts concerned with civil cases and possessing the powers and structure described in the previous chapter.

In 1834 a special Central Criminal Court was established. It was decided that this court would hold twelve sessions a year in the "Old Bailey" or keep of the old Newgate Prison, a solid structure built of gray stone in the neo-classical style. As the reader may be aware, almost all of the unlovely commercial buildings around the Central Criminal Court were destroyed by German bombs in the Second World War. Several parts of the Court itself were badly damaged.

The criminal jurisdiction of the Old Bailey extends over the parts of Middlesex, Essex, Kent and Surrey that are covered by greater London. By a curious fiction the actual power of Old Bailey reaches far beyond the London border counties into strange and distant places. The reasons for this remarkable situation lie far back in the mist of the centuries. In the first place, English common law says that a crime can only be committed in the body of a county. Accordingly, a necessary legal fiction states that the high seas are actually in the body of a county. If a murder is committed abroad on a ship of British registry in the Yellow Sea the law says that the murder occurred in the parish of St. Mary le Bow, in Cheapside, in the county of Middlesex. Hence such cases are tried today in the Old Bailey Central Criminal Court. So also are offenses against such important laws as the Official Secrets Acts and the Corrupt Practices Act and the Treachery Act. Here, for instance, were tried the men accused of betraying their king and country during the Second World War by broadcasting for the enemy, stealing official documents, giving other forms of aid and comfort to the Nazis, the Fascists, the Japanese. In Court No. 1 of the Old Bailey were tried such traitors as John Amery and Dr. Allan Nunn May. Here in the dock stood William Joyce, "who, traitorously contriving and intending to aid and assist the said enemies of our lord the King . . . did traitorously adhere and aid and give comfort to the said enemies in parts beyond the seas without the realm of England, to wit in the realm of Germany." The way of the *perfidus* is hard and just.

Below the Queen's Bench Division in the High Court of Justice and the Old Bailey Central Criminal Court stand the lower courts concerned with crime in England. In all counties and in some boroughs the courts of quarter sessions still exist and function although they try no important cases. In the counties all justices of the peace, who are now usually called "magistrates," still have the right to attend the quarter sessions and to constitute the court under an elected chairman. In the boroughs there is a professional judge called a "Recorder."

Below the quarter sessions courts are the petty sessional divisions of each county. These petty session tribunals are courts of summary jurisdiction in minor cases. In cases where the alleged offenses are indictable it is usual for preliminary investigations to be held and depositions taken by the petty sessions courts. These courts are then in a position to decide whether or not there is sufficient evidence against the accused person to warrant his being held and "committed for trial" or "bound over" or "enlarged on bail" until the next assize court. In the assize court—and sometimes in quarter sessions—a grand jury makes the final decision as to whether or not a true bill should be returned against the accused.

It should be remarked in passing that accused individuals are carefully protected against vexatious or unreasonable indictments. A considerable list of offenses requires the signed order of a judge before there can be any proceeding to trial. Moreover, the provisions of the

Vexatious Indictments acts and the Malicious Prosecutions acts tend to limit the placing of irresponsible charges. Neither a prosecutor nor a complainant wishes to face the prospect of an irate citizen seeking a civil remedy for false arrest or malicious prosecution. The reader who has a special interest in this subject is advised to consult such statutes as the Vexatious Indictments Act of 1859 with its subsequent amendments and the Criminal Law Amendment Act of 1867.

THE PATHS OF POWER 1875–1900

In the election battle of 1874 the Liberals were both out-maneuvered and out-gunned by the Conservatives. Disraeli, then seventy years old, had completely reorganized the Conservative party. He had created an entirely new system, a party organization that was the forerunner of the great modern political machines. A comprehensive National Union had been formed in 1867. Later a Conservative party manager and a large staff had been established in London. Numerous local Conservative associations and workingmen's societies formed a chain of stout political outposts. The days of the faltering and disorderly leadership that had marked the previous twenty-five years was now ended.

It was inevitable that the Liberals should follow the Conservative example. They extended their Birmingham caucus system throughout Britain. Later in the nineteenth century the Liberals, who believed so much in freedom, found that these Liberal and Conservative political machines were in many respects the enemies of freedom and true Parliamentary democracy. They also discovered that their insistence upon free trade had spurred development of a capitalist and industrial system often inimical to the growth of economic democracy and effectively fettering the freedom of individual choice. The Liberals were soon to face another paradox. Their doctrine of free markets in labor, land and money had as its necessary corollary the familiar idea of the self-regulating market. However, the Liberals also believed in advancing public welfare by legislation. Thus they were confronted by a sharp and vivid contrast between theory and practice. Nobody could deny that state intervention, as in the case of the factory laws, checked and altered not only the self-regulation of markets but also the free operation of many other things. Hence the Liberals talked about individualism long after they had in fact ceased to be individualists. The later decline of Liberalism was partly the result of the Liberal failure to swallow the consequences of what they had done. For example, their creation of an impersonal and efficient party machine was certainly expedient. Nevertheless, it could never be explained or defended in terms of declared Liberal ideals.

Before the election of 1874 Disraeli had defined the principles and program of the new "Tory democracy"—the maintenance of the historic institutions of England and the British Empire; the adoption of the ideal of steady social reform and simple, ordered progress. The work of Gladstone had already demonstrated that united and coherent policies brought more political stability and hence better government. In the last quarter of the nineteenth century both the Liberal and the Conservative parties were much more concerned than earlier with the growth and statement of their political policies and philosophies as well as with problems of political organization and political power.

Disraeli said that his legislation would be slow and unheroic; his internal reforms would be of an "honest humdrum" kind. During the six years of his great ministry (1874–1880) there was some useful ecclesiastical and land law legislation. The Artisans Dwelling Act of 1875, for instance, tackled the problem of the housing of the poor. It gave the local authorities of London and certain other large cities the power to condemn and demolish buildings declared unfit for human habitation and to build new and improved dwellings. There was also a considerable body of labor legislation, the broad results of which were twofold. The first was a marked advance in trade union status. The second was a codification of the laws regarding working conditions and hours by the Factory and Workshops Act of 1878. Local taxation was reduced. A new sinking fund was established. The Merchant Shipping Act of 1876 increased the powers of the Board of Trade to deal with ships made unseaworthy by age, damage, or overloading. Despite his great concern with external and Imperial affairs, Disraeli did not neglect or overlook the national importance of social reform legislation. He was well aware, too, of the fact that every piece of legislation helped to modify the economic, social, political, constitutional and legal structure of the state. After all, he had written *Sybil* and *Coningsby*.

The first phases of England's Imperial adventures under Disraeli's leadership did not bring universal satisfaction: the purchase of nearly half the Suez Canal stock; the conferring of the title "Empress of India" upon Queen Victoria; the triumph of Disraeli at the Congress of Berlin in 1878; the wars in Afghanistan and South Africa. On the other hand, a vigorous and spirited Imperial policy, heralded by loud Conservative trumpets, was often welcomed by calculating merchants and financiers. The long depression (1873–1885) helped to turn the eyes of bankers, industrialists, and commercial men towards the colonies. Colonies, surely, were profitable fields for investment capital; sources of raw materials for England's factories; export markets for England's goods. This idea was old, much older than the Liberal opinion that the colonies might well be encouraged to go their own way to early and complete independence. Moreover, to the cold economic approach to Imperialism Disraeli added the romantic and emotional appeal of the new Toryism. He spoke of the destiny of the British race and "the sublime instincts of an ancient people." He viewed with pleasure the export of English goods, English methods, English laws and constitutional procedures, those apparently sure guarantees of ordered liberty.

Gladstone and the Liberals were of a decidedly different opinion. Nor was the English public yet convinced of the wisdom or utility of Disraeli's ranging interference and the costly wars abroad. Imperialism, said Gladstone, had been carried too far. He insisted, with massive moral indignation, that the Conservative proceedings were cynical and unscrupulous, that such events as the seizure of the Transvaal, the wars with the Zulus, the Boers and the Afghans, the pocketing of Cyprus, were sullying England's soul. Like a prophet of old, in speeches of evangelical fire, he implored the people to break the idols in the temple of Baal and to vote for the Liberal party. "The social forces," he said, "moving on in their might and majesty" made inevitable the triumph of middle class Liberalism.

The Liberals won the election of 1880 and Disraeli at once resigned. A year later Disraeli died. He was probably the greatest of the undisputed chiefs of the Conservative party, at least until Sir Winston Churchill became a pilot in more stormy waters and even less happier times.

Gladstone had been elected in 1880 on his indictment of Disraeli's policy. Nevertheless, after he came to power he stood forth as an Empire builder in spite of himself. When economic and strategic interests were clearly challenged steps had to be taken against defiant foreign pressure and outright blackmail. The result was soon to be a series of British political annexations of territories that otherwise might have been seized by Germany, France, Belgium, or other powers. During the second ministry of Gladstone (1880–1885) this process was foreshadowed by the fact that the Liberals were harassed by urgent difficulties in South Africa, Egypt, the Sudan, Afghanistan and Ireland.

The Imperial and foreign problems of these years were dark and clouded. Meanwhile, all the time, the slow expansion of England's power, the pace of which was soon to be accelerated, meant that more men of the East and West were using England's political and constitutional devices, England's laws, England's goods.

Very difficult was the dark and tangled problem of Ireland. Weltering in bitterness, poverty and turmoil, Ireland had cause for grievance. And yet the responsibility for Irish woe was not entirely English. During Gladstone's second ministry blunt demands for Irish self-government came from southern Ireland. The leader of the Home Rule party was Charles Stuart Parnell, the enigmatic and unsociable president of the Irish Land League and soon to be the "uncrowned king of Ireland." The formidable Parnell, who hated England, believed that force, and force alone, would gain for Ireland the freedom so long denied. Talk should be helped by dynamite and guns. Crime and outrage increased. The currents of charity were frozen.

The Liberal government passed a Coercion Bill. Then it passed a new Land Act based upon the Irish Land League's demand for "the three F's": fixity of tenure; free sale of tenants' interests to other tenants; and fair rent, to be decided by the courts. It was hoped that compromise might kill conspiracy. The hope was vain. The Invincibles of Dublin murdered the Chief Secretary for Ireland in Dublin's Phoenix Park. The Liberal government passed a new coercive Crimes Act. Home Rule, disputed and postponed, remained to convulse society and politics with passion and intensity. The southern Catholic Irish were determined to have Home Rule. But the six Protestant counties of Ulster in northern Ireland, fearful of the southern Roman Catholics, obstinately insisted on maintaining the Act of Union of 1801. Thus the legacy of the past, the internal divisions of Ireland, the obstructions of the land-owning Anglican House of Lords, the Liberal schisms and Conservative doubts combined to bring deadlock.

In domestic affairs the second Gladstone ministry carried through a considerable body of legislation. The titles of some of the acts of Parliament will suggest their content: the Bankruptcy Act, the Electric Lighting Act, the Agricultural Holdings Act, the Employers Liability Act, the Ground Game Act.

In 1884 the Representation of the People Act provided for a further reform of Parliament by giving the vote to the agricultural workers. This was done by extending to the counties the "household qualification" established for the boroughs by the third section of the Reform Act of 1867. The right to vote was granted to every male over twenty-one years of age who was the "inhabitant occupier" of a dwelling house, or any part of a house that was occupied as a separate dwelling (subject to a few exceptions) "of a clear yearly value of not less than £10." Thus "a uniform household franchise and a uniform lodger franchise" were established. About 2,000,000 voters were added to the register. After 1884 almost all males who possessed or occupied property had the vote.

The Redistribution of Seats Act of 1885 made radical changes in the distribution of seats. Twelve new members were added to the House of Commons, making a total of 670 (England: 465; Wales: 30; Scotland: 72; Ireland: 103). The new act provided that all boroughs with fewer than 15,000 inhabitants ceased to elect members to Parliament and were merged with the counties. Two-member constituencies with a population of less than 50,000 were deprived of one member. Only the universities and twenty-two boroughs retained two members each. The rest became single member constituencies, approximately equal in population. County and borough boundaries were changed considerably. Although representation in proportion to population was not completely achieved the act of 1885 was a significant step in that direction.

About most of the foreign and domestic policy of the government there was grave dissension in the Cabinet. From 1880 to 1905 the Liberals were to be continuously weakened by disunion. Gladstone was faced by the danger of rupture within his party and by attacks from his opponents. In June, 1885, his ministry was defeated on the budget and resigned. No government, united or not, could have stood the blows to national and Imperial prestige suffered by Gladstone's second administration.

The successor of Disraeli as leader of the Conservatives was Lord Salisbury, an able and resolute representative of the great Cecil family. Salisbury and the Conservatives held office for only a few months and then, as the result of a national election, the Liberals were returned to power and Gladstone became Prime Minister for the third time at the age of seventy-seven. Meanwhile Gladstone had decided to grant Home Rule to Ireland if he could carry the Liberals with him. The consequences of his decision were disastrous for his party. Ninety-three Liberals voted against their leader. A national election decisively proved that England was against Home Rule. Lord Salisbury and the Conservatives returned to hold office for six years. The issue of Home Rule was not settled.

Although the six years of Salisbury's second ministry (1886–1892) were rather barren in domestic legislation there were a few significant internal reforms. One was the passage of the Local Government Act of 1888. This act entirely changed the basis of local government by transferring the administrative authority of the justices of the peace to elected county councils. The justices of the peace continued to keep their judicial functions: "Nothing in this act shall affect the powers, duties, and liabilities of justices of the peace as conservators of the peace." The Technical Instruction Act of 1889 authorized local councils to provide technical education facilities. By these measures, as well as others involving social reforms in agriculture and industry, the Tory democracy of Benjamin Disraeli was continued and extended.

In 1892, as a result of a national election, the Liberals were returned to power and Gladstone, then eighty-three years of age, became Prime Minister for the fourth time. He was handicapped by an unstable majority divided into different groups with different wishes. What legislation was desirable? They could not easily decide. Under pressure from the Irish Nationalists the Cabinet did suspend the operation of the coercive Crimes Act earlier passed by the Conservatives to put down unrest in Ireland. Once more Gladstone entered the lists to battle for the old cause of Home Rule. After many debates and amendments a Home Rule Bill passed the House of Commons but was vetoed by the House of Lords (419 to 41). Gladstone then wanted to fight another election at once on the issue but his colleagues convinced him that the Liberals would be defeated. A strong mandate would be needed to override the mighty power of the House of Lords. It might be given one day by the people, but not in 1893 and not on the question of Home Rule. Gladstone's last crusade had failed. In March, 1894, he resigned as leader of the Liberal party. Lord Rosebery now became Prime Minister and Sir William Harcourt led the Liberals in the House of Commons. Only one important piece of legislation was passed by the Liberals between 1892 and 1894: the Parish Councils Act of 1894 which introduced the elective principle into the small parish units of government.

In June, 1895, Lord Rosebery, the deeply discouraged leader of a weak and divided Liberal party, resigned. The Conservatives returned again under Lord Salisbury. The most dramatic events of the third Salisbury government (1895–1902) lay in the field of foreign and Imperial affairs: the dispute with the United States over the Venezuela boundary; the expansion of British power in the Far East; the quarrels with France and the Fashoda Incident; the Boer War. Upon the domestic scene there was little legislation or other activity of concern to students of legal and constitutional history.

By the end of the century the swollen tide of Imperial sentiment was in full surge, not only in England but in the Dominions and the colonies. The Imperial bond was growing strong and tight. In 1897 Queen Victoria celebrated her Diamond Jubilee. In the same year, the second Colonial Conference was held in London. Discussions among the statesmen ranged over wide areas. Joseph Chamberlain, the Colonial Secretary, explored ways to check centrifugal forces within the Empire. He proposed the creation of an Imperial Council "to which the colonies would send representative plenipotentiaries." The colonial premiers were cool to this proposal and to any idea of Imperial federation. They were content to approve the continuance of periodic conferences to discuss problems of Imperial defense, commerce, and other matters of common interest. In 1907 it was agreed that Imperial conferences should be held regularly every four years. Thus the Victorian period ended with a considerable advance in the realm of Imperial policy.

Meanwhile the Dominions were moving towards complete self-government. Canada had achieved responsible government in domestic affairs fifty years earlier and her stature in foreign affairs was steadily increasing. In January, 1901, the self-governing Australian colonies were united in the Commonwealth of Australia. This new federation embraced the six states of New South Wales, Victoria, Queensland, Tasmania, South Australia and West Australia. So the new Dominion of the antipodes was created, half a world away from Britain but bound to her by the "silken ties" of language, race, culture, institutions and sentiment. New Zealand, twelve hundred miles from Australia, retained her separate identity. As a Dominion today New Zealand is one of the most democratic nations in the world.

PREROGATIVE AND POLITICS

Much has been said and written about the power and influence of Queen Victoria in the political history of her reign and in the development of the modern English constitution. There is available a large body of evidence provided by such varied sources as diaries, letters, memoirs and official papers. Nevertheless, the most competent modern scholars have found impediments standing in the way of final and certain judgments. They have therefore advanced their conclusions with hesitation. There are several reasons for their diffidence and caution. One reason is this: as the symbolic character of the monarchy increased it became more and more difficult to know and to judge the human being who stood behind the symbol. There is a second cause for the reluctance of respectable historians to state final conclusions about the ambiguous influence of Queen Victoria upon the constitution: they cannot be certain about the extent to which Queen Victoria was herself responsible for a slow change and how much that change came from a series of events and attitudes far beyond the queen's control. When, precisely, did Queen Victoria act decisively to shape and fix policy? Only isolated events provide partial and provoking answers.

Professor A. J. P. Taylor has shrewdly remarked that some modern historians have written sternly about Queen Victoria's "unconstitutional" actions, forgetting that the word "unconstitutional" has little meaning in the British world today. "In our flexible system," says Professor Taylor, "any practice is constitutional that is tolerated by contemporaries."

The four Georges and William IV exercised the prerogative of appointing their own Prime Ministers. The young Queen Victoria seemed to look upon Lord Melbourne as an adviser who did not hold his office solely for political and party reasons. Victoria apparently felt that one major reason why Lord Melbourne was Prime Minister was that she approved of him. Only after the general election of 1841 was the issue of Lord Melbourne's departure finally settled—two years after the incident of the Ladies of the Bedchamber described in the previous chapter. John Wilson Croker, that contemporary source of so much fact and fancy, noted that "for the first time the people chose the Prime Minister for the sovereign." It does seem that Queen Victoria was responsible for the existence of Lord Aberdeen's coalition ministry of 1852. That was the last time in British history that the monarch was able and willing to take the initiative and to prevail in the actual formation of a government.

On occasion, of course, the sovereign has not taken the advice of a departing Prime Minister as to his successor. Queen Victoria did not ask Gladstone's advice about his successor in 1894. If Asquith gave

George V any advice in 1916 the king certainly did not follow it when he called upon David Lloyd George to be Prime Minister. It is true, then, that the monarch can and does sometimes choose between individuals.

Although the sovereign clearly possesses the power in theory to choose between parties he cannot do so in fact. The Prime Minister must come from a party or a combination of parties that can control a majority of the votes in the House of Commons. In that respect the individual initiative of the Crown exists no more. The sovereign today exerts a pressure and an influence on the policy of government but not upon the selection of Cabinet personnel.

In Victoria's day, however, the queen in fact shared less in the actual making of policy than some contemporaries and later historians believed. After the death of Albert, the Prince Consort (1861), Victoria withdrew from an active life for several years. Later her erratic interventions caused her Cabinets much concern but did not, in the end, deeply influence national policy. Again, it is true that Victoria intrigued with the Conservative leaders to overthrow the Liberal government in 1893 but there is nothing to show that the royal activities gained or lost support for either party in the world of politics and votes. The Liberal government of 1892–1895 was driven from power mainly because it was divided within itself. From the practical workings of politics Victoria was more and more excluded. So, too, was Edward VII, who did not much care.

George V and George VI, who possessed remarkable gifts of insight and judgment, were able to give invaluable service to their governments by their timely and sagacious comment and advice. Victoria gave way to her prejudices. George V and George VI tried to conquer theirs. Events have proved that these monarchs were often wiser than their Cabinets. In Walter Bagehot's famous phrase, quoted earlier, the monarch continues "to advise, to encourage, and to warn." This is also true in all successful constitutional monarchies, such as those of Sweden and Norway. The new British monarchy of the twentieth century obviously does not carry on the system inherited by Victoria from George III. Hectoring memoranda were penned by Queen Victoria to her Prime Ministers. They do not flow from the desk of Elizabeth II. The strength and prestige of the modern constitutional monarch is different both in quality and kind from the older days. Power is not the same thing as authority.

THE END OF AN ERA

The death of Queen Victoria in 1901 closed the longest reign in English history. The queen and her ministers had travelled far together to advance the interests of England at home and abroad. The great age of progress and liberalism upon which the curtain was now falling had clearly marked a diminution of the constitutional power of the monarch. At the same time, the personal influence of the beloved queen had steadily increased. As a symbol of the continuing British traditions of freedom and ordered law throughout a united Empire and Commonwealth, the Crown was soon to assume a far greater influence in the twentieth century than it ever possessed in the years of its highest prerogative power.

When Edward VII (1901–1910) ascended the throne, increasingly significant changes were being set in train. A multitude of forces born of the ever-rising demands of an industrialized society and a dangerous international situation deranged the structure of Victorian England. The complacency of Britain had been shaken by the Boer War. Isolation might be dangerous as well as splendid. Hence Britain's diplomacy altered its course. Widening discussion of working class conditions and the rise of gospels of political and economic dissent captured public attention as eyes withdrew from contemplating the rewards and burdens of Imperialism. Hence came the great era of social reform in the first decades of the twentieth century. In the early phases of the modern age there were new equations, new winds of change: the growth of socialism and the development of the Labour party; the rise of an altered spirit of Liberalism; the successive steps along the road to two world wars; the slowly changing patterns of the law and the constitution. It was to be the task of anonymous millions in the twentieth century to struggle with sweat and blood to defend the accumulated freedoms of the centuries. It was their destiny to seek, in the face of mingled triumph and tragedy, the distant gates to a world where economic democracy, decency, and social justice might one day prevail.

CHAPTER XXI

The Twentieth Century

THE HARVEST OF LIBERALISM

IN 1902 Lord Salisbury retired from the leadership of the Conservative party. He was succeeded as Conservative chief and Prime Minister by his nephew, the brilliant and fastidious Arthur James Balfour. Balfour carried on until 1906.

Despite the few reform proposals of the Conservatives after 1902 the Balfour government was responsible for the great Education Act of 1902. This act abolished the local school boards. Henceforth local county and borough councils, under the Minister of Education, were to control secular education in all schools, including those established by county councils under the act of 1870 and the voluntary schools founded by religious groups. Thus was taken a long step towards a uniform and compulsory system of education. There nevertheless remained difficult problems of religious education. For example, because the ministers of education appointed only one-third of the managers of voluntary schools, these schools continued to teach religion as they pleased.

The Education Act also contained provisions for secondary and technical education. The new science had increasingly tended to subdue nature and to mould society. Hence men of industry and commerce called for reform of the British educational system. Utilitarian considerations were becoming a national necessity. Technical schools would provide young men with training in useful skills. Highly practical people took the view that students exposed to "utilitarian" training in technical schools would be able to extend and increase their chances of serving themselves and the state successfully.

By the Licensing Act of 1904 the temperance cause was advanced in

England. The Conservatives also established the Committee for the Coordination of Imperial Defense. With these measures the Balfour government stopped. It had neither the time nor the inclination to do more. Heavy squalls were blowing up. The conduct of the Boer War brought adverse criticisms. Commissions produced voluminous reports on the state of the British Army. Several reforms were proposed. Long disputes arose. A suspicious public clamored for less debate and more action. The Liberals also noted that because of labor shortages in South Africa a number of Chinese and Indian laborers had been imported. These workers had complained of labor conditions. Here the Liberals saw an excellent source for election propaganda. Rather startling pictures of Chinese coolies in chains shortly appeared upon Liberal election posters. Meanwhile the decision of the House of Lords in the Taff Vale case had alienated thousands of workingmen from the Conservatives. The House of Lords, acting in its capacity as the highest appeal court, handed down a decision which in effect made trade unions financially responsible for any act committed by their agents. Employers might now sue trade unions for any damage resulting from trade disputes.

The heavily buffeted government was wrecked on an uncharted reef. Startling proposals came from the Colonial Secretary, the Imperialist ex-Liberal Joseph Chamberlain. He advocated an Imperial preferential tariff. He urged that a high protective barrier be established against Europe and the United States and that a preference in duties be given to all Dominions and colonies provided that they were willing to give similar tariff preference to Great Britain. Thus the Empire would be strengthened by new economic bonds; customs revenue would be increased; Great Britain would be less dependent upon foreign nations for food; British manufacturers would be assured of Empire markets; the colonies and Dominions would have sure markets for their wheat, meat, and other foodstuffs.

At once the Conservative party divided. Many wanted a tariff on agricultural products that would protect British landowners; but not one that would give a preference to Australia, Canada, or South Africa. These Dominions were as much competitors with British agriculture as foreign countries. For once Balfour was shaken from his Olympian detachment. When his adroit dialectics failed, he fought passionately to hold his party together. At last Chamberlain resigned from the Cabinet, taking some of his followers with him. The Liberals, always historically a Free Trade party, hastened into the controversy. They created the slogan "Your food will cost you more!" In the face of such defection and intense opposition Balfour could not carry on. In December, 1905, his collapsed Cabinet was forced to resign.

In the election of 1906 Balfour and the Conservatives suffered a heavy defeat. The Liberals, led by Sir Henry Campbell-Bannerman, won 379 seats; the Conservatives, 132; the Irish Nationalists, 83; and the new Labour party, 51. Thus the Liberals, pledged to a policy of vigorous social reform, came to power with a majority over all other parties combined.

In this election, as remarked above, the new Labour party had appeared, a party that claimed it would try to reorganize society in the interests of all the people, rich and poor alike. The history of this party had not been long. Only in 1899 had it been decided that the cause of labor could be more swiftly advanced if all labor groups would cooperate. In 1900 a conference was held by representatives of the Trades Union Congress, the Independent Labour Party, the Social Democratic Federation, and the Fabian Society. A permanent Labour Representation Committee was formed. In 1906 this Committee became the Socialist Labour Party.

The Labour party, so important in Britain today, has never believed that private initiative and competition form the source and motive power of progress. Nor do its members believe in the social or moral justice of the private ownership of "the means of production." They do believe in a planned economy, in organized state action in place of private initiative. They assert that state ownership or the "nationalization" of natural resources, public utilities, key industries, and other "means of production" will remove many of the evils born of ruthless private enterprise in an industrial age. Socialism, says the Labour party, will inevitably come by gradual stages in the natural evolution of society. By such processes the relation between the state and the individual will be entirely changed. Private and free enterprise will yield to collectivism. Such is the point of view of the British Socialists.

Not for eighteen years were the Labourites to control the government. In 1906 the Liberals were triumphant. They have always believed that the power of the state should be used to emancipate private enterprise and to create competitive conditions where all individuals will be stimulated to put forth their best efforts. The policy of the new Liberal government was declared to be social reconstruction, a policy that caused the Conservatives to contemplate the new Cabinet and

Parliament with considerable misgivings. One of these followers of Balfour described the House of Commons as "the most hysterical and ill-informed Parliament that has ever, at a critical moment, determined the fortunes of the nation."

From the Conservative point of view it was fortunate that their party controlled the House of Lords. The veto power of the Lords still remained. The Lords had fought the Whig Reform Bill of 1832; they had scotched Home Rule; they would now protect England from what the Conservatives considered the threatened bruising excesses of the Liberal and Labour zealots in the House of Commons. Within a few years the House of Lords had vetoed such measures as a Liberal Education Bill of 1906; a bill for land reform in the United Kingdom; a Licensing Bill that provided for the revocation of nearly 30,000 licenses for the sale of liquor in the following fourteen years; a Plural Voting Bill designed to prevent individuals from casting ballots in more than one place. The Lords also mauled and mutilated such proposals as an Agricultural Holdings Bill and an Irish Town Tenants Bill. They almost rejected the Old Age Pensions Bill, providing for the payment of five shillings a week to all persons over seventy years of age who had no other means of support, who were not criminals or common loafers, and who had been British subjects for twenty years and British residents for twelve. Smaller weekly sums were to be paid to those whose incomes were very small.

Controversy between the Lords and Commons moved towards a crisis. The Lords, said the Liberals, were "filling up the cup." The spirit of the dispute grew steadily more bitter. Some Liberals declared that they would not "act as caretakers for the party that the country has rejected." Others said that the time for "compromise and temporizing and verbal expostulations" had gone. Balfour asserted that the Liberals had "deliberately picked a quarrel with the House of Lords and deliberately framed bills to get them rejected." David Lloyd George—the Welsh President of the Board of Trade and ideal of the radicals—replied that the House of Lords was not "the watchdog of the British Constitution. It is Mr. Balfour's poodle." Again and again the Liberals declared that the Conservative party was attempting to rule England through its huge majority in the House of Lords.

The Taff Vale decision, mentioned briefly above, had exposed to financial ruin any trade union that undertook or sanctioned a strike. After long discussion a Trade Disputes Bill was passed in the Commons. It granted the unions the right "peaceably to persuade." This meant that unions might boycott and picket if these activities did not involve violence. "It shall be lawful for one or more persons . . . to attend at or near a house where a person resides or works or carries on business or happens to be, if they so attend merely for the purpose of peacefully persuading any person to work or abstain from working." The workers strongly supported this bill and the workers had votes. Hence the bill passed the upper house.[1]

A second measure approved by the Lords was the Workmen's Compensation Act of 1906 which extended the provisions of earlier laws of 1880 and 1897. Under the new enactment most workers receiving less than £250 a year were entitled to compensation from their employers in cases of industrial accidents and occupational diseases. During the period of illness or injury the compensation equalled about half the usual wages. In the event of a worker's death resulting from injury or occupational disease, his dependents received a sum approximately equal to three years' wages. Nearly six million workers were protected under the Workmen's Compensation Act.

There were two important Imperial measures. The first concerned South Africa. Responsible government was granted to the Transvaal in 1906 and to the Orange Free State in 1908. In 1909 the Imperial Parliament passed the Union of South Africa Act which united Cape Colony, Natal, the Orange Free State, and the Transvaal into a centralized state. The Union was not a federation in the Canadian or Australian sense. Each of the four South African units kept its political identity and certain local administrative powers exercised by provincial councils. The legislative capital of the Union is at Capetown; the executive capital is at Pretoria; the judicial capital is at Bloemfontein.

A second significant action in the area of Imperial affairs concerned India. As a part of the Morley-Minto Reforms the Indian Councils Act of 1909 extended the election principle of the Indian Councils Act of 1892 and added more Indian elected members to the legislative councils of the Viceroy and the governors of the provinces. Indian council members were to be elected by the small number of Indians permitted to vote under the restricted franchise. The British government took

---

[1] For the text of the Trade Disputes Act and other legislation and debates discussed in this chapter see Carl Stephenson and F. G. Marcham, *Sources of English Constitutional History*, pp. 817–892.

the position, then and later, that the vote should be given only to those who possessed some education and who understood something of what was meant by a system of representative government.

In 1909 there were three important additions to the body of reform legislation. The first was the Labour Exchanges Act which established 350 labor exchanges in eleven districts as clearing houses for information about jobs available anywhere in the United Kingdom. The second was the Trade Boards Act, which dealt with the problem of sweated labor, especially among unskilled workers. The third was the House and Town Planning Act, which made landlords legally responsible for the condition of their property; it forbade the construction of back-to-back houses; it provided for the demolition of condemned buildings by the municipal authorities and state aid for the construction of new ones. By such slow steps the condition of England's workers was to be lifted above the level permitted by uncontrolled competition.

The Liberal government was able to carry through a number of other important measures. In 1911 an act provided for yearly salary of £400 to all members of the House of Commons. Thus the doors of the Commons were opened to those who did not possess independent means. In the Osborne Case of 1909 the House of Lords had forbidden trades unions to use their funds to help Labour members of Parliament. The Lords had held that members paid by unions were not free to vote as they pleased and the liberties of Parliament were thereby violated. Several Labour members were now relieved of the heavy burdens imposed upon them by the Osborne judgment. Meanwhile, the National Insurance Act of 1911 began the great experiment of compulsory insurance against sickness and unemployment. Nearly 15,000,000 workers earning less than £160 a year were insured.

LORDS *VERSUS* COMMONS

All these unexampled reforms paled beside the budget of 1909 brought down to the Commons by David Lloyd George, who had become Chancellor of the Exchequer in 1908. The cost of an expanding naval program together with the financial demands of the new social reforms made necessary a large tax increase. "Democracy," Gladstone had said, "will prove a very costly mistress." As one of the avowed ends of the new Liberalism had been to redistribute the national income, Lloyd George prepared "the People's Budget" with a view to invading a promising field of taxation. The capitalists and landlords would pay for social reform and battleships. They would discover what democratic finance really meant. In his remarkable budget proposals Lloyd George increased all death duties on estates over £5,000. This included a 10 per cent death duty on all estates valued at £200,000 or more. He placed a super-tax on all income of more than £3,000 a year. He placed a tax of 20 per cent on all increase of urban land values. A tax of a halfpenny per pound was put on "undeveloped" land, by which was meant land intended for building purposes but held up until its value increased. The Budget Bill passed the House of Commons after long debates. Throughout England controversy mounted.

Although the House of Lords had already vetoed important Liberal legislation it was an entirely different matter to quash a budget. By constitutional tradition finance was outside the province of the Lords. Usage dictated that the upper house could not initiate or amend any money bills. Theoretically, of course, the House of Lords did have the right to throw out the budget altogether. If they did that, the Liberals would certainly demand an election. The people might then support Lloyd George and his colleagues. In that event, the Lords would be in for heavy weather. On the other hand, this budget struck at wealth in general and land-holding in particular. For centuries the Lords had been England's greatest landholders; their ranks included the wealthiest men in the country. Under the budget they were liable for the heaviest taxes. Most of them believed in the old order. This budget, they said, was socialistic revolution. Both their pockets and their pride were challenged. Heedless of consequences, they rejected the Liberal budget.

Amidst national concern and bitter debate Mr. H. H. Asquith, who had succeeded Campbell-Bannerman as Prime Minister in 1908, asked for a dissolution of Parliament. The election results of January, 1910, brought a marked decrease in Liberal power. For a majority in the Commons the government was dependent upon Irish Nationalist and Labour votes. The Irish agreed to support the Liberals only on the understanding that the Liberals would support Home Rule. When the Irish obtained that assurance the new House of Commons promptly passed the budget again. This time the Lords accepted it.

Meanwhile the Commons had turned once more to the task of devising legislation to whittle down the powers of the Lords. Violent disputes arose. On May 7, 1910, the death of Edward VII resulted in the accession of his son George V. The new king vainly tried to bring about a settlement. Late in 1910 Asquith brought in a Parliament Bill "for regulating the relations between the Houses of Parliament."

The Parliament Bill provided that the House of Lords could not delay by more than one month any measure certified by the Speaker of the House of Commons to be a money bill. Any other bill passed by the Commons in three consecutive sessions would become law without the assent of the Lords provided that two years had elapsed between the introduction of the bill and its final passage. The life of Parliament was to be limited to five years instead of seven.

Scenes reminiscent of the days of Pym and Hampden occurred in both Houses of Parliament. Opponents of the Liberals accused them of trying to "revise at ten days' notice the constitution of eight hundred years." King George V arranged secret conferences at Lansdowne House between Liberal and Conservative leaders. In November, 1910, Asquith admitted "an apparently irreconcilable divergence of opinion." When the Lords rejected the Parliament Bill a national election was held in December. The Liberals won 272 seats. The Conservatives won 272 seats. The Irish and Labour groups again held the balance of power.

In February, 1911, the Commons passed the Parliament Bill once more. By July the Lords had drawn its teeth by amendments. Asquith then announced that the king had agreed to create about five hundred Liberal peers to force the bill through the upper house. In vain the Lords raged as waves of excited public clamor beat against the walls of Parliament. In the House of Commons Asquith faced his tormentors, his speech punctuated by loud denunciations. When Balfour rose to reply to a speech he had not heard, the Speaker was compelled to adjourn the House, "a state of grave disorder having arisen." At last, under the revolutionary threat of the creation of hundreds of peers, the Lords yielded. The Parliament Bill was passed by a vote of 131 to 114. Many Lords refused to vote at all and simply stayed away.

Thus the Parliament Bill became the Parliament Act. The House of Lords had been shorn of a part of its powers. No longer could it thwart the will of a majority of the House of Commons. Since 1911 there have been many proposals for further reform. In November, 1953, the Conservative government of Sir Winston Churchill announced that it was giving careful consideration to the possibility of constructive alterations in the structure and powers of the upper chamber. By such slow steps has the constitution been made and mended.

HOME RULE AGAIN

To the Irish Nationalists Asquith had promised that the Liberals would embrace Home Rule in return for Irish support in the disputes with the House of Lords. In 1912 he introduced the third Home Rule Bill.

The new Liberal bill provided for a bicameral Irish Parliament in Dublin which was to have full control over all Irish matters not reserved to the British government. Important constitutional and administrative functions were to be retained by Westminster. These included control over the army and navy, foreign affairs, old age pensions, land settlement, the administration of the National Insurance Act, and the collection of taxes. The British government guaranteed religious liberty. The royal veto remained. Forty-two Irish members were still to sit in the English Parliament.

The Liberals insisted that the safeguards provided in the bill were necessary. They pointed to the fact that Britain had many investments and many liabilities in Ireland. British interests, they asserted, must be firmly protected. The southern Irish did not then protest the failure to give them full control of their own affairs. They were willing to support the bill as the first installment of freedom.

From the Protestant industrial counties of northern Ireland came loud and strong objections. They feared domination by the Roman Catholic and agricultural south. Proud of the progressive north, they viewed with anger the prospect of being linked with a south they regarded as being economically backward. The Ulster leader was the famous lawyer Sir Edward Carson, once the prosecutor of Oscar Wilde. Carson called the Home Rule Bill "the most nefarious conspiracy that was ever hatched against a free people." Ulsterites armed and drilled. In the south the Nationalist Volunteers did likewise. In January, 1913, the House of Commons passed the third Home Rule Bill. Despite its rejection by the House of Lords the bill would become law, under the terms of the Parliament Act, if passed by the Commons three times within two years.

In May, 1914, the bill passed the House of Commons again. A conference between Sir Edward Carson of Ulster and John Redmond of southern Ireland failed completely. British troops fired upon Nationalist Volunteers in Dublin. Civil war seemed inevitable. Such a sad event was prevented only by the coming of the First World War. A Suspensory Act was passed by the British Parliament providing that

Home Rule should not become operative in Ireland until hostilities between the Allies and the Central Powers ceased.

Not all southern Irishmen accepted the principle of peaceful co-operation pending the end of the European war. The result was confusion and plotting and, finally, the small-scale Irish rebellion of 1916. When the First World War ended, the bitter issues still remained in an island of much hatred and little room.

WAR AND PEACE

The titanic struggle that is called the First World War brought several significant political developments and constitutional expedients. When the conflict began in August, 1914, Henry Herbert Asquith seemed to hold his office as leader of the Liberals and Prime Minister with a sure and steady hand. His position seemed unassailable. It was not long to be so. Cabinet explosions and military disasters united to weaken the Cabinet, the Liberal party, and the man who led both. In 1915 a coalition government was formed. The coalition Cabinet contained twelve Liberals, eight Conservatives, and one Labourite. In December, 1916, the moderate and calculating Asquith was finally replaced as Prime Minister by a man of quite different nature: David Lloyd George, an efficient and hurrying Welshman. Lloyd George immediately formed the second coalition Cabinet. In it the Conservative element was stronger than before. New ministries of Air, Labor, and Pensions were created. A Food Controller and a Shipping Controller were appointed.

Accompanying these shifts were other important developments, of special significance to the student of legal and constitutional history. In the first place, government power increased with government responsibility in an hour of national danger. The Defence of the Realm Consolidation Act of 1914 and later legislation gave to the king in council vast authority "to issue regulations for securing the public safety." It was in the national interest that individual liberties should be restricted where such restriction contributed to the successful prosecution of the war. Famous judicial decisions—as in the case of the King *v.* Halliday (1917) and the Attorney-General *v.* De Keyser's Royal Hotel (1920)—made it clear that in time of war a great nation could not be governed on the principles of Magna Carta.

In the case of the King *v.* Halliday, Lord Chancellor Finlay, in setting forth the judgment delivered in the House of Lords, dismissed the appeal of a naturalized British subject of German birth who had been interned by the Secretary of State. "At a time of supreme national danger" precautions must be taken "to impose some restriction on the freedom of movement of persons whom there may be any reason to suspect of being disposed to help the enemy."

In the case of the Attorney-General *v.* De Keyser's Royal Hotel the owners of the hotel by a petition of right asked for compensation for the compulsory occupation of a part of their premises by the War Office. The Crown, on the other hand, contested "the right of the suppliants to compensation for such compulsory occupation" and pleaded "that it was an exercise of the royal prerogative and gave no right of compensation." The House of Lords held that the action of compulsory occupation was not an exercise of the royal prerogative. It was, rather, a step taken under statutory powers. Therefore statutory provisions for compensation, such as those stated in the Defence Act of 1842, clearly applied. The owners of De Keyser's Royal Hotel could not have prevented the occupation of their premises but they could and did collect compensation.

There were other problems and developments. For instance, the burden of increasing domestic and war business and the importance of speed and efficiency made a large Cabinet cumbersome and unwieldy. Moreover, the twenty-nine ministers who were heads of Departments had much more work than before the war. Lloyd George therefore created a small, flexible, inner "War Cabinet" of three Conservatives, one Liberal and one Labourite. Mr. Bonar Law, Conservative Chancellor of the Exchequer, was the only one who held a portfolio and had duties in a Department. The rest were completely free to devote their full time and to make swift decisions in matters of policy. The other ministers were outside the regular meetings of the inner circle of the War Cabinet. They carried on their heavy administrative duties and came to the meetings of the War Cabinet only when the interests of their Departments were directly concerned. The flexible nature of the British Cabinet system was clearly shown by the emergence of this new institution. It was further illustrated by a second innovation, simple in operation and important in its implications.

On three occasions in 1917 and in 1918 the War Cabinet expanded into a wider Imperial War Cabinet. To "special and continuous meetings" of the War Cabinet came the Prime Ministers of the Dominions, the Secretary of State for India and Indian representatives, and the Secretary of State for the Colonies. These men were full members of the British Cabinet for questions of Imperial war policy. The Dominion Prime Ministers were not members of the same Parliament. They were not responsible to the same Parliament. They sat in the Imperial War Cabinet for no other reason than that the interests of the Empire demanded it.

Although the main task of the coalition government was the vigorous prosecution of the war, two important measures in the field of domestic legislation were passed in 1918. The first was the Representation of the People Act, a fourth Reform Bill, which gave the vote to all men over twenty-one years of age who had been residents of the constituency for a short, prescribed period and who occupied either a residence or business premises of a yearly value of not less than £10, or held a University degree. The franchise was also extended to include all women over thirty years of age who occupied property of a yearly value of not less than £5 or whose husbands met that occupation qualification. Women over thirty years were also permitted to register as Parliamentary electors if they had passed University residence and examination requirements, which would have given them University degrees had they not been barred from receiving them by reason of their sex.

The provisions of the act of 1918 also stated that no person might vote in more than two of the constituencies where he might be properly qualified and registered. No person was to be disqualified from voting because he had received poor relief. Election expenses of candidates were to be limited. Finally, the ninth schedule to the act contained a complete and amended list of all constituencies in the United Kingdom setting forth the number of members to be returned by each. By a redistribution of seats thirty-seven new members were added to the House of Commons. This redistribution recognized more completely than before the principle of representation by population. There was to be one member of Parliament for every 70,000 persons in Great Britain and one for every 43,000 in Ireland. This act added about 8,000,000 voters to the electorate, including 6,000,000 women. After the passage of the Representation of the People Act of 1918 the total number of voters stood at approximately 18,000,000.

The second important domestic measure of 1918 was the Education Act which increased the educational benefits available to the working classes. All children between the ages of five and fourteen were required to attend school regularly. Children between the ages of fourteen and eighteen were to spend a certain number of hours a week in continuation schools. This act also established nursery schools and schools for mentally defective children. More adequate provision was made for free medical care. Several sections of the act dealt with the problem of raising standards in the training of elementary school teachers and in guaranteeing a higher scale of salaries throughout the teaching profession.

In November, 1918, the First World War ended and a month later the coalition government led by David Lloyd George carried 485 seats in a national election. In the next few years, however, the power and prestige of that government slowly declined. There were many economic problems to be faced. There was trouble in foreign and Imperial affairs: in Egypt, India, Ireland, Russia, Turkey. There were the persistent and tangled questions of reparations and disarmament. In such circumstances the heavily bludgeoned Lloyd George government could not survive a final blow: the withdrawal of the Conservatives from the coalition late in 1922.

In a national election the Conservatives, led by Andrew Bonar Law, were returned to power. They won 344 seats. The Labour party obtained 142. The Liberals, badly divided, numbered 117. Bonar Law had been elected on the slogan of "tranquillity"; in the United States, the slogan of Warren G. Harding was "normalcy." In both Britain and America it seemed that a disillusioned public was demanding "not surgery, but serenity." Thus the Conservatives came into power for the first time since their defeat in 1906.

In May, 1923, Bonar Law retired and was succeeded as leader of the Conservatives and Prime Minister by Stanley Baldwin, shrewd and sound, a man who delighted in being considered "the supremely ordinary man." Baldwin felt that the unemployment level could be reduced by giving the British Dominions preference in British markets provided that the British Dominions gave similar preference to British products. This was the rock upon which Joseph Chamberlain had piloted the Conservatives at the turn of the century. This was also the rock upon which Stanley Baldwin wrecked his supposedly safe majority. All his enemies drew together and made common cause against him. Arguments about protection and free trade have always been strong and bitter in modern Britain. The industrial north stood solid for free trade. Several of the great press barons opposed protection. In the election of December, 1923, the Conservatives won 257 seats; the Labour party 192; and the Liberals 152. At once the Liberals and the Labourites voted Baldwin out of office.

As the Socialist Labour party was now the second largest group in the House of Commons the king asked its leader Ramsay MacDonald to form a Cabinet. MacDonald, assured of the support of the 152 Liberals, formed a Cabinet in January, 1924. Many Conservatives felt that as Britain's first Labour government came into being, a revolution was indeed at hand. Some were pleased to reflect that the great trade unions had never been strongly socialistic. There was also consolation in the fact that the Labourites would continue to depend upon Liberal support for a working majority.

The tide that had swept the Labour party into power rapidly ebbed. Votes fell away from the Labourites by hundreds of thousands. Little was done by the government to improve the domestic situation. Labour troubles grew worse. Trade went down and unemployment went up. Irish patriots shot and pillaged. The political sky was darkened still more by the Labour government's proposal to resume normal trade relations with Russia. When at last the Liberals refused their votes to MacDonald, the Labour government could not carry on.

In a national election late in 1924 the Conservatives were returned with a large majority—they won 415 seats. The Labour power in the Commons was reduced to 152 members. The Liberals, for their part, saw disaster sit upon their banners because they obtained only 42 seats. The strange death of Liberal England—in a phrase made famous by George Dangerfield—was at hand. Thus Stanley Baldwin began his second Conservative ministry. It was to last for five years.

Several important and dramatic events occurred during the period of Conservative rule between 1924 and 1929. Chief among these were the signing of the Locarno pacts (1925) and the great general strike (1926). The student of legal and constitutional history also finds two statutes of special interest. The first is the Trade Disputes and Trade Unions Act of 1927. This piece of legislation—a direct result of the collapse of the general strike of 1926—declared that "any strike is illegal if it has any object other than or in addition to the furtherance of a trade dispute within the trade or industry in which the strikers are engaged, and is a strike designed or calculated to coerce the government, either directly or by inflicting hardship upon the community." The same provisions were applied to lockouts. No person refusing to take part in an illegal strike or lockout could be expelled from a trade union or fined or made subject to any penalty or disadvantage in the union. Civil servants were barred from joining any trade unions. Other clauses of this act made it administratively difficult for trade unions to collect funds from their members for political purposes.

The second significant statute was the Equal Franchise Act of 1928. Its preamble described it as "an act to assimilate the franchise for men and women in respect of Parliament and local government elections." The Equal Franchise Act gave the franchise to all individuals over twenty-one years of age who met short residence requirements and who were not legally disqualified as a result of such things as criminal offenses or lunacy. By this statute about 5,000,000 women were admitted to the vote on equal terms with men. A total of about 8,000,000 persons were added to the list of those eligible to vote in elections. Today there are about 36,000,000 voters in the United Kingdom.

By the terms of the Parliament Act of 1911 the legal life of Parliament had been reduced to five years. Hence a national election was due in 1929. The Conservatives, loud prophets of a bright tomorrow, asked the British people to send them back into office. "Trust Baldwin!" said one slogan. "Safety first!" said another. Meanwhile, the Labour party had been moving steadily towards the right in the late 1920's. Even the Conservatives no longer thought of Ramsay MacDonald as wild and subversive; he was now adorned with the top hat of respectability. The Conservatives, for their part, were becoming more flexible as more of their reactionary leaders left the political scene.

In the elections of 1929 the Labourites won 287 seats. Baldwin's Conservatives held 260. With the support of some 50 Liberals, Ramsay MacDonald formed the second Labour government.

During the next two years there arose a serious situation within the British financial structure. When the world depression came in 1929 all revenues from overseas investments, shipping, and financial services fell sharply. At the same time, the export-import adverse balance increased with the decline of British exports. In 1930 the credit balance fell to £23,000,000. In 1931 the loss of revenue resulted in a net adverse balance of £75,000,000. Meanwhile, too, industrial prices in Britain declined still more with the deepening slump. Would the British pound ride out the storm? Was the British banking system stable? The doubtful answers to these questions helped to hasten panic among foreign depositors and an incipient flight from the pound.

In May, 1931, it was admitted that "the solidarity of the British financial system" was in danger. "Drastic measures will have to be taken if the budget equilibrium is to be maintained and industrial recovery made." In June a government commission reported that the budget would show a deficit of at least £120,000,000. Meanwhile the financial world of all Europe was threatening to slip downwards to disaster. The Austrian Credit Anstalt failed. President Hindenburg of Germany appealed to President Hoover of the United States for aid and Hoover proposed a one-year moratorium on international debts. France and the United States, no longer in receipt of money directly from Germany, withdrew gold more heavily from Britain. Loans from New York and Paris temporarily bulwarked the pound sterling. Nevertheless, the gold reserves of the Bank of England were slipping and shrinking with alarming speed. Could the country be kept solvent? If so, how?

It was clear that drastic financial economies must be effected in the face of dwindling revenues. Some members of the Labour party said that the budget must be balanced, no matter what was sacrificed, no matter what the cost might be. The government, they said, must pay its way. Opposed to them were those who insisted that the social security program must not be cut down or restricted. These men refused to decrease unemployment insurance or reduce any other social security benefits. Along these lines of dispute the Labour party divided. Ramsay MacDonald and ten members of his Cabinet agreed that there must be economy in the social services. They were immediately opposed by the trade union leaders and eight members of the Cabinet. Lacking sufficient strength to carry on a government MacDonald resigned in late August, 1931. Together with fourteen of his sympathizers he was read out of the Labour party.

King George V, after consulting with Conservative and Liberal leaders, commissioned Ramsay MacDonald to form a "National Government," containing members of all three major parties, "to deal with the financial emergency." The new Cabinet included four Labourites, four Conservatives, and two Liberals. The flexibility of the British governmental system is shown by the fact that MacDonald, who was really a man without any party at all when he accepted the king's commission, became Prime Minister at the king's request and with the support of those who had opposed him earlier. The Conservatives, a few days before his strong enemies, were now, in the National government, his constant and chief support.

The National government immediately took drastic steps to deal with the grave financial emergency. Unemployment insurance was reduced by 10 per cent. All pay rates in the armed services and all salaries of Crown servants were cut. Taxes were swiftly raised. The gold standard was abandoned.

On October 27, 1931, the National government went to the country in a general election, asking for "a doctor's mandate" to bring economic recovery. The opponents of the government won only 56 seats. The National government held 556 seats; 473 of these were won by Conservatives. Under various leaders and in various forms the National government was to carry on through fifteen troubled years to the end of the Second World War.

During these years several significant chapters were written in the legal and constitutional history of Great Britain and the British Empire. One of the most important developments in the modern world has been the swiftly changing shape of the British realms beyond the seas. Let us turn to see what major changes have occurred in the lands once ruled from Westminster.

COMMONWEALTH AND EMPIRE

The First World War pointed to the fact that the principles conceded in the granting of responsible government to the British Dominions contained within themselves the basis of a new Imperial unity implying the final growth of the Dominions into independent nations. In 1926 the Imperial Conference stated that "Equality of status, so far as Britain and the Dominions are concerned, is the root principle governing our intra-Imperial relations." This famous Imperial Conference also declared that the self-governing Dominions were to be regarded as "autonomous communities within the British Empire, equal in status, in no way subordinate one to another in any aspect of their domestic or external affairs, though united by a common allegiance to the crown, and freely associated as members of the British Commonwealth of Nations."

As a result of the reports of the Imperial Conferences held in 1926 and 1930 and the recommendations of legal experts, the decisions regarding Dominion status were embodied in the Statute of Westminster, passed by the Imperial Parliament in December, 1931. This statute clearly recognized the sovereign right of each Dominion to control its own domestic and foreign affairs. For example, it was provided that "Any law touching the succession to the throne or the royal style and titles shall hereafter require the assent as well of Parliaments of all the Dominions as of the Parliament of the United Kingdom." It was also stated that "no law hereafter made by the Parliament of the United Kingdom shall extend to any of the said Dominions as part of the law of that Dominion otherwise than at the request and at the consent of that Dominion." It was expressly provided that "no law and no provision of any law made after the commencement of this act by the Parliament of a Dominion shall be void or inoperative on the ground that it is repugnant to the laws of England, or to the provisions of any existing or any future act of Parliament of the United Kingdom or to any order, rule, or regulation made under any such act, and the powers of the Parliament of a Dominion shall include the power to repeal or amend any such act, order, rule, or regulation insofar as the same is part of the law of the Dominion."

Thus the remarkable British experiment in developing political organisms abroad has resulted in this unique Commonwealth of Nations formed of "autonomous communities, in no way subordinate one to another." These freely associated nations, daughters of the slow and unspectacular changes of time, remain bound together by such things as a common interest in freedom, cooperation and Imperial defense, the imponderables of sentiment and tradition and the very real importance of economic self-interest.[2]

Between the formation of the National government in 1931 and the opening phases of the Second World War there were eight years of uneasy peace. Meanwhile many shadows lay across the face of Empire. A series of swiftly shaping events altered still more the structure of the British nations and colonies. In 1937, for instance, the men of southern Ireland succeeded in obtaining a new constitution, ratified by plebiscite. It declared Ireland an "independent and sovereign state" to be called Eire. It asserted that its territory included all Ireland—for obvious reasons, of course, the writ of the government of Eire ran only through the twenty-six counties of the south. Ulster, proudly aloof in the north, was determined to remain an integral part of the United Kingdom. The new constitution of Eire abolished the office of governor-general; it omitted all reference to the Crown. It established a president to be elected by a direct vote every seven years. There remained two houses in the legislative body of government: the dail, or assembly, and the senate. Through the president, the Dail was to appoint the Prime Minister, who, in turn, was to appoint his ministers.

The Government of India Act of 1935 set up an Indian federation to come into being in 1937 with limited responsible government in

---

[2] See the excellent little volume *The Law and the Commonwealth* by R. T. E. Latham (1949).

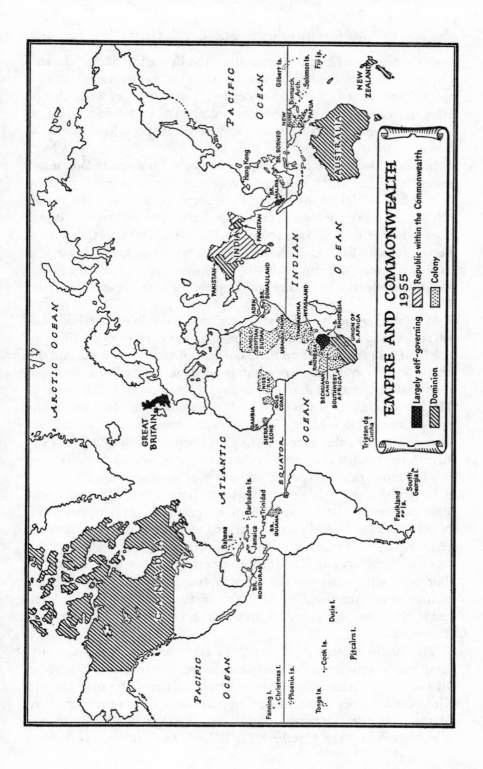

EMPIRE AND COMMONWEALTH 1955

Largely self-governing
Republic within the Commonwealth
Dominion
Colony

both the bicameral federal government and in the provinces. The sections of the act providing for federation never went into effect. The central government operated under the Government of India Act of 1919 until 1947. Only "provincial autonomy" took effect in 1937. The British government retained control of finances, foreign affairs, and the military services.

In India the new act was unpopular. It did not grant Dominion status. It did not grant independence. Amidst ignorance and poverty, cultural and religious divisions, new leaders appeared beside the old. On the eve of the Second World War Jawaharlal Nehru of the predominantly Hindu All-India National Congress Party demanded independence, socialism, and a strong central government for India. On the other hand, Mohamed Ali Jinnah of the Moslem League insisted that the Moslems should have an independent state, separate from the Hindus.

Since the Second World War the political structures of several British realms and territories beyond the seas have been changed. In 1947 the British at last laid down their burdens of empire in India and the result was the creation of two independent nations within the Commonwealth: India and Pakistan. In 1948 the new unified Federation of Malaya was created. It was hoped that this step would "offer the means and prospect of developing Malaya's capacity in the direction of self-government." In the same year Ceylon became a Dominion and the British terminated their rule in Palestine. In November, 1948, southern Ireland became a republic and left the Commonwealth.

In Africa, the British protectorates of Basutoland, Swaziland, and Bechuanaland still stand far from self-government. On the other hand, Nigeria and the Gold Coast are inching towards Dominion status. A central African Federation was established in 1953, comprising the territories of Northern Rhodesia, Southern Rhodesia, and Nyasaland. The possibility of an effective West Indian Federation is now being examined and discussed by Barbados, British Guiana, British Honduras, Jamaica, the Leeward and Windward Islands, Tobago and Trinidad.

The British system is neither static nor stagnant. It is active, dynamic, moving at an accelerated pace towards the unknown tomorrow. In a series of dramatic steps Great Britain is attempting to guide and direct the forces she can no longer fully control. The present structure of the Commonwealth contains seven sovereign nations professing allegiance to Queen Elizabeth II. Indeed, the Commonwealth has seven Queens, as it were, responsible to seven different sets of ministers in Great Britain, Australia, Canada, Ceylon, New Zealand, Pakistan, South Africa. The eighth independent realm is India, which is a republic recognizing Elizabeth II as Head of the Commonwealth.

By the side of the freely associated peoples of the Commonwealth stands the vast Empire of Britain, containing 65 colonies, protectorates and trust territories in various degrees of political and economic development. One-fourth of all the land in the world, containing more than half a billion inhabitants, lies within the boundaries of the Commonwealth and Empire. It is a far cry from a scene such as this to the days of the Witan held by Alfred the Great on a little island at the remote edge of the civilized world.

THE RECENT YEARS

Ramsay MacDonald remained at the helm of the National government for four years. In June, 1935, he was succeeded by Stanley Baldwin, the Conservative leader, who thus became Prime Minister for the third time.

In January, 1936, Britain was saddened by the death of King George V. His eldest son succeeded to the throne as Edward VIII. The new king had many qualities that might have made him a great constitutional monarch. He was popular, conscientious, and genuinely interested in the condition of the poor. All would have judged him worthy of the throne if he had ever ascended it. In December, 1936, to the distress of the British people, Edward VIII made his "final and irrevocable decision" to marry a twice-divorced woman. By an Instrument of Abdication he renounced the throne. The Declaration of Abdication Act, giving effect to his wishes, was passed by both Houses of Parliament in less than three hours. On the night of December 11, 1936, the king who had suddenly become the Duke of Windsor went out into exile. "In the darkness," said the Archbishop of Canterbury, "he left these shores." Fortunately the catastrophe was personal, not public. The new king, George VI, came to the throne prepared to maintain in the highest degree the tradition of his family and position.

In 1937 Stanley Baldwin resigned as Prime Minister and went to the House of Lords. His successor as head of the National government was Neville Chamberlain, who had been Chancellor of the Exchequer. This son of Joseph Chamberlain was at once confronted by tasks with which he was not by ability or temperament fitted to cope. The new Prime Minister was an excellent business man and an admirable financier. In areas of diplomacy and statesmanship he was less successful. On September 3, 1939, Great Britain moved into war against Germany. Australia, Canada, New Zealand, South Africa, and all the British Empire and Commonwealth except southern Ireland moved to do battle against the common foe.

On May 10, 1940, Neville Chamberlain fell from power. He had long been associated in the public mind with "appeasement." His competence as a war leader was doubtful. Faced by Allied disasters Britain turned to Winston Churchill. A new National government was formed, consisting still of Conservative, Labour, and Liberal ministers. This government remained in power until the election of July, 1945. The results of that election drove Winston Churchill and the Conservatives out of office and replaced them by the Labour party, led by Clement Attlee. The new House of Commons contained 393 Labour members. There were 216 Conservatives and 11 Liberals.

In these dramatic years there were no developments of permanent consequence to the history of England's law and constitution. It is certainly worth noting, however, that a steady stream of remarkable legislation began to transform the face of the United Kingdom long before the struggle with Germany and her allies had ended. For instance, the Town and Country Planning Act of 1942 enabled the government to undertake a long-term housing program under the leadership of a new Ministry of Town and Country Planning. In January, 1947, a second Town and Country Planning Act extended the powers of the government to guide and control planned urban living. A second major advance was in education. The Education Act of 1944, superseding all previous acts, provided for a series of comprehensive reforms. The central authority for all education in England and Wales was to be the Ministry of Education. The 145 Local Education Authorities were made responsible for seeing that there was a full range of education in their areas through the three stages of primary, secondary, and further education. All children were to be given a full-time secondary education. New standards of school construction were prescribed. Local Education Authorities were required to supply milk and noon meals to all children. All children were required to attend school until they reached the age of fifteen; as soon as sufficient buildings and teachers were available the school-leaving age was to be raised to sixteen. These selected facts illustrate the way in which Britain prepared to provide inexpensive education for all the youth of the nation, the citizens of tomorrow.

Meanwhile, too, there were remarkable and novel attempts to establish a sound program of employment policy and social security. The National Insurance Act of 1946 provided almost everyone in Great Britain with a large measure of personal protection from childhood to old age. Major clauses of the act included provisions for sickness and unemployment insurance, widows' benefits, maternity benefits, guardian allowances, death grants and retirement pensions. In July, 1948, the National Health Services Act went into effect. It was designed to provide "a universal health service without any insurance qualification of any sort."

In the new "mixed economy" advocated by the Labour party it was necessary to have some of the "commanding heights of industry" taken over by the state. A series of major alterations in the British economic structure resulted from the nationalization plans of the Attlee government. Several sectors of economic enterprise were taken under state control: the Bank of England, the coal mines, the railways, civil aviation, the gas and electricity companies, the iron and steel industry (the latter was returned to private hands in 1953). The nationalization of these industries raised many practical and philosophical problems about the proper relationship of the citizen to the state.

LAWS AND COURTS

The rapidly changing needs of the twentieth century community have resulted in a vast amount of legislation and many alterations in the body of the law. For the sake of simplicity, several branches of the common law have been codified by statutes based on the old judicial case decisions. This tendency was clear in the latter part of the nineteenth century, as is evident in the Bills of Exchange Act (1882), the Partnership Act (1890) and the Sale of Goods Act (1893). Among the most important codifying statutes of the modern age are the Bankruptcy Act (1941), the Larceny Act (1914), the Law Reform (Miscellaneous Provisions) Act (1934), and the Companies Act (1948) which today controls the commercial operations of all joint stock companies. This list of statutes, the nature of whose content is partly indicated by their titles, must not be taken to mean that the movement to put bodies of judicial decisions into statutory form has been uniformly successful. In the sectors of law referred to above it was not difficult to make adequate codes and general principles because the body of case law was already fairly complete and mature. On the other hand, in those areas where the case law remains difficult and complex it is virtually impossible to approach success in shaping a code. Whatever a statute may say, large sections of common law will be left outside the act so long as the doctrine of precedent is maintained and the judges continue to build and change the structure of actions.

Significant pieces of legislation of the twentieth century have been those relating to real property. Most of the enactments have been mainly designed to remove technicalities, to wipe away obsolete practices, to shorten and simplify procedures in such operations as the making of titles to land interests.

A very great deal of the law of property has to do with the practices of conveyancing. The earlier Land Transfer Acts (1875–1897) provided for conveyancing by the voluntary registration of land titles— the entry in a register in effect constituted a title. Transfers were thus accomplished by new entries made according to the rules established by the laws. Under the statutes, mortgages were registered and erased in a similar manner. The Land Registration Act of 1925 made only minor changes in these new title, transfer and mortgage procedures.

Between 1922 and 1925 a series of far-reaching laws (the Birkenhead Code) made numerous changes. For instance, the Administration of Estates Act provided for significant alterations in the laws of estates. Since 1925 only estates in fee simple "absolute in possession and in term of years absolute" are legal estates. A copyhold, for example, is thus no longer a legal estate. The Statute of Uses, now repealed, became unnecessary because it is obviously impossible to create an estate for life or an entailed estate—except by the technical method of "a trust for sale" or the even more complicated trust instrument provided for by the Settled Land Act of 1925. On the other hand, it has been possible since 1925 to entail personal property. Because remainders and reversions are not now legal estates there can be no shifting or springing uses. Nevertheless, it is true that such uses can be created in another way and under another name by an equity arrangement behind a trust—the equitable interest practice of the modern day.

Since the Second World War there has been an increasing awareness of the need for further reforms in the legal machinery and the procedural methods of the courts of England. Probably the most comprehensive and technical report upon the total problem was the one completed in July, 1953, by the Committee on Supreme Court Practice and Procedure. This detailed document contained a careful analysis of existing procedures together with a study of the costs of litigation. "Cheap justice," says the report, "may often be inferior justice, but when justice goes beyond the means of the would-be litigant it is not justice at all." The core of the report was a series of specific recommendations for legal reform:

Almost all actions in English courts are opened by a writ. Then written pleadings are exchanged and a hearing in court follows. The Committee proposed that many actions might be commenced by an originating summons such as that used in the Chancery Division of the High Court of Justice. The advantage of this procedure, in the judgment of the Committee, was that it would permit cases to be heard in the chambers of the judges rather than in the open courts. Thus a judicial decision could be reached swiftly and at minimum cost.

Secondly, the Committee proposed that expert and expensive witnesses should not always be required to give verbal evidence in court. Instead, the Committee recommended that the rules of reception of evidence be changed to permit the exchange between parties of documentary evidence of an expert nature so that highly paid specialists would not be summoned to court and kept in attendance there.

Thirdly, the Committee recommended that in certain cases, especially when the only question was the meaning of a statute, appeals should be channelled directly from the High Court to the House of Lords rather than to the Court of Appeals.

This Committee on Supreme Court Practices and Procedures also made a series of recommendations about the organization and rules of the legal profession. The most outstanding of their proposals were two: (1) a Disciplinary Committee of the Inns of Court and the Bar Council should be established with a special duty to watch and guard the fee levels of the individual members of the legal profession with "power to direct the remission or return of fees in appropriate cases" and (2) the two branches of the legal profession, the barristers and solicitors, should be fused in the interests of efficiency and economy.

No formal action has yet been taken upon this carefully prepared and highly practical report. It is widely hoped that the challenging document may give a new impetus to the contemporary movement for the reform of complex legal machinery and costly court procedure.

THE DUTY OF WESTERN MAN

The assumptions of the nineteenth century were often based upon the firm idea that the stable world our grandfathers knew would not swiftly change. Many Victorians looked confidently towards a sunlit future of abundance and freedom and the gradual creative evolution of societies and governments. These hopes have now been broken under the harsh compulsion of the events of recent years. In 1900 no one foresaw two world wars, the repressive burdens of war debts and tariffs, the cynicism and despair that have embittered so many lives. No one knew that we would see the impatient tides of nationalism racing across our planet and hear the bristling protests of peoples quickening from the ancient torpor of Africa and Asia.

Our century is filled with vibrant leaders and compulsive aspirations, with harsh discords and converging anxieties, with compassion and coercion inextricably mingled together. There have been many major shifts and changes in man's perspectives and methods during his heavy journey through the ages. What view our descendants will take of their sorely tried ancestors we cannot yet know. We are certain only that the future of all mankind hangs upon this question: Does man exist for the state or the state for man? This is one of the classical problems of political and moral science forged long ago. Every generation, it seems, has to answer it.

Man has lifted himself from savagery through long centuries, bitter and barren, filled with carnage, superstition, and atrocity. The dawn of conscience was but yesterday in the history of our race.

As we look back over the chapters of the legal and constitutional history of England we see the prolonged conflict about the location of power in the state, the triumph of compromise and adaptation, the finding of agreed standards of reference. We also see, in the slow shaping of the English civilization, the emergence of a body of law and a judicial system based upon a vital will to decide between right and wrong. From the complex of opposing forces that we call the common will there has emerged, despite the clutter of arguments, an adequate and practicable protection of the individual in the state. It is in the nature of the law and the constitution that one of the great and abiding strengths of England lies. Here are the secrets of liberty in the web of modern society, a web whose threads no eye can follow. "There is a hidden strength in freedom," said Professor James T. Shotwell, "that tyrants never know."

The enemies of all democratic states are ignorance, injustice and intolerance. If free people are to stay free, they must believe in the value and the dignity of the individual human personality. All competing claims must be considered pallid and thin and frustrate. Close adherence to legal form is not enough in the perilous present. Only the spirit gives life. It rests in the hearts of men who agree with Dean Inge that it is better to count heads than to break them. The language of laws and constitutions in free lands shows how far we have travelled since the paleolithic age. Our duty is to preserve, defend, and improve. If we refuse to do battle with the barbarians within and without, if we wince and slink away, then the daylight we now know will be no more. In the darkness all men are blind.

CHAPTER XXII

The State
and the Citizen

THE SPIRIT OF THE LAW

THERE have been many attempts by students of jurisprudence to examine the content of the law as it is and the law as it ought to be. Through the long history of man various standards of justice have appeared and slowly fallen into the shadows. Justice has obviously meant different things to different minds at different times. There have also been numerous expedients for the attainment of equity and justice in various ages and in contrasting social systems.

In our own age, several political theories, contributions to jurisprudence, and critical studies of sovereignty have had their arguments and conclusions buttressed by the use of new criteria based upon the careful consideration of psychological, sociological, and economic factors in human behavior. More and more knowledge about the nature of man and the consequences of human conduct has resulted in the opening of new roads to scientific investigation and new conclusions in jurisprudence and its related fields. Meanwhile, we still have all manner of ideas about the origins, ends and purposes of law derived from the facts and fictions at our command.

The questions and the answers are many. What, for instance, is a just law? Ought just laws to be adapted to changing human wants? Should legal rules be judged empirically with reference to the total aspects of the society in which they exist? When is the content of a rule of law objectively justified? What is the rationale of the so-called "binding force" of law? What principles may be derived from the idea of a social ideal?

Was Dean Roscoe Pound justified in his concept of law as "continually more efficacious social engineering"? Or is the rationalism of the

502

analytical Austinians like Albert V. Dicey defensible when they insist that law is nothing more, and nothing less, than the command of the sovereign? Are the conclusions of the historical school of jurisprudence —led by Sir Henry Sumner Maine, Friedrich Karl von Savigny, and James C. Carter—completely satisfactory when they state that law is still primarily discovered in the consciousness and collective wisdom of the community? Is law the result of the inexorable growth of institutions whose forms and total natures are the result of an inward organic necessity?

Should law be described as "an aggregate of rules" and nothing more? Is it "the system of all the claims society enforces" in any state, in any age? Do all substantive rights come from custom? Is legislation, therefore, only a handmaid to custom? Does the collective mind of peoples and societies decide what rules, doctrines and rights time and experience have proved valuable?

It is questions such as these that have engaged the attention and perplexed the minds of many thoughtful and able men through several centuries. The student who is interested in the growth of the law, the nature of the judicial process and the shifting concepts of justice will find the titles of several books worth reading and possessing listed in the bibliography at the end of this volume. The man who walks very far with such companions as Cardozo, Duguit, Holmes, Kelsen, Krabbe, Pound and Stammler will find that he has undertaken an adventure both exhilarating and difficult. The scenery is beautiful and breath-taking but the traveller must choose carefully at every painful step as he seeks Truth among the rocks.

In ages yet to come England will be praised for her achievements in government and law. In view of this fact it is perhaps remarkable that there has been relatively little philosophical speculation in England about many of the problems of jurisprudence. The name of Thomas Hill Green, of course, comes immediately to mind as a famous Idealist; but he stood almost alone. Sir Henry Sumner Maine was far more concerned with historical fact and the mists of legend than he was with the involutions of abstract theories. John Austin's approach and conclusions were stated concretely enough when he wrote about positive law and superior and inferior beings. Is it entirely an accident that several of England's outstanding scholars in the whole kingdom of legal philosophy have been more interested in the historical and the analytical schools of jurisprudence than in the sociological and philosophical?

There is no doubt of the fact that for law in the abstract most Englishmen would seem to have little use or little patience. They usually fail to consider at length any compact sets of theoretical dogmas. They look upon the law as the expression, mainly, of two things: reason and common consent. In their judgment, law is any rule of rights and obligations that will be enforced by the courts. They insist that their rights and their obligations should be clearly stated and clearly understood. Rudolf von Ihering, the famous Austrian legal philosopher, was once attempting to explain the Englishman's attachment to law and he wrote this: "In the guinea for which the litigious Englishman fights so stubbornly at law lies the explanation of England's constitutional history. No one, however mighty, will dare to rob of its dearest possession, liberty, a people in whose ingrained character it lies to battle boldly for its rights even in the smallest things." Professor von Ihering's words may not be precisely those that we would use but the idea is sound and sure: one of the acid tests of a democracy is the awareness, vivid and continual, of the rights and duties of the citizen, protected by the law.

The Englishman must look to the law of the land for the defense of all his rights and liberties. There are no constitutional guarantees of the kind usually set out in black in written constitutions. There are no "rights of man" mentioned anywhere in English constitutional law. Part of the constitutional law of England is in the statute books, in such documents as the Bill of Rights and the acts relating to *habeas corpus*. Part of it is in the great body of the common law. Likewise, part of the flexible constitution consists of rules and usages that have no legal status at all. These subtle and complex "conventions of the constitution" are very important indeed. For instance, there is no law or case decision stating that Queen Elizabeth II must accept the advice of her Cabinet. No law declares that a government must resign if it fails to hold a majority in the House of Commons. All of these non-legal conventions and usages, scattered over the face of England, seem today to be sensible and reasonable. Moreover, they work. If they ceased to be effective they would be abandoned and they would wither away. So the rules of organic growth continue and the constitution is slowly changed and modified as needs and circumstances require.

To these comments must be added the remark that what Sir Maurice Amos calls the "principles of liberty" are really a part of the English constitution. Deeply embedded in the spirits of Englishmen are the sensitive fibres of feeling about the basic freedoms of conscience, the rules of the game, the fundamental decencies, the rules of tolerance and accommodation. This subtle and imponderable temper defies precise analysis but it remains a constant and vital force. If representative institutions and legal procedures are not strongly buttressed by the potent power of the citizens' hatred of persecution and injustice they will collapse and crumble. Indeed, these attitudes must be widely held in any true democracy. No matter what the letter of the law may say or refrain from saying it is the spirit that gives life and power. No Parliament or Congress can legislate into existence the subtle and mighty forces of toleration, balance, and compromise that alone make democracy an effective way of life and government. No pen can easily describe or explain all the threads, at once so delicate and so tough, that are woven into the complex patterns of democratic states.

It is not surprising that the English constitution has been called "religion without dogma."

THE SUBJECT: RIGHTS AND DUTIES

The laws of England obviously have no place for acts of state. *Lex est rex.* The rule of law prevails at all times and in all places.

On the one hand, it is true that "the queen can do no wrong." On the other hand, let us suppose that a servant of the Crown makes a contract on its behalf and that contract is not fulfilled. Or let us suppose that some property of a subject has been illegally obtained by the Crown. What can the subject do? He cannot, obviously, sue Queen Elizabeth II because the queen may not be prosecuted or condemned in her own courts.

The answer, from a British point of view, is clear, coherent and quite logical. Since 1860, the subject may make a petition of right to the Secretary of State and thus seek redress for the ills allegedly inflicted upon him by the Crown (the Petition of Right Act, 1860). The courts, if the petition is endorsed by the Secretary of State, will treat the case as an ordinary lawsuit and a solicitor of the Treasury appears for the Crown. If the plaintiff is able to support his case to the satisfaction of the court, a declaratory judgment is filed at the Treasury and the Treasury pays the plaintiff the sum specified by the court out of the public purse or returns the property hitherto in dispute. The Crown, in other words, has consented, by an act of grace, to see that right is done.

So far as the law is concerned, the Crown cannot give an unlawful order. No servant of the Crown can plead that he acted illegally under orders from the Crown or shield himself behind his badge or uniform.

The very moment he commits a crime or a tortious act he has ceased to be a representative or official of the Crown. In the doing of any crime or tortious act he is a private citizen and he may be sued or prosecuted as such. In these cases, the doctrine of *respondeat superior* never applies, never is relevant in any judicial sense. Thus the subject is protected by the law, even if an injury comes from the Crown or its servants.

In England there can never be the "suspension of constitutional guarantees" that has sometimes plagued other lands. Nor does English constitutional law make any provision for martial law—it is specifically forbidden in the Petition of Right and elsewhere ("they therefore do humbly pray . . . that the foresaid commissions for proceeding by martial law may be revoked and annulled and that hereafter no commissions of like nature may issue forth to any person or persons whatever. . . ."). Under such legislation as the Defence of the Realm Act (1914) and the Emergency Powers Acts (1920, 1939) provision has been made in the United Kingdom for swift action by government authorities in time of such national emergencies as those arising from war, floods, and the like. Similar laws exist in the other Commonwealth nations. Under these and other pieces of legislation the government and its officers possess wide emergency powers.

The subject, for his part, has a right to protection against violence and the results of violence to his person or his property. It is the duty of the government to make every reasonable effort to give him protection. If the subject suffers from riots or any other kinds of disorder he may submit his claims to the government and, if necessary, he may sue the officials accused of dereliction of duty or other offenses of omission or commission. Of course, as Lord Justice Scrutton once remarked, "While the subject should be protected by the state, the state is entitled to expect the subject to show reasonable self-control and courage."[1]

If democratic government is to be effective, the citizens of the state must possess such rights as those described above: government under the law and protection from violence, arbitrary arrest, imprisonment

---

[1] These remarks about such subjects as the importance of the rule of law, the position of the Crown and its servants, *habeas corpus,* emergency powers, protection from violence, etc., are illustrated by acts and cases cited in Carl Stephenson and F. G. Marcham, *Sources of English Constitutional History* pp. 458, 557, 572, 577, 705, 711, 715, 801, 826, 857, 861, 867, 871, etc.

or punishment by agents of the government. Fundamental liberties must also include the right to assemble freely to discuss and persuade; to speak and write freely, subject to the laws of libel and slander; to move without let or hindrance about the land; to aid in the community election of the central and local governments. These statements mean that a British subject may do what he likes, say what he likes, go where he likes, provided that he does not violate the law as it stands enacted by Parliament or in the common law of the realm. He may, for instance, go to Hyde Park and make the rudest remarks about the Archbishop of Canterbury and no one will stop him—at least, no policemen will stop him—provided that he does not break the laws of libel or slander or does not try to organize a riotous assembly to burn down Westminster Abbey. If his freedoms are infringed, the citizen has immediate access to the courts for remedies. Only an act of Parliament can deprive him of any liberty or any legal remedy.

The subjects of Queen Elizabeth II have duties as well as rights. In the first place, of course, every citizen has a series of responsibilities and obligations towards his fellows in society. A large part of the common and statute law has been built to regulate the relations of the members of the community by declaring the laws of obligation in torts (*non alieno nocere*) and contracts (*suum cuique tribuere*). In the second place, the subject has several duties that he owes to the Crown under the rules of constitutional law.

Every subject of Queen Elizabeth II must, for instance, be loyal. The outright violation of allegiance is treason, a capital offense, the most serious crime recognized by English law. The forms of treason have been clearly stated in a series of statutory enactments, including the Treachery Act of 1940. There is no occasion here to review in detail the legal definitions of treason and it will suffice to say that they include compassing or imagining the death of Queen Elizabeth II or Prince Charles (if accompanied by an overt act), levying war against the queen, adhering to her enemies in her realms, giving aid or comfort to her enemies, slaying such officials as the Chancellor or the justices of the upper courts "being in their places and doing their offices." There is also a series of lesser offenses known as "treason felonies" and "treasonable misdemeanors." These include such actions as unlawful arming or drilling, attacking royal dockyards or arsenals, stirring up disaffection among the soldiers, sailors, airmen, and police. Although these offenses are not technically treason they are considered breaches of the allegiance that binds every British subject to the Crown.[2]

It is also a very ancient duty of a British subject to assist in the maintenance of public order, to aid in the arrest of felons, to help the police whenever requested to do so. He is further bound to do nothing to disturb public order. It will be recalled that once, long ago, an offense "against the peace of our sovereign lord the king" was a serious crime indeed. Today a large and complex body of criminal law illustrates quite well the duty of every subject to "keep the peace," in other words, to obey the laws of England.

If the subject moves to obstruct the administration of justice he is also in some trouble. He may be fined or imprisoned or both for doing such things as tampering with witnesses, purchasing lawsuits with a view to profit (champerty), stirring up cases in which he has no real interest (maintenance), perjuring himself, being guilty of contempt of court.

British subjects must also pay the taxes that have been voted by Parliament or embodied in a statute. They can be compelled to pay no other levies. In a case often cited—Bowles *v.* the Bank of England, 1913—Mr. Bowles successfully sued the Bank of England to recover an income tax payment which had been voted by a resolution of the House of Commons in a Committee of the Whole for Ways and Means but which had not been formally embodied in a Finance Act for the year. Justice Parker stated the law as it was then and is now: "By the statute . . . usually known as the Bill of Rights it was finally settled that there could be no taxation in this country except under authority of an act of Parliament. The Bill of Rights still remains unrepealed, and no practice or custom, however prolonged, or however acquiesced in on the part of the subject, can be ruled on by the Crown as justifying any infringement of its provisions. It follows that, with regard to the powers of the Crown to levy taxation, no resolution, either of the Committee for Ways and Means or of the House itself, has any legal effect whatever."

---

2 Illustrations of cases involving the duties of British subjects under constitutional law are printed in Carl Stephenson and F. G. Marcham, *Sources of English Constitutional History*, pp. 637, 715, 792, 798, 857, 864, 875, etc. Relevant statutes are to be found on pp. 227, 301, 351, 450, 481, 538, 540, 601, 617, 826, etc. The student may obtain succinct statements of facts and problems discussed in this chapter in volume I of *Stephen's Commentaries on the Laws of England,* 20th edition (1938). This volume contains separate sections about the organization of the courts, the history of the courts, civil procedure, the legal profession, constitutional and administrative law, Parliament, government, church and state, etc. See particularly Book II, Part V, Chaps. 25, 26 under the titles "Constitutional Position of the Subject" and "Constitutional Functions of the Judges."

A British subject is forbidden to reveal any state secrets. The Official Secrets Acts (1911, 1920) created many offenses that were not legal offenses at all before they were put upon this statutory footing. Any disclosure or theft of secret papers or any attempt to procure them is an offense under the law. If you trespass upon any "prohibited areas" you are violating one of the clauses of the Official Secrets Acts. In this connection it may be added that no British subject may join in the international quarrels of neutral or friendly governments. It is a penal offense for a British subject, wherever he may be, to enlist in the service of any state which is at war with a nation with which Britain is at peace. Nor may he induce or aid anybody else to enlist in such service or fit out any naval or military expedition against a friendly state.

It would be quite incorrect to suppose that the rights and duties of the citizen have been completely stated in the preceding paragraphs. An enormous number of rights and duties are involved in daily actions throughout the Commonwealth and Empire. The important fact is simply this: all rights and all duties exist under and are protected by a clearly stated and precisely formulated body of law. There are no vague political offenses, no concentration camps, no censorship, no secret police. There are no arbitrary arrests or imprisonments, no pains and penalties ruthlessly dictated and imposed by a totalitarian and allegedly infallible state.

THE QUEEN AND THE CROWN

The Crown is a symbol standing above creeds and parties. It is an emblem of unity, purpose, continuity, mysticism, poetry. The Crown itself is impersonal. The wearer of the Crown is a human being, the blood descendant of kings and queens who have lived and reigned in England for a thousand years. The Anglo-Saxon ancestors of Elizabeth II ruled in a small and primitive world. Today the Crown and the queen who wears it have acquired overwhelming significance as the core and symbol of the unity of the Commonwealth and Empire.

In addition to a heavy burden of social and ceremonial duties Queen Elizabeth II carries many other onerous responsibilities. In the working of the whole intricate constitution the part she plays is essential.

In a formal and technical sense the queen is still the executive authority. She is still "the fountain of justice." The courts function in her name and by her command—she is present in theory in every court. Queen Elizabeth II is the commander of the navy, the army, and the air force in all her realms and territories. The queen in Parliament is the highest legislative authority. She is the Governor of the Established Church. She is the fountain of mercy and exercises the prerogative of mercy in pardoning offenders or commuting death sentences (acting through the Secretary of State for Home Affairs). She is the fountain of honor and all titles, peerages and decorations rise from her (acting normally on the advice of her ministers).

Walter Bagehot once listed some of the steps the monarch could legally take without consulting Parliament: "Not to mention other things, she could disband the Army (by law she cannot engage more than a certain number of men, but she is not obliged to engage any men); she could dismiss all the officers, from the General-Commanding-in-Chief downwards; she could dismiss all the sailors, too; she could sell off all our ships of war and all our naval stores; she could make a peace by the sacrifice of Cornwall, and begin a war for the conquest of Britanny. She could make every citizen in the United Kingdom, male or female, a peer; she could make every parish in the United Kingdom a 'university'; she could dismiss most of the civil servants; she could pardon all offenders."

Queen Elizabeth II could do a great deal more. It is a long task to draw up a complete list of prerogatives of the Crown. Broad and deep powers remain in the prerogative despite the fact that some have fallen into disuse and others raise very difficult questions of constitutional law. Acts of Parliament have also extended Crown powers by statutory measures in several areas where they have now become "various, wide, and growing—all in a superlative degree" (Sir Maurice Amos). From a purely legal standpoint Queen Elizabeth II, as a natural person, possesses manifold rights and powers—some of them precisely defined and some of them discretionary—and the cumulative total of all these rights and powers make up what is called the Crown. As a matter of common usage, however, the words "queen" and "Crown" are used interchangeably.

Since this book is not a detailed study of the complex constitutional law of England we can simply assert that what matters most in the United Kingdom and the Commonwealth and Empire is not the technical questions (of which there are many) but the practical, diamond-hard fact that England is a constitutional or limited monarchy. A large number of the powers of the Crown today are exercised by or on the advice of the queen's ministers. The government is officially and legally Her Majesty's Government. It is usually formed from the party that possesses a majority in the House of Commons. The party that controls the second largest number of votes in the Commons makes up Her Majesty's Loyal Opposition and the leaders of that party, as earlier explained, form a "shadow Cabinet"—that is, they will constitute the government if and when they can command enough votes to control the Commons. (In no other country is the leader of the opposition paid a salary.) The queen herself has no political views or, rather, her views are those of her ministerial servants, the government of the day. She appoints, on the advice of her ministers, most of the higher administrative and judicial officers. All of the departments carry out administrative acts in her name.

The royal assent is necessary for bills passed by Parliament before they become acts or statutes. No bill has been vetoed by the monarch since Queen Anne refused to accept a Scottish Militia Bill in 1707. The veto power, of course, still remains in the Crown. It is not used, and will not be, except in highly improbable circumstances. This is so because, to an increasing extent, the monarch does what the ministers advise. The Queen's Speech at the opening of Parliament is prepared by her ministers and it contains an outline of their program for the approaching session. The Prime Minister advises Queen Elizabeth II about the appointment or dismissal of ministers, about the summoning, prorogation and dissolution of Parliament.

It is the monarch's duty to see that the government is carried on and in exceptional and grave cases the advice of the ministers might not be accepted. Many kinds of contingencies may arise, such as the necessity of choosing a Prime Minister when the leaders of the party in power are not eligible. This happened in 1922 and 1940. In such cases the sovereign must decide what to do. Mr. Walter Bagehot has said, in words widely quoted, that "the Sovereign has, under a constitutional monarchy such as ours, three rights—the right to be consulted, the right to encourage, and the right to warn." There is no doubt that the monarch's judgment is "ripened by a continuous experience of affairs, such as no minister can possibly, under our party system, hope to enjoy." Governments and ministers may come and go but the wearer of the crown remains until life's end.

Through the years the sovereign sees all important Cabinet papers, agenda, despatches, memoranda. Long discussions are held with Cabinet members, especially with the Prime Minister. It is the duty of the Cabinet to keep the sovereign informed of all government policy decisions. Foreign diplomats present their credentials to the ruler in whose name the government exercises authority. The daily appointment lists include the names of eminent men from all over the world. It is inevitable that as the years pass the monarch has an increasing claim to be heard by the transient ministers with more than the formal deference properly accorded the sovereign. Experience ripens wisdom. We know that George V and George VI habitually wielded influence in the formulation of policy, always in a strictly constitutional sense. Despite the fact that almost all of the official acts of the Crown must by usage be carried out by the queen's ministers in the Cabinet, the modern constitutional sovereign is no automaton, no figurehead, no puppet monarch.

HER MAJESTY'S SERVANTS: THE CABINET

The members of the Cabinet, together with the Ministers of the Crown who happen to be outside the Cabinet, are loyal subjects of Queen Elizabeth II and are fittingly called "Her Majesty's Servants." The responsible Cabinet is the bridge between the executive and legislative organs of government, the Crown and the Parliament. Its members are formally appointed by the queen and politically responsible to the House of Commons. The House of Commons, in turn, is periodically elected by the millions of individuals who comprise the electorate. The members of the Cabinet control the various Departments of state. They shape the total policy of the government and are responsible to Parliament and people for the success or failure of all decisions and all policies. In the carrying out of the actual tasks of government and administration the Cabinet is aided by a skilled corps of permanent civil servants.

The reader who recalls certain passages in Chapter XVII will remember that in a strictly legal sense there is no Cabinet at all. There is, rather, a committee of Privy Councillors who are members of Parliament. The members of one or other of the Houses of Parliament who are to be Ministers of the Crown are sworn in as members of the Privy Council. It is the individual who becomes Prime Minister who decides which of these ministers shall be summoned to the meetings of Her Majesty's Servants that are called Cabinet meetings. Usually the Cabinet contains about twenty members, most of them leading members of the dominant party in the House of Commons. The Ministers of the Crown Act (1937) specified definite salaries for certain Ministers of the Crown who are normally in the Cabinet; but the Prime Minister has the final decision as to who will be in and who will be out. The

Lord Chancellor's salary is £10,000 annually. The same salary is paid the Prime Minister who must also be the First Lord of the Treasury in order to have either place, power, or salary.

Many powers of the Crown have been put in commission in the hands of the Cabinet. The authority of the Cabinet, as shown in several passages of this book, is very great indeed. Cabinet ministers introduce legislation. They are responsible for the administration of every Department of the government. They control finance and the armed services. They conduct foreign affairs. Here is concentrated leadership, power and responsibility. Here is the source of initiative in government. Here are made the final decisions on all matters of major policy. So long as the government has and holds a majority in the House of Commons, it carries on. The Crown in practice follows the advice of the Cabinet. In the British system it is of vital importance that this should be so.

Her Majesty's Government must speak with one voice. The responsibility of the Cabinet is collective. The conclusions reached in Cabinet are binding upon all members and the secrecy of Cabinet meetings is protected by the Officials Secrets Acts and the oath each member takes as a Privy Councillor. If a member of the Cabinet cannot agree publicly with his colleagues he must resign or be dismissed on the recommendation of the Prime Minister. In the private discussions of the Cabinet, of course, there are many opinions and many disputes. But once the Cabinet meetings are ended and policy has been agreed upon, the members of the Cabinet must all be in public agreement. A Cabinet minister may bitterly oppose a proposal at a Cabinet meeting in the morning. If the Cabinet accepts that proposal, the same Cabinet member may find himself defending it that afternoon in the House of Commons or elsewhere. Without Cabinet solidarity the English Cabinet system simply would not work.

An immense increase in government business and administration has occurred in recent decades. It has therefore been necessary to do more and more work of the Cabinet through committees. The vast broadening of the scope of the state's activities has made the machinery of government grow daily more complex. For example, every step in the wide programs of social and economic reform means more administration and more control, unhappy aspects of the price of progress. It cannot be pretended that the mounting problems involved in these tendencies are capable of easy or satisfactory solution.

There is no constant number of members in the Cabinet. In the formation of almost every government some portfolios are added and some are taken away. Usually, however, a British Cabinet will contain the following members:

> Prime Minister and First Lord of the Treasury
> Chancellor of the Exchequer
> Lord President of the Council
> Lord Chancellor
> Secretary of State for Home Affairs
> Secretary of State for Foreign Affairs
> Lord Privy Seal
> Secretary of State for Commonwealth Relations
> Secretary of State for the Colonies
> Minister of Defense
> First Lord of the Admiralty
> Secretary of State for War
> Secretary of State for Air
> Secretary of State for Scotland
> President of the Board of Trade
> Minister of Agriculture and Fisheries
> Minister of Education
> Minister of Health
> Minister of Labour
> Minister of Transport
> Chancellor of the Duchy of Lancaster

PARLIAMENT

The English Parliament is composed of the monarch and the two Houses of Parliament: the House of Lords and the House of Commons. Queen Elizabeth II in Parliament is legally sovereign. Parliament possesses "the right to make or unmake any law whatever." Its legal power is absolute and unlimited. To paraphrase a famous comment of Walter Bagehot: Parliament can do anything except make a man a woman, and legally it can do that too. Whenever Parliament assembles it is the supreme authority in the land. No court or any other tribunal can hold its acts unconstitutional for the laws of England have no word to say about constitutions. So far as the "constitution" of England is concerned it is law and custom combined and it is nothing more. Parliament can make any acts on any matter and in furtherance of any policy which a majority of its members approve. It can repeal any acts. Because each Parliament is sovereign no Parliament can bind its successors. The only other limits upon its powers are natural ones: the dictates of practical wisdom, the willingness of the citizens to obey its enactments, the extra-Parliamentary forces of gravitation, electromagnetism, mass and energy. From a legal point of view, to repeat, Parliament is not the agent of the electors or a trustee for the constituents. It is the sovereign legislative power in the state. At the same time, it is "the grand inquest" of the nation. It is a public forum of debate and opinion. Here, in the voices of Her Majesty's Government, Her Majesty's Opposition, the other parties, and the scattered independent members, is heard the authentic judgments of the people of the kingdom.

The House of Commons is composed of 640 members elected by a universal franchise covering both sexes and all classes. Any British subject who is twenty-one years of age may vote unless he is legally disqualified by being a lunatic, a bankrupt, a person convicted of treason or felony and actually in prison, a Parliamentary candidate who has been found guilty of corrupt practices (in such cases the offending individual is forever disqualified from voting in the constituency where the offense was committed, and for seven years anywhere else), a clergyman of the Church of England, the Church of Scotland, and the Roman Catholic Church, a holder of certain specified offices under the Crown, a peer of England, Scotland, or the United Kingdom—but peers of Northern Ireland may run for seats in the House of Commons if they are not representative peers of Ireland having seats in the House of Lords. In order to vote a person must be registered as a voter in a constituency by a specified date before a national election. In the event of a dispute about registration an appeal is possible from the decision of the Returning Officer to the County Court and, in certain cases, to the Court of Appeal.

Any British citizen, not subject to one or more of the legal disqualifications, may be a candidate for election to the House of Commons. Members receive a salary of £1,000 a year and certain additional payments for expenses. No member, as in days of old, may be arrested during a session except on such charges as treason, felony, and breach of the peace. Every member has absolute freedom of speech in the Commons, without any fear of libel or slander penalties. The House controls its own procedure by Standing Orders, by usage and custom. It can punish anyone for contempt or for infringement of its rules and it can send anyone to jail for the duration of the session. Acting through the Speaker of the House it may suspend or expel any member.

The initiative and the final authority in all matters of finance lie with the House of Commons. When Queen Elizabeth II is reading the speech from the throne in the House of Lords at the opening of a session of Parliament, the Commons attending at the Bar, she usually comes to a passage concerning finance. When she does so, she technically ceases to address the House of Lords by dropping the words "My Lords" and substituting "Members of the House of Commons." In this simple way recognition is given to the result of centuries of struggle: the supremacy of the Commons in all financial matters. Only the Commons can authorize the raising of money and its expenditure.

It is obviously impossible to discuss here such complicated things as private bills and public bills or the various procedures of the House of Commons. Nevertheless, mention should certainly be made of the fact that tradition has prescribed the various ways and the number of times that bills must be brought forward for debates and votes. The rules, which vary for different classes of bills, are very peculiar and complicated. The experienced student of constitutional law will recognize that the writer departs, on occasion, from the whole truth. Strictly accurate statements, with the necessary amendments of successive qualifications, are neither possible nor desirable in certain circumstances, and this is one of them. It is sufficient to say that before a bill passes the House of Commons it must travel through three stages, called readings. The first reading introduces the bill. Upon the second reading there is a debate upon the broad and general principles of the proposed legislation. If a motion stating that "the bill be now read a second time" passes the House, the document is sent back to the Standing Committee or Select Committee that referred it out. In the Committee the bill is carefully studied and debated and sometimes revised and amended. When this has been done, the bill returns to the Commons, and the carrying of the motion that the bill "be now read a third time" passes the bill and it is then sent to the House of Lords. If, at any stage, the motion that the bill be read again is amended, the bill stands rejected.

A similar procedure by which bills are read three times is followed in the House of Lords. Bills (except money bills) may originate in either House of Parliament. After a bill has passed through all stages in the Lords and Commons it is submitted to the sovereign for approval. Hence the formula: "Be it enacted by the Queen's Most Excellent Majesty, by and with the advice and consent of the Lords Spiritual and Temporal, and Commons, in this present Parliament assembled and by authority of the same. . . ." These stages of traditional procedure are usually followed with a tenacious adherence to the rules established by time and usage. Only rarely are there evasions or errors: "In 1844 there were two Eastern Counties Railway bills in Parliament; one had passed all its stages, the other was still pending in the House of Lords, when by mistake the Queen expressed her consent to the latter instead of to the former. The mistake was discovered, and another act was passed declaring that the bill to which assent had been given should be deemed not to have received the royal assent."

The House of Lords today consists of more than 800 peers of whom only 100 normally attend regularly. The peers of the House of Lords include the princes of the blood royal; the 26 lords spiritual, including the Archbishops of Canterbury and York and the bishops of London, Winchester and Durham; the hereditary peers of England, whose peerages were created before 1707; the hereditary peers of the United Kingdom, whose peerages were created between 1707 and 1801; the hereditary peers of the United Kingdom of Great Britain and Northern Ireland, whose peerages have been created since 1801; the 16 representative peers of Scotland, elected for each Parliament by the peers of Scotland who do not hold peerages of the United Kingdom; the representative peers of Ireland—the dwindling number of the survivors of the twenty-eight peers elected for life by the peers of Ireland before the establishment of the Irish Free State (1921)—only seven remained in 1954; nine (earlier six) Lords-of-Appeal-in-Ordinary who have been chosen under the Appellate Jurisdiction Act of 1876 to hold life peerages and to bring their great legal knowledge and skill to the highest court in the land.

It may be remarked in passing that women may be peeresses in their own right but they may not sit in the House of Lords. The Committee of Privileges held in 1922 that despite the Sex-Disqualification Removal Act of 1919 Viscountess Rhondda was not entitled to a writ of summons to the Lords. All other members of the peerage not subject to legal disqualifications for different reasons than those existing in the case of Viscountess Rhondda are summoned to the House of Lords, as the ancestors of some of them were called to attend the king in the distant days of the *curia regis*.

The House of Lords represents a great body of industrial and landed wealth. It also contains many men of training and ability in numerous fields of national life. The judgment of the House of Lords is indeed a weighty one. The debates of the members are conducted in an atmosphere free from the tumults and pressures of the Commons. Often the amendments of the Lords are gratefully accepted by the lower house. There is no doubt, too, that the hereditary House of Lords has sometimes acted as a brake upon proposals sent forward too hastily by a popularly elected lower house looking towards the results of elections rather than to the long-term welfare of the state. There are several members of the House of Lords who would probably be heckled off the platform in a modern political meeting. Their abilities and gifts are not those of the fighting politicians. Although the public might sometimes understand the common politician better than the noble lord each has his place, surely, in the service of the state.

No agreement has yet been reached among those who propose a drastic reform of the upper house. It seems possible, however, that some modifications and compromises may be undertaken in keeping with the statement and spirit of the preamble of the Parliament Act of 1911. Any conjecture about the future pattern of policy is alike unnecessary and unwise.

MODERN PROBLEMS

In recent decades the functions of the state have been steadily extended. It has inevitably followed that Parliament has found it impossible to cope with the mounting tide of demands upon its time and comprehension. The scope and complexity of public administration in modern democratic states like Great Britain and the United States almost defies the imagination of the average citizen. Administrative empires proliferate. Bureaus rise and fall. New names appear in the newspapers and new strains are placed upon the resources of alphabet and language. It has been found necessary to employ many administrative agents to administer the laws and sometimes to move into realms beyond the laws. As new philosophies of social welfare have gradually replaced the theory and practice of laissez-faire and individualism, the collectivist state foreseen and feared by Professor A. V. Dicey and others is nearer than in Gladstone's day. Such events as the extension of the state's activities in years of war and the rolling power of Socialist Labour doctrines have changed the face of England.

The problem has arisen of reconciling the demands of technical and administrative efficiency with the long traditions of public responsibility. New methods, more or less efficient, have been devised and used to place experts and others in the service of an expanding bureaucratic system. Many of the new administrative servants and organizations have been relieved of detailed supervision and regular scrutiny by the officials of responsible Departments. The new bureaus and agencies have sometimes tended to operate, once Parliamentary approval has been given upon questions of general policy, in an increasingly independent fashion. Even at key points the degree of actual control by the government has obviously been too spasmodic.

By such devices as the Provisional Order, the Special Order, and the Statutory Scheme the process of delegating legislative authority from Parliament to government Departments and thence to subordinate organs of administration has continued apace. Parliament has found it necessary to lay down general principles and then to leave the responsibility of adequately and properly applying those principles to particular Departments of government. It is true that by steps such as these Parliament has been relieved of tasks of supervision that could not possibly be discharged. Nevertheless, it is still open to doubt that the results of the particular remedies adopted have been to the national advantage.

Several acts of Parliament have conferred upon Ministers or their subordinates the power to supplement the provisions of statutes by issuing Statutory Rules and Orders, either in the form of Orders-in-Council or Departmental Orders or Regulations. The total text of the Statutory Rules and Orders now covers more pages in one year than the total text of the acts of Parliament. There can be little objection to the delegation and devolution of Parliamentary powers provided that limitations and safeguards against an unwise or arbitrary use of authority are carefully provided. The fact that such safeguards have not always been made available has given rise to widespread, serious and responsible comment and criticism.

It is not surprising that careful critics have observed with concern the extensive quasi-judicial powers exercised by such administrative Departments as the Home Office, Labour, Trade, Education, Agriculture, and Health (especially those powers taken over from the Local Government Board when the latter body was abolished in 1919). The administrative tribunals established under existing orders have used wide quasi-judicial powers and from their decisions there has been no appeal to the ordinary courts. Indeed, under the British system of legal machinery, there can never be appeals from such administrative bodies to the courts of law. In recent years it has been frequently remarked that England has never possessed a *droit administratif* and does not need one now. Fortunately the tendencies succinctly described above have been carefully scrutinized by successive governments in recent years. In 1932 a Select Committee on Ministers' Powers reviewed the whole problem. It made several excellent recommendations about protective devices to ward off any threats to the supremacy of law and Parliament or to the rights of the individual. In May, 1944, a Select Committee of the House of Commons was established to examine and to study every Statutory Rule and Order with a view to ensuring its formal regularity and propriety. The Statutory Instruments Act (1945) provided for a uniform procedure in submitting Rules and Orders to the House and in publishing them. Despite these precautionary measures it would seem that the body of constitutional principles threatened by the devolution of executive and legislative powers can best be defended by conscientious Ministers and sensible civil servants. The question is always this: do the Statutory Instruments, Regulations, and Orders achieve what they are intended to do with a minimum of interference with the lives of the citizens?

The problem of what Lord Hewart called "the New Despotism" and the growth of administrative bureaucracy is only one of the difficulties of Parliamentary government in the twentieth century. It is the responsibility of Parliament to control the administrative aspects of government. Whether it can effectively do so, the history of the next few decades will reveal.[3]

THE SUMMING-UP

This book has tried to give an intelligible and intelligent account of the leading features and principles of the constitutional and legal history of England. It is a long road from the Witan to party government and ministerial responsibility, those twin pillars of the modern Parliamentary system. Here is the story of slow and hesitating progress through the rocks and winds of time, of almost constant consolidation and adventurous activity. Earlier generations wrestled with their hydras and prevailed.

In these pages we have described the buttressed growth of the present system of English law and government, often considered so eccentric, insular, mysterious, and impenetrable by the earnest and log-

---

[3] For a more complete discussion of this important topic see Lord Hewart, *The New Despotism* (1929); C. K. Allen, *Bureaucracy Triumphant* (1931), *Law and Orders* (1945); Sir Cecil Carr, *Concerning English Administrative Law* (1941); Committee on Ministers' Powers, *Report*, Command Paper 4060, H. M. Stationery Office, 1932.

ical inhabitants of other lands. Here is a nation, the mother of a great Commonwealth, where the queen reigns but does not rule. At the same time, as Paul de Visscher has remarked, "In the twentieth century, administration is still what it was in its origin: the secret garden of the Crown." The ancient meets the medieval; and the medieval is wedded to the present. New worlds are made out of necessity; but they need not entirely overwhelm the old.

We have seen that in England there is no organic, monolithic, written constitution. The Englishman understands this perfectly. What has been built may sometimes seem inconsistent or inappropriate. Nevertheless, the system works. The tests of experience count for much. Those who want to uproot and make all things new should remember some, at least, of the words of Edmund Burke.

Nor has English law ever been codified. It is all case law, all statute law, custom and precedent. It never deals with right in the abstract. We have noted earlier that it seldom seems to have been interested in philosophical speculations. Notice how blunt and clear Magna Carta is: "to no one will we sell, to no one will we delay or deny, right or justice." English law is, above all, concerned with the rights of the individual man as against those of his neighbor or of the state. Neither monarch nor Prime Minister may come between the judge and the performance of his duty. The laws say that the claims of the many must not yield to the privileges of the few. Many chapters of English history are the tales of the way in which the barriers of privilege were breached so that the interests of all might be served. Again, the law says that no man shall be punished legally unless it can be shown by evidence before independent judges that he has broken a specific law. The moment that rule is destroyed or evaded the democratic state and the citizen are in peril.

The English judicature is separated from the legislature because Englishmen will not trust a government to be at once prosecutor and judge in its own cause. When the courts are safeguarded, the citizen cannot be browbeaten or bribed by the state through the judicial system. "Let others have every liberty, so long as they leave my liberties alone." That is the Englishman's real history and there his abiding home. Hence John Stuart Mill's famous conclusion: "If all mankind minus one were of one opinion, and only one person were of the contrary opinion, mankind would be no more justified in silencing that one person, than he, if he had the power, would be justified in silencing mankind."

Englishmen know that a state can never be regarded as something different from its citizens if a democratic nation is to survive. The citizens make the state and control its course. The individual is, by definition, an essential part of the popular will. In all cases, that popular will is the effective source of power. In all cases, too, the individual must be considered as an end in himself, not a means to an end proclaimed by the state. Those who believe and practice modern political democracy know, as the Greeks once knew, that governments free from popular control degenerate. The individual withers and the state becomes Alpha and Omega, the beginning and the end of all goals, all purposes. If a man has no share in power he usually has none of the benefits of power.

One of the central purposes of civilization is to try to find the secret of combining individual freedom with social order. A vital task of modern democracy is to continue to strive towards that goal, moving with eternal vigilance, swerving neither to the right nor to the left. With the aid of compromise and toleration the citizens of democratic lands upon this planet have travelled far and well. The promises of the future are for those who take them.

At the center of the whole democratic principle is nothing more and nothing less than the everlasting ideal of the ultimate importance of the individual. There may be a better way to ensure the dignity of the human personality than is provided by a democratic system of government. At the present moment in the time scale, however, democracy—with all its faults and all its unrealized ideals—still provides the most satisfactory means of protecting the values cherished by free men everywhere.

Fortunately for themselves and the world, the English people have seldom been apathetic about political matters. They know, as we in the United States know, that democracy is not an easy way of life. The citizen who sleeps at his post may cost his country survival. The wages of political apathy and neglect are usually indecent slavery, chains of steel, and the death of the spirit. "All things excellent," said Spinoza, "are as difficult as they are rare."

TABLES

$\mathcal{T}ables$

KINGS

ANGLO-SAXON KINGDOMS

Northumbria

Elthelfrith, 593-617
Edwin, 617-633
Oswald, 635-642
Oswy, 642-670
Ecgfrith, 670-685

Mercia

Penda, 626-655
Ethelbald, 716-757
Offa II, 757-796
Cenulf, 796-821

Kent

Ethelbert, 560-616

Wessex

Ine, 688-726
Egbert, 802-839
Ethelwulf, 839-858
Ethelbald, 858-860
Ethelbert, 860-866
Ethelred, 866-871

ENGLAND

Alfred, 871-899
Edward, 899-924
Ethelstan, 924-939
Edmund, 939-946
Edred, 946-955
Edwig, 955-959
Edgar, 959-975
Edward, 975-978
Ethelred, 978-1016
Edmund, 1016
Canute, 1017-1035
Harold, 1035-1040
Harthacanute, 1040-1042
Edward, 1042-1066
Harold, 1066

NORMANS

William I, 1066-1087
William II, 1087-1100
Henry I, 1100-1135
Stephen, 1135-1154

ANGEVINS

Henry II, 1154-1189
Richard I, 1189-1199
John, 1199-1216
Henry III, 1216-1272
Edward I, 1272-1307
Edward II, 1307-1327
Edward III, 1327-1377
Richard II, 1377-1399

LANCASTRIANS

Henry IV, 1399-1413
Henry V, 1413-1422
Henry VI, 1422-1461

YORKISTS

Edward IV, 1461-1483
Edward V, 1483
Richard III, 1483-1485

TUDORS

Henry VII, 1485-1509
Henry VIII, 1509-1547
Edward VI, 1547-1553
Mary, 1553-1558
Elizabeth I, 1158-1603

STUARTS

James I, 1603-1625
Charles I, 1625-1649
Commonwealth and Protectorate,
  1649-1660
Charles II, 1660-1685

James II, 1685-1688
William III and Mary, 1688-1702
Anne, 1702-1714

HANOVERIANS

George I, 1714-1727
George II, 1727-1760
George III, 1760-1820

George IV, 1820-1830
William IV, 1830-1837
Victoria, 1837-1901
Edward VII, 1901-1910
George V, 1910-1936
Edward VIII, 1936
George VI, 1936-1952
Elizabeth II, 1952-

PRIME MINISTERS

Sir Robert Walpole, 1721-1742
Lord Wilmington and John Carteret,
 1742-1744
Henry Pelham, 1744-1754
Duke of Newcastle, 1754-1756
Duke of Devonshire and William Pitt,
 1757-1757
Duke of Newcastle and William Pitt,
 1756-1761
Duke of Newcastle and Lord Bute,
 1761-1762
Lord Bute, 1762-1763
George Grenville, 1763-1765
Lord Rockingham, 1765-1766
William Pitt, Earl of Chatham,
 1766-1768
Duke of Grafton, 1768-1770
Lord North, 1770-1782
Lord Rockingham, 1782
Lord Shelburne, 1782-1783
Duke of Portland, Lord North, Charles
 James Fox, 1783
William Pitt, the Younger, 1783-1801
Henry Addington, 1801-1804
William Pitt, the Younger, 1804-1806
Lord Grenville and Charles James Fox,
 1806-1807
Duke of Portland, 1807-1809
Spencer Perceval, 1809-1812
Lord Liverpool, 1812-1827
George Canning, 1827
Lord Goderich, 1827
Duke of Wellington, 1828-1830

Earl Grey, 1830-1834
Lord Melbourne, 1834
Sir Robert Peel, 1834-1835
Lord Melbourne, 1835-1841
Sir Robert Peel, 1841-1846
Lord John Russell, 1846-1852
Lord Derby and Benjamin Disraeli, 1852
Lord Aberdeen, 1852-1855
Lord Palmerston, 1855-1858
Lord Derby and Benjamin Disraeli,
 1858-1859
Lord Palmerston, 1859-1865
Lord John Russell, 1865-1866
Lord Derby and Benjamin Disraeli,
 1866-1868
William Ewart Gladstone, 1868-1874
Benjamin Disraeli, 1874-1880
William Ewart Gladstone, 1880-1885
Lord Salisbury, 1885-1886
William Ewart Gladstone, 1886
Lord Salisbury, 1886-1892
William Ewart Gladstone, 1892-1894
Lord Rosebery, 1894-1895
Lord Salisbury, 1895-1902
Arthur James Balfour, 1902-1905
Henry Campbell-Bannerman, 1905-1908
Herbert Henry Asquith, 1908-1916
David Lloyd George, 1916-1922
Andrew Bonar Law, 1922-1923
Stanley Baldwin, 1923-1924
James Ramsay MacDonald, 1924-1925
Stanley Baldwin, 1925-1929
James Ramsay MacDonald, 1929-1931
 (Labour government)

James Ramsay MacDonald, 1931-1935
  (National government)
Stanley Baldwin, 1935-1937
Neville Chamberlain, 1937-1940
Sir Winston Churchill, 1940-1945
Clement Attlee, 1945-1951
Sir Winston Churchill, 1951-1955

Sir Anthony Eden, 1955-1957
Harold Macmillan, 1957-1963
Sir Alexander Douglas-Home, 1963-1964
Harold Wilson, 1964-1970
Edward Heath, 1970-1974
Harold Wilson, 1974-1976
James Callaghan, 1976-1979
Margaret Thatcher, 1979-

BIBLIOGRAPHY

$\mathcal{B}i\text{ßliograp\text{ßy}}$

GENERAL WORKS

To avoid confronting the reader with an unwieldy bibliography I have endeavored to indicate only the most useful recent works, a number of typical sources, and places where more comprehensive bibliographies may be found.

BIBLIOGRAPHIES. The following are useful bibliographical aids: Cam, H. M., and Turberville, A. S., *A Short Bibliography of English Constitutional History* (*Historical Association Leaflet* No. 75, 1929); Davies, G., *Bibliography of British History, Stuart Period, 1603–1714* (1928); Grose, C. L., *A Select Bibliography of British History 1660–1760* (1939); Gross, G., *The Sources and Literature of English History from the Earliest Times to about 1485* (2nd ed., 1915); Milne, A. T., *Writings on British History* (annually, 1934–   ); Paetow, L. J., *Guide to the Study of Medieval History* (1931); Pargellis, S., and Medley, D. J., *Bibliography of British History: the Eighteenth Century, 1714–1789* (1950), a companion volume to Davies, G., cited above, and Read, Conyers, *Bibliography of British History, Tudor Period, 1485–1603* (1933). Many of the volumes cited below contain excellent bibliographies.

CONSTITUTIONAL AND LEGAL HISTORIES. Outstanding studies in constitutional history include: Anson, W. R., *The Law and Custom of the Constitution* (2 vols., vol. i, 5th ed. 1922, vol. ii, 4th ed. 1935); Bagehot, Walter, *The English Constitution* (rev. ed. 1928 with an introduction by the late Earl Balfour); Dicey, A. V., *Introduction to the Study of the Law of the Constitution* (9th ed. 1939; first pub. 1885). Students would be well advised to read some of the writings of this great nineteenth century English jurist and defender of Parliamentary sovereignty. In this book, for instance, Professor Dicey formulated his famous distinction between legal and political sovereignty. Of enduring reputation is Lowell, A. L., *The Government of England* (2 vols., 1910). Every student should be required to read at least several chapters of Maitland, F. W., *The Constitutional History of England* (8th ed. 1936). Of considerable value is Sir Thomas Erskine May's massive and scholarly *The Constitutional History of England since the Accession of George III* (3 vols., 12th ed. 1912. Vols. i, ii, covering the period 1760–1860 were written by May; vol. iii, covering the years 1860–1911, was written by Francis C. Holland).

The most famous exposition of medieval constitutional history is that of Bishop William Stubbs: *The Constitutional History of England* (3 vols., 1874–83. There are several editions). The unwary student should be warned that many of the premises and conclusions of Bishop Stubbs are no longer considered valid in the light of modern research. See also Petit-Dutaillis, C. E., and Lefebvre, G., *Studies and Notes Supplementary to Stubbs' Constitutional History down to the Great Charter* (vols. i, ii were written by Petit-Dutaillis in

531

1908, 1914; Lefebvre published vol. iii in 1929. The English translation, by W. A. Waugh and W. E. Rhodes, was published in 1930). See further Cam, H. M., "Stubbs Seventy Years After," *Cambridge Historical Journal*, IX, No. 2, 1948. Students interested in the medieval period will read at length in Tout, T. F., *Chapters in the Administrative History of Mediaeval England* (6 vols., 1920–1933) and Chrimes, S. B., *An Introduction to the Administrative History of Mediaeval England* (1952).

Standard and general constitutional histories include: Adams, G. B., *Constitutional History of England* (revised, edited, and expanded by R. L. Schuyler, 1934); Amos, M., *The English Constitution* (1930); Jennings, W. I., *The British Constitution* (1941); Jolliffe, J. E. A., *The Constitutional History of Medieval England from the English Settlement to 1485* (2nd ed. 1947); Keir, D. L., *The Constitutional History of Modern Britain 1485–1937* (4th ed. 1950); Keith, A. B., *The Constitution of England from Queen Victoria to George VI* (2 vols., 1940); Knappen, M. M., *Constitutional and Legal History of England* (1942); Marriott, J. A. R., *English Political Institutions* (1925); Medley, D. J., *A Student's Manual of English Constitutional History* (6th ed. 1950); Morris, W. A., *Constitutional History of England to 1216* (1930); Muir, R., *How Britain Is Governed* (3rd ed. 1935); Ogg, F. A., *English Government and Politics* (1934); Taswell-Langmead, T. P., *Constitutional History of England* (10th ed. rev. by T. F. T. Plucknett, 1946); Thomson, M. A., *Constitutional History of England 1642–1801* (vol. iv, 1938); White, A. B., *The Making of the English Constitution* (1925; this volume covers the period before 1485); Wilkinson, B., *The Constitutional History of Medieval England 1216–1399 with Select Documents* (the first of the projected three volumes, *Politics and the Constitution 1216–1307*, appeared in 1948; the second, *Politics and the Constitution 1307–1399* in 1951). An excellent brief survey is Chrimes, S. B., *English Constitutional History* (1947) in the Home University Library series.

The best books on English constitutional law are: Wade, E. C. S., and Phillips, G. G., *Constitutional Law* (an outline of the law and practice of the constitution including administrative law, English local government, the constitutional relationships of the British Commonwealth and Empire and the Church of England, 3rd ed., 1946); Keir, D. L., and Lawson, F. H. *Cases in Constitutional Law* (3rd ed., 1948); Ridges, E. W., *Constitutional Law of England* (7th ed., revised by A. B. Keith, 1939).

For a study of English legal history the two finest works are Pollock, F., and Maitland, F. W., *A History of English Law before the Time of Edward I* (2 vols., 2nd ed., 1898. See the "List of Texts Used," vol. i, pp. xix–xxii); Holdsworth, W. S., *A History of English Law* (12 vols., 1903–38. There are several editions). The best brief volumes are Jenks, E., *A Short History of English Law* (5th ed., 1938) and Potter, H., *An Historical Introduction to English Law and Its Institutions* (1932). Other standard works are Maitland, F. W., and Montague, F. C., *A Sketch of English Legal History* (1915); Plucknett, T. F. T., *A Concise History of the Common Law* (4th ed., 1948); Carter, A. T., *History of English Legal Institutions* (7th ed., 1944); Radcliffe, G. R. Y., and Cross, G., *The English Legal System* (2nd ed., 1946); Jackson, R. M., *The Machinery of Justice in England* (1940, 1953); Russell, F. F., *Outline of Legal History* (1929). Meriting the attention and perusal of all students are Radin, Max, *A Handbook of Anglo-American Legal History* (1936) and the three volumes entitled *Select Essays in Anglo-American Legal History*, compiled and edited by a committee of the Association of American Law Schools (1907–09). See also Holdsworth, W. S., *The Historians of Anglo-American Law* (1928).

SOURCES. The best one-volume collection of constitutional documents, with a valuable bibliography and excellent notes, is Stephenson, Carl, and Marcham, F. G., *Sources of English Constitutional History* (1937). The essential documents of the medieval constitution are found in the famous *Select Charters* of Bishop Stubbs (10th ed., 1921). Standard and excellent are Lodge, Eleanor C., and Thornton, Gladys A., *English Constitutional Documents 1307–1485* (1935); Adams, G. B., and Stephens, A. M., *Select Documents of English Constitutional History* (1924); Robertson, C. G., *Select Statutes, Cases, and Documents to Illustrate English Constitutional History 1660–1832* (1935, with supplement covering the years 1832–1894); Violette, E. M., *English Constitutional Documents Since 1832* (1936); Dykes, D. O., *Source Book of Constitutional History from 1660* (1930). For the listing of collections embracing shorter periods or special topics see the appropriate chapter bibliographies below. See also Costin, W. C., and Watson, J. S., *The Law and Working of the Constitution: Documents 1660–1914* (2 vols., 1953).

In 1953 *English Historical Documents 1042–1189*, edited by Professor David C. Douglas and Mr. George W. Greenaway, was published by The Oxford University Press. This is the first volume of a large-scale series now being prepared under the general editorship of Professor Douglas. There will be thirteen volumes in the *English Historical Documents* and the period covered will be from 500 to 1776.

In the brief chapter bibliographies occasional reference has been made to a few of the published national and local records. For example, the Pipe Roll Society has edited and published portions of the series of Pipe Rolls—the rolls of the Exchequer which contain the statements of royal rents and profits and run in an almost unbroken stream from 1131 to 1833. From the early years of the thirteenth century come the Chancery series of the Charter, Close, and Patent Rolls. The student who wishes to see for himself how the medieval kings did some of their business will find references in the appropriate chapter bibliographies.

As the machinery of government becomes more diversified and elaborate several new kinds of records appear: journals and records of the houses of Parliament; more council and Chancery records; records of the Star Chamber and the Court of Admiralty; State Papers relating to colonial, foreign, and home affairs; the modern Department records.

Specific reference is made in the chapter bibliographies to some of the great Law books, such as those of Glanville, Bracton, Britton, Fleta, and Fortescue. The Year Books, the law reports of the Middle Ages, run in an almost steady stream from the reign of Edward I to the Tudors; the last Year Book appeared in 1536. To these Year Books a few references appear below, especially to some of the massive achievements in the Rolls Series editions and the Selden Society series begun by Professor F. W. Maitland.

For a clear and scholarly discussion of the origin and importance of the documents mentioned above the student may consult with profit Holdsworth, W. S., *Sources and Literature of English Law* (1925). Here he will also find excellent comments upon the Law Reports of the sixteenth and seventeenth centuries, the Abridgments, the rise of a regular series of Reports, discussions and bibliographical aids on Littleton, Coke, Selden, Hale, and Blackstone.

It has not been feasible to list more than a few of the sources published by H. M. Stationery Office, the Records Commission, etc. Students wishing to consult documents in the series of the Fine Rolls (extending from the reign of John to 1641), the Chancery Warrant series, the Curia Regis Rolls, and similar collections will usually find that the time span covered by the volumes is clearly indicated in library catalogs.

HISTORIES OF ENGLAND. The most complete and authoritative history is the *Oxford History of England* edited by G. N. Clark (14 vols., 1934–   ). Each volume contains an excellent critical bibliography. Several volumes are listed in chapter bibliographies below. For the medieval period the student may consult the appropriate sections of the *Cambridge Medieval History* (8 vols., 1911–1936). The best one-volume survey of English history is still Trevelyan, G. M., *History of England* (1936). Standard and useful are Feiling, K., *History of England* (1950); Lunt, W. E., *History of England* (rev. ed., 1945); Marcham, F. G., *History of England* (rev. ed., 1950) and Smith, Goldwin, *A History of England* (1949), published in the Scribner's Historical Series. Each of these volumes contains critical bibliographies.

SPECIAL STUDIES. The student may find the following of value and interest: Bulmer-Thomas, Ivor, *The Party System in Great Britain* (1953); Dowell, S., *A History of Taxation and Taxes in England* (4 vols., 2nd ed., 1898); Emden, C. S., *Principles of British Constitutional Law* (1925) and *The People and the Constitution* (1933); Howell, T. B., and T. J., *Complete Collection of State Trials* (1809–1828); Lapsley, G., "Some Recent Advances in English Constitutional History (before 1485)," *Cambridge Historical Journal* V, (1936), 119–61; Pike, L. O. A., *A Constitutional History of the House of Lords* (1894); Schramm, P., *The History of the English Coronation* (trans. L. G. Wickham Legg, 1937). Excellent and standard works on local government are the monumental *English Local Government* (6 vols., 1906–29) by Sidney and Beatrice Webb; Redlich, J., and Hirst, F. W., *Local Government in England* (2 vols., 1903); Jackson, W. E., *Local Government in England and Wales* (2nd ed., 1949). Excellent volumes on political theory are Carlyle, R. W., and Carlyle, A. J., *A History of Medieval Political Theory in the West* (6 vols., 1903–36); Gierke, Otto von, *Political Theories in the Middle Age* (trans. F. W. Maitland, 2nd ed., 1927); McIlwain, C. H., *The Growth of Political Thought in the West* (1937); Sabine, G. H., *History of Political Philosophy* (1937); Coker, Francis, *Recent Political Thought* (1934). See also Spahr, Margaret, *Readings in Recent Political Philosophy* (1935); the introductory notes to the sections of the text are excellent.

LEGAL PHILOSOPHY. Of constant and necessary value to all students of the laws of Great Britain and America are numerous works in jurisprudence and legal history. A few of the best one-volume studies are Carter, A. T., *Law: Its Origin, Growth, and Function* (1907); Gray, J. C., *The Nature and Sources of Law* (1921); Keeton, G. W., *The Elementary Principles of Jurisprudence* (1949); Paton, G. W., *A Textbook of Jurisprudence* (1946); Pollock, F., *A First Book of Jurisprudence* (6th ed., 1929); Zane, J. M., *The Story of Law* (1927).

More detailed and advanced works are Berolzheimer, Fritz, *The World's Legal Philosophies* (trans. R. S. Jastrow, 1912); Cardozo, Benjamin N., *Growth of the Law* (1924) and *Nature of the Judicial Process* (1921); see also Cardozo's essay "Our Lady of the Common Law" in *Selected Writings* (1947); Haines, C. G., *The Revival of Natural Law Concepts* (1930); this book contains admirable references to certain phases of American constitutional law; Holdsworth, W. S., *Some Lessons from Our Legal History* (1926) and *Some Makers of English Law* (1938); Holland, T. E., *The Elements of Jurisprudence* (10th ed., 1907); Krabbe, Hugo, *The Modern Idea of the State*, first published in 1915 and translated in 1922 with a brilliant introduction by Sabine, G. H., and Shepard, W. J.; Maitland, F. W., *Selected Essays* (1936); Pound, Roscoe, *The Spirit of the Common Law* (1921), *An Introduction to the Philosophy of Law* (1922), *Interpretations of Legal History* (1923), and *Law and Morals* (1926). Dean Pound, the pioneer in sociological jurisprudence, published many articles among which the following are especially important: "The End of Law as Developed in Legal Rules and Doctrines" and "The End of Law as Developed in Juristic Thought," 27 *Harvard Law Review;* "Theory of the Judicial Decision," 36 *Harvard Law Review;* "Schools of Jurisprudence," 24 *Harvard Law Review;* "Law and Its Limitations," 12 *Harvard Law Review;* "Mechanical Jurisprudence," 8 *Columbia Law Review*. See also Radin, Max, *Law as Logic and Experience* (1940); Sayre, Paul (ed.), *Interpretations of Modern Legal Philosophies: Essays in Honor of Roscoe Pound* (1947); Wigmore, J. H., *Problems of Law* (1920).

Students interested in the analytical school of jurisprudence may consult Austin, John, *Lectures on the Province of Jurisprudence Determined* (1832); Brown, W. J., *The Austinian Theory of Law* (1906). This book is an editing of Austin's *Lectures on Jurisprudence or the Philosophy of Positive Law* (1863) which is an expansion by Austin's widow of the book published by Austin in 1832 cited above. See also Cohen, M. R., "John Austin" in the *Encyclopedia of Social Sciences* (vol. ii, 1930) and *Law and Reason* (1950); Willoughby, W. W., *An Examination of the Nature of the State* (1896) and "The Juristic Theories of Krabbe," *Am. Pol. Sci. Rev.*, August, 1926.

The major conclusions of the historical school of jurisprudence are stated in Maine, Sir Henry Sumner, *Dissertations on Early Law and Custom* (1883); *Lectures on the Early History of Institutions* (1888. See especially Lecture XII, "Sovereignty"); Savigny, Friedrich Karl von, *On the Vocation of Our Age for Legislation and Jurisprudence* (1814); Holmes, O. W., "The Path of the Law" in *Collected Legal Papers* (1920); Allen, C. K., *Law in the Making* (1939). See also Essay VIII in vol. ii of Sir Paul Vinogradoff's *Collected Papers* (1928).

The philosophical jurists are discussed in several of the volumes mentioned earlier. In addition, see Stammler, Rudolf, *The Theory of Justice* (1902, translated in 1925 by Isaac Husik); Dickinson, John, "The Law Behind the Law," 29 *Columbia Law Review;* Duguit, Léon, *The Transformation of the Theory of the State* (1913, translated in 1919 by Frida and Harold Laski under the title *Law in the Modern State*). See also Duguit's "Law and the State," 31 *Harvard Law Review* and his *Treatise on Constitutional Law* (1911); Brown, J. W., "The Jurisprudence of M. Duguit," *Law Quarterly Review* XXXII, (1916).

In recent years much has been written in the sociological school of jurisprudence. In addition to the works mentioned earlier, especially the books and articles of Dean Roscoe Pound, see Frank, Jerome, *Law and the Modern Mind* (1930), especially pp. 3–31, 207–216; Robinson, E. S., *Law and the Lawyers* (1935); Radin, Max, "Legal Realism," 31 *Columbia Law Review;* Arnold, T., *The Symbols of Government* (1935); Pound, Roscoe, "The Scope and Purpose of Sociological Jurisprudence," vols. 24 and 25 *Harvard Law Review*.

CHAPTER I: THE ANGLO-SAXONS: KINGS AND MEN

For this and the following chapter consult these standard works: Stenton, F. M., *Anglo-Saxon England*, vol. ii in the *Oxford History of England* (1943); Hodgkin, R. H., *A History of the Anglo-Saxons* (2 vols., 1939); Maitland, F. W., *Domesday Book and Beyond* (1897); Chadwick, H. M., *Studies in Anglo-Saxon Institutions* (1905).

Other valuable studies are: Cam, H. M., *Local Government in Francia and England* (1912); Corbett, W. J., "The Tribal Hidage," *Trans. Royal Hist. Soc.*, new series, XIV; Jolliffe, J. E. A., *Pre-Feudal England: the Jutes* (1932); Harmer, F. E. (ed.), *Anglo-Saxon Writs* (1952; Miss Harmer published 120 writs and stated for each of them the evidence for regarding it as genuine or spurious. After the Confessor's death, Westminster Abbey was "a factory of forgeries"); Larson, L. M., *The King's Household in England before the Norman Conquest* (1904); Liebermann, F., *The National Assembly in the Anglo-Saxon Period* (1913); Morris, W. A., *The Medieval English Sheriff to 1300* (1927) and "The Office of the Sheriff in the Anglo-Saxon Period," *E. H. R.* XXXI (1916); Stenton, F. M., *Types of Manorial Structure in the Northern Danelaw*, Oxford Studies in Social and Legal History II (1910) and "The Supremacy of the Mercian Kings," *E. H. R.* XXXIII (1918); Vinogradoff, Paul, *Growth of the Manor* (1905).

CHAPTER II: THE ANGLO-SAXONS: LAND AND LAW

The following are of special value for this chapter: Attenborough, F. L., *The Laws of the Earliest English Kings* (1922) and a companion volume by Robertson, Agnes J., *The Laws of the Kings of England from Edmund to Henry I* (1925); Howland, Arthur C., *Ordeals, Compurgation, Excommunication, and Interdict* (1898); Liebermann, F., *Gesetze der Angelsachsen* (3 vols., 1898–1916); Morris, W. A., *The Early English County Court* (1926) and *The Frankpledge System* (1910); Seebohm, F., *Tribal Custom in Anglo-Saxon Law* (1902) and *The English Village Community* (1903); Turner, G. J., "Bookland and Folkland" in *Historical Essays in Honour of James Tait* edited by J. G. Edwards, V. H. Galbraith and E. F. Jacob (1933).

The growth and nature of the borough has been a subject of profound scholarship and prolonged controversy. Many local records have been published. For the convenience of the reader the main references to boroughs and charters have been listed here and appropriate cross-references made in later chapter bibliographies. Everyone interested in the growth of English towns will profit by reading the following:

Stephenson, Carl, *Borough and Town* (1933); Professor Stephenson brings his study of the boroughs down to the beginning of the thirteenth century; Tait, James, *Medieval English Boroughs* (1936); Professor Tait's conclusions are frequently in marked opposition to those of Professor Stephenson; Maitland, F. W., *Township and Borough* (1898) and "The Origin of the Borough," *E. H. R.*, XI (1896). See also Darlington, Reginald R., "The Early History of English Towns," *History*, XXIII (1938).

A large volume of published records include: Cronne, H. M. (ed.), *Bristol Charters 1378–1499*, Bristol Records Society, vol. XI (1946); Markham, C. A. (ed.), *The Records of the Borough of Northampton* (2 vols., 1898); Bateson, M. (ed.), *Borough Customs* (Selden Society, 2 vols., XVIII, XXI, 1904–1906); Bateson, M., and Stocks, H. (eds.), *Records of the Borough of Leicester 1103–1603* (4 vols., 1899–

1923); The Corporation of Nottingham, *Records of the Borough of Nottingham 1155–1835* (8 vols., 1882–1952); Harding, N. D. (ed.), *Bristol Charters 1155–1373,* Bristol Records Society, vol. I (1930); Ballard, A., *Domesday Boroughs* (1904) and (ed.) *British Borough Charters 1042–1216* (1913); Ballard, A., and Tait, J. (eds.), *British Borough Charters 1216–1307* (1923); Weinbaum, M. (ed.), *British Borough Charters 1307–1660* (1943). See also Douglas, David C., and Greenaway, George W., *English Historical Documents 1042–1189* (1953), Part IV, Section D.

CHAPTER III: THE NORMANS: PEACE BY POWER

Students will find that several of the works cited here will help them to understand many aspects of the whole medieval period. The following is a selected list of outstanding books and articles.

Of primary importance for background reading are these: Davis, H. W. C., *England under the Normans and Angevins* (1909); Haskins, C. H., *Norman Institutions* (1918); Painter, Sidney, *The Rise of the Feudal Monarchies* (1951); Poole, A. L., *From Domesday Book to Magna Carta, 1087–1216,* vol. iii in the *Oxford History of England* (1951); Stenton, F. M., *The First Century of English Feudalism 1066–1166* (1932); Petit-Dutaillis, C., *The Feudal Monarchy in France and England from the 10th to the 13th Century* (English translation, 1936); Stephenson, Carl, *Medieval Feudalism* (1942). This excellent little book by Professor Stephenson is in the Berkshire studies; students will find the bibliography of particular value. Pollock, F., and Maitland, F. W., *A History of English Law,* cited above, contains a useful chapter on "Norman Law" (vol. i, chap. iii). See also the chapters on feudalism in Thompson, J. W., *The Middle Ages* (1932) and Painter, S., *French Chivalry* (1940). See further Adams, G. B., *Councils and Courts in Anglo Norman England* (1936); Stephens, W. R., *The English Church from the Norman Conquest to the Accession of Edward I* (1901); Baldwin, J. F., *The King's Council in England during the Middle Ages* (1913), "Beginning of the King's Council," *Trans. Royal Hist. Soc.* XIX (1905), "Early Records of the King's Council," *A. H. R.* XI (1915) and "Antiquities of the King's Council," *E. H. R.* XXI (1906); Round, J. H., *Feudal England* (1895); Vinogradoff, Paul, *Villeinage in England* (1892) and *English Society in the Eleventh Century* (1908).

More specialized modern scholarship has produced many works meriting examination and study. Among the most valuable are Adams, G. B., "Local King's Courts in the Reign of William I," *Yale Law Journal* XXIII (1914), "Private Jurisdiction in England," *A. H. R.* XXIII (1918); Brooke, Z. N., "Pope Gregory VII's Demand for Fealty from William the Conqueror," *E. H. R.* XXVII (1911); Chew, Miss H. M., "Ecclesiastical Tenants in Chief and Writs of Military Summons," *E. H. R.* XLI (1920); Galbraith, V. H., "The Making of Domesday Book," *E. H. R.* LVII (1941); Hoyt, R. S., *The Royal Demesne in English Constitutional History, 1066–1272* (1951); Jeudwine, L. W., *Tort, Crime and Police in Medieval England* (1927); Morris, W. A., "The Office of the Sheriff in the Early Norman Period," *E. H. R.* XXXIII (1918). See also Neilson, Nellie, *Medieval Agrarian Economy.* This little book in the Berkshire series is probably the best account of the manorial system available in English. See further Noyes, A. H., *The Military Obligation in Medieval England* (1930); Painter, S., "Studies in the History of the English Feudal Barony" in the Johns Hopkins University Studies in Historical and Political Science LXI, pp. 337–558 (1943); Stephenson, Carl, "Commendation and Related Problems in Domesday," *E. H. R.* LIX (1944) and "Feudalism and Its Antecedents in England," *A. H. R.* XLVIII (1943). See also Turner, G. J. (ed.), *Select Pleas of the Forest,* Selden Society, XIII (1899).

CHAPTER IV: ENTERPRISE AND DECAY

For this and the following chapters in the medieval period see Chrimes, S. B., *An Introduction to the Administrative History of Mediaeval England* (1952); Norgate, K., *England Under the Angevin Kings* (1908); Sayles, G. O., *The Medieval Foundations of England* (1948); Kern, F., *Kingship and Law in the Middle Ages* (trans. S. B. Chrimes, 1939). Other valuable studies include Haskins, C. H., "The Abacus and the King's Curia," *E. H. R.* XXVII (1912); Lapsley, G. T., *The County Palatine of Durham* (1900); Lunt, W. E., *Financial Relations of the Papacy with England to 1327* (1937); Richardson, H. G., "The English Coronation Oath," *Trans. Royal Hist. Society*, XXIII (1941); Steel, Anthony, "The Place of the King's Household in English Constitutional History," *History*, XV, January, 1931; *Historical Essays in Honour of James Tait*, ed. by J. C. Edwards, V. H. Galbraith, and E. F. Jacob (1933), mentioned earlier.

CHAPTER V: HENRY II: THE MAKING OF ORDER

See Stenton, D. M., "England: King Henry II" in *Cambridge Medieval History*, vol. vii, chap. xvii; Eyton, R. W., *Court Household and Itinerary of King Henry II* (1878); Hughes, A., Crump, C. G., and Johnson, C. (eds.), *Richard Fitznigel's Dialogue on the Exchequer* (1902); Poole, R. L., *The Exchequer in the Twelfth Century* (1912); Woodbine, C. E. (ed.), *Ranulf de Glanville's Treatise on the Laws and Customs of England* (1932).

F. W. Maitland's *Roman Canon Law in the Church of England* (1898) contains an excellent chapter (Chapter IV) on "criminous clerks." See also the essays of Gabriel Le Bras on the canon law and Sir Paul Vinogradoff on customary law in *The Legacy of the Middle Ages*, ed. by C. G. Crump and E. F. Jacob (1926). See further Brooke, Z. N., "The Effect of Becket's Murder on Papal Authority in England," *Cambridge Historical Journal* II, No. 3 (1928).

Students who have the time and opportunity would do well to become acquainted with some of the numerous publications of the Pipe Roll Society. For example, see *Pipe Roll of 31 Henry I*, Record Commission, London, 1833, reprinted by the Pipe Roll Society in 1929; *Pipe Roll of 33 Henry II*, Pipe Roll Society, vol. XXXVII (1915); see also Maitland, F. W. (ed.), *Three Rolls of the King's Court 1194–1195*, Pipe Roll Society, vol. XIV (1891). For examples of other financial documents referred to in the General Bibliography, see some of the volumes in the *Calendar of Treasury Books*, Rolls Series (1904–   ); the *Calendar of the Patent Rolls*, Rolls Series (1891–   ) and the published Charter Rolls and Close Rolls. The Close Rolls begin in John's reign. For example, see *The Close Rolls of the Reign of Henry III*, Rolls Series (1902–   ). See also Lady Stenton's "The Pipe Rolls and the Historians 1600–1883," *Cambridge Historical Journal*, X, No. 3, 1952.

CHAPTER VI: HENRY II: THE MAKING OF LAW

See Keeney, B. C., *Judgment by Peers* (1949); McIlwain, C. H., "The English Common Law, Barrier Against Absolutism," *A. H. R.* October, 1943 and "Our Heritage from the Laws of Rome," *Foreign Affairs*, April, 1941. See further Goodhart, A. L., "Precedent in English and Continental Law," *Law Quarterly Review*, January, 1934; Neilson, Nellie, "Custom and Common Law in Kent," *Harvard Law Review*, XXXVIII (1925) and "The Early Pattern of the Common Law," *A. H. R.* XLIX (1944).

A number of assize rolls and similar documents have been printed by county records societies. For instance, the Lincoln Record Society has published several courts of common pleas records for the twelfth and thirteenth centuries. See also Stenton, D. M., *Earliest Lincolnshire Assize Rolls 1202–1204*, Lincoln Records Society, vol. 22 (1926). Students may also wish to examine such volumes as Jenkinson, H., and Formoy, B. E. R. (eds.), *Select Cases in the Exchequer of Pleas*, Selden Society, vol. XLVIII (1932); Maitland, F. W. (ed.), *Select Pleas of the Crown 1200–1225*, Selden Society, vol. I (1888); Maitland, F. W., and Baildon, W. P. (eds.), *The Court Baron* (1891). Several rolls for the king's courts in addition to the references given here have been printed for the reigns of Richard and John. See also the four volumes of Curia Regis Rolls published by the Record Commission and edited by C. T. Flower (1922–29).

A number of reports of the courts of quarter sessions of the peace have also been published for Cheshire, Derbyshire, Hertford, Lancashire, Lincoln, Northampton, Somerset, Staffordshire, Worcester, etc. See, for example, the accounts of quarter sessions published by the Lincoln Records Society (vol. 30) for the period 1360–1375 (1937) and the *Worcestershire Quarter Sessions Papers* published in Worcestershire County Records, Division I, vol. I (1900).

A few feet of fine records have been published, such as the *Abstract of Feet of Fines Relating to the County of Sussex* compiled by L. F. Salzman, Sussex Record Society, vols. ii, vii, xxiii (1903–1916); the *Feet of Fines for Oxfordshire 1195–1291*, transcribed by H. E. Salter, Oxfordshire Records Society (1930). Since 1912 the Devon and Cornwall Record Society has been publishing feet of fine records for those two counties.

Readers interested in borough developments in the twelfth century will find suggestions for further reading in the works cited in the bibliography for Chapter II.

CHAPTER VII: MAGNA CARTA AND BEYOND

Outstanding are the two superb volumes by Professor Faith Thompson: *The First Century of Magna Carta: Why It Persisted as a Document* (1925) and *Magna Carta, Its Role in the Making of the English Constitution, 1300–1629* (1948). Students will also find of value the classic McKecknie, W. S., *Magna Carta, A Commentary on the Great Charter of King John* (2nd. rev. ed., 1914). See also Bémont, C., *Magna Carta* (trans. by E. F. Jacob, 1930); Malden, H. E. (ed.), *Magna Carta Commemoration Essays* (Royal Historical Society, 1917); in this volume of essays see especially C. H. McIlwain's "Magna Carta and the Common Law" which discusses what was understood by the common law in the 13th and 14th centuries. Other books of authority and interest are Baldwin, J. F., *The Scutage and Knight Service in England* (1897); Norgate, K., *John Lackland* (1907); Painter, S., *The Reign of King John* (1949); Powicke, F. M., *The Loss of Normandy* (1913) and *Stephen Langton* (1928).

Articles of outstanding merit are Painter, S., "Magna Carta" in *A. H. R.* LIII, No. 1 (1947); Fox, J. C., "The Originals of the Great Charter of 1215," *E. H. R.* XXXIX (1924); Denholm-Young, N., "Feudal Service in the Thirteenth Century," *History* XXIX (1944); White, A. B., "Magna Carta" in the *Encyclopaedia of the Social Sciences*, vol. x; Powicke, F. M., "England: Richard I and John" in *Cambridge Medieval History*, vol. vi, chap. vii.

For this and following chapters the student will find of special value Painter, S., *Studies in the History of the English Feudal Barony* (1943); Mitchell, S. K., *Studies in Taxation under John and Henry III* (1914) and *Taxation in Medieval*

England (edited in 1951 by Professor Sidney Painter). In the latter book Professor Mitchell showed in detail the nature of the taxes levied in medieval England and the effect of the taxation system on the development of the constitution and the administrative machinery. See also Powicke, Sir Maurice, *The Thirteenth Century 1216–1307*, vol. iv in the *Oxford History of England* (1953).

CHAPTER VIII: THE RISE OF PARLIAMENT

The following are standard books about the origin and growth of Parliament: McIlwain, C. H., *The High Court of Parliament and Its Supremacy* (1910); Pollard, A. F., *The Evolution of Parliament* (2nd ed., 1926); Thompson, Faith, *A Short History of Parliament, 1295–1642* (1953); White, A. B., *Self-Government at the King's Command* (1933); Haskins, G. L., *The Growth of English Representative Government* (1948); Pasquet, D., *Essay on the Origins of the English House of Commons,* trans. by R. G. D. Laffan, with preface and additional notes by G. T. Lapsley (1925). On the origins of Parliament see also H. M. Cam's brief note in the *Bulletin of the International Committee of Historical Sciences* IX (1937) and the comments of Professor Carl Stephenson in *E. H. R.* LIII (1938). For a bibliography of earlier books and articles about the development of representative assemblies see the *Cambridge Medieval History,* vol. vii, 948–956.

The following are authoritative and excellent articles: Baldwin, J. F., "The King's Council from Edward I to Edward III," *E. H. R.* XXII (1907); Cam, H. M., "From Witness of the Shire to Full Parliament," *Trans. Royal Hist. Society,* 4th series, XXVI (1933); Chew, H. M., "Scutage under Edward I," *E. H. R.* XXXVII (1922); Denholm-Young, N., "Documents of the Barons' Wars," *E. H. R.* XLVIII (October, 1933); Edwards, J. G., "Confirmatio Cartarum and Baronial Grievances," *E. H. R.* LVIII (1943) and "Personnel of the Commons in the Parliaments of Edward I and Edward II" in *Essays in Medieval History Presented to T. F. Tout* (1925) and "The Plena Potestas of the English Parliamentary Representatives" in *Oxford Essays in Medieval History Presented to H. E. Salter* (1934); Haskins, G. L., "The Petitions of Representatives in the Parliaments of Edward I," *E. H. R.* LIII (1938) and "Parliament in the Later Middle Ages," *A. H. R.* LIII (1947); Jacob, E. F., "What Were the 'Provisions of Oxford'?" *History* IX (1934); and "The Complaints of Henry III Against the Baronial Council in 1261," *E. H. R.* XLI (1926); and "The Reign of Henry III; Some Suggestions," *Trans. Royal Hist. Society,* 4th series, X (1927); Johnstone, H., "England: Edward I and Edward II," chapter xiv in *Cambridge Medieval History,* vol. vii; McIlwain, C. H., "Medieval Estates," chapter xxiii in *Cambridge Medieval History,* vol. vii; Powicke, F. M., "Some Observations on the Baronial Council (1258–60) and the Provisions of Westminster" in *Essays in Medieval History Presented to T. F. Tout,* edited by A. G. Little and F. M. Powicke (1925) and "The Chancery During the Minority of Henry III," *E. H. R.* XXIII (1908); Raskell, J. S., "The Medieval Speakers for the Commons in Parliament," *Bulletin Inst. Hist. Research,* XXVII (May, 1950); Richardson, H. G., "The Origins of Parliament," *Trans. Royal Hist. Society,* 4th series, XI (1928); Richardson, H. G., and Sayles, G. O., "The King's Ministers in Parliament, 1272–1377," *E. H. R.* XLVI, XLVII (1931, 1932) and "The Early Records of the English Parliaments," *Bulletin Inst. Hist. Research* V (1928) and VI (1929); Stephenson, Carl, "The Beginnings of Representative Government in England" in *The Constitution Reconsidered* edited by Conyers Read (1938) and "Taxation and Representation in the Middle Ages" in *Haskins Anniversary Essays* (1929); Templeman, Geoffrey, "The History of Parliament to 1400 in the Light of Modern Research," *University of Birmingham Historical Journal,*

I (1940), reprinted in *The Making of English History*, edited by R. L. Schuyler and H. Ausubel (1952); Treharne, R. F., "The Significance of the Baronial Reform Movement 1258–1259," *Trans. Royal Hist. Society*, 4th series, XXV (1943) and "The Knights in the Period of Reform and Rebellion 1258–1267," *Bulletin Inst. Hist. Research*, XXIII (May and November, 1946) and "The Personal Rule of Henry III and the Aims of the Baronial Reformers of 1258," *History* XVI (January, 1932); Turner, H. G., "The Minority of Henry III," *Trans. Royal Hist. Society*, 4th series, XVIII (1935); White, A. B., "Some Early Instances of Concentration of Representatives in England," *A. H. R.* XIX (1914) and "The First Concentration of Juries," *A. H. R.* XVII (1911) and "Was There a Common Council Before Parliament?" *A. H. R.* XXV (1919).

Valuable special studies include Barker, E., *The Dominican Order and Convocation* (1913); Bémont, C., *Simon de Montfort* (trans. by E. F. Jacob, 1930); Ehrlich, L., *Proceedings Against the Crown 1216–1377*, Oxford Studies in Social and Legal History VI (1921); Gibbs, M., and Lang, J., *Bishops and Reform 1215–1272* (1934); Hennings, M. A., *England Under Henry III* (1924); Jacob, E. F., *Studies in the Period of Baronial Reform and Rebellion 1258–67*, Oxford Studies in Social and Legal History VIII (1925); Maitland, F. W. (ed.), *Memoranda de Parliamento*, the records of the Parliament held at Westminster in 1305, Rolls Series (1893); Norgate, K., *The Minority of Henry III* (1912); Painter, S., *William Marshal* (1933); Powicke, F. M., *King Henry III and the Lord Edward: the Community of the Realm in the Thirteenth Century* (2 vols., 1947); Templeman, G., *The Sheriffs of Warwickshire in the Thirteenth Century* (1948); Treharne, R. F., *The Baronial Plan of Reform 1258–63* (1932).

For this and following chapters see Cam, H. M., *Studies in the Hundred Rolls*, Oxford Studies in Social and Legal History V (1920); in this book Miss Cam discusses some aspects of thirteenth century local administration and the famous inquests of 1274–75. Her *The Hundred and the Hundred Rolls* (1930) presents an admirable outline of local government in thirteenth century England with some translations of documents. In *The Legislators of Medieval England* (the Raleigh Lecture on History, British Academy, 1946) Miss Cam described and discussed the relations between law and opinion in medieval England. See also M. V. Clarke, *Medieval Representation and Consent* (1936) and R. W. Hunt, W. A. Pantin, and R. W. Southern (eds.), *Studies in Medieval History Presented to Frederick Maurice Powicke* (1948). In this volume the student will find a complete bibliography of Professor Powicke's publications to 1948 (p. 469). See further Lapsley, G. T., *Crown, Community, and Parliament in the Later Middle Ages*, ed. by H. M. Cam and G. Barraclough (1951); McKisack, Mary, *The Parliamentary Representation of English Boroughs during the Middle Ages* (1932); Riess, Ludwig, *The History of the English Electoral Law in the Middle Ages*, trans. by K. L. Wood-Legh in 1940, first published in German in 1885. Riess took the singular view that Edward I called knights and burgesses mainly to offset the control of the sheriff in local government. In the latter chapters of *The Medieval Foundations of England* (1948) Professor G. O. Sayles treats with skill and clarity the more recent conclusions and interpretations of modern scholars about several phases of the history of Parliament before 1300. Reference to this excellent volume was also made in the bibliography for Chapter IV.

CHAPTER IX: EDWARD I: LAW AND CONSTITUTION

Of special value for this period and chapter are Jenks, E., *Edward Plantagenet*, a book stressing Edward's legal reforms (1902); Tout, T. F., *Edward I* (rev. ed. 1909). See also Holdsworth, W. S., *An Historical Introduction to the Land Law* (1927); Pollock, Sir Frederick, *The Land Laws*, a volume that places particular emphasis upon the changes following Edward I's reign (3rd ed. 1896).

Documents of importance for this and other chapters are Dunham, W. H. (ed.), *Casus Placitorum and Reports of Cases in the King's Courts 1272–1278*, Selden Society, vol. LXIX (1952); Gross, G., *Select Cases from Coroners' Rolls 1270–1638*, Selden Society, vol. IX (1896); Horwood, A. J., and Pike, L. O. (eds.), *Year Books of the Reign of Edward I* (Rolls Series, 1863–79); Illingworth, W. (ed.), *Placita Quo Warranto* (Record Commission, 1818); Leadam, I. S., and Baldwin, J. F. (eds.), *Select Cases before the King's Council 1243–1482*, Selden Society, vol. XXXII (1918); Maitland, F. W. (ed.), *Select Pleas in Manorial and Other Seignioral Courts*, Selden Society, 2 vols. (1888–89); vol. i is for the reigns of Henry III and Edward I; Palgrave, Sir Francis (ed.), *Parliamentary Writs and Writs of Military Summons* (Record Commission, 2 vols., 1818); Sayles, G. O., *Select Cases in the Court of King's Bench under Edward I*, Selden Society, 3 vols. (1936–39); vol. LV (1936) covers the reign of Edward I; Stubbs, W. (ed.), *Chronicles of the Reigns of Edward I to Edward II* (Rolls Series, 2 vols., 1882). Information about the law tracts of Edward I's reign can be found in Holdsworth, W. S., *History of English Law*, vol. ii, pp. 319–336. See also the appropriate volumes listed under *General Works* earlier in this bibliography.

CHAPTER X: BARONS, COURTS, AND PARLIAMENTS

Useful for this chapter are Davies, J. C., *The Baronial Opposition to Edward II* (1918); Haskins, G. L., *The Statute of York and the Interest of the Commons* (1935); Hughes, Dorothy, *A Study of Social and Constitutional Tendencies in the Early Years of Edward III* (1915); Plucknett, T. F. T., *Statutes and Their Interpretation in the First Half of the Fourteenth Century*, Cambridge Studies in English Legal History (1922); Putnam, Bertha H., *The Enforcement of the Statute of Laborers during the First Decade After the Black Death 1349–1359* (1908); *Early Treatises on the Practices of the Justices of the Peace* (1924) and *The Place in Legal History of Sir William Shareshull, Chief Justice of the Court of King's Bench 1350–1361: a Study of Judicial and Administrative Methods in the Reign of Edward III* (1950); Steel, Anthony, *Richard II* (1941); Tout, T. F., and Johnstone, H., *The Place of the Reign of Edward II in English History* (1941); Wilkinson, B., *The Chancery Under Edward III* (1929) and *Studies in the Constitutional History of the Thirteenth and Fourteenth Centuries* (2nd ed. 1952); Willard, J. F., *Parliamentary Taxes on Personal Property 1290–1334*, Monograph No. 19 of the Medieval Academy of America (1934); Willard, J. F., Morris, W. A., and Dunham, W. H. (eds.), *The English Government at Work 1327–1336*, Publications Nos. 37, 48, 56 of the Medieval Academy of America (1930–1950). Volume I of this work is entitled *Central and Prerogative Administration*, Volume II *Fiscal Administration*, and Volume III *Local Administration and Justice*.

See further Maitland, F. W., *Bracton's Notebook* (1887); Woodbine, G. E. (ed.), *Bracton: De Legibus et Consuetudinibus Angliae* (4 vols., 1915–1942). The acute and scholarly work of Professor Woodbine replaces the inadequate edition of

Bracton prepared by Sir Travers Twiss (6 vols., 1878–83, Rolls Series). See also O. W. Holmes' speech on Bracton (1915) in *Collected Legal Papers* (1920) and Professor Woodbine's *Four Fourteenth Century Law Tracts* (1910).

For this and the immediately following chapter the student will find of interest and value Gray, H. L., *The Influence of the Commons on Early Legislation*, Harvard Historical Studies XXXIV (1932); this book is an essential work on the Parliamentary history of the fourteenth and fifteenth centuries. See also Cam, H. M., *Liberties and Communities in Medieval England: Collected Studies in Local Administration and Topography* (1944).

Useful articles include the following: Baldwin, J. F., "The Privy Council of the Time of Richard II," *A. H. R.* XII (1906); Clarke, M. V., "Committees of Estates and the Deposition of Edward II" in *Historical Essays in Honour of James Tait* (1933) and "The Origin of Impeachment" in *Oxford Essays in Medieval History Presented to H. E. Salter* (1934) and (with V. H. Galbraith) "The Deposition of Richard II," *Bulletin of the John Rylands Library XIV;* Graves, E. P., "Legal Significance of the Statute of Praemunire of 1353" in *Anniversary Essays in Medieval History by Students of Charles Homer Haskins* (1929); Johnson, C., "The Exchequer Chamber under Edward II," *E. H. R.* XXI (1906); Lapsley, G. T., "The Commons and the Statute of York," *E. H. R.* XXVII (1913), "Knights of the Shire in the Parliaments of Edward II," *E. H. R.* XXXIV (1919), "Archbishop Stratford and the Parliamentary Crisis of 1341," *E. H. R.* XXX (1915), and "The Parliamentary Title of Henry IV," *E. H. R.* XLIX (1934); Manning, B. L., "England: Edward III and Richard II," in *Cambridge Medieval History,* vol. vii, chap. xv; Pollard, A. F., "Receivers of Petitions and Clerks of Parliament," *E. H. R.* LVI (1941); Richardson, H. G., and Sayles, G. O., "Parliaments of Edward III," *Bulletin Institute Historical Research,* VIII and IX (1931–1932); Waugh, W. T., "The Great Statute of Praemunire," *E. H. R.* XXXVII (1922); Wilkinson, B., "The Coronation Oath of Edward II," in *Historical Essays in Honour of James Tait,* cited earlier. For this and later chapters see Cam, H. M., "The Decline and Fall of English Feudalism," *History* XXV (1940); Galbraith, V. H., "Good Kings and Bad Kings in Medieval English History," *History,* XXX (1945); and Richardson, H. G., "The Commons and Medieval Politics," *Trans. Royal Hist. Soc.,* 4th series, XXVIII (1946).

Studies and documents of special interest are Bolland, W. C. (ed.), *Select Bills in Eyre 1292–1333,* Selden Society (1914); the *Calendars* of the Patent and Close Rolls for the reigns of Edward I, II, and III (*Calendar of State Papers,* 1891–1906) and see the bibliography for Chapter V above; Edwards, Kathleen, *The English Secular Cathedrals in the Middle Ages: a Constitutional Study with Special Reference to the Fourteenth Century* (1949), a study of the nine cathedrals served not by monastic bodies but by seculars—"the Old Foundation"; Hemmant, M. (ed.), *Select Cases in Exchequer Chamber before all the Justices of England 1377–1461,* Selden Society (1933); Maitland, F. W. (ed.), *Eyre of Kent 6 and 7 Edward II,* Rolls Series (1910); Putnam, Miss Bertha H. (ed.), *Proceedings before the Justices of the Peace in the Fourteenth and Fifteenth Centuries, Edward III to Richard III* (2 vols., 1938); Maitland, F. W., et al. (eds.), *Year Books of Edward II* (1903–1934) and Pike, L. O. (ed.), *Year Books of Edward III* (1883–1911); the Year Books of Richard II have been published by the Ames Foundation (1914, 1929, 1937).

For the early history of Chancery see in particular: Goodwin, E. H., *The Equity of the King's Court Before the Reign of Edward I* (1912); Maitland, F. M., *Equity* (ed. by A. H. Chaytor and W. S. Whittaker, 1909); Adams, G. B., "The Origin of English Equity," *Columbia Law Review* XVI (1916). See also the bibliography for Chapter V. The student who wishes to read beyond the general descriptions of

Chancery developments may profitably consult a few of the many volumes published by various English historical societies. See, for example, Baildon, W. P. (ed.), *Select Cases in Chancery 1364–1471*, Selden Society, vol. X (1896); Salzman, L. F. (ed.), *A Calendar of Post Mortem Inquisitions Relating to the County of Sussex 1 to 25 Elizabeth*, Sussex Record Society, vol. III (1904); Vol. XIV (1912) covers the period 1485–1649; see also vol. XXXIII. See further *Index of Persons named in Early Chancery Proceedings Richard II (1385) to Edward IV (1467)*, Harleian Society Publications, vols. LXXVIII and LXXIX (1927–1928). See also the reports for Yorkshire covering the reigns of Henry III and Edward I in the courts of Chancery and of Wards and Liveries in the Yorkshire Record Society Series, vols. XII, XIII, XXXI, XXXVII. Reports for the reigns of Henry IV and V are in vol. LIX of this series (1918); those for the reigns of James I and Charles I are in vol. I (1885).

Other valuable works about this period include Poole, A. L., *Obligations of Society in the XII and XIII Centuries* (1946) and Professor N. Denholm-Young's essay "Feudal Society in the 13th Century: the Knights" in his *Collected Papers on Medieval Subjects* (1946). These references are obviously of value for later chapters. Likewise of importance for a broad time period are such technical studies as Murray, K. M. E., *Constitutional History of the Cinque Ports* (1935) and Cuttino, G. P., *English Diplomatic Administration 1259–1339* in the Oxford Historical Series (1940). Each of these works is an example of specialized scholarship at its best.

CHAPTER XI: THE FIFTEENTH CENTURY: PRECEDENT AND PRIVILEGE

The following is a brief list of useful books: Chrimes, S. B., *English Constitutional Ideas in the Fifteenth Century* (1936) and Fortescue's *De Laudibus Legum Angliae*, translated and edited by Dr. Chrimes (1942); Hastings, Margaret, *The Court of Common Pleas in Fifteenth Century England: A Study of Legal Administration and Procedure* (1947); Kingsford, C. L., *Henry V* (1911) and *Prejudice and Promise in Fifteenth Century England* (1935); Myers, A. R., *England in the Later Middle Ages* (1952); Otway-Ruthven, J., *The King's Secretary and the Signet Office in the XVth Century* (1939); Plummer, Charles (ed.), *Fortescue's The Governance of England* (1885); Scofield, Miss Cora L., *The Life and Reign of Edward IV* (1923); Wedgwood, J. C., *History of Parliament, Register of the Ministers and of the Members of Both Houses, 1439–1509* (1938).

Outstanding articles include Cam, H. M., "Representative Institutions in England and Europe in the Fifteenth Century in Relation to Later Developments," in *Liberalism as a Force in History: Lectures on Aspects of the Liberal Tradition*, ed. Chester McA. Destler (1953); Chrimes, S. B., "Sir John Fortescue and His Theory of Dominion," *Trans. Royal Hist. Soc.*, IVth series, XVII (1934); Plucknett, T. F. T., "The Place of the Council in the Fifteenth Century," *Trans. Royal Hist. Soc.*, IVth series, I (1918) and also by Plucknett, "The Lancastrian Constitution" in *Tudor Studies*, presented to A. F. Pollard and edited by R. W. Seton-Watson (1924) and "The Place of the Legal Profession in the History of English Law," *Law Quarterly Review*, XLVIII (1932); Thrupp, Sylvia L., "The Problem of Conservatism in Fifteenth Century England," *Speculum*, XVIII (1943). On the subject of the legal history see the appropriate sections of the volumes to which reference is made in the division of this bibliography headed *General Works*.

CHAPTER XII: THE EARLY TUDORS: A NEW IMPERIUM

Information about the early Tudors may be found in Mackie, J. D., *The Earlier Tudors, 1485–1558* (1952), vol. vii in the *Oxford History of England*. See also such books as Allen, J. W., *History of Political Thought in the Sixteenth Century* (1928); Baumer, Franklin Le Van, *The Early Tudor Theory of Kingship* (1940); Leadam, I. S. (ed.), *Select Cases in the Court of Requests 1497–1569*, Selden Society (1898), and *Select Cases before the King's Council in Star Chamber 1477–1544*, Selden Society (2 vols., 1903, 1910) also edited by I. S. Leadam with an excellent introduction describing the composition, jurisdiction and procedure of the Star Chamber; Scofield, Miss Cora L., *A Study of the Court of Star Chamber* (1900). Excellent illustrations of the Star Chamber in action may also be found in *Abstracts of Star Chamber Proceedings Relating to the County of Sussex Henry VII to Philip and Mary*, Sussex Records Society, vol. XVI (1913) and *Yorkshire Star Chamber Proceedings*, Yorkshire Records Society (5 vols., 1909–1914). See also Richardson, W. C., *Tudor Chamber Administration 1485–1547* (1952). This is a brilliant study of the extension of conciliar control in the realm of crown revenues. It contains a detailed analysis of the revenue courts established by Henry VII and Henry VIII: the court of wards and liveries, the general surveyors, the court of first fruits and tenths, and the court of augmentations.

Other standard works are: Maitland, F. W., *English Law and the Renaissance* (1901); Pickthorn, K. W. M., *Early Tudor Government Henry VII* (1934) and *Early Tudor Government Henry VIII* (1934); Pollard, A. F., *Henry VIII* (1913); Thorne, Samuel E. (ed.), *Prerogativa Regis* (1949). Professor Thorne has written a wise introduction to this exposition of Robert Constable in 1495 of the *Prerogativa Regis*, first written in the late thirteenth century as a summary of the prerogative rights of the king. This and other "rehearsals" of feudal rights provided the new feudalism of the Tudors with one basis for systematic use of royal feudal powers, especially against tenants-in-chief.

Excellent articles include Dunham, W. H., "Henry VIII's Whole Council and Its Parts," *Huntington Library Quarterly*, November, 1943; Newton, A. P., "The King's Chamber under the Early Tudors," *E. H. R.* XXXVIII (1923) and Perceval, R. W., "Henry VIII and the Origin of Royal Assent by Commission," *Parliamentary Affairs*, Spring, 1950. See also Bell, H. E., *An Introduction to the History and Records of the Court of Wards and Liveries*, Cambridge Studies in English Legal History (1953).

For this and following chapters see further Gardiner, S. R. (ed.), *Reports of Cases in the Courts of Star Chamber and High Commission*, Camden Society, new series, XXXIX (1886); Harcourt, L. W. Vernon, *His Grace the Steward and the Trial of Peers* (1907); Lovell, Colin Rhys, "The Trial of Peers in Great Britain," *A. H. R.* LV (1949); Marsden, R. G. (ed.), *Select Pleas in the Admiralty Court 1527–1602* (2 vols., 1892, 1897); Percy, Lord Eustace, *The Privy Council under the Tudors* (1907); Pollard, A. F., "Council, Star Chamber and Privy Council under the Tudors," *E. H. R.* XXXVII (1922); Read, Conyers, *The Tudors* (1936), a brief and brilliant study of the whole Tudor period; Reid, Rachel, *The King's Council in the North* (1921); Skeel, Caroline A. J., *The Council in the Marches of Wales* (1904), a study in local government during the 16th and 17th centuries; Smith, L. B., *Tudor Prelates and Politics 1536–1558* (1953); Tanner, J. R., *Tudor Constitutional Documents 1485–1603* (1922), with an excellent introductory essay and explanatory comments throughout; Usher, R. G., *The Rise and Fall of the High Commission* (1913).

CHAPTER XIII: ELIZABETH I: THE VITAL BALANCE

In addition to the references for the preceding chapter the following books are important: Black, J. B., *The Reign of Elizabeth, 1558–1603* (1936), vol. viii in the *Oxford History of England;* Evans, F. M. G., *The Principal Secretary of State 1558–1680* (1923); Neale, J. E., *Queen Elizabeth* (1934), *The Elizabethan House of Commons* (1950), and *Elizabeth I and Her Parliaments, 1559–1581* (1953); the Alston edition of Sir Thomas Smith's *De Republica Anglorum* (1906). For the long history and development of the office of the Justice of the Peace, an institution particularly important in the Tudor period, see Beard, C. A., *The Office of the Justice of the Peace in England* (1904). See also the work of Miss Bertha Putnam, an outstanding authority on the fourteenth century referred to in the bibliography for Chapter X, in the history of the Justices of the Peace. Much light on local administration is provided by Mildred C. Campbell's *The English Yeoman under Elizabeth and the Early Stuarts* (1942). See further Trevor-Roper, H. R., *The Gentry 1540–1640* (the *Economic History Review* Supplements, I), 1953. Students interested in the problems of state finance during the late Tudor and early Stuart periods should consult F. C. Dietz, *English Public Finance 1558–1641* (1932).

Useful articles include Bayne, C. G., "The First House of Commons of Queen Elizabeth," *E. H. R.* XXIII (1908); Neale, J. E., "The Commons' Privilege of Free Speech in Parliament" in *Tudor Studies* ed. by R. W. Seton-Watson (1924) and "Peter Wentworth," *E. H. R.* XXXIX (1924); Richardson, W. C., "The Surveyors of the King's Prerogative," *E. H. R.* LVI (1941); Smith, Goldwin, "Elizabeth and the Apprenticeship of Parliament," *University of Toronto Quarterly,* VIII (1939).

For this and the following chapter see Prothero, G. W., *Select Statutes and Other Constitutional Documents Illustrative of the Reigns of Elizabeth and James I* (first published 1894, 4th ed. 1913).

CHAPTER XIV: CROSSROADS OF POWER: PREROGATIVE AND PARLIAMENT

Excellent books about the constitutional and legal history of the early seventeenth century are: Allen, J. W., *English Political Theory 1603–1640* (1938); Gardiner, S. R., *History of England 1625–1642* (2 vols., 1883–1885)—these famous volumes contain much political history; Judson, Miss Margaret A., *The Crisis of the Constitution: an Essay in Constitutional and Political Thought in England 1603–1645* (1949); McIlwain, C. H., *The Political Works of James I,* particularly the introduction (1918); Relf, F. H., *The Petition of Right* (1917); Tanner, J. R., *Constitutional Documents of the Reign of James I* (1930); Willson, D. H. (ed.), *The Parliamentary Diary of Robert Bowyer* (1931) and *The Privy Councillors in the House of Commons 1604–1629* (1940); Wormuth, F. D., *The Royal Prerogative* (1939) and *The Origins of Modern Constitutionalism* (1949). There is at present no adequate biography of James I. For an admirable general treatment of the period see Davies, Godfrey, *The Early Stuarts, 1603–1660,* vol. ix of the *Oxford History of England* (1943).

Useful articles include Adair, E. R., "The Petition of Right," *History,* V (1921); Gordon, M. D., "The Collection of Ship Money in the Reign of Charles I," *Trans.*

Royal Hist. Soc., 3rd series, IV (1910). Published debates include Notestein, W., Relf, F. H., and Simpson, H. (eds.), *Commons Debates, 1621* (1921); Notestein, W., and Relf, F. H. (eds.), *Commons Debates, 1629* (1924); Relf, F. H. (ed.), *Notes of the Debates in the House of Commons in 1621, 1625, 1628*, Royal Historical Society (1929); Gardiner, S. R. (ed.), *Notes of the Debates of the House of Lords . . . 1621*, Camden Society (1870) and *Debates in the House of Commons in 1625*, Camden Society (1873). There are several other accounts of debates and disputes in the 16th and 17th centuries that have not been cited here. Students are referred to the appropriate sections of the bibliographies of Professors Conyers Read and Godfrey Davies listed earlier in Bibliographies under *General Works*.

See also Gardiner, S. R., *Reports on the Cases in Star Chamber 1631–32*, Camden Society, 2nd series, XXXIX (1886); Notestein, W., *The Winning of the Initiative by the House of Commons*, Proceedings of the British Academy, 1924. The finest recent study of its kind is Willcox, W. B., *Gloucestershire: A Study in Local Government 1540–1640* (1940). Students seeking references in the field of local government will profit by consulting Professor Willcox's bibliographical note in this volume.

For this and following chapters see Figgis, J. N., *The Divine Right of Kings* (1922); Gooch, G. P., *History of English Democratic Ideas in the Seventeenth Century* (2nd ed. by Harold Laski, 1927); Tanner, J. R., *English Constitutional Conflicts of the Seventeenth Century 1603–1689* (1928).

CHAPTER XV: CIVIL WAR AND COMMON WEAL

The following books are of special value for the period of the Civil Wars and the Commonwealth and Protectorate: Firth, C. H., and Rait, R. S., *Acts and Ordinances of the Interregnum* (1911); Gardiner, S. R., *A History of the Great Civil War 1642–1649* (4 vols., 1893) and *History of the Commonwealth and Protectorate* (1901); Hexter, J. H., *The Reign of King Pym* (1941); Inderwick, F. A., *The Interregnum* (1901); Jenks, E., *The Constitutional Experiment of the Commonwealth 1649–1660* (1890); Jordan, W. K., *The Development of Religious Toleration in England* (4 vols., 1932–1940); Pease, T. C., *The Leveller Movement* (1916).

More specialized studies and collections of documents include Firth, C. H., *The House of Lords during the Civil War* (1910) and *The Last Years of the Protectorate* (1910); Gardiner, S. R., *The Constitutional Documents of the Puritan Revolution 1625–1660;* Haller, W. (ed.), *Tracts on Liberty in the Puritan Revolution 1638–1647* (3 vols., 1934); Woodhouse, A. S. P., *Puritanism and Liberty, Being the Army Debates (1647–49) from the Clarke Manuscripts* (1938)—note particularly Professor Woodhouse's introduction; Notestein, W. (ed.), *The Journal of Sir Simonds D'Ewes from the beginning of the Long Parliament to the Opening of the Trial of the Earl of Strafford* (1923); Coates, W. H. (ed.), *The Journal of Sir Simonds D'Ewes from the First Recess of the Long Parliament to the Withdrawal of King Charles from London* (1942).

See also Latham, R. C., "English Revolutionary Thought 1640–1660," *History*, March, 1945 and Smith, Goldwin, "The Reform of the Laws of England 1640–1660," *University of Toronto Quarterly*, X (1941). The latter essay is reprinted in *The Making of English History*, ed. R. L. Schuyler and H. Ausubel (1952). For this and the following chapter see Abbott, W. C., *The Writings and Speeches of Oliver Cromwell* (4 vols., 1938–1947); Brown, L. F., *Baptists and Fifth Monarchy Men* (1912); Firth, C. H., *Oliver Cromwell and the Rule of the Puritans in England* (1905, 1953); Wedgwood, C. V., *Oliver Cromwell* (1939).

CHAPTER XVI: CHARLES II AND JAMES II: POLITICAL ARITHMETIC

The following books are standard: Clark, G. N., *The Later Stuarts 1660–1714* (1934), vol. x in the *Oxford History of England;* Feiling, Keith, *British Foreign Policy* (1930); Kent, C. B. R., *The Early History of the Tories* (1908); Ogg, David, *England in the Reign of Charles II* (2 vols., 1934); Plum, H. G., *Restoration Puritanism* (1943)—this study is particularly valuable for its description of the linkage between Puritanism and the continued development of common law, ideas of social reform, and toleration; Trevelyan, G. M., *The English Revolution 1688–1689* (2nd ed., 1946); Turner, G. F., *James II* (1938). There are several interesting biographies of Charles II but none is scholarly or reliable. Of these, Arthur Bryant's *King Charles II,* Tory in bias, is probably the best.

Important articles include: Abbott, W. C., "The Long Parliament of Charles II," *E. H. R.* XXI (1906) and "The Origin of British Political Parties," *A. H. R.* XXIV (1919); Jenks, E., "The Story of Habeas Corpus," in *Select Essays in Anglo-American History,* II, 531–48, cited earlier under *General Works.*

For this and the following chapters see Feiling, Keith, *History of the Tory Party 1640–1714* (1924). See also Bosher, R. S., *The Making of the Restoration Settlement* (1952); W. A. Shaw's introduction to the *Calendar of Treasury Books 1660–1689* (3 vols., 1904–1926) and Clyde L. Grose's comments in *A. H. R.* XLIII (1938). S. A. Peyton has edited the records of the court of quarter sessions of the peace "held for the parts of Kesteven in the county of Lincoln 1674–1695," Lincoln Record Society, vols. 25, 26 (1931). Records of quarter sessions have also been published for the sixteenth and seventeenth centuries for Yorkshire (West Riding) and a few other county areas.

CHAPTER XVII: GROWTH OF THE CABINET SYSTEM: ENDS AND MEANS

Useful works that point the way to further reading are Blauvelt, M. T., *The Development of Cabinet Government in England* (1902); Jenks, E., *Parliamentary England: the Evolution of the Cabinet System* (1903); Laprade, W. T., *Public Opinion and Politics in Eighteenth Century England to the Fall of Walpole* (1936); Morgan, W. M., *English Political Parties and Leaders in the Reign of Queen Anne* (1920); Morley, John, *Sir Robert Walpole* (1889)—see especially chapter seven; Thomson, M. A., *The Secretaries of State 1681–1782* (1932); Trevelyan, G. M. (ed.), *Select Documents for Queen Anne's Reign* (1929) and *England under Queen Anne* (3 vols., 1930–34); Turberville, A. S., *The House of Lords in the Reign of William III* (1926) and *The House of Lords in the Eighteenth Century* (1927); Turner, E. R., *The Cabinet Council of England in the Seventeenth and Eighteenth Centuries 1622–1784* (2 vols., 1930–32)—the bibliography contains a list of the main sources, pp. 413–449—and *The Privy Council of England in the Seventeenth and Eighteenth Centuries 1603–1784* (2 vols., 1927–28); Williams, Basil, *The Whig Supremacy 1714–1760* (1939), vol. xi in the *Oxford History of England.* Of interest also is Witmer, Helen E., *The Property Qualifications of Members of Parliament* (1943). This monograph is a careful study of the history of an act passed by the Tories in 1710–1711 which made the possession of a minimum amount of *landed* property a requirement for members of Parliament. This act was not repealed until 1858.

Among many excellent articles the following are best: Anson, W. R., "The Cabinet in the Seventeenth and Eighteenth Centuries," *E. H. R.* XXIX (1914) and "The Development of the Cabinet 1688–1760," also in *E. H. R.* XXIX (1914); Davies, Godfrey, "Council and Cabinet 1679–88," *E. H. R.* XXXVII (1922); Radice, F. R., "The Reign of Queen Anne," *History*, June, 1935; Sedgwick, R. R., "The Inner Cabinet from 1739 to 1741," *E. H. R.* XXXIV (1919); Temperley, H. W. V., "Inner and Outer Cabinet and Privy Council 1689–1783," *E. H. R.* XXVII (1912) and "A Note on Inner and Outer Cabinets . . . ," *E. H. R.* XXXI (1916) and "Powers of the Privy Council in the Seventeenth Century," *E. H. R.* XXVIII (1913); Turner, E. R., "Lords Justices of England 1695–1755," *E. H. R.* XXIX (1914), "Committees of the Council and the Cabinet," *A. H. R.* XIX (1914), "The Development of the Cabinet," *A. H. R.* XVIII (1913), "The Cabinet in the Eighteenth Century," *E. H. R.* XXXII (1917) and "Committees of the Privy Council 1688–1760," *E. H. R.* XXXI (1916); Williams, E. T., "The Cabinet in the Eighteenth Century," *History*, XXII (1937).

For this and the following chapters see Robertson, C. G., *England under the Hanoverians* (1911).

CHAPTER XVIII: COURTS AND CABINETS: THE POLITICS OF POWER

The following are standard works on the problems and events of the late eighteenth century: Barnes, D. G., *George III and William Pitt 1783–1806* (1939); Butterfield, H., *George III, Lord North and the People 1779–1780* (1949); Davies, A. M., *The Influence of George III on the Development of the Constitution* (1921); Egerton, H. E., *Causes and Character of the American Revolution* (1923); Feiling, K., *The Second Tory Party 1714–1832* (1938); Keith, A. B., *Constitutional History of the First British Empire* (1930); Schuyler, R. L., *Parliament and the British Empire: Some Constitutional Controversies Concerning Imperial Legislative Jurisdiction* (1929).

See also Adams, R. G., *Political Ideas of the American Revolution* (1922); Andrews, C. M., *Colonial Background of the American Revolution* (1924); Beer, G. L., *The Old Colonial System* (1912) and *British Colonial Policy 1754–65* (1907); Bleackley, H. W., *Life of John Wilkes* (1917); Coupland, R., *The American Revolution and the British Empire* (1930); Davies, G., *George III* (1936); Foord, A. S., "The Waning of the 'Influence of the Crown,'" *E. H. R.* LXII (1947); Namier, L. B., *The Structure of Politics at the Accession of George III* (2 vols., 1929), *The Government of England at the Time of the American Revolution* (1930) and *Monarchy and the Party System* (1952)—see also the article "The Namier View of History," in the *Times Literary Supplement*, August 28, 1953; Pares, R., *George III and the Politicians* (1953)—see especially Lecture VI: "The Decline of Personal Monarchy"; Sedgwick, Romney (ed.), *Letters from George III to Lord Bute 1756–1766* (1949); Van Tyne, C. H., *Causes of the War of Independence* (1922); Williams, Basil, "Lord Chatham and the Representation of the Colonies in the Imperial Parliament," *E. H. R.* XXII (1907); Winstanley, D. A., "George III and His First Cabinet," *E. H. R.* XVII (1902) and *Personal and Party Government 1760–1766* (1910) and *Lord Chatham and the Whig Opposition* (1912); Fortescue, J., *The Correspondence of King George the Third* (6 vols., 1927–28).

CHAPTER XIX: REFORM AND DEMOCRACY: THE PRICE OF PROGRESS

The following books are of special value: Bell, K. N., and Morrell, W. P. (eds.), *Select Documents on British Colonial Policy 1830–1860* (1928); Butler, J. R. M., *The Passing of the Great Reform Bill* (1914); Davis, H. W. C., *The Age of Grey and Peel* (1929); Gash, Norman, *Politics in the Age of Peel; a Study in the Technique of Parliamentary Representation 1830–1850* (1953); Hammond, J. L., and Barbara, *The Age of the Chartists 1832–1854* (1930); Keith, A. B., *The British Cabinet 1830–1938* (1939); Kennedy, W. P. M. (ed.), *Documents of the Canadian Constitution 1759–1915* (1928); Thursfield, J. R., *Peel* (1891); Trevelyan, G. M., *Lord Grey of the Reform Bill* (1920); Veitch, G. S., *The Genesis of Parliamentary Reform* (1908)—especially valuable for eighteenth century background; Wallas, G., *Life of Francis Place* (1898).

Excellent articles include Aspinall, A., "English Party Organization in the Early Nineteenth Century," *E. H. R.* XLII (1926); Holdsworth, W. S., "The Movements for Reforms in the Law 1739–1832," *Law Quarterly Review*, April, 1940; Jennings, W. Ivor, "Cabinet Government at the Accession of Queen Victoria," *Economica*, XI (1931) and XII (1932); Turberville, A. S., "The House of Lords and the Advent of Democracy 1837–67," *History*, September, 1944.

For this and the following chapter see Cheyney, E. P., *Modern English Reform* (1931); Seymour, C., *Electoral Reform in England and Wales* (1915); Thomas, J. A., *The House of Commons 1832–1901* (1939); Woodward, E. L., *The Age of Reform 1815–1870* (1946), vol. xiii in the *Oxford History of England*.

For specific and excellent references to the growth of responsible government in the British Empire see the bibliography in Paul Knaplund's *The British Empire 1815–1939* (1941).

CHAPTER XX: THE VICTORIAN AGE

See the suggested references for Chapter XVIII and Chapter XIX. The following standard works may also be consulted: Ensor, R. C. K., *England, 1870–1914*, vol. xiv in the *Oxford History of England* (1936); Marriott, J. A. R., *England Since Waterloo* (1932); Trevelyan, G. M., *British History in the Nineteenth Century and After* (1937). See further Dicey, A. V., *Lectures on the Relation between Law and Public Opinion in England during the Nineteenth Century* (1905); Hardie, F., *The Political Influence of Queen Victoria 1861–1900* (1935); Park, J. H., *The English Reform Bill of 1867* (1920); Morley, John, *Life of William Ewart Gladstone* (3 vols., 1903); Monypenny, W. F., and Buckle, G. E., *Life of Benjamin Disraeli, Earl of Beaconsfield* (rev. ed., 2 vols., 1929). Several of the volumes listed in the General Bibliography contain sections and chapters on various aspects of the legal and constitutional history of this period.

CHAPTER XXI: THE TWENTIETH CENTURY

See the relevant citations in the General Bibliography. Several works listed there are of particular value for the modern period. See also such careful and balanced biographies as Sir Harold Nicolson's *King George the Fifth: His Life and Reign* (1952). Less successful is G. M. Young's *Stanley Baldwin* (1952).

Excellent books and articles about the twentieth century include: Dennis, A. L. P., "Impressions of British Party Politics 1909–1911" and "The Parliament

Act of 1911," in the *Political Science Quarterly*, V, VI (1911–1912); Finer, H., *English Local Government* (1934); Hawgood, J. A., "The British Constitution in 1948," *Parliamentary Affairs*, Autumn, 1949; Jackson, W. E., *The Structure of Local Government in England and Wales* (1949); Schuyler, R. L., "The British War Cabinet," *American Political Science Review*, XXXIII (1918) and "The British Cabinet 1916–1919," *American Political Science Review*, XXXV (1920); Smellie, K. B., *A Hundred Years of English Government* (1937); Stout, H. M., *British Government* (1953); Weidner, E. W., "Trends in English Local Government, 1944," *American Political Science Review*, April, 1945.

On the history of the British Empire and Commonwealth see Dawson, R. M., *The Development of Dominion Status 1900–1936* (1937); Hancock, W. K., *Empire in the Changing World* (1943); Jennings, W. I., *Constitutional Laws of the British Empire* (1938) and *The British Commonwealth of Nations* (1948); Keith, A. B., *The Governments of the British Empire* (1935) and *The Dominions as Sovereign States, Their Constitutions and Governments* (1938); Latham, R. T. E., *The Law and the Commonwealth* (1949); Walker, Eric, *The British Empire* (1944); Wheare, K. C., *The Statute of Westminster and Dominion Status* (2nd ed., 1947) and "Recent Constitutional Developments in the British Commonwealth," *Journal of Comparative Legislation and International Law*, November, 1948; Zimmern, A., *The Third British Empire* (1926). See also reports about Imperial and international affairs published by the Royal Institute of International Affairs and the various publications of H. M. Stationery Office.

CHAPTER XXII: THE STATE AND THE CITIZEN

See the appropriate references for Chapter XXI and the relevant books and articles listed earlier under *General Works*. See also Allen, C. K., *Bureaucracy Triumphant* (1931) and *Law and Orders* (1945); Amery, Leopold, *Thoughts on the Constitution* (1948); Campion, Lord, *et al.*, *British Government Since 1918* (1950), especially D. N. Chester's essay "The Development of the Cabinet, 1914–1949," in this volume; Cohen, E. W., *The Growth of the British Civil Service 1780–1939* (1941); Dale, H. E., *The Higher Civil Service of Great Britain* (1941); Ensor, R. C. K., *Courts and Judges in France, Germany, and England* (1933); Greaves, H. R. G., *The British Constitution* (2nd ed., 1948); Hanbury, H. G., *English Courts of Law* (1944); Hewart, Lord, *The New Despotism* (1929); Jennings, W. I., *Cabinet Government* (1936) and *Parliament* (1939) and *The Law and the Constitution* (3rd ed., 1943); Lawson, F. H., *The Rational Strength of English Law* (1951); Mackenzie, Kenneth, *The English Parliament* (1951), especially the latter sections; Port, F. J., *Administrative Law* (1929); Robson, W. A., *Justice and Administrative Law* (2nd ed., 1947); Salisbury, Mark, *The English Law Courts* (1938); Wickwar, W. H., *The Public Services* (1939); Willis, J., *The Parliamentary Powers of English Government Departments* (1933). Excellent discussions of the present imbalance between Cabinet and Parliament are to be found in *Parliament: A Survey*, by Lord Campion, *et al.* (1952). This volume of thirteen essays emerged from a study group on Parliamentary government in Britain initiated by the University of London in 1947.

INDEX

Index